RADIOSITY

A Programmer's Perspective

IAN ASHDOWN

JOHN WILEY & SONS, INC.

New York • Chichester • Brisbane • Toronto • Singapore

Publisher: Katherine Schowalter
Senior Editor: Diane D. Cerra
Managing Editor: Maureen B. Drexel
Editorial Production & Design: G & H Soho Inc.

Designations used by companies to distinguish their products are often claimed as trademarks. In all instances where John Wiley & Sons, Inc. is aware of a claim, the product names appear in initial capital or all capital letters. Readers, however, should contact the appropriate companies for more complete information regarding trademarks and registration.

This text is printed on acid-free paper.

This publication is designed to provide accurate and authoritative information in regard to the subject matter covered. It is sold with the understanding that the publisher is not engaged in rendering legal, accounting, or other professional service. If legal advice or other expert assistance is required, the services of a competent professional person should be sought.

Library of Congress Cataloging-in-Publication Data

Ashdown, Ian, 1950–
    Radiosity : a programmer's perspective / Ian Ashdown.
      p. cm.
    Includes bibliographical references and index.
    ISBN 0-471-30488-3 (pbk./disk : alk, paper).—ISBN 0-471-30443-3
(disk).—ISBN 0-471-30444-1 (pbk. : alk. paper)
    1. Computer graphics.   I. Title.
T385.A774   1994
006.6'6—dc20   94-9040
                                     CIP

Printed in the United States of America
10 9 8 7 6 5 4 3 2 1

Credits for copyrighted materials are listed on page 497.

Contents

Color plates follow page 210

Foreword

In the last decade three-dimensional computer graphics has emerged from research laboratories and has quickly become a part of our experience. Today it is routine to find realistic, computer-generated images on television and in the movies. Synthetic images are also routinely used in scientific and engineering applications, such as medicine, astronomy, and mechanical engineering. Of particular interest these days is the creation, manipulation, and display of virtual environments such as cities, campuses, buildings, and rooms. These environments have obvious applications in architecture, but they may also be used to organize large information landscapes and virtual communities.

Underlying all these applications is the computer technology, both software and hardware, to create realistic pictures. In the strongest use of the term, realism may be interpreted to mean indistinguishable from the real world. Many of us are routinely fooled into thinking a digital artifact is, in fact, a photo of a real event or place. The goals of realistic rendering, however, go beyond mere duplication. Our perceptual system responds to many complex visual cues, such as perspective, shading, texturing, and shadows, and these are used to perceive attributes and relationships of objects and the environment in which they are embedded. To the designer, these visual cues may be used to communicate space and form. This ability to use visual metaphors to connect to our perceptual system is why there are so many applications of three-dimensional graphics.

The majority of the computer technology revolving around imagery manipulates images directly. Images or drawing primitives are input, and images are output. Three-dimensional graphics is quite different in that the process involves creating a computer model of the scene and running an algorithm to produce an image from that model. To produce an interesting image, the computer model must describe a complex environment with diverse objects. The objects must have interesting shapes and be made from interesting materials. Also input are the position and properties of a digital camera and a set of digital lights. The objects that comprise the computer model are not that different, in principle, from the "objects" that a director manipulates to produce a scene in a real film.

The next step, rendering, produces the images from the model. The rendering process simulates the action of the digital camera: Virtual light is focused onto virtual film to create virtual image. Virtual light is emitted from sources, interacts with material objects, and eventually arrives at the camera's film plane. The key to three-dimensional rendering is modeling light.

Two major techniques have been developed for modeling light on a computer, ray tracing and radiosity. Ray tracing was the first of the two and is well known to anybody interested in computer graphics. Ray-tracing systems model light rays traveling from the eye to the light sources. As the rays propagate they may be blocked by intervening occluders, or they may be reflected or refracted according to the classic laws of optics. Radiosity is a more recent innovation. Radiosity systems model the interreflection of light from matte or diffuse surfaces. A matte surface reflects light equally in all directions. The key advantage of a radiosity algorithm is that multiple bounces of light can be modeled. Thus it is possible to capture very subtle, but dramatic, illumination effects such as soft shadows and indirect light. These lighting effects are what create the ambience of many of the environments in which we live.

This book is the first attempt to bring radiosity algorithms to a wide audience. It provides a lively and accessible description of the basic ideas and techniques. But more important, the book is not merely a collection of formulas and references, but contains C++ source code that implements a complete radiosity system on readily available PCs. If the reader is interested in three-dimensional graphics, and likes to learn through experimenting with real programs, this is the book.

Princeton, New Jersey   Pat Hanrahan

Preface

The soul's radiance in a wintry hour
Flings a sweet summer halo round us
> B. Cornwell
> *Miscellaneous Poems,* 1822

WHAT IS RADIOSITY?

There are two approaches to generating photorealistic images—digital pictures that are difficult to distinguish from real photographs—in computer graphics. The first approach involves ray-tracing techniques; the second approach is *radiosity*.

The use of photorealistic images in television and print advertising has left us somewhat inured to the capabilities of ray-tracing techniques. We see images that look almost, but not quite, like reality every day. Look carefully, however, at the cover and color plates of this book. Notice the accurate rendition of diffuse reflections and color bleeding between surfaces, realistic penumbrae along shadow boundaries, and detailed shading within shadows. These subtle but important visual effects, so difficult to achieve with conventional ray-tracing techniques, are inherent attributes of the radiosity approach.

Radiosity offers more than mere realism, however. Imagine creating a virtual reality stroll through the lobby, halls, and rooms of an international-class hotel. The building exists only as a set of architectural CAD drawings. What you want is an animated sequence of images, a video in which every frame is as richly detailed as the images shown in this book. If you use basic ray-tracing techniques, each frame has to be traced pixel by pixel. Ray-tracing techniques are view dependent; the number of ray-surface intersection calculations can increase geometrically with the complexity of the scene. In contrast, the radiosity approach is view independent. Most of the lighting calculations are performed only once for a given environment. Once they have been completed, it is a relatively simple task to render a view of the environment as seen from any camera position. The effort required to generate a sequence of images can be considerably less than that needed using ray-tracing techniques.

This is not a theoretical example that requires some future supercomputer. The cover of this book is courtesy of the architectural firm of Hellmuth, Obata and Kassabaum, Inc. They are using radiosity-based rendering software that runs on desktop graphics workstations to create promotional stills and videos for their clients. The radiosity approach is being used *today*.

Few of us are rich or fortunate enough to have a $30,000 dollar graphics workstation sitting on our desks. For now at least, we will have to let the professionals create their photorealistic and richly detailed videos. We can, however, create high-resolution color images using nothing more expensive than an off-the-shelf desktop personal computer.

What sorts of images? The color plates in this book imply that the radiosity approach is useful primarily as an architectural design and illustration tool. This emphasis reflects the original development of radiosity as a computer graphics tool. Architectural interiors provided convenient and impressive demonstrations of radiosity's strengths. Since then, the radiosity approach has been applied to entertainment productions, virtual reality systems, diagnostic medicine, scientific research, and engineering studies. Research into the applications of radiosity has really just begun.

RADIOSITY AND RAY TRACING

Radiosity is in a sense the complement of ray tracing. Ray-tracing techniques excel in the rendition of point light sources, specular reflections, and refraction effects. Radiosity methods accurately model area light sources, diffuse reflections, color bleeding effects, and realistic shadows. It follows that the best use of radiosity may lie in a combination of radiosity methods and ray-tracing techniques. Fortunately, most scenes of everyday interest include few specular surfaces and transparent objects. We can potentially use radiosity methods to visualize a scene, followed where necessary by a ray-tracing pass to more accurately render the specular highlights and refraction effects. The number of rays that must be traced is far fewer than if the scene was visualized using ray-tracing techniques alone.

Looking to the future, we can see that virtual reality systems will be expected to offer photorealistic images at real-time display rates. The radiosity approach allows us to create such images using "progressive refinement" techniques, where each image initially appears as an approximate rendering of the scene. The radiosity algorithm is then iterated to progressively "refine" the image. The longer we focus our attention on a scene, the closer the scene will approach reality. We will be able to combine this ability with motion compensation and other video data compression techniques to create seemingly smooth zoom and pan sequences through our virtual worlds.

Critics have argued that radiosity methods require inordinate amounts of memory and processing power. Their complaints were justified when the first of these methods was proposed a decade ago. Times have changed, however, and will continue to do so. We have affordable personal computers with memory, processing power, and video display capabilities undreamed of a decade ago sitting on our desktops. We also have practical radiosity methods that can be easily implemented on these computers. Radiosity is no longer the domain of academic researchers with their multiprocessor workstations and dedicated hardware graphics accelerators. We can experiment and work with radiosity today using off-the-shelf personal computers.

A FEW LIMITATIONS

The radiosity approach has several limitations when compared to ray-tracing techniques. To begin with, radiosity theory is based on the assumption that all surfaces are ideal diffuse reflectors. Accurately modeling specular surfaces and transparent materials requires a combination of radiosity methods and ray-tracing techniques. These combinations—*extended* radiosity methods—offer the best features of radiosity and ray tracing, but often at the expense of impractical processing requirements.

Another limitation involves the representation of surfaces. Whereas ray-tracing techniques can use implicit equations to define curved surfaces, most radiosity methods require all surfaces—curved and flat—to be modeled as typically nonuniform polygon meshes. This is not a fundamental limitation because any flat or curved surface can be approximated by a polygon mesh. Nevertheless, a complex curved surface defined as a mesh usually requires a fair amount of memory. The same surface represented by an implicit equation (e.g., a Bézier or quadric surface) requires memory for only a few parameters.

A more serious limitation is that these polygon meshes must be carefully chosen to avoid aliasing artifacts in the rendered images. Choosing an appropriate mesh for each surface is a nontrivial problem that depends on the geometrical relationship between surfaces, the placement of light sources, and surface reflectance properties. Fortunately, the meshing process can be automated to some extent using "adaptive subdivision" techniques.

On the positive side, there is a popular misconception that the radiosity approach requires a closed environment, where every ray of light must eventually intersect at least one surface. In fact, it is just that—a misconception. Radiosity can model any environment that ray tracing can.

Given these limitations, the radiosity approach is clearly not a panacea for generating photorealistic images of arbitrary scenes. As a rule of thumb, it is best suited for those applications where the majority of objects have surfaces that are flat, opaque, and diffusely reflective. Many architectural scenes fall nicely into this category, which explains why most artistic examples of radiosity feature office interiors and the like. Scenes featuring mostly curved objects with specular or semispecular surfaces and transparent materials such as glass are more appropriately rendered using ray-tracing techniques.

This is not to say that the radiosity approach should be considered only for architectural design and illustration. More esoteric applications include thermal engineering analysis, solar atmospheric studies, computer-aided tomography, and virtual reality simulations. After ten years of research, we are just beginning to see radiosity methods applied to real-world problems. It will be interesting to see where future work will take us.

HIGHER MATHEMATICS NOT REQUIRED

Radiosity is very much a computer graphics *tool*. Consequently, this book examines the gamut of radiosity methods in depth, beginning with the basics of radiosity theory and ending somewhere in the frontiers of current research. The algorithms are rigorously and clearly explained; implementation details are examined at length; and C++ source code is presented for a complete radiosity-based renderer—*HELIOS*— that runs under Microsoft Windows 3.1 and Windows NT. Moreover, most of the code is platform independent and designed for 32-bit environments, which means that it can be ported to other development and target platforms with minimal effort. In short, this book is itself a programmer's tool for exploring radiosity.

Many advanced computer graphics techniques rely heavily on sophisticated mathematics; this is not true for radiosity. Understanding radiosity requires no more than a basic knowledge of vectors and matrices, plus an ability to visualize in three dimensions. Please do not let the brief excursions into higher mathematics deter you. If you remember your high school algebra, you have all the mathematical tools you need. The occasional text box provides a brief explanation of possibly unfamiliar mathematical notation and concepts. At worst, the mathematics can be skipped altogether with minimal loss of continuity.

This book is aimed at computer science undergraduates and computer enthusiasts of all ages. There are no classroom exercises to spoil the fun—we all learn best by *doing*. The radiosity renderer presented in this book offers endless opportunities. Take it apart, see how it works, and rebuild it . . . add features, experiment with different algorithms, and profile their performance. Learn from your experiences and discoveries, and above all else enjoy what you are doing. Remember: radiosity is easy to understand and fascinating to experiment with.

WHAT YOU NEED

In terms of today's personal desktop computer technology, what you need to compile and run *HELIOS* is minimal:

- an IBM PC-AT clone with a 386 CPU and 4 megabytes of RAM and a 387 floating-point coprocessor (486 or Pentium CPU recommended).
- minimum 256-color display adapter and color monitor (65,536 or 16.7 million [24-bit] colors recommended).
- Microsoft Windows 3.1 or Windows NT.
- a C++ compiler capable of generating Windows 3.1 or Windows NT executables.

These are *minimum* requirements. An IBM PC-AT clone with a 66-MHz 486-DX2 CPU rendered the photorealistic image shown in Color Plate 1 in 35 seconds. A computer with a 16-MHz 386-SX CPU will take considerably longer.

HELIOS uses Microsoft's BMP graphics file format to both display and store 24-bit color images. It can also generate color dithered images suitable for 16-bit (65,356 color) and 15-bit (32,768 color) displays. However, it does not directly support 256-color displays. The images it does display on computers with these adapters will appear posterized.

Nevertheless, a computer with a 256-color display adapter can be used. The diskette that accompanies this book includes a standalone utility (with fully documented C++ source code) for generating 8-bit (256-color) BMP files from the 24-bit BMP files that *HELIOS* produces. (It would take very little work to add this capability to *HELIOS* itself. However, both programs require a fair amount of memory. On a machine with 4 megabytes of memory, it is probably better to run each program separately to avoid those dreaded "out of memory" error messages.)

This book is about radiosity and the implementation of radiosity methods in C++. It is not about programming in or for any particular environment. There are some 7,000 lines of draft ANSI C++ source code, of which only 1,700-odd lines are devoted to the graphical user interface provided by MS-Windows. The remainder focus on the underlying computer graphics software needed to implement the radiosity renderer.

The MS-Windows interface is written in ANSI C and compiles without modification under either Microsoft Visual C++ Version 1.5 or Borland C++ Version 4.0. No use whatsoever is made of any compiler-specific functions or class libraries other than those required for generic MS-Windows programs. More important, the interface code is completely encapsulated in its own set of classes.

Are you programming for another environment? HELIOS also compiles as a Microsoft Win32s or Windows NT program without modification. You only need to specify a global *#define* to create a 32-bit executable. As such, the platform-independent C++ radiosity code should properly compile under any C++ compiler. All you have to add is a graphical user interface.

A radiosity algorithm can be written in about a dozen lines of pseudocode. A functional radiosity-based rendering program, on the other hand, requires much more. In particular, it requires the support of a complete three-dimensional viewing system. Although the algorithms have been published before, few computer graphics programming texts have attempted to address the complexities of writing the necessary code. The effort needed to develop a ray-tracing program pales in comparison. Neverthless, it is all here.

FROM BEGINNING TO END

Radiosity is both simple and subtle. It is not enough to provide a few brief explanations, wave our hands with magic incantations, and implement some pseudocode in C++. If we are to understand radiosity in any useful sense, we must approach the subject with patience and discipline. This philosophy is reflected in the organization of this book, which is divided into three parts:

Part I: Radiosity Models Light

Our understanding of radiosity must begin with its fundamental principles. While the basics of radiosity can be explained in five hundred words or less—see the Introduction—we need a deeper appreciation of its theoretical basis. We will see that radiosity theory and its underlying principles can be expressed in one unifying phrase: *radiosity models light.*

Chapter 1, "Measuring Light," begins with an overview of light—what is light and how do we measure it? The chapter examines the parallel sciences of radiometry and photometry in detail, with a brief excursion into radiometric field theory. The concepts are simple but extremely important to what follows.

Chapter 2, "Radiosity Theory," explains radiosity in terms of the geometrical nature of light, using a minimum of mathematics. Mathematical proofs of key concepts are provided as optional reading.

Radiosity models light. This is a crucial detail that has been so far overlooked in the computer graphics literature. In recognizing this point, we can more easily grasp the full significance of radiosity as a computer graphics tool.

Part II: Tools of the Trade

Speaking of tools, we shall need a graphics toolkit for *HELIOS*, our radiosity renderer. Most radiosity methods expect only one type of graphic primitive: three-dimensional polygons. Chapter 3, "Building An Environment," presents the basic algorithms needed to represent these polygons. These algorithms are not part of the radiosity approach per se. Nevertheless, they are needed to describe complex three-dimensional scenes and to view them afterward. Fortunately, they are simple to understand and straightforward to implement.

We will also need many of the basic algorithms used in three-dimensional CAD programs. Chapter 4, "A Viewing System," reviews synthetic cameras, windowing and clipping, hidden-surface elimination, scan conversion, and incremental shading techniques. From these, it builds a complete three-dimensional viewing system for MS-Windows 3.1 and Windows NT. With it we will be able to view wireframe images, shaded three-dimensional models, and photorealistic renderings.

You might argue that these two chapters consume an inordinate amount of space within a book devoted to radiosity. Perhaps. Unfortunately, they are necessary. While expensive desktop workstations may offer hardware and software support for three-dimensional graphics, our personal desktop computers and their operating systems are far less capable.

Part III: Radiosity and Realism

We can now address radiosity in depth, beginning with form factors. In a sense, these the heart and soul of radiosity theory. Imagine two polygons floating in space. If one polygon is emitting light, how much of its light will be intercepted by the other one? This is a simple question with no easy answer. Believe it or not, it took mathematicians over 230 years to find a equation that solves for the general case of two arbitrarily oriented polygons! Fortunately, there are much simpler solutions for our needs. Chapter 5, "Form Factor Determination," looks at a number of efficient calculation methods, including hemicubes, cubic tetrahedrons, and ray casting.

Chapter 6, "Solving the Radiosity Equation," presents several radiosity algorithms and associated techniques that have been developed over the past ten years. The first method, full radiosity, was an academic curiosity derived from radiant heat-transfer theory. The subsequent improvements and modifications represent a fascinating *tour de force* of mathematical insight and programming ingenuity. The chapter concludes with three fully functional versions of *HELIOS*.

Aliasing is an ever-present problem for the radiosity approach. Surfaces are described as polygon meshes. If the mesh is too coarse, the mesh outline will be visible in the rendered surface. If the mesh is too fine, the radiosity methods must perform unnecessary calculations. Chapter 7, "Meshing Strategies," examines the issues involved and explores substructuring techniques that attempt to create optimal meshes for surfaces. Be forewarned, however, that automatic meshing algorithms are currently one of the open questions of radiosity research.

Finally, Chapter 8, "Looking to the Future," proposes a number of enhancements for *HELIOS* that you might consider as programming projects. These projects range from texture mapping to creating your own radiosity-based videos. The chapter concludes with a brief look at the "bleeding edge" of radiosity research. If nothing else, it shows that there is much more to come!

This book offers a programmer's perspective of radiosity. It implements a radiosity-based rendering program with the intention that you, the reader, will extend the program's capabilities to suit your needs and desires. With this in mind, the conclusion of this book is that most valuable of resources: an extensive bibliography that lists almost every radiosity-related paper published to date. If you have an idea for extending *HELIOS*, these papers may prove to be worth be their weight in gold.

ACKNOWLEDGMENTS

My debts of gratitude extend in several directions. First, I am indebted to the many computer graphics researchers who found radiosity as fascinating a topic as I have. More to the point, it is their investigative work that has provided the foundations for this book. There are too many names to acknowledge here; I can only hope my interpretations have done justice to their contributions.

Second, I am indebted to a number of researchers in other fields. There are many interwoven threads leading to the development of radiosity, including geometrical optics, astronomy, photometry and radiometry, radiant heat and illumination engineering, field theory, and nuclear physics. They include forgotten and neglected names such as Fock, Yamauti, Gershun, and Moon, whose pioneering work in photometric and radiometric theory was fifty to one hundred years before its time. Their efforts are implicitly acknowledged throughout this book.

Third, I owe personal debts to a number of people. They include Peter Murphy of Ledalite Architectural Products for financial support and an unending interest in the impossible, Domina Eberle Spencer of the University of Connecticut for inspiration and helios, David DiLaura at the University of Colorado for providing an unattainable goal and sharing his love of higher mathematics, and Peter Ngai of Peerless Lighting for ten years of unwitting but friendly incentive. I also thank Peter Franck of Ledalite Architectural Products for his careful review of the draft manuscript and Eric Haines of 3D/Eye for his insightful comments and for sharing his radiosity bibliography.

The radiosity research community is small and friendly. I am extremely grateful to Stuart Feldman, Filippo Tampieri, and Rod Recker of Lightscape Technologies and David Munson of Hellmuth, Obata and Kassabaum for providing their exquisite color images. Thanks are also due to Holly Rushmeier, Michael Cohen, Pat Hanrahan, Richard Mistrick, Greg Ward, Mark Pavicic, Nelson Max, John Wallace, Alain Fournier, Pierre Poulin, and numerous others for their collective assistance and many small but important contributions.

Writing a program as complicated as a radiosity renderer from scratch is not for the faint of heart. Aside from the mathematics and technical issues involved, it requires a great deal of careful thought, detailed planning, and discipline. For this, I thank my friends at Glenayre Research and Development and Josef Roehrl of Stonehenge Software Technologies, who collectively spent four years teaching me the difference between programming and software engineering. One million-plus lines of C and 680x0 assembly code for electronic voice mail and radio telecommunications—now there is a program to be proud of!

As for this book, we must all be thankful for Diane Cerra of John Wiley & Sons with her initial shot-in-the-dark inquiry and enduring faith thereafter, and to Fran Bartlett and her patient staff at G & H Soho for their crossed eyes and dotty tees. Writing the manuscript for a book may be hard work, but it pales in comparison to the dogged effort needed to prepare it for publication.

Finally, I thank the following for their encouragement, moral support, and love: my wife Janet, my parents Frank and Marjorie Ashdown, and last but not least, Annie Ballyk for endlessly repeating her favorite phrase: "Have you finished your book yet?"

Never underestimate the power of a grandmother's words. Yes, Annie, I finally have!

West Vancouver, British Columbia   I. E. A.

Introduction

I.0   RADIOSITY: A TENTH ANNIVERSARY

The year 1994 marks the tenth anniversary of radiosity as recognized by the computer graphics community. It began more or less as a mathematical curiosity that could laboriously render the interior of an empty box (Goral et al. 1984). Today radiosity is entering the marketplace as a powerful computer graphics tool for synthesizing photorealistic images from architectural drawings.

Despite this inherent power, radiosity has remained almost exclusively a university research topic. Each passing year has seen the publication of more effective and ingenious radiosity-based algorithms. Nevertheless, the number of radiosity-based rendering programs available to individual computer graphics enthusiasts has remained almost insignificant. As of 1994, there are apparently only two public domain packages for UNIX-based machines, both available on the Internet from their authors. (There are also several implementations of *RADIANCE*, a superlative public domain ray-tracing program with radiosity-related effects.) None of these programs, however, explores the radiosity approach in depth.

Why is this? There is certainly no shortage of public domain ray-tracing programs. *DKBTrace* (e.g., Lindley 1992) and its successor, *Persistence of Vision* (Wells and Young 1993), are two well-known examples that can produce outstanding ray-traced imagery. These are complex programs with many options and capabilities. The effort put into their development likely exceeds that needed to develop a fully functional radiosity-based rendering program by an order of magnitude. If this is so, why are there so few radiosity programs available?

1

Perhaps the answer can be found in this quotation from Shenchang Eric Chen (1991) of Apple Computer, Inc:

> While a naive ray tracer can be implemented fairly easily and compactly (as in the case of Paul Heckbert, who has a ray tracer printed on his business card), implementing a radiosity program is generally regarded as an enormous task. This is evident in that there still is no public domain radiosity code available . . .

This sounds reasonable; public domain programs usually begin as small weekend programming projects that quietly grow into major undertakings. The critical factor is that first tentative release. If it has any merit whatsoever, a cadre of loyal users will prompt the author to fix one more bug and add another handful of features. The project soon becomes a group effort that continues to grow until it rivals its commercial counterparts.

A radiosity-based renderer, on the other hand, is not something you do in a weekend. It is a major undertaking that requires many long and tedious hours of planning, design, development, and testing. Worse, there are no intermediate stages of development. The first synthesized image appears only when the entire project nears completion.

This is saddening. The widespread availability of affordable ray-tracing programs has brought us many captivating images by talented artists, both amateur and professional. They have also captured the imagination of many young students, encouraging them to pursue their interests in computer graphics and related fields. A capable radiosity-based rendering program can only encourage this pool of talented individuals.

In celebration then of radiosity's tenth anniversary: *HELIOS*, an affordable radiosity-based renderer, complete with over 7,000 lines of C++ source code and 500 pages of documentation (this book).

HELIOS is both a celebration and a challenge. The celebration is twofold: radiosity's anniversary and *HELIOS*'s own marriage of radiosity with Microsoft Windows 3.1 and Windows NT. The challenge . . . well, we will get to that in a moment.

Shenchang Chen got it right—developing *HELIOS* was indeed "an enormous task." As such, it deserves more than a few pages of hastily prepared user documentation. It needs every page of the book you are now holding to properly describe its underlying algorithms and design philosophy.

This book was written concurrently with the program's development. Each paragraph bears with it the immediate (and often frustrating) experience of having implemented the algorithms being discussed. The subtitle "A Programmer's Perspective" means precisely what it says.

The challenge in writing the program was to ensure that the code remained as generic as possible. True, *HELIOS* has been implemented as an MS-Windows program. However, very little of the code is specific to MS-Windows. This comes from the first draft specification for the program's design:

> [The program] shall be implemented such that the display device and environment dependencies are minimized. Wherever possible, these dependencies shall be encapsulated in clearly defined and well-documented C++ classes.

Most of the code in this book is written in draft ANSI C++. More important, it was expressly designed for ease of porting to other computer environments. It compiles without any errors or warnings for both 16-bit (Windows 3.1) and 32-bit (Windows NT and Win32s) target environments. The goal was to develop a radiosity renderer that could be implemented on any platform that supports bitmap graphics displays. *HELIOS* explicitly supports this design philosophy.

The real challenge is to you. This book provides an abundance of radiosity algorithms and implementations. Some features are discussed but not implemented. Others are implemented but not incorporated into *HELIOS*. They range from small but significant performance enhancements to major software development projects. Although *HELIOS* is a fully functional program, it lacks some of the bells and whistles we normally associate with a commercial product. This is an opportunity: You can enhance *HELIOS* and learn while you do so.

First, however, we should examine what radiosity is.

I.1 CAPTURING REALITY

Think of an empty and darkened room. It has a fluorescent light fixture mounted on the ceiling and a table sitting on the floor underneath it. The light fixture is turned off. There are no windows, open doors, or any other source of illumination. Now turn on the light.

We all know what happens next. Light *flows* from the light fixture, filling every corner of the room at the speed of . . . well, light. It directly illuminates the walls, floor, and tabletop (Fig. I.1). The sides of the table are in shadow, and the ceiling is not directly illuminated. Depending on the surface reflectances, some of the light will be reflected back into the room; the rest will be absorbed. The reflected light will "bounce" from surface to surface until it is completely absorbed. In the process, it will indirectly illuminate the entire room, including the table sides and ceiling.

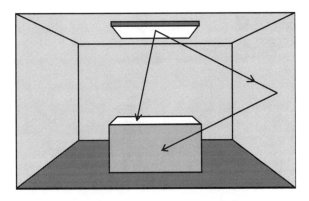

Figure I.1   Modeling the flow of light in a room

Within this simple model is the realm of our visual experience. Of this light, an almost infinitesimal portion will find its way to our eye's retina. Converted into electrochemical signals, it provides images to our brain: We perceive the room in all its visual complexity.

Note the term "perceive." It represents an important but often neglected point. We visually *see* light that impinges on our retina; electrochemical reactions generate nerve impulses that travel along the optic nerves to the visual cortex in our brain. From this, we consciously *perceive* the information it conveys.

If you think about it for a moment, we are surrounded by a three-dimensional field of light that we can never directly see or perceive. A flashlight beam is invisible until it is reflected by a surface, shines through translucent glass, or passes through smoke or airborne dust. We can experience only those material objects that direct light toward our eye; the light itself is an invisible agent in this process.

We commonly think in terms of *rays* of light that are emitted by a light source. Each ray follows a straight line through space, possibly bouncing from surface to surface, until it is either completely absorbed or enters our eye (Fig. I.2). Those rays we see are focused by the cornea onto the retina; together they form an image of the objects we perceive.

From this, it should be evident that we can look at a photograph and perceive the objects it portrays. If each ray of light reflected from the photograph toward our eye exactly mimics those rays we see from the original scene, then we should not be able to tell the difference between the photograph and the original objects.

Of course, nature is rarely so kind. Our binocular vision immediately tells us that the photograph is a two-dimensional surface with no perceptual depth. The relative positions of the objects in the photograph remain unchanged as we move our heads. These and a thousand other visual cues tell us that a photograph is a photograph and not the objects it portrays.

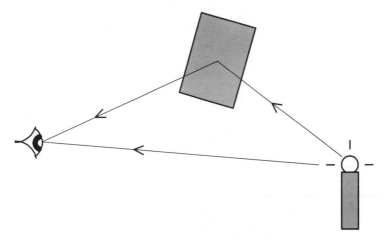

Figure I.2   Perceiving objects through rays of light

Nevertheless, we appreciate these images and value them for both their aesthetic and informational content. They take us to places where we cannot go, remind us of past events, and convey images of reality we cannot see or otherwise imagine. More recently, they have shown us images of virtual realities—photorealistic renditions of imaginary worlds that exist only as bits of information in the memory of our computers.

We value these images most when they portray the world as we think it should be. A view of an architectural interior should exhibit all the characteristics of the real world. Specular reflections from glass and polished wood, diffuse reflections from matte finishes, fine details and textures in every object, and realistic shadows are but a few of these. Capturing these nuances is a considerable challenge to the computer scientist and artist alike. Although much progress has been made since the first crude line drawings were displayed on the cathode ray tube screen of MIT's WhirlWind I computer in 1950 (Newmann and Sproull 1979), the current state of the art reveals that we still have far to go.

In the meantime, we have the knowledge and computing power to synthesize photorealistic images using nothing more than our artistic sense and a personal desktop computer. We might say that these images allow us to capture reality. It will take several hundred pages of higher mathematics and some rather convoluted source code to explain how, but the results will be rewarding and extremely satisfying.

I.2 RAYS OF LIGHT

The first attempts to capture reality in the form of photorealistic images relied on the basic principles of geometric optics. Using Figure I.1 as an example, we see that each ray of light emitted by the light source is faithfully followed as it traversed the room (Whitted 1980). At each point where it intersects a surface, the physical properties of that surface determine how much of the ray is absorbed and the direction and color of the remainder. A black surface will obviously reflect much less light than a white one. Similarly, a red surface will reflect mostly red light, even though the color of the light source may have been white. A transparent object behaves in the same manner except that the remaining light is transmitted through its volume rather than reflected from its surface.

The problem with this approach is that it is shockingly inefficient. Most of the rays will be fully absorbed before they ever reach our eye. Why follow them if they cannot be seen? This leads to the concept of *backward ray tracing*. Knowing how a ray is reflected or transmitted by each object it encounters on its path from the light source to our eye, we can trace it backward through space and time from our eye (Fig. I.3). We then have to consider only those rays that we can actually see.

Unfortunately, this leads to a second problem. Figures I.2 and I.3 show a single ray being reflected from the surface, but this is a gross simplification. Physical surface finishes vary from microscopically smooth to roughly textured. A smooth and

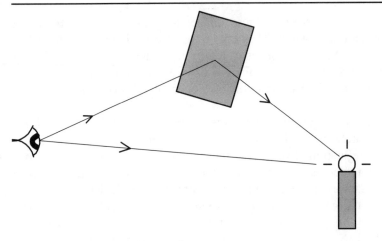

Figure I.3   Backwards ray tracing

polished surface acts much like a mirror—it is a specular reflector of light. A single ray of light incident on the surface will be reflected as a single ray. This is a trivial event for a ray-tracing program, because the angle of reflection can be calculated very easily.

More often, however, physical surfaces will act as semispecular and diffuse reflectors (Fig. I.4). Here, an incident ray is reflected as an *infinite number* of rays. The intensity of each reflected ray will vary, depending on the angle of the incident ray, the angle of the reflected ray, and the surface reflectance properties. This makes ray tracing somewhat more difficult, to say the least.

The overall effect of light being repeatedly reflected from semispecular and diffuse surfaces is to fill the room with rays going in every direction. This *fill light*, to use the artist's term, provides the soft shadows and subtle shadings we associate with realistic images. Without it, most shadows are black and featureless.

It becomes computationally infeasible to trace any significant number of these diffusely reflected rays for complex scenes (or *environments*) involving hundreds or thousands of nonspecular surfaces. This highlights an important limitation of ray-tracing techniques: They have difficulty in accurately modeling semispecular and diffuse reflections.

Most ray-tracing programs do not attempt to model these reflections directly. Instead, numerous techniques have been developed to simulate their contribution to

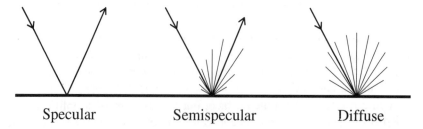

Specular   Semispecular   Diffuse

Figure I.4   Reflection from specular and diffuse surfaces

indirect illumination. One popular approach is simply to assume that all surfaces are evenly illuminated by a completely diffuse but hidden light source. This *ambient lighting term* has no physical basis; it simply attempts to make the objects in the environment look more realistic.

Other, more sophisticated ray-tracing algorithms can be used to simulate soft shadows and diffuse reflections. Again, however, they are often ad hoc techniques without a firm physical basis. The results are not always satisfactory—many ray-traced images exhibit the characteristic signature of plastic-looking surfaces, and their shadows may be less than convincing.

This is not to disparage ray-tracing techniques. Computer graphics practitioners have been extremely successful in using these techniques to create an astounding assortment of realistic images. What we need to recognize is that they have their limitations, and to consider the possible alternatives where necessary. These are our radiosity methods, a fundamentally different approach to photorealistic image synthesis.

I.3   RADIOSITY EXPLAINED

Figure I.5 shows our empty room again but with three significant refinements: (1) all surfaces are assumed to be ideal diffuse and opaque reflectors; (2) the light source is an ideal diffuse *emitter* of light; and (3) each surface is subdivided into a mesh of elements called *patches*.

The assumption that all surfaces are ideal diffuse (or *Lambertian*) reflectors is important. These reflectors have a unique and very interesting property: They reflect light equally in all directions, regardless of the angle of the incident ray or rays of light illuminating the surface.

Look at the paper this page is printed on—it is a reasonable approximation of an ideal diffuse reflector. Try holding it under an incandescent desk lamp and tilting the book back and forth. If you keep it at a constant distance from the lamp, the

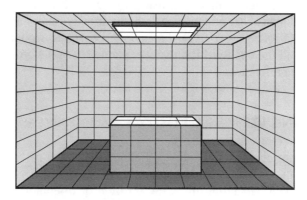

Figure I.5   A room with subdivided surfaces

visual "brightness" of the paper will not change significantly. A spot light meter will tell you the same thing; the amount of light reflected in any direction is independent of the angle of the incident light.

This principle will prove extremely useful to us. The total quantity of light reflected from a Lambertian surface is equal to the quantity of the incident light times the surface reflectance. Period. A gray Lambertian surface with a surface reflectance of 20 percent reflects precisely 20 percent of any incident light, and distributes it equally in all directions.

An ideal diffuse emitter is identical to a Lambertian reflector except that it *emits* light equally in all directions. Some fluorescent light fixtures are reasonable approximations of ideal diffuse emitters. Most light sources, however, are not. Neverthless, it is a useful concept that will help us understand the radiosity approach.

So what does this give us? Well, consider that it is very easy to calculate how much light is emitted in any given direction by a Lambertian emitter or reflector. (The details are presented in Chapter 1.) If we know the geometry of the room and the constituent elements of its surfaces, we can determine how much light each element receives from the light source. Note that we do *not* have to trace individual rays, since all the information we need is contained in the room and element geometry. (See Chapter 5 for a detailed exposition.) Most of the elements will receive some light. A few, however, will be hidden from view (as seen from the light source) by other elements, and so they receive no direct illumination.

So far, so good. Now, each of these elements will absorb some of the light it receives and reflect the remainder back into the room. If we know the reflectance of each surface, we can calculate the precise amount. Each illuminated element now becomes a secondary ideal diffuse emitter that "sends" its light to those elements visible to it.

This process is clearly iterative and proceeds until all of the reflected light from all of the elements is finally absorbed. If we keep a tally of how much light each element reflects and/or emits, we end up knowing how "bright" the element will appear when viewed from any direction. Loosely speaking, this is the element's *radiosity*.

Finally, we know the geometry of each element in the room—in computer graphics parlance, it is a three-dimensional *polygon*. If we know its brightness, we can use a three-dimensional graphics package to directly render a photorealistic image of the room (as a collection of three-dimensional polygons) from any viewpoint.

That's all there is to it! Radiosity explained in 500 words or less. Mark this section for future reference.

I.4   RAY TRACING VERSUS RADIOSITY

There are both obvious and subtle differences between ray tracing and radiosity. In ray tracing, the viewer is paramount. All rays are traced from the view position into the environment. Changing the view position or orientation by more than a small amount usually requires repeating the entire ray-tracing process from scratch. As such, most ray-tracing techniques represent a *view-dependent* process.

Radiosity is the exact opposite. Our light-transfer calculations are based solely on the geometry of the environment. There is no view position or viewer. Radiosity considers only the interaction of light with surfaces in the environment.

This has an important consequence. Given an environment, we can calculate the visual brightness of each of its surface elements. These calculations may take some time, but we only need to perform them once. After that, we can position and orient ourselves anywhere in the environment and synthesize a photorealistic image almost as quickly as we can draw and shade three-dimensional polygons on our computer screen. Radiosity methods therefore represent a *view-independent* process.

On the other side of the coin, efficient radiosity methods are limited to modeling Lambertian surfaces. They can model semispecular surfaces but only with roughly the same amount of effort as is required by ray-tracing techniques. Also, radiosity methods fail completely to model those specular reflections that are ray tracing's forte.

In short, we should consider ray tracing and radiosity as complementary approaches to photorealistic image synthesis. Researchers are still refining existing algorithms and developing new ones. In the future, we will likely rely on a hybrid approach that combines the best features of both—radiosity for diffuse reflections and ray tracing for specular highlights. Here, our interest is in radiosity, its theory and implementation.

I.5   RADIOSITY MODELS LIGHT

There is a fundamental aspect of the radiosity approach that has been so far over-looked in the computer graphics literature. Consider that ray-tracing techniques model *objects*. An individual ray must interact with objects in the environment before it can convey any information. Without detailed knowledge of these objects, their geometry and physical properties, we cannot create an image.

Radiosity is different. Yes, we still need to know the geometry and physical properties of the objects. However, radiosity allows us to render an image of the environment from any viewpoint. Seen thus, it is evident that radiosity is not model-ing the objects within the environment. Instead, it is modeling the three-dimensional *field of light* that permeates the environment. More to the point, we will see in Chapter 1 that radiosity can in theory model this field exactly and completely. This then becomes a central theme of this book: *Radiosity models light.*

I.6   A PROGRAMMER'S PERSPECTIVE

In explaining the radiosity approach, we necessarily had to gloss over a few minor implementation details . . . well, maybe not so minor. In fact, it will take the remainder of this book to discuss them. It will involve the occasional excursion into higher mathematics, including analytic geometry, elementary calculus, matrix theory, four-dimensional . . . come back here! It will not be as difficult as you might think. If anything, the sheer volume of C++ source code will prove to be more of challenge. Implementing a functional radiosity-based renderer is no easy task, as the length of this book attests. Besides, all of the key mathematical concepts and terminology are explained in strategically positioned text boxes.

The radiosity approach is firmly based on simple geometrical concepts that can be explained without the aid of mathematics. The mathematics are included because we have to explain these simple concepts to some very stupid acquaintances: our computers. Read the text first so that you understand the principles involved. The reasoning behind the mathematics should readily follow.

Enough, however, of generalities; it is time to begin.

REFERENCES

Arvo, J., ed. 1991. *Graphics Gems II*. San Diego, CA: Academic Press.

Chen, S. E. 1991. "Implementing Progressive Radiosity with User-Provided Polygon Display Routines," in Arvo (1991), pp. 295–298, 583–597.

Goral, C. M., K. E. Torrance, D. P. Greenberg, and B. Battaile. 1984. "Modeling the Interaction of Light between Diffuse Surfaces," *Computer Graphics* 18:(3):213–222 (ACM SIGGRAPH '84 Proc.).

Lindley, C. A. 1992. *Practical Ray Tracing in C*. New York: John Wiley.

Newmann, W. M., and R. F. Sproull. 1979. *Principles of Interactive Computer Graphics*, 2nd ed. New York: McGraw-Hill.

Wells, D., and C. Young. 1993. *Ray Tracing Creations*. Corte Madera, CA: Waite Group Press.

Whitted, T. 1980. "An Improved Illumination Model for Shaded Display," *Communications of the ACM* 23(6): 343–349.

RADIOSITY MODELS LIGHT

Here there be dragons. Beware!

Radiosity models light. To appreciate fully the significance of this contention, we first need to understand what light is and how it is measured. Chapter 1 examines the concepts of radiometry and photometry, with a brief excursion into radiometric field theory. These concepts provide a foundation for Chapter 2, which explains radiosity in terms of the geometrical nature of light.

For some readers, there may indeed be dragons here. Differential equations, area integrals, and other topics from college-level mathematics are not everyday fare for most programmers. Fear not, however. The accompanying text boxes tame them with high school algebra and trigonometry.

CHAPTER 1

Measuring Light

light, n. **1.** The natural agent that stimulates the sense of light. **2.**
Medium or condition of space in which sight is possible.

The Concise Oxford English Dictionary
Fifth edition, 1964

1.0   INTRODUCTION

There have been many theories concerning the nature of light. Aristotle (384–322 B.C.)
believed that light consisted of "corpuscles" that emanated from the eye to illuminate
the world. Today we favor the theory of quantum mechanics (e.g., Hecht and Zajac
1987) or perhaps the possibility that light may be vibrations in the fifth dimension of
ten-dimensional hyperspace (e.g., Kaku 1994). Even so, the true nature of light remains
a mystery. It is perhaps appropriate that the preeminent dictionary of the English language describes light so loosely: "the natural agent that stimulates the sense of sight."

Whatever it may be, our interest in light is much more parochial. We simply
want to model what we see and perceive. Whereas we may think in terms of objects,
what we see is light. Ray-tracing models objects; radiosity models light. The distinc-
tion is subtle but important. If we are to understand radiosity, we must first understand the basics. What is light, and how do we measure it?

The material in this chapter is somewhat removed from the computer graphics main-
stream. Nevertheless, it is vitally important to understand what it is we are trying to
model. The key concepts in radiosity are *radiant exitance* (also known as *radiosity*) and
luminance. Unfortunately, these concepts must be carefully described in fairly rigorous
terms. So, grab a cup of coffee or another mental stimulant and we can begin.

1.1   WHAT IS LIGHT?

Light is *electromagnetic radiation*. What we see as visible light is only a tiny fraction of the electromagnetic spectrum, extending from very-low-frequency radio waves through microwaves, infrared, visible, and ultraviolet light to x-rays and ultraenergetic gamma rays. Our eyes respond to visible light; detecting the rest of the spectrum requires an arsenal of scientific instruments ranging from radio receivers to scintillation counters.

A rigorous and exact description of electromagnetic radiation and its behavior requires a thorough knowledge of quantum electrodynamics and Maxwell's electromagnetic field equations. Similarly, a complete understanding of how we perceive the light our eyes see delves deeply into the physiology and psychology of the human visual system. There is an enormous body of literature related to the physical aspects of light as electromagnetic radiation (e.g., Hecht and Zajac 1987) and an equally enormous amount devoted to how we perceive it (e.g., Cornsweet 1977). Fortunately, our interests are extremely modest. We simply want to measure what we see and perceive.

1.2   RADIOMETRY

Radiometry is the science of measuring light in any portion of the electromagnetic spectrum. In practice, the term is usually limited to the measurement of infrared, visible, and ultraviolet light using optical instruments.

There are two aspects of radiometry: theory and practice. The practice involves the scientific instruments and materials used in measuring light, including radiation thermocouples, bolometers, photodiodes, photosensitive dyes and emulsions, vacuum phototubes, charge-coupled devices, and a plethora of others. What we are interested in, however, is the theory.

Radiometric theory is such a simple topic that most texts on physics and optics discuss it in a few paragraphs. Unfortunately, a certain historical bias has left us with a theory that is conceptually simple but sometimes difficult to understand. In essence, the problem is one of separating light from objects. To appreciate this bias, we first need to review the fundamental radiometric concepts.

1.2.1   Radiant Energy

Light is *radiant energy*. Electromagnetic radiation (which can be considered both a wave and a particle, depending on how you measure it) transports energy through space. When light is absorbed by a physical object, its energy is converted into some other form. A microwave oven, for example, heats a glass of water when its microwave radiation is absorbed by the water molecules. The radiant energy of the microwaves is converted into thermal energy (heat). Similarly, visible light causes an electric current to flow in a photographic light meter when its radiant energy is transferred to the electrons as kinetic energy.

Radiant energy is measured in joules.

1.2.2 Radiant Flux (Radiant Power)

Energy per unit time is power, which we measure in joules per second, or watts. A laser beam, for example, has so many milliwatts or watts of *radiant power*. Light "flows" through space, and so radiant power is more commonly referred to as the "time rate of flow of radiant energy," or *radiant flux*. It is defined as:

$$\Phi = dQ/dt \tag{1.1}$$

where Q is radiant energy and t is time.

> If your background doesn't include college-level calculus, think of the above *differential equation* as follows. You might walk m meters in t minutes. The velocity v at which you walk may vary, but your average velocity v_{avg} is the distance m divided by the time t, or:
>
> $$v_{avg} = m/t$$
>
> In each minute, you may walk Δm meters, where Δm varies from minute to minute. Your average velocity for each minute is given by:
>
> $$v_{avg} = \Delta m/\Delta t$$
>
> where Δt is the interval of time over which Δm is measured. We can clearly shorten the interval of time (seconds, milliseconds, etc.) until it is infinitesimally small. The distance traveled is then infinitesimally short. If we denote the time interval as dt (indicating a *differential* interval of time) and the distance as dm, we have the *instantaneous* velocity v:
>
> $$v = dm/dt$$
>
> Looking again at Equation 1.1, we see that the radiant energy Q is the total "amount of work done" (the definition of energy). The radiant flux Φ is the infinitesimal amount of work done (dQ) in a differential amount of time (dt).

In terms of a photographic light meter measuring visible light, the instantaneous magnitude of the electric current is directly proportional to the radiant flux. The total amount of current measured over a period of time is directly proportional to the radiant energy absorbed by the light meter during that time. This is how a photographic flash meter works—it measures the total amount of radiant energy received from a camera flash.

The flow of light through space is often represented by geometrical rays of light such as those used in computer graphics ray tracing. They can be thought of as infinitesimally thin lines drawn through space that indicate the direction of flow of radiant energy (light). They are also mathematical abstractions—even the thinnest laser beam has a finite cross section. Nonetheless, they provide a useful aid to understanding radiometric theory.

1.2.3 Radiant Flux Density (Irradiance and Radiant Exitance)

Radiant flux density is the radiant flux per unit area at a point on a surface, where the surface can be real or imaginary (i.e., a mathematical plane). There are two possible conditions. The flux can be arriving at the surface (Fig. 1.1a), in which case the radiant flux density is referred to as *irradiance*. The flux can arrive from any direction above the surface, as indicated by the rays. Irradiance is defined as:

$$E = d\Phi/dA \qquad\qquad (1.2)$$

where Φ is the radiant flux arriving at the point and dA is the differential area surrounding the point.

The flux can also be leaving the surface due to emission and/or reflection (Fig. 1.1b). The radiant flux density is then referred to as *radiant exitance*. As with irradiance, the flux can leave in any direction above the surface. The definition of radiant exitance is:

$$M = d\Phi/dA \qquad\qquad (1.3)$$

where Φ is the radiant flux leaving the point and dA is the differential area surrounding the point.

The importance of a "real or imaginary" cannot be overstated. It means that radiant flux density can be measured anywhere in three-dimensional space. This includes on the surface of physical objects, in the space between them (e.g., in air or a vacuum), and inside transparent media such as water and glass.

Radiant flux density is measured in watts per square meter.

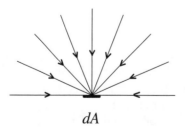

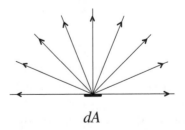

dA dA

Figure 1.1a Irradiance   **Figure 1.1b** Radiant exitance

1.2.4   Radiance

Radiance is best understood by first visualizing it. Imagine a ray of light arriving at or leaving a point on a surface in a given direction. Radiance is simply the infinitesimal amount of radiant flux contained in this ray. Period.

A more formal definition of radiance requires that we think of the ray as being an infinitesimally narrow ("elemental") cone with its apex at a point on a real or imaginary surface. This cone has a differential solid angle $d\omega$ that is measured in steradians.

A *solid angle* is the three-dimensional analog of a two-dimensional angle. Figure 1.2a shows two lines radiating from the center of a circle of radius r. The angle θ between the lines can be measured in terms of the length of the chord c between them. If $c = r$, then the angle is one *radian*. The circumference of a circle is $2\pi r$; therefore, there are 2π radians in a circle.

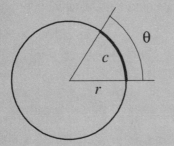   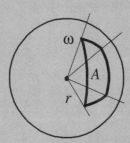

Figure 1.2a   Two-dimensional angle   **Figure 1.2b**   Three-dimensional solid angle

Similarly, Figure 1.2b shows a cone radiating from the center of a sphere of radius r. The solid angle ω of the cone (which can have any cross-sectional shape) can be measured in terms of the surface area A of the sphere it intersects as $\omega = A/r^2$. If $A = r^2$, then the solid angle is one *steradian*. The area of a sphere is $4\pi r^2$; therefore, there are 4π steradians in a sphere.

We must also note that the ray is intersecting the surface at an angle. If the area of intersection with the surface has a differential cross-sectional area dA, the cross-sectional area of the ray is $dA\cos\theta$, where θ is the angle between the ray and the surface normal, as shown in Figure 1.3. (The ray cross-sectional area $dA\cos\theta$ is called the *projected area* of the ray-surface intersection area dA. The same term is used when referring to finite areas ΔA.)

With these preliminaries in mind, we can imagine an elemental cone $d\omega$ containing a ray of light that is arriving at or leaving a surface (Figs. 1.4a and 1.4b). The definition of radiance is then:

$$L = d^2\Phi / \left[dA(d\omega \cos\theta) \right] \tag{1.4}$$

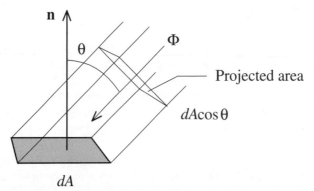

Figure 1.3 A ray of light intersecting a surface

where Φ is the radiant flux, dA is the differential area surrounding the point, $d\omega$ is the differential solid angle of the elemental cone, and θ is the angle between the ray and the surface normal **n** at the point.

The superscript "2" in Equation 1.4 does not mean that anything is being squared. Rather, it indicates that the infinitesimal amount of flux $d\Phi$ is divided by the differential area dA *and* the differential solid angle $d\omega$.

Unlike radiant flux density, the definition of radiance does not distinguish between flux arriving at or leaving the surface. In fact, the formal definition of radiance (ANSI/IES 1986) states that it can be "leaving, passing through or arriving at" the surface.

Another way of looking at radiance is to note that the radiant flux density at a point on a surface due to a single ray of light arriving (or leaving) at an angle θ to the surface normal is $d\Phi/(dA\cos\theta)$. The radiance at that point for the same angle is then $d^2\Phi/[d\omega(dA\cos\theta)]$, or radiant flux density per unit solid angle.

Radiance is measured in watts per square meter per steradian.

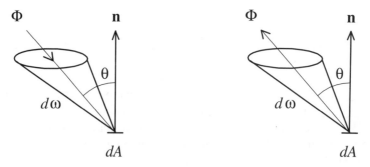

Figure 1.4a Radiance (arriving)   **Figure 1.4b** Radiance (leaving)

1.2.5   Radiant Intensity

We can imagine an infinitesimally small *point source* of light that emits radiant flux in every direction. The amount of radiant flux emitted in a given direction can be represented by a ray of light contained in an elemental cone. This gives us the definition of *radiant intensity*:

$$I = d\Phi/d\omega \tag{1.5}$$

where $d\omega$ is the differential solid angle of the elemental cone containing the given direction. From the definition of a differential solid angle ($d\omega = dA/r^2$), we get:

$$E = d\Phi/dA = d\Phi/r^2 \, d\omega = I/r^2 \tag{1.6}$$

where the differential surface area dA is on the surface of a sphere centered on and at a distance r from the source and E is the irradiance at that surface. More generally, the radiant flux will intercept dA at an angle θ (Fig. 1.5). This gives us the *inverse square law* for point sources:

$$E = I \cos\theta/d^2 \tag{1.7}$$

where I is the intensity of the source in the given direction and d is the distance from the source to the surface element dA.

We can further imagine a real or imaginary surface as being a continuum of point sources, where each source occupies a differential area dA (Fig. 1.6). Viewed at an angle θ from the surface normal **n**, the source has a projected area of $dA\cos\theta$. Combining the definitions of radiance (Eq. 1.4) and radiant intensity (Eq. 1.5) gives us an alternative definition of radiance:

$$L = dI/(dA \cos\theta) \tag{1.8}$$

where dI is the differential intensity of the point source in the given direction.

Radiant intensity is measured in watts per steradian.

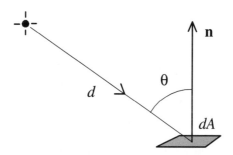

Figure 1.5 Inverse square law for point sources

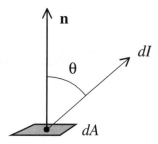

Figure 1.6 Radiance of a point source

1.3   ILLUMINATION VERSUS THERMAL ENGINEERING

The definitions just given are those commonly used in illumination engineering and are in accordance with the American National Standard Institute publication *Nomenclature and Definitions for Illuminating Engineering* (ANSI/IES 1986). Unfortunately, these definitions differ somewhat from those used in thermal engineering (e.g., Siegel and Howell 1981). Radiative heat-transfer theory (i.e., infrared light) does not use the point source concept. Thermal engineers instead use the term "radiant intensity " to describe *radiance* (watts per unit area per unit solid angle).

The different terminology was of little consequence until the computer graphics community adapted the concepts of radiative heat transfer to create radiosity theory. In the process of doing so it adopted thermal engineering's terminology. This is an unfortunate situation, because computer graphics also relies on the point source concept for ray tracing.

This book defines *radiant intensity* as "watts per unit solid angle" and *radiance* as "watts per unit area per unit solid angle" to maintain consistency between radiosity and ray-tracing theory. Note, however, that many papers and texts on radiosity theory and some computer graphics texts define "radiant intensity" as "watts per unit area per unit solid angle."

1.4   PHOTOMETRY

Photometry is the science of measuring visible light in units that are weighted according to the sensitivity of the human eye. It is a quantitative science based on a statistical model of the human visual response to light—that is, our *perception* of light—under carefully controlled conditions.

The human visual system is a marvelously complex and highly nonlinear detector of electromagnetic radiation with wavelengths ranging from about 380 to 770 nanometers (nm). We see light of different wavelengths as a continuum of colors ranging through the visible spectrum: 650 nm is red, 540 nm is green, 450 nm is blue, and so on.

The sensitivity of the human eye to light varies with wavelength. A light source with a radiance of one watt/m²-steradian of green light, for example, appears much brighter than the same source with a radiance of one watt/m²-steradian of red or blue light. In photometry, we do not measure watts of radiant energy. Rather, we attempt to measure the subjective impression produced by stimulating the human eye–brain visual system with radiant energy.

This task is complicated immensely by the eye's nonlinear response to light. It varies not only with wavelength but also with the amount of radiant flux, whether the light is constant or flickering, the spatial complexity of the scene being perceived, the adaptation of the iris and retina, the psychological and physiological state of the observer, and a host of other variables.

Nevertheless, the subjective impression of seeing can be quantified for "normal" viewing conditions. In 1924, the *Commission Internationale d'Eclairage* (International Commission on Illumination, or CIE) asked over one hundred observers to visually match the "brightness" of monochromatic light sources with different wavelengths under controlled conditions. The statistical result—the so-called CIE photometric curve shown in Figure 1.7—shows the *photopic luminous efficiency* of the human visual system as a function of wavelength. It provides a weighting function that can be used to convert radiometric into photometric measurements.

Photometric theory does not address how we perceive colors. The light being measured can be monochromatic or a combination or continuum of wavelengths; the eye's response is determined by the CIE weighting function. This underlines a crucial point: *The only difference between radiometric and photometric theory is in their units of measurement*. With this thought firmly in mind, we can quickly review the fundamental concepts of photometry.

1.4.1 Luminous Intensity

The foundations of photometry were laid in 1729 by Pierre Bouguer. In his "L'Essai d'Optique," Bouguer discussed photometric principles in terms of the convenient

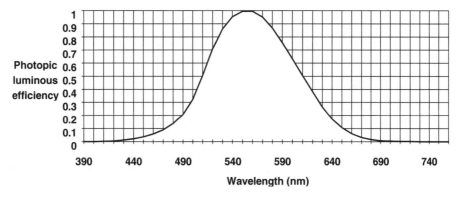

Figure 1.7 CIE photometric curve

light source of his time: a wax candle. This became the basis of the point source concept in photometric theory.

Wax candles were used as national light source standards in the 18th and 19th centuries. England, for example, used spermaceti (a wax derived from sperm whale oil). These were replaced in 1909 by an international standard based on a group of carbon filament vacuum lamps and again in 1948 by a crucible containing liquid platinum at its freezing point. Today the international standard is a theoretical point source that has a *luminous intensity* of one *candela* (the Latin word for "candle"). It emits monochromatic radiation with a frequency of 540×10^{12} Hertz (or approximately 555 nm, corresponding with the wavelength of maximum photopic luminous efficiency) and has a radiant intensity (in the direction of measurement) of 1/683 watts per steradian.

Together with the CIE photometric curve, the candela provides the weighting factor needed to convert between radiometric and photometric measurements. Consider, for example, a monochromatic point source with a wavelength of 510 nm and a radiant intensity of 1/683 watts per steradian. The photopic luminous efficiency at 510 nm is 0.503. The source therefore has a luminous intensity of 0.503 candela.

1.4.2   Luminous Flux (Luminous Power)

Luminous flux is photometrically weighted radiant flux (power). Its unit of measurement is the *lumen*, defined as 1/683 watts of radiant power at a frequency of 540×10^{12} Hertz. As with luminous intensity, the luminous flux of light with other wavelengths can be calculated using the CIE photometric curve.

A point source having a uniform (isotopic) luminous intensity of one candela in all directions (i.e., a uniform *intensity distribution*) emits one lumen of luminous flux per unit solid angle (steradian).

1.4.3   Luminous Energy

Luminous energy is photometrically weighted radiant energy. It is measured in lumen seconds.

1.4.4   Luminous Flux Density (Illuminance and Luminous Exitance)

Luminous flux density is photometrically weighted radiant flux density. *Illuminance* is the photometric equivalent of irradiance, whereas *luminous exitance* is the photometric equivalent of radiant exitance.

Luminous flux density is measured in lumens per square meter.

1.4.5 Luminance

Luminance is photometrically weighted radiance. In terms of visual perception, we perceive luminance. It is an approximate measure of how "bright" a surface appears when we view it from a given direction. Luminance used to be called photometric brightness. This term is no longer used in illumination engineering because the subjective sensation of visual brightness is influenced by many other physical, physiological, and psychological factors.

Luminance is measured in lumens per square meter per steradian.

1.5 LAMBERTIAN SURFACES

A *Lambertian surface* is a surface that has a constant radiance or luminance that is independent of the viewing direction. In accordance with the definition of radiance (luminance), the radiant (luminous) flux may be emitted, transmitted, and/or reflected by the surface.

A Lambertian surface is also referred to as an *ideal diffuse* emitter or reflector. In practice there are no true Lambertian surfaces. Most matte surfaces approximate an ideal diffuse reflector but typically exhibit semispecular reflection characteristics at oblique viewing angles. Nevertheless, the Lambertian surface concept will prove useful in our development of radiosity theory.

Lambertian surfaces are unique in that they reflect incident flux in a completely diffuse manner (Fig. 1.8). It does not matter what the angle of incidence θ of an incoming geometrical ray is—the distribution of light leaving the surface remains unchanged.

We can imagine a differential area dA of a Lambertian surface. Being infinitesimally small, it is equivalent to a point source, and so the flux leaving the surface can

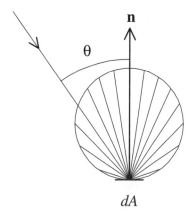

Figure 1.8   Reflection from a Lambertian surface

be modeled as geometrical rays. The intensity I_θ of each ray leaving the surface at an angle θ from the surface normal is given by *Lambert's cosine law*:

$$I_\theta = I_n \cos \theta \tag{1.9}$$

where I_n is the intensity of the ray leaving in a direction perpendicular to the surface.

The derivation of Equation 1.9 becomes clear when we remember that we are viewing dA from an angle θ. For a differential area dA with a constant radiance or luminance, its intensity must vary in accordance with its projected area, which is $dA\cos\theta$. This give us:

$$L = dI/(dA \cos \theta) = dI_n/dA \tag{1.10}$$

for any Lambertian surface.

There is a very simple relation between radiant (luminous) exitance and radiance (luminance) for flux leaving a Lambertian surface:

$$M = \pi L \tag{1.11}$$

where the factor of π is a source of endless confusion to students of radiometry and photometry. Fortunately, there is an intuitive explanation. Suppose we place a differential Lambertian emitter dA on the inside surface of an imaginary sphere S (Fig. 1.9). The inverse square law (Eq. 1.6) provides the irradiance E at any point P on the inside surface of the sphere. However, $d = D\cos\theta$, where D is the diameter of the sphere. Thus:

$$E = I_\theta \cos \theta/(D \cos \theta)^2 = I_\theta/D^2 \cos \theta \tag{1.12}$$

and from Lambert's cosine law (Eq. 1.9), we have:

$$E = I_N \cos \theta/D^2 \cos \theta = I_n/D^2 \tag{1.13}$$

which simply says that the irradiance (radiant flux density) of any point P on the inside surface of S is a constant.

This is interesting. From the definition of irradiance (Eq. 1.2), we know that $\Phi = EA$ for constant flux density across a finite surface area A. Since the area A of the surface of a sphere with radius r is given by:

$$A = 4\pi r^2 = \pi D^2 \tag{1.14}$$

we have:

$$\Phi = EA = \pi I_n D^2/D^2 = \pi I_n \tag{1.15}$$

Given the definitions of radiant exitance (Eq. 1.3) and radiance for a Lambertian surface (Eq. 1.10), we have:

$$M = d\Phi/dA = \pi dI_n/dA = \pi L \tag{1.16}$$

This explains, clearly and without resorting to integral calculus, where the factor of π comes from.

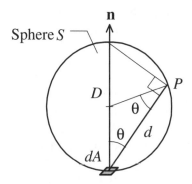

Figure 1.9 A Lambertian emitter illuminating the interior of a sphere

1.7 VOLUME LIGHT SOURCES

We see light only through its effects on physical objects. In looking at the world, we "see" physical objects. More precisely, we perceive the luminance of their surfaces. Bouguer and other early investigators made this apparent truism an integral part of photometric theory by defining illuminance, luminous exitance, and luminance in terms of physical surfaces.

Physicists later became interested in other aspects of light, including that emitted by plasmas. What is the luminous exitance or luminance of an electric arc? The glowing gas has no definable surface! The same goes for the sky overhead, where the blue light we see is due to sunlight scattered by air and dust molecules from the ground to the outer reaches of the atmosphere. These are clearly *volume* sources of light. The definitions of luminous flux density and luminance do not seem to apply.

This problem was overcome by introducing the concept of an imaginary surface, a mathematical plane drawn in space. It can be positioned and oriented in three-dimensional space as required, including inside a volume light source. The traditional photometric definitions were thus retained intact.

The question is, why? Photometric and radiometric theory does not address the properties of any surface, real or imaginary. Is it necessary to consider surfaces at all? The answer is simple and unequivocal: no.

1.8 RADIOMETRIC FIELD THEORY

Field theory is one of the most powerful mathematical methods used in physics today. At the time of its development, however, most of our present-day radiometric and photometric theory was already firmly established. Based mainly on the work of Johann Heinrich Lambert (1760) and geometrical optics, radiometry and photometry make no use of field theory.

Mehmke (1898) was the first to suggest that field theory might have applications in illumination engineering. His suggestion was later developed into a formal theoretical framework for radiometric field theory by Yamauti (1932) and Gershun (1936). Moon and Spencer continued to develop this theory for another forty-odd years, culminating in their publication of *The Photic Field* (1981).

Radiometric field theory does not address light coming from point sources. Rather, it considers a *field of light* that permeates three-dimensional space. Yamauti and Gershun referred to this field as a "light field," whereas Moon and Spencer (1981) called it a "photic" field. Photic fields are rigorously described by Maxwell's electromagnetic field equations for the special case of zero wavelength (Moon and Spencer (1981). They are also five-dimensional scalar fields, where scalar measurements (irradiance and radiance) are made in five dimensions: three axes for position (x, y, and z) and two axes for orientation (vertical and horizontal).

As you might have guessed, the full mathematical details of radiometric field theory are complex and abstract. This complexity has made it more of a curiosity than a useful tool for everyday illumination engineering. Very few illumination engineers are even aware of its existence.

Nevertheless, radiometric field theory has something to offer: a different view of radiometry and photometry. This becomes evident when we reconsider radiometry (and by extension photometry) from first principles.

1.9   RADIOMETRY RECONSIDERED

The validity of radiant energy and radiant flux is self-evident because they do not refer to surfaces. Electromagnetic radiation transports energy through space. We can therefore imagine a field of light—a photic field—in three-dimensional space, with geometrical rays indicating its direction of flow.

We can monitor this flow with an instrument that detects the radiant flux incident on a small surface area (its "active surface"). The flux is converted into an electric current I that we can measure with an ammeter M (Fig. 1.10). By dividing the measured flux by the surface area, we can calculate the average irradiance at the surface.

Our instrument can be placed anywhere in space; the amount of radiant flux it measures clearly depends on its position and orientation. If we make the active surface area infinitesimally small, we can in theory measure irradiance at a mathematical point.

The radiant flux must come from physical objects, either directly from emissive sources or indirectly through reflection, refraction, diffraction, or scattering. Remember, however, that we are measuring *light*; where it comes from is immaterial. We are interested only in measuring radiant flux and irradiance at a point in space.

In measuring irradiance, our instrument "sees" an entire hemisphere of space. That is, it is sensitive to rays of light arriving from any direction above the surface of the imaginary plane defined by the position and orientation of the instrument's active surface. However, we are measuring irradiance as a property of a photic field. We do not need to relate this measurement to any surface, real or imaginary.

This is a subtle but very important point. Radiometric field theory does not

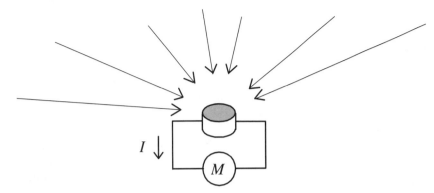

Figure 1.10   An irradiance meter

change the definition of radiant flux density (irradiance and radiant exitance). Instead, it changes the way we interpret it. Radiant flux density is an intrinsic property of a photic field. Its relation to any physical surface is almost coincidental. We should therefore refer to irradiance or radiant exitance *at* a surface rather than *of* a surface.

1.10   RADIANCE REDEFINED

This interpretation of radiant flux density can be extended to the definition of radiance with interesting results. Suppose we use an opaque shield (oriented perpendicular to the active surface) to restrict our irradiance meter's field of view to a finite solid angle ω (Fig. 1.11). It then measures the average radiance at the active surface for the directions contained within the field of view.

By using a differential solid angle $d\omega$ and a differential active surface area dA, we can in theory measure the radiance at a mathematical point for radiant flux arriving from directly above the surface. Since the solid angle $d\omega$ defines a geometrical ray of light that is perpendicular to the active surface, the area dA coincides with the differential cross-sectional area of the ray. In other words, our instrument measures the radiance of a ray of light at a point in space. The interpretation is clear: Radiance is an intrinsic property of a geometrical ray of light. It is not a property of any surface, real or imaginary.

Radiometric field theory simplifies the definition of radiance. It becomes:

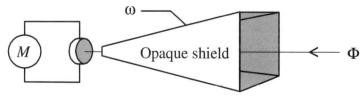

Figure 1.11   A radiance meter

1.10.1 Radiance (of a Geometrical Ray)

The radiance of a geometrical ray at a point in space is defined as:

$$L = d^2\Phi/dAd\omega \tag{1.17}$$

where Φ is the radiant flux of the ray at the point, dA is the differential cross-sectional area *of the ray,* and $d\omega$ is the differential solid angle of an elemental cone containing the ray.

Moon (1942) referred to this definition of radiance as *helios.* However, it is merely a special case of the more general definition of radiance (Eq. 1.4). In particular, it considers only radiant flux arriving at a point, and it has an implicit divisor of $\cos\theta$ (where the angle θ is zero).

To answer the obvious question, the name of the radiosity-rendering program presented in this book—*HELIOS*—is in honor of the pioneering work done by Moon and Spencer in the fields of photometry and radiometry.

1.11   FIELD THEORY AND RADIOSITY

If nothing else, radiometric field theory clearly demonstrates the following axiom:

> *Radiometry and photometry measure intrinsic properties of a field of light in space. These measurements are independent of any surface, real or imaginary.*

There is an interesting corollary to this axiom: *radiometric and photometric theory does not require a point source.* This was implicitly demonstrated in the order of presentation of the radiometric definitions, where radiant intensity was presented almost as an afterthought. Without a point source, we would not need to define radiant intensity at all.

The photometric definitions began with luminous intensity only because photometric theory defines the candela as a basic unit of measurement and derives the definition of lumens from it. This is a historical artifact from the time of Pierre Bouguer and his wax candles. (We still draw point sources as a candle with geometrical rays radiating from the flame!) The lumen can be defined from first principles without resorting to point sources; the candela is just another name for lumens per steradian.

The inconsequential nature of the point source is important for two reasons. First, there are no point sources in nature. Even the distant stars have a finite width that can be measured if the telescope aperture is large enough. We will see in Chapter 2 that radiosity theory does not require a point source. In this sense, radiometric field theory provides a clearer understanding of radiosity.

Second, point sources are objects. Ray-tracing techniques rely on point sources as the ultimate source of radiant flux within an environment. The illuminance at a surface due to a point source can be determined using Lambert's inverse square law, but only if we know the exact distance from the surface to the source. This is simple enough for single point sources, but it becomes difficult for extended line and area sources and intractable for volume sources if they are modeled as an array or continuum of point sources.

The radiosity approach emphasizes light over objects. As we shall see in the next chapter, the geometrical relations between objects in an environment are required only to determine their mutual "form factors." Radiosity then models the photic field within the environment with no further reference to these objects. This is the proof of our contention: Radiosity models light.

1.12 WHAT IS RADIOSITY?

ANSI/IES (1986) does not define or even mention the term "radiosity." This is not unusual—there are many photometric and radiometric terms whose use is no longer encouraged. "Illuminance", for example, used to be called "illumination." It was changed to "illuminance" to avoid confusion with "the act of illuminating or the state of being illuminated" (ANSI/IES 1986).

When Moon wrote *The Scientific Basis of Illumination Engineering* in 1936, luminous exitance was called luminosity. Curiously, there was no equivalent term for "radiant exitance," so he coined the term "radiosity" to describe the density of radiant flux leaving a surface.

The illumination engineering community ignored Moon's proposal. Luminosity was changed to "luminous emittance" and later to "luminous exitance," with "radiant exitance" following as a consequent. Meanwhile, the thermal engineering community adopted "radiosity" (e.g., Siegel and Howell 1981).

It's all very confusing. Fortunately, we only need to remember that:

> *Radiosity* is *radiant exitance.*

This book takes exception, perhaps unwisely, to the computer graphics community's use of the term "radiosity" to describe *radiant exitance*. Whereas it is an accepted term within the thermal engineering community, it is not acceptable to illumination engineers for a variety of historical reasons. The computer graphics and illumination engineering communities have many common interests. If we are to communicate effectively, we must use a common lexicon of definitions. That lexicon is ANSI/IES (1986).

1.13 MEASURING AND PERCEIVING COLOR

An irradiance or radiance meter is carefully designed to respond equally to light of any wavelength within the visible spectrum. As such, the meter measures radiant flux, regardless of whether we are measuring sunlight, monochromatic laser radiation, or any other source of visible light.

Suppose that we are using a radiance meter to measure sunlight reflected from a surface, where the radiant flux consists of a continuum of wavelengths across the visible spectrum (e.g., Fig. 1.12). We can filter this light such that it has a very narrow band width. For example, we can use a "multilayer interference" filter that is only transparent to light with wavelengths between 632 nm and 633 nm. If we could make the filter band width infinitesimally narrow (a physical impossibility), we could measure *spectral radiance*, which is expressed in watts per square meter per steradian per nanometer (ANSI/IES 1986). Following Equation 1.4, we see that *spectral radiance* is expressed mathematically as:

$$L_\lambda = d^3\Phi \big/ \left[dA (d\omega \cos\theta) d\lambda \right] \qquad\qquad (1.18)$$

where λ is the wavelength. (On second thought, it might be better to remember the concept rather than the equation!)

The sum of spectral radiance for each infinitesimally narrow band across the visible spectrum is, of course, equal to the radiance we would measure without a filter. In practice, we can divide the spectrum into bands of finite width and achieve approximately the same result. Suppose we measure average spectral radiance through red, green, and blue filters, where each filter is almost transparent within its band width and the amount of overlap between the color bands is minimized. The sum of these averages will closely approximate the measured radiance.

In measuring the distribution of spectral radiance across the visible spectrum, we are measuring the physical "color" of the radiant flux. The relative amounts of spectral radiance determine what we perceive as the color of the surface. Red, for example, indicates a preponderance of spectral radiance at wavelengths between 580 nm and 700 nm, whereas blue indicates a preponderance of spectral radiance between 400 nm and 480 nm. According to Figure 1.12, our surface will appear to be distinctly reddish.

Measuring the color of radiant flux is a relatively straightforward task. However, it is often difficult to determine what our *perception* of the color will be. As

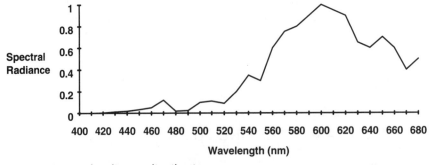

Figure 1.12   Spectral radiance distribution

with photometric quantities, our response to spectral radiance distribution (color) depends on a host of physical and psychological variables. The subjective impression of color perception can be quantified (in a statistical sense) only for carefully controlled "normal" viewing conditions.

A full discussion of how we perceive color requires at least a book in itself (e.g., Judd and Wyszecki 1975 or Burnham et al. 1963). For the purposes of photorealism, however, our viewing environment is somewhat controlled—typically a color monitor, a photographic print, or a color transparency. Foley et al. (1990), Hill (1990), Watt (1990), and other tutorial and reference texts offer informative overviews of color theory for the computer graphics enthusiast. Perhaps the best reference on the subject, however, is Hall (1989).

You might question the brevity of this discussion on color theory, especially since this book is devoted to the subject of photorealistic images. If so, you are absolutely correct. Unfortunately, the topic of radiosity and its implementation fills a book in itself. As interesting and important as the topic of color theory is, there is simply no space here to discuss it in any greater depth.

1.14 SPECTRAL RADIANT EXITANCE

Given the definition of spectral radiance, we can compare it with the definition of radiant exitance and derive the definition of *spectral radiant exitance* as:

$$M_\lambda = d^2\Phi/(dAd\lambda) \tag{1.19}$$

which is measured in watts per square meter per nanometer.

This is one of the two key concepts in radiosity theory (the other is luminance). More specifically, it is the concept of an *average* spectral radiant exitance that is measured through a red, green, or blue filter. The importance of these concepts will become evident in the next chapter.

We can remember this concept in a colloquial sense: The average spectral radiant exitance of a real or imaginary surface is simply the amount of radiant flux—visible light—per square meter leaving the surface, where the light is within a given band of colors (e.g., red, green, or blue).

1.15 REFLECTANCE AND TRANSMITTANCE

Having seen that radiometric and photometric quantities are intrinsic properties of a field of light in space, we must remind ourselves that:

Reflectance and transmittance are intrinsic properties of physical objects. They are independent of any surrounding field of light.

In the simplest case, we have opaque objects with ideal diffuse or ideal specular surfaces. Here, reflectance is a dimensionless number that indicates the percentage of incident radiant flux reflected from each surface.

The reflectance of any given surface typically varies with wavelength. Thus, we can refer to inherent *spectral reflectance* as the reflectance of a surface within an infinitesimally narrow band of wavelengths. We can further refer to the spectral reflectance distribution as the "color" of the surface. Defined in this manner, color is an intrinsic property of physical surfaces that is independent of any surrounding field of light. We know from experience that the *perceived* color of an object can vary, depending on the spectral irradiance distribution of the light illuminating it. For example, an object that appears blue in sunlight will be jet black when viewed under a monochromatic red light. This, however, is a consequence of the surrounding photic field, not the object itself.

There is more to reflectance than this, of course. In general, the reflectance of an opaque object with semispecular surfaces is a function of the angle of incidence of the illuminating flux and the viewing angle. This must be expressed as a multidimensional *bidirectional reflectance distribution function*, or BRDF.

Transparent and translucent objects complicate matters even further, especially when the objects are inhomogeneous. We can easily measure and express the transmittance of an ideal transparent object with specular surfaces. For ideal transparent objects with semispecular surfaces, we can express transmittance as a multidimensional *bidirectional transmittance distribution function* (BTDF). In real life, the problem becomes more intractable. Reflection, refraction, diffraction, scattering, and polarization effects all contribute to the distribution of radiant flux within and through transparent and translucent objects. Accurately modeling these effects typically requires a physically accurate model of the object being illuminated.

We shall find in the Chapter 2, however, that the radiosity approach is best suited to modeling environments with opaque and ideally diffuse surfaces. Thus, although we should be aware of the reflectance and transmittance of physical objects, we can consider reflectance in its simplest form: the percentage of (spectral) radiant flux reflected from an ideal diffuse surface.

1.15 CONCLUSIONS

The material in this chapter is unquestionably tedious reading for someone interested solely in computer programming. Clearly though, the fundamental definitions of radiometry and photometry are prerequisites to a full understanding of radiosity theory.

The very brief introduction to radiometric field theory is recommended reading. Defining radiometric and photometric theory in terms of a photic field is more than mere semantic juggling; it offers a new paradigm for lighting research and radiosity studies. More important, it clarifies the contention that radiosity models light.

REFERENCES

ANSI/IES. 1986. *Nomenclature and Definitions for Illuminating Engineering*, ANSI/IES RP-16-1986. New York: Illuminating Engineering Society of North America

Bouguer, P. 1729. *L'Essai d'Optique*. Paris.

Burnham, R. W., R. M. Hanes, and C. J. Bartleson 1963. *Color: A Guide to Basic Facts and Concepts*. New York: John Wiley & Sons, Inc.

Cornsweet, T. N. 1977. *Visual Perception*. New York: Academic Press.

Foley, J. D., A. van Dam, S. K. Feiner, and J. F. Hughes. 1990. *Computer Graphics: Principles and Practice* (2nd ed.). Reading, MA: Addison-Wesley.

Gershun, A. 1936. *Svetovoe Pole* (The Light Field), Moscow. P. Moon and G. Timoshenko, trans., in *Journal of Mathematics and Physics* (Massachusetts Institute of Technology). XVIII (1939):51–151.

Hall, R. 1989. *Illumination and Color in Computer Generated Imagery*. New York: Springer-Verlag.

Hecht, E., and A. Zajac. 1987. *Optics* (2nd ed.) Reading, MA: Addison-Wesley.

Hill, F. S., Jr. 1990. *Computer Graphics*. New York: Macmillan.

Judd, D., and G. Wyszecki. 1975. *Color in Business, Science and Industry*. New York: John Wiley & Sons, Inc.

Kaku, M. 1994 *Hyperspace*. Oxford, England: Oxford University Press.

Lambert, J. H. 1760. *Photometria sive de mensura et gradibus luminus, colorum et umbrae*. German translation with annotations by E. Anding (1892), *Ostwalds Klassiker der Exakten Wissenschaften*, Nos. 31–33, Leipzig.

Mehmke, R. 1898. "Über die mathematische bestimmung der helligkeit in räumen mit tagesbeleuchtung, insbesondere gemäldesälen mit deckenlict," *Zs. für Math. u. Phys.* 43:41–57.

Moon, P. 1936. *The Scientific Basis of Illumination Engineering*. New York: McGraw-Hill.

Moon, P. 1942. "A System of Photometric Concepts," *Journal of the Optical Society of America* 32:348 –362 (June).

Moon, P., and D. E. Spencer 1981. *The Photic Field*. Cambridge, MA: MIT Press.

Siegel, R., and J. R. Howell. 1981. *Thermal Radiation Heat Transfer*. Washington, DC: Hemisphere Publishing.

Yamauti, Z. 1932. "Theory of Field of Illumination" (in English), *Researches of the Electrotechnical Laboratory*, No. 339 (October). Tokyo, Japan: Ministry of Communications.

Watt, A. 1989. *Fundamentals of Three-Dimensional Computer Graphics*. Reading, MA: Addison-Wesley.

Radiosity Theory

INTRODUCTION

Radiosity models light. More specifically, the radiosity approach models the field of light—the photic field—within an environment. We saw this on an informal basis in the Introduction; it is now time to develop a firm mathematical foundation for our intuition.

Our understanding of how light is measured allows us to consider both ray tracing and radiosity in greater detail. Returning to our empty room (Fig. 2.1), we can now ask how we might model both the flow of light *and* the photic field within it.

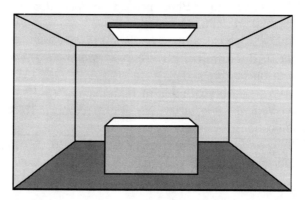

Figure 2.1   Modeling the flow and field of light in an empty room

2.1 **RAY-TRACING TECHNIQUES**

Light *flows* through space and optically homogeneous media (air, water, glass, and so forth) in a straight line, which we model as a geometrical ray. This is the essence of the ray-tracing approach.

We can model the direct illumination in an environment using conventional ray-tracing techniques. We know that the illuminance at a point on any surface due to a single point source can be calculated using the inverse square law (Eq. 1.7). We can model the light fixture (an *area* source) as a finite two-dimensional array of n point sources (e.g., Verbeck and Greenberg 1984), as shown in Figure 2.2. The illuminance at a point on a surface is then given by:

$$E = \sum_{i=1}^{n} \left(I_i \cos \theta_i / d_i^2 \right) \tag{2.1}$$

where I_i is the luminous intensity of point source S_i in its given direction. In other words, we simply add together the contributions of the n point sources to determine the illuminance E.

> Another quick note on mathematical terminology. The "Σ" symbol ("sigma") indicates summation. If, for example, we have n variables x_i, where $1 \leq i \leq n$, then the expression:
>
> $$y = \sum_{i=1}^{n} x_i$$
>
> means that y is equal to the sum of the variables x_i, or $y = x_1 + x_2 + x_3 + \ldots + x_n$. The lower and upper subscripts correspond to the lower and upper limits of the summation.
>
> You may sometimes see the sigma symbol without these limits, but only when they are obvious and therefore are implied.

There are a few complications, of course. We need to determine whether each point source i is visible from the surface being illuminated (that is, its *visibility*), and

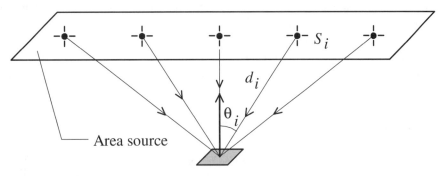

Figure 2.2 Modeling an area source as an array of point sources

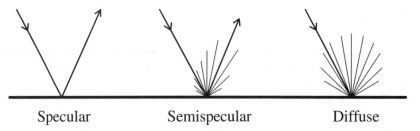

Specular   Semispecular   Diffuse

Figure 2.3   Reflection from specular and diffuse surfaces

we need to know its distance d_i from the point on the surface. We also need to know the luminous intensity I_i for each source in its given direction. Modeling an area source as a two-dimensional array of point sources is a straightforward but computationally expensive technique.

Modeling the indirect illumination is more challenging. A ray of light reflected from an ideal specular surface remains a single ray. In general, however, most physical surfaces are semispecular or diffuse reflectors. This means that a single ray of light will be reflected as an infinite number of rays (Fig. 2.3).

We saw in the Introduction that this represents a nearly intractable computation problem. We can trace as many rays as we want or have time for, but this will still represent a vanishingly small portion of the number of rays actually in the environment. Yes, ray tracing accurately models the *flow* of light in an environment. However, it provides at best an almost insignificant sampling of the *field* of light that permeates it.

Backward ray tracing (e.g., Glassner 1989) provides a partial solution by tracing a finite number of rays from the eye to the objects being modeled. As such, it attempts to sample the photic field at a specific point in space. Consider, however, what this means. A ray of light is traced backward from the eye to the object it is originated from. In Figure I.2, the ray luminance at the point of intersection is due to two rays from the point source and a specular surface. In reality, however, life is more complex. The ray luminance at the point of intersection is due to the direct illuminance from the source (which is, in general, an area or volume source) and the indirect illuminance due to multiple reflections from many semispecular and diffuse objects in the environment (Fig. 2.4).

This is the dilemma of ray-tracing techniques. Each and every reflection from a diffuse or semispecular surface results in an infinity of rays from a single incident ray. The ray-tracing approach can only sample these rays at each surface. Each reflection results in a geometric decrease in the overall size of the sample (infinity, infinity square, infinity cubed, . . .). As such, it cannot accurately model the photic field at a specific point in space, since in general *the entire field contributes to its value at any point in space*.

This explains the inability of ray-tracing techniques to model accurately soft shadows and other subtle effects of lighting (such as color bleeding). These effects can be achieved only through the use of ad hoc techniques that are better at generating visually appealing imagery than they are at modeling the physical reality of light.

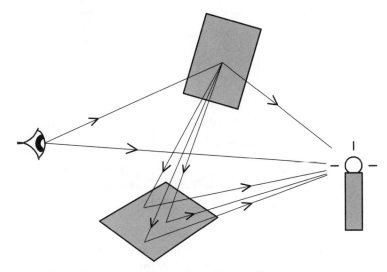

Figure 2.4 Backward ray tracing through multiple reflections

Once again, this is not to disparage ray-tracing techniques. The dual of the above argument is that specular highlights are essential to truly photorealistic images. In a sense, however, they represent the luminance of individual rays of light. Considering Figure 2.2 and Equation 2.1, we see that the illuminance at a point in space (i.e., our eye) is due to the sum of many rays. The contribution of any single ray is minuscule. Nevertheless, we may perceive one or more individual rays as being dazzlingly luminous against a muted background.

This is where the ray-tracing approach excels. We see—at least to within the limits of resolution of the human eye—the *luminance* of individual rays of light; we do not see or perceive the *illuminance* of our retinas. The ray-tracing approach is essential if we are to model accurately the luminance of specularly reflected rays.

In summary, ray tracing accurately models the flow of light in an environment. Unfortunately, it does not and cannot model the field of light with the same degree of accuracy. For this, we need a fundamentally different approach.

2.2 THE RADIOSITY APPROACH

And so we return to our empty room, with each surface neatly divided into a mesh of elements that we shall call *patches* (Fig. 2.5). We also assume that each surface is a Lambertian reflector and that the light source is a Lambertian emitter.

The assumption that all surfaces are Lambertian is important—remember that these surfaces have a constant luminance (or, more generally, radiance) that is independent of the viewing direction. For a Lambertian reflector, the reflected luminous (radiant) flux is independent of the angle of the incident flux. From the point of view of a single patch, it does not matter where the light is coming from—if we know its illumi-

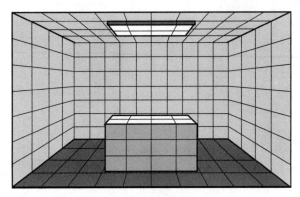

Figure 2.5   An empty room with surfaces subdivided into patches

nance (irradiance) and reflectance, we can calculate its luminous (radiant) exitance and luminance (radiance). For the sake of convenience, we shall henceforth discuss radiosity in radiometric terms; the substitution of photometric quantities is inconsequential.

We know that the distribution of flux leaving a Lambertian surface is given by Lambert's cosine law (Eq. 1.9). We can therefore calculate the flux emitted in any given direction by the light source patch. Simple geometry allows us to determine which patches are visible from each light source patch; this allows us to determine their irradiances. Each irradiated patch in turn reflects some of its incident flux back into the room. Again using Lambert's cosine law, we can determine the irradiances of all the patches visible to it.

This process is clearly iterative and proceeds until all of the reflected flux is finally absorbed. If we keep a record of how much flux each patch reflects and/or emits, we end up knowing its radiant exitance M. Since the patch is Lambertian, we can divide M by π to determine its radiance L (from Eq. 1.11).

Confused? Read "Radiosity Explained" in the Introduction and try again. The two explanations are equivalent, except that the one just given uses the more rigorous terminology we developed in Chapter 1.

Finally, we know the geometry of each patch in the room. If we know its radiance (and consequently its luminance), we can use a three-dimensional graphics package to directly render a photorealistic image of the room (as a collection of shaded three-dimensional polygons) from any viewpoint.

The restriction of Lambertian surfaces is not fundamental. As presented above, it simply allows us to employ Lambert's cosine law as a computational convenience. Suppose, for example, that we have a non-Lambertian light source whose spatial flux distribution characteristics are known. Again using the room geometry, we can determine the flux (i.e., the direct illumination) incident on any given patch. If the projected width of the patch as seen from the source is small enough in comparison to the distance between them, we can "shoot" a ray from the source to the center of the patch. The luminance of this ray will be approximately the same as the infinite number of other source rays that directly illuminate the patch, and so we can approximate the incident flux as the ray luminance times the patch's projected area (with appropriate allowances for occluding objects). By considering any nonemitting patch that reflects flux as a "secondary light source," we can generalize this concept to any semispecular or specular surface.

That's all there is to it! We have exactly paraphrased our discussion in the Introduction, this time adding the proper radiometric/photometric terminology and a few explanatory comments. True, we have necessarily glossed over a few minor implementation details . . . well, maybe not so minor. We will examine these details in depth in the following chapters.

Summarizing once again, we see that radiosity accurately models the field of light within an environment. The contribution of the entire photic field is taken into account at every point in space, and so the subtle lighting effects of soft shadows and color bleeding are naturally accounted for. Moreover, the radiosity approach solves for the entire photic field at all points in space. We can choose any point and direction in the environment and generate a photorealistic view without having to repeat the radiosity calculations.

In that ray-tracing techniques model the flow of light in an environment, we might visualize ray tracing as a dynamic process that follows photons of light as they interact with objects in the environment. In contrast, radiosity is a static process. The incessant generation and flow of photons results in a static field that permeates the environment. Radiosity models the intrinsic nature of this photic field.

Radiosity and ray tracing are in a sense dual processes (Smits et al. 1992). In practical terms, radiosity models the field of light that determines the wide brush of lighting and its subtle nuances. Ray tracing, its indispensable complement, is needed to provide the specular highlights as finishing touches. Only together are they capable of providing truly photorealistic images . . . with a few exceptions.

2.3   WHAT RADIOSITY CANNOT DO

To be honest, existing radiosity methods model the field of light in a purely reflective environment. Nowhere in the above discussion is there any mention of the refraction of light through transparent objects. There is also no mention of scattering, diffraction, or other optical phenomena that are easily modeled with ray-tracing techniques.

If you think about it, these phenomena are most often localized to the objects and their immediate environs. A prism casts a rainbow of light on a surface; a glass sphere projects a circle of light on a tabletop and presents a topsy-turvy view of the environment seen through it. Although we see and perceive these phenomena as prominent visual effects, they rarely influence the surrounding photic field to any significant extent. Their effect on the global environment is localized to those rays of light that directly interact with them.

There are hybrid techniques that combine radiosity methods with ray-tracing techniques to model these phenomena accurately (e.g., Wallace et al. 1987, Rushmeier and Torrance 1990, and Chen et al. 1991). Once you understand both approaches, it is not difficult to create a hybrid rendering program.

These, however, are future challenges for the motivated reader. In this book, our concern is to understand and implement the radiosity approach.

2.4   AN ASIDE: LOCAL VERSUS GLOBAL ILLUMINATION

The computer graphics community has traditionally divided the problem of modeling the flow of light into two separate subproblems: *local* and *global* illumination. Local illumination is light that travels directly from the source to the surface being illuminated—in other words, direct illumination. Global illumination is light that has been reflected, refracted, scattered, diffracted, or whatever by one or more objects—in other words, indirect illumination.

To some extent, this division reflects the viewpoint and heritage of ray-tracing techniques and their emphasis on point sources and objects. If we approach the problem in terms of a photic field, the division between local and global illumination becomes less important.

The radiosity approach is often characterized in the literature as a solution to the global illumination problem. In a sense it is. However, it is more productive to remember that ray-tracing models objects, whereas radiosity models light.

2.5   FORM FACTORS

Perhaps the greatest surprise in developing a radiosity-rendering program comes from realizing that its most difficult aspect has nothing whatsoever to do with light per se. The claim in Section 2.2 that "simple geometry allows us to determine which patches are visible from each patch" is true, but only in an intuitive sense. Solving this problem analytically is anything but simple!

Stated in more formal terms, the problem is this: Knowing the radiant exitance of one Lambertian patch, what portion of its flux will be received by a second patch in an environment?

Figure 2.6 shows this problem in its simplest form. The relative position and orientation of the two patches E_i and E_j is entirely arbitrary. Patch E_i is a Lambertian emitter that is emitting some quantity of flux Φ_i, whereas patch E_j is receiving a portion of its emitted flux, Φ_{ij}. The dimensionless fraction Φ_{ij}/Φ_i is called the *form factor* from E_i to E_j and is denoted as either F_{Ei-Ej} or, more compactly, F_{ij}.

The problem is deceptively simple. The total flux emitted by patch E_i is $\Phi_i = M_i A_i$, where M_i is its radiant exitance and A_i is its area. The flux received by E_j is $\Phi_{ij} = F_{ij}\Phi_i$. Unfortunately, calculating F_{ij} can be an extremely difficult problem in analytic geometry. It is so difficult, in fact, that a general solution was not found until

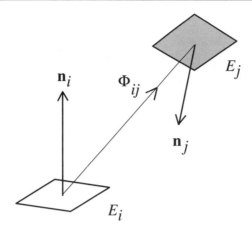

Figure 2.6   Patch E_j receiving flux Φ_{ij} from patch E_i

1993 (Schröder and Hanrahan 1993), over 260 years after the problem was first formulated by Johann Lambert!

Chapter 5 is devoted to calculating the form factor between two patches in an environment. In the following section, we will develop the underlying mathematics that we will need later.

2.5.1   Form Factor Geometry

A word of encouragement. Although the following equations involve rudimentary calculus, you do not need any knowledge of this subject to understand them. Look carefully: The terms of these equations are treated no differently than any others in algebra.

Remember also that these equations describe physical concepts. As long as you understand these concepts, the formal mathematics are of secondary importance.

Consider the two differential area (that is, infinitesimally small) patches dE_i and dE_j shown in Figure 2.7, where dE_i is a Lambertian emitter. The fraction of flux emitted by dE_i that is received by dE_j is the *differential* form factor from dE_i to dE_j, denoted as $dF_{dEi-dEj}$.

Recalling the discussion of solid angles and projected areas from the previous chapter, we see that the solid angle $d\omega$ subtended by dE_j as seen from dE_i is:

$$d\omega = \cos\theta_j \, dA_j / r^2 \tag{2.2}$$

where dA_j is the differential area of dE_j. From Equation 1.4, we find that the differential flux $\Phi(\theta_i)$ leaving dE_i in the direction θ_i is:

$$\Phi(\theta_i) = L(\theta_i)\cos\theta_i \, dA_i \, d\omega = \Phi_{ij} \tag{2.3}$$

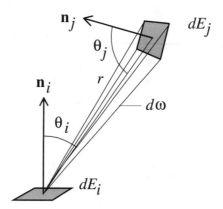

Figure 2.7   Form factor geometry between two differential elements

where $L(\theta_i)$ is the radiance of dE_i in the direction θ_i. Since dE_i is a Lambertian emitter, $L(\theta_i) = L_i$ (a constant) for all directions θ_i. Substituting this and Equation 2.2 for $d\omega$ gives:

$$\Phi_{ij} = L_i \cos \theta_i \cos \theta_j dA_i dA_j / r^2 \qquad (2.4)$$

Since dE_i is a Lambertian emitter, the *total* emitted flux Φ_i is given by Equation 1.16, or:

$$\Phi_i = M_i dA_i = \pi L_i dA_i \qquad (2.5)$$

The form factor $dF_{dEi-dEj}$ for two differential area patches is thus:

$$dF_{dEi-dEj} = \frac{L_i \cos \theta_i \cos \theta_j dA_i dA_j}{\pi L_i dA_i r^2} = \cos \theta_i \cos \theta_j dA_j / \pi r^2 \qquad (2.6)$$

which is a satisfying simple result.

Now, suppose that dE_j is the Lambertian emitter and dE_i is receiving its flux, namely Φ_{ji}. We can determine the *reciprocal* differential form factor $dF_{dEj-dEi}$ by simply reversing the patch subscripts in Equation 2.6. Doing so illustrates the *reciprocity relation* for form factors between any two differential areas dE_i and dE_j:

$$dA_i dF_{dEi-dEj} = dA_j dF_{dEj-dEi} \qquad (2.7)$$

This is an *extremely* important result for radiosity theory. We will see why this is so in the next section and again in Chapter 6.

Now the fun begins. We can compute the form factor F_{dEi-Ej} from a differential Lambertian emitter dE_i to a finite area E_j by integrating over the area of E_j:

$$F_{dEi-Ej} = \int_{A_j} dF_{dEi-dEj} = \int_{A_j} \frac{\cos \theta_i \cos \theta_j}{\pi r^2} dA_j \qquad (2.8)$$

Equation 2.8 is an *area integral equation*. What it says is this: Divide the finite area E_j into an infinite number of differential areas, calculate their differential form factors, and add the results together to obtain F_{dEi-Ej} for the finite area E_j (Fig. 2.8). It is equivalent to:

$$F_{dEi-Ej} = \sum_{jn=1}^{\infty} \frac{\cos \theta_{in} \cos \theta_{jn}}{\pi r_{jn}^2} dA_{jn}$$

where E_j is divided into an infinite number of infinitesimal areas dE_{jn}, each with its own angles θ_{in} and θ_{jn} and distance r_{jn}.

This is all you need to know about integral F_{Ei-dEj} calculus in order to understand radiosity theory!

Next, we need to determine the form factor F_{Ei-dEj} from a finite area Lambertian emitter E_i with a uniform radiance distribution across its surface to a differential area patch dE_j. We note that the total flux Φ_i emitted by E_i is:

$$\Phi_i = M_i A_i \tag{2.9}$$

whereas the flux Φ_{ij} received by dE_j is:

$$\Phi_{ij} = M_i \int_{A_i} dF_{dEi-dEj} dA_i \tag{2.10}$$

(Note that we are now integrating over the area of E_i rather than E_j.)

From our definition of a form factor, we then have:

$$F_{Ei-dEj} = \frac{\Phi_{ij}}{\Phi_i} = \frac{M_i \int_{A_i} dF_{dEi-dEj} dA_i}{M_i A_i} = \frac{1}{A_i} \int_{A_i} dF_{dEi-dEj} dA_i \tag{2.11}$$

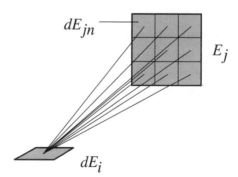

Figure 2.8 Determining the form factor F_{dEi-Ej} by area integration over E_j

which yields:

$$F_{Ei-dEj} = \frac{dA_j}{A_i} \int_{A_i} \frac{\cos\theta_i \cos\theta_j}{\pi r^2} dA_i \qquad (2.12)$$

Of course, our interest is in patch-to-patch form factors, or the form factor from a finite area E_i to another finite area E_j. For this, we need to integrate over the areas of E_i and E_j. (In physical terms, we need to consider the contribution of each differential area of E_i to the illuminance of E_j.) The flux received by E_j is then:

$$\Phi_{ij} = M_i \int_{A_i} F_{dEi-Ej} dA_i \qquad (2.13)$$

so that the form factor F_{Ei-Ej} is:

$$F_{Ei-Ej} = \frac{M_i \int_{A_i} F_{dEi-Ej} dA_i}{M_i A_i} = \frac{1}{A_i} \int_{A_i} F_{dEi-Ej} dA_i \qquad (2.14)$$

From Equation 2.8, this yields the double area integral equation:

$$F_{Ei-Ej} = \frac{1}{A_i} \int_{A_i} \int_{A_j} \frac{\cos\theta_i \cos\theta_j}{\pi r^2} dA_j dA_i \qquad (2.15)$$

The reciprocal form factor F_{Ej-Ei} is obtained by reversing the patch subscripts. This demonstrates that the reciprocity relation (Eq. 2.7) also holds true for finite area patches. In other words:

$$A_i F_{ij} = A_j F_{ji} \qquad (2.16)$$

The importance of the reciprocity relation cannot be overstated. It says that if we can somehow calculate the form factor F_{ij} from a patch E_i to another patch E_j, then we can trivially calculate the reciprocal form factor F_{ji}. This is a key concept in radiosity theory.

The equations just given implicitly assume that the two patches E_i and E_j are fully visible to each other. In a complex environment, two patches may be partially hidden by one or more occluding objects. If so, then a suitable term must be added to account for the occlusions, such as:

$$F_{Ei-Ej} = \frac{1}{A_i} \int_{A_i} \int_{A_j} \frac{\cos\theta_i \cos\theta_j}{\pi r^2} HID_{ij} dA_j dA_i \qquad (2.17)$$

where the term HID_{ij} accounts for the possible occlusion of each point of patch E_j as seen from each point of patch E_i.

We now know the relation between the geometry of two patches and their form factors. However, equations involving double integration are often difficult to solve, and Equation 2.17 is no exception, with or without occlusion. For our needs, there are no practical analytic solutions for this equation. This leaves us with numerical integration, which will be the primary topic of Chapter 5.

As a final comment, Equation 2.17 does not consider the *medium* separating the two patches. In the example of our empty room, the medium is air. Each ray of light traveling from patch to patch does so in a straight line without absorption, refraction, or scattering. In other words, the medium is considered to be *nonparticipating*. This is not always the case; airborne dust, smoke, and fog are a few examples of *participating* media. These introduce complications that the radiosity approach can handle only with severe computational difficulty (e.g., Rushmeier and Torrance 1987). The issues involved are, unfortunately, well beyond the scope of this book.

To summarize:

1. The form factor from a differential area dE_i to another differential area dE_j is given by:

$$dF_{dEi-dEj} = \cos \theta_i \cos \theta_j \, dA_j / \pi r^2$$

where θ_i and θ_j are the angles between a line connecting dE_i and dE_j and their respective surface normals (Fig. 2.7), and dA_j is the differential area of dE_j.

2. The form factor from a finite area patch E_i to another finite area patch E_j is given by:

$$F_{ij} = \frac{1}{A_i} \int_{A_i} \int_{A_j} \frac{\cos \theta_i \cos \theta_j}{\pi r^2} \, dA_j \, dA_i$$

There are no practical analytic solutions for this equation. It must typically be solved using numerical methods (see Chap. 5).

3. The *reciprocity relation* states that:

$$A_i F_{ij} = A_j F_{ji}$$

applies for both differential and finite area patches E_i and E_j.

4. The form factor concept assumes that the medium separating the patches does not absorb, refract, or scatter light. In other words, it is a *nonparticipating* medium.

2.5.2 Form Factor Properties

A form factor is a dimensionless constant representing the fraction of flux emitted by one surface patch that is received by another—*and no more*. It takes into account the shape and relative orientation of both surfaces and the presence of any obstructions but is otherwise independent of any surface properties.

Form factors were first developed for use in thermal and illumination engineering (see Section 2.7), where they have been variously called *shape, configuration, angle,* and *view* factors. The thermal engineering literature is filled with discussions of *form factor algebra*, of which the reciprocity relation is only one example. Most of these discussions relate to a time when form factors were calculated by hand. Some properties, however, are still useful. For example, the *summation relation* states that:

$$\sum_{j=1}^{n} F_{ij} = 1 \tag{2.18}$$

for any patch E_i in a *closed* environment with n patches. (A closed environment is one in which all of the flux emitted by any one patch must be received by one or more patches in the environment. In other words, none of it can escape into space.) This summation includes the form factor F_{ii}, which is defined as the fraction of flux emitted by E_i that is also directly received by E_i. Clearly, F_{ii} can be nonzero only if E_i is concave. Thus:

$F_{ii} = 0$ if E_i is planar (i.e., flat) or convex, and

$F_{ii} \neq 0$ if E_i is concave

Most radiosity methods model surfaces as two-dimensional grids of planar polygons (see Chap. 3), so that F_{ii} is always zero.

2.6   THE RADIOSITY EQUATION

If patches E_i and E_j are both Lambertian surfaces, the form factor F_{ij} indicates the fraction of flux emitted by E_i that is received by E_j. Similarly, the reciprocal form factor F_{ji} indicates the fraction of flux emitted by E_j that is received by E_i. However, form factors in themselves do not consider the flux that is subsequently reflected from these receiving patches.

Remember that we are trying to determine the radiant exitance M_i of each patch E_i in an n-patch environment. This exitance is clearly due to the flux initially emitted by the patch *plus* that reflected by it. The reflected flux comes from all of the other patches E_j visible to E_i in the environment.

Consider any patch E_j that is fully visible to E_i. The flux-leaving patch E_j is $\Phi_j = M_j A_j$. The fraction of this flux received by patch E_i is $\Phi_{ji} = M_j A_j F_{ji}$. Of this, the flux subsequently reflected by E_i is $\rho_i M_j A_j F_{ji}$, where ρ_i is the reflectance of E_i. This gives us:

$$M_{ij} = \rho_i M_j A_j F_{ji} / A_i \tag{2.19}$$

where M_{ij} is defined as the exitance of E_i due to the flux received from E_j. Using the reciprocity relation, we can rewrite this as:

$$M_{ij} = \rho_i M_j F_{ij} \tag{2.20}$$

To calculate the final exitance M_i of patch E_i, we must consider the flux received by E_i from all other patches E_j. Thus:

$$M_i = M_{oi} + \rho_i \sum_{j=1}^{n} M_j F_{ij} \tag{2.21}$$

where M_{oi} is the initial exitance of patch E_i due to its emitted flux only. Rearranging terms results in:

$$M_{oi} = M_i - \rho_i \sum_{j=1}^{n} M_j F_{ij} \tag{2.22}$$

We can express this equation for all the patches E_1 through E_n as a set of n simultaneous linear equations:

$$M_{o1} = M_1 - \left(\rho_1 M_1 F_{11} + \rho_1 M_2 F_{12} + \ldots + \rho_n M_n F_{1n}\right)$$

$$M_{o2} = M_2 - \left(\rho_2 M_1 F_{21} + \rho_2 M_2 F_{22} + \ldots + \rho_2 M_n F_{2n}\right) \tag{2.23}$$

$$\ldots$$

$$M_{on} = M_n - \left(\rho_n M_1 F_{n1} + \rho_n M_2 F_{n2} + \ldots + \rho_n M_n F_{nn}\right)$$

which we can write in matrix form as:

$$\begin{bmatrix} M_{o1} \\ M_{o2} \\ \ldots \\ M_{on} \end{bmatrix} = \begin{bmatrix} 1 - \rho_1 F_{11} & -\rho_1 F_{12} & \ldots & -\rho_1 F_{1n} \\ -\rho_2 F_{21} & 1 - \rho_2 F_{22} & \ldots & -\rho_2 F_{2n} \\ \ldots & \ldots & \ldots & \ldots \\ -\rho_n F_{n1} & -\rho_n F_{n2} & \ldots & 1 - \rho_n F_{nn} \end{bmatrix} \begin{bmatrix} M_1 \\ M_2 \\ \ldots \\ M_n \end{bmatrix} \tag{2.24}$$

In matrix notation, this can be succinctly expressed as:

$$\mathbf{M}_o = (\mathbf{I} - \mathbf{T})\mathbf{M} \tag{2.25}$$

where $\mathbf{I}$ is the $n \times n$ identity matrix, $\mathbf{M}$ is the final $n \times 1$ exitance vector, $\mathbf{M}_o$ is the initial $n \times 1$ exitance vector, and $\mathbf{T}$ is an $n \times n$ matrix whose i,jth element is $\rho_i F_{ij}$. (If you find this terminology confusing, see Section 3.10 for a quick review of elementary matrix theory.)

This is the elegantly simple *radiosity equation*: a set of simultaneous linear equations involving only surface reflectances,[1] patch form factors, and patch exitances. Solving these equations provides us with the radiant exitance, radiance, and ultimately luminance of every patch in the environment it describes.

It is evident that we first require the initial patch exitances M_{oi}. Clearly, only those patches that emit radiant flux will have nonzero values, which we can obtain from the description of the light sources.

Second, we must determine the form factors F_{ij} for each pair of patches in the environment. Equation 2.22 implies that we must determine n^2 form factors for an environment with n patches. However, the reciprocal form factors F_{ji} can be trivially determined using the reciprocity relation, thus providing $n(n-1)/2$ factors. Also, if the patches are flat or convex, the form factors F_{ii} are zero. We are then left with:

---

[1]The reflectance of a surface generally varies according to the wavelength of light. This is what gives a surface its color when it is viewed under "white light" illumination. Recalling the discussion of spectral reflectance distribution from Chapter 1, we can divide the spectrum into three component bands—red, green, and blue—and determine an average spectral reflectance value for each band. (This approach maps directly onto the familiar red-green-blue (RGB) color model of computer graphics. Other, more sophisticated color models may use four or more spectral bands.) The radiosity equation can then be solved *independently* for each color band.

$$n^2 - n(n-1)/2 - n = n(n-3)/2 \approx n^2/2 \qquad (2.26)$$

form factors that must be determined from the patch geometries. To put this into perspective, a reasonably complex environment with 10,000 patches requires some *fifty million* form factor determinations.

This is a *very* big number for desktop computers. Allowing four bytes per floating-point number for each form factor means we need some 190 megabytes of random access memory. Even if we had this amount of memory, it would take a very long time to calculate 50 million numbers.

Fortunately, there are a variety of acceleration techniques for form factor determination that allow us to circumvent these time and memory constraints. We will closely examine several of these techniques in Chapter 5. Even so, you should be aware that form factor determination typically consumes some 90 percent of the CPU time required to render a radiosity-based image.

On the other hand, there is no reason to be discouraged by these numbers. A personal desktop computer with four megabytes of RAM is more than adequate for producing photorealistic images in a few minutes or less. The image shown in Color Plate 1 took 35 seconds to render on a 66 MHz 486 IBM PC-AT clone. Compare this to the hours of computation time often needed to render a single ray-traced image!

Our problem, then, is to solve the radiosity equation for the final patch exitances M_i. The matrix is typically too large for direct methods such as Gaussian elimination. However, it is ideally suited for iterative techniques such as the Jacobi and Gauss-Seidel methods (e.g., Golub and Van Loan 1983, Varga 1962). These methods are guaranteed to converge to a solution, since the matrix is always strictly diagonally dominant for flat and convex patches. That is, $\rho_i F_{ij}$ is always less than one, whereas F_{ii} is always zero. Furthermore, the methods converge very quickly, typically in six to eight iterations (Cohen and Greenberg 1985). We will examine these methods and a more powerful and useful variation called *progressive refinement* in Chapter 6

This then is our basic *radiosity algorithm*: any one of several iterative techniques that solve the radiosity equation. There are strong connections between these techniques and the physical flow of light in an environment. Again, however, we will have to wait until Chapter 6 before we can examine them in detail.

2.6.1   Understanding the Radiosity Equation

Solving the radiosity equation for an environment is equivalent to determining its "energy balance." The amount of radiant flux reflected and absorbed by a patch must equal the amount of flux incident on its surface. Flux is energy per unit time. If this balance is not maintained, the patch will steadily accumulate or lose energy over time. The final solution to the radiosity equation therefore ensures that the flow of energy is balanced for all patches in the environment.

The radiosity equation reveals why most radiosity methods are view independent. Once we have determined the form factors for an environment and solved for the final patch exitances, we can quickly render a photorealistic image of the environment as a collection of three-dimensional polygons from any viewpoint. The solution to the radiosity equation thus describes the photic field permeating the environment. In doing so, it allows us to move anywhere within this field and visualize it in any direction.

Equation 2.24 also shows that radiosity methods model light rather than objects. The radiosity equation solves for the field of light—the photic field—within an environment. The only contribution made by the objects comprising the environment is in defining the form factors and surface reflectances.

Recall from Section 1.9 that we can place an irradiance meter (Fig. 1.10) anywhere in physical space and orient it in any direction. We can then measure the irradiance at that point in space. Here we have a virtual space defined by the description of patches in a computer file. Virtual or not, we can place a differential patch with zero reflectance anywhere in this space and orient it as we please. By determining the form factors from the surrounding environment to this patch, we can calculate its irradiance.

We can similarly calculate the radiance at any point P in any direction in a virtual space with the mathematical analogue of a radiance meter (Fig. 1.11). If we assume that the normal of our differential patch intersects a point Q on some surface in the environment, the radiance at the point P in the given direction is equal to the radiance of the ray of light emanating from the point Q and intersecting our patch.

A photic field is completely characterized by its radiance at any point and direction in the space containing the field. In physical space, we can measure irradiance and radiance. In virtual space, we can calculate these properties by solving the radiosity equation. Clearly then, radiosity models light.

One problem with the radiosity approach in general is that each patch must necessarily have a finite area. An implicit assumption of the radiosity equation is that each patch then has a uniform irradiance and radiant exitance distribution across its surface. This is not true in real life: Illuminated surfaces exhibit continuous gradations of radiance. Accurately modeling these smooth changes within the radiosity equation requires the use of extremely small patches—and an ever larger matrix to solve. (There are a number of elegant solutions to this problem. However, they are at the forefront of current radiosity research and so are beyond the scope of this book. The best that can be done is to provide a brief survey in Chapter 8.)

On a more positive note, it is evident that we need to determine the form factors for a particular environment only once. The radiosity equation then allows us quickly to change the patch reflectances and initial patch exitances without any further calculations other than solving the equation. In more colloquial terms, we can quickly dim, brighten, and turn off lights; change the light source colors; change the surface reflectance and color of any object in the environment; and even redefine which objects emit light. The details of this magic—which can be difficult at best using raytracing techniques—are also discussed in Chapter 8.

2.6.2   Time and Space Considerations

We need to discuss one more concept regarding radiosity theory, this time from computer science. Actually, there are two closely related concepts to consider: *time* and *space complexity*.

Time complexity is a measure of how long it will take a computer to solve a problem using a specific algorithm. It is not a measure of time per se, but rather a measure of how many elementary CPU operations (add, multiply, divide, and so forth) must be performed to solve the problem. Similarly, space complexity is a measure of the maximum amount of memory the algorithm requires in order to solve the problem.

The radiosity equation solves for the final exitances of n patches. Solving this equation using (for example) Gaussian elimination would require cn^3 operations, where c is a constant. However, constant factors are not considered in complexity calculations. This ensures that the time and space complexity measures are independent of the CPU or compiled program used to implement the algorithm. The time complexity of Gaussian elimination is thus expressed as $O(n^3)$. This so-called big-O notation is thus a measure of how much time is required to solve the problem relative to the number of patches n.

This also demonstrates one reason why Gaussian elimination is ill suited to solving the radiosity equation. If an environment with 10,000 patches requires t minutes to solve its corresponding radiosity equation, an environment with 100,000 patches (which is a large but not unreasonable number for complex architectural scenes) will require approximately *1,000 times* as long to solve. We might with clever programming reduce this to 500 times, but the basic issue remains—the Gaussian elimination method does not "scale well" to larger problems.

The Gauss-Seidel method is somewhat better in that its time complexity is $O(n^2)$ or one iteration (see Chap. 6 for details). However, its space complexity is determined by the number of form factors that must be stored in memory, which is approximately $n^2/2$. Ignoring the constant factor, we find that this is a space complexity of $O(n^2)$. Clearly, the Gauss-Seidel method also does not scale well to problems involving complex environments with many thousands of patches.

How bad is this? Given an environment with 100,000 patches, solving the corresponding radiosity equation using Gauss-Seidel iteration would require the solution of one billion floating-point equations and four gigabytes of memory. At least one iteration is required before an initial approximation of the final exitance values becomes available. Without these, we cannot generate an image.

The good news is that there are progressive refinement algorithms that solve the radiosity equation in reasonable time. Those we will examine in Chapter 6 have time and space complexities of $O(n)$. That is, they need memory to store at most n form factors at any one time, and they can generate an *initial* image in $O(n)$ time. Subsequent images become progressively more refined, quickly approaching the photorealistic quality of the final image.

Although there are some disadvantages to these algorithms (see Chap. 6 for details), they make radiosity a practical approach to photorealistic image generation.

More important, they scale well as the environment becomes increasingly more complex.

2.7   RADIOSITY HISTORY

The radiosity approach to photorealistic image generation was independently introduced to the computer graphics community by Goral et al. (1984) and Nishita and Nakamae (1985), who based their work on radiative heat-transfer theory and thermal engineering techniques (e.g., Siegel and Howell 1992). At that time, various radiosity algorithms had been employed by the thermal engineering community for some thirty years (e.g., Hottel 1954). Hottel referred to his algorithm as the "zone method" (Hottel and Sarofim 1967), calling "radiosity" an "undesirable word." However, Sparrow (1963) had earlier noted that the algorithms proposed by Hottel (1954), Eckbert and Drake (1959), and Gebhart (1961) were essentially equivalent and had labeled them "radiosity methods." By 1967, the term had become part of thermal engineering's lexicon.

This is not the beginning of the story, however. The fundamental equation of radiant flux transfer between ideal diffuse surfaces (Eq. 2.22) was apparently first recognized by Yamauti (1926) and Buckley (1927). It was Ziro Yamauti who first suggested solving this *Fredholm integral of the second kind* (e.g., Heckbert 1991) using finite difference equations. His suggestion was formalized as a lighting calculation technique in H. H. Higbie's (1934) *Lighting Calculations*. In the absence of computers, however, the technique was not widely practiced by illumination engineers.

One exception was the work of Parry Moon and Domina Eberle Spencer in the 1940s. They used Yamauti's technique (which they called the "interflection method") to study lighting in empty rooms (Moon and Spencer 1946). Credit for the first photorealistic images created using radiosity methods must go to Moon and Spencer: They exhibited synthetic photographs of empty rooms with luminous ceilings at the 1946 National Technical Conference of the Illuminating Engineering Society of North America (O'Brien and Howard 1959). In the absence of computers, they calculated the luminance of each patch by hand, cut out paper squares from Munsell color charts, and pasted them together to form their images, which were then photographed (Spencer 1993). These photographs are reproduced in Moon and Spencer (1948).

The introduction of digital computers in the 1950s saw an international resurgence of interest in Yamauti's work. Numerous papers were presented to the illumination engineering community, including those by Caracciolo (1952), Centeno and Zagustin (1953), Dourgnon (1955), O'Brien (1955), Phillips (1957), and O'Brien and Howard (1959). Radiosity theory research has continued within this community to the present day (e.g., DiLaura and Franck 1993).

The illumination and thermal engineering communities have variously referred to radiosity theory and methods as "interflection," "interreflection," "lumped parameter," "network," "finite difference," "lumped sum," "zone," "zonal cavity," "zone analysis," and "radiative transfer." Today illumination engineers use the term "radiative transfer theory," whereas thermal engineers and the computer graphics community use "radiosity theory." Terminology aside, the two theories are equivalent.

2.8   CONCLUSIONS

In modeling an environment, the radiosity theory we have developed makes the following assumptions:

1. All surfaces are Lambertian.
2. Each patch has a uniform exitance distribution.
3. Each patch has a uniform irradiance distribution.
4. The intervening medium is nonparticipating.

Although none of these assumptions represents fundamental constraints for radiosity theory, they make solving the radiosity equation a computationally tractable problem for personal desktop computers.

Of course, much more can be said about radiosity theory. For instance, reducing the patches from finite to differential areas leads to the *Neumann series* and a generalization of the Jacobi iteration method. It also leads to *Fredholm integrals of the second kind*, *Galerkin* and *point collocation* methods (an adaptation of *finite element* techniques), and other mathematical esoterica. There are also much more sophisticated methods for representing the radiosity equation. (See Chap. 8 for a brief survey of the relevant literature.)

Readers interested in pursuing this topic are strongly advised to read Cohen and Wallace (1993). There is no better reference text to be found on the subject. Be forewarned, however, that portions of this text are aimed at graduate-level computer science students and researchers. You will need a strong background in integro-differential equations and other fields of higher mathematics to understand it completely. On the other hand, it includes a wealth of technical details that, while beyond the scope of this book, are easily understood.

We have seen in this chapter that radiosity does in truth model light. We have also seen the elegant simplicity of the approach, both in its intuitive concepts and in its mathematical foundations. With this understanding, we can now develop the tools and techniques needed for a radiosity-based rendering program.

REFERENCES

Buckley, H. 1927. "On the Radiation from the Inside of a Circular Cylinder," *Philosophical Magazine* (London) 4:753.

Caracciolo, F. B. 1952. "Calcolo dell'illuminazione artificiate degli ambienti chiusi," *L'Ingegnere* 10 (Italy).

Centeno, M., and A. Zagustin. 1953. "Interflectance in Two Dimensions," Universidad Central de Venezuela, Caracas, Venezuela.

Chen, S. E., H. E. Rushmeier, G. Miller, and D. Turner. 1991. "A Progressive Multi-Pass Method for Global Illumination," *Computer Graphics* 25(4):165–174 (ACM SIGGRAPH '91 Proc.).

Cohen, M. F., and D. P. Greenberg. 1985. "The Hemi-Cube—A Radiosity Solution for Complex Environments," *Computer Graphics* 19(3):31–40 (ACM SIGGRAPH '85 Proc.)

Cohen, M. F., and J. Wallace. 1993. *Radiosity and Realistic Image Synthesis.* San Diego, CA: Academic Press.

DiLaura, D. L., and P. Franck. 1993. "On Setting Up and Solving Large Radiative Transfer Systems," *Journal of the Illuminating Engineering Society* 22(2):3–7 (Summer).

Dourgnon, J. 1955. "La Théorie des Réflexions Mutuelles Appliquée sur Calcul du Facteur d'Utilisation," *Cahiers du Centre Scientifique Technique du Bâtiment* 27 (September).

Eckbert, E. R. G., and R. M. Drake. 1959. *Heat and Mass Transfer.* New York: McGraw-Hill.

Gebhart, B. 1961. *Heat Transfer.* New York: McGraw-Hill.

Glassner, A. S., ed. 1989. *An Introduction to Ray Tracing.* San Diego, CA: Academic Press.

Golub, G. H., and C. F. Van Loan. 1983. *Matrix Computations.* Baltimore, MD: John Hopkins University Press.

Goral, C. M., K. E. Torrance, D. P. Greenberg, and B. Battaile. 1984. "Modeling the Interaction of Light between Diffuse Surfaces," *Computer Graphics* 18(3):213–222 (ACM SIGGRAPH '84 Proc.).

Heckbert, P. S. 1991. "Simulating Global Illumination Using Adaptive Meshing," Ph.D. thesis, University of California Berkeley, Technical Report UCB/CSD 91/636.

Higbie, H. H. 1934. *Lighting Calculations.* New York: John Wiley.

Hottel, H. C. 1954. "Radiant Heat Transmission," in W. H. McAdams, ed., *Heat Transmission.* New York: McGraw-Hill.

Hottel, H. C., and A. F. Sarofim. 1967. *Radiative Transfer.* New York: McGraw-Hill.

Moon, P., and D. E. Spencer. 1946. "Lighting Design by the Interflection Method," *Journal of the Franklin Institute* 242:465.

Moon, P., and D. E. Spencer 1948. *Lighting Design.* Cambridge, MA: Addison-Wesley.

Nishita, T., and E. Nakamae. 1985. "Continuous Tone Representation of Three-Dimensional Objects Taking Account of Shadows and Interreflection," *Computer Graphics* 19(3):23–30 (ACM SIGGRAPH '85 Proc.).

O'Brien, P. F. 1955. "Interreflections in Rooms by a Network Method," *Journal of the Optical Society of America* 45(6):419–424 (June).

O'Brien, P. F., and J. A. Howard. 1959. "Predetermination of Luminances by Finite Difference Equations," *Illuminating Engineering* 64(4):209–218 (April).

Phillips, R. O. 1957. "The Calculation of Interreflected Illumination and Luminances in Rooms, Using an Electronic Computer," School of Architecture, New South Wales University.

Rushmeier, H. E., and K. E. Torrance. 1987. "The Zonal Method for Calculating Light Intensities in the Presence of a Participating Medium," *Computer Graphics* 21(4):293–302 (ACM SIGGRAPH '87 Proc.).

Rushmeier, H. E., and K. E. Torrance. 1990. "Extending the Radiosity Method to Include Specularly Reflecting and Translucent Materials," *ACM Transactions on Graphics* 9(1):1–27.

Schröder, P., and P. Hanrahan. 1993. "On the Form Factor between Two Polygons," *Computer Graphics Proceedings* (SIGGRAPH '93 Conference), pp.163 –164.

Siegel, R., and J. R. Howell. 1992. *Thermal Radiation Heat Transfer,* 3rd ed. Washington, DC: Hemisphere Publishing.

Smits, B. E., J. R. Arvo, and D. H. Salesin. 1992. "An Importance-Driven Radiosity Algorithm," *Computer Graphics* (ACM SIGGRAPH '92 Proc.). 26(2):273–282.

Sparrow, E. M. 1963. "On the Calculation of Radiant Interchange between Surfaces," in W. Ibele, ed., *Modern Developments in Heat Transfer*. New York: Academic Press.

Spencer, D. E. 1993. Private communication.

Varga, R. S. 1962. *Matrix Iterative Analysis*. Englewood Cliffs, NJ: Prentice-Hall.

Verbeck, C. P., and D. P. Greenberg. 1984. "A Comprehensive Light-Source Description for Computer Graphics," *IEEE Computer Graphics & Applications* 4(7):66–75.

Wallace, J. R., M. F. Cohen, and D. P. Greenberg. 1987. "A Two-Pass Solution to the Rendering Equation: A Synthesis of Ray Tracing and Radiosity Methods," *Computer Graphics* (ACM SIGGRAPH '87 Proc.). 21(4):311–320.

Yamauti, Z. 1926. "The Light Flux Distribution of a System of Interreflecting Surfaces," *Journal of the Optical Society of America* 13(5):561 (November).

TOOLS
OF THE
TRADE

But what Trade art thou? Answer me directly . . .
William Shakespeare
Julius Caesar, 1601

The tools of the trade are one: a graphics package to manage and display three-dimensional polygons. Chapter 3 examines polygon representations and view transformations. Chapter 4 reviews viewing systems, polygon clipping, hidden-surface elimination, scan conversion, and incremental shading algorithms.

These tools are not part of the radiosity approach per se and may be available as callable library functions in certain environments. Even so, it's always a good idea to know your tools before embarking on a major project.

Building an Environment

3.0 INTRODUCTION

Having laid the theoretical foundations of radiosity, we can now begin writing a radiosity-based rendering program. From Chapter 2, we see that our program will have to perform the tasks listed in Figure 3.1.

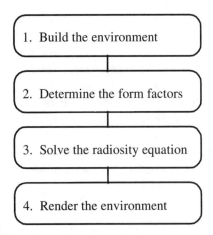

Figure 3.1 Radiosity-based rendering program outline

In this and the following chapter we consider the tasks of building and rendering environments. These are not part of the radiosity approach per se. However, our photic fields are due to and defined by their environments. To model a field of light, then, we first need to model its environment. For most radiosity methods, this means representing objects as collections of three-dimensional polygons.

Our tools for doing so—that is, algorithms and data structures—include vector mathematics, view transformations, polygon clipping, hidden-surface elimination, and polygon scan conversion. These are familiar tools of the trade for three-dimensional computer graphics programming of any sort. Indeed, many high-end graphics programming environments include them as callable library functions, and some desktop workstations and advanced video display subsystems offer them as built-in hardware or firmware features. In general, however, we must assume that they are not available. We shall build—and in doing so better understand—our own set of tools.

The goal of this chapter is to develop a three-dimensional graphics toolkit for building environments. The coverage given the underlying algorithms and data structures is neither rigorous nor comprehensive; if it were it would fill the remainder of this book and more. Instead, the emphasis is on developing a set of C++ classes sufficient to model collections of three-dimensional polygons. Readers interested in a more definitive approach to three-dimensional computer graphics are encouraged to consult one of the many excellent reference texts, including Foley et al. (1990) Hill (1990), Watt (1989), and Rogers and Adams (1976).

We must also take a minimalist approach to user interface design. In particular, we will develop a simple parsing program that reads an ASCII text file and translates it into a representation of an environment in memory. The complexity of our environments is therefore limited to those we can generate by hand using a text editor.

Of course, ultimately we will want to create complex and visually interesting environments consisting of thousands to hundreds of thousands of polygons. In practical terms, this is a task best performed with a commercial computer-aided drafting (CAD) program such as AutoCAD. Fortunately, we do not need most of the features of this expensive product; there are more reasonably priced CAD programs that offer all of the functionality we need. Specifically, we require three features: (1) the ability to draw in three dimensions; (2) a command that renders curved surfaces as polygon meshes; and (3) the ability to generate AutoCAD-compatible DXF files.

The DXF graphics file format is a de facto standard in the CAD industry. Although it has several deficiencies that limit its usefulness for radiosity-rendering applications, these can be overcome with some discipline on the part of the draftsperson. We can create complex environments using a commercial CAD program, generate a DXF file, and use it as a basis for generating input files for our radiosity renderer.

We will develop a data file format later in this chapter that is optimized for radiosity applications. A program (including an explanatory text file and full C++ source code) that partially converts DXF files into this format is included with the diskette accompanying this book. That, however, comes later; right now we need to design and code our graphics toolkit.

3.1   GLOBAL DEFINITIONS

We begin with an include file that defines a few global *typedefs* and constants. Yes, it's trivial and boring, but we have to start somewhere.

Listing 3.1

```
// GENERAL.H - General Definitions

#ifndef _GENERAL_H
#define _GENERAL_H

#ifndef _NOT_WIN_APP
#define STRICT            // Win32 API compatibility
#include <windows.h>      // MS-Windows application
#endif

#include <stdio.h>
#include <stdlib.h>
#include <math.h>

#ifdef _NOT_WIN_APP
#define FALSE   0
#define TRUE    1

typedef int BOOL;                  // Boolean flag
typedef unsigned char BYTE;
typedef unsigned short WORD;
typedef unsigned long DWORD;
#endif

#ifndef max
#define max(a,b)  (((a) > (b)) ? (a) : (b))
#endif

#ifndef min
#define min(a,b)  (((a) < (b)) ? (a) : (b))
#endif

#define PI              3.141592654
#define MIN_VALUE       1.0e-10        // Minimum value
#define MAX_VALUE       1.0e10         // Maximum value
inline double RadToDeg( double r )
{ return r * 180.0 / PI; }

inline double DegToRad( double d )
{ return d * PI / 180.0; }
```

(continued)

Listing 3.1   *(continued)*

```
inline double GetNormRand()
{ return (double) rand() / (double) RAND_MAX; }

#endif
```

GENERAL.H assumes MS-Windows 3.1 or Windows NT to be its target environment. If you have another environment in mind, be sure to define *_NOT_WINAPP* somewhere for your compiler. (Most C++ compilers allow you to specify global definitions from the command line or workplace shell.)

3.2   VECTOR MATHEMATICS

Next, we need two C++ classes to define and manipulate three-dimensional points and vectors. Many C programmers create a *Point* structure and then typedef a *Vector* structure as follows:

```
typedef struct Point
{ float x, y, z; }
Point;

typedef Point Vector;
```

Although this method works, it obscures the mathematical definition of a vector. In particular, a point defines a *position* in space; a vector defines a *direction*. This has important consequences for properly defined point and vector classes. There are mathematical operations we can perform on points that have no meaning for vectors, and vice versa. For instance, we can determine the distance between two points but not between two vectors. Thus, a vector class cannot—or at least should not—be derived from a point class, despite the similarities between these classes.

On the other hand, we can and should define an abstract base class for points and vectors that encapsulates their similarities. Thus:

Listing 3.2

```
// VECTOR3.H - 3-D Vector and Point Classes

#ifndef _VECTOR3_H
#define _VECTOR3_H

#include <math.h>
#include "general.h"

class Vector3;   // Forward reference
```

```
class Space3      // 3-D co-ordinates
{
  protected:
    float x;      // X-axis co-ordinate
    float y;      // Y-axis co-ordinate
    float z;      // Z-axis co-ordinate

  public:
    Space3() { };
    Space3( double xval, double yval, double zval )
    {
      x = (float) xval;
      y = (float) yval;
      z = (float) zval;
    }

    double GetX() { return x; }
    double GetY() { return y; }
    double GetZ() { return z; }

    void SetX( double xval ) { x = (float) xval; }
    void SetY( double yval ) { y = (float) yval; }
    void SetZ( double zval ) { z = (float) zval; }
};

class Point3 : public Space3     // 3-D point
{
  public:
    Point3() : Space3() { };

    Point3( double xval, double yval, double zval ) :
        Space3 ( xval, yval, zval )
    { };

    // Add vector v to point p
    friend Point3 operator+( Point3 p, Vector3 v );

    // Add point p to vector v
    friend Point3 operator+( Vector3 v, Point3 p );

    friend class Vector3;
};

class Vector3 : public Space3    // 3D vector
{
  public:
    Vector3() : Space3() { };

    Vector3( double xval, double yval, double zval ) :
        Space3 ( xval, yval, zval )
    { };
```

(continued)

Listing 3.2   *(continued)*

```
Vector3( Point3 &p ) : Space3()
{ x = p.x; y = p.y; z = p.z; }

Vector3( Point3 &start, Point3 &end ) : Space3()
{
  x = end.x - start.x;
  y = end.y - start.y;
  z = end.z - start.z;
}

// Return vector length
double Length()
{ return sqrt(x * x + y * y + z * z); }

// Assign scalar
Vector3 &operator=( double s )
{
  x = (float) s;
  y = (float) s;
  z = (float) s;

  return *this;
}

// Add/assign vector v
Vector3 &operator+=( Vector3 &v )
{ x += v.x; y += v.y; z += v.z; return *this; }

// Subtract/assign vector v
Vector3 &operator-=( Vector3 &v )
{ x -= v.x; y -= v.y; z -= v.z; return *this; }

// Multiply/assign by scalar s
Vector3 &operator*=( double s )
{
  x *= (float) s;
  y *= (float) s;
  z *= (float) s;

  return *this;
}

// Divide/assign by scalar s
Vector3 &operator/=( double s )
{
  x /= (float) s;
  y /= (float) s;
  z /= (float) s;

  return *this;
}
```

```
// Negation
Vector3 operator-()
{
  Vector3 temp;      // Temporary 3-D vector

  temp.x = -x;
  temp.y = -y;
  temp.z = -z;

  return temp;
}

// Add vector v2 to vector v1
friend Vector3 operator+( Vector3 v1, Vector3 v2 )
{
  Vector3 temp;      // Temporary 3-D vector

  temp.x = v1.x + v2.x;
  temp.y = v1.y + v2.y;
  temp.z = v1.z + v2.z;

  return temp;
}

// Subtract vector v2 from vector v1
friend Vector3 operator-( Vector3 v1, Vector3 v2 )
{
  Vector3 temp;      // Temporary 3-D vector

  temp.x = v1.x - v2.x;
  temp.y = v1.y - v2.y;
  temp.z = v1.z - v2.z;

  return temp;
}

// Multiply vector v by scalar s
friend Vector3 operator*( Vector3 v, double s )
{
  Vector3 temp;      // Temporary 3-D vector

  temp.x = v.x * (float) s;
  temp.y = v.y * (float) s;
  temp.z = v.z * (float) s;

  return temp;
}

// Multiply scalar s by vector v
friend Vector3 operator*( double s, Vector3 v )
{ return v * s; }
```

(continued)

Listing 3.2   *(continued)*

```cpp
      // Divide vector v by scalar s
      friend Vector3 operator/( Vector3 v, double s )
      {
        Vector3 temp;       // Temporary 3-D vector

        temp.x = v.x / (float) s;
        temp.y = v.y / (float) s;
        temp.z = v.z / (float) s;

        return temp;
      }

      // Divide scalar s by vector v
      friend Vector3 operator/( double s, Vector3 v )
      { return v / s; }

      // Normalize
      Vector3 &Norm()
      {
        double len = Length();

        if (len < MIN_VALUE)
          len = 1.0;

        x /= (float) len;
        y /= (float) len;
        z /= (float) len;

        return *this;
      }

      // Return dot product of vectors v1 and v2
      friend double Dot( Vector3 &v1, Vector3 &v2 )
      { return (v1.x * v2.x + v1.y * v2.y + v1.z * v2.z); }

      // Return cross product of vectors v1 and v2
      friend Vector3 Cross( Vector3 &v1, Vector3 &v2 )
      {
        Vector3 temp;       // Temporary 3-D vector

        temp.x = v1.y * v2.z - v1.z * v2.y;
        temp.y = v1.z * v2.x - v1.x * v2.z;
        temp.z = v1.x * v2.y - v1.y * v2.x;

        return temp;
      }
};

#endif
```

and:

Listing 3.3

```
// VECTOR3.CPP - 3-D Point and Vector Classes

#include "vector3.h"

// Add vector v to point p
Point3 operator+( Point3 p, Vector3 v )
{
  Point3 temp;  // Temporary 3-D point

  temp.x = p.x + (float) v.GetX();
  temp.y = p.y + (float) v.GetY();
  temp.z = p.z + (float) v.GetZ();

  return temp;
}

// Add point p to vector v
Point3 operator+( Vector3 v, Point3 p )
{ return p + v; }
```

The above *Vector3* class includes two friend functions—*Dot* and *Cross*—that may not be familiar to you. They aren't difficult to understand, and they are incredibly useful in computer graphics. Remembering that vectors represent directions, we see that the *dot product* of two vectors $\mathbf{v}_1$ and $\mathbf{v}_2$ is related to the cosine of the angle θ between them (Fig. 3.2a). Mathematically, it is defined as:

$$\mathbf{v}_1 \cdot \mathbf{v}_2 = |\mathbf{v}_1||\mathbf{v}_2|\cos\theta$$

where $|\mathbf{v}_1|$ and $|\mathbf{v}_2|$ indicate the lengths of vectors $\mathbf{v}_1$ and $\mathbf{v}_2$ respectively. If both vectors are *normalized* (i.e., have unit lengths), then their dot product is equal to the cosine of the angle θ between them. A dot product of two vectors is a *scalar* (a single number).

The dot product of two vectors is easily calculated as the sum of the products of their component coordinates, or:

$$\mathbf{v}_1 \cdot \mathbf{v}_2 = v_{1x} * v_{2x} + v_{1y} * v_{2y} + v_{1z} * v_{2z}$$

The *cross product* of two vectors $\mathbf{v}_1$ and $\mathbf{v}_2$ is a third vector $\mathbf{v}_C$ in a direction perpendicular to the plane of $\mathbf{v}_1$ and $\mathbf{v}_2$ and with a length $|\mathbf{v}_C|$ equal to the area of the parallelogram described by them (Fig. 3.2b). Mathematically, the cross product is defined as:

$$\mathbf{v}_1 \times \mathbf{v}_2 = \mathbf{v}_C$$

where the length is:

$$|\mathbf{v}_C| = |\mathbf{v}_1||\mathbf{v}_2|\sin\theta$$

and its three component coordinates are given by:

(continued)

$$\mathbf{v}_{C_x} = v_{1y} * v_{2z} - v_{1z} * v_{2y}$$

$$\mathbf{v}_{C_y} = v_{1z} * v_{2x} - v_{1x} * v_{2z}$$

$$\mathbf{v}_{C_z} = v_{1x} * v_{2y} - v_{1y} * v_{2x}$$

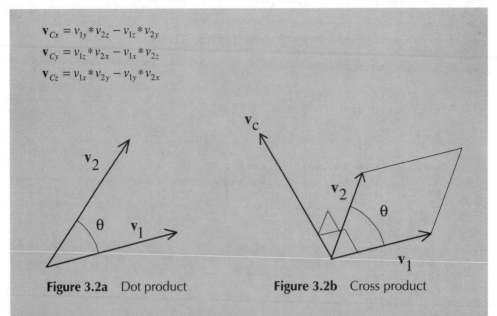

Figure 3.2a Dot product   **Figure 3.2b** Cross product

The direction of the cross-product vector can be quickly determined without mathematics using the *right-hand rule* mnemonic. Look at Figure 3.2b and imagine grasping $\mathbf{v}_C$ in your right hand such that your thumb points in its direction. Your fingers will then always curl around $\mathbf{v}_C$ from $\mathbf{v}_1$ to $\mathbf{v}_2$. (This assumes a *right-handed* coordinate system; a *left-handed* coordinate system would have $\mathbf{v}_C$ pointing in the opposite direction.)

Finally, the class constructors *Vector3(Point3 &)* and *Vector3(Point3 &, Point3 &)* define *bound* vectors, which have both a direction and a starting position. There is no need to create a separate data type for bound vectors because we can model them using our *Vector3* class. Their starting positions are implied by their context.

3.3   RECTANGULAR AND SPHERICAL COORDINATES

Although our *Vector3* class is based on the commonly used rectangular coordinate system, it is sometimes more convenient and even necessary to specify three-dimensional vectors in spherical coordinates. For example, in Chapter 4 we will need to specify a direction of view from a point in the environment. Spherical coordinates allow a more intuitive user interface for this task, particularly if the direction must be specified from the keyboard.

We could store both rectangular and spherical coordinates in the *Vector3* class. However, this redundant information would consume inordinate amounts of memory if applied to every *Vector3* object. Since we shall rarely need both coordinate types for the same object, we shall instead define a separate C++ class for spherical coordinate vectors and convert between coordinate systems as necessary.

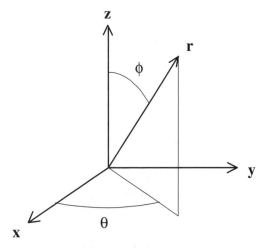

Figure 3.3 Rectangular and spherical coordinates

Converting from spherical to rectangular coordinates is the easier of the two tasks. Given the length |**r**|, the horizontal angle (or *colatitude*) θ, and the vertical angle (or *azimuth*) ϕ of a vector **r** (Fig. 3.3), its equivalent rectangular coordinates $\{r_x, r_y, r_z\}$ can be determined from:

$$r_x = |\mathbf{r}|\sin\phi\cos\theta$$
$$r_y = |\mathbf{r}|\sin\phi\sin\theta \qquad\qquad (3.1)$$
$$r_z = |\mathbf{r}|\cos\phi$$

Determining the spherical coordinates of a vector **r** from its rectangular representation requires a bit more care. The requisite formulas are:

$$|\mathbf{r}| = \sqrt{r_x^{\,2} + r_y^{\,2} + r_z^{\,2}}$$
$$\phi = \arccos(r_z\ |\mathbf{r}|) \qquad\qquad (3.2)$$
$$\theta = \arctan(r_y, r_x)$$

where $|\mathbf{r}|$ is the vector length and the function arctan(*y*, *x*) is the two-argument form of the arctangent function. It returns:

$$\arctan(y/x) \qquad \text{if } x > 0$$
$$\arctan(y/x) + \pi \quad \text{if } x < 0$$
$$\pi/2 \qquad\qquad \text{if } x = 0 \text{ and } y > 0$$
$$-\pi/2 \qquad\qquad \text{if } x = 0 \text{ and } y < 0$$

This function is available in most C++ implementations as the standard library function *atan2(y, x)*.

Encapsulating these formulas in a class gives us:

Listing 3.4

```cpp
// SPHERIC3.H - 3-D Spherical Co-ordinate System Class

#ifndef _SPHERIC3_H
#define _SPHERIC3_H

#include "vector3.h"

class Spheric3        // 3-D spherical co-ordinate system
{
  private:
    double length;        // Vector length
    double horz;          // Horizontal angle (in radians)
    double vert;          // Vertical angle (in radians)

  public:
    Spheric3( double len = 1.0, double h = 0.0, double v =
        0.0 )
    { length = len; horz = h; vert = v; }

    double GetHorz() { return horz; }
    double GetLength() { return length; }
    double GetVert() { return vert; }
    void SetHorz( double h ) { horz = h; }
    void SetLength( double len ) { length = len; }
    void SetVert( double v ) { vert = v; }

    // Convert spherical to rectangular co-ordinates
    void SpherToRect( Vector3 *pv )
    {
      pv->SetX(length * sin(vert) * cos(horz));
      pv->SetY(length * sin(vert) * sin(horz));
      pv->SetZ(length * cos(vert));
    }

    // Convert rectangular to spherical co-ordinates
    void RectToSpher( Vector3 &v )
    {
      length = v.Length();
      vert = acos(v.GetZ() / length);
      horz = atan2(v.GetY(), v.GetX());
    }
};

#endif
```

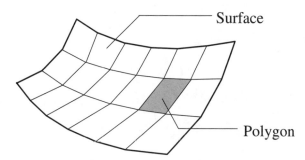

Figure 3.4 Polygon mesh representation of a surface

3.4 POLYGONS

We saw in the Chapter 2 that the radiosity approach subdivides each surface of an environment into a mesh of elements called patches, where each patch is a three-dimensional polygon. A polygon mesh is the simplest mathematical representation of a surface (Fig. 3.4).

Most three-dimensional CAD programs model curved surfaces as polygon meshes. Unfortunately, many of them do not allow the user to specify which side of the surface is exterior to an object. Clearly, only one side of the surface is visible. Nevertheless, programs such as AutoCAD can distinguish sides (and their subsequent visibility) only by inference from the surface's placement in an environment. This is a nuisance, to say the least. For our purposes, we will consider each surface and its constituent polygons to have two sides, only one of which is exterior to an object.

Polygons can be flat (i.e., planar), convex, or concave (i.e., nonplanar). Unfortunately, nonplanarity introduces a number of unwelcome complexities. For instance, the direction of the normal vector varies across the polygon surface, and the curve of the surface must be represented somehow. Since most radiosity methods assume flat patches, we will ignore these complexities and consider only planar polygons.

A planar polygon can be uniquely represented by an ordered list of *vertices* (Fig. 3.5), where by definition the vertices all lie on the same two-dimensional plane. Looking at the visible side of the polygon, we see that the vertices are ordered such that they follow a counterclockwise path around the polygon edges. *This is essential!* We can then use the vertices to define the polygon normal **n**. If we define vectors $\mathbf{v}_1$ and $\mathbf{v}_2$ as $p_1 - p_0$ and $p_3 - p_0$ respectively, then **n** is given by the cross product of the two vectors:

$$\mathbf{n} = \mathbf{v}_1 \times \mathbf{v}_2 \tag{3.3}$$

or, to use an example of our *Point3* and *Vector3* class notation:

```
Point3 p0(0.0, 0.0, 0.0);
Point3 p1(1.0, 0.0, 0.0);
Point3 p2(1.0, 1.0, 0.0);
Point3 p3(0.0, 1.0, 0.0);
```

(continued)

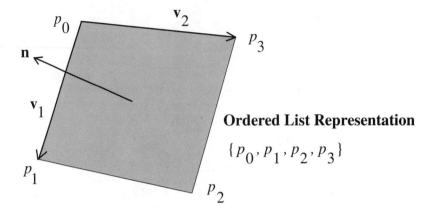

Figure 3.5   Ordered list representation of planar polygon

```
Vector3 v1(p0, p1);
Vector3 v2(p0, p3);

Vector3 n = Cross(v1, v2));
n.Norm();    // Normalize vector
```

Although a polygon can have any number of vertices, it becomes awkward to manage the data structures needed to represent them. For our purposes, we need consider only two polygon primitives: triangles and quadrilaterals. All of our polygons will have four vertices—triangles will be represented as having equal third and fourth vertices. We will also assume that our polygons are *simple* (i.e., none of their edges cross one another, thereby forming two triangular polygons from a quadrilateral polygon) and that they are not *degenerate* (i.e., they have finite areas).

A polygon can also be convex or concave in another sense, as shown in Figure 3.6. A convex planar polygon is one in which you can stretch an imaginary rubber band around it and not have any gaps between it and the polygon edges.

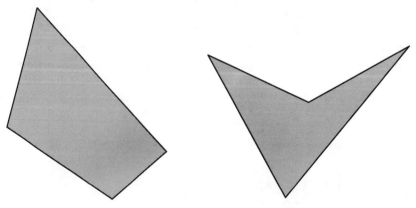

Figure 3.6a   Convex planar polygon   **Figure 3.6b**   Concave planar polygon

Concave planar polygons are somewhat more difficult to deal with in computer graphics. Rather than address these difficulties in this book, we shall simply issue a fiat to ourselves: All quadrilateral polygons must be convex.

3.4.1 Polygon Visibility

Since a polygon has only one visible side (its *face*), we can ask whether we can see it from a given point in space. A visibility test called backface elimination or culling allows us quickly to identify which polygons face away from our viewing position (Fig. 3.7).

The test is very simple: the polygon face is visible only if the angle θ between the polygon normal **n** and the line of sight vector **s** is less than ± 90 degrees. Recalling the formula for the dot product of two vectors $\mathbf{v}_1$ and $\mathbf{v}_2$ and noting that **s** is pointing in the opposite direction from **n**), we see that the angle θ between **n** and **s** will be less than ± 90 degrees only if the their dot product is less than zero. Thus:

IF n · s = 0
    Polygon is visible
ELSE
    Polygon is not visible
ENDIF

In terms of our *Vector3* class notation, this becomes:

```
Vector3 normal, sight;

if (Dot(normal, sight) < (float) 0.0)
  return TRUE;
else
  return FALSE;
```

Our dot-product function *Vector3::Dot* requires only three multiplication and two addition operations, making polygon-visibility determination very fast. This is an important consideration, since we will be viewing many thousands of polygons in

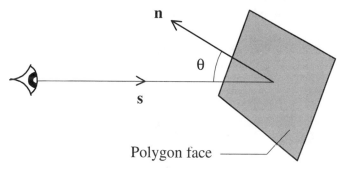

Polygon face

Figure 3.7   Polygon visibility test

a complex three-dimensional environment. Backface culling allows us quickly to eliminate roughly half the polygons from further consideration before performing the computationally expensive operations of view transformation, clipping, hidden-surface elimination, and scan conversion (to be discussed in Chap. 4).

We can now see why we must define the vertices of a polygon in counterclockwise order: Doing so ensures that the polygon normal points away from the visible face. Without this ordering, our simple backface culling algorithm wouldn't work.

3.4.2 Polygon Areas

We shall later need to know the area of a polygon. If we limit our attention to planar triangles (Fig. 3.8), there is a very elegant answer given by the cross product:

$$A = |\mathbf{v}_1 \times \mathbf{v}_2|/2 \tag{3.4}$$

where A is the area and $\mathbf{v}_1$ and $\mathbf{v}_2$ are vectors defined by the polygon vertices. (Any convex planar quadrilateral can, of course, be decomposed into two triangles.)

Why this works becomes clear when we consider the physical interpretation of the cross-product operation. Remember that the magnitude of the cross product of two vectors is equal to the area of the parallelogram described by them (Fig 3.2b). Our triangle is exactly one half of the parallelogram, regardless of which vertices we use to define the vectors.

An example using our *Point3* and *Vector3* classes is:

```
Point3 p0(0.0, 0.0, 0.0);
Point3 p1(1.0, 0.0, 0.0);
Point3 p2(0.0, 1.0, 0.0);

Vector3 v1(p0, p1);
Vector3 v2(p0, p3);

Vector3 temp = Cross(v1, v2);
area = temp.Length() / (float) 2.0;
```

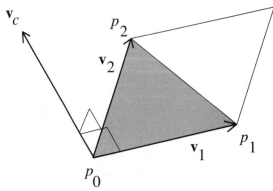

Figure 3.8 Area of a triangular polygon

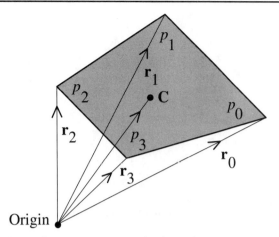

Figure 3.9 Determining the center (centroid) of a polygon

3.4.3 Polygon Centers

We shall also later need to know the *center* of a polygon. More specifically, we will need to know its center of gravity, or *centroid*. Imagine a physical polygon cut from a piece of stiff, flat cardboard. It will balance on the tip of a needle only if it is supported at its centroid.

Given a polygon with *m* vertices, its centroid **C** is defined as:

$$\mathbf{C} = \sum_{i=1}^{m} \mathbf{r}_i / m \tag{3.5}$$

where $\mathbf{r}_i$ is a bound vector from the origin to vertex p_i (Fig 3.9).

The centroid **C** is a three-dimensional point located on the surface of the polygon. However, we can add only vectors, so Equation 3.5 considers **C** to be a bound vector from the origin to the centroid. Its *x*, *y*, *z* coordinates are the same as the centroid's position in three-dimensional space, and so we can simply copy them to a *Point3* object after we calculate them as a *Vector3* object.

3.4.4 Vertex Normals

Although we can model a curved surface as an array of planar polygons, we have to pay careful attention to the surface normal. The direction of the true surface normal varies continuously as we move across a curved surface. Each polygon normal, on the other hand, has a constant direction. Moving across the polygonal approximation of the surface results in discontinuous changes in the direction of the surface normal.

These discontinuities are of particular concern in ray-tracing applications, where the ray tracer needs to know the true normal of a specular surface (or a close approximation) in order to determine the direction of a reflected ray. In contrast,

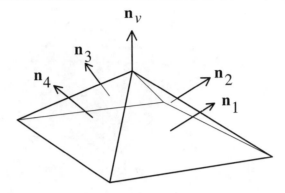

Figure 3.10   Determining the vertex normal from adjacent polygon normals

most radiosity applications are concerned with diffuse surfaces. As such, they only need to know about the individual polygon normals.

There are radiosity applications, however, in which it is necessary to know the surface normal at the polygon vertices (see Chap. 5). Looking at Figure 3.10, we can approximate the true normal at the vertex as the average of the normals for the polygons sharing it. In other words, we have:

$$\mathbf{n}_v = \sum_{i=1}^{m} \mathbf{n}_i / m \tag{3.6}$$

where $\mathbf{n}_v$ is the vertex normal and $\mathbf{n}_i$ is the normal of the ith of m polygons.

3.5   REFLECTANCE AND COLOR

We have so far represented polygons as three-dimensional geometrical objects with no intrinsic physical properties. To be useful for anything other than wireframe models, we need to add surface reflectances to our model.

As was noted in Chapter 1, the physical reflectance properties of a surface usually depend on wavelength. However, they can be approximated by specifying the average spectral reflectance within three or more color bands. Subtle color aliasing effects can occur in photorealistic renderings when only three bands are used (Hall 1989). However, these are usually apparent only when compared to the physical objects they are modeling. For most purposes, a choice of red, green, and blue bands is sufficient. Together the three reflectance values define the intrinsic color of the polygon surface.

How many bits are needed for each value? Under optimal viewing conditions, we can distinguish at most several hundred thousand colors. This implies that the 16.7 million colors offered by a 24-bit representation (using one byte for each primary color) are quite adequate for display purposes.

Spectral radiant exitance, on the other hand, requires much greater precision.

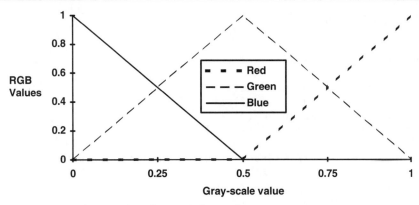

Figure 3.11 A simple pseudocolor encoding scheme

Our radiosity methods require us repeatedly to update a polygon's exitance, possibly as many as several hundred times in the course of solving the radiosity equation. Each update requires that we multiply the flux received by the polygon by its average spectral reflectance for each color band. A single byte per spectral band is clearly inadequate here; we have to use a floating-point representation.

We may also want to create and display gray-scale images. Since our eyes are more sensitive to green light than they are to red or blue (Fig. 1.7), we will need to take a weighted average of the three color band values. A set of weights suitable for most display devices is:

$$value = 0.30R + 0.59G + 0.11B \tag{3.7}$$

where *value* is the gray-scale value and *R*, *G,* and *B* are the red, green, and blue color band values respectively. Assigning this value to each color band produces a monochromatic shade of gray.

We may also want to display pseudocolor images, with each color representing a given range of surface exitance values. We have an almost infinite variety of choices when it comes to assigning colors. One simple but useful approach is offered by the color scheme shown in Figure 3.11, where the colors range from blue through green to red in order of increasing exitance. This allows us to perform color mapping on the fly without having to store a potentially large color look-up table.

The following *ColorRGB* and *Spectra* classes incorporate these ideas in a simple but effective representation:

Listing 3.5

```
// COLOR.H - Color Model Classes

#ifndef _COLOR_H
#define _COLOR_H
```

(continued)

Listing 3.5   *(continued)*

```cpp
#include <limits.h>
#include "general.h"

// Grayscale color band weights
#define C_RedWeight     (float) 0.30
#define C_GreenWeight   (float) 0.59
#define C_BlueWeight    (float) 0.11

class Spectra    // Average spectral radiant exitance
{
  private:
    float red_band;
    float green_band;
    float blue_band;

  public:
    float GetBlueBand() { return blue_band; }
    float GetGreenBand() { return green_band; }
    float GetRedBand() { return red_band; }
    void Reset()
    { red_band = green_band = blue_band = 0.0; }
    void SetBlueBand( float b ) { blue_band = b; }
    void SetGreenBand( float g ) { green_band = g; }
    void SetRedBand( float r ) { red_band = r; }

    Spectra &Add( Spectra &a )  // Add color
    {
      red_band += a.red_band;
      green_band += a.green_band;
      blue_band += a.blue_band;

      return *this;
    }

    Spectra &Subtract( Spectra &a )     // Subtract color
    {
      red_band -= a.red_band;
      green_band -= a.green_band;
      blue_band -= a.blue_band;

      return *this;
    }

    // Blend colors
    friend Spectra Blend( Spectra &s1, Spectra &s2, double
        alpha )
    {
      Spectra temp;     // Temporary spectrum
```

```
        // Linear interpolation
        temp.red_band = s1.red_band + (s2.red_band -
            s1.red_band) * (float) alpha;
        temp.green_band = s1.green_band + (s2.green_band -
            s1.green_band) * (float) alpha;
        temp.blue_band = s1.blue_band + (s2.blue_band -
            s1.blue_band) * (float) alpha;

        return temp;
    }

    double GetMaxColor()           // Get maximum color
    {
        float maximum = 0.0;

        maximum = max(maximum, red_band);
        maximum = max(maximum, green_band);
        maximum = max(maximum, blue_band);

        return (double) maximum;
    }

    void Scale( double value )  // Scale color
    {
        red_band *= (float) value;
        green_band *= (float) value;
        blue_band *= (float) value;
    }
};

class ColorRGB  // 24-bit RGB color model
{
    private:
        BYTE red;
        BYTE green;
        BYTE blue;

    public:
        BYTE GetBlue() { return blue; }
        BYTE GetGreen() { return green; }
        BYTE GetRed() { return red; }
        void SetBlue( BYTE b ) { blue = b; }
        void SetGreen( BYTE g ) { green = g; }
        void SetRed( BYTE r ) { red = r; }

        // Set 24-bit grayscale
        void SetColor( Spectra &c )
        {
            red = (BYTE) (c.GetRedBand() * (float) UCHAR_MAX);
            green = (BYTE) (c.GetGreenBand() * (float) UCHAR_MAX);
            blue = (BYTE) (c.GetBlueBand() * (float) UCHAR_MAX);
        }
```

(continued)

Listing 3.5   *(continued)*

```
    // Set 24-bit grayscale
    void SetMono( Spectra &c )
    {
      red = green = blue =  (BYTE) ((c.GetRedBand() *
          C_RedWeight + c.GetGreenBand() * C_GreenWeight +
          c.GetBlueBand() * C_BlueWeight) * (float)
          UCHAR_MAX);
    }

    // Set 24-bit pseudocolor
    void SetPseudo( Spectra &c )
    {
      double gsv;         // Grayscale value

      // Convert color to grayscale
      gsv = (double) (c.GetRedBand() * C_RedWeight +
          c.GetGreenBand() * C_GreenWeight + c.GetBlueBand()
          * C_BlueWeight);

      // Convert grayscale to pseudocolor
      if (gsv < 0.5)
      {
        red = (BYTE) 0;
        green = (BYTE) (2.0 * gsv * (double) UCHAR_MAX);
        blue = (BYTE) ((1.0 - 2.0 * gsv) * (double)
            UCHAR_MAX);
      }
      else
      {
        red = (BYTE) ((2.0 * gsv - 1.0) * (double)
            UCHAR_MAX);
        green = (BYTE) ((2.0 - 2.0 * gsv) * (double)
            UCHAR_MAX);
        blue = (BYTE) 0;
      }
    }
};

#endif
```

Spectra is used for two purposes: to represent surface reflectances and average spectral radiant exitances. When used for surface reflectance, the three color band values *red_band, green_ban,* and *blue_band* must range from 0.0 to 1.0 inclusive. For average spectral radiant exitance, however, they can assume any nonnegative number. This allows us to add bright light source patches to an environment without adjusting the exitances of existing light source patches. However, *ColorRGB* implicitly assumes that *red_band, green_band,* and *blue_band* range from 0.0 to 1.0. This means that we need to scale appropriately all *Spectra* objects before calling *ColorRGB::SetColor* to convert them to a 24-bit RGB representation. (The same applies for *ColorRGB::SetMono* and *ColorRGB::SetPseudo*.) To do this, each *Spectra* object is examined to determine the maximum color band value for the set of objects (by calling *Spectra::GetMaxColor*). The inverse of this value becomes the parameter to be passed to *Spectra::Scale*. (More sophisticated conversion algorithms can also be used; see, for example Hall 1989).

3.5.1 Gamma Correction

Specifying a color as a 24-bit *ColorRGB* object is not enough for photorealistic display purposes. Most video monitors (monochrome and color), photographic films, four-color printing processes, and other display media have nonlinear responses that we must compensate for.

Consider, for example, a typical color video monitor. The video display adapter in our computer converts each color value into a discrete voltage for the three electron guns inside the cathode ray tubes. The resultant beams of electrons are directed to a pixel on the screen, where rare earth phosphors convert their energy into the visible (i.e., red, green, and blue) light that we see.

The problem is that there is a nonlinear relation between electron gun voltage and light output. This relation can be expressed as:

$$L = kv^{\gamma} \tag{3.8}$$

where L is the phosphor spectral radiance, k is a constant, v is the input voltage to the electron gun, and the exponent γ ("gamma") determines the degree of nonlinearity. The value of this exponent varies between monitors but generally ranges from 2.2 to 2.5 (Foley et al. 1990). In visual terms, a displayed image displayed "as is" will appear to have too much contrast.

We can compensate for this nonlinear behavior through *gamma correction*. Given an input value v_{input} (such as one of the members of a *ColorRGB* object), the linearized output value v_{output} is given by:

$$v_{output} = \left(\frac{v_{input}}{k} \right)^{\frac{1}{\gamma}} \tag{3.9}$$

In critical color-rendition applications, it may be necessary to determine experimentally a value of γ for each primary color. In most instances, however, the same gamma correction can be applied equally to all three members of a *ColorRGB* object.

Since each *ColorRGB* member has a limited range of discrete values it can assume, it will be convenient to precompute the equivalent output values and store them in a look-up table. This gives us:

Listing 3.6   GAMMA.H

```
// GAMMA.H - Gamma Correction Class

#ifndef _GAMMA_H
#define _GAMMA_H

#include "color.h"

static const int G_Domain = 256;        // Input domain
static const int G_Range = 256;         // Output range

class Gamma        // Gamma correction
{
  private:
    // Gamma correction lookup table
    static BYTE GammaTable[256];

    double g_value;      // Gamma value

    void InitTable()
    {
      int i;     // Loop index

      // Calculate gamma correction lookup table entries
      for (i = 0; i < G_Domain; i++)
        GammaTable[i] = (BYTE) ((double) G_Range *
            pow((double) i / (double) G_Domain, 1.0 /
            g_value));
    }

  public:
    Gamma( double g = 2.2 )
    {
      g_value = g;
      InitTable();
    }

    double GetGamma() { return g_value; }

    void Correct( ColorRGB &c )
    {
      c.SetRed(GammaTable[c.GetRed()]);
      c.SetGreen(GammaTable[c.GetGreen()]);
      c.SetBlue(GammaTable[c.GetBlue()]);
    }

    void SetGamma( double g )
    {
      g_value = g;
      InitTable();
    }
};

#endif
```

and:

Listing 3.7

```
// GAMMA.CPP - Gamma Correction Class

#include "gamma.h"

// Gamma correction lookup table
BYTE Gamma::GammaTable[G_Domain];
```

Actually, this class can provide more than gamma correction. The defined constants *G_Domain* and *G_Range* specify the range of the input and output values respectively. For *ColorRGB*, these are both assumed to be 8-bit *BYTE* data types. However, some video display adapters (the IBM-PC's VGA and 256-color SuperVGA adapters, for example) support only six bits per primary color. *Gamma* can support these devices if *G_Range* is redefined to be 64. The gamma-correction look-up table values will then be calculated such that the output values are within the range 0 to 63.

The *g_value* member specifies the gamma correction to be applied and defaults to 2.2. Other values can be used for specific video monitors or other display media. It can be updated at any time by calling *SetGamma* with any positive gamma value.

Gamma is something of an oddball class. It belongs with *ColorRGB*, but it has nothing to do with building an environment. It's one of the joys of trying to shoehorn the real world into a hierarchy of neatly defined classes: Sometimes you have bits and pieces left over. *Gamma* is one of those pieces. Having developed it, we can put it aside until the next chapter.

3.5.2 Color-Reduction Techniques

While 24-bit color display adapters with their 16.7 million colors are becoming increasingly common, there are still many personal desktop computers without such capabilities. Since our radiosity renderer will inherently generate 24-bit color images, we need to consider *color-reduction* techniques that match our images to the display capabilities of these computers.

Many of the more recent personal computers support a maximum of 32,768 or 65,536 colors. This includes those with display adapters that offer 24-bit support for their lower-resolution modes only. Displaying 24-bit color images is possible if the software reduces the gamut of image colors to those that can be displayed. In most cases, this is done simply by dividing the 16.7 million possible colors into 32,768 or 65,536 equally spaced regions. Unfortunately, this usually results in annoying color bands appearing on what should be smoothly shaded surfaces.

One solution is to employ one of several *dithering* techniques (e.g., Foley et al. 1990). Although often effective, a discussion of color-dithering algorithms is beyond the scope of this book (see Thomas and Bogart 1991 for two examples, including C source code). Fortunately, we can use a simpler approach that produces nearly equal results: color *jittering*.

The basic principle is that the human eye is fairly insensitive to random pixel-by-pixel variations in color or shading—we tend to see the average color instead. This is useful: We can introduce a small amount of random "noise" to an image without noticeably degrading its appearance. At worst, the image appears to have a somewhat "grainy" appearance, much like a photograph taken with a high-speed color film.

By itself, adding noise does nothing to improve the appearance of a displayed 24-bit color image. However, the noise very effectively masks the color bands we would otherwise see. Given a choice, observers invariably choose images with random noise over those with visible color banding.

Bragg 1992 presented a simple color-reduction "filter" that capitalizes on this effect by jittering each color component of an RGB pixel by a small random amount. This random noise is weighted such that the average RGB color of any small group of pixels closely approximates the average color of their original 24-bit colors. Each RGB component is then masked to produce a 5-bit value, resulting in a total of 32,768 (i.e., $32 \times 32 \times 32$) possible colors.

In detail, Bragg's algorithm begins by dividing each 8-bit RGB color-component value into 32 equally spaced regions and saving the remainder. Each region represents one of 32 output values. This value is divided by 8; its remainder is in the range of 0 to 7. A random number in the range of 0 to 8 is then chosen. If the second remainder is less than or equal to this number, the original 8-bit RGB component value is incremented by 8. The effect of this procedure is to produce a randomized component value that is weighted toward the nearest 5-bit output value.

The component value is further randomized by adding another small random value. The range of this noise is user-defined by a "noise level" parameter that can range from 0 (no noise) to 8. A value of 1 or 2 is sufficient to mask any color banding in most images; 8 produces very grainy images. Finally, a 5-bit output value is produced by masking off the three least significant bits.

We can implement this algorithm with the following C++ class:

Listing 3.8

```
// C_JITTER.H - Color Reduction Filter Class

#ifndef _C_JITTER_H
#define _C_JITTER_H

// Adapted from: Bragg, D. [1992]. "A Simple Color Reduction
//               Filter", in Graphics Gems III (D. Kirk,
//               Ed.), Academic Press, San Diego, CA, 20 -
//               22, 429 - 431

#include <stdlib.h>
#include "color.h"
```

```
static const int C_LargeNum = 1024;
static const int C_TableSize = 1024;
static const int C_Mask = C_TableSize - 1;

class ColorJitter          // Color reduction filter
{
  private:
    double *pxrand;        // Jitter lookup table pointer
    double *pyrand;        // Jitter lookup table pointer
    int noise;             // Noise level ( 0 - 8 )
    int *pirand;           // Jitter lookup table pointer
    BOOL status;           // Object status

    double JitterX( int x, int y, int band )
    {
      return pxrand[((x + (y << 2)) + pirand[(x + band) &
        C_Mask]) & C_Mask];
    }

    double JitterY( int x, int y, int band )
    {
      return pyrand[((y + (x << 2)) + pirand[(y + band) &
        C_Mask]) & C_Mask];
    }

  public:
    ColorJitter();

    ~ColorJitter();

    BOOL GetStatus() { return status; }
    int GetNoiseLevel() { return noise; }
    void SetNoiseLevel( int n ) { noise = n % 9; }
    void Reduce( ColorRGB *, int, int );
};

#endif
```

and:

Listing 3.9

```
// C_JITTER.CPP - Color Reduction Filter Class

// Adapted from: Bragg, D. [1992]. "A Simple Color Reduction
//               Filter", in Graphics Gems III (D. Kirk,
//               Ed.), Academic Press, San Diego, CA, 20 -
//               22, 429 - 431

#include "c_jitter.h"

ColorJitter::ColorJitter()       // Class constructor
{
```

(continued)

Listing 3.8   *(continued)*

```
  int i;    // Loop index

  status = TRUE;

  // Initialize jitter lookup table pointers
  pirand = NULL;
  pxrand = NULL;
  pyrand = NULL;

  noise = 1;    // Set default noise level

  // Allocate jitter lookup tables
  if ((pirand = new int[C_TableSize]) == NULL)
  {
    status = FALSE;
    return;
  }

  if ((pxrand = new double[C_TableSize]) == NULL)
  {
    status = FALSE;
    return;
  }

  if ((pyrand = new double[C_TableSize]) == NULL)
  {
    status = FALSE;
    return;
  }

  // Initialize jitter lookup tables
  for (i = 0; i < C_TableSize; i++)
  {
    pirand[i] = (int) ((double) C_TableSize * ((double)
        (rand() % C_LargeNum) / (double) C_LargeNum));
    pxrand[i] = (double) (rand() % C_LargeNum) / (double)
        C_LargeNum;
    pyrand[i] = (double) (rand() % C_LargeNum) / (double)
        C_LargeNum;
  }
}

ColorJitter::~ColorJitter()    // Class destructor
{
  // Release jitter lookup tables
  if (pirand != NULL)
    delete [] pirand;

  if (pxrand != NULL)
    delete [] pxrand;
```

```
    if (pyrand != NULL)
      delete [] pyrand;
}

// Perform color reduction by jittering color values
void ColorJitter::Reduce( ColorRGB *pc, int x, int y )
{
  int i;              // Loop index
  int p, q;           // Temporary variables
  BYTE color[3];      // Color band values

  // Get color band values
  color[0] = pc->GetRed();
  color[1] = pc->GetGreen();
  color[2] = pc->GetBlue();

  for (i = 0; i < 3; i++)
  {
    if (color[i] < 248)
    {
      // Map color band value to one of 32 possible output
      // values and determine remainder
      p = (int) (color[i] % 8);

      // Look up random jitter value based on color band
      // index and pixel x-y co-ordinates
      q = (int) (JitterX(x, y, i) * 9.0);

      // Jitter color band value
      if (p >= q)
        color[i] += 8;

      // Calculate second jitter value and add to color
      // band value
      q = 8 * ((int) ((JitterY(x, y, i) * (double) (2 *
          noise)) + 0.5) - noise) + (int) color[i];

      // Ensure jittered color band value is within
      // allowable range
      if (q >= 0 && q <= 255)
        color[i] = q;
    }

    // Mask off lowest three bits to create 5-bit value
    color[i] &= 0xf8;
  }

  // Set jittered color band values
  pc->SetRed(color[0]);
  pc->SetGreen(color[1]);
  pc->SetBlue(color[2]);
}
```

The *ColorJitter* class constructor precalculates and stores random jitter values in three look-up tables. The table look-up functions *JitterX* and *JitterY* are admittedly somewhat convoluted. However, they have the valuable property that the returned random number always has the same magnitude for any given pair of pixel coordinates (*x* and *y*). This is important if *ColorJitter* is to be used to color reduce a sequence of 24-bit images for an animation. Using *rand* for each jitter value would result in the animated sequence displaying a highly objectionable amount of "snow." A detailed explanation and analysis of the look-up tables and their access functions is given in Cychosz (1990).

What about older-model desktop computers that offer a maximum of 256 colors? Attempting to display 24-bit color images with these systems usually produces unacceptably garish and posterized results. Nevertheless, it is evident that they are quite capable of displaying reasonable-quality photorealistic images.

The saving grace of these computers is that their 256-color display adapters feature programmable palettes. At six bits per color channel, there are 262,144 ($64 \times 64 \times 64$) colors to choose from. Since most scenes are dominated by relatively few colors, often fewer than 256 colors are needed to provide a reasonable approximation of a 24-bit color image. All we have to do is to find those colors!

Unfortunately, finding the colors is not a simple problem. Basically, we need to group common colors together and represent them with one averaged color for each group. There are several *color-quantization* techniques that we can use, but a full discussion would take us too far afield. The diskette accompanying this book includes a text file that discusses the octree color-quantization algorithm (Gervautz and Purgathofer 1990) and presents full C++ source code for a stand-alone color-quantization utility. Here we simply note the problem and continue with our primary interest: building an environment.

3.6   ENTITIES AND INSTANCES

Many ray-tracing and CAD programs model complex three-dimensional environments as a hierarchy of objects, volumes, surfaces, and polygons. That is, an environment consists of a collection of objects, each of which is modeled as a set of volume primitives such as boxes, spheres, cylinders, and tori. In the case of CAD programs, the merged surfaces of these volumes are then approximated with polygon meshes.

This approach has numerous advantages. For example, we might be modeling an office that has several identical tables located about the room. A hierarchical representation allows us to model one table as an *entity*. Each table in the room then becomes an *instance* of this entity. We can scale, rotate, and translate these instances as required (see Section 3.11) to position them individually in the room.

The approach we must take is regrettably more common. Developing a three-dimensional CAD interface that would enable us to model interactively objects as volume primitives and polygon meshes is beyond the scope of this book. Instead, we will have to model entities as a hierarchy of surfaces and polygons by hand. (Again, however, the accompanying diskette includes a data file translator for readers with access to a three-dimensional CAD program that can generate AutoCAD-compatible DXF files. A considerable amount of hand work still has to be done, but at least you are spared the necessity of having to enter manually innumerable vertex coordinates.)

3.7   POLYGONS AND RADIOSITY

Recalling Section 2.2, we realize that the solution of the radiosity equation is expressed in terms of patch (polygon) exitances. Now exitance—as was emphasized in Section 1.9—is not a property of a polygon surface per se. Nevertheless, it will be convenient to store this information as a *Spectra* data type in the polygon data structure. This will allow us to solve the radiosity equation independently for each of the three spectral color bands.

We will also see in Chapter 5 that the time needed to solve the radiosity algorithm can be reduced by modeling surfaces as a two-level hierarchy of polygons. A surface is first divided into a coarse grid of polygons called *patches*. Each patch is then divided into a smaller grid of polygons called *elements* (Fig. 3.12).

Other radiosity methods go further, dividing the surfaces into a multilevel hierarchy of polygons; the reasons for this will be explained in Chapter 8. For our purposes, a two-level hierarchy is sufficient.

3.8   MODELING AN ENVIRONMENT

There are many possible ways to describe polygons in a complex three-dimensional environment. Cohen et al. (1986), for example, used a *winged-edge* data structure to provide access to polygon data in constant time. Winged-edge data structures (e.g., Baumgart 1975) offer several computational advantages when manipulating polygons. They are also quite complex and difficult to implement properly (Glassner 1991). We will therefore limit our attention to a simpler but still efficient and flexible linked list representation.

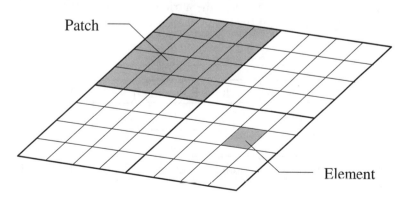

Figure 3.12   Subdividing a surface into a hierarchy of patches and elements

It is very important to ensure that we can access the information we need in an environment with a minimum of effort. This leads to the linked list representation shown in Figure 3.13.

An environment consists of a linked list of instances. The purpose of the links is as follows:

Object	Link	Comments
Instance	Surface	Each instance consists of one or more surfaces.
	Vertex	Provides immediate access to linked list of vertices.
	Next Instance	
Surface	Patch	Each surface consists of one or more patches.
	Next Surface	
Patch	Element	Each patch consists of one or more elements.
	Vertex[4]	Each patch has three or four vertices.
	Parent surface	Each patch belongs to a parent surface.
	Next Patch	
Element	Vertex[4]	Each element has three or four vertices.
	Parent patch	Each element belongs to a parent patch.
	Next Element	
Vertex	ElemList	Each vertex is shared by one or more elements.
	Next vertex	
ElemList	Element	Each ElemList member points to an element.
	Next ElemList	

To expand on this explanation, all the vertices defining a surface are stored once in memory as a linked list. This list is owned by the instance, which provides it with access to the vertices without having to traverse the linked lists of surfaces, patches, and elements.

The patches and elements each point to three or four of these vertices, depending on whether they represent triangles or quadrilaterals. Each vertex is shared by one or more elements and patches.

Later we will want to access the attributes of the elements sharing a given vertex as quickly as possible. Each vertex therefore points to a linked list of *ElemList*

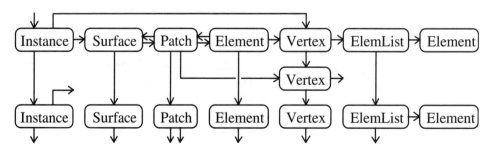

Figure 3.13   Modeling the environment as a linked list data structure

objects, each of which points to an element sharing the vertex. (The patches sharing a vertex are not important.)

Finally, each element has a pointer to its parent patch, and each patch has a pointer to its parent surface. These will be used to access patch and surface attributes from an element without having to traverse the environment data structure.

One disadvantage of linked lists is that they have a voracious appetite for memory, especially when relatively small objects must be allocated from C++'s free store (also referred to as *global* or *heap* memory). This concerns memory management, which is discussed at length in Appendix B. For our current purposes, we can allocate and release memory as required using C++'s default *new* and *delete* operators. A production-quality program, however, really should provide its own class-specific memory-management functions.

3.8.1 Modeling Polygons

Beginning at the bottom of our hierarchy of entities, surfaces, and polygons, we can represent patches and elements with the following C++ class:

Listing 3.10

```
// PATCH3.H - 3-D Patch Classes

#ifndef _PATCH3_H
#define _PATCH3_H

#include "vector3.h"
#include "color.h"

#define QUAD_FLAG    0x01    // Quadrilateral flag

class Surface3;             // External reference

class ElemList              // Element list
{
  private:
    class Element3 *pelem;  // Element pointer
    ElemList *pnext;        // Next element list pointer

  public:
    ElemList( Element3 *pe, ElemList *pel )
    { pelem = pe; pnext = pel; }

    Element3 *GetElemPtr() { return pelem; }
    ElemList *GetNext() { return pnext; }
};
```

(continued)

Listing 3.10   *(continued)*

```cpp
class PatchList            // Patch list
{
  private:
    class Patch3 *ppatch;   // Patch pointer
    PatchList *pnext;       // Next patch list pointer

  public:
    PatchList( Patch3 *pp, PatchList *ppl )
    { ppatch = pp; pnext = ppl; }

    Patch3 *GetPatchPtr() { return ppatch; }
    PatchList *GetNext() { return pnext; }
};

class Vertex3            // 3-D vertex
{
  private:
    Point3 posn;          // Vertex co-ordinates
    Vector3 normal;       // Vertex normal
    Spectra exitance;     // Vertex exitance
    ElemList *pelhd;      // Element list head pointer
    Vertex3 *pnext;       // Next vertex pointer

  public:
    Vertex3( Point3 &coord )
    {
      posn = coord;
      normal = 0.0;
      pelhd = NULL;
      pnext = NULL;
      exitance.Reset();
    }

    ~Vertex3()
    {
      ElemList *pel = pelhd;
      ElemList *pelnext;

      // Delete element list
      while (pel != NULL)
      {
        pelnext = pel->GetNext();
        delete pel;
        pel = pelnext;
      }
    }
```

```
      ElemList *GetElemListPtr() { return pelhd; }
      Point3 &GetPosn() { return posn; }
      Point3 *GetPosnPtr() { return &posn; }
      Spectra &GetExitance() { return exitance; }
      Vector3 &GetNormal() { return normal; }
      Vertex3 *GetNext() { return pnext; }
      void CalcNormal();
      void SetExitance( Spectra &e ) { exitance = e; }
      void SetElemListPtr( ElemList *ppl) { pelhd = ppl; }
      void SetNext( Vertex3 *pn ) { pnext = pn; }
      void SetPosn( Point3 &p ) { posn = p; }
};

class Element3                      // 3-D element
{
  protected:
    BYTE flags;                     // Flags bitmap
    float area;                     // Element area
    Patch3 *ppatch;                 // Parent patch pointer
    Spectra exitance;               // Spectral exitance
    Vector3 normal;                 // Normal vector
    Vertex3 *pvertex[4];            // Vertex pointer array
    Element3 *pnext;                // Next element pointer

  public:
    Element3( Vertex3 *pvtx[4], Patch3 *pp )
    {
      int index;            // Array index

      ppatch = pp;
      area = 0.0;
      flags = (BYTE) 0;
      pnext = NULL;
      exitance.Reset();

      for (index = 0; index < 4; index++)
        pvertex[index] = pvtx[index];
    }

    BOOL IsQuad() { return (flags & QUAD_FLAG); }
    double GetArea() { return area; }
    int GetNumVert()
    { return (flags & QUAD_FLAG) ? 4 : 3; }
    Element3 *GetNext() { return pnext; }
    Patch3 *GetParentPtr() { return ppatch; }
    Spectra &GetExitance() { return exitance; }
    Vector3 &GetNormal() { return normal; }
    Vertex3 *GetVertexPtr( int i ) { return pvertex[i]; }
    void CalcArea();
    void CalcNormal();
    void SetExitance( Spectra &e ) { exitance = e; }
    void SetNext( Element3 *pn ) { pnext = pn; }
    void SetQuad() { flags |= QUAD_FLAG; }
};
```

(continued)

Listing 3.10 *(continued)*

```
class Patch3 : public Element3   // 3-D patch
{
  private:
    Point3 center;        // Patch center
    Element3 *pelhd;      // Element list head ptr
    Surface3 *psurf;      // Parent surface pointer

  public:
    Patch3( Vertex3 *pvtx[4], Surface3 *ps ) :
        Element3( pvtx, NULL )
    {
      pelhd = NULL;
      psurf = ps;
    }

    ~Patch3()
    {
      Element3 *pe = pelhd;
      Element3 *penext;

      while (pe != NULL)          // Delete elements
      {
        penext = pe->GetNext();
        delete pe;
        pe = penext;
      }
    }

    double GetUnsentFlux()
    {
      return ((exitance.GetRedBand() +
          exitance.GetGreenBand() + exitance.GetBlueBand())
          * (double) area);
    }

    Element3 *GetElementPtr() { return pelhd; }
    Patch3 *GetNext() { return (Patch3 *) pnext; }
    Point3 &GetCenter() { return center; }
    Surface3 *GetParentPtr() { return psurf; }
    void CalcCenter();
    void SetElementPtr( Element3 *pe ) { pelhd = pe; }
};

#endif
```

and:

Listing 3.11

```cpp
// PATCH3.CPP - 3-D Patch Classes

#include "patch3.h"

void Vertex3::CalcNormal()        // Calculate vertex normal
{
  ElemList *pelist = pelhd;        // Element list pointer

  // Sum element normals
  while (pelist != NULL)
  {
    normal += pelist->GetElemPtr()->GetNormal();
    pelist = pelist->GetNext();
  }

  normal.Norm();            // Normalize vector
}

void Element3::CalcArea()         // Calculate element area
{
  Vector3 temp;        // Temporary 3-D vector

  Vector3 va(pvertex[0]->GetPosn(), pvertex[1]->GetPosn());
  Vector3 vb(pvertex[0]->GetPosn(), pvertex[2]->GetPosn());

  temp = Cross(va, vb);
  area = (float) (temp.Length() / 2.0);

  if (IsQuad() == TRUE)
  {
    Vector3 vc(pvertex[3]->GetPosn(),
        pvertex[0]->GetPosn());

    temp = Cross(vb, vc);
    area += (float) (temp.Length() / 2.0);
  }
}

void Element3::CalcNormal()       // Calculate element normal
{
  Vector3 va(pvertex[0]->GetPosn(), pvertex[1]->GetPosn());
  Vector3 vb(pvertex[0]->GetPosn(), pvertex[2]->GetPosn());

  normal = Cross(va, vb);
  normal.Norm();
}

void Patch3::CalcCenter()          // Calculate patch centroid
{
```

(continued)

Listing 3.11   *(continued)*

```
int i;              // Loop index
int num_vert;       // Number of vertices
Vector3 cv;         // Centroid vector

num_vert = GetNumVert();

// Initialize centroid vector to origin
cv = Vector3(0.0, 0.0, 0.0);

// Determine patch centroid
for (i = 0; i < num_vert; i++)
  cv += Vector3(pvertex[i]->GetPosn());

cv /= (double) num_vert;

// Convert centroid vector to 3-D point
center.SetX(cv.GetX());
center.SetY(cv.GetY());
center.SetZ(cv.GetZ());
}
```

ElemList is self-explanatory: Each object of the class provides a singly linked list element that points to an *Element3* object and the next *ElemList* element. *ElemList::GetNext* returns *NULL* for the last element of the list. *PatchList* provides the same services for *Patch3* objects. We don't use linked lists of patches in our environment data structure, but we will need them later in this chapter when we build environments from data file descriptions.

The *Vertex3* class is slightly more interesting. Its private data members include the vertex coordinates and normal, its color (to be used in Chap. 4), a pointer to a linked list of elements that share the vertex, and a pointer to the next *Vertex3* list element. Again, *Vertex3::GetNext* returns *NULL* for the last element of the vertex list.

Vertex3::CalcNormal calculates the vertex normal according to Equation 3.6; normalizing the sum of the polygon normals is equivalent to dividing by the number of polygons sharing the vertex. These normals are not available when the *Vertex3* object is constructed, which is why *CalcNormal* is not part of the class constructor.

The *Element3* class can represent triangular and quadrilateral polygons. Each *Element3* object is a singly linked list element whose private data members include the polygon area and normal, a quadrilateral flag, an array of four *Vertex3* pointers, a pointer to its parent patch, and a pointer to the next *Element3* list element. If the polygon is a triangle, the third and fourth *Vertex3* pointers should be equal; otherwise *Element3::SetQuad* must be called to set the quadrilateral bit flag in *flags*.

Element3::CalcArea and *Element3::CalcNormal* calculate the polygon area and normal. Note that these values are not calculated by the *Element3* constructor; an object of this class initially belongs to an entity with default values for its dimensions, orientation, and position in space. Only when we create an instance of this entity by scaling, rotation, and translation (see Section 3.11) will we have the information necessary to calculate the polygon area and normal.

Patch3 is derived from *Element3* and so inherits its members and functions. To this it adds the patch center, a pointer to a linked list of elements, and a pointer to its parent surface. Like the *CalcArea* and *CalcNormal* functions, *Patch3::CalcCenter* should be called only after we've created an instance of the entity.

Patch3 also provides *Patch3::GetUnsentFlux* to calculate the patch's "unsent" flux. All this function does is sum the patch's spectral radiant exitances and multiply the value by the patch area. The result—the amount of radiant flux leaving and/or reflected by the patch—will be used in Chapter 6 when we solve the radiosity equation.

You may question the complexity of these data structures, particularly the *Element3* and *Patch3* classes. Keep in mind, however, that we want our data structures to (1) conserve memory; (2) provide quick and easy access to the polygon data members; and (3) allow for the dynamic addition, deletion, and modification of polygons and their vertices. The current C++ class designs, although perhaps not perfect, substantially achieve these goals.

3.8.2 Modeling Surfaces

Moving up our hierarchy, we next consider the representation of surfaces. Their physical geometry is described by their patches and elements; all we need to add are reflectance and initial spectral radiant exitance.

In theory, we should specify exitance values in units of watts per square meter for each color band. However, we are rarely interested in actual radiometric or photometric quantities when rendering radiosity images. It's like a camera, where you adjust the exposure and/or lens aperture to properly expose the film. Our interest is in the relative distribution of spectral radiant exitance in the environment. Accordingly, we can choose any convenient floating-point range—say 0.0 to 1.0—where the maximum value represents the maximum *initial* spectral radiant exitance in the environment. (Final calculated exitances may exceed this value if the light source also reflects light.)

One other point about surfaces: They do not share vertices where they join other surfaces. This allows us to set vertex colors according to the color of their parent polygons and surfaces.

Our *Surface3* class is thus:

Listing 3.12

```
// SURFACE3.H - 3-D Surface Class

#ifndef _SURFACE3_H
#define _SURFACE3_H

#include "patch3.h"
```

(continued)

Listing 3.12   *(continued)*

```
class Surface3  // 3-D surface
{
  private:
    Spectra reflectance;     // Spectral reflectance
    Spectra emittance;       // Initial radiant exitance
    Patch3 *pplhd;           // Patch list head pointer
    Surface3 *pnext;         // Next surface pointer

  public:
    Surface3( Spectra reflect, Spectra emit )
    {
      reflectance = reflect;
      emittance = emit;

      pplhd = NULL;
      pnext = NULL;
    }

    ~Surface3()
    {
      Patch3 *pp = pplhd;
      Patch3 *ppnext;

      while (pp != NULL)          // Delete patches
      {
        ppnext = pp->GetNext();
        delete pp;
        pp = ppnext;
      }
    }

    Spectra &GetReflectance() { return reflectance; }
    Spectra &GetEmittance() { return emittance; }
    Patch3 *GetPatchPtr() { return pplhd; }
    Surface3 *GetNext() { return pnext; }
    void SetNext( Surface3 *pn ) { pnext = pn; }
    void SetPatchPtr( Patch3 *pp ) { pplhd = pp; }
};

#endif
```

   Each *Surface3* object is a singly linked list element that points to a linked list of *Patch3* objects and the next *Surface3* element. As before, *Surface3::GetNext* returns NULL for the last element of the list.

3.8.3   Modeling Entities and Instances

Finally, we need a C++ class to represent entities, the top level of our hierarchy. We will later copy and transform each entity into instances for our environment. Although the transformation process may modify the size, orientation, and position of the entity in the environment, it does not result in any change in the underlying data structure. In other words, an entity is morphologically equivalent to an instance. We can therefore use the following *Instance* class to represent both entities and instances:

Listing 3.13

```
// INSTANCE.H - Instance Class

#ifndef _INSTANCE_H
#define _INSTANCE_H

#include "surface3.h"

class Instance              // Instance (also entity)
{
  private:
    Surface3 *pshead;       // Surface list head pointer
    Vertex3 *pvhead;        // Vertex list head pointer
    Instance *pnext;        // Next instance pointer

  public:
    Instance( Vertex3 *pv, Surface3 *ps )
    {
      pvhead = pv;
      pshead = ps;
      pnext = NULL;
    }

    ~Instance()
    {
      Surface3 *psnext;
      Surface3 *ps = pshead;
      Vertex3 *pvnext;
      Vertex3 *pv = pvhead;

      // Delete surfaces
      while (ps != NULL)
      {
        psnext = ps->GetNext();
        delete ps;
        ps = psnext;
      }

      // Delete vertices
      while (pv != NULL)
      {
        pvnext = pv->GetNext();
        delete pv;
        pv = pvnext;
      }
    }
```

(continued)

Listing 3.13   *(continued)*

```
    Instance *GetNext() { return pnext; }
    Surface3 *GetSurfPtr() { return pshead; }
    Vertex3 *GetVertPtr() { return pvhead; }
    void SetNext( Instance *pn ) { pnext = pn; }
    void SetSurfPtr( Surface3 *ps ) { pshead = ps; }
    void SetVertPtr( Vertex3 *pv ) { pvhead = pv; }
};

#endif
```

Each *Instance* object is a singly linked list element. Its private data members include a pointer to a linked list of *Surface3* objects, a pointer to a linked list of *Vertex3* elements, and a pointer to the next *Instance* element. A linked list of *Instance* elements fully describes a complex three-dimensional environment.

3.9   MODELING AN ENVIRONMENT

The last requirement for our environment is a class that can provide some statistics about it, such as the number of instances, surfaces, and so forth. It should also provide a pointer to the first instance and delete the memory allocated to the environment when we are through with it. This becomes:

Listing 3.14

```
// ENVIRON.H - Environment Class

#ifndef _ENVIRON_H
#define _ENVIRON_H

#include "instance.h"

class Environ    // Environment
{
  private:
    Instance *pinsthd;   // Instance list pointer
    WORD num_inst;       // Number of instances
    WORD num_surf;       // Number of surfaces
    WORD num_patch;      // Number of patches
    WORD num_elem;       // Number of elements
    WORD num_vert;       // Number of vertices

    friend class Parse;

  public:
    Environ() { pinsthd = NULL; }
```

```
~Environ() { DeleteEnv(); }

Instance *GetInstPtr() { return pinsthd; }
WORD GetNumInst() { return num_inst; }
WORD GetNumSurf() { return num_surf; }
WORD GetNumPatch() { return num_patch; }
WORD GetNumElem() { return num_elem; }
WORD GetNumVert() { return num_vert; }
void DeleteEnv()
{
  Instance *pinst;   // Instance pointer
  Instance *pnext;   // Next instance pointer

  pinst = pinsthd;
  while (pinst != NULL)
  {
    pnext = pinst->GetNext();
    delete pinst;
    pinst= pnext;
  }
  pinsthd = NULL;
}
};

#endif
```

3.10 A RUDIMENTARY DATA FILE FORMAT

Having designed a hierarchical data structure, we need a data file format that will allow us to store and retrieve our representations to and from disk, and possibly to transfer them across computer platforms.

Our first thought should be to consider one of the device-independent graphics standards, such as IGES, GKS-3D, or PHIGS. On the microcomputer front is the popular AutoCAD DXF graphics file format. However, these graphics standards all have complex specifications that cover far more than we need. All we want is a data file format that supports polygons, surfaces, and entities. There's little sense in choosing a graphics standard that includes scalable text, multiple fonts, polylines, linetype patterns, bicubic and Bezier surfaces, constructive solid geometry, and a host of other features that we'll never use. Lacking any existing standards for radiosity-rendering programs, we shall simply have to create our own.

Actually, we shall require two data file formats: one to describe individual entities and another to describe the transformations necessary to create instances of them in an environment. The entity file format will be considered here; the environment file format will be addressed later.

We begin by specifying our entity data file structure as in Figure 3.14.

```
COMMENT Entity Data File
ENTITY entity_name
VERTEX
< x1 y1 z1 >
< x2 y2 z2 >
...
< xm ym zm >
END_VERT
SURFACE
[ rr1 rg1 rb1 ] [ er1 eg2 eb1 ]
[ rr2 rg2 rb2 ] [ er2 eg2 eb2 ]
...
[ rrn rgn rbn ] [ ern egn ebn ]
END_SURF
PATCH
s1 { v10 v11 v12 v13 }
s2 { v20 v21 v22 v23 }
...
sp { vp0 vp1 vp2 vp3 }
END_PATCH
ELEMENT
p1 { v10 v11 v12 v13 }
p2 { v20 v21 v22 v23 }
...
pp { vp0 vp1 vp2 vp3 }
END_ELEM
END_ENTITY
```

Figure 3.14   Entity data file structure

The syntactic rules for our nameless file format specification are:

1. The data file consists of ASCII characters.
2. Each line must be terminated with an environment-specific "newline" character (typically <CR><LF> for MS-DOS and <CR> for UNIX systems).
3. The maximum length of a line is 256 characters, including the newline character(s).
4. Multiple whitespace (ASCII space and horizontal tab) characters between data values and separators are ignored.
5. Comment lines beginning with the keyword "COMMENT" are ignored.
6. The data file consists of one ENTITY section.
7. The ENTITY section header begins with the "ENTITY" keyword, followed on the same line by an optional *entity_name* character string that identifies the entity. Any printable ASCII character is permitted in the string.
8. The ENTITY section header is followed by a VERTEX subsection. It begins with the "VERTEX" keyword, followed on subsequent lines by a list of four or more vertex vectors. A maximum of 65,536 vertex vectors are allowed. Each vertex is implicitly assigned an index number according to its position

in the list, beginning with zero. The "END_VERT" keyword terminates the subsection

9. Each vertex vector consists of a '<' separator, followed by three floating-point numbers representing the *x*, *y*, and *z* values of the vertex coordinates respectively, followed by a '>' separator.

10. The VERTEX subsection is followed by a SURFACE subsection. It begins with the "SURFACE" keyword, followed on subsequent lines by a list of one or more RGB color vector pairs. The first vector of each pair represents the surface reflectance for the entity; the second vector represents the surface's initial surface spectral radiant exitance. A maximum of 65,536 surfaces are allowed. Each surface and its associated reflectance and initial exitance vectors is implicitly assigned an index number according to its position in the list, beginning with zero. The "END_SURF" keyword terminates the subsection.

11. Each reflectance vector consists of a '[' separator, followed by three floating-point numbers representing the *red*, *green,* and *blue* primary color values respectively, followed by a ']' separator. The color values must be in the range 0.0 to 1.0.

12. Each initial exitance vector consists of a '[' separator, followed by three floating-point numbers representing the *red*, *green*, and *blue* primary color values respectively, followed by a ']' separator. The color values must be equal to or greater than 0.0.

13. The SURFACE subsection is followed by a PATCH subsection. It begins with the keyword "PATCH," followed on subsequent lines by one or more patch identifiers. A maximum of 65,536 polygon identifiers are allowed. The "END_PATCH" keyword terminates the subsection.

14. Each patch identifier consists of an integer number indicating the index number of the surface to which the patch belongs, followed by a '{' separator, followed by four integer numbers indicating the indices of the four patch vertices *v0*, *v1*, *v2*, and *v3* respectively, followed by a '}' separator. If the patch is a triangle, the third and fourth vertex indices must be identical.

15. The PATCH subsection is followed by an ELEMENT subsection. It begins with the keyword "ELEMENT," followed on subsequent lines by one or more element identifiers. A maximum of 65,536 element identifiers are allowed. The "END_ELEM" keyword terminates the subsection.

16. Each element identifier consists of an integer number indicating the index number of the patch to which the element belongs, followed by a '{' separator, followed by four integer numbers indicating the indices of the four element vertices *v0*, *v1*, *v2*, and *v3* respectively, followed by a '}' separator. If the element is a triangle, the third and fourth vertex indices must be identical.

17. The ELEMENT subsection is followed by an "END_ENTITY" keyword, which terminates the file.

To clarify the rules just given, here's an example of a small entity data file that describes a colored cube:

Listing 3.15   COL.CUBE.ENT

```
ENTITY colored cube
VERTEX
< 0.0 0.0 0.0 >
< 1.0 0.0 0.0 >
< 1.0 0.0 1.0 >
< 0.0 0.0 1.0 >
< 1.0 0.0 0.0 >
< 1.0 1.0 0.0 >
< 1.0 1.0 1.0 >
< 1.0 0.0 1.0 >
< 1.0 1.0 0.0 >
< 0.0 1.0 0.0 >
< 0.0 1.0 1.0 >
< 1.0 1.0 1.0 >
< 0.0 1.0 0.0 >
< 0.0 0.0 0.0 >
< 0.0 0.0 1.0 >
< 0.0 1.0 1.0 >
< 0.0 0.0 0.0 >
< 0.0 1.0 0.0 >
< 1.0 1.0 0.0 >
< 1.0 0.0 0.0 >
< 0.0 0.0 1.0 >
< 1.0 0.0 1.0 >
< 1.0 1.0 1.0 >
< 0.0 1.0 1.0 >
END_VERT
SURFACE
[ 0.0 0.0 1.0 ] [ 0.0 0.0 0.0 ]
[ 1.0 1.0 0.0 ] [ 0.0 0.0 0.0 ]
[ 1.0 1.0 1.0 ] [ 0.0 0.0 0.0 ]
[ 0.0 1.0 1.0 ] [ 0.0 0.0 0.0 ]
[ 1.0 0.0 0.0 ] [ 0.0 0.0 0.0 ]
[ 0.0 1.0 0.0 ] [ 0.0 0.0 0.0 ]
END_SURF
PATCH
0 {  0  1  2  3 }
1 {  4  5  6  7 }
2 {  8  9 10 11 }
3 { 12 13 14 15 }
4 { 16 17 18 19 }
5 { 20 21 22 23 }
END_PATCH
ELEMENT
0 {  0  1  2  3 }
1 {  4  5  6  7 }
2 {  8  9 10 11 }
3 { 12 13 14 15 }
4 { 16 17 18 19 }
5 { 20 21 22 23 }
END_ELEM
END_ENTITY
```

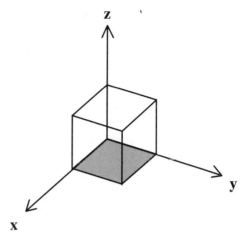

Figure 3.15 Cube in a right-handed coordinate system

For the sake of simplicity, the surfaces described here consist of one patch each. Similarly, each patch consists of only one element. Clearly though, any surface or patch can be subdivided into multiple patches and elements by defining additional vertices and patch or element identifiers.

3.11 THREE-DIMENSIONAL TRANSFORMATIONS

We have so far defined an entity as an object floating in its own *local coordinate space*, independent of all other entities. Our colored cube, for example (Listing 3.15), is aligned with the coordinate axes and has one corner at the origin. Following the usual computer graphics conventions, it's a right-handed coordinate system, as shown in Figure 3.15.

What we want, of course, is to place instances of our entities in the *world coordinate space* of our three-dimensional environment. In general, this requires that we (1) *scale* the entity dimensions to that required for the instance; (2) *rotate* the instance to properly align it with respect to the world coordinate axes; and (3) *translate* the instance to its proper position in the world space. Taken together, these operations are referred to as *linear three-dimensional transformations*.

The subject of three-dimensional transformations, linear and otherwise, deserves an entire book. Some of the more accessible texts include Watt (1990), Harrington (1987), and Foley et al. (1990). Thorough coverage is provided by Hill (1990) and Rogers and Adams (1976). The best we can afford here is to review the basics necessary for our three-dimensional graphics toolkit.

3.11.1 Translation, Scaling, and Rotation

Imagine we have a vertex $\mathbf{v}_1$ in space whose coordinates are $\{x_1, y_1, z_1\}$ and that we want to move (translate) it to another position $\mathbf{v}_2$ with coordinates $\{x_2, y_2, z_2\}$. Expressing the vertex coordinates in matrix notation as:

$$\mathbf{v} = \begin{bmatrix} x \\ y \\ z \end{bmatrix}$$

we can represent the translation as $\mathbf{v}_2 = \mathbf{v}_1 + \mathbf{t}$, where:

$$\mathbf{t} = \begin{bmatrix} x_2 - x_1 \\ y_2 - y_1 \\ z_2 - z_1 \end{bmatrix}$$

We can clearly apply the same translation to every vertex of an object to move it anywhere in space.

Now suppose we want to scale the same object, either enlarging or reducing it in size. Our colored cube has unit dimensions along each edge; we might want to change it into a rectangular box with say $x = 2.0$, $y = 1.5$, $z = 3.0$. For any vertex $\mathbf{v}_1$, we must multiply each of its coordinates by the appropriate scaling factor for that dimension. Again using matrix notation, we have $\mathbf{v}_2 = \mathbf{s}\mathbf{v}_1$, where:

$$\mathbf{s} = \begin{bmatrix} s_x & 0 & 0 \\ 0 & s_y & 0 \\ 0 & 0 & s_z \end{bmatrix}$$

is the *scaling matrix*.

We can express our vertex coordinates in four-dimensional *homogeneous coordinates* as the matrix:

$$\begin{bmatrix} V_x \\ V_y \\ V_z \\ w \end{bmatrix}$$

where w can be any value other than zero, and where:

$$\begin{aligned} v_x &= V_x/w \\ v_y &= V_y/w \\ v_z &= V_z/w \end{aligned} \tag{3.10}$$

In computer graphics, w is usually taken to be unity, so that the homogeneous coordinates of our vertex reduce to:

$$\begin{bmatrix} v_x \\ v_y \\ v_z \\ 1 \end{bmatrix}$$

One advantage of homogeneous coordinates is that they allow us to unify the linear transformation operations. Whereas translation required matrix addition and scaling required matrix multiplication, the homogeneous coordinates representation allows us to do the following:

Translation:
$$\begin{bmatrix} x_2 \\ y_2 \\ z_2 \\ 1 \end{bmatrix} = \begin{bmatrix} 1 & 0 & 0 & t_x \\ 0 & 1 & 0 & t_y \\ 0 & 0 & 1 & t_z \\ 0 & 0 & 0 & 1 \end{bmatrix} \begin{bmatrix} x_1 \\ y_1 \\ z_1 \\ 1 \end{bmatrix} = \mathbf{T} \begin{bmatrix} x_1 \\ y_1 \\ z_1 \\ 1 \end{bmatrix} \qquad (3.11)$$

Scaling:
$$\begin{bmatrix} x_2 \\ y_2 \\ z_2 \\ 1 \end{bmatrix} = \begin{bmatrix} s_x & 0 & 0 & 0 \\ 0 & s_y & 0 & 0 \\ 0 & 0 & s_z & 0 \\ 0 & 0 & 0 & 1 \end{bmatrix} \begin{bmatrix} x_1 \\ y_1 \\ z_1 \\ 1 \end{bmatrix} = \mathbf{S} \begin{bmatrix} x_1 \\ y_1 \\ z_1 \\ 1 \end{bmatrix} \qquad (3.12)$$

Anyone who has taken a formal course in matrix theory knows it is not for the mathematically timid. Fortunately, matrix scaling, addition, and multiplication are much easier to understand.

A matrix is a rectangular array of elements. A matrix with m horizontal rows and n vertical columns is called an $m \times n$ matrix. A matrix with a single row or column of elements is called a *row* or *column vector*. Thus, our vertex expressed in homogeneous coordinates is a 4×1 column vector. A *square* matrix has the same number of rows and columns (e.g., 4×4).

We can *scale* any matrix $\mathbf{A}$ by a number s by multiplying each element of $\mathbf{A}$ by s. For example, if $\mathbf{A}$ is a 2×2 matrix, then:

$$s\mathbf{A} = s \begin{bmatrix} a_{00} & a_{01} \\ a_{10} & a_{11} \end{bmatrix} = \begin{bmatrix} sa_{00} & sa_{01} \\ sa_{10} & sa_{11} \end{bmatrix}$$

We can *add* two matrices $\mathbf{A}$ and $\mathbf{B}$ to produce a third matrix $\mathbf{C}$ only if the matrices have the same number of rows and columns (i.e., they have the same *shape*). Each element of $\mathbf{C}$ is the sum of its corresponding elements in $\mathbf{A}$ and $\mathbf{B}$. For example:

$$\mathbf{C} = \begin{bmatrix} c_{00} & c_{01} \\ c_{10} & c_{11} \end{bmatrix} = \mathbf{A} + \mathbf{B} = \begin{bmatrix} (a_{00} + b_{00}) & (a_{01} + b_{01}) \\ (a_{10} + b_{10}) & (a_{11} + b_{11}) \end{bmatrix}$$

(continued)

Two matrices $\mathbf{A}$ and $\mathbf{B}$ can be *multiplied* only if the number of columns of $\mathbf{A}$ equals the number of rows of $\mathbf{B}$. For example, a 2×3 matrix $\mathbf{A}$ can be multiplied by a 3×2 matrix $\mathbf{B}$ to produce the 2×2 matrix $\mathbf{C} = \mathbf{AB}$.

Given $\mathbf{C} = \mathbf{AB}$, the *ij*th element of $\mathbf{C}$ (that is, the element from the *i*th row and *j*th column) is the dot product (Section 3.2) of the *i*th row of $\mathbf{A}$ with the *j*th column of $\mathbf{B}$. For example:

$$\mathbf{C} = \begin{bmatrix} c_{00} & c_{01} \\ c_{10} & c_{11} \\ c_{20} & c_{21} \end{bmatrix} = \mathbf{AB} = \begin{bmatrix} a_{00} & a_{01} & a_{02} \\ a_{10} & a_{11} & a_{12} \\ a_{20} & a_{21} & a_{22} \end{bmatrix} \begin{bmatrix} b_{00} & b_{01} \\ b_{10} & b_{11} \\ b_{20} & b_{21} \end{bmatrix}$$

$$= \begin{bmatrix} \left(a_{00}b_{00} + a_{01}b_{10} + a_{02}b_{20} \right) \left(a_{00}b_{01} + a_{01}b_{11} + a_{02}b_{21} \right) \\ \left(a_{10}b_{00} + a_{11}b_{10} + a_{12}b_{20} \right) \left(a_{10}b_{01} + a_{11}b_{11} + a_{12}b_{21} \right) \\ \left(a_{20}b_{00} + a_{21}b_{10} + a_{22}b_{20} \right) \left(a_{20}b_{01} + a_{21}b_{11} + a_{22}b_{21} \right) \end{bmatrix}$$

Stated more succinctly, matrix multiplication $\mathbf{C} = \mathbf{AB}$ is defined as:

$$c_{ik} = \sum_{k=0}^{k<j} a_{ij}b_{jk}$$

for each element c_{ij} of C.

Note, however, that $\mathbf{B}$ cannot be multiplied by $\mathbf{A}$. That is, $\mathbf{C} = \mathbf{AB}$ is undefined for this example. Since, in general, the order of $\mathbf{A}$ and $\mathbf{B}$ cannot be reversed in multiplication (square matrices being the exception), we say that for $\mathbf{C} = \mathbf{AB}$, $\mathbf{B}$ *postmultiplies* $\mathbf{A}$ or $\mathbf{A}$ *premultiplies* $\mathbf{B}$.

We define the *identity* matrix $\mathbf{I}$ as a square matrix whose elements are all zero except for those along the *main diagonal*, which are one. For example, the 3×3 identity matrix is:

$$I = \begin{bmatrix} 1 & 0 & 0 \\ 0 & 1 & 0 \\ 0 & 0 & 1 \end{bmatrix}$$

The identity matrix has the property that $\mathbf{A} = \mathbf{AI}$. That is, multiplying a matrix by an identity matrix does not change the original matrix.

From this, we can define the *inverse* of a matrix $\mathbf{M}$ as $\mathbf{M}^{-1}$, where:

$$\mathbf{MM}^{-1} = \mathbf{M}^{-1}\mathbf{M} = \mathbf{I}$$

Some matrices (called *singular* matrices) do not have definable inverses. Those of interest to us, however, are *nonsingular* matrices with easily determined inverses.

Finally, we can interchange the rows and columns of a matrix $\mathbf{A}$. This gives us the *transpose* of $\mathbf{A}$, denoted as $\mathbf{A}^{\mathrm{T}}$, where $a_{ij}^{\mathrm{T}} = a_{ji}$. This also means that we can represent three- and four-dimensional homogeneous coordinates as 1×3 and 1×4 row vectors. In fact, some computer graphics textbooks (e.g., Hill 1990) use this notational style. It's a matter of personal preference, since the following two representations produce equivalent results:

$$\mathbf{C} = \begin{bmatrix} c_0 \\ c_1 \\ c_2 \end{bmatrix} = \mathbf{AB} = \begin{bmatrix} a_{00} & a_{01} & a_{02} \\ a_{10} & a_{11} & a_{12} \\ a_{20} & a_{21} & a_{22} \end{bmatrix} \begin{bmatrix} b_0 \\ b_1 \\ b_2 \end{bmatrix}$$

$$= \begin{bmatrix} (a_{00}b_0 + a_{01}b_1 + a_{02}b_2) \\ (a_{10}b_0 + a_{11}b_1 + a_{12}b_2) \\ (a_{20}b_0 + a_{21}b_1 + a_{22}b_2) \end{bmatrix}$$

and:

$$\mathbf{C}^T = \begin{bmatrix} c_0 & c_1 & c_2 \end{bmatrix} = \mathbf{B}^T\mathbf{A}^T = \begin{bmatrix} b_0 & b_1 & b_2 \end{bmatrix} \begin{bmatrix} a_{00} & a_{10} & a_{20} \\ a_{01} & a_{11} & a_{21} \\ a_{02} & a_{12} & a_{22} \end{bmatrix}$$

$$= \begin{bmatrix} (b_0 a_{00} + b_1 a_{01} + b_2 a_{02}) & (b_0 a_{10} + b_1 a_{11} + b_2 a_{12}) & (b_0 a_{20} + b_1 a_{21} + b_2 a_{22}) \end{bmatrix}$$

There is a vast body of literature available on matrix mathematics. However, the information provided in this box is all we need in order to understand the radiosity approach.

Translation and scaling are now in identical form, being a single matrix multiplication. Although multiplication is more time consuming than addition, there is an advantage to homogeneous coordinates that more than compensates for the additional time expended. We will address this matter shortly; in the meantime, the three examples in Figure 3.16 should clarify how these transformations work.

The same mathematical form applies to rotation about one of the coordinate axes:

$$x \text{ axis:} \quad \begin{bmatrix} x_2 \\ y_2 \\ z_2 \\ 1 \end{bmatrix} = \begin{bmatrix} 1 & 0 & 0 & 0 \\ 0 & \cos\theta & -\sin\theta & 0 \\ 0 & \sin\theta & \cos\theta & 0 \\ 0 & 0 & 0 & 1 \end{bmatrix} \begin{bmatrix} x_1 \\ y_1 \\ z_1 \\ 1 \end{bmatrix} = \mathbf{R}_x \begin{bmatrix} x_1 \\ y_1 \\ z_1 \\ 1 \end{bmatrix} \tag{3.13}$$

$$y \text{ axis:} \quad \begin{bmatrix} x_2 \\ y_2 \\ z_2 \\ 1 \end{bmatrix} = \begin{bmatrix} \cos\theta & 0 & \sin\theta & 0 \\ 0 & 1 & 0 & 0 \\ -\sin\theta & 0 & \cos\theta & 0 \\ 0 & 0 & 0 & 1 \end{bmatrix} \begin{bmatrix} x_1 \\ y_1 \\ z_1 \\ 1 \end{bmatrix} = \mathbf{R}_y \begin{bmatrix} x_1 \\ y_1 \\ z_1 \\ 1 \end{bmatrix} \tag{3.14}$$

$$z \text{ axis:} \quad \begin{bmatrix} x_2 \\ y_2 \\ z_2 \\ 1 \end{bmatrix} = \begin{bmatrix} \cos\theta & -\sin\theta & 0 & 0 \\ \sin\theta & \cos\theta & 0 & 0 \\ 0 & 0 & 1 & 0 \\ 0 & 0 & 0 & 1 \end{bmatrix} \begin{bmatrix} x_1 \\ y_1 \\ z_1 \\ 1 \end{bmatrix} = \mathbf{R}_z \begin{bmatrix} x_1 \\ y_1 \\ z_1 \\ 1 \end{bmatrix} \qquad (3.15)$$

where θ is the angle of rotation measured counterclockwise about the axis when looking toward the origin. Two examples are shown in Figure 3.17.

The advantage of having one common mathematical form for translation, scaling, and rotation is that any sequence of these transformations can be *concatenated* (i.e., premultiplied) to yield a single net transformation matrix. Matrix multiplication is *associative*, so we can group matrix multiplications as we please. That is, rather

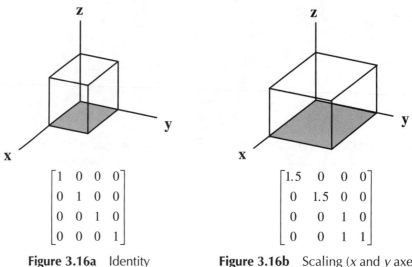

$$\begin{bmatrix} 1 & 0 & 0 & 0 \\ 0 & 1 & 0 & 0 \\ 0 & 0 & 1 & 0 \\ 0 & 0 & 0 & 1 \end{bmatrix}$$

Figure 3.16a Identity

$$\begin{bmatrix} 1.5 & 0 & 0 & 0 \\ 0 & 1.5 & 0 & 0 \\ 0 & 0 & 1 & 0 \\ 0 & 0 & 1 & 1 \end{bmatrix}$$

Figure 3.16b Scaling (*x* and *y* axes)

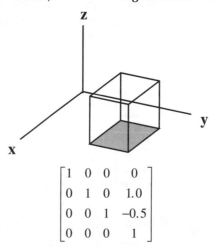

$$\begin{bmatrix} 1 & 0 & 0 & 0 \\ 0 & 1 & 0 & 1.0 \\ 0 & 0 & 1 & -0.5 \\ 0 & 0 & 0 & 1 \end{bmatrix}$$

Figure 3.16c Translation

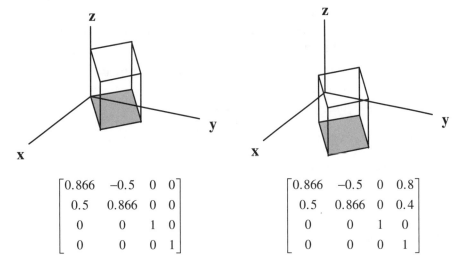

$$\begin{bmatrix} 0.866 & -0.5 & 0 & 0 \\ 0.5 & 0.866 & 0 & 0 \\ 0 & 0 & 1 & 0 \\ 0 & 0 & 0 & 1 \end{bmatrix} \qquad \begin{bmatrix} 0.866 & -0.5 & 0 & 0.8 \\ 0.5 & 0.866 & 0 & 0.4 \\ 0 & 0 & 1 & 0 \\ 0 & 0 & 0 & 1 \end{bmatrix}$$

Figure 3.17a $30°$ rotation about z axis   **Figure 3.17b**   Rotation and translation

than separately translating, scaling, and rotating each vertex, we can successively premultiply the transformation matrices together, as in:

$$\mathbf{v}_2 = \big(\mathbf{R}(\mathbf{ST})\big)\mathbf{v}_1 = \mathbf{M}\mathbf{v}_1 \tag{3.16}$$

where the net transformation matrix $\mathbf{M}$ has the general form:

$$\mathbf{M} = \begin{bmatrix} a_{11} & a_{12} & a_{13} & t_x \\ a_{21} & a_{22} & a_{23} & t_y \\ a_{31} & a_{32} & a_{33} & t_z \\ 0 & 0 & 0 & 1 \end{bmatrix} \tag{3.17}$$

Note that the 3×3 upper-left submatrix $\mathbf{A}$ determines the net rotation and scaling, whereas the three elements t_x, t_y, and t_z determine the net translation.

Any number of translation, scaling, and rotation matrices can be concatenated in any order. However, the results depend on the order of concatenation. Rotations, for example, are not *commutative*. Given any two rotation matrices $\mathbf{R}_1$ and $\mathbf{R}_2$, $\mathbf{R}_1\mathbf{R}_2$ $\neq \mathbf{R}_2\mathbf{R}_1$. (Try rotating an object 90 degrees vertically, then 90 degrees horizontally. Note its orientation, return it to its original orientation, and then rotate it 90 degrees in the same horizontal direction before rotating it 90 degrees vertically.) Similarly, scaling and then translating a vertex's coordinates is not the same as translating the coordinates before scaling.

Any transformation can be reversed by multiplying the transformation $\mathbf{M}$ matrix by its inverse $\mathbf{M}^{-1}$. $\mathbf{T}^{-1}$ is obtained by negating t_x, t_y, t_z, $\mathbf{S}^{-1}$ replaces s_x, s_y, and s_z by their inverses, and $\mathbf{R}^{-1}$ negates the rotation angle θ.

Remember too that rotation is defined with respect to the coordinate system origin. Therefore, in creating an instance of an entity for an environment, we typically want to compute a transformation matrix that will do the following:

1. Scale the entity vertices.
2. Rotate the vertices counterclockwise about the *x*, *y*, and *z* axes.
3. Translate the vertices.

In practice, this computation requires a single net transformation matrix **M** that is applied to all the vertices belonging to the entity.

The following *Transform3* class implements the tools we need:

Listing 3.16

```
// TRANSFM3.H - 3-D Linear Transformation Class

#ifndef _3D_TRANS_H
#define _3D_TRANS_H

#include "vector3.h"

class Transform3          // 3-D linear transformation
{
  private:
    double scale_x;       // x-axis scaling factor
    double scale_y;       // y-axis scaling factor
    double scale_z;       // z-axis scaling factor
    double trans_x;       // x-axis translation distance
    double trans_y;       // y-axis translation distance
    double trans_z;       // z-axis translation distance
    double rot_x;         // x-axis rotation (in radians)
    double rot_y;         // y-axis rotation (in radians)
    double rot_z;         // z-axis rotation (in radians)
    double m[3][4];       // Transformation matrix

    void Identity()       // Initialize identity matrix
    {
      int i, j;           // Loop indices

      for (i = 0; i < 3; i++)
        for (j = 0; j < 4; j++)
        {
          if (i == j)
            m[i][j] = 1.0;
          else
            m[i][j] = 0.0;
        }
    }

    // Note: s_val is sine of rotation angle
    //       c_val is cosine of rotation angle

    // Rotate counterclockwise about x-axis
    void RotateX( double s_val, double c_val )
    {
      int i;            // Loop index
      double temp;      // Temporary variable
```

```cpp
    for (i = 0; i < 4; i++)
    {
      temp = m[1][i] * c_val - m[2][i] * s_val;
      m[2][i] = m[1][i] * s_val + m[2][i] * c_val;
      m[1][i] = temp;
    }
  }

  // Rotate counterclockwise about y-axis
  void RotateY( double s_val, double c_val )
  {
    int i;         // Loop index
    double temp;   // Temporary variable

    for (i = 0; i < 4; i++)
    {
      temp = m[0][i] * c_val + m[2][i] * s_val;
      m[2][i] = -m[0][i] * s_val + m[2][i] * c_val;
      m[0][i] = temp;
    }
  }

  // Rotate counterclockwise about z-axis
  void RotateZ( double s_val, double c_val )
  {
    int i;         // Loop index
    double temp;   // Temporary variable

    for (i = 0; i < 4; i++)
    {
      temp = m[0][i] * c_val - m[1][i] * s_val;
      m[1][i] = m[0][i] * s_val + m[1][i] * c_val;
      m[0][i] = temp;
    }
  }

  void Scale()
  {
    m[0][0] *= scale_x;
    m[1][1] *= scale_y;
    m[2][2] *= scale_z;
  }

  void Translate()
  {
    m[0][3] += trans_x;
    m[1][3] += trans_y;
    m[2][3] += trans_z;
  }

public:
  Transform3()
  {
```

(continued)

Listing 3.16   *(continued)*

```
      scale_x = scale_y = scale_z = 1.0;
      trans_x = trans_y = trans_z = 0.0;
      rot_x = rot_y = rot_z = 0.0;

      Identity();
   }

   // Set scaling factors
   void SetScale( double sx, double sy, double sz )
   { scale_x = sx; scale_y = sy; scale_z = sz; }

   // Set translation distances
   void SetTranslation( double tx, double ty, double tz )
   { trans_x = tx; trans_y = ty; trans_z = tz; }

   // Set rotation angles
   void SetRotation( double rx, double ry, double rz )
   { rot_x = rx; rot_y = ry; rot_z = rz; }

   void BuildTransform()
   {
      Identity();          // Initialize identity matrix

      Scale();             // Concatenate scale matrix

      // Concatenate rotation matrices
      RotateX(sin(rot_x), cos(rot_x));
      RotateY(sin(rot_y), cos(rot_y));
      RotateZ(sin(rot_z), cos(rot_z));

      Translate();         // Concatenate translation matrix
   }

   // Premultiply point by 3-D transformation matrix
   void Transform( Point3 *pp )
   {
      Point3 temp;         // Temporary 3-D point

      temp.SetX(m[0][0] * pp->GetX() + m[0][1] * pp->GetY()
         + m[0][2] * pp->GetZ() + m[0][3]);
      temp.SetY(m[1][0] * pp->GetX() + m[1][1] * pp->GetY()
         + m[1][2] * pp->GetZ() + m[1][3]);
      temp.SetZ(m[2][0] * pp->GetX() + m[2][1] * pp->GetY()
         + m[2][2] * pp->GetZ() + m[2][3]);

      pp->SetX(temp.GetX());
      pp->SetY(temp.GetY());
      pp->SetZ(temp.GetZ());
   }
};

#endif
```

There are two items of interest here. First, the transformation matrix m is stored as a 3×4 rather than a 4×4 matrix. As Equation 3.17 indicates, the fourth row of the transformation matrix is always the same for scaling, translation, and rotation. We can therefore ignore it in our calculations.

Second, the user is allowed to specify the net transformation matrix only in terms of scaling factors, translation distances, and rotation angles. Calling *Build-Transform* results in the transformation matrix being recalculated based on the current set of parameters. Note that the private member functions responsible for scaling, translation, and rotation are designed for this specific use. That is, they modify the identity matrix in a given order to produce the net transformation matrix. Equivalent public functions to perform scaling, translation, and rotation by premultiplying an arbitrary three-dimensional transformation matrix would each have to perform a full matrix multiplication.

3.12 BUILDING AN ENVIRONMENT

Building an environment consists of copying and transforming entities into instances. For this, we need an environment data file format to describe which entities are to be copied and what three-dimensional linear transformations are to be applied to them.

The general outline of the data file format is given in Figure 3.18.

```
WORLD world_name
COMMENT Environment Data File
entity_file_name
< sx sy sz >
< rx ry rz >
< tx ty tz >
entity_file_name
...
END_FILE
```

Figure 3.18   Environment data file format

Similar to our entity data file format, the following syntax rules apply:

1. The data file consists of ASCII characters.
2. Each line must be terminated with an environment-specific "newline" character (typically <CR><LF> for MS-DOS and <CR> for UNIX systems).
3. The maximum length of a line is 256 characters, including the newline character(s).
4. Multiple whitespace (ASCII space and horizontal tab) characters between data values and separators are ignored.
5. Comment lines beginning with the keyword "COMMENT" are ignored.
6. The data file begins with the keyword "WORLD," followed on the same line by an optional *world_name* character string that identifies the environ-

ment. Any printable ASCII character is permitted in the string.

7. The remainder of the data file consists of one or more entity sections, followed by the "END_FILE" keyword. Any lines after this keyword are ignored.

8. An entity section consists of an *entity_file_name* character string, followed in sequence by a scaling vector, a rotation vector, and a translation vector.

9. The *entity_file_name* is an environment-specific file name that uniquely identifies the entity data file.

10. A scaling vector consists of a '<' separator, followed by three floating-point numbers representing the *x*-axis, *y*-axis, and *z*-axis scaling factors respectively, followed by a '>' separator.

11. A rotation vector consists of a '<' separator, followed by three floating-point numbers representing the *x*-axis, *y*-axis, and *z*-axis rotation angles (in degrees) respectively, followed by a '>' separator.

12. A translation vector consists of a '<' separator, followed by three floating point numbers representing the *x*-axis, *y*-axis, and *z*-axis translation values respectively, followed by a '>' separator.

Here's an example of a data file that places two instances of our previously defined colored cube entity in a world environment:

Listing 3.17   COL_CUBE.WLD

```
WORLD colored cube
COMMENT first instance
col_cube.ent
< 2.0 3.0 1.0 >
< 30.0 45.0 0.0 >
< 2.0 0.0 0.0 >
COMMENT second instance
col_cube.ent
< 1.5 1.0 0.5 >
< 30.0 45.0 30.0 >
< 0.0 0.0 1.0 >
END_FILE
```

3.13   AN ENVIRONMENT DATA FILE PARSER

Our final requirement is for a C++ class that can read an environment data file and build an equivalent data structure in memory. In terms of programming languages and compiler theory, we want to *parse* the data file. Unlike even the smallest programming language, however, parsing our data file formats will be a trivial exercise. At the highest level, we want to do something like that shown in Figure 3.19 where most of the work will be handled by our previously defined classes.

```
Open environment file
WHILE more entity sections
  Read entity file
  Create entity
  Read transformation matrix
  Transform entity to instance
  Add instance to linked list
ENDWHILE
Close environment file
```

Figure 3.19   Environment file parser program pseudocode

So why is the following *Parse* class so lengthy? Most of its code is devoted to manipulating linked lists and converting ASCII character strings into meaningful data primitives such as *int* and *float*. If you ignore the bookkeeping, *PARSE.CPP* is fairly straightforward. Keeping this in mind, we have the following header file:

Listing 3.18

```
// PARSE.H - Environment Data File Parser Class

#ifndef _PARSE_H
#define _PARSE_H

#include "environ.h"
#include "transfm3.h"
#include "win_text.h"

#define MaxLine 256      // Maximum line length

typedef Patch3 *PatchPtr;      // Patch pointer data type
typedef Surface3 *SurfacePtr;  // Surface pointer data type
typedef Vertex3 *VertexPtr;    // Vertex pointer data type

class Parse      // Environment data file parser
{
  private:
    WORD elem_cnt;             // Instance element count
    WORD patch_cnt;            // Instance patch count
    WORD surf_cnt;             // Instance surface count
    WORD vert_cnt;             // Instance vertex count
    char ent_buff[MaxLine];    // Entity file name buffer
    char line_buff[MaxLine];   // Line buffer
    char msg_buff[MaxLine];    // Message buffer
    Environ *penv;             // Environment pointer
    PatchPtr *pp_array;        // Patch pointer array ptr
    SurfacePtr *ps_array;      // Surface pointer array ptr
    Transform3 tm;             // 3-D transformation matrix
    VertexPtr *pv_array;       // Vertex pointer array ptr
    WinText efile;             // Entity file
    WinText ifile;             // Instance file
```

(continued)

Listing 3.18 *(continued)*

```
    BOOL ParseElements();
    BOOL ParsePatches();
    BOOL ReadVector( WinText &, double *, double *,
       double * );
    Instance *ParseEntityFile();
    Surface3 *ParseSurfaces();
    Surface3 *ReadSurface();
    Vertex3 *ParseVertices();
    Vertex3 *ReadVertex();
    void ReadLine( WinText & );
    void ReadTransform();
    void TransformInstance( Instance * );

  public:
    BOOL ParseFile( char *, char *, Environ * );
};

#endif
```

If your target environment is not MS-Windows, you should note the MS-DOS-specific file path separator '\'. A UNIX-based implementation, for example, would require this to be '/'.

Another platform-dependent issue to watch out for is text file handling, which is handled in PARSE.H by an MS-Windows-specific class called *WinText* (described below). MS-Windows uses a 256-character extended ASCII character set. It also provides no built-in functions for reading text files. You can use the C++ *iostream* or *stdio.h* file functions, but you have to be careful about casting character strings and *FILE* pointers if you're using them in conjunction with MS-Windows functions (which typically expect *_far* pointers).

We can sidestep these issues by using the large memory model when compiling our MS-Windows application program and encapsulating the file-handling functions in a separate class. While the following *WinText* class is nominally specific to MS-Windows, it can applied without change to most other environments.

Listing 3.19

```
// WIN_TEXT.H - MS-Windows Text File Class

#ifndef _WIN_TEXT_H
#define _WIN_TEXT_H

#include <string.h>
#include "general.h"

// NOTE: Requires LARGE memory model for Win16

class WinText    // MS-Windows text file
{
```

```
  private:
    FILE *pfile;            // File pointer

  public:

    // Close file
    void Close() { (void) fclose(pfile); }

    // Read next line from file
    void GetLine( char *pline, int max )
    {
      char *pstr;           // String pointer

      if ((pstr = fgets(pline, max, pfile)) != NULL)
        pstr = strchr(pline, '\n');

      if (pstr == NULL)
        pstr = pline;

      *pstr = '\0';         // Strip off newline
    }

    BOOL Open( char *fname )     // Open text file
    {
      if ((pfile = fopen(fname, "r")) != NULL)
        return TRUE;
      else
        return FALSE;
    }
};

#endif
```

The remainder of our Parse class consists of:

Listing 3.20   PARSE.CPP

```
// PARSE.CPP - Environment Data File Parser Class

#include <string.h>
#include "error.h"
#include "parse.h"

// File path separator (MS-DOS specific)
static const char PathSeparator[] = "\\";

// Data file keywords
static const char EndFileStr[] = "END_FILE";
static const char CommentStr[] = "COMMENT";
```

(continued)

Listing 3.20 *(continued)*

```
// Parse world file
BOOL Parse::ParseFile( char *fname, char *fpath, Environ
    *pe )
{
  char *pefp;          // Entity file path pointer
  Instance *pinst;     // Instance pointer
  Instance *pinsthd;   // Instance list head pointer

  penv = pe;     // Save environment pointer

  // Delete previous environment (if any)
  penv->DeleteEnv();

  pinst = pinsthd = NULL;

  // Initialize environment statistics
  penv->num_inst = (WORD) 0;
  penv->num_surf = (WORD) 0;
  penv->num_patch = (WORD) 0;
  penv->num_elem = (WORD) 0;
  penv->num_vert = (WORD) 0;

  // Build file path string
  pefp = ent_buff;
  if (*fpath != '\0')
  {
    strcpy(ent_buff, fpath);
    if (fpath[strlen(ent_buff) - 1] != *PathSeparator)
      strcat(ent_buff, PathSeparator);
    pefp += strlen(ent_buff);
  }

  if (ifile.Open(fname) != TRUE)     // Open instance file
  {
    sprintf(msg_buff, "Could not open world file %s",
        fname);
    ReportError(msg_buff);
    return FALSE;
  }

  ReadLine(ifile);       // Read world name

  for ( ; ; )
  {
    ReadLine(ifile);     // Read entity file name

    // Check for end of file
    if (strcmp(line_buff, EndFileStr) == 0)
      break;

    // Build full entity file name
    strcpy(pefp, line_buff);
```

```
    // Read entity file
    if ((pinst = ParseEntityFile()) == NULL)
    {
      ifile.Close();
      return FALSE;
    }

    // Read 3-D transformation matrix
    ReadTransform();

    // Transform entity into instance
    TransformInstance(pinst);

    // Link instance to instance list
    pinst->SetNext(pinsthd);
    pinsthd = pinst;
    penv->num_inst++;
  }
  ifile.Close();
  penv->pinsthd = pinsthd;
  return TRUE;
}

// Parse entity data file
Instance *Parse::ParseEntityFile()
{
  BOOL status;            // Return status
  Instance *pinst;        // Instance pointer
  Surface3 *ps;           // Surface pointer
  Vertex3 *pv;            // Vertex pointer

  pinst = NULL;
  ps = NULL;
  pv = NULL;

  surf_cnt = patch_cnt = elem_cnt = vert_cnt = (WORD) 0;

  // Open entity file
  if (efile.Open(ent_buff) != TRUE)
  {
    sprintf(msg_buff, "Could not open entity file %s",
        ent_buff);
    ReportError(msg_buff);
    return NULL;
  }

  ReadLine(efile);        // Read file description

  pv = ParseVertices();
  ps = ParseSurfaces();
  status = ParsePatches();

  if (status == TRUE)
    status = ParseElements();
```

(continued)

Listing 3.20 *(continued)*

```
    // Delete temporary pointer arrays
    delete [] pv_array;
    delete [] ps_array;
    delete [] pp_array;

    // Create new entity
    if (status == TRUE)
      pinst = new Instance(pv, ps);

    efile.Close();
    return pinst;
}

// Parse vertices
Vertex3 *Parse::ParseVertices()
{
    WORD v_index;            // Vertex pointer array index
    Vertex3 *pv;             // Vertex pointer
    Vertex3 *pvhd;           // Vertex list head ptr

    pv = pvhd = NULL;

    ReadLine(efile);        // Read vertex section header

    // Build vertex linked list
    for ( ; ; )
    {
      // Read vertex vector
      if ((pv = ReadVertex()) == NULL)
        break;

      // Link vertex to vertex list
      pv->SetNext(pvhd);
      pvhd = pv;
      penv->num_vert++;
      vert_cnt++;
    }

    // Build vertex pointer array
    pv = pvhd;
    pv_array = new VertexPtr[vert_cnt];
    v_index = vert_cnt - (WORD) 1;
    while (pv != NULL)
    {
      pv_array[v_index-] = pv;
      pv = pv->GetNext();
    }
    return pvhd;
}

// Parse surfaces
Surface3 *Parse::ParseSurfaces()
{
```

```
    WORD s_index;                // Surface pointer array index
    Surface3 *ps;                // Surface pointer
    Surface3 *pshd;              // Surface list head ptr

    ps = pshd = NULL;

    ReadLine(efile);        // Read surface section header

    // Build surface linked list
    for ( ; ; )
    {
      // Read surface identifier
      if ((ps = ReadSurface()) == NULL)
        break;

      // Link surface to surface list
      ps->SetNext(pshd);
      pshd = ps;
      penv->num_surf++;
      surf_cnt++;
    }

    // Build surface pointer array
    ps = pshd;
    ps_array = new SurfacePtr[surf_cnt];
    s_index = surf_cnt - (WORD) 1;
    while (ps != NULL)
    {
      ps_array[s_index--] = ps;
      ps = ps->GetNext();
    }
    return pshd;
}

// Read surface identifier
Surface3 *Parse::ReadSurface()
{
    char start[2], end[2];          // Vector separators
    float ered, egreen, eblue;      // Exitance components
    float rred, rgreen, rblue;      // Reflectance components
    Spectra reflect;                // Spectral reflectance
    Spectra emit;                   // Spectral radiant exitance

    ReadLine(efile);        // Read color vector

    if (sscanf(line_buff, "%1s %f %f %f %1s %1s %f %f %f %1s",
        start, &rred, &rgreen, &rblue, end, start, &ered,
        &egreen, &eblue, end) == 10)
    {
      // Set reflectance
      reflect.SetRedBand(rred);
      reflect.SetGreenBand(rgreen);
      reflect.SetBlueBand(rblue);
```

(continued)

Listing 3.20   *(continued)*

```
    // Set initial spectral radiant exitance
    emit.SetRedBand(ered);
    emit.SetGreenBand(egreen);
    emit.SetBlueBand(eblue);

    return new Surface3(reflect, emit);
  }
  else
    return NULL;           // Must be terminator
}

// Parse patch identifiers
BOOL Parse::ParsePatches()
{
  char start[2], end[2];     // List separators
  int v_index;               // Vertex pointer array index
  BOOL status = TRUE;        // Status flag
  WORD p_index;              // Patch pointer array index
  WORD s_index;              // Surface index
  WORD ivtx[4];              // Vertex indices
  Patch3 *pp;                // Patch pointer
  Patch3 *pphd;              // Patch head pointer
  PatchList *ppl = NULL;     // Patch list pointer
  PatchList *pplnext;        // Next patch list pointer
  Vertex3 *pv[4];            // Vertex pointers array

  ReadLine(efile);        // Read patch section header

  for ( ; ; )
  {
    ReadLine(efile);      // Read patch identifier

    if (sscanf(line_buff, "%d %1s %d %d %d %d %1s",
        &s_index, start, &ivtx[0], &ivtx[1], &ivtx[2],
        &ivtx[3], end) == 7)
    {
      // Validate surface index
      if (s_index >= surf_cnt)
      {
        sprintf(msg_buff,
            "Entity file: %s\nPatch # %u\nSurface index "
            "error: %s", ent_buff, patch_cnt + 1,
            line_buff);
        ReportError(msg_buff);
        status = FALSE;
        break;
      }

      // Validate vertex array indices
      for (v_index = 0; v_index < 4; v_index++)
      {
```

```
          if (ivtx[v_index] >= vert_cnt)
          {
            sprintf(msg_buff,
                "Entity file: %s\nPatch # %u\nVertex index "
                "error: %s", ent_buff, patch_cnt + 1,
                line_buff);
            ReportError(msg_buff);
            status = FALSE;
            break;
          }
        }

        if (status == FALSE)
          break;

        // Get vertex pointers
        for (v_index = 0; v_index < 4; v_index++)
          pv[v_index] = pv_array[ivtx[v_index]];

        // Update surface patch linked list
        pp = new Patch3(pv, ps_array[s_index]);
        pphd = ps_array[s_index]->GetPatchPtr();
        pp->SetNext(pphd);
        ps_array[s_index]->SetPatchPtr(pp);

        // Determine whether triangle or quadrilateral
        if (ivtx[2] != ivtx[3])
          pp->SetQuad();
      }
      else
        break;

      // Link patch to temporary patch list
      ppl = new PatchList(pp, ppl);
      penv->num_patch++;
      patch_cnt++;
    }

    // Build patch pointer array and delete patch list
    pp_array = new PatchPtr[patch_cnt];
    p_index = patch_cnt - (WORD) 1;
    while (ppl != NULL)
    {
      pp_array[p_index-] = ppl->GetPatchPtr();
      pplnext = ppl->GetNext();
      delete ppl;
      ppl = pplnext;
    }

    return status;
}
```

(continued)

Listing 3.20 *(continued)*

```
// Parse element identifiers
BOOL Parse::ParseElements()
{
  char start[2], end[2];    // List separators
  int nvert;                // Number of vertices
  int v_index;              // Vertex pointer array index
  BOOL status = TRUE;       // Status flag
  WORD p_index;             // Patch array index
  WORD ivtx[4];             // Vertex indices
  Element3 *pe;             // Element pointer
  Element3 *pehd;           // Element head pointer
  ElemList *pel;            // Element list pointer
  ElemList *pelhd;          // Element list head pointer
  Vertex3 *pv[4];           // Vertex pointers array

  ReadLine(efile);          // Read element section header

  for ( ; ; )
  {
    ReadLine(efile);        // Read element identifier

    if (sscanf(line_buff, "%d %1s %d %d %d %d %1s",
        &p_index, start, &ivtx[0], &ivtx[1], &ivtx[2],
        &ivtx[3], end) == 7)
    {
      // Validate patch index
      if (p_index >= patch_cnt)
      {
        sprintf(msg_buff,
            "Entity file: %s\nElement # %u\nPatch index "
            "error: %s", ent_buff, elem_cnt + 1,
            line_buff);
        ReportError(msg_buff);
        status = FALSE;
        break;
      }

      // Validate vertex array indices
      for (v_index = 0; v_index < 4; v_index++)
      {
        if (ivtx[v_index] >= vert_cnt)
        {
          sprintf(msg_buff,
              "Entity file: %s\nElement # %u\nVertex index "
              "error: %s", ent_buff, elem_cnt + 1,
              line_buff);
          ReportError(msg_buff);
          status = FALSE;
          break;
        }
      }
```

```
            if (status == FALSE)
              break;

            // Get vertex pointers
            for (v_index = 0; v_index < 4; v_index++)
              pv[v_index] = pv_array[ivtx[v_index]];

            // Update patch element linked list
            pe = new Element3(pv, pp_array[p_index]);
            pehd = pp_array[p_index]->GetElementPtr();
            pe->SetNext(pehd);
            pp_array[p_index]->SetElementPtr(pe);
            penv->num_elem++;
            elem_cnt++;

            // Determine whether triangle or quadrilateral
            if (ivtx[2] != ivtx[3])
            {
              nvert = 4;
              pe->SetQuad();
            }
            else
              nvert = 3;

            for (v_index = 0; v_index < nvert; v_index++)
            {
              // Update vertex element linked list
              pelhd = pv[v_index]->GetElemListPtr();
              pel = new ElemList(pe, pelhd);
              pv[v_index]->SetElemListPtr(pel);
            }
          }
        else
          break;
      }

  return status;
}

void Parse::ReadTransform()
{
  double sx, sy, sz;    // Scaling parameters
  double rx, ry, rz;    // Rotation parameters
  double tx, ty, tz;    // Translation parameters

  // Read transformation vectors
  ReadVector(ifile, &sx, &sy, &sz);
  ReadVector(ifile, &rx, &ry, &rz);
  ReadVector(ifile, &tx, &ty, &tz);
```

(continued)

Listing 3.20 *(continued)*

```
  // Convert rotation angles to radians
  rx = DegToRad(rx);
  ry = DegToRad(ry);
  rz = DegToRad(rz);

  // Calculate vertex transformation matrix
  tm.SetScale(sx, sy, sz);
  tm.SetRotation(rx, ry, rz);
  tm.SetTranslation(tx, ty, tz);
  tm.BuildTransform();
}

// Read vertex identifier
Vertex3 *Parse::ReadVertex()
{
  double xval, yval, zval;      // Vertex coordinates

  if ((ReadVector( efile, &xval, &yval, &zval)) == TRUE)
    return new Vertex3(Point3(xval, yval, zval));
  else
    return NULL;
}

// Read vector
BOOL Parse::ReadVector( WinText &file, double *px, double
    *py, double *pz )
{
  float x, y, z;               // Temporary variables
  char start[2], end[2];       // Data separators

  ReadLine(file);        // Read vector

  if (sscanf(line_buff, "%1s %f %f %f %1s", start, &x, &y,
      &z, end) == 5)
  {
    *px = x;
    *py = y;
    *pz = z;

    return TRUE;
  }
  else
    return FALSE;
}

// Transform entity into instance
void Parse::TransformInstance( Instance *pinst )
{
  Element3 *pe;          // Element pointer
  Patch3 *pp;            // Patch pointer
  Surface3 *ps;          // Surface pointer
  Vertex3 *pv;           // Vertex pointer
```

```
  // Transform vertex co-ordinates
  pv = pinst->GetVertPtr();
  while (pv != NULL)
  {
    tm.Transform(pv->GetPosnPtr());
    pv = pv->GetNext();
  }

  // Calculate patch attributes
  ps = pinst->GetSurfPtr();
  while (ps != NULL)
  {
    pp = ps->GetPatchPtr();
    while (pp != NULL)
    {
      // Calculate element attributes
      pe = pp->GetElementPtr();
      while (pe != NULL)
      {
        pe->CalcArea();
        pe->CalcNormal();
        pe = pe->GetNext();
      }

      pp->CalcArea();
      pp->CalcCenter();
      pp->CalcNormal();
      pp = pp->GetNext();
    }
    ps = ps->GetNext();
  }

  // Calculate vertex normals
  pv = pinst->GetVertPtr();
  while (pv != NULL)
  {
    pv->CalcNormal();
    pv = pv->GetNext();
  }
}

// Read next line from file
void Parse::ReadLine( WinText &file )
{
  for ( ; ; )
  {
    file.GetLine(line_buff, MaxLine);

    // Skip comment lines
    if (strncmp(line_buff, CommentStr, strlen(CommentStr))
        != 0)
      break;
  }
}
```

Our program outline (Fig. 3.19) is handled by *ParseFile*, which accepts as its parameters an environment data file name and an optional file path name to where the entity files are stored.

ParseFile extracts each entity file name from the environment data file and appends it to the entity file path name (if one was specified). Using this fully expanded file name, it calls *ParseEntityFile* to read each entity file, after which it calls *ReadTransform* to read the associated transformation matrix. Each entity returned by *ParseEntityFile* is transformed into an instance by *TransformInstance*.

If *ParseFile* is successful, a pointer to the environment can be obtained by calling *GetEnv*. The memory allocated to this data structure can be released at any time by calling *DeleteEnv*. This memory is also released if *ParseFile* is called again; each *Parse* object can point only to a single environment.

Finally, *ParseFile* calls *ReportError* if it can't open an environment or entity file. This global function is defined by:

Listing 3.21

```
// ERROR.H- Error Reporting Functions

#ifndef _ERROR_H
#define _ERROR_H

#ifndef _NOT_WIN_APP
#include <windows.h>
#else
#include <iostream.h>
#endif

extern void OutOfMemory();
extern void ReportError( char * );

#endif
```

and:

Listing 3.22

```
// ERROR.CPP - Error Reporting Functions

#include "error.h"

void OutOfMemory()        // Report out of memory error
{
#ifndef _NOT_WIN_APP
  MessageBox(GetFocus(), "Out of memory", NULL, MB_OK |
      MB_ICONEXCLAMATION);
#else
  cerr << "ERROR: out of memory" << endl;
#endif
}
```

```
// Report error message
void ReportError( char *msg )
{
#ifndef _NOT_WIN_APP
  MessageBox(GetFocus(), msg, NULL, MB_OK |
      MB_ICONEXCLAMATION);
#else
  cerr << "ERROR: " << msg << endl;
#endif
}
```

Note the use of the externally defined _NOT_WIN_APP to choose between a character-mode and an MS-Windows application. *MessageBox* is an MS-Windows function that displays the error message in a popup window.

PARSE.CPP and ERROR.CPP are not exactly laudable examples of robust user interface code. Unlike the previous classes, *Parse* has to accept input from the outside world. Done properly, it should exhaustively validate these data, provide meaningful error messages, and exit gracefully. As a rule of thumb, the error-checking code should double the size of PARSE.CPP.

3.14 A CHARACTER-MODE TEST PROGRAM

Using the example data files COL_CUBE.ENT and COL_CUBE.WLD (Listings 3.15 and 3.17), we can exercise the code we've developed to date with:

Listing 3.23

```
// TEST_1.CPP - Environment Data File Parser Test Program

// NOTE: _NOT_WIN_APP must be globally defined for this
//       program to be successfully compiled

#include <stdio.h>
#include <iostream.h>
#include "parse.h"

// Default entity directory path
static char NoEntityDir[] = "";

static Parse Parser;          // World file parser
static Environ Environment;   // Environment

int main( int argc, char **argv )
{
```

(continued)

Listing 3.23   *(continued)*

```
int inst_num;          // Instance number
WORD surf_num;         // Surface number
WORD patch_num;        // Patch number
WORD elem_num;         // Element number
WORD vert_num;         // Vertex number
WORD list_num;         // Polylist number
char *pentdir;         // Entity directory path
Instance *pinst;       // Instance pointer
Surface3 *psurf;       // Surface pointer
ElemList *pelist;      // Element list pointer
Patch3 *ppatch;        // Polygon pointer
Element3 *pelem;       // Element pointer
Vertex3 *pvert;        // Vertex pointer
Spectra color;         // Temporary color
Point3 posn;           // Point co-ordinates
Vector3 normal;        // Normal vector

// Get entity directory path (if any)
if (argc > 2)
  pentdir = argv[2];
else
  pentdir = NoEntityDir;

// Parse the environment file
if (Parser.ParseFile(argv[1], pentdir, &Environment) ==
    FALSE)
  return 1;

// Get environment pointer
pinst = Environment.GetInstPtr();

// Walk the instance list
inst_num = 1;
while (pinst != NULL)
{
  cout << "Instance #" << inst_num++ << endl;

  // Walk the surface list
  surf_num = 1;
  psurf = pinst->GetSurfPtr();
  while (psurf != NULL)
  {
    cout << "  Surface #" << surf_num++ << endl;
    color = psurf->GetReflectance();
    cout << "    reflectance = [ " << color.GetRedBand()
        << " " << color.GetGreenBand() << " " <<
        color.GetBlueBand() << " ]" << endl;
    color = psurf->GetEmittance();
    cout << "    emittance = [ " << color.GetRedBand() <<
        " " << color.GetGreenBand() << " " <<
        color.GetBlueBand() << " ]" << endl;
```

```
// Walk the patch list
patch_num = 1;
ppatch = psurf->GetPatchPtr();
while (ppatch != NULL)
{
  cout << "     Patch #" << patch_num++ << endl;
  cout << "        area = " << ppatch->GetArea() <<
      endl;
  posn = ppatch->GetCenter();
  cout << "        center = < " << posn.GetX() << " "
      << posn.GetY() << " " << posn.GetZ() << " >" <<
      endl;
  normal = ppatch->GetNormal();
  cout << "        normal = < " << normal.GetX() << " "
      << normal.GetY() << " " << normal.GetZ() <<
      " >" << endl;
  color = ppatch->GetExitance();
  cout << "        exitance = [ " << color.GetRedBand()
      << " " << color.GetGreenBand() << " " <<
      color.GetBlueBand() << " ]" << endl;

  // Walk the patch element list
  elem_num = 1;
  pelem = ppatch->GetElementPtr();
  while (pelem != NULL)
  {
    cout << "       Element #" << elem_num++ << endl;
    cout << "          area = " << pelem->GetArea() <<
        endl;
    normal = pelem->GetNormal();
    cout << "          normal = < " << normal.GetX() <<
        " " << normal.GetY() << " " << normal.GetZ()
        << " >" << endl;
    color = pelem->GetExitance();
    cout << "          exitance = [ " <<
        color.GetRedBand() << " " <<
        color.GetGreenBand() << " " <<
        color.GetBlueBand() << " ]" << endl;

    pelem = pelem->GetNext();
  }
  ppatch = ppatch->GetNext();
}
psurf = psurf->GetNext();
}

// Walk the vertex list
vert_num = 1;
pvert = pinst->GetVertPtr();
while (pvert != NULL)
{
```

(continued)

Listing 3.23   *(continued)*

```
      cout << "   Vertex #" << vert_num++ << endl;
      posn = pvert->GetPosn();
      cout << "      position = < " << posn.GetX() << " " <<
          posn.GetY() << " " << posn.GetZ() << " >" << endl;
      normal = pvert->GetNormal();
      cout << "      normal = < " << normal.GetX() << " " <<
          normal.GetY() << " " << normal.GetZ() << " >" <<
          endl;
      color = pvert->GetExitance();
      cout << "      color = [ " <<  color.GetRedBand() << " "
          << color.GetGreenBand() << " " <<
          color.GetBlueBand() << " ]" << endl;

      // Walk the vertex element list
      list_num = 0;
      pelist = pvert->GetElemListPtr();
      while (pelist != NULL)
      {
        list_num++;
        pelist = pelist->GetNext();
      }
      cout << "      vertex shared by " << list_num <<
          " elements" << endl;
      pvert = pvert->GetNext();
    }
    pinst = pinst->GetNext();
  }

  return 0;
}
```

TEST_1 is a character-mode application that sends its output to the user console. As such, *_NOT_WIN_APP* must be globally defined in order to correctly compile ERROR.CPP.

To run *TEST_1*, make sure that both data files are in the current directory, then enter the following command:

```
TEST_1 COL_CUBE.WLD
```

Alternatively, you can have COL_CUBE.ENT in a separate directory, say "C:\RADIANT\ENTITIES," and enter:

```
TEST_1 COL_CUBE.WLD C:\RADIANT\ENTITIES
```

The output in either case will be a detailed listing of the surfaces, polygons, and vertices belonging to the two instances in the environment, along with their properties (surface colors, polygon normals, vertex coordinates, and so on).

3.14 CONCLUSIONS

With *Parse* and its associated classes, we have the three-dimensional graphics toolkit necessary to build an environment. There are, of course, opportunities for improvement. The RGB model used in the *ColorRGB* class, for example, could be augmented with a more sophisticated representation such as the HSV (hue-saturation-value) or HLS (hue-lightness-saturation) models (e.g., Foley et al. 1990, Hall 1989, Hill 1990, and Watt 1990). These models are particularly useful for interactive control of surface colors, where equal changes in the color space parameters produce approximately equal changes in the perceived color. Foley et al. (1990) and Watt (1990) both offer Pascal code for converting between HLS and HSV color models and the RGB color model.

A second approach is to use four or more color bands (Hall 1989) for more accurate color rendition. Chen (1991) offers C source code for mapping between such models and the simpler RGB color model. The only problem is that there is very little information available on the spectral reflectance distribution of most materials. Architectural finishes in particular are most often characterized using the subjective *Munsell color specification system* (e.g., Burnham et al. 1963, Judd and Wyszecki 1975, and Munsell 1946.) with its hue, value ,and chroma parameters. A Munsell color can be mapped only to the three color bands of the RGB and similar color models.

The *Element3*, *Patch3,* and *Surface3* classes are candidates for improvement. The winged-edge data structure (Baumgart 1974, 1975 and Glassner 1991) for polygon representation is one possibility, although developing a robust winged-edge class in C++ is not for the timid. Another possibility is to replace the polygon-based representation of surfaces with the edge-based representation described in Mitchell (1990; see also Watt and Watt 1992). This approach results in a data structure that is simpler than *Element3* and that consumes less memory. Unfortunately, it requires different rendering techniques than are presented in the next chapter.

Finally, the *Parse* class could be made more robust for use in a stand-alone application. Given the widespread availability of reasonably priced three-dimensional CAD packages, however, it is probably more reasonable to develop an Auto-CAD DXF file translator (see the accompanying diskette for a simple example) to generate complex environment descriptions. For our purposes, *Parse* and its associated classes are more than adequate.

REFERENCES

Arvo, J., ed. 1991. *Graphics Gems I.* San Diego, CA: Academic Press.

Baumgart, B. G. 1974. "Winged-Edge Polyhedron Representation." Palo Alto, CA: Stanford University, *Technical Report* STAN-CS-320.

Baumgart, B. G. 1975. "A Polyhedron Representation for Computer Vision," *Proc. National Computer Conference '75*, pp. 589–596.

Bragg, D. 1992. "A Simple Color Reduction Filter," in Kirk (1992), pp. 20–22, 429–431.

Burnham, R. W., R. M. Hanes, and C. J. Bartleson. 1963. *Color: A Guide to Basic Facts and Concepts*. New York: John Wiley & Sons, Inc.

Chen, S. E. 1991. "Implementing Progressive Radiosity with User-Provided Polygon Display Routines," in Arvo (1991), pp. 295 - 298.

Cychosz, J. M. 1990. "Efficient Generation of Sampling Jitter Using Look-Up Tables," in Glassner (1990), pp. 64–74, 660 –661.

Foley, J. D., A. van Dam, S. K. Feiner, and J. F. Hughes. 1990. *Computer Graphics: Principles and Practice (*2nd ed.). Reading, MA: Addison-Wesley.

Gervautz, M., and W. Purgathofer. 1990. "A Simple Method for Color Quantization: Octree Quantization," in Glassner (1990), pp. 287–293.

Glassner, A. S. 1990. *Graphics Gems*. San Diego, CA: Academic Press.

Glassner, A. S. 1991. "Maintaining Winged-Edge Models," in Arvo (1991), pp.191–201.

Hall, R. 1989. *Illumination and Color in Computer Generated Imagery*. New York: Springer-Verlag.

Harrington, S. 1987. *Computer Graphics: A Programming Approach*. New York: McGraw-Hill.

Hill, F. S., Jr. 1990. *Computer Graphics*. New York: Macmillan.

Judd, D., and G. Wyszecki. 1975. *Color in Business, Science and Industry*. New York: John Wiley & Sons, Inc.

Kirk, D., ed. 1992. *Graphics Gems III*. San Diego, CA: Academic Press.

Mitchell, D. P. 1990. *Fast Algorithms for 3D Computer Graphics*, Ph.D. thesis, University of Sheffield, England.

Munsell, A. H. 1946. *A Color Notation*. Baltimore, MD: Munsell Color Co.

Rogers, D. F., and J. A. Adams. 1976. *Mathematical Elements for Computer Graphics*. New York: McGraw-Hill.

Thomas, S. W,. and R. G. Bogart. 1991. "Color Dithering," in Arvo (1991), pp. 72 –77, 509–513.

Watt, A. 1989. *Fundamentals of Three-Dimensional Computer Graphics*. Reading, MA: Addison-Wesley

Watt, A., and M. Watt.1992. *Advanced Animation and Rendering Techniques*. Reading, MA: Addison-Wesley.

CHAPTER 4

A Viewing System

INTRODUCTION

Our environment consists of a complicated arrangement of data structures and pointers residing somewhere in memory. Examining its contents is not easy; even a pair of colored cubes floating in space presents us with an overwhelming stream of instance, surface, polygon, and vertex values. Before doing anything else, we need to develop a *viewing system* to display three-dimensional environments on our two-dimensional computer screens.

What is a viewing system? Think of a computer screen as being a glass window looking into the environment (Fig. 4.1). Examining the image on the screen from a fixed position with one eye closed, we cannot say (with a bit of poetic license) whether we are viewing a three-dimensional environment or a two-dimensional representation of it.

That's all there is to it! By tracing rays from a three-dimensional object to our eye position, we can "project" the object onto the two-dimensional window. The ray luminances determine the luminances of the window at the points of intersection. Looking at this window, we see a two-dimensional *perspective projection* of the three-dimensional environment.

Do not be misled by some of the more complex discussions of viewing systems in the computer graphics literature. A viewing system—*any* viewing system—consists of one eye and a window. The viewing system we will develop in this chapter is a slightly simplified version of the GKS-3D (ISO 1988) and PHIGS (ANSI 1988) systems. The principles of these industry standards are described at length in Singleton (1987), with more generalized descriptions available in Foley et al. (1990) and Hill (1990).

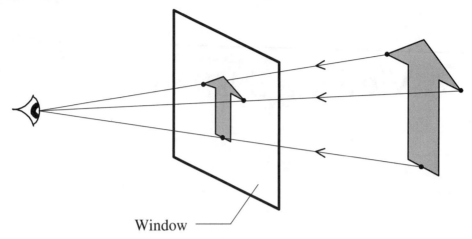

Window

Figure 4.1   Projecting a three-dimensional object onto a two-dimensional window

The differences between our viewing system and GKS-3D or PHIGS are minimal and relatively unimportant. Our system can show us everything we could see and photograph with a 35-mm camera in real life. In fact, the only advantage GKS-3D and PHIGS offer is their ability to model a professional photographer's view camera with its tilting lens holder. This is useful only if you want to correct for perspective distortion (such as a tall building photographed from street level with a wide-angle lens). Few of us own one of these cameras, so why bother implementing its equivalent in software?

The advantage of our viewing system is that it is conceptually simple. Don't let the mathematics intimidate you. Look at the illustrations first and remind yourself that the equations are nothing more than a formalized description of what you see. Taken one step at a time, they are actually quite easy to follow and understand.

4.1   A MINIMAL VIEWING SYSTEM

Imagine our window as being part of an infinite *view plane* that is some distance (called the *view distance*) in front of our eye and perpendicular to our line of sight (Fig. 4.2). We can position this *view-plane window* anywhere in an environment and orient it such that we can look in any direction.

To simplify our understanding of what we see, we can define a left-handed-*view-plane coordinate system* (or "view space") whose origin lies at the center of our window. In accordance with computer graphics convention, we label its axes *u, v,* and *n*. The *n* axis indicates the direction in which we are looking, whereas the *v* axis establishes our local "up" direction. Expressing the view-space origin in world coordinates (i.e., o_x, o_y, o_z) establishes our position; expressing the *n* axis and *v* axis as vectors in world coordinates uniquely orients our view space with respect to the environment. The *n*-axis unit vector **n** is called the *view-direction vector*, and the *v*-axis unit vector **v** is referred to as the *view-up vector*.

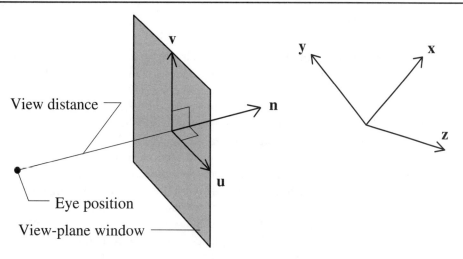

Figure 4.2 View-plane coordinate system

Our view-plane window is a square with dimensions 2 units wide by 2 units high. What the units actually represent—inches, feet, or meters—is not important. Looking through the window, we can see that the set of rays traced from its four corners to the eye position define an imaginary pyramidal cone (the *view pyramid*) that delimits our angular *field of view* (Fig. 4.3). We can change this field of view by varying the view distance. The effect is the same as that we achieve by changing the focal length setting of a zoom lens on a camera—objects appear larger through the view-plane window as the view distance is increased.

Actually, the "window" analogy is somewhat misleading. Unlike a physical window, we will not see an object that is in front of the window (i.e., between the view plane and our eye position) but outside the view pyramid. Conversely, any object contained within the view pyramid will be visible, regardless of whether it is behind or in front of the window. A more accurate description of the view-plane window is that of an imaginary square, defined on the equally imaginary view plane, that determines the shape of the view pyramid.

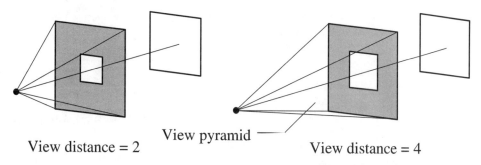

View distance = 2   View pyramid

View distance = 4

Figure 4.3 Changing the field of view by varying the view distance

4.1.1   The View Volume

We need two more components to make our minimal viewing system a useful tool. Suppose we want to look at the interior of a room somewhere inside a large building. If the eye position we need to obtain the proper perspective is located outside the room, we must somehow remove the intervening walls and objects. Even if our eye position is within the room, we will still want to ignore anything that lies beyond the far walls.

A simple but effective solution is to define two additional planes (called *clipping planes*) that are perpendicular to the view-direction vector (Fig. 4.4). Together with the view pyramid, these planes delimit a *view volume* (also known as a *view frustum*). Only objects that are contained within this volume are visible through the view-plane window; those that lie partially or wholly outside the volume are *clipped* from our field of view. In our example, we would likely set the front clipping plane to be just inside the room and the back clipping plane to lie just beyond the far room walls.

Given a viewing system position and orientation within an environment, we may find that the nearest objects of interest are between the eye position and the view-plane window. This is not a problem! The front clipping plane can be placed as close to the eye position as necessary, including in front of the view-plane window. We can always trace rays backward from the eye position through the objects to the view plane.

4.1.2   Specifying the View-Up Vector

Later in developing a user interface for our viewing system we will need to specify its position and orientation in world coordinates. Whereas specifying the position is trivial, orienting the viewing system presents a minor problem. Designing an intu-

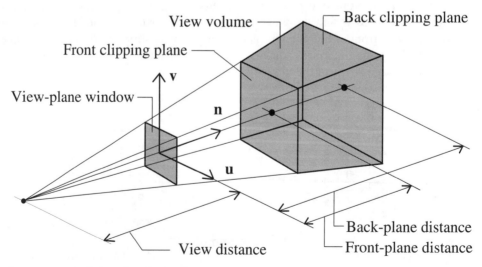

Figure 4.4   Defining the view volume

itive interface suggests that the view-direction vector **n** and view-up vector **v** should be specified using spherical coordinates. However, **v** must be exactly perpendicular to **n**. Once we specify **n**, how can we accurately specify **v**?

One reasonable approach is to indicate an approximate view-up vector **v'**. The true view-up vector **v'** can then be determined by projecting **v'** onto the view plane (Fig. 4.5) and normalizing the resultant vector. This can be done by calculating:

$$\mathbf{v} = norm\left(\mathbf{v'} - (\mathbf{v'} \cdot \mathbf{n})\mathbf{n}\right) \tag{4.1}$$

where the only restriction is that **v'** cannot point in the same or opposite direction as **n**. In other words, **v'** cannot be *collinear* with **n**.

Knowing **v** and **n**, we can determine the world coordinates of the unit vector **u** from:

$$\mathbf{u} = \mathbf{n} \times \mathbf{v} \tag{4.2}$$

where **n** comes before **v** in the cross product only because **u**, **v,** and **n** comprise a left-handed coordinate system.

4.2 FROM WORLD TO VIEW COORDINATES

The objects in our environment are defined in terms of three-dimensional polygons with world coordinates. To project them onto the view-plane window, we first need to transform their coordinates into those of our view space. This problem is similar to that of transforming an entity into an instance (Section 3.9), except that no scaling is required. We are also dealing with an environment (a "world space") rather than a single entity. Nevertheless, the same principles apply.

Imagine that we have an environment consisting of a cube and a viewing system as shown in Figure 4.6a. We need a linear three-dimensional transformation that will perform two operations. First, it should translate the world space such that its origin coincides with our view-space origin (Fig 4.6b). In other words, the world coordinates of every object in the environment are shifted a distance equal to that between the two origins.

Second, the transformation should rotate the world space such that its axes are aligned with those of our view space (Fig. 4.6c). Remember, however, that the world

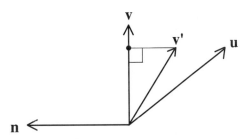

Figure 4.5 Determining the view-up vector **v** from an approximate vector **v'**

space has a right-handed coordinate system, whereas our view space is left-handed. This means that when the x-axis unit vector is aligned with the u-axis unit vector and the y-axis and v-axis unit vectors are similarly aligned, the z-axis unit vector will point in the opposite direction to that of its n-axis counterpart.

In terms of homogeneous coordinates, this transformation can be expressed as:

$$\begin{bmatrix} u \\ v \\ n \\ 1 \end{bmatrix} = \mathbf{RT} \begin{bmatrix} x \\ y \\ z \\ 1 \end{bmatrix} = \mathbf{M} \begin{bmatrix} x \\ y \\ z \\ 1 \end{bmatrix} \tag{4.3}$$

where $\mathbf{T}$ is the translation matrix, $\mathbf{R}$ is the rotation matrix, and $\mathbf{M}$ is the net *view-space transformation* matrix.

The translation component is quite simple:

$$\mathbf{T} = \begin{bmatrix} 1 & 0 & 0 & -o_x \\ 0 & 1 & 0 & -o_y \\ 0 & 0 & 1 & -o_z \\ 0 & 0 & 0 & 1 \end{bmatrix} \tag{4.4}$$

where o_x, o_y, and o_z are the world coordinates of the view-space origin. The rotation component is somewhat more complicated. We have the view-space axes as unit vectors $\mathbf{u}$, $\mathbf{v}$, and $\mathbf{n}$ expressed in world space coordinates (e.g., $u = \{u_x, u_y, u_z\}$ for the u-axis vector). We want a three-dimensional transformation matrix $\mathbf{R}$ that will rotate them into the following view-space coordinates:

$$\mathbf{u} = \{1, 0, 0\}$$
$$\mathbf{v} = \{0, 1, 0\} \tag{4.5}$$
$$\mathbf{n} = \{0, 0, 1\}$$

Expressed in homogeneous coordinates, these become:

$$\mathbf{R} \begin{bmatrix} u_x \\ u_y \\ u_z \\ 1 \end{bmatrix} = \begin{bmatrix} 1 \\ 0 \\ 0 \\ 1 \end{bmatrix}$$

$$\mathbf{R} \begin{bmatrix} v_x \\ v_y \\ v_z \\ 1 \end{bmatrix} = \begin{bmatrix} 0 \\ 1 \\ 0 \\ 1 \end{bmatrix} \tag{4.6}$$

$$\mathbf{R} \begin{bmatrix} n_x \\ n_y \\ n_z \\ 1 \end{bmatrix} = \begin{bmatrix} 0 \\ 0 \\ 1 \\ 1 \end{bmatrix}$$

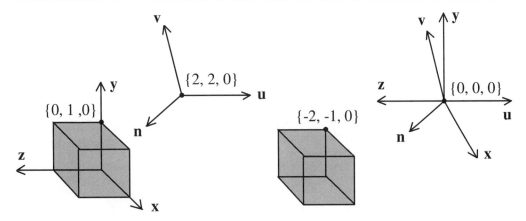

Figure 4.6a   Viewing system in world space

Figure 4.6b   Translate world coordinates to view-space origin

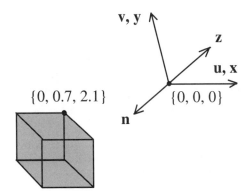

Figure 4.6c   Rotate world coordinates into view space

It can be shown (e.g., Hill 1990) that the matrix $\mathbf{R}$ must have the form:

$$\mathbf{R} = \begin{bmatrix} u_x & u_y & u_z & 0 \\ v_x & v_y & v_z & 0 \\ n_x & n_y & n_z & 0 \\ 0 & 0 & 0 & 1 \end{bmatrix} \tag{4.7}$$

where u_x, u_y, and u_z are the world coordinates of the u-axis unit vector, and similarly for the v-axis and n-axis unit vectors. For our purposes, it is sufficient to confirm that $\mathbf{R}$ satisfies Equation 4.6 (since $u_x^2 + u_y^2 = u_z^2 = 1$ for $\mathbf{u}$, and similarly for $\mathbf{v}$ and $\mathbf{n}$).

Concatenating these two matrices gives us the view-space transformation matrix:

$$\mathbf{M} = \mathbf{RT} = \begin{bmatrix} u_x & u_y & u_z & t_x \\ v_x & v_y & v_z & t_y \\ n_x & n_y & n_z & t_z \\ 0 & 0 & 0 & 1 \end{bmatrix} \tag{4.8}$$

where:

$$\begin{aligned} t_x &= -o_x * u_x - o_y * u_y - o_z * u_z \\ t_y &= -o_x * v_x - o_y * v_y - o_z * v_z \\ t_z &= -o_x * n_x - o_y * n_y - o_z * n_z \end{aligned} \tag{4.9}$$

from the definition of matrix multiplication. Put more succinctly, each of the components of the submatrix $\mathbf{t}$ is the dot product of the view-space origin $\mathbf{o}$ (expressed as a vector in world space coordinates) and one of the vectors $\mathbf{u}$, $\mathbf{v}$, or $\mathbf{n}$. In other words:

$$\mathbf{t} = \begin{bmatrix} -\mathbf{o} \cdot \mathbf{u} \\ -\mathbf{o} \cdot \mathbf{v} \\ -\mathbf{o} \cdot \mathbf{n} \end{bmatrix} \tag{4.10}$$

Referring to Figure 4.6 as an example, suppose we have chosen a view space whose position and orientation in world coordinates are: $\mathbf{o} = \{2, 2, 0\}$, $\mathbf{u} = \{0, 0, -1\}$, $\mathbf{v} = \{-1/\sqrt{2}, 1/\sqrt{2}, 0\}$, and $\mathbf{n} = \{-1/\sqrt{2}, -1/\sqrt{2}, 0\}$. This gives us the following view-space transformation matrix:

$$\mathbf{M} = \begin{bmatrix} 0 & 0 & -1 & 0 \\ -1/\sqrt{2} & 1/\sqrt{2} & 0 & 0 \\ -1/\sqrt{2} & -1/\sqrt{2} & 0 & 2\sqrt{2} \\ 0 & 0 & 0 & 1 \end{bmatrix} \tag{4.11}$$

If we then have (for example) a point in our environment with world coordinates $\{0, 1, 0\}$, premultiplying its homogeneous coordinates representation:

$$\begin{bmatrix} 0 \\ 1 \\ 0 \\ 1 \end{bmatrix}$$

by $\mathbf{M}$ gives its view-space coordinates of $\{0, -1/\sqrt{2}, 3/\sqrt{2}\}$.

In summary, we can position and orient our viewing system anywhere in an environment. Having done so, Equations 4.8 and 4.9 show us how to compute its transformation matrix. Applying this matrix to the world coordinates of any point in the environment gives us its equivalent view-space coordinates.

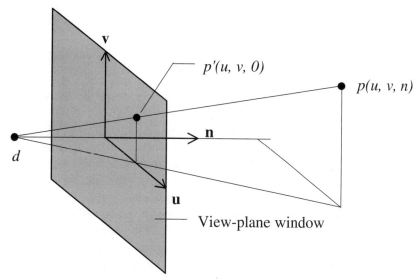

Figure 4.7 Perspective projection

4.3 PERSPECTIVE PROJECTION

The objects in our environment consist of collections of three-dimensional polygons. Having transformed the world coordinates of their vertices into view-space coordinates, it remains to project these vertices onto the view plane. At first glance, this appears to be a problem involving elementary geometry.

From Figure 4.7, we see that the coordinates of the projected point p' can be determined from the coordinates of p according to the equations:

$$p'_u = p_u/w$$
$$p'_v = p_v/w$$

(4.12)

where $w = 1 - (p_n/d)$, with d being the view distance (and where $d < 0$).

This is reminiscent of our definition of homogeneous coordinates (Eq. 3.10). Suppose we expand Equation 4.12 to include the n-axis coordinate:

$$p'_u = p_u/w$$
$$p'_v = p_v/w$$
$$p'_n = p_n/w$$

(4.13)

where again $w = 1 - (p_n/d)$. Expressed in terms of homogeneous coordinates, this becomes:

$$\text{Perspective:} \quad \begin{bmatrix} P_u \\ P_v \\ P_n \\ w \end{bmatrix} = \begin{bmatrix} 1 & 0 & 0 & 0 \\ 0 & 1 & 0 & 0 \\ 0 & 0 & 1 & 0 \\ 0 & 0 & -1/d & 1 \end{bmatrix} \begin{bmatrix} u \\ v \\ n \\ 1 \end{bmatrix} = \mathbf{P} \begin{bmatrix} u \\ v \\ n \\ 1 \end{bmatrix}$$

(4.14)

where the projected coordinates are given by:

$$p'_u = P_u/w$$
$$p'_v = P_v/w \qquad\qquad (4.15)$$
$$p'_n = P_n/w$$

(The division of the first three homogeneous coordinates by the fourth coordinate is called the *perspective divide* operation.)

This approach offers several advantages. First, it allows us to perform perspective projection as a three-dimensional transformation using homogeneous coordinates. Recalling Section 3.11, we can concatenate the perspective transformation matrix **P** with our view-space transformation matrix **M** (Eq. 4.8), thereby performing two transformations with one matrix multiplication.

Second, the projected n-axis coordinate p'_n has a physical meaning. It represents the *perspective depth* (or *pseudodepth*) of the vertex. Given two vertices p_1 and p_2 where $p_{1n} > p_{2n}$, the projected n-axis coordinates are such that $p'_{1n} > p'_{2n}$. In other words, the perspective transformation preserves the depth ordering of the vertices relative to the view plane. (It does not preserve the true n-axis depth, however. Plotting p'_n versus p_n will show that the n-axis scale is stretched as it approaches the back clipping plane.) We will need this information later to determine whether an object is hidden by any other objects in front of it.

Third and most important, the perspective transformation preserves straight lines and planes. That is, a straight line between two vertices in our view space is projected onto the view plane as a straight line while retaining the proper depth ordering of each point along the line. The same applies to points on a plane. This is essential if we are to interpolate edges and planar polygon surfaces between vertices after a perspective transformation of their coordinates.

The four homogeneous coordinates represent four dimensions. Unfortunately, the words "four dimensions" bring to mind thoughts of general relativity and curved space-time, following which most of us respond to social conditioning and switch our minds into neutral. To avoid this syndrome, we should consider the simpler case of three dimensions.

The diagram in Figure 4.8 illustrates two points (p_0 and p_1) on a three-dimensional line being projected onto the u-v plane. The projected points are p'_0 and p'_1 respectively. Notice that the two horizontal axes are labeled u and v, whereas the vertical axis is labeled w. Notice also that $p'_0 = p'_1/w$. This applies for any point along the line.

There are two crucial concepts here: First, the w axis plots our fourth coordinate and therefore represents the fourth dimension. It clearly shows that the coordinate w is nothing more than a scaling factor that converts the u, v coordinates of a point to their projected coordinates on the view plane. This same scaling factor converts the n-axis coordinate to its perspective depth.

Second, the fourth homogeneous dimension is no different from the other three dimensions. We can plot points, lines, and planes in four dimensions as easily as we can in two or three. Moreover, the usual rules of geometry and trigonometry apply. For example, the length of a four-dimensional vector is given by $\sqrt{u^2 + v^2 + n^2 + w^2}$.

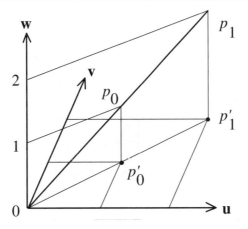

Figure 4.8   Avoiding the "general relativity" syndrome

There is one point to remember, however. Since w represents a scaling factor (as shown by Eq. 4.13), any line or plane plotted along the w axis must intersect the origin. There are exceptions to this rule in computer graphics, but they do not occur in any area of concern to us.

What happens if a point p is *behind* our eye position? Even though p_n has a negative value, Equations 4.14 and 4.15 yield valid results. They can be interpreted by tracing a ray from the point through the eye position to the view plane (Fig. 4.9). This emphasizes the need for our view volume. Without it, objects behind the eye position are projected onto the view plane. Another reason is that any attempt to project a point on the plane parallel to the view plane and intersecting the eye position (i.e., $p_n = d$) will result in a division-by-zero error.

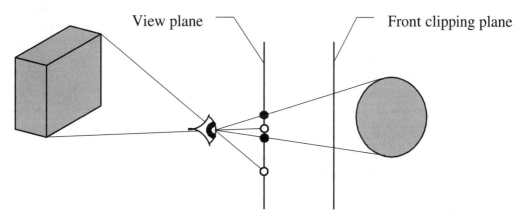

Figure 4.9   Projecting points from behind the eye position

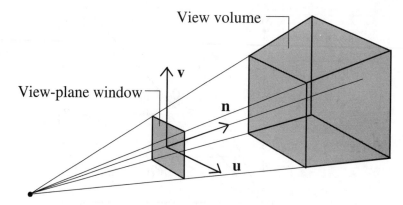

Figure 4.10a   Perspective view volume (before perspective divide)

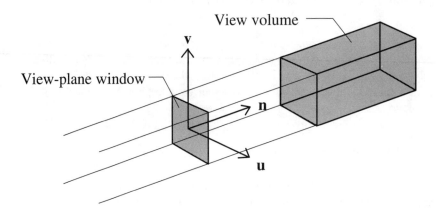

Figure 4.10b   Parallel view volume (after perspective divide)

The perspective division distorts the truncated pyramid of our *perspective* view volume (Fig. 4.10a) into the *parallel* view volume shown in Figure 4.10b.

The view volume is now a rectangular box with parallel sides, with our eye position removed to minus infinity along the *n* axis. Of course, all the points in the view space have been similarly distorted—we have transformed our perspective projection of the world space into an equivalent parallel projection (Fig. 4.11). The projection of any point onto the view plane can now be performed by tracing a ray parallel to the *n* axis from the point to the view plane. The spatial distortions we have introduced with the perspective transformation make this projection of the environment onto the view-plane window look like our original perspective projection.

4.4   SCREEN-SPACE COORDINATES

Our view-plane window is a square. From the beginning of this chapter we recall that our goal is to display two-dimensional projected images of a three-dimensional envi-

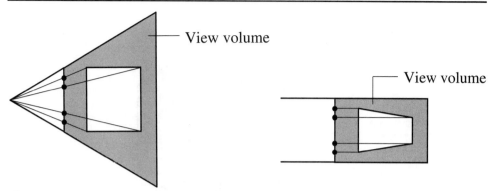

Figure 4.11a   Before perspective division   **Figure 4.11b**   After perspective division

ronment. These images will typically be rectangular. We can think of them having a left-handed *screen-space* coordinate system (Fig. 4.12), with the x axis and y axis representing the image width and height, respectively and the z axis representing the depth "behind" the screen. The question is, once we project a point onto the square view-plane window, how can we scale its u, v view-space coordinates to the x, y, z screen-space coordinates of a rectangular image?

We could, of course, simply crop the projected image before scaling. However, this entails an unnecessary amount of work. We still have to clip, shade, and perform hidden-surface elimination calculations for each polygon (discussed in the following sections) before we can scale it.

The *aspect ratio* of an image is defined as the ratio of its width to its height. What if we redefined our view-plane window as a rectangle with the same aspect ratio as the image we want to display? Unfortunately, this complicates both our definition of a view volume and the following algorithms for clipping, shading, and hidden-surface elimination. In particular, the algorithms must be made aware of the relative dimensions of the image.

The preferred solution is to scale our entire view space. Suppose we want to

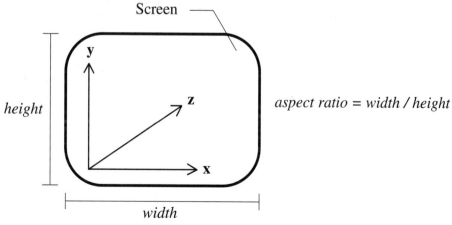

aspect ratio = width / height

Figure 4.12   Screen-space coordinates

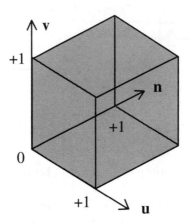

Figure 4.13   Canonical parallel-view volume

display a rectangular image that measures 320 pixels horizontally and 240 pixels vertically on a computer screen with square pixels. The aspect ratio of this image is approximately 1.33. By multiplying (i.e., scaling) the view-space v-axis coordinates by this ratio, we can stretch our view space vertically such that the rectangular image becomes a square. This allows us to continue to use our square view-plane-window. (If the aspect ratio were less than one—that is, if we wanted a vertically oriented image—we would have to scale the u-axis coordinates instead.)

We can now perform our clipping, shading, and hidden-surface elimination calculations for each polygon in this distorted view space. More important, the algorithms do not need to know about the aspect ratio. We need only divide the distorted v-axis or u-axis coordinates by this ratio when we are ready to scale to screen-space coordinates.

What about the front and back clipping plane distances? As a result of perspective division, the front plane is now located at $F/(1 - F/d)$ units along the n axis, where F is the front-plane distance and d is the view distance (with $d < 0$). Similarly, the back plane is located at $B/(1 - B/d)$ units, where B is the back-plane distance. By translating and then scaling our view volume in the n-axis direction prior to perspective division, we can change these distances to 0 and +1 units respectively. By appropriately translating and scaling in the u-axis and v-axis directions as well, we can create the *canonical* parallel-view volume shown in Figure 4.13, where $0 \leq u \leq 1$ and $0 \leq v \leq 1$. These are *normalized* view-space coordinates.

The required translation and scaling can be performed with one *normalization* transformation, expressed in homogeneous coordinates as:

$$\text{Normalization:} \quad \begin{bmatrix} u' \\ v' \\ n' \\ 1 \end{bmatrix} = \begin{bmatrix} s_u & 0 & 0 & 1/2 \\ 0 & s_v & 0 & 1/2 \\ 0 & 0 & s_n & r_n \\ 0 & 0 & 0 & 1 \end{bmatrix} \begin{bmatrix} u \\ v \\ n \\ 1 \end{bmatrix} = \mathbf{N} \begin{bmatrix} u \\ v \\ n \\ 1 \end{bmatrix} \quad (4.16)$$

where:

$$s_u = \frac{a}{2}$$

$$s_v = \frac{b}{2}$$

$$s_n = \left(\frac{B}{1 - B/d} - \frac{F}{1 - F/d} \right)^{-1} = \frac{(d - B)(d - F)}{d^2(B - F)} \qquad (4.17)$$

$$r_n = -\left(\frac{F}{1 - F/d} \right) s_n = \frac{F(d - B)}{d(F - B)}$$

and where:

$$a = 1$$

$$b = aspect$$

if $aspect \geq 1$, otherwise:

$$a = 1/aspect$$

$$b = 1$$

with *aspect* being the image aspect ratio.

Later we will need the pseudodepth n' of our normalized view-space coordinates to determine the relative depth of objects in the view volume. Meanwhile, we can scale u' and v' to four screen-space coordinates using:

$$x = \min\big((\text{int})(u' * width), \quad width - 1 \big)$$

$$y = \min\big((\text{int})(v' * height), \quad height - 1 \big) \qquad (4.18)$$

where x is the horizontal position in pixels from the left edge of the screen and y is the vertical position in scan lines from the bottom. Similarly, the screen *width* is measured in pixels and its *height* is measured in scan lines. Since u' and v' can range from 0.0 to 1.0 inclusive, the *min* function is needed to ensure that the screen-space coordinates stay within their upper bounds.

There are some differences of opinion in the computer graphics community regarding the coordinates of a pixel. Our normalized view-space coordinates are floating-point values, implying a *continuous* image. Our screen, on the other hand, is an array of pixels, which implies a *discrete* image. The question is, are these pixels centered on integer coordinates or halfway between? Given a floating-point value of 3.75, do we round it to the nearest integer value of 4.0 or truncate it to 3.0?

Heckbert (1990a) argues for the latter, stating that "the pixel with discrete coordinates (x, y) has its center at continuous coordinates $(x + 1/2, y + 1/2)$." That is, we should truncate using the C++ math library *floor* function. This is done implicitly when the compiler converts a floating-point value to its integer representation (Plauger and Brodie 1989) through the cast to *int* in Equation 4.18.

4.5   THREE-DIMENSIONAL PROJECTIVE TRANSFORMATIONS

Summarizing our viewing system transformations then, we have:

$$
\begin{bmatrix} P_u \\ P_v \\ P_n \\ w \end{bmatrix} = \mathbf{NPM} \begin{bmatrix} p_x \\ p_y \\ p_z \\ 1 \end{bmatrix}
\tag{4.19}
$$

where $\{p_x, p_y, p_z\}$ are the world coordinates of a point p, $\mathbf{M}$ is the view-space transformation matrix (Eq. 4.8), $\mathbf{P}$ represents the perspective transformation (Eq. 4.14), and $\mathbf{N}$ performs the normalization transformation (Eqn. 4.16). The perspective division (Eq. 4.15) then recovers the three-dimensional projected coordinates $\{p'_u, p'_v, p'_n\}$. The net transformation matrix $\mathbf{NPM}$ is called the three-dimensional *projective transformation* matrix.

The beauty of homogeneous coordinates is that for any given set of viewing system parameters, these three matrices can be concatenated to form a single 4×4 transformation matrix. This allows us to accomplish our view-space, normalization, and perspective transformations with a single matrix multiply operation, and to apply the identical operation to each point in the environment.

To illustrate Equation 4.19, assume we have a viewing system with view distance $d = -4.0$, front-plane distance $F = 2.0$, and back-plane distance $B = 10.0$. Our image has an aspect ratio *aspect* = 1.33 If we orient this system such that its origin is located at the world coordinate space origin, its view-direction vector is $n = \{0, 0, 1\}$ and its view-up vector is $v = \{0, 1, 0\}$, then its u-axis coordinates will be $u = \{-1, 0, 0\}$. This gives us the view-space transformation matrix:

$$
\mathbf{M} = \begin{bmatrix} -1 & 0 & 0 & 0 \\ 0 & 1 & 0 & 0 \\ 0 & 0 & 1 & 0 \\ 0 & 0 & 0 & 1 \end{bmatrix}
\tag{4.20}
$$

which *in this case only* does nothing more than convert right-handed world space coordinates into those of the left-handed view-space coordinate system.

Premultiplying by the perspective transformation matrix $\mathbf{P}$, we have:

$$
\mathbf{PM} = \begin{bmatrix} 1 & 0 & 0 & 0 \\ 0 & 1 & 0 & 0 \\ 0 & 0 & 1 & 0 \\ 0 & 0 & 1/4 & 1 \end{bmatrix} \mathbf{M} = \begin{bmatrix} -1 & 0 & 0 & 0 \\ 0 & 1 & 0 & 0 \\ 0 & 0 & 1 & 0 \\ 0 & 0 & 1/4 & 1 \end{bmatrix}
\tag{4.21}
$$

From Equation 4.17, we have $s_u = 1/2$, $s_v = 2/3$, $s_n = 21/32$, and $r_n = -7/8$. Premultiplying by the normalization matrix $\mathbf{N}$, we get:

$$\mathbf{NPM} = \begin{bmatrix} 1/2 & 0 & 0 & 1/2 \\ 0 & 2/3 & 0 & 1/2 \\ 0 & 0 & 21/32 & -7/8 \\ 0 & 0 & 0 & 1 \end{bmatrix} \mathbf{PM} = \begin{bmatrix} -1/2 & 0 & 1/8 & 1/2 \\ 0 & 2/3 & 1/8 & 1/2 \\ 0 & 0 & 7/16 & -7/8 \\ 0 & 0 & 1/4 & 1 \end{bmatrix}$$

(4.22)

Applying this transformation matrix to a point with world space coordinates {4, 3, 7}, we obtain its equivalent view-space coordinates:

$$w = 1 + z/4 = 11/4$$

$$u = \left(-\frac{1}{2}x + \frac{1}{8}z + \frac{1}{2} \right) \bigg/ w = -5/22$$

$$v = \left(\frac{2}{3}y + \frac{1}{8}z + \frac{1}{2} \right) \bigg/ w = 27/22$$

(4.23)

$$n = \left(\frac{7}{16}z - \frac{7}{8} \right) \bigg/ w = 35/44$$

Substituting the front and back clipping plane values of 2 and 10 for the point's z-axis coordinate will demonstrate that its perspective depth n becomes 0 and 1 respectively. Similar substitutions can be used to confirm the normalized u-axis and v-axis limits.

4.6 BACKFACE CULLING

We saw in the previous chapter (Section 3.4.1) that a polygon is visible only if the angle between its normal and our line-of-sight vector is less than ±90 degrees, or equivalently if their dot product is less than zero. Backface culling employs this concept to eliminate those polygons we cannot see before we perform our projective transformations.

We already have the polygon normal in world coordinates. What we need is the *view vector* from our eye position to any point on the polygon (Fig. 4.14). The polygon's first vertex makes as good a choice as any. The view vector is then defined as

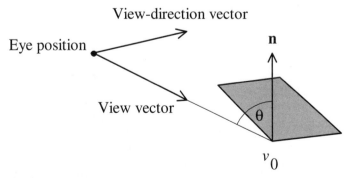

Figure 4.14 Backface culling in world space

the vector from our eye position to this vertex. (Note that this vector is not our view-*direction* vector. The polygon may not even be in our field of view.)

We do not have the eye position in world coordinates. However, we do have the view system origin **o** and view-direction vector **n**. Given the view distance d, the eye position coordinates are given by:

$$e_x = o_x + d*n_x$$
$$e_y = o_y + d*n_y \qquad\qquad (4.24)$$
$$e_z = o_z + d*n_z$$

or in vector notation, **e** = **o** + d***n**. (Note that this applies only when the eye position is on the n axis. Whereas this is always true for our viewing system, it may not be true for a more generalized viewing system such as GKS-3D or PHIGS.)

The view vector has to be calculated for each polygon, which may seem like a fair amount of work. Could we not perform backface culling after the projective transformations have been applied? The eye position will have been removed to minus infinity, and so every view vector will be parallel to the view-direction vector. A polygon will be visible only if its normal in-view space points toward the eye position. Unfortunately, the amount of work involved in the projective transformation of a polygon is greater than that of backface culling the polygon in world space.

4.7   A VIEWING SYSTEM CLASS

We can neatly encapsulate the preceding equations and parameters of our minimal viewing system in the following class:

Listing 4.1

```
// VIEW_SYS.H - Viewing System Class

#ifndef _VIEW_SYS_H
#define _VIEW_SYS_H

#include "patch3.h"

class ViewSys            // Viewing system
{
  private:
    double bpd;          // Back plane distance
    double eye;          // View distance
    double fpd;          // Front plane distance
    Point3 origin;       // View space origin
    Point3 eye_posn;     // Eye position
    Vector3 vdv;         // View direction vector
    Vector3 vuv;         // View-up vector
    double ptm[4][4];    // Projective transformation matrix
```

```
  protected:
    double aspect;        // Aspect ratio

    BOOL BackFaceCull( Patch3 *);
    double (*GetProjMatrix())[4];
    void BuildTransform();

  public:
    ViewSys()
    {
      aspect = 1.0;
      fpd = -0.99;
      bpd = 10000.0;
      eye = -1.0;
      eye_posn = Point3(-1.0, 0.0, 0.0);
      origin = Point3(0.0, 0.0, 0.0);
      vdv = Vector3(-1.0, 0.0, 0.0);
      vuv = Vector3(0.0, 0.0, 1.0);

      BuildTransform();          // Initialize matrix
    }

    double GetBackDist() { return bpd; }
    double GetFrontDist() { return fpd; }
    double GetViewDist() { return -eye; }
    Point3 &GetOrigin() { return origin; }
    Point3 &GetEyePosn() { return eye_posn; }
    Vector3 &GetViewDir() { return vdv; }
    Vector3 &GetViewUp() { return vuv; }
    void SetBackDist( double b ) { bpd = b; }
    void SetEyePosn( Point3 &e ) { eye_posn = e; }
    void SetFrontDist( double f ) { fpd = f; }
    void SetOrigin( Point3 &o ) { origin = o; }
    void SetViewDir( Vector3 &v ) { vdv = v; }
    void SetViewDist( double e ) { eye = -e; }
    void SetViewUp( Vector3 & );
};

// Return projective transformation matrix pointer
inline double (*ViewSys::GetProjMatrix())[4]
{ return ptm; }

#endif
```

and:

Listing 4.2

```
// VIEW_SYS.CPP - Viewing System Class

#include "view_sys.h"
```

(continued)

Listing 4.2   *(continued)*

```cpp
// Build projective transformation matrix and eye position
void ViewSys::BuildTransform()
{
  double rn;              // Translation factor
  double su, sv, sn;      // Scaling factors
  Vector3 o;              // Origin vector
  Vector3 u;              // u-axis vector

  // Set view space origin
  origin.SetX(eye_posn.GetX() - eye * vdv.GetX());
  origin.SetY(eye_posn.GetY() - eye * vdv.GetY());
  origin.SetZ(eye_posn.GetZ() - eye * vdv.GetZ());

  o = Vector3(origin);  // Initialize origin vector
  u = Cross(vdv, vuv);  // Calculate u-axis vector

  // Initialize view transformation matrix
  ptm[0][0] = u.GetX();
  ptm[0][1] = u.GetY();
  ptm[0][2] = u.GetZ();
  ptm[0][3] = -(Dot(o, u));

  ptm[1][0] = vuv.GetX();
  ptm[1][1] = vuv.GetY();
  ptm[1][2] = vuv.GetZ();
  ptm[1][3] = -(Dot(o, vuv));

  ptm[2][0] = vdv.GetX();
  ptm[2][1] = vdv.GetY();
  ptm[2][2] = vdv.GetZ();
  ptm[2][3] = -(Dot(o, vdv));

  ptm[3][0] = 0.0;
  ptm[3][1] = 0.0;
  ptm[3][2] = 0.0;
  ptm[3][3] = 1.0;

  // Premultiply by perspective transformation matrix
  ptm[3][0] -= ptm[2][0] / eye;
  ptm[3][1] -= ptm[2][1] / eye;
  ptm[3][2] -= ptm[2][2] / eye;
  ptm[3][3] -= ptm[2][3] / eye;

  // Premultiply by normalization matrix

  if (aspect >= 1.0)
  {
    su = 0.5;
    sv = 0.5 * aspect;
  }
```

```
    else
    {
      su = 0.5 / aspect;
      sv = 0.5;
    }

    sn = (eye - bpd) * (eye - fpd) / (eye * eye * (bpd -
        fpd));
    rn = fpd * (eye - bpd) / (eye * (fpd - bpd));

    ptm[0][0] = su * ptm[0][0] + 0.5 * ptm[3][0];
    ptm[0][1] = su * ptm[0][1] + 0.5 * ptm[3][1];
    ptm[0][2] = su * ptm[0][2] + 0.5 * ptm[3][2];
    ptm[0][3] = su * ptm[0][3] + 0.5 * ptm[3][3];

    ptm[1][0] = sv * ptm[1][0] + 0.5 * ptm[3][0];
    ptm[1][1] = sv * ptm[1][1] + 0.5 * ptm[3][1];
    ptm[1][2] = sv * ptm[1][2] + 0.5 * ptm[3][2];
    ptm[1][3] = sv * ptm[1][3] + 0.5 * ptm[3][3];

    ptm[2][0] = sn * ptm[2][0] + rn * ptm[3][0];
    ptm[2][1] = sn * ptm[2][1] + rn * ptm[3][1];
    ptm[2][2] = sn * ptm[2][2] + rn * ptm[3][2];
    ptm[2][3] = sn * ptm[2][3] + rn * ptm[3][3];
}

// Set view-up vector
void ViewSys::SetViewUp( Vector3 &approx )
{
  Vector3 temp = vdv;    // Temporary vector

  // Project approximate view-up vector onto view plane
  temp *= Dot(approx, vdv);
  vuv = approx - temp;

  vuv.Norm();    // Normalize view-up vector
}

// Perform backface culling
BOOL ViewSys::BackFaceCull( Patch3 *ppatch )
{
  Vector3 view;           // View vector

  // Calculate view vector (first vertex to eye position)
  view = Vector3(ppatch->GetVertexPtr(0)->GetPosn(),
      eye_posn);

  // Indicate whether patch is backface
  return (Dot(ppatch->GetNormal(), view) < MIN_VALUE) ?
      TRUE : FALSE;
}
```

Only one instance of *ViewSys* is required for our radiosity renderer. Its constructor positions the viewing system at the world space origin with its view-direction vector aligned with the *x* axis in the negative direction and its view-up vector aligned with the *z* axis. The eye position is set at −1.0, and the front- and back-plane distances are set to very small and large values respectively. The constructor then calls *BuildTransform* to initialize the three-dimensional projective transformation matrix and determine the eye position.

ViewSys also presents the view distance to the user as a positive number through the functions *GetViewDist* and *SetViewDist*. This is more for the user's convenience than anything else; its internal representation and mathematics remain unchanged.

The viewing system parameters can be changed at any time by calling the appropriate class-member functions. However, any change to *SetViewDir* must be followed with a call to *SetViewUp*. This call is not included in *SetViewDir*, since the user must specify an approximate view-up vector that is not collinear with the new view-direction vector. Once the parameters have been updated, *BuildTransform* must be called to calculate the new transformation matrix elements and update the eye position.

One final comment: The function *GetProjMatrix* represents one of the least elegant aspects of C++. All it does is return a pointer to the projective transformation matrix *ptm*. Unfortunately, C++ function declarations involving pointers to multidimensional arrays are something only a compiler writer can love.

4.8   POLYGON CLIPPING

Again, the objects in our environment consist of collections of three-dimensional polygons. Although we want to project these polygons onto the view plane, we must consider that a polygon may not be wholly within the view volume. If it is completely outside, we can simply ignore it. However, it may be only partly within the volume (e.g., Fig. 4.15). In this case we must somehow *clip* the portion that is outside the view volume before projecting its remainder onto the view-plane window.

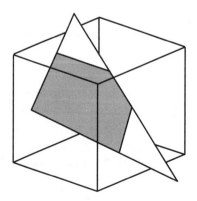

Figure 4.15   Clipping a polygon to the canonical view volume

4.8.1   The Sutherland-Hodgman Algorithm

There are many different polygon clipping algorithms described in the literature, including Liang and Barsky (1983), Weiler and Atherton (1980), Burkett and Noll (1988), and Vatt (1992). For our purposes, however, we need look no further than the classic Sutherland-Hodgman algorithm (Sutherland and Hodgman 1974).

Looking at our view volume, we can imagine it as being the intersection of six clipping planes (Section 4.1.1). The Sutherland-Hodgman algorithm accepts as its input an n-sided polygon modeled as an ordered list of vertices $p_0, \ldots, p_{n-1}$ and clips it against each of these planes in sequence. Vertices within the view volume are retained, and new vertices are created wherever a polygon edge intersects one of the clipping planes. The algorithm's output is a new set of vertices $q_0, \ldots, q_{m-1}$ that represents the clipped polygon.

We can best see how the algorithm works by first examining how it clips a polygon against a single plane. It considers the vertices $p_0, \ldots, p_{n-1}$ one vertex at a time, beginning with p_0. Each vertex p_i is considered to be the end vertex E of an edge of the polygon; the start vertex S is the preceding vertex p_{i-1}. The algorithm may generate zero, one, or two output vertices of the clipped polygon for each input vertex, depending on the relation of the edge to the clipping plane.

The plane divides the view-plane space into two regions: a "visible" region that contains the view volume and an "invisible" region. This leads to the four possibilities shown in Figure 4.16. First, the edge may have both vertices in the visible region (Fig 4.16a), in which case the end vertex E is output (the start vertex will have been previously output). (A vertex actually on the plane is assumed to be in the visible region.) Second, the edge may have both vertices in the invisible region (Fig. 4.16b), in which case no vertex is output. Third, the edge may leave the visible region (Fig. 4.16c),

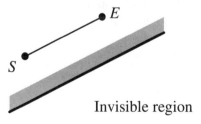

Figure 4.16a   Edge in visible region

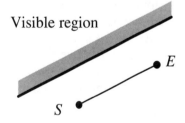

Figure 4.16b   Edge in invisible region

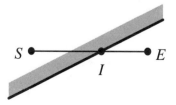

Figure 4.16c   Edge leaving visible region

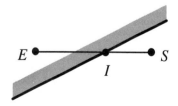

Figure 4.16d   Edge entering visible region

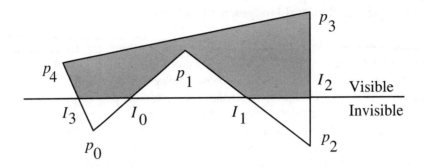

Figure 4.17   Clipping a polygon against a single plane

with only the start vertex in the visible region. In this case, the intersection I between the edge and the plane is determined and output as a vertex. Fourth, the edge may enter the visible region (Fig. 4.16d), with only the end vertex in the visible region. Here two vertices are output: the intersection I between the edge and the plane, followed by the end vertex E.

Looking at Figure 4.17, we can follow the vertices of an arbitrary polygon intersected by a plane to see that this algorithm works with one exception: The edge from p_4 to p_0 is not considered. If it crosses the plane, we miss the final intersection vertex I_3.

The solution is to save the first vertex p_0 and "close" the polygon by examining the edge from p_{n-1} to p_0 after all the input vertices have been considered. A final output vertex is generated only if the edge crosses the plane. (We could instead simply access p_0 directly if the vertices are stored in an array. However, one of the primary advantages of the Sutherland-Hodgman algorithm is that it does not need intermediate storage for an indeterminate number of input or output vertices. All it needs to store for clipping against a plane is the first and previous vertices p_0 and p_{i-1}.)

Expressed in pseudocode, the above becomes as in Figure 4.18, where *polygon* is an ordered list of vertices $p_0, \ldots, p_{n-1}$, *plane* describes the clipping plane, *Intersect* computes the intersection of the polygon edge and the plane, and *Output* generates an output vertex that is placed in an output vertex array.

```
static F                              // First vertex
static S                              // Start vertex
BOOL fflag                            // First vertex seen flag

PolyClip(polygon, plane)              // Clip entire polygon
fflag = FALSE
FOR each vertex p_i
  Clip p_i, plane)
ENDFOR
Close(plane)                          // Close polygon
```

```
Clip(E, plane)                          // Clip polygon edge
IF (fflag == FALSE)
  F = E
  fflag = TRUE
ELSE IF (edge SE intersects plane)
  I = Intersect(S, E, plane)
  Output(I)
ENDIF
IF (E in visible region)
  Output(E)
ENDIF
S = E

Close(plane)                            // Close polygon
IF (fflag == TRUE)
  IF (edge SF intersects plane)
    I = Intersect(S, F, plane)
    Output(I)
  ENDIF
ENDIF
```

Figure 4.18   Sutherland-Hodgman algorithm (single plane)

4.8.2   Clipping-Plane Intersections

To determine the intersection of a polygon edge and an arbitrary plane, we first need to describe both objects mathematically. Given an edge with start vertex S and end vertex E, we can define the vector $\mathbf{r} = E - S$. The *parametric* equation of the polygon edge is then:

$$p(t) = S + t * \mathbf{r} \tag{4.25}$$

where $0 \le t \le 1$ is the parameter that describes the set of points $p(t)$ between S and E. For example, if $S = \{1, 2, 0\}$, $E = \{-2, 3, 1\}$, and $t = 0.7$, then the point $p(0.7)$ has the coordinates $\{-1.1, 2.7, 0.7\}$.

We can similarly define an arbitrary plane (shown in cross section in Figure 4.19) using the equation:

$$n_x x + n_y y + n_z z = d \tag{4.26}$$

where the coefficients n_x, n_y, and n_z are the coordinates of the plane normal $\mathbf{n}$ and d is the distance from the origin to the nearest point on the plane. Expressed in vector notation, this gives us the *point normal* equation of a plane:

$$\mathbf{n} \cdot \mathbf{p} = d \tag{4.27}$$

where $\mathbf{p}$ is the bound vector from the origin to any point p on the plane.

We adopt the convention that the visible region of the plane contains the plane normal $\mathbf{n}$. An arbitrary vertex p represented by the bound vector $\mathbf{p}$ from the origin to the vertex is then:

1. In the visible region if $\mathbf{n} \cdot \mathbf{p} > d$.
2. On the plane (and in the visible region) if $\mathbf{n} \cdot \mathbf{p} = d$.
3. In the invisible region if $\mathbf{n} \cdot \mathbf{p} < d$.

For example, given a plane with normal $\mathbf{n} = \{2, -1, 3\}$ and distance $d = 3$, its point normal equation is $\{2, -1, 3\} \cdot \{x, y, z\} = 3$. The vertex $\mathbf{p} = \{2, 5, -1\}$ is in the invisible region, since $\mathbf{n} \cdot \mathbf{p} = -4$.

A polygon edge intersects a plane only if its start and end vertices S and E are on opposite sides. If we substitute Equation 4.25 into Equation 4.26, we get:

$$n_x * (S_x + r_x * t) + n_y * (S_y + r_y * t) + n_z * (S_z + r_z * t) = d \qquad (4.28)$$

Rearranging terms to solve for t gives us:

$$t = \frac{d - (n_x * S_x + n_y * S_y + n_z * S_z)}{n_x * r_x + n_y * r_y + n_z * r_z} \qquad (4.29)$$

Expressed in vector notation, this becomes:

$$t = \frac{d - \mathbf{n} \cdot \mathbf{S}}{\mathbf{n} \cdot \mathbf{r}} \qquad (4.30)$$

where $\mathbf{S}$ is the vector from the origin to vertex S and $\mathbf{r} = E - S$. Substituting t into Equation 4.25 gives us the coordinates of the intersection point. For example, suppose we have a plane with normal $n = \{2, -1, 3\}$ and distance $d = 3$. The polygon edge described by the vertices $S = \{2, 5, -1\}$ and $E = \{4, 7, 3\}$ intersects the plane at the point $I = \{3, 6, 1\}$.

4.8.3   Clipping Against Multiple Planes

Another advantage of the Sutherland-Hodgman algorithm is the ease with which it can be extended to clip against multiple planes. We could, of course, clip against each of our six view-volume clipping planes in sequence, saving the intermediate polygon as an ordered list of vertices $q_0, \ldots, q_{m-1}$ at each stage. However, the Sutherland-Hodgman algorithm allows a more elegant approach. Apart from the

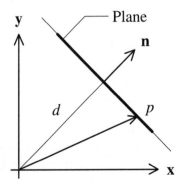

Figure 4.19   Determining the equation of a plane

Intersect function, the code is identical for each plane. We can make the *Clip* function reentrant by defining separate static *F* and *S* vertices for each plane. More important, we can modify *Output* such that it recursively calls *Clip* for the current vertex and the next plane. In other words, the next clipping stage can begin as soon as the current stage finds an acceptable vertex. This approach is often used to advantage in hardware graphics accelerators, where the vertices can be processed in a "pipeline" without the need for intermediate storage of the output vertices.

The revised algorithm for clipping against *m* multiple planes becomes as given in Figure 4.20, where the function *Put* generates the output vertex. The additional logic in *Close* is needed to ensure that the first vertex for the current plane is valid.

```
static F[m]                        // First vertices array
static S[m]                        // Start vertices array
static fflag[m]                    // First vertex seen flags array

PolyClip(polygon)                  // Clip polygon
FOR each plane
  fflag[plane] = FALSE
ENDFOR
FOR each vertex p_i
  Clip(p_i, first_plane)
ENDFOR
Close(first_plane)

Clip(E, plane)                     // Clip polygon against plane
IF (fflag[plane] == FALSE)
  F[plane] = E
  fflag[plane] = TRUE
ELSE
  S = S[plane]
  IF (edge SE intersects plane)
    I = Intersect(S, E, plane)
    Output(I, plane)
  ENDIF
ENDIF
IF (E in visible region)
  Output(E, plane)
ENDIF
S[plane] = E

Output(vertex, plane)              // Output vertex
IF (no more planes)
  Put(vertex)
ELSE
  Clip(vertex, next_plane)
ENDIF

Close(plane)                       // Close polygon
IF (fflag[plane] == TRUE)
  S = S[plane]
  F = F[plane]
  IF (edge SF intersects plane)
    I = Intersect(S, F, plane)
    Output(I, plane)
  ENDIF
```

(continued)

Figure 4.20   *(continued)*

```
IF (more planes)
   Close(next_plane)
   ENDIF
ENDIF
```

Figure 4.20   Recursive Sutherland-Hodgman algorithm (multiple planes)

4.8.4   Clipping a Polygon—An Example

The behavior of the Sutherland-Hodgman algorithm is quite subtle. Even the authors (Sutherland and Hodgman 1974) admitted that they were "somewhat chagrined that the obvious extension of work on line clipping with which we have been involved kept us so long from seeing the simplicity of the present approach." With this in mind, it may help to see the algorithm in action where a polygon is being clipped against a rectangle in two dimensions (Fig. 4.21).

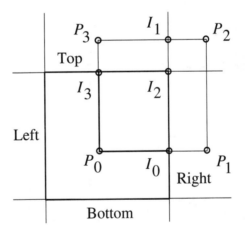

Figure 4.21   Clipping a polygon against a rectangle

Ordering the four clipping planes as *Left*, *Right*, *Top*, and *Bottom*, we see that the algorithm proceeds as in Figure 4.22.

```
Clip(P0, Left)                       // Clip P0
   first[Left] = P0
   Clip(P0, Right)
      first[Right] = P0
      Clip(P0, Top)
         first[Top] = P0
         Clip(P0, Bottom)
            first[Bottom] = P0
            Output(P0)               // Output P0
```

```
           S[Bottom] = P0
         S[Top] = P0
       S[Right] = P0
     S[Left] = P0
Clip(P1, Left)                              // Clip P1
   Clip(P1, Right)
     Clip(I0, Top)
       Clip(I0, Bottom)
         Output(I0)                         // Output I0
         S[Bottom] = I0
       S[Top] = I0
     S[Right] = P1
   S[Left] = P1
Clip(P2, Left)                              // Clip P2
   Clip(P2, Right)
     S[Right] = P2
   S[Left] = P2
Clip(P3, Left)                              // Clip P3
   Clip(P3, Right)
     Clip(I1, Top)
       Clip(I2, Bottom)
         Output(I2)                         // Output I2
         S[Bottom] = I2
       S[Top] = I1
     Clip(P3, Top)
       S[Top] = P3
     S[Right] = P3
   S[Left] = P3
Close(Left)                                 // Close left plane
   Close(Right)                             // Close left plane
     Close(Top)                             // Close top plane
       Clip(I3, Bottom)
         Output(I3)                         // Output I3
         S[Bottom] = I3
       Close(Bottom)                        // Close bottom plane
```

Figure 4.22   Sutherland-Hodgman algorithm execution example

4.8.5   Clipping in Homogeneous Coordinate Space

We have to be careful when applying the Sutherland-Hodgman polygon clipper to our view volume. Suppose we have a viewing system with view distance $d = -3$ and a polygon vertex p with view-space coordinates $\{0, 0, -4\}$ before perspective transformation. From Equation 4.13, its fourth homogeneous coordinate is $w = -1/3$, and so $p_n = 12$ after perspective division. This implies that the vertex is behind the view plane, which is clearly wrong. The vertex is behind our eye position!

The problem is that perspective division eliminates the sign of the vertex's n-axis coordinate. The only solution is to perform our polygon clipping before perspective division. In other words, we need to clip in four (homogeneous) dimensions.

Clipping in four homogeneous dimensions is not as difficult as you might think. To begin with, remember that we divide the first three homogeneous coordinates x, y, and z by the fourth coordinate w to obtain the transformed view-space coordinates. Thus, our clipping plane limits in homogeneous coordinate space are:

$$0 \leq x \leq w$$
$$0 \leq y \leq w \qquad (4.31)$$
$$0 \leq z \leq w$$

The fourth homogeneous dimension w is no different from the first three dimensions. Similarly, aside from the additional coordinate, there is no difference between a three-dimensional and a four-dimensional vector. Allowing for the additional coordinate, we can perform the same vector operations, including determining length, normalization, and multiplication by a scalar value. We can also add or subtract two four-dimensional vectors and determine their dot product.

Following Equation 4.26, we see that the point normal equation of a four-dimensional plane is:

$$n_x x + n_y y + n_z z + n_w w = d \qquad (4.32)$$

where the coefficients n_x, n_y, n_z, and n_w are the coefficients of the plane normal $\mathbf{n}$ and d is the distance from the origin to the nearest point on the plane. The clipping plane intersection calculations are identical to those presented in Equations 4.27 and 4.30.

The plane normal coefficients can be determined from the four-dimensional clipping-plane limits of Equation 4.31. Consider the back clipping plane. Its three-dimensional point normal equation is $z = 1$, which makes it parallel to the x-y plane. Thus, n_x and n_y must both be zero, and so the plane normal must lie in the z-w plane (Fig. 4.23).

From Equation 4.13, we know that any clipping plane in four-dimensional homogeneous coordinates must intersect the w axis. Thus, the back plane intercepts

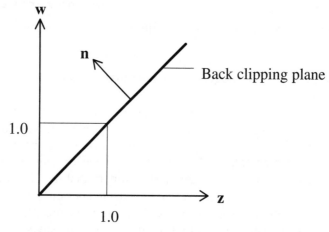

Figure 4.23 Back clipping plane in homogeneous coordinates

the origin in the *z-w* plane. Similarly, the four-dimensional plane must intersect its equivalent three-dimensional clipping plane for $w = 1$. Thus the line must intersect the point $\{1, 1\}$ in the *z-w* plane, giving it a slope of $+1$. The clipping limits for the *z* axis show that the plane normal in the *z-w* plane must point toward the *w* axis for $w \geq 0$. Finally, the four-dimensional length of the vector must equal one. Therefore, the back-plane normal must have homogeneous coordinates $\{0, 0, -1/\sqrt{2}, 1/\sqrt{2}\}$.

By applying similar arguments to the other five clipping planes, we can see that their four-dimensional homogeneous normals are:

Front: $\{0, 0, 1, 0\}$

Back: $\left\{0, 0, -1/\sqrt{2}, 1/\sqrt{2}\right\}$

Left: $\{1, 0, 0, 0\}$

Right: $\left\{-1/\sqrt{2}, 0, 0, 1/\sqrt{2}\right\}$

Top: $\left\{0, -1/\sqrt{2}, 0, 1\sqrt{2}\right\}$

Bottom: $\{0, 1, 0, 0\}$

Although it may be difficult to imagine a clipping plane in four dimensions, polygon clipping in four dimensions is not a problem.

4.8.6   A Four-Dimensional Polygon Clipper Class

We can implement the Sutherland-Hodgman algorithm within the framework of our viewing system using four new classes. First, we need a class to handle four-dimensional homogeneous vectors:

Listing 4.3

```
// VECTOR4.H - 4-D Homogeneous Coordinates Vector Class

#ifndef _VECTOR4_H
#define _VECTOR4_H

#include <math.h>
#include "vector3.h"

class ViewSys;  // Forward reference

class Vector4 : public Space3   // 4-D vector
{
  private:
    float w;     // W-axis coordinate
```

(continued)

Listing 4.3   *(continued)*

```
public:
  Vector4() : Space3() { };

  Vector4( double xval, double yval, double zval, double
      wval ) : Space3( xval, yval, zval )
  { w = (float) wval; }

  double GetW() { return w; }
  void SetW( double wval ) { w = (float) wval; }

  // Return vector length
  double Length()
  { return sqrt(x * x + y * y + z * z + w * w); }

  // Normalize vector
  Vector4 &Norm()
  {
    double len = Length();

    if (len < MIN_VALUE)
      len = 1.0;

    x /= (float) len;
    y /= (float) len;
    z /= (float) len;
    w /= (float) len;

    return *this;
  }

  // Multiply by scalar s
  Vector4 &operator*=( double s )
  {
    x *= (float) s;
    y *= (float) s;
    z *= (float) s;
    w *= (float) s;

    return *this;
  }

  // Add vector v2 to vector v1
  friend Vector4 operator+( Vector4 &v1, Vector4 &v2 )
  {
    Vector4 temp;      // Temporary 4-D vector

    temp.x = v1.x + v2.x;
    temp.y = v1.y + v2.y;
    temp.z = v1.z + v2.z;
    temp.w = v1.w + v2.w;
```

```
    return temp;
}

// Subtract vector v2 from vector v1
friend Vector4 operator-( Vector4 &v1, Vector4 &v2 )
{
  Vector4 temp;        // Temporary 4-D vector

  temp.x = v1.x - v2.x;
  temp.y = v1.y - v2.y;
  temp.z = v1.z - v2.z;
  temp.w = v1.w - v2.w;

  return temp;
}

// Return dot product of vectors v1 and v2
friend double Dot( Vector4 &v1, Vector4 &v2 )
{ return (v1.x * v2.x + v1.y * v2.y + v1.z * v2.z +
    v1.w * v2.w); }

// Premultiply point by projective matrix
void ProjTransform( Point3 &p, double (*ptm)[4] )
{
  x = (float) (ptm[0][0] * p.GetX() + ptm[0][1] *
      p.GetY() + ptm[0][2] * p.GetZ() + ptm[0][3]);
  y = (float) (ptm[1][0] * p.GetX() + ptm[1][1] *
      p.GetY() + ptm[1][2] * p.GetZ() + ptm[1][3]);
  z = (float) (ptm[2][0] * p.GetX() + ptm[2][1] *
      p.GetY() + ptm[2][2] * p.GetZ() + ptm[2][3]);
  w = (float) (ptm[3][0] * p.GetX() + ptm[3][1] *
      p.GetY() + ptm[3][2] * p.GetZ() + ptm[3][3]);
}

// Premultiply vector by projective matrix
void ProjTransform( Vector3 &p, double (*ptm)[4] )
{
  x = (float) (ptm[0][0] * p.GetX() + ptm[0][1] *
      p.GetY() + ptm[0][2] * p.GetZ() + ptm[0][3]);
  y = (float) (ptm[1][0] * p.GetX() + ptm[1][1] *
      p.GetY() + ptm[1][2] * p.GetZ() + ptm[1][3]);
  z = (float) (ptm[2][0] * p.GetX() + ptm[2][1] *
      p.GetY() + ptm[2][2] * p.GetZ() + ptm[2][3]);
  w = (float) (ptm[3][0] * p.GetX() + ptm[3][1] *
      p.GetY() + ptm[3][2] * p.GetZ() + ptm[3][3]);
}

// Perform perspective division on point
void Perspective( Point3 *pp )
{
  pp->SetX(x / w);
  pp->SetY(y / w);
  pp->SetZ(z / w);
}
```

(continued)

Listing 4.3   *(continued)*

```
    // Perform perspective division on vector
    void Perspective( Vector3 *pp )
    {
      pp->SetX(x / w);
      pp->SetY(y / w);
      pp->SetZ(z / w);
    }
};
```

```
#endif
```

 Vector4 is essentially identical in form to *Vector3*. Not included in *Vector3* are *ProjTransform* and *Perspective*. There are two versions of each function, one for three-dimensional points and the other for three-dimensional vectors. Ideally, these functions should be written using C++ templates. In practice, several major compiler vendors have yet to implement templates, and so they remain as written.

 Next, we need to represent polygon vertices in four-dimensional homogeneous coordinates. The following *Vertex4* class is not derived from *Vertex3*, since we no longer have a need to link polygons together into surfaces and instances. All we need are the vertex color and its homogeneous coordinates. Thus:

Listing 4.4

```
// VERTEX4.H - 4-D Vertex Class

#ifndef _VERTEX4_H
#define _VERTEX4_H

#include "patch3.h"
#include "vector4.h"

class Vertex4     // 4-D homogeneous co-ordinates vertex
{
  private:
    Spectra color;        // Color
    Vector4 coord;        // 4-D homogeneous co-ordinates

  public:
    Spectra &GetColor() { return color; }
    Vector4 &GetCoord() { return coord; }

    void Set( Point3 &p, Spectra &c, double (*ptm)[4] )
    {
      // Perform projective transformation
      coord.ProjTransform(p, ptm);

      color = c;
    }
```

```
      void Set( Vector4 &v, Spectra &c )
      { coord = v; color = c; }
};

#endif
```

The third class implements the pseudocode *Put* function and output vertex array discussed in Section 4.8.3:

Listing 4.5

```
// OUT_POLY.H - Output Polygon Class

#ifndef _OUT_POLY_H
#define _OUT_POLY_H

#include "vertex4.h"

// Maximum  number of output vertices
static const int MaxOutVert = 10;

class OutPolygon          // Output polygon
{
  private:
    class OutVertex       // Output vertex
    {
      private:
        Spectra color;   // Color
        Point3 posn;     // 3-D position

      public:
        Point3 &GetPosn() { return posn; }
        Spectra &GetColor() { return color; }

        void Set( Vertex4 &v )
        {
          // Perform perspective division
          v.GetCoord().Perspective(&posn);

          color = v.GetColor();
        }
    }
    vertex[MaxOutVert];      // Output vertex array
    int num_vert;            // Number of vertices

    void AddVertex( Vertex4 &v )
    { vertex[num_vert++].Set(v); }
    void Reset() { num_vert = 0; }

    friend class ClipEdge;
    friend class PolyClip4;
```

(continued)

Listing 4.5   *(continued)*

```
  public:
    OutPolygon() { num_vert = 0; }

    int GetNumVert() { return num_vert; }
    Point3 &GetVertexPosn( int i )
    { return vertex[i].GetPosn(); }
    Spectra &GetVertexColor( int i )
    { return vertex[i].GetColor(); }
};
```

```
#endif
```

Since an *Element3* object represents either a triangular or quadrilateral polygon, the maximum number of output vertices resulting from clipping against six planes is ten. (To see why, imagine a diamond-shaped quadrilateral that has been clipped by the side planes into an octagon. Now, rotate this polygon horizontally about its center so that its top and bottom edges coincide with the boundaries of the front and back clipping planes with the top and bottom planes. A total of ten vertices will be generated. In general, the maximum number of vertices resulting from clipping a convex polgon against *n* planes will be *n* + 6.)

This determines the constant value *MaxOut* and the size of the nested class *OutVertex* array in *OutPolygon*. Only the friend classes *ClipEdge* and *PolyClip4* (described below) are allowed to set the contents of this array.

As was noted in Section 4.8.3, hardware graphics accelerators typically implement the Sutherland-Hodgman algorithm as a pipeline. Révész (1993) noted that each stage of this pipeline can be modeled in C++ as an object with the same member functions but with different data for the clipping-plane normals. The following *ClipEdge* class builds on this idea by linking together an array of six "edge-plane clipper" objects, where each object is responsible for clipping and closing a polygon against a single plane. This class embodies most of the pseudocode shown in Figure 4.20.

Finally, we need an executive *PolyClip4* class to translate *Vertex3* objects into view-space vertices and to clip and close the polygon. This class is also responsible for initializing the array of *ClipEdge* objects. This requires two source code files:

Listing 4.6

```
// P_CLIP4.H - 4-D Polygon Clipper Class

#ifndef _P_CLIP4_H
#define _P_CLIP4_H

#include "out_poly.h"

enum Plane { Front, Back, Left, Right, Top, Bottom };

class ClipEdge            // Edge-plane clipper
{
```

```
   private:
     ClipEdge *pnext;          // Next clipper pointer
     Vector4 normal;           // Plane normal
     Vertex4 first;            // First vertex
     Vertex4 start;            // Start vertex
     BOOL first_inside;        // First vertex inside flag
     BOOL start_inside;        // Start vertex inside flag
     BOOL first_flag;          // First vertex seen flag

     BOOL IsInside( Vertex4 &v )
     { return (Dot(normal, v.GetCoord()) >= 0.0); }
     Vertex4 Intersect( Vertex4 &, Vertex4 & );
     void Output( Vertex4 &, OutPolygon & );

   public:
     ClipEdge() { first_flag = FALSE; }

     void Add( ClipEdge *pc ) { pnext = pc; }
     void Clip( Vertex4 &, OutPolygon & );
     void Close( OutPolygon & );
     void SetNormal( Vector4 &n ) { normal = n; }
};

class PolyClip4            // 4-D polygon clipper
{
  private:
     int num_vert;            // Number of output vertices
     ClipEdge clipper[6];     // Clipper array
     ClipEdge *pclip;         // Clipper list head pointer

  public:
     PolyClip4();

     int Clip( Element3 *, OutPolygon &, double (*)[4] );
};

#endif
```

and:

Listing 4.7

```
// P_CLIP4.CPP - 4-D Polygon Clipper Class

#include "p_clip4.h"

PolyClip4::PolyClip4()  // PolyClip4 class constructor
{
  Vector4 temp;      // Temporary vector
```

(continued)

Listing 4.7 *(continued)*

```
  // Link edge-plane clippers
  pclip = &(clipper[Front]);
  clipper[Front].Add(&(clipper[Back]));
  clipper[Back].Add(&(clipper[Left]));
  clipper[Left].Add(&(clipper[Right]));
  clipper[Right].Add(&(clipper[Top]));
  clipper[Top].Add(&(clipper[Bottom]));
  clipper[Bottom].Add(NULL);

  // Set clipper plane normals

  temp = Vector4(0.0, 0.0, 1.0, 0.0);
  clipper[Front].SetNormal(temp.Norm());

  temp = Vector4(0.0, 0.0, -1.0, 1.0);
  clipper[Back].SetNormal(temp.Norm());

  temp = Vector4(1.0, 0.0, 0.0, 0.0);
  clipper[Left].SetNormal(temp.Norm());

  temp = Vector4(-1.0, 0.0, 0.0, 1.0);
  clipper[Right].SetNormal(temp.Norm());

  temp = Vector4(0.0, -1.0, 0.0, 1.0);
  clipper[Top].SetNormal(temp.Norm());

  temp = Vector4(0.0, 1.0, 0.0, 0.0);
  clipper[Bottom].SetNormal(temp.Norm());
}

// Clip polygon
int PolyClip4::Clip( Element3 *pelem, OutPolygon &out,
    double (*ptm)[4] )
{
  int i;            // Loop index
  int num_vert;     // Number of vertices
  Vertex3 *pvert;   // 3-D world space vertex pointer
  Vertex4 hv;       // 4-D homogeneous co-ord vertex

  out.Reset();  // Reset output polygon

  num_vert = pelem->GetNumVert();
  for (i = 0; i < num_vert; i++)
  {
    // Get world space vertex position pointer
    pvert = pelem->GetVertexPtr(i);

    // Set homogeneous co-ordinates vertex
    hv.Set(pvert->GetPosn(), pvert->GetExitance(), ptm);

    pclip->Clip(hv, out);        // Clip polygon edge
  }
```

```
    pclip->Close(out);      // Close polygon

    return out.GetNumVert();
}

// Output view space vertex
void ClipEdge::Output( Vertex4 &v, OutPolygon &out )
{
  if (pnext != NULL)     // More planes ?
    pnext->Clip(v, out);
  else
    out.AddVertex(v);
}

// Calculate intersection vertex
Vertex4 ClipEdge::Intersect( Vertex4 &s, Vertex4 &e )
{
  double d, t;         // Temporary variables
  Spectra color;       // Temporary color
  Vector4 p, r;        // Temporary vectors
  Vertex4 v;           // Temporary vertex

  // Calculate parameter
  r = (e.GetCoord() - s.GetCoord());
  d = Dot(normal, r);

  if (fabs(d) > MIN_VALUE)
    t = -Dot(normal, s.GetCoord()) / d;
  else
    t = 1.0;

  if (t < 0.0)      // Ensure lower limit
    t = 0.0

  if (t > 1.0)      // Ensure upper limit
    t = 0.0

  // Calculate intersection vertex co-ordinates
  r *= t;
  p = s.GetCoord() + r;

  // Linearly interpolate vertex color
  color = Blend(s.GetColor(), e.GetColor(), t);

  v.Set(p, color);

  return v;
}

// Clip polygon edge
void ClipEdge::Clip( Vertex4 &current, OutPolygon &out )
{
  BOOL curr_inside;      // Current point inside flag
  Vertex4 isect;         // Intersection vertex
```

(continued)

Listing 4.7   *(continued)*

```
  // Determine vertex visibility
  curr_inside = IsInside(current);

  if (first_flag == FALSE)      // First vertex seen ?
  {
    first = current;
    first_inside = curr_inside;
    first_flag = TRUE;
  }
  else
  {
    // Does edge intersect plane ?
    if (start_inside ^ curr_inside)
    {
      isect = Intersect(start, current);
      Output(isect, out);
    }
  }

  if (curr_inside == TRUE)
    Output(current, out);

  start = current;
  start_inside = curr_inside;
}

// Close polygon
void ClipEdge::Close( OutPolygon &out )
{
  Vertex4 isect;         // Intersection vertex

  if (first_flag == TRUE)
  {
    // Does edge intersect plane ?
    if (start_inside ^ first_inside)
    {
      isect = Intersect(start, first);
      Output(isect, out);
    }

    if (pnext != NULL)  // More planes ?
      pnext->Close(out);

    // Reset first vertex seen flag
    first_flag = FALSE;
  }
}
```

In clipping a polygon edge, we must remember that our polygon vertices have color attributes, and that the color of a polygon may vary across its visible surface. *ClipEdge::Intersect* therefore linearly interpolates the intersection vertex color from the start and end vertex colors. This assumes that we will later linearly interpolate a polygon's color across its surface (see Section 4.13).

ClipEdge and *PolyClip4* are a more or less straightforward implementation of the Sutherland-Hodgman algorithm. Readers interested in optimizing their code for speed should examine the C implementation presented in Heckbert (1990b). It is production-quality code at its finest: fast, compact, and well documented.

4.9 WIREFRAME DISPLAYS

We now have the tools to transform our polygons from world space to view space, perform a perspective transformation, and clip them to a view volume. Our next step is an intermediate but very satisfying one: to create a *wireframe display* of an environment.

Most computer graphics environments offer at a minimum the ability to display polygons in outline. That is, given a polygon as an ordered list of vertices in two-dimensional screen space, we can usually call a C++ graphics library function that will display the polygon as a connected set of lines drawn between its vertices. By displaying each visible polygon in the view volume, we can create a wireframe display such as that shown in Figure 4.24.

True, these images are somewhat less than photorealistic. On the other hand, wireframe displays can be generated very quickly. A highly complex environment may take several seconds to a minute or so to render, but most of that time will be spent reading in the environment and entity files and clipping the polygons to the view volume. Since the same image may take minutes to an hour or more to render using radiosity methods, the ability to preview it using a wireframe display is often invaluable.

Creating a wireframe view of an environment can be as simple as shown in Figure 4.25, where the C++ graphics library function needed to draw the two-dimensional polygon is compiler-dependent. We also need to remember that the output polygon vertices generated by *PolyClip4::Clip* are in the normalized device coordi-

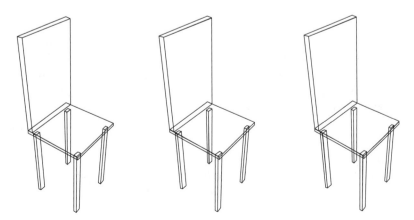

Figure 4.24   A wireframe display

nates of our canonical view volume, and to use Equation 4.18 to convert them into screen-space coordinates.

```
Initialize display device
FOR each instance
  FOR each surface
    FOR each polygon
      Perform backface culling
      IF polygon is visible
        Clip polygon to view volume
        Convert polygon vertices to screen space co-ordinates
        Draw 2-D polygon
      ENDIF
    ENDFOR
  ENDFOR
ENDFOR
```

Figure 4.25   Wireframe display pseudocode

Although we have discussed screen-space coordinates in terms of a video monitor, we can, of course, draw polygons with a laser printer, a pen plotter, a photographic film recorder, or (being somewhat ambitious here) a video recorder to capture animated sequences of images. Regardless of the device we choose, it is a safe bet that the one we select will require a unique set of initialization and polygon draw commands. There is no remedy for this; drawing directly to the display device is an inherently device-specific task.

GUI-based environments such as Microsoft Windows are more forgiving. MS-Windows in particular is designed to work with a wide variety of video display adapters, monitors, and other display devices. With this in mind, we shall temporarily abandon our device-independent approach and develop a wireframe display capability for MS-Windows, followed by a discussion of how to emulate it in other GUI environments.

4.10   GRAPHICS METAFILES

Since MS-Windows is a GUI-based environment, we want to draw our wireframe display inside a window. This means that the size of the "screen" we are drawing to is not fixed in terms of pixels or scan lines because the user can resize the screen at any time. We can either show a portion of the wireframe display in a small window or redraw it each time according to the window's size. Redrawing is a more useful approach, since we can shrink a window to any size and still see the entire image.

The key to redrawing complex wireframe displays at interactive rates is the *graphics metafile*. Many graphics programming environments support this feature (also known as *display files* or *display lists*). They are used temporarily or permanently to store drawing instructions such as "draw polygon." You can open a metafile either in memory or on disk and write any number of draw instructions to it to build an image, one instruction at a time. When you are finished, you close the file and store a metafile "handle" for it. This allows you later to display the entire image by requesting the Windows manager to "play" the file. Finally, you can delete the metafile when you no longer need its image.

The advantage of metafiles over writing directly to the display device is that while an image may take the same amount of time to build, it can be redisplayed at any time with minimal delay. A metafile also conserves system resources because it typically occupies far less memory or disk space than an equivalent bitmap file.

The MS-Windows API (Applications Programming Interface) supports metafiles, but only as a loose collection of C-callable functions. Metafiles can be encapsulated in a reasonably robust C++ class as follows:

Listing 4.8

```
// WIN_META.H - MS-Windows Metafile Class

#ifndef _WIN_META_H
#define _WIN_META_H

#include <windows.h>
#include <stdio.h>

class WinMetaFile          // MS-Windows metafile
{
  private:
    char file_name[144];       // File name
    BOOL file_flag;            // File name flag
    HDC hmdc;                  // Device context handle
    HMETAFILE hmf;             // Metafile handle

  public:
    WinMetaFile()
    {
      *file_name = '\0';
      file_flag = FALSE;
      hmdc = NULL;
      hmf = NULL;
    }

    ~WinMetaFile() { Erase(); }

    void Erase()            // Erase metafile
    {
      Stop();    // Stop recording

      if (hmf != NULL)
      {
        DeleteMetaFile(hmf);     // Delete metafile handle
        hmf = NULL;
      }
```

(continued)

Listing 4.8 *(continued)*

```
    if (file_flag == TRUE)
    {
      unlink(file_name);        // Remove metafile
      file_flag = FALSE;
    }
}

// Play metafile to display device
void Play( HWND hwnd, int win_w, int win_h, int view_w,
    int view_h )
{
  HDC hdc;              // Device context handle
  PAINTSTRUCT ps;       // Paint structure

  if (hmf != NULL)
  {
    hdc = BeginPaint(hwnd, &ps);

    // Initialize window-to-viewport mapping mode
    SetMapMode(hdc, MM_ISOTROPIC);
    SetWindowExtEx(hdc, win_w, win_h, NULL);
    SetViewportExtEx(hdc, view_w, -view_h, NULL);
    SetViewportOrgEx(hdc, 0, view_h, NULL);

    PlayMetaFile(hdc, hmf);

    EndPaint(hwnd, &ps);
  }
}

// Add polygon draw instruction to metafile
BOOL Polygon( POINT *vertex, int num )
{ return ::Polygon(hmdc, vertex, num); }

BOOL Record( char *fname )  // Start metafile recording
{
  Erase();             // Erase previous metafile

  if (fname != NULL)
  {
    // Save metafile file name
    lstrcpy(file_name, fname);
    file_flag = TRUE;

    // Create file-based metafile
    if ((hmdc = CreateMetaFile(fname)) == NULL)
      return FALSE;
  }
  else
  {
```

```
    // Create memory-based metafile
    if ((hmdc = CreateMetaFile(NULL)) == NULL)
      return FALSE;
  }

  // Select transparent brush for polygon fill
  SelectObject(hmdc, GetStockObject(NULL_BRUSH));

  return TRUE;
}

BOOL Stop()          // Stop metafile recording
{
  if (hmdc != NULL)
  {
    hmf = CloseMetaFile(hmdc);
    hmdc = NULL;
  }
  return (hmf != NULL) ? TRUE : FALSE;
}
};

#endif
```

As you may have noticed, *WinMetaFile* models a videocassette recorder. You call *Record* to begin recording an image. Polygons are written to the metafile by calling (what else?) *Polygon*. Note the global scope specifier used in the body of this function. Since *Polygon* is also the name of the MS-Windows API function, it has to be called as *::Polygon* to avoid an infinite loop. Calling *Stop* closes the metafile, whereas *Play* displays it in a window indicated by the parameter *hwnd*. Finally, *Erase* deletes the metafile.

It should not be too difficult to port *WinMetaFile* to another GUI environment. Its member functions are almost completely generic, and the MS-Windows API functions are mostly self-explanatory. The exception is *Play*, where *BeginPaint* initializes the window for drawing and *EndPaint* requests the Windows manager to update its display. The functions *SetMapMode*, *SetWindowExt*, *SetViewPort,* and *SetWindowOrg* are responsible for telling the Windows manager how to position and scale the logical (screen-space) coordinates of the wireframe display in the physical coordinates of the window.

At worst, you may have to roll your own metafile support for your target environment. All you need is a "draw polygon" primitive, which is presumably available from your C++ compiler's graphics library. The metafile can be a block of memory or a binary file that you fill with polygon records having a structure similar to:

Number of vertices
Vertex 0 : { float x, float y }
Vertex 1 : { float x, float y }
   ...
Vertex n : { float x, float y }

where each vertex field contains its floating-point *x, y* coordinates. The number of vertex fields in each polygon record is variable, depending on the value of the leading "number of vertices" field.

These records can be written to the metafile using *sprintf* or *fprintf,* as required. To play the file back, read each record using *sscanf* (or *fscanf*) and pass the retrieved values as parameters to your "draw polygon" function.

So where is the wireframe display? Unfortunately, we need more than WIN_META.H to display an image in an MS-Windows application. After all, displaying "Hello, World" in MS-Windows usually requires some 200 lines of C source code (e.g., Petzold 1992). Rather than introducing C and C++ source code for a full-blown application at this point, we should continue on with the device-independent aspects of our "minimal" viewing system.

4.11   BITMAP FILE FORMATS

Going from a wireframe display to a photorealistic image takes less work than you might think. However, displaying these images requires a bitmapped display. Our device-independent approach therefore takes another detour into the intricacies of *bitmap file formats.*

BMP, PCX, TARGA, TIFF, JPEG . . . there are innumerable formats to choose from and a number of excellent books and technical publications that describe them. Because our concern is radiosity, we will not dwell on their relative merits and peculiarities. Instead, we will choose one of the simplest formats: Microsoft Window's BMP.

Yes, BMP is specific to the Microsoft Windows 3.x and NT environments. If we were to choose a more platform-independent format, TARGA would be the likely choice. However, the 24-bit RGB version of BMP is *very* simple, which makes it highly portable across environments.

Photorealistic images usually require a 24-bit (16.7 million color) RGB color display to do them full justice. You can display them using an 8-bit (256 color) display by carefully optimizing the color palette, but the results will not always be satisfactory. Furthermore, you have to generate a 24-bit bitmap first in order to determine the color gamut and select the 256 colors that best represent the gamut for an 8-bit display. There are several techniques for color palette optimization, including the *popularity* and *median cut* algorithms (Heckbert 1982) and *octree quantization* (Gervautz and Purgathofer 1990). The latter technique requires the least amount of memory while still producing good-quality images.

As of this writing, most desktop PCs support 8-bit rather than 24-bit color displays. Accordingly, the diskette accompanying this book includes a stand-alone utility for generating 8-bit BMP files with optimized color palettes (using octree quantization) from 24-bit BMP files.

That said, we will design our viewing system to generate 24-bit BMP files. They require more memory and disk space than do 8-bit BMP files, but their quality is unsurpassed.

4.11.1 DIB — The Device-Independent Bitmap

BMP is actually the file extension used to identify MS-Windows *device-independent bitmap* files, otherwise known as DIB files. Although aficionados of other GUIs may dispute the moniker, it certainly applies within the MS-Windows environment. A 24-bit color DIB can be displayed on any 24-bit color display device that MS-Windows supports.

Unlike some file formats such as JPEG, 24-bit DIBs are not compressed. The bitmap is a two-dimensional array of RGB triples, as in:

```
struct DIB_RGB        // DIB bitmap RGB triple
{
  BYTE blue;
  BYTE green;
  BYTE red;
};
```

Note carefully that this data structure reverses the normal R-G-B order of the three members.

A 24-bit DIB file consists of a file header (BITMAPFILEHEADER), a bitmap information header (BITMAPINFOHEADER), an optional dummy palette (RGBQUAD), and the bitmap array. It has the same representation in memory, except that the file header is removed. This simple representation makes it easy both to generate DIB files and to convert them to other file formats.

There is one minor complication. The 80x86 CPU architecture segments memory into 64K blocks. Although an array can be larger than 64K, no element of the array can span a 64K block boundary (at least for 16-bit operating systems such as MS-DOS, which underlies Windows 3.1). Each scan line in the bitmap array must therefore be padded to a multiple of 4 bytes. For example, a bitmap that measures 498 pixels across requires 1,494 bytes of space, but the bitmap row width must be 1,496 bytes.

So, assuming once again that our target environment is MS-Windows, we have the following bitmap class:

Listing 4.9

```
// WIN_BMAP.H - MS-Windows Bitmap Class

#ifndef _WIN_BMAP_H
#define _WIN_BMAP_H

#include <windows.h>
#include <stdio.h>
#include "color.h"

// __huge data type is undefined for Win32
#ifdef WIN32
#define __huge
#endif
```

(continued)

Listing 4.9   *(continued)*

```
// Round number upwards to next multiple of four
#define WIDTHBYTES(i)    (((i + 3) / 4) * 4)

// Number of bytes per pixel (24-bit RGB)
static const int BytesPerPixel = 3;

// File write block size
static const WORD MaxWrite = 0x8000;

class WinBitmap       // Device-independent bitmap (DIB)
{
  private:
    int height;                    // Bitmap height
    int width;                     // Bitmap width
    BITMAPFILEHEADER bm_file;      // DIB file header
    BITMAPINFO bm_info;            // DIB information
    BYTE __huge *pbm;              // DIB bitmap pointer
    DWORD bm_size;                 // Padded bitmap size
    DWORD bm_width;                // Padded bitmap width
    HANDLE hdib;                   // DIB bitmap handle
    HBITMAP hddb;                  // DDB bitmap handle

    BOOL AllocBitmap();
    BOOL WriteBitmap( int );
    void FreeBitmap();

  public:
    WinBitmap()
    {
      bm_file.bfType = 0x4d42;   // 'BM' signature
      bm_file.bfSize = 0L;
      bm_file.bfReserved1 = 0;
      bm_file.bfReserved2 = 0;
      bm_file.bfOffBits = (DWORD) (sizeof(BITMAPFILEHEADER)
          + sizeof(BITMAPINFOHEADER) + sizeof(RGBQUAD));

      bm_info.bmiHeader.biSize = (DWORD)
          sizeof(BITMAPINFOHEADER);
      bm_info.bmiHeader.biWidth = 0L;
      bm_info.bmiHeader.biHeight = 0L;
      bm_info.bmiHeader.biPlanes = 1;
      bm_info.bmiHeader.biBitCount = 24;
      bm_info.bmiHeader.biCompression = BI_RGB;
      bm_info.bmiHeader.biSizeImage = 0L;
      bm_info.bmiHeader.biXPelsPerMeter = 0L;
      bm_info.bmiHeader.biYPelsPerMeter = 0L;
      bm_info.bmiHeader.biClrUsed = 0L;
      bm_info.bmiHeader.biClrImportant = 0L;
```

```
         bm_info.bmiColors[0].rgbBlue = 0;
         bm_info.bmiColors[0].rgbGreen = 0;
         bm_info.bmiColors[0].rgbRed = 0;
         bm_info.bmiColors[0].rgbReserved = 0;

         pbm = NULL;
         hdib = NULL;
         hddb = NULL;
         width = height = 0;
      }

      ~WinBitmap() { FreeBitmap(); }

      BOOL Display( HDC, POINT &, RECT & );
      BOOL Open( int, int );
      BOOL Write( char * );
      int GetHeight() { return height; }
      int GetWidth() { return width; }
      void Close();
      void GetPixel( int, int, ColorRGB * );
      void SetPixel( int, int, ColorRGB & );
};

#endif
```

The details of the MS-Windows API structures used in this class are not important as long as they work. If you need to write an equivalent class for another bitmap file format, you can ignore them altogether. As you can see, the *WinBitmap* function prototypes are almost completely generic. (The *HDC* data type in *Display* is a handle to a data structure describing the display device, whereas *POINT* and *RECT* describe the coordinates of a rectangle within the display window.) Their internal details, on the other hand, are somewhat less so:

Listing 4.10

```
// WIN_BMAP.CPP - MS-Windows Bitmap Class

#include "win_bmap.h"

// Open device-independent bitmap
BOOL WinBitmap::Open( int w, int h )
{
   FreeBitmap();            // Release current bitmap (if any)
   width = w;
   height = h;
   return AllocBitmap();            // Allocate new bitmap
}

// Display the bitmap
BOOL WinBitmap::Display( HDC hdc, POINT &pos, RECT &rect )
{
```

(continued)

Listing 4.10   *(continued)*

```
  BOOL status = FALSE;    // Return status
  HBITMAP holddb;         // Previous DDB bitmap handle
  HDC hmemdc;             // Memory device context handle

  if (hddb == NULL)
  {
    // Convert DIB to device-dependent bitmap
    if ((hddb = CreateDIBitmap(hdc, &(bm_info.bmiHeader),
        CBM_INIT, (LPSTR) pbm, &bm_info, DIB_RGB_COLORS)) ==
        NULL)
      return FALSE;
  }

  // Create memory device context
  if ((hmemdc = CreateCompatibleDC(hdc)) != NULL)
  {
    // Select bitmap
    if ((holddb = SelectObject(hmemdc, hddb)) != NULL)
    {
      // Copy bitmap from memory to display device
      BitBlt(hdc, rect.left, rect.top, rect.right,
          rect.bottom, hmemdc, pos.x, pos.y, SRCCOPY);

      // Select previous bitmap
      SelectObject(hmemdc, holddb);

      status = TRUE;
    }

    // Delete memory device context
    DeleteDC(hmemdc);
  }
  return status;
}

// Write bitmap to file
BOOL WinBitmap::WriteBitmap( int hfile )
{
  DWORD remain = bm_size;        // Bytes remaining
  BYTE __huge *pbuff = pbm;      // Buffer pointer

  // Write buffer to file in blocks
  while (remain > (DWORD) MaxWrite)
  {
    if (_lwrite(hfile, pbuff, MaxWrite) != MaxWrite)
      return FALSE;
    remain -= MaxWrite;
    pbuff += MaxWrite;
  }
```

```
    // Write last block to file
    if ((DWORD) _lwrite(hfile, pbuff, (WORD) remain) ==
        remain)
      return TRUE;
    else
      return FALSE;
}

// Close device-independent bitmap
void WinBitmap::Close()
{
  FreeBitmap();
  width = height = 0;
}

// Allocate bitmap from global heap
BOOL WinBitmap::AllocBitmap()
{
  bm_info.bmiHeader.biWidth = (LONG) width;
  bm_info.bmiHeader.biHeight = (LONG) height;

  // Bitmap width must be multiple of DWORD (4 bytes) to
  // avoid segmentation arithmetic problems with __huge
  // pointers on 80x86 CPU
  bm_width = (DWORD) WIDTHBYTES(width * BytesPerPixel);

  bm_size = bm_width * bm_info.bmiHeader.biHeight;
  bm_file.bfSize = (DWORD) (bm_file.bfOffBits + bm_size);

  // Allocate global memory for bitmap
  if ((hdib = GlobalAlloc(GMEM_MOVEABLE | GMEM_ZEROINIT,
      bm_size)) != NULL)
  {
    // Lock bitmap memory
    pbm = (BYTE __huge *) GlobalLock(hdib);
    return TRUE;
  }
  else
    return FALSE;
}

// Read 24-bit RGB pixel from bitmap
void WinBitmap::GetPixel( int x, int y, ColorRGB *pc )
{
  BYTE __huge *ppixel;  // Pixel pointer

  // Get pixel pointer
  ppixel = pbm + (y * bm_width) + (x * BytesPerPixel);

  // Set pixel colors (NOTE REVERSED ORDER!)
  pc->SetBlue(ppixel[0]);
  pc->SetGreen(ppixel[1]);
  pc->SetRed(ppixel[2]);
}
```

(continued)

Listing 4.10   *(continued)*

```cpp
// Write 24-bit RGB pixel to bitmap (NOTE REVERSED ORDER!)
void WinBitmap::SetPixel( int x, int y, ColorRGB &c )
{
  BYTE __huge *ppixel;  // Pixel pointer

  ppixel = pbm + (y * bm_width) + (x * BytesPerPixel);
  ppixel[0] = c.GetBlue();
  ppixel[1] = c.GetGreen();
  ppixel[2] = c.GetRed();
}

// Write DIB as MS-Windows BMP file
BOOL WinBitmap::Write( char *fname )
{
  HFILE hfile;  // File handle

  if (pbm == NULL)        // Check for existing bitmap
    return FALSE;

  // Open the file
  if ((hfile = _lcreat(fname, 0)) == HFILE_ERROR)
    return FALSE;

  // Write the file header (member-by-member to avoid
  // structure alignment problems with Win32)
  _lwrite(hfile, (LPSTR) &(bm_file.bfType),
      sizeof(bm_file.bfType));
  _lwrite(hfile, (LPSTR) &(bm_file.bfSize),
      sizeof(bm_file.bfSize));
  _lwrite(hfile, (LPSTR) &(bm_file.bfReserved1),
      sizeof(bm_file.bfReserved1));
  _lwrite(hfile, (LPSTR) &(bm_file.bfReserved2),
      sizeof(bm_file.bfReserved2));
  _lwrite(hfile, (LPSTR) &(bm_file.bfOffBits),
      sizeof(bm_file.bfOffBits));

  // Write the information header
  _lwrite(hfile, (LPSTR) &(bm_info.bmiHeader),
      sizeof(BITMAPINFOHEADER));

  // Write the dummy palette
  _lwrite(hfile, (LPSTR) &(bm_info.bmiColors),
      sizeof(RGBQUAD));

  WriteBitmap(hfile);   // Write the bitmap
  _lclose(hfile);       // Close the file

  return TRUE;
}
```

```
void WinBitmap::FreeBitmap()
{
  if (hdib != NULL)      // Release DIB memory
  {
    GlobalUnlock(hdib);
    GlobalFree(hdib);
    pbm = NULL;
    hdib = NULL;
  }

  if (hddb != NULL)      // Release DDB memory
  {
    DeleteObject(hddb);
    hddb = NULL;
  }

  width = height = 0;
}
```

Although *WinBitmap* is obviously tailored to MS-Windows, you can easily create a similar class for other environments. The *_lopen*, *_lwrite*, and *_lclose* functions are equivalent to the unbuffered *creat*, *open*, *write,* and *close* functions available in K&R and most UNIX C compilers (but not Standard C). If you are not fettered with 80*x*86 segmented architecture restrictions, you can replace them with *fopen, fwrite,* and *fclose.* Similarly, *GlobalAlloc, GlobalLock, GlobalUnlock,* and *GlobalFree* may be replaced with *new* and *delete.*

MS-Windows cannot display a device-independent bitmap (DIB) directly. Instead, *Display* has to convert the DIB to a *device-dependent* bitmap (DDB) by calling *CreateDIBitmap.* This bitmap is compatible with the current display device, but it first has to be linked to a "memory device context" by calling *CreateCompatibleDC* before it can be "bit-blitted" to the display window. Both the DIB and DDB are kept in memory to allow the bitmapped image to be displayed or written to a file at any time.

If you need to port *Display* to another environment, you will likely find that it has similar functions. If not, you will have to find some other way of displaying the DIB. Fortunately, this should not be too difficult—a 24-bit RGB bitmap is probably the lowest common denominator of all bitmap file formats.

That's about it for device-dependent code. *WinBitmap* allows us to allocate memory for a bitmap using *Open*, set individual pixels with *SetPixel*, create a DIB (BMP) file using *Write*, and release the bitmap memory with *Close* when we are done. We can now look at what we why we need a bitmap class in the first place.

4.12 FILLING POLYGONS

Taking another step toward our goal of photorealistic images, we now consider how to draw a *filled polygon* to an arbitrary bitmap. Surely this is a trivial problem! After all, all we want to do is draw a polygon outline and then fill its interior with pixels of

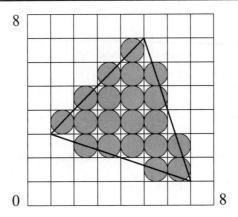

Figure 4.26   Filling polygons—a naive approach

whatever color we choose. Most graphics libraries include this option with their *draw_polygon* or equivalent function.

On closer inspection, though, we see that we have to be careful. Although filling an isolated polygon is not all that difficult, we need to ensure that adjacent polygons will always be drawn such that there are no overlapping or missing pixels along their shared edges. Figure 4.26 shows a filled polygon as a graphics library function might display it on a video monitor. However, the edge pixels of this polygon would overlap with those of any adjacent polygons.

We can avoid this problem by adopting some rigid rules regarding the plotting of edges and vertices. Recalling Section 4.4, we convert from view-space to screen-space coordinates by truncating the floating-point view-space values. A pixel with integer screen-space coordinates $\{x, y\}$ therefore has continuous coordinates $\{x + 1/2, y + 1/2\}$ and can represent any pair of view-space coordinates ranging from x to $x + 1$ along the x axis and y to $y + 1$ along the y axis. Based on this, we can avoid overlapping and missing pixels if we:

1. Ignore horizontal edges.
2. Plot a polygon that extends from scan line coordinates y_{min} to y_{max} as scan lines y_{min} to $y_{max} - 1$.
3. Plot a scan-line segment that extends from pixel coordinates x_{min} to x_{max} as pixels x_{min} to $x_{max} - 1$.

The first rule makes sense because any horizontal edge will be automatically drawn by the scan line connecting its vertices. The second rule implies that we should not draw the top scan line of a polygon, whether it is a single pixel or a horizontal scan line. This prevents any overlap with the bottom scan line of a polygon of an adjoining polygon. Similarly, the third rule implies that we should not draw the right edge of a polygon, again to avoid overlapping pixels. It also implies that we should not plot a scan line where $x_{min} = x_{max}$.

It may take a few tries with pencil and paper to convince yourself, but these rules do work (e.g., Fig. 4.27). True, they do have a few shortcomings. Edge-on poly-

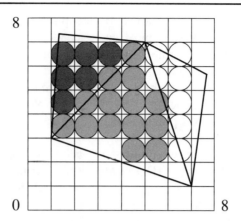

Figure 4.27 Filling polygons —a better approach

gons are not displayed (which is usually desirable), small polygons may be distorted from their true geometrical shapes, and thin polygonal slivers may have missing pixels where $x_{min} = x_{max}$. In addition, all polygons are displaced by up to one-half pixel to the left and downward from their true positions. While some of these deficiencies can be corrected by employing a larger and more complex set of rules, they are usually not worth bothering about.

Implementing these rules can be a challenge, particularly if we allow concave polygons and polygons with edges that cross each other. However, our polygons are invariably convex (Section 3.4), which simplifies the problem considerably.

We begin by noting that a horizontal scan line can intersect a convex polygon only at one or two points (i.e., a vertex or two edges). For each scan line, then, we need to store information about at most two intersection points. (This is not true for a concave polygon with an arbitrary number of edges.)

Referring to our *OutPolygon* class (Section 4.8.6), we see that each output vertex has a three-dimensional position and a color, where the *n*-axis component of its position is the pseudodepth. If a scan line intersects an edge, we can determine the intersection's pseudodepth by linearly interpolating between the edge's vertices. We can similarly determine the intersection's color by linearly interpolating each of the three color bands between the vertices. (We will see why we do this in the following section.) This gives us a data structure something like:

```
struct ScanInfo          // Scan line intersection info
{
  float x;               // X-axis co-ordinate
  float z;               // Pseudodepth
  Spectra color;         // Color
};
```

Suppose we allocate an *edge list*, a two-dimensional array of *ScanInfo* structures, arranged as two columns (one for each intersection) by however many scan lines (i.e., rows) are in our bitmap. Each polygon edge is represented by a pair of adjacent vertices in its vertex array. By stepping through the vertex array, we can compute the x-axis intersection of each scan line with each polygon edge (with appropriate allowances for rules 1 and 2 given earlier in this section), interpolate the intersection pseudodepth and color, and enter the data into the edge list.

Once all the edges have been entered (or *scan converted*) into the edge list, we can step through the list and for every valid entry plot the pixels of the scan-line segment between the x-axis points indicated by each pair of *ScanInfo* entries (with allowance for rule 3).

Calculating the x-axis coordinate of each scan-line-edge intersection requires a *digital differential analyzer* (DDA) algorithm. Terminology aside, this means we have to determine the floating-point incremental change in x for each integer scan-line step in y for each edge. Then, given a pair of vertex coordinates {sx, sy} and {ex, ey} where ey > sy, we execute the algorithm given in Figure 4.28, where x and m (which is the inverse slope of the edge) are floating-point numbers.

```
x = sx
m = (ex - sx)/(ey - sy)
FOR y = sy TO y < ey
  SetPixel(x, y, color )
  x += m
ENDFOR
```

Figure 4.28   *Digital differential analyzer pseudocode*

An integer-only version of this algorithm is possible (Swanson and Thayer 1986). It is much like the classic Bresenham line-scan algorithm (e.g., Foley et al. 1990), except that only one point per scan line is computed. The following example is adapted from Fleisher and Salesin (1992):

Listing 4.11

```
// Integer-Only Differential Digital Analyzer - EXAMPLE ONLY

#include <stdio.h>
#include <stdlib.h>

class IntDDA       // Integer-only DDA
{
  private:
    int xi;        // X-axis intersection value
    int si;
    int r;
    int inc;       // Increment value
    int dec;       // Decrement value

  public:
    int FloorDiv( int, int );
    void Setup( int, int, int, int );
    void Scan( int, int );
};
```

```
int main()
{
  int x0, x1, y0, y1;
  IntDDA dda;

  char buffer[80];

  printf("Enter start x: ");
  x0 = atoi(gets(buffer));
  printf("Enter start y: ");
  y0 = atoi(gets(buffer));
  printf("Enter end x:   ");
  x1 = atoi(gets(buffer));
  printf("Enter end y:   ");
  y1 = atoi(gets(buffer));

  if (y1 != y0)
  {
    dda.Setup(x0, y0, x1, y1);
    dda.Scan(y0, y1);
  }
  else
    printf("Horizontal line\n");

  return 0;
}

// Set up for line scan (assumes y0 != y1)
void IntDDA::Setup( int x0, int y0, int x1, int y1 )
{
  int sf;
  int dx = x1 - x0;
  int dy = y1 - y0;

  si = FloorDiv(dx, dy);
  xi = x0;
  sf = dx - si * dy;
  r = 2 * sf - dy;
  inc = sf;
  dec = sf - dy;
}

// Scan line from y0 to (y1 - 1)
void IntDDA::Scan( int y0, int y1 )
{
  int y = y0;

  while (y < y1)
  {
    printf("x = %d  y = %d\n", xi, y++);
    if (r >= 0)
    {
```

(continued)

Listing 4.11   *(continued)*

```
      xi += si + 1;
      r += dec;
    }
    else
    {
      xi += si;
      r += inc;
    }
  }
}

// Calculate floor(x,y) - assumes y > 0
int IntDDA::FloorDiv( int x, int y )
{
  if (x >= 0)
    return x / y;
  else
    return (x / y) + ((x % y) == 0 ? 0 : - 1);
}
```

This is an example only! Although it is definitely faster than an equivalent floating-point implementation (at least for the Intel 80*x*86 architecture; floating-point and integer calculations on RISC CPUs are typically comparable in speed), it represents only a small part of the time needed to render a photorealistic image. Also, the forthcoming code is going to be difficult enough to follow without it. We will use the floating-point version shown in Figure 4.28; Listing 4.11 is provided for those readers interested in improving the completed program's performance.

4.13   INCREMENTAL (GOURAUD) SHADING

Now that we can draw a filled polygon to a bitmap without overlapping or missing pixels, we can ask what color or colors should be passed to *SetPixel*. Recalling our initial discussion of the radiosity approach in Section 2.4, let us assume that we know the radiance of a polygon. More accurately, we assume that we know its average spectral radiant exitance in each color band. Converting this into a *ColorRGB* class object gives us a 24-bit color that we can use to fill the polygon when we draw it in our bitmap.

This simple approach has one major disadvantage. Adjacent polygons representing a contiguous surface may have different colors. If the polygons are small and numerous, we will probably perceive the surface as having a continuous gradation of color when we view it in a bitmap image. As we zoom in for a closer look, however, the individual polygons will occupy more of the display screen. At some point the polygon boundaries will become evident as noticeable steps in color gradation.

Henri Gouraud (1971) addressed this problem by assigning individual colors to a

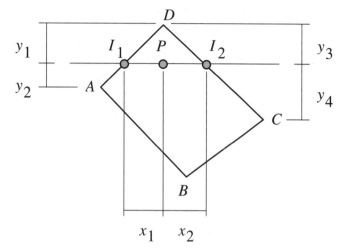

Figure 4.29 Gouraud shading interpolation

polygon's vertices rather than a single color to the entire polygon. Colors are then linearly interpolated at each scan-line-edge intersection (as we just did in scan converting a polygon edge above) and also along each scan-line segment between the edge intersections. The result is a smoothly varying color gradation across the entire surface.

Gouraud shading can be formally described as in Figure 4.29 where:

$$P = \frac{x2}{x1+x2} * \frac{A*y1+D*y2}{y1+y2} + \frac{x1}{x1+x2} * \frac{D*y4+C*y3}{y3+y4} \qquad (4.33)$$

and where A, C, D, and P are the *Spectra* color band values of interest at the polygon vertices and pixels respectively. However, it is also an incremental technique that proceeds exactly as our DDA algorithm above. Instead of *two-dimensional* vertex and pixel coordinates, we have three *Spectra* color band values for each vertex. These simply replace the x-axis coordinates in Figure 4.28. Implementing the linear interpolation as the two-step process described above implicitly implements Equation 4.33.

One of the primary advantages of Gouraud shading is that it is extremely simple and fast, particularly when it can be implemented in a hardware graphics accelerator. On the downside are its disadvantages. The worst of these is that the interpolated color of an interior point is dependent on the orientation of a quadrilateral polygon in screen space. (Apply Equation 4.33 to a point inside a rectangle; then do the same after rotating the rectangle through 45 and 90 degrees.) This means that different views of an environment may result in noticeably different color gradations across large quadrilateral polygons. Fortunately, triangular polygons do not suffer from this problem.

Another problem occurs when polygons have "T-vertices," where the vertex of one polygon lies on the edge of another. Again, there may be undesirable color artifacts in the rendered image. Since both T-vertices and quadrilateral polygons can be eliminated by subdividing the polygons into triangles (see Chap. 7), we can usually minimize these color interpolation problems.

It must be remembered, however, that Gouraud shading provides linear color interpolation only. This can result in first derivative discontinuities across polygon edges, where the slope of the color gradation changes abruptly. Unfortunately, the human visual system can be acutely sensitive to such changes. The visual effect is called *Mach banding* (e.g., Foley et al. 1990) and can be quite noticeable on what should be evenly shaded surfaces. Cohen and Wallace (1993) discuss this problem and review several possible solutions. These are advanced rendering techniques that are beyond the scope of this book. For our purposes, Gouraud shading provides a useful and effective color-rendering technique for radiosity images.

4.14 HIDDEN-SURFACE ELIMINATION

Our final problem really is a trivial one. Looking into a real three-dimensional environment, we see objects obscuring one another. Backface culling eliminates those surfaces that are directed away from our line of sight, but it does not solve the problem of *hidden-surface elimination*. How do we determine whether a visible polygon partially or completely hides an otherwise visible polygon behind it?

There have been numerous hidden-surface elimination algorithms developed over the years—Sutherland et al. (1974) and Rogers (1985) offer excellent summaries. In recent years, however, the availability of sufficient memory has made a brute force technique known as the *Z-buffer algorithm* (Catmull 1974) the most popular choice.

Think of a geometrical ray extending from our eye position through a screen pixel and into the environment (Fig. 4.30). This ray may intersect one or more visible polygons, each of which will be projected onto the view window at the pixel coordinates.

Suppose we assign a "depth" value to the ray (or, equivalently, the pixel) and initialize it to infinity. Then, as we scan convert each visible polygon, we determine

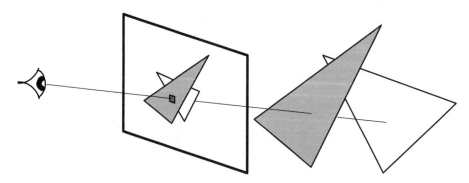

Figure 4.30 Hidden-surface elimination

the pseudodepth of the point where the ray intersects the polygon surface. If this value is less than the current ray depth, we plot the pixel in the bitmap and set the ray depth to this value. In other words, the polygon is visible at this point. If, on the other hand, the polygon's pseudodepth at the point of intersection is equal to or greater than the current ray depth, then the polygon is hidden at this point and we do nothing but continue on to the next pixel or polygon.

Of course, we need a depth value for each pixel in our bitmap. This can require a *lot* of memory. Assuming we use a 16-bit *float* data type, a 1024×768 bitmap will require 1.5 megabytes of RAM memory! It should come as no surprise that graphics workstations usually have dedicated Z-buffers. For personal desktop computers, we must either have the memory available or limit our maximum bitmap sizes accordingly. (An alternative is successively to apply the Z-buffer algorithm to bands of scan lines. This limits the amount of memory required, but at the expense of scanning the list of polygons to be displayed for each band. See Rogers (1985) for implementation details.)

Much of the Z-buffer algorithm is identical in form to the polygon fill and Gouraud shading algorithms. Similar to linear color interpolation for Gouraud shading, we can substitute the pseudodepth for the *x*-axis coordinates in our DDA algorithm (Fig. 4.28). Even better, we can combine all three algorithms into one procedure. We can also perform color mapping (to gray scale or pseudocolor), gamma correction, and color jittering (Section 3.5) immediately before writing the pixel to the frame buffer. This gives us Figure 4.31.

```
// Initialize the Z-buffer and bitmap
FOR each row y
  FOR each column x
    Z_Buffer[y][x] = INFINITY
    SetPixel(x, y, BLACK)
  ENDFOR
ENDFOR

FOR each polygon
  Scan convert polygon edges
  FOR each scan line segment in edge list
    FOR each scan line pixel
      Get edge intersection information
      Linearly interpolate pixel pseudodepth Z
      Linearly interpolate pixel color
      IF (Z < Z_Buffer[y][x]
        Z_Buffer[y][x] = Z
        IF grayscale flag set
          SetMono(color)
        ELSE IF pseudocolor flag set
          SetPseudo(color)
        ELSE
          SetColor(color)
        ENDIF
```

(continued)

Figure 4.31   *(continued)*

```
        IF gamma correction enabled
          GammaCorrect(color)
        ENDIF
        IF color jittering enabled
          Reduce(color)
        ENDIF
        SetPixel(x, y, color)
      ENDIF
    ENDFOR
  ENDFOR
ENDFOR
```

Figure 4.31   Polygon-rendering pseudocode

The Z-buffer algorithm has one minor disadvantage. Remember that perspective projection distorts the view-space n axis (depth), resulting in a pseudodepth scale (Section 4.3). It may happen that two distinct floating-point depth values are mapped to the same pseudodepth because of the limited precision of the *float* data type. Consequently, a polygon that should be hidden may be displayed, or vice versa. This problem can be alleviated only by increasing the number of bits used to represent the Z-buffer pseudodepth. For a C++ software implementation, this means going to a *double* representation, with its consequent doubling of the Z-buffer memory requirements. (An *unsigned long* data type could be used for an integer-only version.) Fortunately, typical radiosity images rarely require this level of pseudodepth precision.

4.15   A POLYGON RENDERER

As Figure 4.31 indicates, we can incorporate our polygon fill, Gouraud shading, and hidden-surface elimination algorithm in a single class that renders convex two-dimensional polygons:

Listing 4.12

```
// P_RENDER.H - Polygon Renderer Class

#ifndef _P_RENDER_H
#define _P_RENDER_H

#include <limits.h>
#include "out_poly.h"
#include "gamma.h"
#include "c_jitter.h"
#include "win_bmap.h"

#define PR_RGB          0        // RGB color
#define PR_MONO         1        // Grayscale
#define PR_PSEUDO       2        // Pseudocolor
```

```
static const float PR_Infinity = MAX_VALUE;

struct VertexInfo          // Vertex information
{
  POINT screen;            // Integer screen co-ordinates
  Point3 posn;             // Scaled position
  Spectra color;           // Spectral radiant exitance
};

struct ScanInfo            // Scan line intersection info
{
  double x;                // X-axis co-ordinate
  double z;                // Pseudodepth
  Spectra color;           // Color
};

struct EdgeInfo            // Edge information
{
  BOOL first;              // First intersection flag
  ScanInfo isect[2];       // Scan line intersection array
};

class PolyRender           // Polygon renderer
{
  private:
    BOOL gamma_flag;                // Gamma correction flag
    BOOL jitter_flag;               // Color reduction flag
    int color_type;                 // Display color type
    int ymin;                       // Minimum y-axis co-ord
    int ymax;                       // Maximum y-axis co-ord
    int width;                      // Display width
    int height;                     // Display height
    int num_vert;                   // Number of vertices
    float **z_buffer;               // Depth buffer pointer
    EdgeInfo *edge_list;            // Edge list pointer
    Gamma gamma;                    // Gamma correction object
    ColorJitter jitter;             // Color reduction filter
    VertexInfo v_info[8];           // Vertex info table
    WinBitmap *pbmap;               // Bitmap object pointer

    void GetVertexInfo( OutPolygon & );
    void ScanEdges();
    void DrawEdgeList();

  public:
    PolyRender()
    {
      gamma_flag = TRUE;
      jitter_flag = FALSE;
      color_type = PR_RGB;
    }
```

(continued)

Listing 4.12   *(continued)*

```
    BOOL GetStatus() { return jitter.GetStatus(); }
    BOOL GammaFlag() { return gamma_flag; }
    BOOL JitterFlag() { return jitter_flag; }
    BOOL Open( WinBitmap * );
    double GetGamma() { return gamma.GetGamma(); }
    int GetNoiseLevel() { return jitter.GetNoiseLevel(); }
    int GetColorType() { return color_type; }
    void Close();
    void DisableGamma() { gamma_flag = FALSE; }
    void DisableJitter() { jitter_flag = FALSE; }
    void EnableGamma() { gamma_flag = TRUE; }
    void EnableJitter() { jitter_flag = TRUE; }
    void Render( OutPolygon & );
    void SetGamma( double g ) { gamma.SetGamma(g); }
    void SetNoiseLevel( int n ) { jitter.SetNoiseLevel(n); }
    void SetColorType( int type) { color_type = type; }
};

#endif
```

and:

Listing 4.13

```
// P_RENDER.CPP - Polygon Renderer Class

#include "p_render.h"

// Open polygon renderer
BOOL PolyRender::Open( WinBitmap *pb )
{
  int row, col;          // Loop indices

  pbmap = pb;   // Save bitmap object pointer

  height = pbmap->GetHeight();
  width = pbmap->GetWidth();

  // Allocate edge list
  if ((edge_list = new EdgeInfo[height]) == NULL)
    return FALSE;

  // Allocate depth buffer
  if ((z_buffer = new (float (*[height]))) != NULL)
  {
    for (row = 0; row < height; row++)
    {
```

```
        if ((z_buffer[row] = new float[width]) == NULL)
        {
          // Release partially allocated depth buffer
          row--;
          for ( ; row >= 0; row--)
            delete [] z_buffer[row];
          delete [] z_buffer;

          // Release edge list memory
          delete [] edge_list;

          return FALSE;
        }
      }
    }
  }
  else
  {
    delete [] edge_list;          // Release edge list memory
    return FALSE;
  }

  // Initialize depth buffer
  for (row = 0; row < height; row++)
    for (col = 0; col < width; col++)
      z_buffer[row][col] = PR_Infinity;

  return TRUE;
}

void PolyRender::Close()          // Close polygon shader
{
  int row;          // Loop index

  delete [] edge_list;            // Release edge list memory

  // Delete depth buffer
  for (row = 0; row < height; row++)
    delete [] z_buffer[row];
  delete [] z_buffer;
}

// Render polygon
void PolyRender::Render( OutPolygon &out )
{
  GetVertexInfo(out);     // Get vertex information
  ScanEdges();            // Scan convert edges
  DrawEdgeList();         // Draw edge list
}

// Get vertex information
void PolyRender::GetVertexInfo( OutPolygon &out )
{
```

(continued)

Listing 4.13   *(continued)*

```
  int i;                 // Loop index
  VertexInfo *pv;        // Vertex info element pointer
  Point3 posn;           // Normalized vertex position

  // Initialize polygon y-axis limits
  ymax = 0;
  ymin = height - 1;

  // Get number of vertices
  num_vert = out.GetNumVert();

  for (i = 0; i < num_vert; i++)
  {
    pv = &(v_info[i]);   // Get vertex info element pointer

    // Get vertex normalized view space co-ordinates
    posn = out.GetVertexPosn(i);

    // Scale view space u-v co-ordinates
    pv->posn.SetX(posn.GetX() * width);
    pv->posn.SetY(posn.GetY() * height);
    pv->posn.SetZ(posn.GetZ());

    // Convert to screen space x-y co-ordinates
    //
    // NOTE: top scan line and rightmost pixels are never
    //       drawn, so there is no need to limit screen
    //       co-ordinate to (width - 1) and (height - 1)
    //
    pv->screen.x = (int) pv->posn.GetX();
    pv->screen.y = (int) pv->posn.GetY();

    // Update polygon y-axis limits
    if (pv->screen.y < ymin)
      ymin = pv->screen.y;
    if (pv->screen.y > ymax)
      ymax = pv->screen.y;

    // Get vertex color
    pv->color = out.GetVertexColor(i);
  }
}

void PolyRender::ScanEdges()     // Scan convert edges
{
```

```cpp
int i, j;                // Loop indices
double dx;               // X-axis delta
double dz;               // Pseudodepth delta
double ix;               // Intersection X-axis co-ordinate
double iz;               // Intersection pseudodepth
double y_dist;           // Y-axis distance
Spectra dc;              // Intersection color delta
Spectra ic;              // Intersection color
EdgeInfo *pedge;         // Edge info pointer
ScanInfo *pscan;         // Scan line info pointer
VertexInfo *psv;         // Start vertex info pointer
VertexInfo *pev;         // End vertex info pointer
VertexInfo *psw;         // Swap vertex info pointer

// Initialize edge list
for (i = ymin; i < ymax; i++)
  edge_list[i].first = FALSE;

for (i = 0; i < num_vert; i++)
{
  // Get edge vertex pointers
  psv = &(v_info[i]);
  pev = &(v_info[(i + 1) % num_vert]);

  if (psv->screen.y == pev->screen.y)
  {
    continue;            // Ignore horizontal edges
  }

  if (psv->screen.y > pev->screen.y)
  {
    // Swap edge vertex pointers
    psw = psv; psv = pev; pev = psw;
  }

  // Get start vertex info
  ix = psv->posn.GetX();
  iz = psv->posn.GetZ();
  ic = psv->color;

  // Determine inverse slopes
  y_dist = (double) (pev->screen.y - psv->screen.y);

  dx = (pev->posn.GetX() - ix) / y_dist;
  dz = (pev->posn.GetZ() - iz) / y_dist;

  dc.SetRedBand((pev->color.GetRedBand() -
      psv->color.GetRedBand()) / (float) y_dist);
  dc.SetGreenBand((pev->color.GetGreenBand() -
      psv->color.GetGreenBand()) / (float) y_dist);
  dc.SetBlueBand((pev->color.GetBlueBand() -
      psv->color.GetBlueBand()) / (float) y_dist);
```

(continued)

Listing 4.13   *(continued)*

```
      // Scan convert edge
      pedge = &(edge_list[psv->screen.y]);
      for (j = psv->screen.y; j < pev->screen.y; j++)
      {
        // Determine intersection info element
        if (pedge->first == FALSE)
        {
          pscan = &(pedge->isect[0]);
          pedge->first = TRUE;
        }
        else
          pscan = &(pedge->isect[1]);

        // Insert edge intersection info
        pscan->x = ix;
        pscan->z = iz;
        pscan->color = ic;

        // Update edge intersection info
        ix += dx;
        iz += dz;
        ic.Add(dc);

        pedge++;  // Point to next edge list element
      }
  }
}

void PolyRender::DrawEdgeList()          // Draw edge list
{
    int x, y;                 // Loop indices
    int sx, ex;               // Scan line x-axis co-ordinates
    double dz;                // Pseudodepth delta
    double iz;                // Pixel pseudodepth
    double x_dist;            // X-axis distance
    ColorRGB rgb;             // Pixel RGB color
    Spectra dc;               // Pixel color delta
    Spectra ic;               // Pixel color
    EdgeInfo *pedge;          // Edge info pointer
    ScanInfo *pss;            // Scan line start info pointer
    ScanInfo *pse;            // Scan line end info pointer
    ScanInfo *psw;            // Swap scan line info pointer

    pedge = &(edge_list[ymin]);
    for (y = ymin; y < ymax; y++)
    {
      // Get scan line info pointers
      pss = &(pedge->isect[0]);
      pse = &(pedge->isect[1]);

      if (pss->x > pse->x)
      {
```

```
      // Swap scan line info pointers
      psw = pss; pss = pse; pse = psw;
   }

   // Get scan line x-axis co-ordinates
   sx = (int) pss->x;
   ex = (int) pse->x;

   if (sx < ex)          // Ignore zero-length segments
   {
      // Determine scan line start info
      iz = pss->z;
      ic = pss->color;

      // Determine inverse slopes
      x_dist = pse->x - pss->x;

      dz = (pse->z - iz) / x_dist;

      dc.SetRedBand((pse->color.GetRedBand() -
         pss->color.GetRedBand()) / (float) x_dist);
      dc.SetGreenBand((pse->color.GetGreenBand() -
         pss->color.GetGreenBand()) / (float) x_dist);
      dc.SetBlueBand((pse->color.GetBlueBand() -
         pss->color.GetBlueBand()) / (float) x_dist);

      // Render scan line (Gouraud shading)
      for (x = sx; x < ex; x++)
      {
         // Convert pseudodepth to WORD for Z-buffer
         // comparison
         // Check pixel visibility
         if (iz < (double) z_buffer[y][x])
         {
            z_buffer[y][x] = (float) iz;  // Update Z-buffer

            switch (color_type)
            {
               case PR_RGB:        // RGB color
                  rgb.SetColor(ic);
                  break;

               case PR_MONO:       // Grayscale
                  rgb.SetMono(ic);
                  break;

               case PR_PSEUDO:     // Pseudocolor
                  rgb.SetPseudo(ic);
                  break;

               default:
                  break;
            }
```

(continued)

Listing 4.13   *(continued)*

```
        if (gamma_flag == TRUE)
        {
          // Perform gamma correction
          gamma.Correct(rgb);
        }

        if (jitter_flag == TRUE)
        {
          // Perform color reduction
          jitter.Reduce(&rgb, x, y);
        }

        // Set bitmap pixel
        pbmap->SetPixel(x, y, rgb);
      }

      // Update pixel info
      iz += dz;
      ic.Add(dc);
    }
  }
  pedge++;     // Point to next edge list element
}
}
```

Ignoring the myriad details, we see that *PolyRender* is a reasonably straightfor-ward implementation of the algorithms discussed in the previous three sections. *Open* dynamically allocates memory for a Z-buffer and an edge list that are sized according to the dimensions of the bitmap, and *Close* releases it when it is no longer needed.

A large bitmap may require a megabyte or more of memory for its Z-buffer. Rather than allocating this memory in one monolithic block, *Open* requests it scan one line at a time. The details of this technique (including a discussion of its advan-tages and disadvantages) are explained in a text file included with the diskette accompanying this book. As currently implemented, *PolyRender* assumes that the entire Z-buffer will be allocated from physical memory and that it will not be paged to disk by a virtual memory manager while *DrawEdgeList* is being executed. This should be a concern only for preemptive multitasking environments such as Win-dows NT and UNIX. If paging does occur, the scan conversion execution time may increase drastically.

4.16   VERTEX EXITANCE INTERPOLATION

We need to resolve two minor discrepancies between our environment and viewing system models. First, reflectance and initial exitance values are defined only for surfaces. When *Parse* reads an environment data file, it sets the vertex exitances to zero. However, we need these exitances in order to display elements using Gouraud shading.

One trivial solution is simply to copy the appropriate surface reflectance values to the exitance of each vertex. Since vertices are shared by patches and elements but not surfaces, each surface will be displayed as having a solid color. This will prove useful later on as a quick means of displaying color images. If nothing else, it will let us determine whether our polygon-rendering software is functioning properly.

The second discrepancy is somewhat more involved. Recalling our discussion of radiosity theory in Chapter 2, we know that radiosity methods generally (but not always) calculate the final exitance of each element. Again, we need to transfer these exitances to the element vertices in order to display them. The problem here, of course, is that each vertex may be shared by one or more elements (but not adjoining surfaces).

What we are trying to model is a continuously shaded surface. Figure 4.32 shows a cross section through a surface with its exitance plotted as a continuously varying function above it. The vertex exitances sample this function at the position of each vertex on the surface. Similarly, the element exitances sample the function at the center of each element. Given only the element exitances as a result of our radiosity calculations, we need somehow to determine the vertex exitances.

This is a common problem in many different fields of mathematics and engineering (particularly *finite element* methods, which are closely related to the radiosity problem). Of course, we do not know the exact exitance distribution across the surface. All we can do is interpolate a reasonable approximation.

The easiest solution is to use *piecewise linear interpolation*. In the one-dimensional example shown in Figure 4.32, we simply draw a straight line between each pair of element exitances and interpolate the vertex exitances where they intersect the lines (Fig. 4.33). We can clearly extend this approach to two-dimensional surfaces by using piecewise *bilinear* interpolation. This can be applied to both triangular and quadrilateral elements, even if they have unequal areas.

An even simpler approach is to assume that the elements form a regularly spaced grid across the surface. If this is true, then each vertex exitance can be inter-

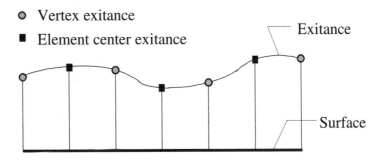

Figure 4.32 Sampling the continuous exitance distribution across a surface

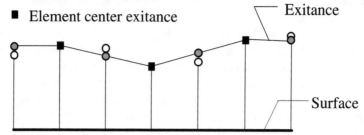

Figure 4.33 Piecewise linear interpolation of vertex exitances

polated by averaging the exitances of the elements that share the vertex (Fig. 4.34). The technique is called *nodal averaging*. It has an advantage over bilinear interpolation in that we do not need to account for the dimensions of each element.

One problem with piecewise bilinear interpolation is that the surface shading becomes discontinuous at the element boundaries. This may lead to visible Mach bands (see Section 4.13) extending across what should be smoothly shaded surfaces. There are several solutions to this problem, but they are beyond the scope of this book. See Cohen and Wallace (1993) for a detailed discussion and references to the associated literature. For our purposes, nodal averaging will generally provide quite adequate results.

4.17 TONE -REPRODUCTION PROBLEMS

Another problem we have to address is *tone reproduction*. The human eye is capable of adapting to a very wide range of average-scene luminances. We can see during

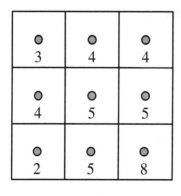

Element exitances

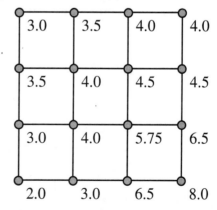

Interpolated vertex exitances

Figure 4.34 Interpolating vertex exitances using nodal averaging

broad daylight as well as by starlight—a truly astounding luminance range of nearly ten trillion to one. Unfortunately, our methods of reproducing these scenes have luminance scales ranging from 50:1 (four-color printing) to 1,000:1 (photographic transparencies). Most computer display terminals have a dynamic range of 100:1.

Our radiosity methods will accurately calculate the exitances that we need to display a photorealistic image. However, if these images include any light sources, that is likely all we will see. Their exitances may be in excess of the other surfaces by a factor of 100:1 or more, in which case our display devices will be unable to render them and the surfaces at the same time. This is not what we see when we look at a typical scene in real life. We need to devise a tone-reproduction technique that compensates for this problem.

One ad hoc but usually satisfactory solution is to scale the vertex exitances according to the vertex with the greatest *reflected* exitance. That is, each exitance value is scaled such that the greatest reflected exitance (in whichever color band of the *Spectra* data type) is assigned a value of slightly less than 1.0. If the exitance of a light source exceeds this value, it is individually scaled to equal 1.0 (again in whichever color band) as well. This ensures that the light sources will be displayed in their proper colors. They will also appear as the "brightest" objects in the image, closely approximating what we would expect to see. We might refer to this process as *exitance normalization*.

With this, we can develop the following tone-reproduction class:

Listing 4.14

```
// TONE_REP.H - Tone Reproduction Class

#ifndef _TONE_REP_H
#define _TONE_REP_H

#include "instance.h"

// Maximum reflected exitance value
#define T_MaxExitance   ((double) 254 / 255)

class ToneRep   // Tone reproduction
{
  public:
    void Interpolate( Instance * );
    void Normalize( Instance * );
    void Shade( Instance * );
};

#endif
```

and:

Listing 4.15   TONE_REP.CPP

```cpp
// TONE_REP.CPP - Tone Reproduction Class

#include "tone_rep.h"

// Shade the vertex exitances
void ToneRep::Shade( Instance *penv )
{
  Instance *pinst;
  Vertex3 *pvert;

  // Walk the instance list
  pinst = penv;
  while (pinst != NULL)
  {
    // Walk the vertex list
    pvert = pinst->GetVertPtr();
    while (pvert != NULL)
    {
      // Set vertex exitance to parent surface reflectance
      pvert->SetExitance(pvert->GetElemListPtr()->
          GetElemPtr()->GetParentPtr()->GetParentPtr()->
          GetReflectance());

      pvert = pvert->GetNext();
    }
    pinst = pinst->GetNext();
  }
}

// Interpolate vertex reflected exitances
void ToneRep::Interpolate( Instance *penv )
{
  int num_elem;          // Number of elements
  Element3 *pelem;       // Element pointer
  ElemList *pel;         // Element list pointer
  Instance *pinst;       // Instance pointer
  Vertex3 *pvert;        // Vertex pointer

  // Walk the instance list
  pinst = penv;
  while (pinst != NULL)
  {
    // Walk the vertex list
    pvert = pinst->GetVertPtr();
    while (pvert != NULL)
    {
      // Initialize vertex reflected exitance
      pvert->GetExitance().Reset();
```

```
      // Walk the element list
      pel = pvert->GetElemListPtr();
      num_elem = 0;
      while (pel != NULL)
      {
        // Get the element pointer
        pelem = pel->GetElemPtr();

        // Add element reflected exitance
        pvert->GetExitance().Add(pelem->GetExitance());

        pel = pel->GetNext();
        num_elem++;
      }

      // Scale vertex reflected exitance according to number
      // of shared elements
      pvert->GetExitance().Scale(1.0 / (double) num_elem);

      pvert = pvert->GetNext();
    }
    pinst = pinst->GetNext();
  }
}

// Normalize vertex exitances
void ToneRep::Normalize( Instance *penv )
{
  double rmax = 0.0;      // Maximum reflected color
  double emax;            // Maximum color
  Instance *pinst;        // Instance pointer
  Spectra emit;           // Surface emittance
  Vertex3 *pvert;         // Vertex pointer

  // Walk the instance list
  pinst = penv;
  while (pinst != NULL)
  {
    // Walk the vertex list
    pvert = pinst->GetVertPtr();
    while (pvert != NULL)
    {
      // Find maximum reflected color band value
      rmax = max(pvert->GetExitance().GetMaxColor(), rmax);

      pvert = pvert->GetNext();
    }
    pinst = pinst->GetNext();
  }

  // Check for non-zero maximum vertex exitance
  if (rmax > MIN_VALUE)
  {
```

(continued)

Listing 4.15   *(continued)*

```
// Walk the instance list
pinst = penv;
while (pinst != NULL)
{
  // Walk the vertex list
  pvert = pinst->GetVertPtr();
  while (pvert != NULL)
  {
    // Get parent surface emittance
    emit = pvert->GetElemListPtr()->GetElemPtr()->
        GetParentPtr()->GetParentPtr()->GetEmittance();

    // Add surface initial exitance to reflected vertex
    // exitance
    pvert->GetExitance().Add(emit);

    // Scale vertex exitance
    pvert->GetExitance().Scale(T_MaxExitance / rmax);

    // Clip vertex exitance to unity
    if ((emax = pvert->GetExitance().GetMaxColor()) >
        1.0)
      pvert->GetExitance().Scale(1.0 / emax);

    pvert = pvert->GetNext();
  }
  pinst = pinst->GetNext();
}
}
}
```

ToneRep is a catch-all class that also implements the vertex shading and exitance interpolation discussed in Section 4.16. In that it has no data members, *ToneRep* should not even be an independent class at all. Unfortunately, there are no other classes that these functions can be logically assigned to.

Exitance normalization has no physical justification—it simply produces results that are visually appealing. The reality is much more complicated. We can clearly sense whether a room is dark or brightly lit, and we can definitely tell the difference between starlight and sunlight! Unfortunately, our approach completely ignores this ability.

Fortunately, there is a growing body of literature on tone-reproduction algorithms that takes the observer into account. Two papers of particular interest are Meyer (1986) and Tumblin and Rushmeier (1993); see also Barbour and Meyer (1992). This will undoubtedly become a more important topic as photorealistic imagery becomes more commonplace.

Finally, it is possible to store floating-point color representations using 32 bits (four bytes) per pixel (Ward 1991). Each color is represented by an 8-bit mantissa,

Color Plate 1 View of ROOM environment with 22 surfaces, 48 patches, and 197 elements. Rendered with cubic tetrahedral version of *HELIOS* in 35 seconds on a 66-MHz 486 PC.

Data file : ROOM.WLD

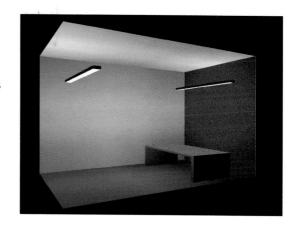

Color Plate 2 View of PIC_ROOM environment with 27 surfaces, 176 patches, and 205 elements. Wall picture colors achieved by Gouraud shading of four polygons sharing a common vertex. Rendered with hemicube version of *HELIOS* in 81 seconds on a 66-MHz 486 PC.

Data file: PIC_ROOM.WLD

Color Plate 3 View of CORNELL environment (the Cornell University "Cornell Room") with 9 surfaces, 112 patches, and 166 elements. Note the diffuse shadows and marked color bleeding between surfaces. Rendered with cubic tetrahedral version of *HELIOS*.

Data file: CORNELL.WLD

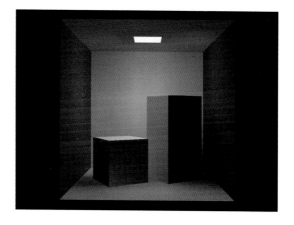

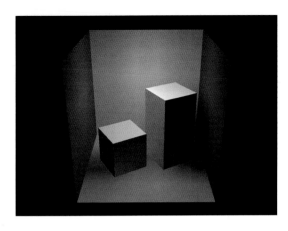

Color Plate 4 Another view of CORNELL environment. The room ceiling was removed automatically by hidden-surface removal. Rendered with cubic tetrahedral version of *HELIOS* in 58 seconds on a 66-MHz 486 PC.

Data file: CORNELL.WLD

Color Plate 5 View of COR-NELL environment rendered with ray-casting version of *HELIOS* in 383 seconds on a 66-MHz 486 PC. Note the strong shadowing effects characteristic of the ray-casting approach.

Data file: CORNELL.WLD

Color Plate 6 View of Frank Lloyd Wright's Unity Temple, Oak Park, Illinois, designed in 1904. The environment included 27,000 polygons and 69 light sources in AutoCAD DXF format. Rendered on a Silicon Graphics Indy workstation in 6 hours using Lightscape Technologies' *Lightscape Visualization System*. Changing viewpoint requires 30 seconds to regenerate image.

Color Plate 7 View of the main lobby of the Ontario Legislature Building, Toronto. The environment included over 450,000 elements. Note the texture-mapped paintings. Rendered on an SGI Indy workstation (no hardware graphics acceleration) in 15 hours with the *Lightscape Visualization System.*

Color Plate 8 View of Jerusalem City Hall main council chambers, Israel. Architects: A. J. Diamond, Donald Schmitt and Company. The environment included 33,000 elements and 60 light sources. Rendered on an SGI Indy in 4 hours with the *Lightscape Visualization System.*

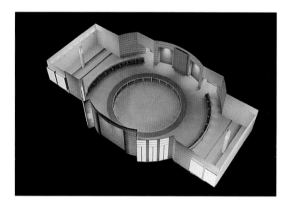

Color Plate 9 Cross-section of auditorium-lecture hall at CIBC Training Centre, King City, Ontario. Architects: A. J. Diamond, Donald Schmitt and Company. The environment included 19,000 original polygons and 57,000 mesh elements after adaptive subdivision. Rendered on an SGI Indy in 5 hours with the *Lightscape Visualization System.*

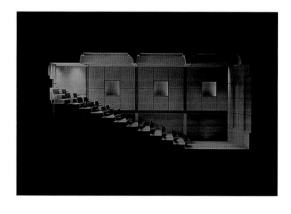

Color Plate 10 View of data entry terminals, Société Générale Bank, New York, New York. Architects: Hellmuth, Obata and Kassabaum, Inc. The environment included over 225,000 elements and required 60 hours to render on an SGI workstation with 128 MB of RAM using in-house radiosity-rendering software.

Color Plate 11 View of hallway, New York Hospital, New York, New York. Architects: Hellmuth, Obata and Kassabaum, Inc. The environment included 120,000 elements and required 20 hours to render on an SGI workstation using in-house radiosity-rendering software.

Color Plate 12 View of Centro Commercial Plaza, Santa Fe, Mexico City. Architects: Hellmuth, Obata and Kassabaum, Inc. Rendered in 12 hours on an SGI workstation using in-house radiosity-rendering software. Elan hardware graphics accelerator displayed the image in 1.5 seconds.

followed by an 8-bit exponent. Although this does not address the limited dynamic range of most display media, it does allow the user to correct the image presentation using only a stored bitmap image.

4.18 A SYNTHETIC CAMERA

That's it—we finally have all the components we need to construct our viewing system! We can model this system as a *synthetic camera*, with a wireframe display as its viewfinder and a bitmap file as its film. As we saw in Section 4.1, changing the view distance is equivalent to changing the focal length setting of a zoom lens.

The viewfinder image lets us preview our image and adjust the camera's position and orientation. Once we have the desired composition, we can "shoot" a fully rendered view of the environment. We can even "crop" the image by specifying the bitmap width and height, and we can choose our film (RGB, gray scale, or pseudo-color display, plus color jittering and gamma correction).

Implementing this model requires *ViewSys* for the viewing system, *PolyClip4* for clipping the polygons, *PolyRender* to render them, *WinMetaFile* for the wireframe display, and WinBitmap for the bitmap file manager. The following *SynCamera* class provides a wrapper that makes it easier to access these classes from our application code (which is still to come).

Listing 4.16

```
// SYN_CAM.H - Synthetic Camera Class

#ifndef _SYN_CAM_H
#define _SYN_CAM_H

#include "instance.h"
#include "p_clip4.h"
#include "p_render.h"
#include "win_meta.h"
#include "win_bmap.h"
#include "view_sys.h"

#ifdef _NOT_WINAPP
struct POINT     // Raster display point
{
  int x;         // X-axis co-ordinate
  int y;         // Y-axis co-ordinate
};
#endif

class SynCamera : public ViewSys        // Synthetic camera
{
```

(continued)

Listing 4.16   *(continued)*

```
private:
  // Note: angles are in degrees
  double vdv_horz;          // View direction horz angle
  double vdv_vert;          // View direction vert angle
  double vup_horz;          // View-up vector horz angle
  double vup_vert;          // View-up vector vert angle
  int height;               // Window height
  int width;                // Window width
  PolyClip4 clipper;        // Polygon clipper
  PolyRender renderer;      // Polygon renderer

public:
  SynCamera( int w, int h, double vdvh, double vdvv,
      double vuph, double vupv ) : ViewSys()
  {
    width = w; height = h;
    vdv_horz = vdvh; vdv_vert = vdvv;
    vup_horz = vuph; vup_vert = vupv;
    aspect = (double) w / (double) h;

    SetViewDirVector(vdvh, vdvv);
    SetViewUpVector(vuph, vupv);

    UpdateViewSystem();

    EnableGamma();
  }

  BOOL GammaFlag() { return renderer.GammaFlag(); }
  BOOL GetStatus() { return renderer.GetStatus(); }
  BOOL JitterFlag() { return renderer.JitterFlag(); }
  BOOL Preview( Instance *, WinMetaFile * );
  BOOL Shoot( Instance *, WinBitmap * );
  double GetGamma() { return renderer.GetGamma(); }
  double GetViewDirHorz() { return vdv_horz; }
  double GetViewDirVert() { return vdv_vert; }
  double GetViewUpHorz() { return vup_horz; }
  double GetViewUpVert() { return vup_vert; }
  int GetColorType() { return renderer.GetColorType(); }
  int GetHeight() { return height; }
  int GetWidth() { return width; }
  int GetNoiseLevel()
  { return renderer.GetNoiseLevel(); }
  void DisableGamma() { renderer.DisableGamma(); }
  void DisableJitter() { renderer.DisableJitter(); }
  void EnableGamma() { renderer.EnableGamma(); }
  void EnableJitter() { renderer.EnableJitter(); }
  void SetColorType( int type )
  { renderer.SetColorType(type); }
```

```
    void SetGamma( double g ) { renderer.SetGamma(g); }
    void SetHeight( int h ) { height = h; }
    void SetNoiseLevel( int n )
    { renderer.SetNoiseLevel(n); }
    void SetViewDirVector( double, double );
    void SetViewUpVector( double, double );
    void SetWidth( int w ) { width = w; }
    void UpdateViewSystem();
};

#endif
```

Our *ViewSys* class represents the viewing system's orientation in rectangular coordinates. To this *SynCamera* adds a set of spherical coordinates, mostly as a convenience for the application program's user interface and information about the width and height of the bitmap.

SynCamera also adds to *ViewSys* the ability to preview and shoot a view of an environment:

Listing 4.17

```
// SYN_CAM.CPP - Synthetic Camera Class

#include "spheric3.h"
#include "syn_cam.h"

// Record wireframe display in metafile format
BOOL SynCamera::Preview( Instance *pinst, WinMetaFile
    *pmeta )
{
  int i;                 // Loop index
  int num_vert;          // Number of vertices
  Element3 *pelem;       // Element pointer
  OutPolygon out;        // Output polygon
  POINT vertex[8];       // Polygon vertex array
  Point3 posn;           // Point co-ordinates
  Patch3 *ppatch;        // Patch pointer
  Surface3 *psurf;       // Surface pointer

  // Start wireframe metafile recording
  if (pmeta->Record(tmpnam(NULL)) == FALSE)
    return FALSE;

  // Walk the instance list
  while (pinst != NULL)
  {
    // Walk the surface list
    psurf = pinst->GetSurfPtr();
    while (psurf != NULL)
    {
```

(continued)

Listing 4.17 *(continued)*

```
      // Walk the patch list
      ppatch = psurf->GetPatchPtr();
      while (ppatch != NULL)
      {
        // Determine patch visibility
        if (BackFaceCull(ppatch) == FALSE)
        {
          // Walk the element list
          pelem = ppatch->GetElementPtr();
          while (pelem != NULL)
          {
            // Clip the 3-D element (polygon)
            num_vert = clipper.Clip(pelem, out,
                GetProjMatrix());

            // Initialize the 2-D polygon vertices array
            for (i = 0; i < num_vert; i++)
            {
              posn  = out.GetVertexPosn(i);

              // Convert normalized device co-ordinates to
              // screen space co-ordinates
              vertex[i].x = (int) (posn.GetX() * width);
              vertex[i].y = (int) (posn.GetY() * height);
            }

            // Add 2-D polygon draw command to metafile
            if (pmeta->Polygon(vertex, num_vert) == FALSE)
            {
              pmeta->Erase();   // Erase metafile recording
              return FALSE;
            }

            pelem = pelem->GetNext();
          }
        }
        ppatch = ppatch->GetNext();
      }
      psurf = psurf->GetNext();
    }
    pinst = pinst->GetNext();
  }
  return pmeta->Stop();              // Stop metafile recording
}

// Record rendered display as bitmap file
BOOL SynCamera::Shoot( Instance *pinst, WinBitmap *pbmap )
{
```

```
  Element3 *pelem;        // Element pointer
  OutPolygon out;         // Output polygon
  Patch3 *ppatch;         // Patch pointer
  Surface3 *psurf;        // Surface pointer

  // Initialize polygon renderer
  if (renderer.Open(pbmap) == FALSE)
    return FALSE;

  // Walk the instance list
  while (pinst != NULL)
  {
    // Walk the surface list
    psurf = pinst->GetSurfPtr();
    while (psurf != NULL)
    {
      // Walk the patch list
      ppatch = psurf->GetPatchPtr();
      while (ppatch != NULL)
      {
        // Determine patch visibility
        if (BackFaceCull(ppatch) == FALSE)
        {
          // Walk the element list
          pelem = ppatch->GetElementPtr();
          while (pelem != NULL)
          {
            // Clip the 3-D polygon
            (void) clipper.Clip(pelem, out,
                GetProjMatrix());

            // Render the 2-D polygon
            renderer.Render(out);

            pelem = pelem->GetNext();
          }
        }
        ppatch = ppatch->GetNext();
      }
      psurf = psurf->GetNext();
    }
    pinst = pinst->GetNext();
  }

  renderer.Close();       // Close the polygon renderer
  return TRUE;
}

// Set view system parameters
void SynCamera::UpdateViewSystem()
{
```

(continued)

Listing 4.17   *(continued)*

```
   aspect = (double) width / (double) height;
   BuildTransform();
}

// Set view direction vector
void SynCamera::SetViewDirVector( double h, double v )
{
   Spheric3 angle;        // View direction angles (radians)
   Vector3 view_dir;      // View direction vector

   vdv_horz = h; vdv_vert = v;

   angle.SetVert(DegToRad(v));
   angle.SetHorz(DegToRad(h));
   angle.SpherToRect(&view_dir);

   SetViewDir(view_dir);
}

// Set view-up vector
void SynCamera::SetViewUpVector( double h, double v )
{
   Spheric3 angle;        // View-up vector angles (radians)
   Vector3 view_up;       // View-up vector

   vup_horz = h; vup_vert = v;

   angle.SetVert(DegToRad(v));
   angle.SetHorz(DegToRad(h));
   angle.SpherToRect(&view_up);

   SetViewUp(view_up);
}
```

Preview implements the wireframe display pseudocode presented in Figure 4.25 with one difference: The "display device" is a metafile. It sets the metafile to record mode, then walks through the linked list of polygons representing the parsed environment, performing backface culling, clipping, and coordinate conversion before drawing the visible polygons to the metafile. The metafile recording is stopped when all of the polygons have been processed. Playing the completed metafile afterward is the responsibility of the application program.

Shoot is almost identical to *Preview*. Instead of drawing the visible polygons to a metafile, however, it renders them in a bitmap. (The *PolyRender* class performs its own coordinate conversion.) Again, the application program is responsible for saving the bitmap to a file.

Finally, *UpdateViewSystem* should be called to update the view system's aspect ratio and transformation matrix whenever any of the view system parameters are changed, either through *SetViewDirVector* or *SetViewUpVector* or through calling one of the *ViewSys* public member functions such as *ViewSys::SetOrigin*.

4.19 A VIEWING SYSTEM FOR MS-WINDOWS

We have written some 2,500 lines of C++ source code so far, but does it work? The only way to answer this question—and to provide a nontrivial example of its use—is to build an application around it. Rather than write a demonstration program, we might as well bite the bullet and develop a complete user interface for our radiosity renderer.

> Our program development and target environments will be the same: Microsoft MS-Windows. The following code is therefore completely and unabashedly concerned with MS-Windows programming. In that this book is not about MS-Windows programming tricks and techniques, the commentary will not address Windows-specific programming issues or belabor porting the code to other environments.
>
> The good news is that the following application program does little more than provide pull-down menus and popup dialog boxes for the user. If you need to write a user interface for another platform, your best bet is to emulate the interface of the MS-Windows executable provided on the accompanying diskette. Porting MS-Windows source code verbatim to another GUI environment is not recommended unless you are fully familiar with the MS-Windows API (see Petzold 1992).

A few specifications before we begin. Naturally, our program should display both wireframe and bitmapped images. MS-Windows does this with relative ease, with the added bonus that it is device independent. Unlike its underlying MS-DOS operating system, MS-Windows 3.1 is fully cognizant of its display device's capabilities. We thankfully do not have to concern ourselves with the many varieties of video display adapters and their arcane programming requirements. (The same capabilities are, of course, available with MS-Windows NT.)

Beyond this, we should take full advantage of the graphical user interface provided MS-Windows. In particular, we should have pull-down menus and the options shown in Figure 4.35.

Menu	Options
File	*Open File* dialog box to open world (environment) files.
	Save As dialog box to save the displayed bitmapped image as a BMP file.
	Directories dialog box to specify a path to where the entity files can be found.
Camera	*Camera Parameters* dialog box to set the view distance, the front and back clipping-plane distances, and the bitmap image width and height.
View	*View Parameters* dialog box to set the eye position, view direction, vector, and view-up vector (using spherical coordinates).

(continued)

Figure 4.35   *(continued)*

Menu	Options
Render	*Wireframe* menu item to display a wireframe image of the specified view of the environment. *Shaded* menu item to display a full-color (but not photorealistic) view of the environment. *Rendering* menu item to perform the radiosity calculations and display a photorealistic view of the environment. *Redisplay* menu item to redisplay the bitmapped image without having to repeat the radiosity calculations.
Options	*Convergence* dialog box to specify the maximum number of allowed iterations for solving the radiosity equation (see Chap. 6), to specify a "stopping criterion" (see below), and to toggle the "ambient exitance" and "positive overshoot" features (see Chap. 6). *Display Parameters* dialog box to enable or disable gamma correction and to specify a gamma-correction value (see Section 3.5.1), to enable or disable color jittering and to specify a "noise-level" value (see Section 3.5.2), and choose 24-bit color, gray-scale, or pseudocolor display (see Section 3.5).
Help	*About* dialog box to identify the program.

Figure 4.35   Viewing system menu specification

This short list completely describes our user interface requirements. It accepts an environment files, allows us to specify a view of the environment, and displays both wireframe and bitmapped images. We can optionally save the bitmapped image as a BMP file.

As for the *Rendering* and *Convergence* menu items, we have yet to develop our radiosity-rendering code. All we can do for now is provide the following do-nothing base class:

Listing 4.18

```
// RAD_EQN.H - Radiosity Equation Solver Base Class

#ifndef _RAD_EQN_H
#define _RAD_EQN_H

#include "environ.h"
#include "tone_rep.h"

class RadEqnSolve    // Radiosity equation solver
{
```

```
    protected:
      int step_count;           // Step count
      int max_step;             // Maximum number of steps
      double stop_criterion;    // Stopping criterion
      double convergence;       // Convergence
      double total_area;        // Total patch area
      double total_flux;        // Total environment flux
      double total_unsent;      // Total unsent exitance
      BOOL amb_flag;            // Ambient exitance flag
      Environ *penv;            // Environment pointer
      Patch3 *pmax;             // Maximum unsent flux patch ptr
      Spectra ambient;          // Ambient exitance
      Spectra irf;              // Interreflection factors
      ToneRep tone;             // Tone reproduction object

      void CalcAmbient();
      void CalcInterReflect();
      void InitExitance();
      void UpdateUnsentStats();

    public:
      RadEqnSolve()
      {
        amb_flag = FALSE;
        max_step = 100;
        stop_criterion = 0.001;
      }

      virtual ~RadEqnSolve() { Close(); }

      BOOL AmbientFlag() { return amb_flag; }
      BOOL Calculate() { return TRUE; }
      BOOL GetStatus() { return TRUE; }
      BOOL Open( Environ * ) { return TRUE; }
      BOOL OverShootFlag() { return FALSE; }
      double GetStopCriterion() { return stop_criterion; }
      double GetConvergence() { return convergence; }
      int GetMaxStep() { return max_step; }
      int GetStepCount() { return step_count; }
      void Close() { }
      void DisableAmbient() { amb_flag = FALSE; }
      void DisableOverShoot() { }
      void EnableAmbient() { amb_flag = TRUE; }
      void EnableOverShoot() { }
      void SetMaxStep( int max ) { max_step = max; }
      void SetStopCriterion( double s )
      { stop_criterion = s; }
      void Shade( Instance *pinst ) { tone.Shade(pinst); }
};

#endif
```

A quick preview: *RadEqnSolve* will later serve as a base class for one of several radiosity equation solvers (described in Chap. 6). It will accept a pointer to a parsed environment and then compute the polygon vertex colors needed to generate a photo-realistic image. We call *GetStatus* to ensure that the derived class object was properly constructed. If so, we call *Open* to initialize the equation solver. If this function returns *TRUE*, we then repeatedly call *Calculate* until it returns *TRUE*.

The radiosity equation solvers are iterative procedures that begin with a trial solution and successively refine it with each call to *Calculate*. The *max_pass* member specifies the maximum number of allowed iterations before the derived *Calculate* function returns *TRUE*. The *stop_criterion* member provides a single quantity that *Calculate* will use to determine whether the latest solution is "close enough."

Once *Calculate* returns *TRUE,* we can call *ToneRep::Interpolate* (if necessary) and *ToneRep::Normalize* to generate element vertex exitances that are suitable for viewing purposes. The details of *Calculate* are discussed in Chapter 6.

Shade is not really part of a radiosity equation solver, since it only calls *ToneRep::Shade* to set the vertex exitances to their parent surface reflectances (Section 4.17). Nevertheless, it is convenient to include it with *RadEqnSolve*.

Finally, calling *Close* releases any memory that was dynamically allocated to the equation solver.

RadEqnSolve has a number of other functions whose purpose will become evident in Chapter 6. In this base class, they essentially return dummy values that we can ignore. This requires the following set of "stub" functions:

Listing 4.19

```
// RAD_TMP.CPP - Dummy Radiosity Equation Solver Base Class

// NOTE: This file provides TEMPORARY function stubs for the
//       RadEqnSolve class.

#include "rad_eqn.h"

void RadEqnSolve::CalcAmbient() { }
void RadEqnSolve::CalcInterReflect() { }
void RadEqnSolve::InitExitance() { }
void RadEqnSolve::UpdateUnsentStats() { }
```

which do nothing other than allow us to continue our development without having to come back and change the code later. RAD_TMP.CPP is a temporary file that will be replaced by RAD_EQN.CPP in Chapter 6.

That's it for platform-independent code in this chapter. The rest of our application program is entirely concerned with user interface details.

4.19.1 A Scroll Bar Class

Our bitmapped image can be whatever size we choose, subject only to the limits of available memory. As such, it may be larger than our display screen. To view the image in its entirety, we need to implement scroll bars. These are traditionally implemented in C within the dreaded "big switch" statement of *WinMain*. (e.g., Petzold 1992). However, the same code must be repeated for every child window that requires scroll bars. In C++, it makes more sense to create a scroll bar control class:

Listing 4.20

```
// WIN_SBAR.H - MS-Windows Scroll Bar Control Class

#ifndef _WIN_SBAR_H
#define _WIN_SBAR_H

#include "general.h"

class WinScroll           // Scroll bar control
{
  private:
    HWND hwnd;            // Client window handle
    POINT curr_pos;      // Current scroll position
    POINT max_range;     // Maximum scroll range
    POINT inc;           // Scroll increment
    POINT size;          // Client window size

  public:
    WinScroll( HWND hw)
    {
      RECT rect;         // Rectangle structure

      curr_pos.x = curr_pos.y = 0;
      max_range.x = max_range.y = 0;
      inc.x = inc.y = 0;

      hwnd = hw;
      GetClientRect(hwnd, &rect);
      size.x = rect.right;
      size.y = rect.bottom;

      Hide();
    }

    POINT Pos() { return curr_pos; }
    void Hide();
    void Horz( WPARAM, WORD );
    void Init( int, int );
    void Set( int, int );
    void Vert( WPARAM, WORD );
};

#endif
```

where a *WinScroll* object is dynamically created for each window when the *WM_CREATE* message is processed and deleted under *WM_DESTROY*.

As for the public member functions, *Pos* returns the current scroll bar button positions, *Hide* hides the scroll bars from view, *Init* initializes the scroll bars for a given bitmap image, *Set* reinitializes the scroll bars after the window has been resized, and *Horz* and *Vert* process messages from the mouse and keyboard. These functions are implemented as:

Listing 4.21

```
// WIN_SBAR.CPP - MS-Windows Scroll Bar Control Class

#include "win_sbar.h"

// Set scroll bar positions and ranges
void WinScroll::Set( int width, int height )
{
  RECT rect;

  GetClientRect(hwnd, &rect);
  size.x = rect.right;
  size.y = rect.bottom;

  max_range.x = max(0, width - size.x);
  curr_pos.x = min(curr_pos.x, max_range.x);

  SetScrollRange(hwnd, SB_HORZ, 0, max_range.x, FALSE);
  SetScrollPos(hwnd, SB_HORZ, curr_pos.x, TRUE);

  max_range.y = max(0, height - size.y);
  curr_pos.y = min(curr_pos.y, max_range.y);

  SetScrollRange(hwnd, SB_VERT, 0, max_range.y, FALSE);
  SetScrollPos(hwnd, SB_VERT, curr_pos.y, TRUE);
}

// Initialize scroll bar positions and ranges
void WinScroll::Init( int width, int height )
{
  curr_pos.x = curr_pos.y = 0;
  Set(width, height);
}

void WinScroll::Hide()   // Hide scroll bars
{
  SetScrollRange(hwnd, SB_HORZ, 0, 0, TRUE);
  SetScrollRange(hwnd, SB_VERT, 0, 0, TRUE);
}

// Process vertical scroll bar message
void WinScroll::Vert( WPARAM sb_code, WORD sb_pos )
{
  switch (sb_code)
  {
```

```
        case SB_LINEUP:
          inc.y = -1;
          break;
        case SB_LINEDOWN:
          inc.y = 1;
          break;
        case SB_PAGEUP:
          inc.y = min(-1, -size.y >> 2);
          break;
        case SB_PAGEDOWN:
          inc.y = max(1, size.y >> 2);
          break;
        case SB_TOP:
          inc.y = -inc.y;
          break;
        case SB_BOTTOM:
          inc.y = max_range.y - curr_pos.y;
          break;
        case SB_THUMBPOSITION:
          inc.y = sb_pos - curr_pos.y;
          break;
        default:
          inc.y = 0;
    }

    if ((inc.y = max(-curr_pos.y, min(inc.y, max_range.y -
        curr_pos.y))) != 0)
    {
      curr_pos.y += inc.y;
      ScrollWindow(hwnd, 0, -inc.y, NULL, NULL);
      SetScrollPos(hwnd, SB_VERT, curr_pos.y, TRUE);
      UpdateWindow(hwnd);
    }
}

// Process horizontal scroll bar message
void WinScroll::Horz( WPARAM sb_code, WORD sb_pos )
{
  switch (sb_code)
  {
    case SB_LINEUP:
      inc.x = -1;
      break;
    case SB_LINEDOWN:
      inc.x = 1;
      break;
    case SB_PAGEUP:
      inc.x = min(-1, -size.x >> 2);
      break;
    case SB_PAGEDOWN:
      inc.x = max(1, size.x >> 2);
      break;
```

(continued)

Listing 4.21 *(continued)*

```
    case SB_THUMBPOSITION:
      inc.x = sb_pos - curr_pos.x;
      break;
    default:
      inc.x = 0;
  }

  if ((inc.x = max(-curr_pos.x, min(inc.x, max_range.x -
      curr_pos.x))) != 0)
  {
    curr_pos.x += inc.x;
    ScrollWindow(hwnd, -inc.x, 0, NULL, NULL);
    SetScrollPos(hwnd, SB_HORZ, curr_pos.x, TRUE);
    UpdateWindow(hwnd);
  }
}
```

WinScroll can be considered much like any other set of library functions: a black box. As long as it works, we need not concern ourselves with the details. We will see an example of its use shortly, but first we have to consider something more general.

4.19.2 An Aside: MS-Windows Programming Issues

Developing MS-Windows applications is at heart an exercise in C programming. The MS-Windows API is not designed for C++. Worse, the dreaded "big switch" statement in *WinMain* can be hidden but not ignored. Several C++ compiler vendors market class libraries designed to make Windows development in C++ easier, but these are at best proprietary solutions.

Lacking an industry-standard C++ compiler for MS-Windows (there are currently two strong contenders and several dark horses), we must take the traditional approach of programming in C. We thankfully do not have to abandon our C++ code, since C and C++ can (by design) coexist quite nicely.

In fact, the only real problem lies in C++'s delightful habit of "name mangling." Although this may be necessary in order for the linker and debugger to distinguish between class functions with the same name, it wreaks havoc with *callback functions* (i.e., functions that are called by Windows rather than your own code). You declare your callback functions (such as *MainWndProc*) in the *EXPORTS* section of your module definition (.DEF) files. If the C++ compiler changes the names of these functions from "func_name" to something like "?func_name@@YAHH@Z," your linker will be unable to resolve (i.e., find) them later.

There are two solutions. First, you can add the *_export* keyword to the function prototypes and remove the function declarations from your .DEF file. Unfortunately, this precludes using *ordinals* to identify the exported functions to Windows, as in:

```
EXPORTS
  MainWndProc     @1
  About           @2
```

Ordinals serve two purposes. One, Windows can process them faster, since it can use the ordinal directly to index a function pointer table instead of first matching a text string when calling the function. Two, they hide the function names from people doing reverse engineering—an important issue for commercial applications.

You could write your program using _export, then use the EXEHDR utility to look up the C++ mangled function names, add them to your .DEF file with accompanying ordinals, remove the _export references, and recompile. That's the hard way.

The second and simpler solution is to write the callback functions in C and declare them as such using C++'s extern "C" mechanism. The C++ compiler considers them to be C functions and compiles them without name mangling. This allows you to declare them in your module definition file as is and with ordinals.

No, this book is not about MS-Windows programming. However, finding this particular information in the MS-Windows API documentation can be a painful experience. Enough said.

One more comment regarding programming issues. Many older books on MS-Windows 3.x programming recommend using the medium memory model. This advice made sense when MS-Windows 3.0 could run in real mode on an Intel 80286 or 8088 CPU. However, support for this mode was thankfully dropped from MS-Windows 3.1, which runs in standard or enhanced mode only. (Of course, there are no memory models to worry about in the 32-bit Windows NT operating system.)

Another argument is that by using near rather than far pointers, a medium model program runs faster. Although this may be true, the difference is usually minimal. Moreover, the source code becomes exponentially unintelligible with endless typecasts to far pointers. Worst of all, many otherwise standard C library functions are not usable in the medium model. You either have to copy function arguments between far and near memory or write your own far code versions that accept near data. What a mess!

This leads to one simple recommendation for all nontrivial 16-bit MS-Windows programs:

> **16-BIT MS-WINDOWS: COMPILE USING THE LARGE MEMORY MODEL**

4.19.3 *HELIOS*—A Radiosity Renderer for MS-Windows

HELIOS is our "minimal" viewing system for MS-Windows 3.1 and MS-Windows NT. None of the following pertains directly to radiosity rendering. For readers familiar with MS-Windows programming, it is an entirely straightforward implementation of a user interface. Otherwise, it is an imposingly large block of inscrutable code.

Fortunately, we can view it as the proverbial black box. It works, and it provides all the user interface support we need for our radiosity renderer. As we saw in Listing 4.18, its relation to our radiosity renderer per se consists of a few function calls. If you must understand its details, a copy of Petzold (1992) and the MS-Windows API documentation are highly recommended as tour guides.

With this, we have:

Listing 4.22

```
// HELIOS.H - Radiosity Renderer for MS-Windows

#ifndef _HELIOS_H
#define _HELIOS_H

static const int MaxLen = 256;
static const int Offset = 2;

// Display type
#define H_NONE  0        // None
#define H_WIRE  1        // Wireframe
#define H_BMAP  2        // Bitmap

#ifdef WIN32
// WIN32 message cracking macros
#define GET_WM_COMMAND_ID(wp, lp)    LOWORD(wp)
#define GET_WM_HSCROLL_POS(wp, lp)   HIWORD(wp)
#define GET_WM_VSCROLL_POS(wp, lp)   HIWORD(wp)
#else
// WIN16 message cracking macros
#define GET_WM_COMMAND_ID(wp, lp)    (wp)
#define GET_WM_HSCROLL_POS(wp, lp)   LOWORD(lp)
#define GET_WM_VSCROLL_POS(wp, lp)   LOWORD(lp)
#endif

int WINAPI WinMain( HINSTANCE, HINSTANCE, LPSTR, int );

static BOOL InitApplication( HINSTANCE );
static BOOL InitInstance( HINSTANCE, int );
static double GetDlgItemFloat( HWND, int );
static void CalcWireDim( short, short, short *, short * );
static void DoKeyDown( HWND, WPARAM );
static void SetDlgItemFloat( HWND, int, double );

extern "C"
{
  LRESULT WINAPI MainWndProc( HWND, UINT, WPARAM,
      LPARAM );
  LRESULT WINAPI WireWndProc( HWND, UINT, WPARAM,
      LPARAM );
```

```
    BOOL CALLBACK About( HWND, UINT, WPARAM, LPARAM );
    BOOL CALLBACK SetCamera( HWND, UINT, WPARAM, LPARAM );
    BOOL CALLBACK SetConverge( HWND, UINT, WPARAM, LPARAM );
    BOOL CALLBACK SetDisplay( HWND, UINT, WPARAM, LPARAM );
    BOOL CALLBACK SetEntityDir( HWND, UINT, WPARAM, LPARAM );
    BOOL CALLBACK SetView( HWND, UINT, WPARAM, LPARAM );
}

#endif
```

Note the use of the *extern "C"* mechanism. This is the one C++ language feature that makes writing MS-Windows applications using (mostly) generic C++ possible.

Next, and with no apologies for its length, is the (again, mostly) C source for *HELIOS*. Thanks to the intimate relation between C and C++, HELIOS.CPP can be compiled as a C++ program.

Listing 4.23

```
// HELIOS.CPP - Radiosity Renderer for MS-Windows

#include <windows.h>
#include <windowsx.h>
#include <commdlg.h>
#include <stdio.h>
#include <math.h>
#include <time.h>
#include "error.h"
#include "spheric3.h"
#include "parse.h"
#include "syn_cam.h"
#include "win_meta.h"
#include "win_bmap.h"
#include "win_sbar.h"

#if (defined(_HEMI_CUBE) || defined(_CUBIC_TETRA))
#include "prog_rad.h"
#elif defined(_RAY_CAST)
#include "ray_rad.h"
#else
#include "rad_eqn.h"
#endif

#include "resource.h"
#include "helios.h"

static char EntityDir[MaxLen];      // Entity directory
static char WorldName[MaxLen];      // World file name buffer
static char BitmapName[MaxLen];     // Bitmap file name buffer
static char FileTitle[MaxLen];      // File title buffer
static char StrBuffer[MaxLen];      // Temporary string buffer
static HINSTANCE hInst;             // Current instance handle
static OPENFILENAME Ofn;            // Open filename structure
```

(continued)

Listing 4.23   *(continued)*

```
// Synthetic camera
static SynCamera Camera(640, 480, -180.0, 90.0, 0.0, 0.0);

static Environ Environment;      // Environment
static Parse Parser;             // World file parser
static WinMetaFile Wire;         // Metafile manager
static WinBitmap Bitmap;         // Bitmap file manager

// Radiosity equation solver
#if (defined(_HEMI_CUBE) || defined(_CUBIC_TETRA))
static ProgRad Radiosity;        // Progressive radiosity
#elif defined(_RAY_CAST)
static RayRad Radiosity;         // Ray cast radiosity
#else
static RadEqnSolve Radiosity;    // Dummy equation solver
#endif

static const char AppName[] = "HELIOS";
static const char BitmapSection[] = "Bitmap";
static const char EyeDistError[] = "Front distance is "
    "behind eye position";
static const char FrontDistError[] = "Front distance must "
    "be greater than zero";
static const char GammaError[] = "Gamma value must be "
    "greater than zero";
static const char HeightEntry[] = "Height";
static const char HorzError[] = "Horizontal angles must be "
    "between -180 and 180 degrees";
static const char InitFileName[] = "HELIOS.INI";
static const char MaxStepError[] = "Maximum number of "
    "steps must be between 1 and 2000";
static const char NoiseError[] = "Noise level must be "
    "between 0 and 8";
static const char PixelError[] = "Pixel values must be "
    "between 32 and 1024";
static const char StopError[] = "Stopping criterion must be"
    "between 0.0 and 1.0";
static const char WidthEntry[] = "Width";
static const char VertError[] = "Vertical angles must be "
    "between 0 and 180 degrees";
static const char ViewDirName[] = "View Direction";
static const char ViewDistError[] = "View distance must be "
    "greater than zero";
static const char ViewUpName[] = "View Up Vector";
static const char ViewUpError[] = "View-up vector is "
    "collinear with view direction vector";
static const char WireClass[] = "WIRE";
```

```
// File type filters
static const char InputFilterSpec[128] =
    "World Files (*.WLD)\0*.WLD\0All Files (*.*)\0*.*\0";
static const char OutputFilterSpec[128] =
    "BMP Files (*.BMP)\0*.BMP\0All Files (*.*)\0*.*\0";

static const int MaxStep = 2000;
static const int MinPixel = 32;
static const int MaxPixel = 1024;

int WINAPI WinMain( HINSTANCE hinstance, HINSTANCE hpinst,
    LPSTR pcmdline, int cmdshow )
{
  MSG msg;        // Window message

  // Other instances of application running ?
  if (!hpinst)
    if (!InitApplication(hinstance))
      return FALSE;

  // Initialize current instance
  if (!InitInstance(hinstance, cmdshow))
      return FALSE;

  // Process window messages
  while (GetMessage(&msg, NULL, NULL, NULL))
  {
    TranslateMessage(&msg);
    DispatchMessage(&msg);
  }
  return (int) msg.wParam;
}

// Initialize window data and register window classes
static BOOL InitApplication( HINSTANCE hinstance )
{
  WNDCLASS wc;  // Window class

  // Register main window class
  wc.style = CS_VREDRAW | CS_HREDRAW;
  wc.lpfnWndProc = (WNDPROC) MainWndProc;
  wc.cbClsExtra = 0;
  wc.cbWndExtra = 0;
  wc.hInstance = hinstance;
  wc.hIcon = LoadIcon(NULL, IDI_APPLICATION);
  wc.hCursor = LoadCursor(NULL, IDC_ARROW);
  wc.hbrBackground = GetStockObject(LTGRAY_BRUSH);
  wc.lpszMenuName = "HeliosMenu";
  wc.lpszClassName = AppName;

  if (!RegisterClass(&wc))
    return FALSE;
```

(continued)

Listing 4.23   *(continued)*

```
  // Register wireframe window class
  wc.lpfnWndProc = (WNDPROC) WireWndProc;
  wc.hIcon = NULL;
  wc.hbrBackground = GetStockObject(WHITE_BRUSH);
  wc.lpszClassName = WireClass;

  return (RegisterClass(&wc) ? TRUE : FALSE);
}

// Save instance handle and create main window
static BOOL InitInstance( HINSTANCE hinstance, int
    cmdshow )
{
  HWND hwnd;     // Main window handle

  hInst = hinstance;     // Save current instance handle

  // Create main window for current instance
  hwnd = CreateWindow(AppName, "HELIOS Radiosity "
      "Renderer", WS_OVERLAPPEDWINDOW | WS_VSCROLL |
      WS_HSCROLL, CW_USEDEFAULT, CW_USEDEFAULT,
      CW_USEDEFAULT, CW_USEDEFAULT, NULL, NULL, hinstance,
      NULL);

  if (hwnd == 0)
    return FALSE;

  // Initialize open filename structure
  Ofn.lStructSize = sizeof(OPENFILENAME);
  Ofn.hwndOwner = hwnd;
  Ofn.lpstrFilter = NULL;
  Ofn.lpstrCustomFilter = NULL;
  Ofn.nMaxCustFilter = 0;
  Ofn.nFilterIndex = 1;
  Ofn.lpstrFile = NULL;
  Ofn.nMaxFile = MaxLen;
  Ofn.lpstrInitialDir = NULL;
  Ofn.lpstrFileTitle = FileTitle;
  Ofn.nMaxFileTitle = MaxLen;
  Ofn.lpstrTitle = NULL;
  Ofn.lpstrDefExt = NULL;
  Ofn.Flags = 0;

  ShowWindow(hwnd, cmdshow);     // Show the window
  UpdateWindow(hwnd);            // Paint the client area

  return TRUE;
}
```

```
// Main window message handler
LRESULT WINAPI MainWndProc( HWND hwnd, UINT msg, WPARAM
    wparam, LPARAM lparam )
{
  static short xclient;           // Client area width
  static short yclient;           // Client area height
  static short xwire;             // Wireframe window width
  static short ywire;             // Wireframe window height
  static int d_type = H_NONE;     // Display type
  static HWND hwnd_wire;          // Wireframe window handle
  static WinScroll *pscroll;      // Scroll bar manager ptr
  BOOL redraw;                    // Redraw flag
  FARPROC pfunc;                  // Exported fcn prolog ptr
  HCURSOR hcursor;                // Cursor handle
  HDC hdc;                        // Device context handle
  HMENU hmenu;                    // Menu handle
  PAINTSTRUCT ps;                 // Window paint structure
  POINT pos;                      // Point co-ordinates
  RECT rc;                        // Rectangle co-ordinates

  switch (msg)
  {
    case WM_CREATE:      // Create window
      // Instantiate scroll bar manager
      pscroll = new WinScroll(hwnd);
      break;
    case WM_SIZE:        // Get client area dimensions
      xclient = LOWORD(lparam);
      yclient = HIWORD(lparam);
      switch (d_type)
      {
        case H_WIRE:
          // Update wireframe display
          CalcWireDim(xclient, yclient, &xwire, &ywire);
          MoveWindow(hwnd_wire, Offset, Offset, xwire,
              ywire, TRUE);
          break;
        case H_BMAP:
          // Set scroll bar manager
          pscroll->Set(Camera.GetWidth(),
              Camera.GetHeight());
          break;
        default:
          break;
      }
      break;
    case WM_PAINT:       // Paint client area
      hdc = BeginPaint(hwnd, &ps);
      if (d_type == H_BMAP)            // Display bitmap ?
      {
```

(continued)

Listing 4.23   *(continued)*

```
      GetClientRect(hwnd, &rc);
      pos = pscroll->Pos();
      if (Bitmap.Display(hdc, pos, rc) == FALSE)
      {
        d_type = H_NONE;
        pscroll->Hide();
      }
    }
    EndPaint(hwnd, &ps);
    break;
  case WM_HSCROLL:      // Process horz scroll bar message
    pscroll->Horz(wparam, GET_WM_HSCROLL_POS(wparam,
        lparam));
    break;
  case WM_VSCROLL:      // Process vertical scroll bar msg
    pscroll->Vert(wparam, GET_WM_VSCROLL_POS(wparam,
        lparam));
    break;
  case WM_KEYDOWN:      // Process key down message
    DoKeyDown(hwnd, wparam);
    break;
  case WM_COMMAND:      // Process window message
    hmenu = GetMenu(hwnd);      // Get menu handle
    switch (GET_WM_COMMAND_ID(wparam, lparam))
    {
      case IDM_FILEOPEN:        // Open file
        Ofn.lpstrDefExt = "WLD";
        Ofn.lpstrFilter = InputFilterSpec;
        Ofn.lpstrFile = WorldName;
        Ofn.Flags = OFN_HIDEREADONLY | OFN_READONLY;
        if (GetOpenFileName((LPOPENFILENAME) &Ofn))
        {
          switch (d_type)
          {
            case H_WIRE:
              // Erase wireframe metafile
              Wire.Erase();
              d_type = H_NONE;

              // Destroy wireframe window
              DestroyWindow(hwnd_wire);
              break;
            case H_BMAP:
              Bitmap.Close();        // Close bitmap
              d_type = H_NONE;
              pscroll->Hide();       // Hide scroll bars

              // Disable Save As menu item
              EnableMenuItem(hmenu, IDM_SAVEAS,
                  MF_GRAYED);
```

```
                    InvalidateRect(hwnd, NULL, TRUE);
                    break;
                default:
                    break;
            }

            // Parse environment file
            if ((Parser.ParseFile(Ofn.lpstrFile, EntityDir,
                &Environment)) == TRUE)
            {
                // Display environment statistics
                wsprintf(StrBuffer, "Number of Instances = "
                    "%u\nNumber of Surfaces = %u\nNumber of"
                    " Patches = %u\nNumber of Elements = %u\n"
                    "Number of Vertices = %u",
                    Environment.GetNumInst(),
                    Environment.GetNumSurf(),
                    Environment.GetNumPatch(),
                    Environment.GetNumElem(),
                    Environment.GetNumVert());
                MessageBox(hwnd, StrBuffer,
                    "Environment Statistics", MB_OK |
                    MB_ICONINFORMATION);

                // Update window title
                wsprintf(StrBuffer, "HELIOS - %s",
                    Ofn.lpstrFile);
                SetWindowText(hwnd, StrBuffer);

                // Enable rendering menu items
                EnableMenuItem(hmenu, IDM_WIREFRAME,
                    MF_ENABLED);
                EnableMenuItem(hmenu, IDM_SHADED,
                    MF_ENABLED);
                EnableMenuItem(hmenu, IDM_RENDER,
                    MF_ENABLED);

                // Disable Redisplay menu item
                EnableMenuItem(hmenu, IDM_REDISPLAY,
                    MF_GRAYED);
            }
        }
        break;
    case IDM_SAVEAS:          // Save BMP file
        Ofn.lpstrDefExt = "BMP";
        Ofn.lpstrFilter = OutputFilterSpec;
        Ofn.lpstrFile = BitmapName;
        Ofn.Flags = OFN_OVERWRITEPROMPT |
            OFN_HIDEREADONLY;
        if (GetSaveFileName((LPOPENFILENAME) &Ofn))
        {
            // Write bitmap file
            if (Bitmap.Write(Ofn.lpstrFile) == FALSE)
            {
```

(continued)

Listing 4.23 *(continued)*

```
              sprintf(StrBuffer, "Could not save file %s",
                  Ofn.lpstrFile);
              ReportError(StrBuffer);
          }
      }
      break;
  case IDM_EXIT:                // Exit application
      DestroyWindow(hwnd);
      break;
  case IDM_SETCAMERA:          // Set camera parameters
      pfunc = (DLGPROC) MakeProcInstance((FARPROC)
          SetCamera, hInst);
      redraw = DialogBox(hInst, "SetCamera", hwnd,
          pfunc);
      FreeProcInstance((FARPROC) pfunc);
      if (redraw == TRUE)
      {
        if (d_type == H_BMAP)
        {
          Bitmap.Close();     // Close bitmap
          d_type = H_NONE;
          pscroll->Hide();    // Hide scroll bars

          // Disable Save As menu item
          EnableMenuItem(hmenu, IDM_SAVEAS, MF_GRAYED);

          InvalidateRect(hwnd, NULL, TRUE);
        }

        if (d_type == H_WIRE)
        {
          // Record wireframe display
          Camera.Preview(Environment.GetInstPtr(),
              &Wire);

          // Resize and redraw wireframe window
          InvalidateRect(hwnd_wire, NULL, TRUE);
          CalcWireDim(xclient, yclient, &xwire, &ywire);
          MoveWindow(hwnd_wire, Offset, Offset, xwire,
              ywire, TRUE);
        }
      }
      break;
  case IDM_SETVIEW:            // Specify view direction
      pfunc = (DLGPROC) MakeProcInstance((FARPROC)
          SetView, hInst);
      redraw = DialogBox(hInst, "SetView", hwnd,
          pfunc);
      FreeProcInstance((FARPROC) pfunc);
      if (redraw == TRUE)
      {
```

```
      if (d_type == H_BMAP)
      {
        Bitmap.Close();    // Close bitmap
        d_type = H_NONE;
        pscroll->Hide();   // Hide scroll bars

        // Disable Save As menu item
        EnableMenuItem(hmenu, IDM_SAVEAS, MF_GRAYED);

        InvalidateRect(hwnd, NULL, TRUE);
      }

      if (d_type == H_WIRE)
      {
        // Record wireframe display
        Camera.Preview(Environment.GetInstPtr(),
            &Wire);
        InvalidateRect(hwnd_wire, NULL, TRUE);
      }
    }
    break;
  case IDM_WIREFRAME:     // Wireframe display
    if (d_type != H_WIRE)
    {
      if (d_type == H_BMAP)
      {
        Bitmap.Close();    // Close bitmap
        d_type = H_NONE;
        pscroll->Hide();   // Hide scroll bars

        // Disable Save As menu item
        EnableMenuItem(hmenu, IDM_SAVEAS, MF_GRAYED);

        InvalidateRect(hwnd, NULL, TRUE);
      }

      // Create wireframe window
      CalcWireDim(xclient, yclient, &xwire,
          &ywire);
      hwnd_wire = CreateWindow(WireClass, NULL,
          WS_CHILD | WS_VISIBLE | WS_BORDER |
          WS_DISABLED, Offset, Offset, xwire, ywire,
              hwnd, NULL, hInst, NULL);
      d_type = H_WIRE;

      // Record wireframe display
      if (Camera.Preview(Environment.GetInstPtr(),
          &Wire) == FALSE)
        OutOfMemory();
    }
```

(continued)

Listing 4.23   *(continued)*

```
      break;
   case IDM_SHADED:          // Shaded display
   case IDM_RENDER:          // Radiosity rendering
     // Display hourglass cursor
     hcursor = SetCursor(LoadCursor(NULL, IDC_WAIT));

     if (wparam == IDM_RENDER)
     {
       // Confirm radiosity equation solver status
       if (Radiosity.GetStatus() == FALSE)
       {
         OutOfMemory();
         break;
       }

       // Initialize equation solver
       if (Radiosity.Open(&Environment) == FALSE)
       {
         OutOfMemory();
         break;
       }

       // Perform radiosity calculations
       while (Radiosity.Calculate() == FALSE)
         ;

       // Close radiosity equation solver
       Radiosity.Close();

       // Disable Rendering menu item
       EnableMenuItem(hmenu, IDM_RENDER, MF_GRAYED);
     }
     else
     {
       // Set vertice exitances to parent surface
       // reflectances
       Radiosity.Shade(Environment.GetInstPtr());

       // Enable Rendering menu item
       EnableMenuItem(hmenu, IDM_RENDER, MF_ENABLED);
     }

     // Open bitmap
     if (Bitmap.Open(Camera.GetWidth(),
         Camera.GetHeight()) == TRUE)
     {
       // Record shaded display
       if (Camera.Shoot(Environment.GetInstPtr(),
           &Bitmap) == TRUE)
       {
         if (d_type == H_WIRE)
         {
```

```
                   // Erase wireframe metafile (if any)
                   Wire.Erase();

                   // Destroy wireframe window
                   DestroyWindow(hwnd_wire);
                 }

                 d_type = H_BMAP;

                 // Initialize scroll bar manager
                 pscroll->Init(Camera.GetWidth(),
                     Camera.GetHeight());

                 // Enable bitmap Redisplay menu item
                 EnableMenuItem(hmenu, IDM_REDISPLAY,
                     MF_ENABLED);

                 // Enable Save As menu item
                 EnableMenuItem(hmenu, IDM_SAVEAS, MF_ENABLED);

                 // Display bitmap (via WM_PAINT)
                 InvalidateRect(hwnd, NULL, TRUE);
               }

               SetCursor(hcursor);       // Redisplay old cursor

               if (d_type == H_BMAP)     // Check for error
               {
                 if (wparam == IDM_RENDER)
                 {
                   MessageBeep(MB_OK);        // Signal completion

                   // Display convergence statistics
                   sprintf(StrBuffer, "Number of Steps = %d\n"
                       "Convergence = %f",
                   Radiosity.GetStepCount(),
                   Radiosity.GetConvergence());

                   MessageBox(hwnd, StrBuffer, "Convergence "
                       "Statistics", MB_OK |
                       MB_ICONINFORMATION);
                 }
               }
               else
                 OutOfMemory();
             }
             break;
           case IDM_REDISPLAY:      // Redisplay bitmap
             // Display hourglass cursor
             hcursor = SetCursor(LoadCursor(NULL, IDC_WAIT));

             // Open bitmap
             if (Bitmap.Open(Camera.GetWidth(),
                 Camera.GetHeight()) == TRUE)
             {
```

(continued)

Listing 4.23   *(continued)*

```
                // Record shaded display
                if (Camera.Shoot(Environment.GetInstPtr(),
                    &Bitmap) == TRUE)
                {
                  if (d_type == H_WIRE)
                  {
                    // Erase wireframe metafile (if any)
                    Wire.Erase();

                    // Destroy wireframe window
                    DestroyWindow(hwnd_wire);
                  }

                  d_type = H_BMAP;

                  // Initialize scroll bar manager
                  pscroll->Init(Camera.GetWidth(),
                      Camera.GetHeight());

                  // Enable Save As menu item
                  EnableMenuItem(hmenu, IDM_SAVEAS, MF_ENABLED);

                  // Display bitmap (via WM_PAINT)
                  InvalidateRect(hwnd, NULL, TRUE);
                }

                SetCursor(hcursor);        // Redisplay old cursor
              }
              break;
            case IDM_DIRECTORY:        // Set entity directory
              pfunc = (DLGPROC) MakeProcInstance((FARPROC)
                  SetEntityDir, hInst);
              DialogBox(hInst, "SetEntityDir", hwnd, pfunc);
              FreeProcInstance((FARPROC) pfunc);
              break;
            case IDM_SETCONVERGE:      // Set convergence
              pfunc = (DLGPROC) MakeProcInstance((FARPROC)
                  SetConverge, hInst);
              redraw = DialogBox(hInst, "SetConverge", hwnd,
                  pfunc);
              FreeProcInstance((FARPROC) pfunc);
              if (redraw == TRUE)
              {
                // Enable Rendering menu item
                EnableMenuItem(hmenu, IDM_RENDER, MF_ENABLED);
              }
              break;
            case IDM_SETDISPLAY:       // Set display parameters
              pfunc = (DLGPROC) MakeProcInstance((FARPROC)
                  SetDisplay, hInst);
              DialogBox(hInst, "SetDisplay", hwnd, pfunc);
              FreeProcInstance((FARPROC) pfunc);
              break;
```

```
          case IDM_ABOUT:              // Display About box
            pfunc = (DLGPROC) MakeProcInstance((FARPROC)
                About, hInst);
            DialogBox(hInst, "AboutBox", hwnd, pfunc);
            FreeProcInstance((FARPROC) pfunc);
            break;
          default:
            break;
        }
        break;
      case WM_DESTROY:      // Destroy window
        delete pscroll;              // Delete scroll bar manager
        Wire.Erase();                // Erase wireframe metafile
        Bitmap.Close();              // Release bitmap memory
        PostQuitMessage(0);
        break;
      default:
        return DefWindowProc(hwnd, msg, wparam, lparam);
    }
    return NULL;
}

// Wireframe window message handler
LRESULT WINAPI WireWndProc( HWND hwnd, UINT msg, WPARAM
    wparam, LPARAM lparam )
{
  static short xclient;         // Client area width
  static short yclient;         // Client area height

  switch (msg)
  {
    case WM_SIZE:
      xclient = LOWORD(lparam);
      yclient = HIWORD(lparam);
      break;
    case WM_PAINT:        // Paint client area
      Wire.Play(hwnd, Camera.GetWidth(), Camera.GetHeight(),
          xclient, yclient);
      break;
    default:
      return DefWindowProc(hwnd, msg, wparam, lparam);
  }
  return NULL;
}

// Set entities directory
BOOL CALLBACK SetEntityDir( HWND hdlg, UINT msg, WPARAM
    wparam, LPARAM lparam )
{
  switch (msg)
  {
```

(continued)

Listing 4.23   *(continued)*

```
    case WM_INITDIALOG:
        SetDlgItemText(hdlg, IDC_ENTITY, EntityDir);
      return TRUE;
    case WM_COMMAND:
      switch (GET_WM_COMMAND_ID(wparam, lparam))
      {
        case IDOK:
          GetDlgItemText(hdlg, IDC_ENTITY, EntityDir,
              sizeof(EntityDir));
          EndDialog(hdlg, TRUE);
          return TRUE;
        case IDCANCEL:
          EndDialog(hdlg, FALSE);
          return TRUE;
        default:
          break;
      }
      break;
    default:
      break;
  }
  return FALSE;
}

// Set camera parameters
BOOL CALLBACK SetCamera( HWND hdlg, UINT msg, WPARAM
    wparam, LPARAM lparam )
{
  double vpd, fpd, bpd;        // Camera distances
  int w, h;                    // Bitmap window dimensions
  BOOL dummy;                  // Dummy parameter

  switch (msg)
  {
    case WM_INITDIALOG:
      // Get camera distances
      SetDlgItemFloat(hdlg, IDC_VDIST,
          Camera.GetViewDist());
      SetDlgItemFloat(hdlg, IDC_FDIST,
          Camera.GetFrontDist());
      SetDlgItemFloat(hdlg, IDC_BDIST,
          Camera.GetBackDist());

      // Get bitmap window dimensions
      SetDlgItemInt(hdlg, IDC_HPIXSZ, Camera.GetWidth(),
          FALSE);
      SetDlgItemInt(hdlg, IDC_VPIXSZ, Camera.GetHeight(),
          FALSE);
```

```
    return TRUE;
case WM_COMMAND:
  switch (GET_WM_COMMAND_ID(wparam, lparam))
  {
    case IDOK:
      // Validate distances
      vpd = GetDlgItemFloat(hdlg, IDC_VDIST);
      fpd = GetDlgItemFloat(hdlg, IDC_FDIST);
      bpd = GetDlgItemFloat(hdlg, IDC_BDIST);

      if (vpd <= 0.0)
      {
        MessageBox(hdlg, ViewDistError, AppName,
            MB_ICONEXCLAMATION | MB_OK);
        return FALSE;
      }

      if (fpd >= bpd)
      {
        MessageBox(hdlg, FrontDistError, AppName,
            MB_ICONEXCLAMATION | MB_OK);
        return FALSE;
      }

      if (fpd < -(vpd - MIN_VALUE))
      {
        MessageBox(hdlg, EyeDistError, AppName,
            MB_ICONEXCLAMATION | MB_OK);
        return FALSE;
      }

      // Validate bitmap window dimensions
      w =  (int) GetDlgItemInt(hdlg, IDC_HPIXSZ, &dummy,
          FALSE);
      h =  (int) GetDlgItemInt(hdlg, IDC_VPIXSZ, &dummy,
          FALSE);
      if (w < MinPixel || w > MaxPixel || h < MinPixel
          || h > MaxPixel)
      {
        MessageBox(hdlg, PixelError, AppName,
            MB_ICONEXCLAMATION | MB_OK);
        return FALSE;
      }

      // Set distances
      Camera.SetViewDist(vpd);
      Camera.SetFrontDist(fpd);
      Camera.SetBackDist(bpd);

      // Set bitmap window dimensions
      Camera.SetWidth(w);
      Camera.SetHeight(h);
```

(continued)

Listing 4.23   *(continued)*

```
            // Update view system parameters
            Camera.UpdateViewSystem();

            EndDialog(hdlg, TRUE);
            return TRUE;
          case IDCANCEL:
            EndDialog(hdlg, FALSE);
            return TRUE;
          default:
            break;
      }
      break;
    default:
      break;
  }
  return FALSE;
}

// Set camera view direction
BOOL CALLBACK SetView( HWND hdlg, UINT msg, WPARAM
    wparam, LPARAM lparam )
{
  double vdvv;          // View dir vert angle (degrees)
  double vdvh;          // View dir horz angle (degrees)
  double vupv;          // View-up vert angle (degrees)
  double vuph;          // View-up horz angle (degrees)
  Point3 eye_posn;      // Camera eye position
  Vector3 view_dir;     // View direction vector
  Vector3 view_up;      // View-up vector
  Spheric3 vdv_angle;   // View direction angles (radians)
  Spheric3 vup_angle;   // View-up vector angles (radians)

  switch (msg)
  {
    case WM_INITDIALOG:
      // Get camera eye position
      eye_posn = Camera.GetEyePosn();
      SetDlgItemFloat(hdlg, IDC_XPOS, eye_posn.GetX());
      SetDlgItemFloat(hdlg, IDC_YPOS, eye_posn.GetY());
      SetDlgItemFloat(hdlg, IDC_ZPOS, eye_posn.GetZ());

      // Get view direction vector angles
      SetDlgItemFloat(hdlg, IDC_VDVV,
          Camera.GetViewDirVert());
      SetDlgItemFloat(hdlg, IDC_VDVH,
          Camera.GetViewDirHorz());

      // Get view-up vector angles
      SetDlgItemFloat(hdlg, IDC_VUPV,
          Camera.GetViewUpVert());
      SetDlgItemFloat(hdlg, IDC_VUPH,
          Camera.GetViewUpHorz());
```

```
      return TRUE;
case WM_COMMAND:
  switch (GET_WM_COMMAND_ID(wparam, lparam))
  {
    case IDOK:
      // Get eye position
      eye_posn.SetX(GetDlgItemFloat(hdlg, IDC_XPOS));
      eye_posn.SetY(GetDlgItemFloat(hdlg, IDC_YPOS));
      eye_posn.SetZ(GetDlgItemFloat(hdlg, IDC_ZPOS));

      // Validate view direction angles
      vdvv = GetDlgItemFloat(hdlg, IDC_VDVV);
      vdvh = GetDlgItemFloat(hdlg, IDC_VDVH);

      if (vdvv < 0.0 || vdvv > 180.0)
      {
        MessageBox(hdlg, VertError, ViewDirName, MB_OK |
            MB_ICONEXCLAMATION);
        return FALSE;
      }

      if (vdvh < -180.0 || vdvh > 180.0)
      {
        MessageBox(hdlg, HorzError, ViewDirName, MB_OK
            | MB_ICONEXCLAMATION);
        return FALSE;
      }

      vdv_angle.SetVert(DegToRad(vdvv));
      vdv_angle.SetHorz(DegToRad(vdvh));
      vdv_angle.SpherToRect(&view_dir);

      // Validate view-up angles
      vupv = GetDlgItemFloat(hdlg, IDC_VUPV);
      vuph = GetDlgItemFloat(hdlg, IDC_VUPH);

      if (vupv < 0.0 || vupv > 180.0)
      {
        MessageBox(hdlg, VertError, ViewUpName, MB_OK |
            MB_ICONEXCLAMATION);
        return FALSE;
      }

      if (vuph < -180.0 || vuph > 180.0)
      {
        MessageBox(hdlg, HorzError, ViewUpName, MB_OK |
            MB_ICONEXCLAMATION);
        return FALSE;
      }

      vup_angle.SetVert(DegToRad(vupv));
      vup_angle.SetHorz(DegToRad(vuph));
```

(continued)

Listing 4.23 *(continued)*

```
            // Check for collinear vectors
            vup_angle.SpherToRect(&view_up);

            if ((1.0 - fabs(Dot(view_dir, view_up))) <
                MIN_VALUE)
            {
              MessageBox(hdlg, ViewUpError, AppName, MB_OK |
                  MB_ICONEXCLAMATION);
              return FALSE;
            }

            // Set camera view parameters
            Camera.SetEyePosn(eye_posn);
            Camera.SetViewDirVector(vdvh, vdvv);
            Camera.SetViewUpVector(vuph, vupv);

            // Update view system parameters
            Camera.UpdateViewSystem();

            EndDialog(hdlg, TRUE);
            return TRUE;
          case IDCANCEL:
            EndDialog(hdlg, FALSE);
            return TRUE;
          default:
            break;
        }
      break;
    default:
      break;
  }
  return FALSE;
}

// Set radiosity rendering convergence parameters
BOOL CALLBACK SetConverge( HWND hdlg, UINT msg, WPARAM
    wparam, LPARAM lparam )
{
  int mp;        // Maximum number of steps
  double sc;     // Stopping criterion
  BOOL dummy;    // Dummy parameter

  switch (msg)
  {
```

```
case WM_INITDIALOG:
  SetDlgItemInt(hdlg, IDC_MSTEP, Radiosity.GetMaxStep(),
      FALSE);
  SetDlgItemFloat(hdlg, IDC_STOPC,
      Radiosity.GetStopCriterion());
  CheckDlgButton(hdlg, IDC_AMBIENT_EN,
      Radiosity.AmbientFlag());
  if (Radiosity.OverShootFlag() == TRUE)
    CheckDlgButton(hdlg, IDC_OVER_EN, TRUE);
  return TRUE;
case WM_COMMAND:
  switch (GET_WM_COMMAND_ID(wparam, lparam))
  {
    case IDOK:
      // Validate parameters
      mp = GetDlgItemInt(hdlg, IDC_MSTEP, &dummy, TRUE);
      sc = GetDlgItemFloat(hdlg, IDC_STOPC);

      if (mp < 1 || mp > MaxStep)
      {
        MessageBox(hdlg, MaxStepError, AppName,
            MB_ICONEXCLAMATION | MB_OK);
        return FALSE;
      }

      if (sc <= 0.0 || sc > 1.0)
      {
        MessageBox(hdlg, StopError, AppName,
            MB_ICONEXCLAMATION | MB_OK);
        return FALSE;
      }

      // Set convergence parameters
      Radiosity.SetMaxStep(mp);
      Radiosity.SetStopCriterion(sc);

      if (IsDlgButtonChecked(hdlg, IDC_AMBIENT_EN) != 0)
        Radiosity.EnableAmbient();
      else
        Radiosity.DisableAmbient();

      if (IsDlgButtonChecked(hdlg, IDC_OVER_EN) != 0)
        Radiosity.EnableOverShoot();
      else
        Radiosity.DisableOverShoot();

      EndDialog(hdlg, TRUE);
      return TRUE;
    case IDCANCEL:
      EndDialog(hdlg, FALSE);
      return TRUE;
    default:
      break;
  }
```

(continued)

Listing 4.23   *(continued)*

```
        break;
    default:
        break;
    }
    return FALSE;
}

// Set display parameters
BOOL CALLBACK SetDisplay( HWND hdlg, UINT msg, WPARAM
    wparam, LPARAM lparam )
{
    double gamma;          // Gamma value
    int noise;             // Noise level
    BOOL dummy;            // Dummy parameter
    static int c_type;     // Display color type

    switch (msg)
    {
      case WM_INITDIALOG:
        c_type = Camera.GetColorType();
        CheckDlgButton(hdlg, IDC_GAMMA_EN,
            Camera.GammaFlag());
        SetDlgItemFloat(hdlg, IDC_GAMMA, Camera.GetGamma());
        CheckDlgButton(hdlg, IDC_JITTER_EN,
            Camera.JitterFlag());
        SetDlgItemInt(hdlg, IDC_JITTER,
            Camera.GetNoiseLevel(), FALSE);
        CheckRadioButton(hdlg, IDC_RGB, IDC_PSEUDO, c_type +
            IDC_RGB);
        return TRUE;
      case WM_COMMAND:
        switch (GET_WM_COMMAND_ID(wparam, lparam))
        {
          case IDC_RGB:
          case IDC_MONO:
          case IDC_PSEUDO:
            c_type = wparam - IDC_RGB;
            CheckRadioButton(hdlg, IDC_RGB, IDC_PSEUDO,
                wparam);
            break;
          case IDOK:
            if (IsDlgButtonChecked(hdlg, IDC_GAMMA_EN) != 0)
              Camera.EnableGamma();
            else
              Camera.DisableGamma();

            gamma = GetDlgItemFloat(hdlg, IDC_GAMMA);

            if (gamma <= 0.0)
            {
```

```
                MessageBox(hdlg, GammaError, AppName,
                    MB_ICONEXCLAMATION | MB_OK);
                return FALSE;
            }

            // Set gamma correction parameter
            Camera.SetGamma(gamma);

            if (IsDlgButtonChecked(hdlg, IDC_JITTER_EN) != 0)
                Camera.EnableJitter();
            else
                Camera.DisableJitter();

            noise = GetDlgItemInt(hdlg, IDC_JITTER, &dummy,
                TRUE);

            if (noise < 0 || noise > 8)
            {
                MessageBox(hdlg, NoiseError, AppName,
                    MB_ICONEXCLAMATION | MB_OK);
                return FALSE;
            }

            // Set noise level parameter
            Camera.SetNoiseLevel(noise);

            // Set display color type
            Camera.SetColorType(c_type);

            EndDialog(hdlg, TRUE);
            return TRUE;
        case IDCANCEL:
            EndDialog(hdlg, FALSE);
            return TRUE;
        default:
            break;
        }
        break;
    default:
        break;
    }
    return FALSE;
}

// Display About dialog box
BOOL CALLBACK About( HWND hdlg, UINT msg, WPARAM wparam,
    LPARAM lparam )
{
    switch (msg)
    {
```

(continued)

Listing 4.23 *(continued)*

```
    case WM_INITDIALOG:
      return TRUE;
    case WM_COMMAND:
      if (wparam == IDOK || wparam == IDCANCEL)
      {
        EndDialog(hdlg, TRUE);
        return TRUE;
      }
      break;
    default:
      break;
  }
  return FALSE;
}

// Get floating point dialog item
static double GetDlgItemFloat( HWND hdlg, int id )
{
  (void) GetDlgItemText(hdlg, id, StrBuffer,
      sizeof(StrBuffer));
  return atof(StrBuffer);
}

// Set floating point dialog item
static void SetDlgItemFloat( HWND hdlg, int id, double num )
{
  sprintf(StrBuffer, "%6.5f", num);
  SetDlgItemText(hdlg, id, StrBuffer);
}

// Calculate wireframe window dimensions
void CalcWireDim( short xclient, short yclient, short
    *pxchild, short *pychild )
{
  double client_aspect;
  double child_aspect;

  if (yclient > 0)
  {
    client_aspect = (double) xclient / (double) yclient;
    child_aspect = (double) Camera.GetWidth() / (double)
        Camera.GetHeight();
    if (client_aspect >= child_aspect)
    {
      *pychild = (short) max(yclient - Offset * 2, Offset);
      *pxchild = (short) ((double) *pychild * child_aspect);
    }
    else
    {
```

```
      *pxchild = (short) max(xclient - Offset * 2, Offset);
      *pychild = (short) ((double) *pxchild / child_aspect);
    }
  }
  else
    *pxchild = *pychild = Offset;
}

// Process WM_KEYDOWN message
void DoKeyDown( HWND hwnd, WPARAM wparam )
{
  switch (GET_WM_COMMAND_ID(wparam, lparam))
  {
    case VK_HOME:
      SendMessage(hwnd, WM_VSCROLL, SB_TOP, 0L);
      break;
    case VK_END:
      SendMessage(hwnd, WM_VSCROLL, SB_BOTTOM, 0L);
      break;
    case VK_PRIOR:
      SendMessage(hwnd, WM_VSCROLL, SB_PAGEUP, 0L);
      break;
    case VK_NEXT:
      SendMessage(hwnd, WM_VSCROLL, SB_PAGEDOWN, 0L);
      break;
    case VK_UP:
      SendMessage(hwnd, WM_VSCROLL, SB_LINEUP, 0L);
      break;
    case VK_DOWN:
      SendMessage(hwnd, WM_VSCROLL, SB_LINEDOWN, 0L);
      break;
    case VK_LEFT:
      SendMessage(hwnd, WM_HSCROLL, SB_PAGEUP, 0L);
      break;
    case VK_RIGHT:
      SendMessage(hwnd, WM_HSCROLL, SB_PAGEDOWN, 0L);
      break;
  }
}
```

Being an MS-Windows program, *HELIOS* needs a few additional files. Its menus and dialog boxes are defined in its "resource script" file, HELIOS.RC. This file is compiled separately and appended to the executable file during the linking process.

RESOURCE.H is an include file for HELIOS.RC:

Listing 4.24

```
// RESOURCE.H - HELIOS.RC Include File

#ifndef _RESOURCE_H
#define _RESOURCE_H

#define IDM_FILEOPEN     100
#define IDM_SAVEAS       101
#define IDM_EXIT         102
#define IDM_DIRECTORY    103
#define IDM_SETCAMERA    104
#define IDM_SETVIEW      105
#define IDM_WIREFRAME    106
#define IDM_SHADED       107
#define IDM_RENDER       108
#define IDM_REDISPLAY    109
#define IDM_SETCONVERGE  110
#define IDM_SETDISPLAY   111
#define IDM_ABOUT        112
#define IDC_XPOS         1000
#define IDC_YPOS         1001
#define IDC_ZPOS         1002
#define IDC_VDVV         1003
#define IDC_VDVH         1004
#define IDC_VUPV         1005
#define IDC_VUPH         1006
#define IDC_VDIST        1007
#define IDC_FDIST        1008
#define IDC_BDIST        1009
#define IDC_HPIXSZ       1010
#define IDC_VPIXSZ       1011
#define IDC_ENTITY       1012
#define IDC_GAMMA        1013
#define IDC_GAMMA_EN     1014
#define IDC_JITTER       1015
#define IDC_JITTER_EN    1016
#define IDC_MSTEP        1017
#define IDC_STOPC        1018
#define IDC_AMBIENT_EN   1019
#define IDC_OVER_EN      1020
#define IDC_RGB          1021
#define IDC_MONO         1022
#define IDC_PSEUDO       1023
#define IDC_STATIC       -1

#endif
```

The resource script itself is:

Listing 4.25

```
// HELIOS.RC - Resource Script

#include <windows.h>
#include "resource.h"

HELIOSMENU MENU DISCARDABLE
BEGIN
  POPUP "&File"
  BEGIN
    MENUITEM "&Open...",            IDM_FILEOPEN
    MENUITEM "&Save As...",         IDM_SAVEAS, GRAYED
    MENUITEM SEPARATOR
    MENUITEM "&Directories...",     IDM_DIRECTORY
    MENUITEM SEPARATOR
    MENUITEM "&Exit",               IDM_EXIT
  END
  POPUP "&Camera"
  BEGIN
    MENUITEM "Set &Parameters...",  IDM_SETCAMERA
  END
  POPUP "&View"
  BEGIN
    MENUITEM "Specify &View...",    IDM_SETVIEW
  END
  POPUP "&Render"
  BEGIN
    MENUITEM "&Wireframe",          IDM_WIREFRAME, GRAYED
    MENUITEM "&Shaded",             IDM_SHADED, GRAYED
    MENUITEM "&Rendering",          IDM_RENDER, GRAYED
    MENUITEM "Re&display",          IDM_REDISPLAY, GRAYED
  END
  POPUP "&Options"
  BEGIN
    MENUITEM "&Set Convergence...", IDM_SETCONVERGE
    MENUITEM "&Set Display...",     IDM_SETDISPLAY
  END
  POPUP "&Help"
  BEGIN
    MENUITEM "&About HELIOS...",    IDM_ABOUT
  END
END

SETENTITYDIR DIALOG DISCARDABLE  32, 32, 255, 52
STYLE DS_MODALFRAME | WS_CAPTION | WS_SYSMENU
CAPTION "Directories"
FONT 8, "MS Sans Serif"
BEGIN
  LTEXT           "Entities File Path:",IDC_STATIC,6,10,60,8
  EDITTEXT        IDC_ENTITY,73,8,118,12,ES_AUTOHSCROLL
  DEFPUSHBUTTON   "OK",IDOK,199,6,48,16
  PUSHBUTTON      "Cancel",IDCANCEL,199,26,48,16
END
```

(continued)

Listing 4.25   *(continued)*

```
SETCAMERA DIALOG DISCARDABLE  32, 32, 202, 154
STYLE DS_MODALFRAME | WS_CAPTION | WS_SYSMENU
CAPTION "Camera Parameters"
FONT 8, "MS Sans Serif"
BEGIN
    GROUPBOX        "Camera Distances",IDC_STATIC,6,6,131,76
    LTEXT           "View Distance:",IDC_STATIC,12,22,72,8
    LTEXT           "Front Plane Distance:",IDC_STATIC,12,42,72,
                    8
    LTEXT           "Back Plane Distance:",IDC_STATIC,12,62,72,
                    8
    GROUPBOX        "Window Dimensions",IDC_STATIC,6,88,131,56
    LTEXT           "Horizontal Pixels:",IDC_STATIC,12,104,82,8
    LTEXT           "Vertical Pixels:",IDC_STATIC,12,124,82,8
    EDITTEXT        IDC_VDIST,86,20,42,12,ES_AUTOHSCROLL
    EDITTEXT        IDC_FDIST,86,40,42,12,ES_AUTOHSCROLL
    EDITTEXT        IDC_BDIST,86,60,42,12,ES_AUTOHSCROLL
    EDITTEXT        IDC_HPIXSZ,108,102,20,12,ES_AUTOHSCROLL
    EDITTEXT        IDC_VPIXSZ,108,122,20,12,ES_AUTOHSCROLL
    DEFPUSHBUTTON   "OK",IDOK,146,10,48,16
    PUSHBUTTON      "Cancel",IDCANCEL,146,30,48,16
END

SETVIEW DIALOG DISCARDABLE  32, 32, 152, 192
STYLE DS_MODALFRAME | WS_CAPTION | WS_SYSMENU
CAPTION "View Parameters"
FONT 8, "MS Sans Serif"
BEGIN
    GROUPBOX        "Eye Position",IDC_STATIC,6,6,81,64
    LTEXT           "X-Axis:",IDC_STATIC,11,20,24,8
    LTEXT           "Y-Axis:",IDC_STATIC,11,36,24,8
    LTEXT           "Z-Axis:",IDC_STATIC,11,52,24,8
    GROUPBOX        "View Direction",IDC_STATIC,6,78,120,48
    LTEXT           "Vertical:",IDC_STATIC,11,108,36,8
    LTEXT           "Horizontal:",IDC_STATIC,11,92,36,8
    LTEXT           "Degrees",IDC_STATIC,92,92,28,8
    LTEXT           "Degrees",IDC_STATIC,92,108,28,8
    GROUPBOX        "View-Up Vector",IDC_STATIC,6,134,120,48
    LTEXT           "Horizontal:",IDC_STATIC,11,148,36,8
    LTEXT           "Vertical:",IDC_STATIC,11,164,36,8
    LTEXT           "Degrees",IDC_STATIC,92,148,28,8
    LTEXT           "Degrees",IDC_STATIC,92,164,28,8
    EDITTEXT        IDC_XPOS,36,18,42,12,ES_AUTOHSCROLL
    EDITTEXT        IDC_YPOS,36,34,42,12,ES_AUTOHSCROLL
    EDITTEXT        IDC_ZPOS,36,50,42,12,ES_AUTOHSCROLL
    EDITTEXT        IDC_VDVH,48,90,38,12,ES_AUTOHSCROLL
    EDITTEXT        IDC_VDVV,48,106,38,12,ES_AUTOHSCROLL
    EDITTEXT        IDC_VUPH,48,146,38,12,ES_AUTOHSCROLL
    EDITTEXT        IDC_VUPV,48,162,38,12,ES_AUTOHSCROLL
    DEFPUSHBUTTON   "OK",IDOK,96,10,48,16
    PUSHBUTTON      "Cancel",IDCANCEL,96,30,48,16
END
```

```
#ifdef _RAY_CAST
SETCONVERGE DIALOG DISCARDABLE  32, 32, 178, 74
STYLE DS_MODALFRAME | WS_CAPTION | WS_SYSMENU
CAPTION "Convergence Parameters"
FONT 8, "MS Sans Serif"
BEGIN
    LTEXT           "Maximum Steps:",IDC_STATIC,6,14,69,8
    LTEXT           "Stopping Criterion:",IDC_STATIC,6,34,69,8
    EDITTEXT        IDC_MSTEP,78,12,32,12,ES_AUTOHSCROLL
    EDITTEXT        IDC_STOPC,78,32,32,12,ES_AUTOHSCROLL
    CONTROL         "Ambient Exitance",IDC_AMBIENT_EN,"Button",
                    BS_AUTOCHECKBOX | WS_TABSTOP,6,54,122,10
    DEFPUSHBUTTON   "OK",IDOK,122,10,48,16
    PUSHBUTTON      "Cancel",IDCANCEL,122,30,48,16
END
#else
SETCONVERGE DIALOG DISCARDABLE  32, 32, 178, 94
STYLE DS_MODALFRAME | WS_CAPTION | WS_SYSMENU
CAPTION "Convergence Parameters"
FONT 8, "MS Sans Serif"
BEGIN
    LTEXT           "Maximum Steps:",IDC_STATIC,6,14,69,8
    LTEXT           "Stopping Criterion:",IDC_STATIC,6,34,69,8
    EDITTEXT        IDC_MSTEP,78,12,32,12,ES_AUTOHSCROLL
    EDITTEXT        IDC_STOPC,78,32,32,12,ES_AUTOHSCROLL
    CONTROL         "Ambient Exitance",IDC_AMBIENT_EN,"Button",
                    BS_AUTOCHECKBOX | WS_TABSTOP,6,54,122,10
    CONTROL         "Positive Overshoot",IDC_OVER_EN,"Button",
                    BS_AUTOCHECKBOX | WS_TABSTOP,6,74,122,10
    DEFPUSHBUTTON   "OK",IDOK,122,10,48,16
    PUSHBUTTON      "Cancel",IDCANCEL,122,30,48,16
END
#endif

SETDISPLAY DIALOG DISCARDABLE  32, 32, 152, 192
STYLE DS_MODALFRAME | WS_CAPTION | WS_SYSMENU
CAPTION "Display Parameters"
FONT 8, "MS Sans Serif"
BEGIN
    GROUPBOX        "Gamma Correction",IDC_STATIC,6,6,81,48
    LTEXT           "Gamma:",IDC_STATIC,12,20,36,8
    EDITTEXT        IDC_GAMMA,46,18,32,12,ES_AUTOHSCROLL
    CONTROL         "Enabled",IDC_GAMMA_EN,"Button",
                    BS_AUTOCHECKBOX | WS_TABSTOP,12,36,40,10
    GROUPBOX        "Color Reduction",IDC_STATIC,6,61,81,48
    LTEXT           "Noise Level:",IDC_STATIC,12,75,49,8
    EDITTEXT        IDC_JITTER,66,73,12,12,ES_AUTOHSCROLL
    CONTROL         "Enabled",IDC_JITTER_EN,"Button",
                    BS_AUTOCHECKBOX | WS_TABSTOP,12,91,40,10
    GROUPBOX        "Color Display",IDC_STATIC,5,116,81,66
    CONTROL         "RGB Color",IDC_RGB,"Button",
                    BS_AUTORADIOBUTTON,10,130,62,10
```

(continued)

Listing 4.25 *(continued)*

```
   CONTROL         "Grayscale",IDC_MONO,"Button",
                   BS_AUTORADIOBUTTON,10,147,62,10
   CONTROL         "Pseudocolor",IDC_PSEUDO,"Button",
                   BS_AUTORADIOBUTTON,10,165,62,10
   DEFPUSHBUTTON "OK",IDOK,96,10,48,16
   PUSHBUTTON      "Cancel",IDCANCEL,96,30,48,16
END

ABOUTBOX DIALOG DISCARDABLE  32, 32, 148, 98
STYLE DS_MODALFRAME | WS_CAPTION | WS_SYSMENU
CAPTION "About HELIOS"
FONT 8, "MS Sans Serif"
BEGIN
   CTEXT           "HELIOS Radiosity Renderer",IDC_STATIC,26,8,
                   96,8
#if defined(_HEMI_CUBE)
   CTEXT           "Version 1.00A/HC",IDC_STATIC,26,24,96,8
#elif defined(_CUBIC_TETRA)
   CTEXT           "Version 1.00A/CT",IDC_STATIC,26,24,96,8
#elif defined(_RAY_CAST)
   CTEXT           "Version 1.00A/RC",IDC_STATIC,26,24,96,8
#else
   CTEXT           "Version 1.00A/SH",IDC_STATIC,26,24,96,8
#endif
   CTEXT           "Copyright 1994 byHeart Software Ltd.",
                   IDC_STATIC,8,40,132,8
   CTEXT           "All Rights Reserved",IDC_STATIC,39,56,70,8
   DEFPUSHBUTTON "OK",IDOK,50,72,48,16
END
```

Finally, we need a "module definition" file, HELIOS.DEF, to instruct the linker on how *HELIOS* is to be linked:

Listing 4.26

```
NAME              Helios
DESCRIPTION       'HELIOS Radiosity Renderer'
EXETYPE           WINDOWS
STUB              'WINSTUB.EXE'
CODE              PRELOAD MOVEABLE DISCARDABLE
DATA              PRELOAD MOVEABLE MULTIPLE
STACKSIZE         5120
EXPORTS
   MAINWNDPROC    @1
   WIREWNDPROC    @2
   SETENTITYDIR   @3
   SETCAMERA      @4
   SETVIEW        @5
   SETCONVERGE    @6
   SETDISPLAY     @7
   ABOUT          @8
```

4.19.4 C++ Compiler Quirks and Foibles

A few comments regarding compiling and linking *HELIOS* may be helpful. First, you need to specify the large memory model—*this is essential!* The *WinText* class (Section 3.13) in particular assumes that its functions use far pointers.

Second, be sure to compile and link the necessary files, using either a "make" file or a project file from within an integrated development environment (IDE). The complete list is shown in Figure 4.36.

HELIOS Version 1.00A/SH

16-bit memory model: Large

Source code file list:

```
c_jitter.cpp      error.cpp       gamma.cpp       helios.cpp
helios.def        helios.rc       p_clip4.cpp     p_render.cpp
parse.cpp         patch3.cpp      rad_tmp.cpp     syn_cam.cpp
tone_rep.cpp      vector3.cpp     view_sys.cpp    win_bmap.cpp
win_sbar.cpp
```

Figure 4.36   *HELIOS* project files

Other files will be added to this list in later chapters. However, no changes to HELIOS.CPP will be needed because the necessary hooks have already been included via the conditional compilation directives *_HEMI_CUBE* and *_CUBIC_TETRA* (in HELIOS.CPP) and *_RAY_CAST* (in HELIOS.CPP and HELIOS.RC). *None of these directives should be defined at this time!*

Third, a C++ compiler run from an IDE may assume a default stack size that conflicts with that specified in HELIOS.DEF. If so, the linker will be certain to complain about it. You can either clear this value or remove the *STACKSIZE* statement from HELIOS.DEF.

Fourth, but not finally, you may see inscrutable error messages such as:

Fatal error RW1031: Segment 1 and its relocation information is too large for load optimization. Make the segment LOADONCALL or rerun RC using the -K switch if the segment must be preloaded.

This particular message came from an IDE resource compiler. It occurred using the default compiler settings when the build mode was set to include debugging information. Setting the build mode to "release" (i.e., no debugging information) allowed the program to compile and link successfully. It took an unreasonably long time to find that load optimization could be turned off from within the IDE. On the other hand, the compiler then made an incorrect assumption about pointer aliasing that caused the program to fail at run time. The joys of software development . . .

HELIOS was developed and tested using the Microsoft Visual C++ Version 1.5 and Borland C++ Version 4.0 compilers. Command-line "make" files for these compilers are included on the diskette accompanying this book. If you use either of these products, you should have no problems. Otherwise, you may encounter an embarrassment of error messages when you first attempt to compile and link *HELIOS*. As MS-Windows programmers, it is a price we all have to pay. Curse freely, try different options, and perhaps even read the printed IDE documentation. Take heart, for it will compile eventually.

4.19.5 Using *HELIOS*

We now have some 3,700 lines of C and C++ source code. Once you successfully compile and link *HELIOS*, you can use it to view both wireframe and full-color bitmap images on any personal computer that can run MS-Windows 3.1 or MS-Windows NT, including monochrome laptops (in gray scale, of course).

What is there to view? Well, COL_CUBE.WLD (Listing 3.17) presents two colored cubes floating in space. For something with a bit more visual interest (one of the chairs shown in Fig. 4.24), you can try the following:

Listing 4.27   CHAIR.WLD

```
WORLD chair
COMMENT seat
col_cube.ent
< 2.0 2.0 0.1>
< 0.0 0.0 0.0 >
< -1.0 -1.0 -0.05 >
COMMENT back
col_cube.ent
< 2.0 0.2 3.0 >
< 0.0 0.0 0.0 >
< -1.0 -1.0 0.05 >
COMMENT leg #1
col_cube.ent
< 0.2 0.1 2.5 >
< 0.0 0.0 0.0 >
< -0.85 -0.8 -2.55 >
COMMENT leg #2
col_cube.ent
< 0.2 0.1 2.5 >
< 0.0 0.0 0.0 >
< -0.85 0.8 -2.55 >
COMMENT leg #3
col_cube.ent
< 0.2 0.1 2.5 >
< 0.0 0.0 0.0 >
< 0.75 -0.8 -2.55 >
COMMENT leg #4
```

```
col_cube.ent
< 0.2 0.1 2.5 >
< 0.0 0.0 0.0 >
< 0.75 0.8 -2.55 >
END_FILE
```

To display a wireframe image of this chair, first make sure that COL_CUBE.ENT and CHAIR.WLD are in the same directory, then run *HELIOS* as an MS-Windows program. Once its main window is displayed, you can:

1. Choose *File* from the menu bar.
2. Choose the *Open…* menu item to display the *Open* common dialog box.
3. Select the CHAIR.WLD file.

An *Environment Statistics* dialog box will then appear with an enumeration of the instances, surfaces, polygons, and vertices in the environment.

If the *COL_CUBE.ENT* file is not in the same directory as CHAIR.WLD, an error message will appear in a dialog box. Rather than exiting *HELIOS*, you can:

1. Choose *File* from the menu bar.
2. Choose the *Directories…* menu item to display the *Directories* dialog box.
3. Enter the correct file path in the *Entities File Path* edit control.

and follow the above three steps to select the CHAIR.WLD file again.

With the environment file parsed and loaded into memory, you can now:

1. Choose *Camera* from the menu bar.
2. Choose the *Set Parameters* menu item to display the *Camera Parameters* dialog box.
3. Enter "2.5" in the *View Distance* edit control.
4. Enter "240" in the *Horizontal Pixels* edit control.
5. Enter "320" in the *Vertical Pixels* edit control.

This sets the camera view distance at 2.5 units, giving a field of view roughly equivalent to a 50-mm lens on a 35-mm camera. It also tells *HELIOS* to display the image as a vertically oriented bitmap of 240 × 320 pixels. You can change this to whatever size you want, from a minimum of 32 pixels to a maximum of 2,048 pixels.

The synthetic camera's position and orientation must be specified next:

1. Choose *View* from the menu bar.
2. Choose the *Specify View…* menu item to display the *View Parameters* dialog box.
3. Enter "4" in the *Eye Position X-Axis* edit control.
4. Enter "5" in the *Eye Position Y-Axis* edit control.
5. Enter "6" in the *Eye Position Z-Axis* edit control.
6. Enter "–25" (note the minus sign) in the *View Direction Horizontal Degrees* edit control.
7. Enter "130" in the View Direction Vertical Degrees edit control.

The *View-Up Vector* edit controls remain unchanged.

The synthetic camera is now set up to display an image, starting with:

1. Choose *Render* from the menu bar.
2. Choose the *Wireframe* menu item.

(Note that the *Render* menu items are grayed (deactivated) until an environment data file is read into memory.)

A wireframe image of the chair will be displayed. This image will automatically resize itself whenever the display window size is changed. You can also go back and change any of the previous entries to change the view or camera parameters; the wireframe image will update itself accordingly.

To display a full-color bitmap image:

1. Choose *Render* from the menu bar.
2. Choose the *Shaded* menu item.

It may take a few seconds to display the image, depending on the CPU speed and whether a math coprocessor is present. If the window's client (display) area is smaller than the specified horizontal or vertical pixels, scroll bars will appear.

To redisplay the image in gray scale or pseudocolor, you can:

1. Choose *Options* from the menu bar.
2. Choose the *Set Display...* menu item to display the *Display Parameters* dialog box.
3. Select either the *Grayscale* or *Pseudocolor* radio button.
4. Select the *OK* button.
5. Choose *Render* from the menu bar.
6. Choose the *Redisplay* menu item.

(The other parameters in the *Display Parameters* dialog box and the parameters in the *Convergence Parameters* dialog box accessible from the *Set Convergence...* menu item do not have any discernible effect for shaded images.)

You can also choose *Rendering* from the *Render* menu item. However, only a blank bitmap will appear on the screen, along with a *Convergence Statistics* dialog box. Choose *Render* and *Shaded* again to redisplay the image.

To save this image to a BMP file:

1. Choose *File* from the menu bar.
2. Choose the *Save As...* menu item to display the *Save As* common dialog box, and specify an appropriate directory and file name. The file can later be viewed using Microsoft Paintbrush or any other BMP-compatible graphics program.

Finally, you can:

1. Choose *Help* from the menu bar.
2. Choose the *About Helios...* menu item to display the *About HELIOS* dialog

box to view the program's copyright notice, version number (which should be "1.00A/SH," where "SH" stands for "SHaded"), and so forth.

If all of the above actions work as described, congratulations! *HELIOS* is alive and well.

4.20 CONCLUSIONS

What began as a "minimal" viewing system somehow grew into a major component of this book. Even so, our MS-Windows implementation is far from being production quality. It lacks any sort of on-line help, it provides a minimal number of error messages, and it does not offer the currently fashionable "chiseled-in-steel" look for its dialog boxes.

The platform-independent portions of our code are also less than perfect. No attempt has been made to profile the code to identify those components that should be rewritten by hand using assembly language. *PolyRender* should be rewritten using integer-only DDA algorithms (see Section 4.12) for the Intel $80x86$ platform and other CPUs with slow floating-point implementations. This includes not only scan conversion for the polygon edges but also pseudodepth and RGB color interpolation for Gouraud shading. (See also Blinn 1992 for further details and comments on Gouraud shading and perspective projection.)

There is more, of course. Support should be added for other bitmap file formats. Antialiasing should be added to minimize the "jaggies" on diagonally oriented polygon edges (Fleisher and Salesin 1992 offer a very effective solution for polygons, including C source code). The list goes on and on.

Somewhere, however, we have to stop. *HELIOS* is a minimal but effective viewing system that can help us investigate a variety of radiosity methods. It's time to move on.

REFERENCES

ANSI. 1988. *American National Standard for Information Processing Systems—Programmer's Hierarchical Interactive Graphics System (PHIGS) Functional Description, Archive File Format, Clear-Text Encoding of Archive File*, ANSI X3.144-1988. New York: American National Standards Institute.

Arvo, J. 1991. *Graphics Gems II*. San Diego, CA: Academic Press.

Barbour, C. G., and G. W. Meyer. 1992. "Visual Cues and Pictorial Limitations for Computer Generated Photorealistic Images," *The Visual Computer* 9:151–165.

Blinn, J. F. 1992. "Hyperbolic Interpolation," *IEEE Computer Graphics & Applications* 12(4):89–94.

Bono, P. R., and I. Herman, eds. 1987. *GKS Theory and Practice*. Berlin, Germany: Springer-Verlag.

Bresenham, J. E. 1965. "Algorithm for Computer Control of a Digital Plotter," *IBM Systems Journal* 4(1): 25–30.

Burkett, A., and S. Noll. 1988. "Fast Algorithm for Polygon Clipping with 3D Windows," *Eurographics '88* (Proc. European Computer Graphics Conference and Exhibition), D. A. Duce and P. Jancene, eds. Amsterdam: Elsevier Sciences Publishers B.V. (North-Holland), pp. 405–419.

Cohen, M. F., and J. R. Wallace. 1993. *Radiosity and Realistic Image Synthesis*. San Diego, CA: Academic Press.

Fleisher, K., and D. Salesin. 1992. "Accurate Polygon Scan Conversion Using Half-Open Intervals," in Kirk (1992), pp. 362–365, 599–605.

Foley, J. D., A. van Dam, S. K. Feiner, and J. F. Hughes. 1990. *Computer Graphics: Principles and Practice* (2nd ed.). Reading, MA: Addison-Wesley.

Gervautz, M., and W. Purgathofer. 1990. "A Simple Method for Color Quantization: Octree Quantization," in Glassner (1990), pp. 287–293.

Glassner, A. S. 1990. *Graphics Gems*. San Diego, CA: Academic Press.

Gouraud, H. 1971. "Illumination for Computer Generated Pictures," *Communications of the ACM* 18(6):311–317.

Heckbert, P. S. 1982. "Color Image Quantization for Frame Buffer Display," *Computer Graphics* 16(3):297–307. (ACM SIGGRAPH '82 Proc.).

Heckbert, P. S. 1990a. "What Are the Coordinates of a Pixel?" in Glassner (1990), pp. 246–248.

Heckbert, P. S. 1990b. "Generic Convex Polygon Scan Conversion and Clipping," in Glassner (1990), pp. 84–86, 667–680.

Hill, F. S., Jr. 1990. *Computer Graphics*. New York: Macmillan,.

ISO. 1988. *International Standard Information Processing Systems—Computer Graphics—Graphical Kernel System for Three Dimensions (GKS-3D) Functional Description*, ISO Document Number 8805:1988(E). New York: American National Standards Institute.

Kirk, D. 1992. *Graphics Gems III*. San Diego, CA: Academic Press.

Liang, Y., and B. A. Barsky. 1983. "An Analysis and Algorithm for Polygon Clipping," *Communications of the ACM* 26(11):868–877, and Corrigenda, *Communications of the ACM* 27(2):151 and *Communications of the ACM* 27(4):383.

Meyer , G. W., H. E. Rushmeier, M. F. Cohen, D. P. Greenberg, and K. E. Torrance. 1986. "An Experimental Evaluation of Computer Graphics Imagery," *ACM Transactions on Graphics* 5(1):30–50.

Newman, W. M., and R. F. Sproull. 1979. *Principles of Interactive Computer Graphics* (2nd ed.). New York: McGraw-Hill.

Petzold, C. 1992. *Programming Windows 3.1* (3rd ed.) Redmond, WA.: Microsoft Press.

Plauger, P. J. and J. Brodie. 1989. *Standard C*. Redmond, WA.: Microsoft Press.

Révész, T. 1993. "Clipping Polygons with Sutherland-Hodgman's Algorithm," *The C Users Journal* 11(8):23–34 (August) and 11(9):135–136 (September).

Rogers, D. F. 1985. *Procedural Elements for Computer Graphics*. New York: McGraw-Hill.

Singleton, K. 1987. "An Implementation of the GKS-3D/PHIGS Viewing Pipeline," in Bono and Herman (1987).

Sutherland, I. E., and G. W. Hodgman. 1974. "Reentrant Polygon Clipping," *Communications of the ACM* 17(1):32 –42.

Sutherland, I. E., R. F. Sproull, and R. Schumacker. 1974. "A Characterization of Ten Hidden-Surface Algorithms," *Computing Surveys* 6(1):1–55.

Swanson, R. W., and L. J. Thayer. 1986. "A Fast Shaded-Polygon Renderer," *Computer Graphics* 20(4):107–116 (ACM SIGGRAPH '86 Proc.).

Tumblin, J., and H. E. Rushmeier. 1993. "Tone Reproduction for Realistic Images," *IEEE Computer Graphics & Applications* 13(6):42–48.

Vatti, B. R. 1992. "A Generic Solution to Polygon Clipping," *Communications of the ACM* 35(7):57–63.

Ward, G. 1991. "Real Pixels," in Arvo (1991), pp. 80–83.

Weiler, K., and P. Atherton. 1977. "Hidden Surface Removal Using Polygon Area Sorting," *Computer Graphics* 11(2):214–222 (ACM SIGGRAPH '77 Proc.).

RADIOSITY AND REALISM

This world is but a canvas to our imaginations.
Henry David Thoreau
A Week on the Concord and Merrimack Rivers, 1849

Our canvas is a three-dimensional viewing system, carefully constructed to support the needs of radiosity-based rendering. We can now begin to paint . . .

Chapter 5 investigates the art and science of form factor determination as an essential component of the radiosity approach. If the way seems long and tortuous, it is. The problem of form factor determination is simply stated but not easily solved.

Chapter 6 looks at the variety of approaches we can take to solving the radiosity equation. From them are derived not one but three fully functional radiosity-based rendering programs. Our dragons reappear in the form of matrix mathematics, but they are harmless.

And yes, there is art in radiosity, or rather an art to it. More than anything else, choosing an appropriate polygon mesh for radiosity-based images requires experience and skill. Chapter 7 considers the conundrums of meshing and substructuring techniques for complex environments.

Finally, Chapter 8 looks at extending the capabilities of our tools and the future of radiosity. There are still exciting times to come.

Radiosity does indeed . . . model light.

Form Factor Determination

5.0   INTRODUCTION

Having developed a graphics toolkit to manage and display three-dimensional polygons, we can take some satisfaction in being halfway to our goal of a functional radiosity-based rendering program (Fig. 5.1). This chapter addresses the problem of determining form factors between polygons in our environments.

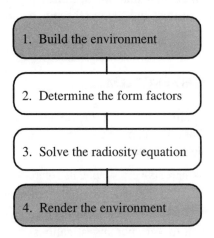

1. Build the environment

2. Determine the form factors

3. Solve the radiosity equation

4. Render the environment

Figure 5.1   Radiosity-based rendering program outline

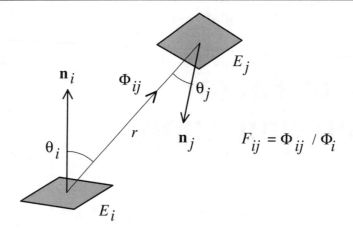

Figure 5.2   Patch E_j receiving flux Φ_{ij} from Lambertian emitter E_i (from Fig. 2.6)

Form factors are an essential component of the radiosity approach, as much so as geometrical rays are essential to ray tracing. As we saw in Chapter 2, a form factor F_{ij} is a dimensionless constant representing the fraction of radiant flux leaving a Lambertian emitter E_i that is intercepted by another surface element (or *patch*) E_j (Fig. 5.2). It is based solely on the geometry and geometric relation between the two surface patches; no surface properties are involved.

Successfully solving the radiosity equation requires accurate form factors. Unfortunately, form factor determination for a complex environment containing several thousand possibly occluded patches can be difficult and extremely time consuming. Pietrek (1993) and others have commented that form factor calculations can consume up to 90 percent of the time required to solve the radiosity equation. It is therefore vitally important that we optimize these calculations, first through a careful choice of algorithms, and second through a carefully crafted C++ implementation.

5.1   SOLVING A KNOTTED PROBLEM

Despite their apparent simplicity, form factors are notoriously difficult to solve using analytic methods. Johann Lambert, a pioneer researcher in photometry and likely the first person to consider the problem, wrote (Lambert 1760):

> Although this task appears very simple, its solution is considerably more knotted than one would expect . . . the highly laborious computation would fill even the most patient with disgust and drive them away.

This does not bode well for our own investigations!

Lambert expressed this opinion in reference to the problem (discussed below) of two perpendicular rectangles sharing a common edge. However, his comments apply equally well to form factor determination in general. As we saw in Section 2.5, the form factor from a finite area patch E_i to another finite area patch E_j is given by the double area integral equation:

$$F_{ij} = \frac{1}{A_i} \int_{A_i} \int_{A_j} \frac{\cos\theta_i \cos\theta_j}{\pi r^2} dA_j dA_i \qquad (5.1)$$

where A_i and A_j are the areas of patches E_i and E_j respectively (Fig. 5.2). *This equation cannot be solved directly.* Instead, we must either find an analytic solution (that is, transform Equation 5.1 into one that does not involve integration) or solve it using numerical integration techniques.

We will examine a few analytic (or "closed-form") solutions, but only to see why numerical integration is the more useful approach. *Don't let the mathematics deter you!* If nothing else, keep in mind that:

> Form factor determination requires no more than high school trigonometry.

5.2   CONTOUR INTEGRATION

Following Lambert's pioneering efforts, it took 230 years to find an exact solution for the general case of two arbitrary but unoccluded polygons (Schröder and Hanrahan 1993). Schröder reported that it took Mathematica (a symbolic mathematics program) only fifteen minutes to solve 90 percent of the problem; the remaining 10 percent took eight months of research. As you might have guessed, their "nonelementary" solution is far too complex for practical use.

Sparrow (1963) found that by applying Stokes's theorem to Equation 5.1, it could be converted to a double contour integral, namely:

$$F_{ij} = \frac{1}{2\pi A_i} \oint_{C_i} \oint_{C_j} \ln(r)dx_i dx_j + \ln(r)dy_i dy_j + \ln(r)dz_i dz_j \qquad (5.2)$$

where C_i and C_j are the patch boundaries. Although this equation can be solved for many polygons and other shapes (see, for example, Siegel and Howell 1992), it is quite impracticable for our purposes. It does, however, have some historical interest: It was used in one of the two papers that introduced radiosity to the computer graphics community (Goral et al. 1984).

Note that Equations 5.1 and 5.2 assume that patches E_i and E_j are fully visible to one another. In other words, the form factor determination method used by Goral et al. (1984) is applicable only to simple unoccluded environments. It cannot be extended to handle our complex environments with possibly occluded polygons.

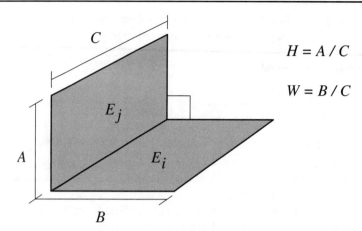

$$H = A / C$$

$$W = B / C$$

Figure 5.3 Form factor geometry between perpendicular rectangles

SPECIAL CASES

A second approach is to consider special cases for which closed-form solutions to Equation 5.1 can be derived. Mechanical and aeronautics engineers have long used published tables of formulas for specific area-to-area geometries in their radiant heat transfer studies, including those by Howell (1982), Siegel and Howell (1992), and Sparrow and Cess (1978). These include simple shapes such as parallel and perpendicular rectangles, circles, and hollow tubes. More complex geometries can be analyzed using *form factor algebra* (Section 2.5) to geometrically add and subtract these shapes and their associated form factors.

Despite their availability, these tables are not particularly useful for complex environments. Consider one of the simplest geometries, that of two adjoining and perpendicular rectangles (Fig. 5.3).Whereas the geometry may be simple, the following equation for its form factor F_{ij} from E_i to E_j is anything but!

$$F_{ij} = \frac{1}{\pi W} \left(W * \arctan\left(\frac{1}{W}\right) + H * \arctan\left(\frac{1}{H}\right) - \sqrt{H^2 + W^2} * \arctan\left(\frac{1}{\sqrt{H^2 + W^2}}\right) \right.$$

$$\left. + \frac{1}{4} \ln\left\{ \frac{\left(1 + W^2\right)\left(1 + H^2\right)}{1 + W^2 + H^2} * \left[\frac{W^2\left(1 + W^2 + H^2\right)}{\left(1 + W^2\right)\left(W^2 + H^2\right)} \right]^{W^2} * \left[\frac{H^2\left(1 + W^2 + H^2\right)}{\left(1 + H^2\right)\left(W^2 + H^2\right)} \right]^{H^2} \right\} \right) \quad (5.3)$$

Remember, this is a "simple" example! Lambert (1760) was clearly justified in his comments. Not shown is the equation for two adjoining but nonperpendicular rectangles—it fills an entire page.

Even if we had closed-form solutions for a useful set of patch geometries, it would not do us much good. Like the contour-integration approach, these solutions assume that the patches are fully visible to one another. This makes them generally unsuitable for complex environments.

5.4 A SIMPLIFIED APPROACH

We can simplify our problem by considering the form factor from a differential area patch dE_i to a finite area patch E_j. In other words, we can model our luminous surface emitter as a point source of light. As we saw in Section 2.5, the form factor F_{dEi-Ej} is given by the area integral equation:

$$F_{dEi-Ej} = \int_{A_j} dF_{dEi-dEj} = \int_{A_j} \frac{\cos\theta_i \cos\theta_j}{\pi r^2} dA_j \tag{5.4}$$

Again, this equation cannot be solved directly for an arbitrary patch E_j. However, there is a surprisingly simple analytic solution for planar convex polygons (Lambert 1760), which is just what we need. Referring to Figure 5.4, we see it is:

$$F_{dEi-Ej} = \frac{1}{2\pi} \sum_{k=0}^{n-1} \beta_k \cos\alpha_k \tag{5.5}$$

or equivalently:

$$F_{dEi-Ej} = \frac{1}{2\pi} \sum_{k=0}^{n-1} \beta_k \mathbf{n}_i \cdot \left(\mathbf{r}_k \times \mathbf{r}_{(k+1)\%n}\right) \tag{5.6}$$

where n is the number of polygon edges, β_k is the angle (in radians) between the vectors $\mathbf{r}_k$ and $\mathbf{r}_{(k+1)\%n}$ defined from dE_i to each pair of vertices k and $(k+1)\%n$ (where "%" is the modulo arithmetic operator), α_k is the angle (again in radians) between the plane of dE_i and the triangle formed by dE_i and the kth edge, and $\mathbf{n}_i$ is the normal of dE_i.

Actually, Equation 5.6 is the contour-integration approach applied to the special case of a differential area emitter and a planar convex polygon receiver. It was used to calculate form factors in the second paper that introduced radiosity to the computer graphics community (Nishita and Nakamae 1984). Although it is certainly simpler than the general contour-integration approach used by Goral et al. (1984), it too assumes that the patches are fully visible to one another (Fig. 5.4).

But wait! The emitting patch dE_i is an infinitesimally small point source. If an intervening polygon partially occludes E_j, we can subdivide E_j into convex polygons that are either fully visible to or completely hidden from dE_i (e.g., Fig. 5.5). We can then apply Equation 5.6 to each visible polygon; the form factor from dE_i to E_j is the sum of their individual form factors.

This is essentially a hidden-surface problem. Seen from dE_i, what polygons in the environment are visible to it, and what other polygons partially or fully occlude each one? What we need is an *area subdivision* algorithm for hidden-surface elimination, such as Warnock's algorithm (e.g., Sutherland et al. 1974), that successively

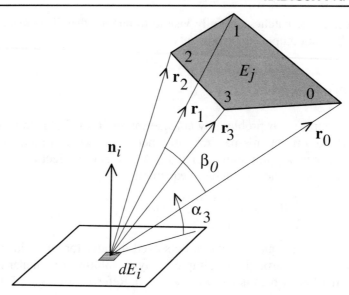

Figure 5.4   Differential area dE_i to polygon E_j form factor geometry

divides polygons into smaller and smaller polygons until each one is either fully visible or completely hidden from some reference point.

Unfortunately, area subdivision algorithms are at least an order of magnitude more complex than the Z-buffer algorithm presented in Chapter 4 (see Rogers 1985 for implementation details of Warnock's algorithm). Whereas Nishita and Nakamae

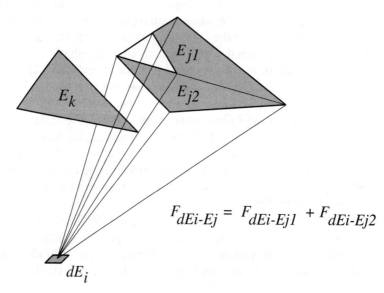

Figure 5.5   Area subdivision of partially occluded polygon E_j into E_{j1} and E_{j2}

(1984) demonstrated that their technique works for complex environments with partially occluded polygons, numerical integration offers a simpler approach.

5.5   THE FIVE-TIMES RULE

Our simplified approach led to an analytic solution for planar convex polygons. Given two arbitrary patches, however, are we justified in modeling the emitter as a point source?

In general, no. If a small but finite polygon is placed parallel to and an infinitesimal distance above a large emitter, it will clearly intercept only a small fraction of the emitted flux. Modeling the emitter as a point source, however, would lead us to conclude that it intercepts nearly all of the emitted flux. Wrong!

So, our simplified approach is an approximation. We therefore need to consider the consequences of this approximation and under what conditions we are justified in modeling a luminous patch as a point source.

It is a thorny question, because the differences between approximate and actual form factors are not directly manifested in the rendered image. The predicted distribution of light within the environment will be subtly different from what it would be in real life, but there are many other approximations in the rendering process that can overshadow these differences (e.g., Meyer et al. 1986).

Murdoch (1981) investigated this problem as part of a theoretical study in illumination engineering. He demonstrated that modeling a Lambertian luminous rectangle as a point source results in worst-case illuminance prediction errors (using the inverse square law) of less than ± 1 percent if the distance from the illuminated point to the rectangle is at least five times its maximum projected width. In other words, the luminous rectangle should subtend an angle of less than 0.2 radians, or approximately 11.5 degrees, as seen from the illuminated point. (Note the caveat *projected* width: A long but narrow light source will subtend a smaller angle when viewed from one end.)

This *five-times rule* (Fig. 5.6) has been used by illumination engineers for nearly a century. If the maximum dimension of a lighting fixture is less than five times its distance from a surface being illuminated, then the fixture is modeled as a point source and the inverse square law for point sources (Eq. 1.7) can be applied.

There have been several other detailed studies of form factor calculation errors, including Saraiji and Mistrick (1992), Emery et al. (1991), Baum et al. (1989), Max and Troutman (1993), and Sbert (1993). Although there is no firm consensus on the topic, it appears that the five-times rule can be applied to form factor calculations as follows:

> **The five-times rule:**
>
> A finite area Lambertian emitter should be modeled as a point source only when the distance to the receiving surface is greater than five times the maximum projected width of the emitter.

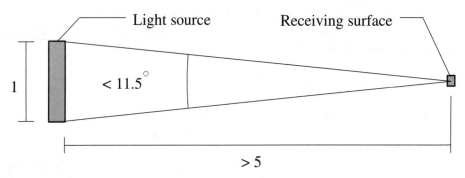

Figure 5.6   Illumination engineering's five-times rule

We should keep in mind that this does not limit the applicability of our simplified approach. If the five-times rule is violated for any two patches, we can always subdivide the emitting patch until the rule is satisfied for each subdivided area. Of course, this fails for the two adjoining patches shown in Figure 5.3—we would be subdividing forever as we approach their common edge. We need a heuristic rule that stops subdividing when the patches become too small to be significant in any rendered image of the environment. These, however, are details for Chapter 7.

5.6   NUSSELT'S ANALOGY

We can take yet another approach to solving Equation 5.4. Imagine dE_i being centered on the base of an imaginary hemisphere with unit radius (Fig. 5.7). Tracing geometric rays from dE_i to E_j, we can project the outline of E_j onto the surface of the hemisphere. We can then trace rays from this projection directly down onto the base of the hemisphere to outline the area A. From this, the form factor F_{ij} is given by:

$$F_{dEi-Ej} = \frac{A}{\pi} \tag{5.7}$$

This entirely geometric solution is known as *Nusselt's analogy* (Nusselt 1928). Although it strictly applies only when dE_i is a differential area, it serves as a useful approximation for any two finite patches E_i and E_j where E_i is much smaller than either E_j or the distance between them (i.e., the five-times rule applies).

Nusselt's analogy works as follows. Suppose E_j is a differential patch, dE_j. Recalling once again the discussion of solid angles and projected areas from Chapter 1, we can see that the solid angle $d\omega$ subtended by dE_j as seen from dE_i (Fig. 5.8) is:

$$d\omega = \cos\theta_j dA_j / r^2 \tag{5.8}$$

where dA_j is the differential area of dE_j. (This is in part the discussion presented in Section 2.5, but it bears repeating here.)

The solid angle $d\omega$ is equal to the area of the projection of dE_j onto the unit

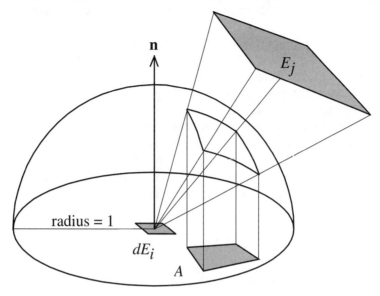

Figure 5.7 Nusselt's analogy

hemisphere's surface; this accounts for the factor $\cos\theta_j/r^2$ in Equation 5.4. The $\cos\theta_i$ term comes from the second projection onto the base. Thus:

$$dA = \cos\theta_i d\omega = \cos\theta_i \cos\theta_j dA_j / r^2 \tag{5.9}$$

where dA is the (now differential) projected area on the hemisphere base. Finally, the denominator of π comes from the base's area (a unit circle). We obtain the finite projected area A by integrating Equation 5.9 over the finite area of E_j.

Unlike our previous contour-integration approach, Nusselt's analogy applies to *any* finite area patch E_j, regardless of its outline. Unfortunately, it leaves us with the

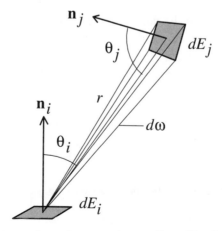

Figure 5.8 Differential area form factor geometry (from Fig. 2.6)

problem of projecting the polygon's outline onto the hemisphere's surface and thence onto its base.

In the past, illumination engineers have relied on mechanical and photographic contrivances (e.g., Cherry et al. 1939 and O'Brien 1963) to perform these projections and measure form factors for real-life objects such as windows and building skylights. More usefully, Bian (1992) and Bian et al. (1992) show how to project n-sided polygons onto the surface of a hemisphere and analytically calculate their form factors. Once again, however, we need an accompanying area subdivision algorithm to solve the hidden-surface elimination problem for partially occluded polygons.

To summarize, analytic solutions require complicated hidden-surface elimination algorithms to determine form factors in complex environments. Rather than pursue this issue further, we should investigate numerical integration techniques.

5.7   THE HEMICUBE ALGORITHM

In considering Nusselt's analogy, Cohen and Greenberg (1985) realized which patches that have the same projected area on a hemisphere will occupy the same solid angle as seen from the emitting patch (Fig. 5.9). In other words, *both patches have the same form factor*. This is perfectly sensible, since both patches will receive the same emitted flux if either one has an unobstructed view of the emitter.

Suppose then that we replace Nusselt's hemisphere with a *hemicube*.[1] As Figure 5.10 shows, we can equally well project a patch onto the surface of the hemicube. Suppose further that each surface (or *face*) of the hemicube is divided into a grid of small *cells*.[2] If we can determine their individual form factors (called *delta form factors*, ΔF), we can determine the form factor of the projected patch simply by summing the delta form factors of those cells it covers.

That is, we have:

$$F_{dEi-Ej} \approx \sum \Delta F_{covered} \tag{5.10}$$

where $\Delta F_{covered}$ refers to the delta form factors of those cells covered by the projection of E_j onto one or more of the hemicube faces.

The accuracy of Equation 5.10 is clearly dependent on the hemicube's grid spacing. This spacing is measured in terms of the number of cells on the top face (256×256 cells, for example) and is referred to as the hemicube's *resolution*. Typical

---

[1]If a *hemisphere* is half of a sphere, then a *hemicube* is half of a cube. There are two commonly used spellings: "hemi-cube" and "hemicube." Cohen and Greenberg (1985) used "hemi-cube" in their original paper, but Cohen and Wallace (1993) later chose "hemicube" for their book. The spelling used here was chosen by flipping a coin.

[2]The computer graphics literature also confusingly refers to hemicube cells as "elements," "pixels," and "patches." The terms "elements" and "patches" are unfortunate because they are easily confused with the surface elements and patches introduced in Chapter 3. The term "cells" follows Cohen and Wallace (1993).

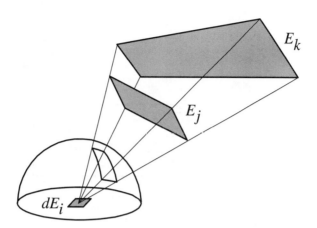

Figure 5.9 Patches E_j and E_k have same form factor from patch dE_i

resolutions used by researchers have ranged from 32×32 to 1024×1024 cells (Cohen and Wallace 1993).

The hemicube algorithm is a classic example of a numerical integration technique known as *numerical quadrature*, where function $f(x)$ is integrated over some interval a to b as:

$$\int_a^b f(x)dx \approx \sum_{j=0}^{n-1} w_j f(x_j) \tag{5.11}$$

and where $f(x)$ (called the *kernel* of the integral function) is evaluated at a series of n distinct sample points $\{x_0, \ldots, x_{n-1}\}$, with w_i being a "weight" determined by the size of the interval between the sample points. The approximation clearly improves as the interval between the sample points decreases. (Further details are available in any good text on numerical analysis.) Substituting Equation 5.9 into Equation 5.7, we get:

$$\Delta F_{dEi-Ej} \approx \frac{\cos \theta_i \cos \theta_j}{\pi r^2} \Delta A_j \tag{5.12}$$

where E_j now refers to a hemicube cell and ΔA_j is its area as a finite fraction of the entire face. The approximation is due to the substitution of the finite cell area ΔA_j for the differential area dA_j in Equation 5.9. (See Section 2.5 for an alternate derivation.) The kernel $f(x)$ of Equation 5.11 is composed of the two cosine terms, the square of the distance r, and the factor π; the weight w_j is the cell's area, ΔA_j.

Cohen and Wallace (1993) examine a number of fascinating mathematical properties relating to form factors and numerical integration. Fortunately, these issues are not essential to our understanding of the hemicube algorithm's theory.

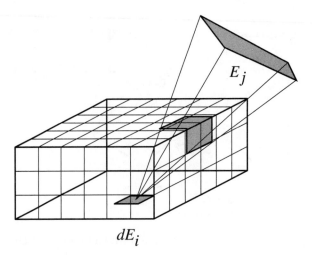

dE_i

Figure 5.10   Projecting patch E_j onto the cells of a hemicube

Indeed, all we need to remember is that the hemicube is analogous to Nusselt's hemisphere. Given this and an understanding of the reasoning behind Figures 5.9 and 5.10, what remains are mostly implementation details.

5.7.1   Delta Form Factors

The hemicube algorithm will be useful only if we can easily calculate its delta form factors. Happily, we can. Consider the hemicube cell shown on the top face[3] in Figure 5.11. It does not matter what the actual dimensions of the hemicube are, because we are interested only in the solid angle subtended by each cell. If we choose a height of one unit for computational convenience, we can see that:

$$r = \sqrt{u^2 + v^2 + 1} \tag{5.13}$$

and

$$\cos \theta_i = \cos \theta_j = 1/r \tag{5.14}$$

---

[3]It should be noted that most discussions of hemicubes use a right-handed x, y, z coordinate system. However, since we are "looking" outward from the surface of dE_i into the environment, we instead use a left-handed u, v, n coordinate system to emphasize that we are in the patch's "view space." Apart from a change of axis labels, the equations remain the same. The origin, however, is located at dE_i rather than at the hemicube face (see Section 5.11).

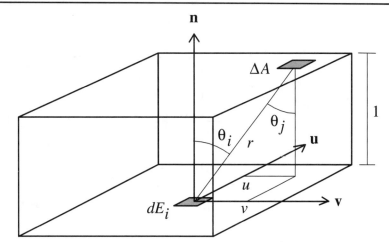

Figure 5.11 Top face hemicube cell form factor

From Equation 5.12, then, we have:

$$\Delta F_{top} \approx \frac{\cos \theta_i \cos \theta_j}{\pi r^2} \Delta A_{top} = \frac{\Delta A_{top}}{\pi \left(u^2 + v^2 + 1\right)^2} \tag{5.15}$$

where ΔA_{top} is the hemicube cell area as a fraction of the top face area of four square units.

For side face cells where $v = \pm 1$ (Fig. 5.12), we have:

$$r = \sqrt{u^2 + n^2 + 1} \tag{5.16}$$

and

$$\cos \theta_i = n/r \\ \cos \theta_j = 1/r \tag{5.17}$$

Thus:

$$\Delta F_{side} \approx \frac{\cos \theta_i \cos \theta_j}{\pi r^2} \Delta A_{side} = \frac{n \Delta A_{side}}{\pi \left(u^2 + n^2 + 1\right)^2} \tag{5.18}$$

and similarly for side face cells where $u = \pm 1$ by substituting v for u. The hemicube cell area ΔA_{side} is once again a fraction of the *full* side face area of four square units, including the bottom half hidden below the hemicube base plane.

Figures 5.11 and 5.12 show that the hemicube's n axis is always aligned with the plane normal of dE_i. By the same token, the orientation of u and v with respect to the world coordinate system is entirely arbitrary. That is, we can arbitrarily rotate the hemicube about its n axis when positioning it over a patch in the environment. Having chosen an orientation, we can substitute the world coordinates of u, v, and n axes into Equations 4.8 and 4.9 to derive a view-space transformation matrix for the hemicube.

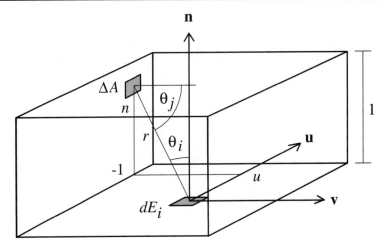

Figure 5.12   Side face hemicube cell form factor ($v = -1$)

This allows us to transform the world coordinates of any other patch E_j into the hemi-cube's "view space."

One of the advantages of the hemicube algorithm is that the delta form factors can be precalculated and stored in a look-up table (Cohen and Greenberg 1985). Even better, the hemicube top has an eightfold symmetry, whereas each side has twofold symmetry. That is, the delta form factors in each octant of the hemicube top face are identical, and similarly for each vertical half of the four side faces. If we add these up and consider a hemicube resolution of $n \times n$ cells, we can see that we need to store only $3n^2/8$ floating-point values.

The hemicube algorithm is probably the most widely used and most popular method of form factor determination among radiosity researchers. This is not to say, however, that it is the most efficient or even the most elegant algorithm available. In keeping with our promise of "a careful choice of algorithms," we should investigate at least one alternative in depth. Besides providing further insights into the hemicube algorithm, implementing both algorithms will give us a valuable sanity check. Although the two algorithms will not provide identical form factor estimates, their answers should at least be comparable within some reasonable error limit for any given pair of polygons.

5.8   THE CUBIC TETRAHEDRAL ALGORITHM

Compared to Nusselt's hemisphere, Cohen and Greenberg's hemicube provides a very simple geometry for polygon projection and form factor determination. However, there is one nagging asymmetry: The top face and the four side faces have different geometries and delta form factor equations. This means that we have to project every polygon onto five separate faces—a considerable nuisance for a complex envi-

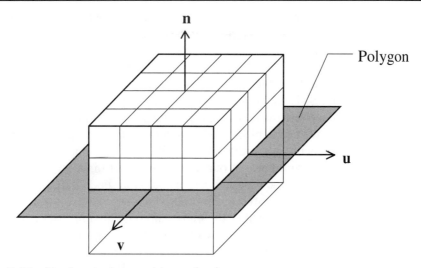

Figure 5.13   The hemicube as a bisected cube

ronment with thousands of polygons. It also means that we will probably need different sets of functions for the top and side faces.

Can we remedy this situation? Yes! There is nothing sacrosanct about the
hemicube. All we need is a simple geometrical object with planar surfaces to project
our polygons onto. The simplest possible three-dimensional object is a triangular
pyramid, otherwise known as a *tetrahedron*.

Beran-Koehn and Pavicic (1991) observed that we can think of the hemicube as a
cube that has been bisected by the polygon it rests on (Fig. 5.13). Suppose we rotate this
cube and its view-space coordinate system such that the polygon intersects three of its
vertices (Fig. 5.14). This results in a geometrical object known as a *cubic tetrahedron*.

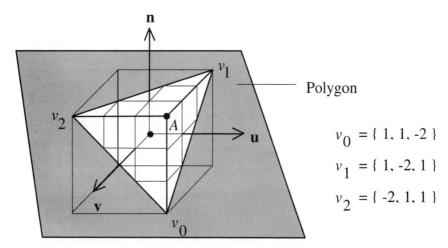

$$v_0 = \{ 1, 1, -2 \}$$

$$v_1 = \{ 1, -2, 1 \}$$

$$v_2 = \{ -2, 1, 1 \}$$

Figure 5.14   Rotating the cube creates a cubic tetrahedron

Again, we are interested only in the solid angle subtended by each cell, and so the size of the cube is immaterial. It will be convenient to use a cube measuring 3 units across each face. This places the cubic tetrahedron's base vertices v_0, v_1, and v_2 at $\{1, 1, -2\}$, $\{1, -2, 1\}$, and $\{-2, 1, 1\}$ respectively. Its apex vertex A is exactly one unit directly above the cubic tetrahedron center at $\{1, 1, 1\}$. (Note that the origin—the polygon center—is not at the center of the cube.)

We now have three identical but triangular faces to project our polygons onto. More important, we accomplished this without unduly complicating the underlying theory of the hemicube algorithm. All else being equal, this result should substantially increase the performance of our form factor determination code.

How much of an increase we can expect is an open question that depends in part on how carefully we craft our C++ code.

Although we could quantify the maximum possible improvement on theoretical grounds, it will be easier to perform experimental timing measurements on our completed implementations. Before then, we need to examine a few details, beginning with delta form factor calculations for cubic tetrahedrons.

5.8.1   Delta Form Factors Revisited

The geometry of a cubic tetrahedron cell is shown in Figure 5.15, where dE_i is the differential patch located at the center of the cubic tetrahedron (that is, the polygon's view-space origin) and E_j is the cell whose form factor we are interested in. Recalling Equation 5.12, we have:

$$\Delta F_{dEi-Ej} \approx \frac{\cos \theta_i \cos \theta_j}{\pi r^2} \Delta A_j \tag{5.19}$$

where ΔA_j is the area of E_j.

Following the development presented in Beran-Koehn and Pavicic (1992), the term $\cos \theta_i$ is given by:

$$\cos \theta_i = \frac{\mathbf{S} \cdot \mathbf{n}_j}{|\mathbf{S}|} = \frac{\mathbf{S} \cdot \mathbf{n}_j}{r} \tag{5.20}$$

where $\mathbf{S}$ is the bound vector from the origin to the cell center and r is its length. Expressed in terms of the cubic tetrahedron's view-space coordinate system, the polygon normal $\mathbf{n}_j$ is described by the vector $\{1/\sqrt{3}, 1/\sqrt{3}, 1/\sqrt{3}\}$. This means that:

$$\cos \theta_i = \frac{s_u + s_v + s_n}{r\sqrt{3}} \tag{5.21}$$

For cells on the cubic tetrahedron face perpendicular to the v axis, the term $\cos \theta_j$ is given by:

$$\cos \theta_j = \frac{-\mathbf{S} \cdot \mathbf{n}_j}{|\mathbf{S}|} = \frac{-\mathbf{S} \cdot \mathbf{n}_j}{r} \tag{5.22}$$

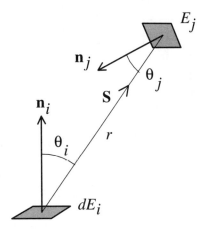

Figure 5.15   Cubic tetrahedron cell geometry

where the cell normal $\mathbf{n}_j$ is described by the vector $\{0, -1, 0\}$. Also, the face lies on the plane $v = 1$. Thus:

$$\cos \theta_j = \frac{s_v}{r} = \frac{1}{r} \tag{5.23}$$

The same result can be derived for the other two faces. Thus, for any cubic tetrahedron cell E_j, we have:

$$\Delta F_{dEi-Ej} = \frac{s_u + s_v + s_n}{\pi r^4 \sqrt{3}} \Delta A_j \tag{5.24}$$

However, $r^2 = s_u^2 + s_v^2 + s_n^2$, and for each face, one of s_u, s_v, or s_n will always be one. Thus:

$$\Delta F_{dEi-Ej} = \frac{x + y + 1}{\pi \left(x^2 + y^2 + 1 \right)^2 \sqrt{3}} \Delta A_j \tag{5.25}$$

where x and y range from 1 to -2 (Fig. 5.14). (Note that these coordinates do not refer to the world x, y, z coordinate system.)

Equation 5.25 describes the delta form factors for square cubic tetrahedron cells. It does not consider the triangular cells at the base of each face (Fig. 5.16). Beran-Koehn and Pavicic (1992) noted that we have two choices. If our resolution is sufficiently high, we can simply ignore these cells—their contribution to the summed form factor will be minuscule. Otherwise, we must include them, but recognize that their areas (ΔA in Eq. 5.25) are half that of the other cells.

The symmetry of the cubic tetrahedron is such that we need to store delta form factors for only one half of one face. For a resolution of $n \times n$ cells on one full face of the underlying cube, we need to store $n^2/4$ floating-point values. This is less than the $3n^2/8$ values required for a hemicube with the same resolution. Moreover, the cubic tetrahedron has $3n^2/2$ cells; the equivalent hemicube has $3n^2$ cells.

But are they equivalent? Beran-Koehn and Pavicic (1992) noted that a hemicube

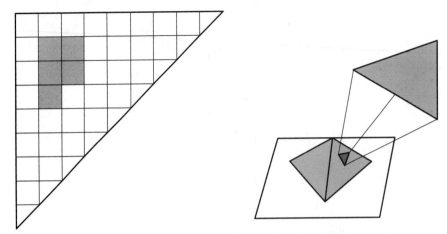

Figure 5.16   Polygon projection onto a cubic tetrahedron face

samples its environment with twice the number of cells as a cubic tetrahedron with the same resolution. It can be shown that the average delta form factor is the same for both geometries when they have the same number of cells. Thus, a cubic tetrahedron must have a resolution of $\sqrt{2} * n \times \sqrt{2} * n$ cells in order to be equivalent to a hemicube with a resolution of $n \times n$ cells.

> Details aside, the cubic tetrahedron is an uncomplicated variant of the hemicube. Except where noted, the following discussions referring to hemicubes and the hemicube algorithm also apply to cubic tetrahedrons.

5.9   NUMERICAL INTEGRATION ERRORS

Before eulogizing either the hemicube or cubic tetrahedral algorithm as *the* solution to form factor determination, we should consider their limitations. Most important, we must remember that these algorithms can only estimate the form factor between any two patches. There will always be some error due to the approximate nature of numerical integration.

A very thorough study of this problem with respect to hemicubes (but not cubic tetrahedrons) is presented in Max and Troutman (1993). We will not attempt to review this study or otherwise quantify these errors here. Instead, we will examine their causes and effects. This knowledge will later prove useful in visually assessing the results of our radiosity renderer. It will also highlight some of the fundamental limitations of the hemicube and similar numerical quadrature algorithms.

If we choose a hemicube or cubic tetrahedron resolution that is too coarse, we

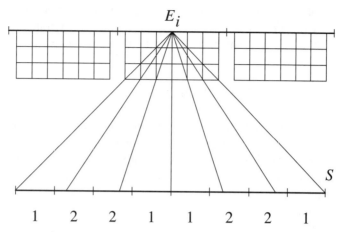

Figure 5.17 Hemicube aliasing

may end up with annoyingly visible aliasing artifacts in our images. Consider Figure 5.17, where the surface S is discretized into a regular array of patches and projected onto a hemicube centered over patch E_i. (A cubic tetrahedron could also be used; the following arguments remain the same.) Some of the patches cover two cells, whereas the others cover only one each. If the hemicube patch is emitting light, these patches may "receive" (according to their calculated form factors) approximately twice as much flux as their neighbors.

This problem is particularly evident when the discretization of a surface into polygons is such that their projection onto the hemicube nearly matches that of the spacing of the hemicube cells. It can be further aggravated by moving the hemicube to patches adjacent to E_i and repeating the process. Depending on the spacing between these patches relative to S, the erroneous distribution of flux on S may be reinforced. Displayed in an image, the surface will appear to have a distinctly plaid-like variation in shading.

A partial solution is to randomly vary the hemicube's orientation about the surface normal as it is moved from patch to patch (Wallace et al. 1987). Although this will not solve the aliasing problem for individual patches, the likelihood of their shading patterns reinforcing one another will be greatly diminished. The sum of these patterns will appear as low-contrast, random noise, to which our eyes are fairly insensitive.

A second, more serious problem is that small patches may cover less than one cell, in which case they will be missed entirely. This can seriously affect small but highly luminous patches in an environment, particularly high-intensity light sources. Reversing roles with the patch beneath the hemicube as a receiver, we see that it may "receive" no flux at all from the emitting patch, even though both are fully visible to one another.

We can, of course, alleviate this problem by increasing the hemicube resolution. However, the hemicube algorithm has a time complexity (Section 2.6) of approximately $\mathbf{O}(n^2)$, where n is the hemicube resolution (e.g., Vilaplana and Pueyo 1992).

In other words, doubling the hemicube resolution approximately quadruples the algorithm's execution time. This also applies to the cubic tetrahedral algorithm. It is the inevitable trade-off in radiosity rendering between image quality and rendering time.

5.10 FORM FACTORS AND RADIOSITY

Before proceeding any further, we should consider the role of form factors in solving the radiosity equation. Figure 5.18 shows one surface (labeled source) illuminating another (labeled receiver). Both surfaces are divided into patches and elements, as explained in Section 3.7. So far, it appears as if we must determine the form factors between each pair of elements. For an environment with 50,000 elements, this means 2,500 million form factors!

The surfaces in an environment should be discretized into patches and elements such that Gouraud shading each element does not result in objectionable aliasing artifacts. The elements must be closely spaced in order to capture the fine shading details across surfaces in a rendered image, particularly at shadow boundaries. (This topic is discussed in detail in Chapter 7.) We will eventually have to calculate the radiant exitance of each of these elements.

However, this topic is primarily a visual criterion. In terms of calculating the flux transfer between two surfaces, we need to apply the five-times rule (Section 5.5). Suppose the receiving surface in Figure 5.18 is discretized into patches and elements such that each patch of the emitting surface satisfies the five-times rule. If so, then we can safely model each patch as a point source. This means that we need to determine only the form factor from the source *patch* to the receiving element. There is no point in considering element-to-element form factors; the calculated flux transfer between the elements of a source patch and a receiving element will be (approximately) the same as that calculated between the patch itself and the receiving element (Cohen et al. 1986).

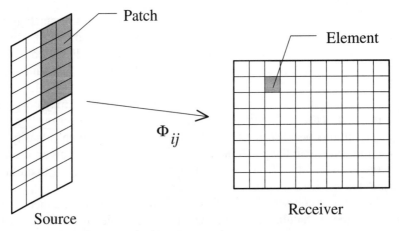

Figure 5.18 Radiant flux transfer between surfaces

This explains why we created a two-level hierarchy of patches and elements in Section 3.7. If we have an environment consisting of m patches and n elements, we need to determine only $m \times n$ form factors between patches and elements. As an example, an environment with 5,000 patches and 50,000 elements requires "only" 250 million form factors.

Fortunately, this is not as bad as it looks: the hemicube algorithm calculates form factors from a patch to all elements in the environment in parallel. An environment with 5,000 patches therefore requires only one hemicube calculation per patch. Furthermore, we will see in the next chapter that we need to store only one form factor per element.

There are other computational advantages to using a two-level hierarchy of patches and elements, and these are examined in Chapter 6. Before then, however, we need to implement the hemicube and cubic tetrahedral algorithms.

5.11 JUST ANOTHER VIEWING SYSTEM

The hemicube algorithm is much easier to explain than it is to implement in software. Seen in isolation, the myriad details tend to overshadow and obscure the underlying algorithm. Like our viewing system, it becomes difficult to see the logic for the code.

Fortunately, we have already seen most of these details before—it's our viewing system! Consider the similarities:

Hemicube Algorithm	Viewing System
Differential area emitter dE_i	Eye position
Hemicube face	View-plane window/screen
Hemicube cell	Screen pixel

The hemicube algorithm is essentially a polygon scan conversion process. Suppose we want to determine the form factor F_{ij} from a polygon E_i to another polygon E_j in an environment. Each hemicube face defines a view volume whose back clipping plane is at plus infinity and whose front clipping plane is (almost) at the hemicube's center (Fig. 5.19a). In other words, it defines an essentially infinite four-sided pyramid. (The cubic tetrahedron's view volume, shown Figure 5.19b, is similar except that it defines a three-sided pyramid.)

If we position the hemicube over E_i, we can perform a perspective projection of E_j onto each of its faces. Filling the projected polygon on each face allows us to determine which hemicube cells are covered by the projection. Once this is done, the approximate form factor F_{ij} is given by Equation 5.10.

One difference is that the viewing system described in Chapter 4 has its origin centered on the view-plane window, whereas the hemicube's u, v, n coordinate system is centered on the eye position (Fig 5.20). A moment's reflection, however, will

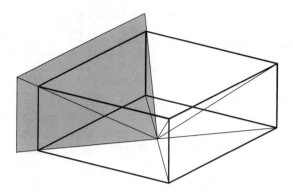

Figure 5.19a   Hemicube face view volumes

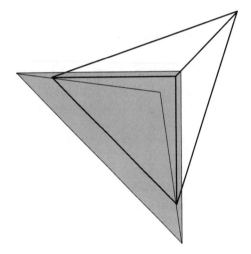

Figure 5.19b   Cubic tetrahedron view volumes

reveal that the two systems are essentially equivalent; the only difference is that the hemicube's origin has been translated a distance of one unit along the n axis with respect to our viewing system's origin. Allowing for this, we can treat the hemicube face no differently from a view-plane window. In particular, we can reuse much of our viewing system code from Chapter 4 to implement the hemicube algorithm.

Unlike our previous attempts at form factor determination, the hemicube algorithm trivially solves the polygon occlusion problem by using a variation of the Z-buffer algorithm presented in Section 4.14. Instead of storing the closest polygon color for each screen pixel in a frame buffer, we can store an identifier for the closest polygon in an equivalent *item buffer*, with one entry for each hemicube cell. A depth-array entry is similarly assigned to each cell.

Suppose we assign a unique identifier to each polygon in the environment, after which we initialize the depth array to *INFINITY* and set the item buffer entries to

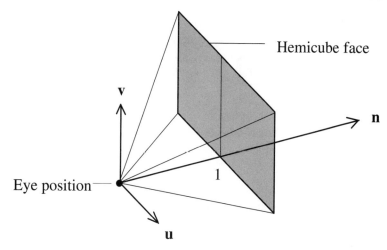

v

n

Hemicube face

Eye position

1

u

Figure 5.20 Hemicube face coordinate system

NONE. As we project each visible polygon in the environment onto the hemicube, we compare its depth at each covered hemicube cell with the current depth-array entry. If it is closer than the current depth, we update the entry and assign the polygon identifier to the item buffer entry. When all of the polygons in the environment have been considered, we scan the item buffer and calculate the form factor for each polygon using Equation 5.10.

Thus, given a polygon E_i, the hemicube algorithm calculates the form factors F_{ij} from E_i to all other polygons E_j in the environment. We can express this algorithm in the pseudocode shown in Figure 5.21 (from Rushmeier et al. 1991).

```
FOR each hemicube cell k              // Precalculate delta form factors
   Calculate delta form factor ΔF_k
ENDFOR

FOR each hemicube face                // Initialize hemicube cells
   FOR each hemicube cell k
      cell_depth(k) = INFINITY
      polygon_id(k) = NONE
   ENDFOR
ENDFOR

FOR each polygon E_ji                 // Initialize polygon form factors
F_ij = 0
ENDFOR

FOR each hemicube face
   FOR each polygon E_j               // Scan convert polygon E_j
      Transform E_j coordinates to E_j (hemicube) view space
      IF E_j is visible
         Clip E_j to hemicube face view volume
         IF clipped polygon is inside view volume
            Project polygon onto hemicube face
```

(continued)

Figure 5.21   *(continued)*

```
        FOR each hemicube face cell k
          IF cell k is covered
            IF depth of E_j at cell k < cell_depth(k)
              cell_depth(k) = depth of E_j at cell k
              polygon_id(k) = j
            ENDIF
          ENDIF
        ENDFOR
      ENDIF
    ENDIF
  ENDFOR

  FOR each hemicube face cell k   // Sum delta form factors
    m = polygon_id(k)
    F_im = F_im + ΔF_k
  ENDFOR
ENDFOR
```

Figure 5.21   Hemicube algorithm

The pseudocode for the cubic tetrahedral algorithm is essentially identical. All we have to do is substitute the words "cubic tetrahedron" where "hemicube" appears. This similarity will be reflected in our C++ implementation, where the common features will be encapsulated in an abstract "form factor" class.

<h2>5.12   DELTA FORM FACTOR CALCULATIONS</h2>

Our first requirement is to precalculate the delta form factors and store the results in a look-up table. For a resolution of $n \times n$ cells, we need to store a minimum of $3n^2/8$ floating-point values for hemicubes. The equivalent cubic tetrahedron has a resolution of $m \times m$ cells, where $m = \sqrt{2} * n$. It therefore requires $m^2/4 = n^2/2$ values. Assuming $n = 100$ and four-byte *float* data type as an example, this translates to 15 Kbytes and 20 Kbytes of memory respectively.

These are minimum values, however. For the hemicube, we need a square array of $n^2/4$ cells to store the delta form factors for the side faces. Unfortunately, the $n^2/8$ delta form factors for the top face of the hemicube form a triangular array. We will want to access this array using a cell's integer u, v coordinates as quickly as possible. Rather than perform a complex mapping between these coordinates and offsets into some sort of compacted array, it is usually better to allocate memory for two quadrants of delta form factors (one for the top face and another for the side faces). This requires $n^2/2$ floating-point values, or 20 Kbytes for the above example. This is a fairly insignificant amount of memory, at least for a radiosity-rendering program. We can allocate a static array in memory and initialize it at program startup.

The cubic tetrahedron is more problematic. We need to store delta form factors for only one half of one face, but this again leads to a triangular array. Storing these

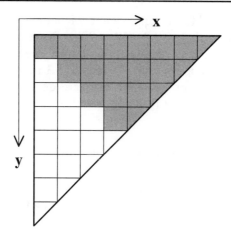

Figure 5.22   Unique delta form factor values for a cubic tetrahedron face

values in a static array implies that we must allocate 40 Kbytes for the above example. If we increased the resolution to $n = 400$ (that is, 566×566 cells), we would be wasting 313 Kbytes of memory. (In fact, we need to store slightly more than $m^2/4$ values. Figure 5.22 demonstrates that for $m = 8$, we need to allocate space for $m^2/4 + m/2 = 20$ unique values. The array remains triangular with $m/2$ rows of varying size.)

Fortunately, one of the more subtle features of the C++ programming language comes to our rescue. We can easily allocate a static (or, if we prefer, dynamic) triangular array with no wasted memory and relatively little overhead. All we have to do is allocate a one-dimensional array for each row and an array of pointers to the rows. C++ (and its progenitor, C) allow us to access this construct exactly as if it were a two-dimensional array. The details are described in a text file on the accompanying diskette.

For now, we have our first C++ code:

Listing 5.1

```
// FF_DELTA.H- Delta Form Factors

#ifndef _FF_DELTA_H
#define _FF_DELTA_H

// Delta form factor resolution (must be an even number)
#if defined(_CUBIC_TETRA)
static const int FF_ArrayRes = 142;
#else
static const int FF_ArrayRes = 100;
#endif

#endif
```

A resolution of 100×100 cells for hemicubes provides a reasonable trade-off between execution speed and minimization of aliasing artifacts. (A resolution of 142

× 142 cells is required for an equivalent cubic tetrahedron.) You can experiment with different resolutions (such as 50×50 or 200×200 cells) by redefining *FF_ArrayRes* and recompiling. The only restriction is that *FF_ArrayRes* must be an even number. (A further restriction applies to MS-Windows 3.1 in that the allocated array size cannot exceed 64 Kbytes unless the arrays are declared as *_huge*—something that should be done only as a last resort.)

5.12.1 Hemicube Form Factor Calculations

FF_DELTA.H simply specifies the delta form factor resolution. We can use the following C++ class to precalculate and store the delta form factors for our hemicube:

Listing 5.2

```
// HC_DELTA.H - Hemicube Delta Form Factor Class

#ifndef _HC_DELTA_H
#define _HC_DELTA_H

#include "general.h"
#include "ff_delta.h"

static const int HC_ArrayDim = FF_ArrayRes / 2;

class HemiDelta          // Hemicube delta form factors
{
  private:
    static float side_array[HC_ArrayDim][HC_ArrayDim];
    static float top_array[HC_ArrayDim][HC_ArrayDim];

  public:
    HemiDelta();

    // Get top face cell form factor
    float GetTopFactor( int row, int col )
    {
      if (row >= HC_ArrayDim)
        row -= HC_ArrayDim;
      else
        row = HC_ArrayDim - row - 1;

      if (col >= HC_ArrayDim)
        col -= HC_ArrayDim;
      else
        col = HC_ArrayDim - col - 1;

      return top_array[row][col];
    }
```

```
      // Get side face cell form factor
      float GetSideFactor( int row, int col )
      {
        if (col >= HC_ArrayDim)
          col -= HC_ArrayDim;
        else
          col = HC_ArrayDim - col - 1;

        return side_array[row - HC_ArrayDim][col];
      }
};

#endif
```

GetTopFactor and *GetSideFactor* map a cell's integer coordinates to indices for the static delta form factor arrays before returning the appropriate value. The arrays are initialized at program startup by:

Listing 5.3

```
// HC_DELTA.CPP - Hemicube Delta Form Factor Class

#include "hc_delta.h"

// Static delta form factor arrays
float HemiDelta::side_array[HC_ArrayDim][HC_ArrayDim];
float HemiDelta::top_array[HC_ArrayDim][HC_ArrayDim];

HemiDelta::HemiDelta()  // Class constructor
{
  int i, j;             // Loop indices
  double da;            // Cell area
  double dx, dy, dz;    // Cell dimensions
  double r, x, y, z;    // Cell coordinates

  // Initialize cell dimensions and area
  dx = dy = dz = 2.0 / (float) FF_ArrayRes;
  da = 4.0 / ((float) FF_ArrayRes * (float) FF_ArrayRes);

  // Calculate top face delta form factors
  x = dx / 2.0;
  for (i = 0; i < HC_ArrayDim; i++)
  {
    y = dy / 2.0;
    for (j = 0; j < HC_ArrayDim; j++)
    {
      r = x * x + y * y + 1.0;
      top_array[i][j] = (float) (da / (PI * r * r));
      y += dy;
    }
    x += dx;
  }
```

(continued)

Listing 5.3 *(continued)*

```
// Calculate side face delta form factors
x = dx / 2.0;
for (i = 0; i < HC_ArrayDim; i++)
{
  z = dz / 2.0;
  for (j = 0; j < HC_ArrayDim; j++)
  {
    r = x * x + z * z + 1.0;
    side_array[i][j] = (float) (z * da / (PI * r * r));
    z += dy;
  }
  x += dx;
}
}
```

Only one global instance of *HemiDelta* is required in a radiosity-rendering program. If you want to experiment with different hemicube resolutions without recompiling, *HemiDelta* should be modified such that it dynamically allocates and initializes its delta form factor arrays.

5.12.2 Cubic Tetrahedron Form Factor Calculations

Our C++ code for precalculating and later accessing delta form factor values for cubic tetrahedrons is based on a C implementation presented in Beran-Koehn and Pavicic (1992). Translated into C++, the code becomes:

Listing 5.4

```
// CT_DELTA.H- Cubic Tetrahedron Delta Form Factor Class

#ifndef _CT_DELTA_H
#define _CT_DELTA_H

#include "general.h"
#include "ff_delta.h"

// Delta form factor array size
static const CT_DeltaDim = FF_ArrayRes / 2;
static const int CT_FormDim = CT_DeltaDim * CT_DeltaDim +
    CT_DeltaDim;

// Cubic tetrahedron face coordinate limits
static const double CT_MinCoord = -2.0;
static const double CT_MaxCoord = 1.0;

class CubicDelta    // Cubic tetrahedron delta form factors
{
```

```
  private:
    // Delta form factor row pointer array
    static float *delta_array[CT_DeltaDim];

    // Delta form factor array
    static float ff_array[CT_FormDim];
  public:
    CubicDelta();

    // Get delta form factor
    float GetFactor( int row, int col )
    {
      int temp;            // Temporary variable

      if (row > col)
      {
        temp = row;
        row = col;
        col = temp;
      }

      return delta_array[row][col - row];
    }
};

#endif
```

and:

Listing 5.5

```
// CT_DELTA.CPP- Cubic Tetrahedron Delta Form Factor Class

#include "ct_delta.h"

// Static delta form factor row pointer array
float *CubicDelta::delta_array[CT_DeltaDim];

// Static delta form factor array
float CubicDelta::ff_array[CT_FormDim];

CubicDelta::CubicDelta()            // Class constructor
{
  int i = 0;                        // Form factor array index
  int left, right, top, bottom;     // Index boundaries
  int row, col;                     // Current indices
  double delta;                     // Cell width
  double diag_delta;                // Diagonal cell width
  double area;                      // Cell area
  double diag_area;                 // Diagonal cell area
  double y, z;                      // Cell center
  double diag_y, diag_z;            // Diagonal cell center
  double r2;                        // Cell distance squared
```

(continued)

Listing 5.5   *(continued)*

```
// Initialize index boundaries
left = top = 0;
right = FF_ArrayRes - 1;
bottom = FF_ArrayRes / 2;

// Initialize cell values
delta = (CT_MaxCoord - CT_MinCoord) / FF_ArrayRes;
diag_delta = delta / 2.0;
area  = delta * delta;
diag_area  = area / 2.0;
y = z = CT_MaxCoord - diag_delta;

// Calculate delta form factors
for (row = top; row < bottom; row++)
{
  // Save delta form factor array row pointer
  delta_array[row] = &(ff_array[i]);

  for (col = left; col < right; col++)
  {
    // Calculate square of cell distance
    r2 = y * y + z * z + 1;

    // Calculate cell delta form factor
    ff_array[i++] = (float) (area * (y + z + 1) / (PI * r2
        * r2 * sqrt(3.0)));

    y -= delta;
  }

  // Calculate square of diagonal cell distance
  diag_y = y + diag_delta;
  diag_z = z + diag_delta;
  r2 = diag_y * diag_y + diag_z * diag_z + 1;

  // Calculate diagonal cell delta form factor
  ff_array[i++] = (float) (diag_area * (diag_y + diag_z +
      1) / (PI * r2 * r2 * sqrt(3.0)));

  left++;
  right-;
  y = z -= delta;
  }
}
```

Unlike *HemiDelta*, *CubicDelta* dynamically allocates a two-dimensional triangular array for its delta form factor values. The details of this technique are discussed in a text file on the accompanying diskette. A similar discussion is presented in Ashdown (1988).

Like our previous *HemiDelta* class, only one global instance of *CubicDelta* is required in a radiosity-rendering program. Moreover, we should choose between the two at some point, because only one is required for form factor determination. Now we have more work to do.

5.13 A POLYGON VERTEX ARRAY CLASS

In an ideal world with truly intelligent optimizing compilers, we could simply derive an implementation of the hemicube algorithm from our previous implementation of the Sutherland-Hodgman algorithm in *PolyClip4* (Section 4.8.6). The C++ compiler would then rewrite our code to remove the extraneous components, reorder our mathematical calculations for improved efficiency, and so forth. In more realistic terms, the two applications are sufficiently different that we are better off rewriting *PolyClip4* expressly for clipping polygons against hemicubes and cubic tetrahedrons.

Following the development of *PolyClip4*, we first need a polygon vertex array class that is very similar to our *OutPolygon* class in Listing 4.5. This becomes:

Listing 5.6

```
// FF_POLY.H - Form Factor Polygon Class

#ifndef _FF_POLY_H
#define _FF_POLY_H

#include "patch3.h"
#include "vector4.h"

// Maximum number of output vertices
static const int MaxVert = 10;

class FormPoly            // Form factor polygon
{
  private:
    Point3 posn[MaxVert];       // Output vertex array
    int num_vert;               // Number of vertices
    WORD ident;                 // Polygon identifier

    void AddVertex( Vector4 &v )
    { v.Perspective(&(posn[num_vert++])); }

    void Reset( WORD id )
    {
      num_vert = 0;
      ident = id;
    }

    friend class FormClipEdge;
    friend class FormClip;
```

(continued)

Listing 5.6   *(continued)*

```
public:
  FormPoly()
  {
    num_vert = 0;
    ident = 0;
  }

  int GetNumVert() { return num_vert; }
  Point3 &GetVertex( int i )
  { return posn[i]; }
  WORD GetPolyId() { return ident; }
};

#endif
```

The *ident* member holds the identifier of the polygon currently being projected onto the hemicube. Unlike our *OutPolygon* class, we need to store only the position for each polygon vertex. This considerably simplifies the class's internal details.

We will need five instances of *FormPoly*, one for each hemicube face. Thus:

Listing 5.7

```
// HC_POLY.H - Hemicube Polygon Class

#ifndef _HC_POLY_H
#define _HC_POLY_H

#include "ff_poly.h"

// Hemicube face identifiers
enum HC_Face
{
  HC_TopFace   = 0,   // n = +1.0
  HC_FrontFace = 1,   // v = +1.0
  HC_RightFace = 2,   // u = +1.0
  HC_BackFace  = 3,   // v = -1.0
  HC_LeftFace  = 4    // u = -1.0
};

#endif
```

HC_POLY.H defines the enumerated *HC_Face* data type. Its values are used arbitrarily but consistently to label the hemicube faces according to their orientation with respect to the hemicube's view-space coordinate system, as shown in Figure 5.23.

We will similarly need three instances of *FormPoly* for our cubic tetrahedron. This becomes:

Listing 5.8

```
// CT_POLY.H - Cubic Tetrahedron Polygon Class

#ifndef _CT_POLY_H
#define _CT_POLY_H

#include "ff_poly.h"

// Cubic tetrahedron face identifiers
enum CT_Face
{
  CT_TopFace = 0,   // n = +1.0
  CT_RightFace = 1, // u = +1.0
  CT_LeftFace = 2   // v = +1.0
};

#endif
```

where the cubic tetrahedron faces are labeled according to the conventions shown in Figure 5.24.

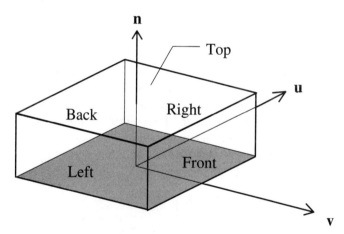

Figure 5.23 Hemicube face naming conventions

5.14 HEMICUBE ORIENTATION

We saw in Section 5.9 that the hemicube should be randomly oriented (or *jittered*) about its *n* axis when it is placed over the center of a polygon in order to minimize aliasing artifacts. We can do this by first generating a random vector **r** using C++'s *rand* function for each coordinate. From this, we derive a random *u*-axis vector $\mathbf{u}_{HC}$, with:

$$\mathbf{u}_{HC} = \mathbf{n}_P \times \mathbf{r} \tag{5.26}$$

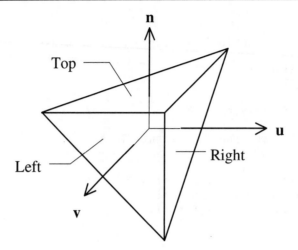

Figure 5.24   Cubic tetrahedron face-naming conventions

where $\mathbf{n}_P = \mathbf{n}_{HC}$ is the polygon normal. (We may have to generate another random vector and repeat this calculation if the length of $\mathbf{u}_{HC}$ is zero.) After normalizing $\mathbf{u}_{HC}$, the v-axis vector $\mathbf{v}_{HC}$ is calculated from:

$$\mathbf{v}_{HC} = \mathbf{u}_{HC} \times \mathbf{n}_{HC} \tag{5.27}$$

This gives us the hemicube's view space in world coordinates. We will need to reorient this system to align it with each face before we can project polygons against them. Fortunately, the hemicube's symmetry makes this particularly easy to do. Following a suggestion by Vilaplana and Pueyo (1992), we can simply swap coordinates and change signs as required for our viewing axes; no other floating-point operations are necessary. Given a hemicube's view-space axes $\mathbf{u}_{HC}$, $\mathbf{v}_{HC}$, and $\mathbf{n}_{HC}$ expressed in world coordinates (Fig. 5.23), the hemicube face-view spaces can be determined from:

Top: $\mathbf{u}_T = \mathbf{u}_{HC},\quad \mathbf{v}_T = \mathbf{v}_{HC},\quad \mathbf{n}_T = \mathbf{n}_{HC}$

Front: $\mathbf{u}_F = -\mathbf{u}_{HC},\quad \mathbf{v}_F = \mathbf{n}_{HC},\quad \mathbf{n}_F = \mathbf{v}_{HC}$

Right: $\mathbf{u}_R = \mathbf{v}_{HC},\quad \mathbf{v}_R = \mathbf{n}_{HC},\quad \mathbf{n}_R = \mathbf{u}_{HC}$ (5.28)

Back: $\mathbf{u}_B = \mathbf{u}_{HC},\quad \mathbf{v}_B = \mathbf{n}_{HC},\quad \mathbf{n}_B = -\mathbf{v}_{HC}$

Left: $\mathbf{u}_L = -\mathbf{v}_{HC},\quad \mathbf{v}_L = \mathbf{n}_{HC},\quad \mathbf{n}_L = -\mathbf{u}_{HC}$

Positioning and orienting the cubic tetrahedron's viewing system is a more involved procedure than it is for the hemicube. We can use Equations 5.26 and 5.27 to generate a randomly oriented viewing system whose normal is collinear with the polygon normal and whose origin coincides with the polygon center. We can think of this as the polygon's view space, with its axes expressed in world coordinates as the unit vectors $\mathbf{u}_P$, $\mathbf{v}_P$, and $\mathbf{n}_P$.

From here, we need to align the cubic tetrahedron's view space such that the polygon normal has the view-space coordinates $\{1/\sqrt{3}, 1/\sqrt{3}, 1/\sqrt{3}\}$. In terms of the polygon's view space, the tetrahedron's view-space axes then have the coordinates:

$$\mathbf{u}_{CT} = \left\{ \frac{1}{2\sqrt{3}}+1, \quad \frac{1}{2\sqrt{3}}-1, \quad \frac{1}{\sqrt{3}} \right\}$$

$$\mathbf{v}_{CT} = \left\{ \frac{1}{2\sqrt{3}}-1, \quad \frac{1}{2\sqrt{3}}+1, \quad \frac{1}{\sqrt{3}} \right\} \tag{5.29}$$

$$\mathbf{n}_{CT} = \left\{ \frac{-1}{\sqrt{3}}, \quad \frac{-1}{\sqrt{3}}, \quad \frac{1}{\sqrt{3}} \right\}$$

Expressed in world coordinates, these become:

$$\mathbf{u}_{CT} = a*\mathbf{u}_P + b*\mathbf{v}_P - c*\mathbf{n}_P$$

$$\mathbf{v}_{CT} = b*\mathbf{u}_P + a*\mathbf{v}_P - c*\mathbf{n}_P \tag{5.30}$$

$$\mathbf{n}_{CT} = c*\mathbf{u}_P + c*\mathbf{v}_P - c*\mathbf{n}_P$$

where the constants a, b, and c are:

$$a = \frac{1}{2\sqrt{3}}+1$$

$$b = \frac{1}{2\sqrt{3}}-1 \tag{5.31}$$

$$c = \frac{-1}{\sqrt{3}}$$

This gives us the cubic tetrahedron's view space in world coordinates. Looking out from the polygon center through each face, we see a triangular view-plane window (Fig. 5.25a). It will be convenient when later we come to polygon scan conversion to have this window oriented as shown in Figure 5.25b. This can be done by negating the u-axis and v-axis coordinate values.

Combining this with our earlier approach for hemicubes, we can reorient the cubic tetrahedron's view space to that of each face with the following:

$$\text{Top:} \quad \mathbf{u}_T = -\mathbf{u}_{CT}, \quad \mathbf{v}_T = -\mathbf{v}_{CT}, \quad \mathbf{n}_T = \mathbf{n}_{CT}$$

$$\text{Left:} \quad \mathbf{u}_L = -\mathbf{u}_{CT}, \quad \mathbf{v}_L = -\mathbf{n}_{CT}, \quad \mathbf{n}_L = \mathbf{v}_{CT} \tag{5.32}$$

$$\text{Right:} \quad \mathbf{u}_R = -\mathbf{v}_{CT}, \quad \mathbf{v}_R = -\mathbf{n}_{CT}, \quad \mathbf{n}_R = \mathbf{u}_{CT}$$

5.15 VIEW-SPACE TRANSFORMATIONS

We now have a hemicube or cubic tetrahedron face view space expressed as vectors **u**, **v**, and **n** in world coordinates. With these, we can use Equations 4.8 and 4.9 to

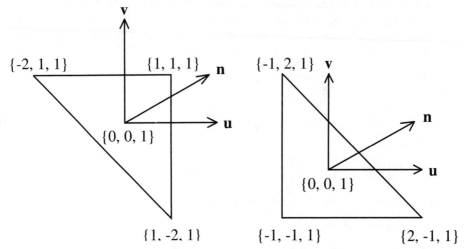

Figure 5.25a   Top-view window   **Figure 5.25b**   Rotated top-view window

determine the view-transformation matrix **M** needed to transform a polygon vertex's world coordinates to this view space. To repeat those equations here:

$$\mathbf{M} = \begin{bmatrix} u_x & u_y & u_z & t_x \\ v_x & v_y & v_z & t_y \\ n_x & n_y & n_z & t_z \\ 0 & 0 & 0 & 1 \end{bmatrix} \tag{5.33}$$

where:

$$t_x = -o_x * u_x - o_y * u_y - o_z * u_z$$
$$t_y = -o_x * v_x - o_y * v_y - o_z * v_z \tag{5.34}$$
$$t_z = -o_x * n_x - o_y * n_y - o_z * n_z$$

and where the bound vector **o** (expressed in world coordinates) represents the view-space origin (i.e., the polygon center).

Recalling that the origin lies at the eye position (Fig. 5.20), we need to translate the view space one unit along the n axis to place the origin in the center of the face. From Equation 4.4, the necessary translation matrix is:

$$\mathbf{T} = \begin{bmatrix} 1 & 0 & 0 & 0 \\ 0 & 1 & 0 & 0 \\ 0 & 0 & 1 & -1 \\ 0 & 0 & 0 & 1 \end{bmatrix} \tag{5.35}$$

We also need to perform the usual perspective and normalization transformations. The perspective-transformation matrix is given by Equation 4.14. Since the view distance is exactly minus one, we have:

$$\mathbf{P} = \begin{bmatrix} 1 & 0 & 0 & 0 \\ 0 & 1 & 0 & 0 \\ 0 & 0 & 1 & 0 \\ 0 & 0 & 1 & 1 \end{bmatrix} \tag{5.36}$$

The normalization matrix is given by Equations 4.16 and 4.17. However, we have to be careful here because the hemicube and cubic tetrahedron faces will require different normalization transformations.

Consider the hemicube faces: Our view-plane window is a square, even for the side faces—we are simply choosing to ignore the bottom half of the view from these windows. Therefore, the aspect ratio is unity, and so $s_u = s_v = 1/2$. This gives us:

$$\mathbf{N}_{HC} = \begin{bmatrix} 1/2 & 0 & 0 & 1/2 \\ 0 & 1/2 & 0 & 1/2 \\ 0 & 0 & s_n & r_n \\ 0 & 0 & 0 & 1 \end{bmatrix} \tag{5.37}$$

where s_n and r_n are determined by our choices for the front and back clipping-plane distances F and B.

Unlike our viewing system in Chapter 4, there is no reason to clip against a front and back plane. If we set the back clipping-plane distance to plus infinity (represented in our code as *MAX_VALUE*), we can dispense with a back-plane clipping operation altogether.

The front clipping-plane distance is more problematic. Ideally, we should locate it as close to the eye position as possible in order to include in the view volume everything above the polygon surface. This suggests a value of *MIN_VALUE* − 1 to ensure that we will not have a divide-by-zero error for a point exactly on or behind the polygon surface. Recalling Section 4.3, however, we are reminded that perspective projection distorts the n-axis values. In particular, placing the front-plane distance too close to the eye position degrades the Z-buffer pseudodepth resolution (Section 4.14). A more reasonable value is −0.99 units, assuming that no two polygons in our environment will be closer together than this. (This is generally a reasonable assumption, at least for form factor calculations.)

These arguments for the front and back clipping planes also apply to the cubic tetrahedron faces. However, Equation 4.16 no longer applies. We have instead:

$$\mathbf{N}_{CT} = \begin{bmatrix} 1/3 & 0 & 0 & 1/3 \\ 0 & 1/3 & 0 & 1/3 \\ 0 & 0 & s_n & r_n \\ 0 & 0 & 0 & 1 \end{bmatrix} \tag{5.38}$$

where s_n and r_n are as given before (Eq. 4.17). Referring to Figure 5.25b, we see that

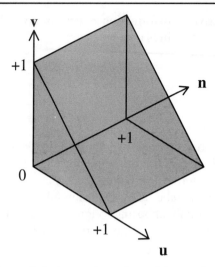

Figure 5.26   Canonical parallel-view volume for cubic tetrahedrons

this transformation translates the view-plane window one unit along the u axis and v axis and scales it in these directions by one third. The view volume is scaled along the n axis as before, resulting in the canonical parallel-view volume shown in Figure 5.26.

We can concatenate these transformation matrices to obtain the three-dimensional projective transformation matrix for our hemicube or cubic tetrahedron faces. That is, similar to Equation 4.19, we have:

$$\begin{bmatrix} P_u \\ P_v \\ P_n \\ w \end{bmatrix} = \mathbf{NPTM} \begin{bmatrix} p_x \\ p_y \\ p_z \\ 1 \end{bmatrix} \tag{5.39}$$

where $\{p_x, p_y, p_z\}$ are the world coordinates of a polygon vertex p. This provides us with the four-dimensional homogeneous coordinates we need for polygon clipping. All we need now is a framework in which to implement these equations.

5.16   POLYGON CLIPPING REVISITED

It is clear that we shall need separate polygon-clipping strategies for our hemicube and cubic tetrahedron view volumes, if only because of their different clipping planes. At the same time, these strategies will have much in common. It makes sense then to develop an abstract polygon clipper class and derive our two polygon clippers from it.

Much of the following code is an adaptation of *PolyClip4*, with the addition of components from our *ViewSys* class (Listings 4.1 and 4.2). Thus:

Listing 5.9

```
// FF_CLIP.H - Form Factor Polygon Clipper Class

#ifndef _FF_CLIP_H
#define _FF_CLIP_H

#include "ff_poly.h"

// View normalization parameters
static const double FPD = -0.99;
static const double BPD = MAX_VALUE;
static const double EYE = -1.0;
static const double SN = (EYE - BPD) * (EYE - FPD) / (EYE *
    EYE * (BPD - FPD));
static const double RN = FPD * (EYE - BPD) / (EYE * (FPD -
    BPD));

class FormClipEdge        // Edge-plane clipper
{
  private:
    FormClipEdge *pnext;         // Next clipper pointer
    Vector4 normal;              // Plane normal
    Vector4 first;               // First vertex
    Vector4 start;               // Start vertex
    BOOL first_inside;           // First vertex inside flag
    BOOL start_inside;           // Start vertex inside flag
    BOOL first_flag;             // First vertex seen flag

    BOOL IsInside( Vector4 &v )
    { return (Dot(normal, v) >= 0.0); }
    Vector4 Intersect( Vector4 &, Vector4 & );
    void Output( Vector4 &, FormPoly & );

  public:
    FormClipEdge() { first_flag = FALSE; }

    void Add( FormClipEdge *pc ) { pnext = pc; }
    void Clip( Vector4 &, FormPoly & );
    void Close( FormPoly & );
    void SetNormal( Vector4 &n ) { normal = n; }
};

class FormClip  // Form factor polygon clipper
{
  protected:
    int num_vert;                // # of polygon vertices
    Vector3 u, v, n;             // View system coordinates
    double vtm[4][4];            // Transformation matrix
    FormClipEdge clipper[5];     // Clipper array
    FormClipEdge *pclip;         // Clipper list head pointer
    Point3 center;               // Polygon center
```

(continued)

Listing 5.9 *(continued)*

```
   Vector3 RandomVector()        // Generate random vector
   {
     Vector3 temp;      // Temporary vector

     temp.SetX(GetNormRand() * 2.0 - 1.0);
     temp.SetY(GetNormRand() * 2.0 - 1.0);
     temp.SetZ(GetNormRand() * 2.0 - 1.0);

     return temp;
   }

 public:
   BOOL BackFaceCull( Patch3 *ppatch )
   {
     Vector3 view;      // View vector

     // Calculate view vector
     view = Vector3(ppatch->GetVertexPtr(0)->GetPosn(),
         center);

     // Indicate whether patch is backface
     return (Dot(ppatch->GetNormal(), view) < MIN_VALUE) ?
         TRUE : FALSE;
   }

   int Clip( Element3 *, FormPoly &, WORD );
};

#endif
```

FF_CLIP.H is very similar to P_CLIP4.H (Listing 4.6). The only major changes are in the derivation of *FormClipEdge* from the *ClipEdge* class. These are:

- The polygon center (*center*), the view system axis coordinates (*u*, *v*, and *n*), and a view-transformation matrix (*vtm*) have been added to assist in reorienting the view system for each hemicube or cubic tetrahedron face.
- Backface culling of patches to be projected onto a face is provided by *Back-FaceCull*, which is an adaptation of *ViewSys::BackFaceCull* from Listing 4.2. (If a planar surface patch faces away from the eye position, then logically all of its elements will do the same.)
- Random vectors are generated by *RandomVector.*

Since the view distance and front and back clipping-plane distances are now constant, *EYE, FPD,* and *BPD* are provided to compute *SN* and *RN* in accordance with Equation 4.17. These constants will be used later to implement the normalization transformations (Eqs. 5.37 and 5.38).

The remainder of our abstract polygon clipper class is adapted from P_CLIP4.CPP (Listing 4.7):

Listing 5.10

```
// FF_CLIP.CPP - Form Factor Polygon Clipper Class

#include "ff_clip.h"

// Clip element
int FormClip::Clip( Element3 *pelem, FormPoly &out, WORD
    poly_id )
{
  int i;              // Loop index
  int num_vert;       // Number of vertices
  Vertex3 *pvert;     // 3-D world space vertex pointer
  Vector4 hv;         // 4-D homogeneous coord vertex

  out.Reset(poly_id);    // Reset output polygon

  num_vert = pelem->GetNumVert();
  for (i = 0; i < num_vert; i++)
  {
    // Get world space vertex position pointer
    pvert = pelem->GetVertexPtr(i);

    // Set homogeneous coordinates vertex
    hv.ProjTransform(pvert->GetPosn(), vtm);

    pclip->Clip(hv, out);       // Clip polygon edge
  }

  pclip->Close(out);    // Close polygon

  return out.GetNumVert();
}

// Output view space vertex
void FormClipEdge::Output( Vector4 &v, FormPoly &out )
{
  if (pnext != NULL)    // More planes ?
    pnext->Clip(v, out);
  else
    out.AddVertex(v);
}

// Calculate intersection vertex
Vector4 FormClipEdge::Intersect( Vector4 &s, Vector4 &e )
{
  double d, t;  // Temporary variables
  Vector4 r;    // Temporary vector

  // Calculate parameter
  r = (e - s);
  d = Dot(normal, r);
```

(continued)

Listing 5.10   *(continued)*

```
    if (fabs(d) > MIN_VALUE)
      t = -Dot(normal, s) / d;
    else
      t = 1.0;

    if (t < 0.0)       // Ensure lower limit
      t = 0.0;

    if (t > 1.0)       // Ensure upper limit
      t = 1.0;

    // Calculate intersection vertex coordinates
    r *= t;

    return (s + r);
}

// Clip polygon edge
void FormClipEdge::Clip( Vector4 &current, FormPoly &out )
{
    BOOL curr_inside;      // Current point inside flag
    Vector4 isect;         // Intersection vertex

    // Determine vertex visibility
    curr_inside = IsInside(current);

    if (first_flag == FALSE)        // First vertex seen ?
    {
      first = current;
      first_inside = curr_inside;
      first_flag = TRUE;
    }
    else
    {
      // Does edge intersect plane ?
      if (start_inside ^ curr_inside)
      {
        isect = Intersect(start, current);
        Output(isect, out);
      }
    }

    if (curr_inside == TRUE)
      Output(current, out);

    start = current;
    start_inside = curr_inside;
}

// Close polygon
void FormClipEdge::Close( FormPoly &out )
{
    Vector4 isect;         // Intersection vertex
```

```
  if (first_flag == TRUE)
  {
    // Does edge intersect plane ?
    if (start_inside ^ first_inside)
    {
      isect = Intersect(start, first);
      Output(isect, out);
    }

    if (pnext != NULL)  // More planes ?
      pnext->Close(out);

    // Reset first vertex seen flag
    first_flag = FALSE;
  }
}
```

The changes here are relatively minor. The class constructor *PolyClip4::Poly-Clip4* has been removed because it depends on the number and orientation of the clipping planes. Also, *FormClip::Intersect* has been simplified by removing the vertex color interpolation that was performed by *PolyClip4::Intersect*.

5.16.1 A Polygon Clipping Class for Hemicubes

We can now derive a polygon clipping class expressly for hemicubes from *FormClip* as follows:

Listing 5.11

```
// HC_CLIP.H - Hemicube Polygon Clipper Class

#ifndef _HC_CLIP_H
#define _HC_CLIP_H

#include "hc_poly.h"
#include "ff_clip.h"

// Clipping plane identifiers
enum HC_Plane
{ HC_Front, HC_Left, HC_Right, HC_Top, HC_Bottom };

// Hemicube polygon clipper
class HemiClip : public FormClip
{
  private:
    void BuildTransform( Vector3 &, Vector3 &, Vector3 & );

  public:
    HemiClip();
```

(continued)

Listing 5.11   *(continued)*

```
    void SetView( Patch3 * );
    void UpdateView( int );
};
```

```
#endif
```

and:

Listing 5.12

```cpp
// HC_CLIP.CPP - Hemicube Polygon Clipper Class

#include "hc_clip.h"

HemiClip::HemiClip()     // HemiClip class constructor
{
  Vector4 temp;      // Temporary vector

  // Link edge-plane clippers
  pclip = &(clipper[HC_Front]);
  clipper[HC_Front].Add(&(clipper[HC_Left]));
  clipper[HC_Left].Add(&(clipper[HC_Right]));
  clipper[HC_Right].Add(&(clipper[HC_Top]));
  clipper[HC_Top].Add(&(clipper[HC_Bottom]));
  clipper[HC_Bottom].Add(NULL);

  // Set clipper plane normals

  temp = Vector4(0.0, 0.0, 1.0, 0.0);
  clipper[HC_Front].SetNormal(temp.Norm());

  temp = Vector4(1.0, 0.0, 0.0, 0.0);
  clipper[HC_Left].SetNormal(temp.Norm());

  temp = Vector4(-1.0, 0.0, 0.0, 1.0);
  clipper[HC_Right].SetNormal(temp.Norm());

  temp = Vector4(0.0, -1.0, 0.0, 1.0);
  clipper[HC_Top].SetNormal(temp.Norm());

  temp = Vector4(0.0, 1.0, 0.0, 0.0);
  clipper[HC_Bottom].SetNormal(temp.Norm());
}

// Choose random hemicube orientation
void HemiClip::SetView( Patch3 *ppatch )
{
  Vector3 rv;    // Random vector

  // Get eye position (hemicube center)
  center = ppatch->GetCenter();
```

```
    // Select random vector for hemicube orientation
    rv = RandomVector();

    n = ppatch->GetNormal();      // Get patch normal

    do    // Get valid u-axis vector
    {
      u = Cross(n, rv);
    }
    while (u.Length() < MIN_VALUE);

    u.Norm();               // Normalize u-axis
    v = Cross(u, n);        // Determine v-axis
}

void HemiClip::BuildTransform( Vector3 &nu, Vector3 &nv,
    Vector3 &nn)
{
  Vector3 origin;          // View space origin

  origin = Vector3(center);

  // Set view transformation matrix
  vtm[0][0] = nu.GetX();
  vtm[0][1] = nu.GetY();
  vtm[0][2] = nu.GetZ();
  vtm[0][3] = -(Dot(origin, nu));

  vtm[1][0] = nv.GetX();
  vtm[1][1] = nv.GetY();
  vtm[1][2] = nv.GetZ();
  vtm[1][3] = -(Dot(origin, nv));

  vtm[2][0] = nn.GetX();
  vtm[2][1] = nn.GetY();
  vtm[2][2] = nn.GetZ();
  vtm[2][3] = -(Dot(origin, nn));

  vtm[3][0] = 0.0;
  vtm[3][1] = 0.0;
  vtm[3][2] = 0.0;
  vtm[3][3] = 1.0;

  // Premultiply by translation matrix
  vtm[2][3] -= 1.0;

  // Premultiply by perspective transformation matrix
  vtm[3][0] += vtm[2][0];
  vtm[3][1] += vtm[2][1];
  vtm[3][2] += vtm[2][2];
  vtm[3][3] += vtm[2][3];

  // Premultiply by normalization matrix
```

(continued)

Listing 5.12   *(continued)*

```
   vtm[0][0] = 0.5 * (vtm[0][0] + vtm[3][0]);
   vtm[0][1] = 0.5 * (vtm[0][1] + vtm[3][1]);
   vtm[0][2] = 0.5 * (vtm[0][2] + vtm[3][2]);
   vtm[0][3] = 0.5 * (vtm[0][3] + vtm[3][3]);

   vtm[1][0] = 0.5 * (vtm[1][0] + vtm[3][0]);
   vtm[1][1] = 0.5 * (vtm[1][1] + vtm[3][1]);
   vtm[1][2] = 0.5 * (vtm[1][2] + vtm[3][2]);
   vtm[1][3] = 0.5 * (vtm[1][3] + vtm[3][3]);

   vtm[2][0] = SN * vtm[2][0] + RN * vtm[3][0];
   vtm[2][1] = SN * vtm[2][1] + RN * vtm[3][1];
   vtm[2][2] = SN * vtm[2][2] + RN * vtm[3][2];
   vtm[2][3] = SN * vtm[2][3] + RN * vtm[3][3];
}

// Update hemicube view transformation matrix
void HemiClip::UpdateView( int face_id )
{
   Vector3 nu, nv, nn;    // View space co-ordinates

   switch (face_id )      // Exchange coordinates
   {
     case HC_TopFace:
       nu = u; nv = v; nn = n;
       break;
     case HC_FrontFace:
       nu = -u; nv = n; nn = v;
       break;
     case HC_RightFace:
       nu = v; nv = n; nn = u;
       break;
     case HC_BackFace:
       nu = u; nv = n; nn = -v;
       break;
     case HC_LeftFace:
       nu = -v; nv = n; nn = -u;
       break;
     default:
       break;
   }

   // Build new view transformation matrix
   BuildTransform(nu, nv, nn);
}
```

The derivation of *HemiClip* from our abstract *FormClip* class completes the adaptation of *PolyClip4*. The class constructor is identical to *PolyClip4::PolyClip4*, except that the back clipping plane has been removed.

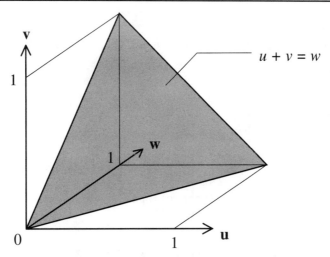

Figure 5.27 Diagonal clipping plane for cubic tetrahedron face

In addition to the functionality provided by its progenitor, *HemiClip* provides several functions specific to hemicubes. *SetView* positions the hemicube over the polygon center and chooses a random orientation about the polygon normal, then stores the hemi-cube view system axis world coordinates in the protected members *u*, *v*, and *n*. *UpdateView* reorients these axes to the current face before calling *Build-Transform*, which initializes the view-transformation matrix.

BuildTransform is an adaptation of *ViewSys::BuildTransform* (Listing 4.2). The only changes are the addition of a translation transformation (Eq. 5.35) to shift the origin from the polygon center to the hemicube face and the replacement of the front and back clipping-plane distance variables with the constants *SN* and *RN*.

In terms of production-quality code, *BuildTransform* should really be rewritten to concatenate the view, translation, perspective, and normalization transformations into one matrix. On the other hand, the function is not called all that often, and its present form is more amenable to debugging.

5.16.2 A Polygon Clipping Class for Cubic Tetrahedrons

Our polygon clipping class for cubic tetrahedrons will be almost—but not quite—like *HemiClip*. The most notable difference is the canonical view volume shown in Figure 5.26. We need to know the normal coordinates of the diagonal clipping plane, but what does it look like in four homogeneous dimensions?

The answer comes from realizing that this plane is parallel to the *n* axis. This means that the third coordinate of the plane normal must be zero. It also means that we can plot the plane in three dimensions, as shown in Figure 5.27. It has the plane equation $u + v = w$, and we can see by inspection that the plane normal in four-dimensional homogeneous coordinates must be $\{-1/\sqrt{3}, -1/\sqrt{3}, 0, -1/\sqrt{3}\}$.

With this, our polygon clipping class becomes:

Listing 5.13

```
// CT_CLIP.H - Cubic Tetrahedron Polygon Clipper Class

#ifndef _CT_CLIP_H
#define _CT_CLIP_H

#include "ct_poly.h"
#include "ff_clip.h"

// Clipping plane identifiers
enum CT_Plane { CT_Front, CT_Left, CT_Bottom, CT_Diag };

// Cubic tetrahedron polygon clipper
class CubicClip : public FormClip
{
  private:
    void BuildTransform( Vector3 &, Vector3 &, Vector3 & );

  public:
    CubicClip();

    void SetView( Patch3 * );
    void UpdateView( int );
};

#endif
```

and:

Listing 5.14

```
// CT_CLIP.CPP - Cubic Tetrahedron Polygon Clipper Class

#include "ct_clip.h"

CubicClip::CubicClip()  // CubicClip class constructor
{
  Vector4 temp;      // Temporary vector

  // Link edge-plane clippers
  pclip = &(clipper[CT_Front]);
  clipper[CT_Front].Add(&(clipper[CT_Left]));
  clipper[CT_Left].Add(&(clipper[CT_Bottom]));
  clipper[CT_Bottom].Add(&(clipper[CT_Diag]));
  clipper[CT_Diag].Add(NULL);

  // Set clipper plane normals

  temp = Vector4(0.0, 0.0, 1.0, 0.0);
  clipper[CT_Front].SetNormal(temp.Norm());
```

```
    temp = Vector4(1.0, 0.0, 0.0, 0.0);
    clipper[CT_Left].SetNormal(temp.Norm());

    temp = Vector4(0.0, 1.0, 0.0, 0.0);
    clipper[CT_Bottom].SetNormal(temp.Norm());

    temp = Vector4(-1.0, -1.0, 0.0, 1.0);
    clipper[CT_Diag].SetNormal(temp.Norm());
}

// Choose random cubic tetrahedron orientation
void CubicClip::SetView( Patch3 *ppatch )
{
    double a, b, c;    // Temporary variables
    Vector3 rv;        // Random vector
    Vector3 patch_u;   // Patch view space u-axis vector
    Vector3 patch_v;   // Patch view space v-axis vector
    Vector3 patch_n;   // Patch view space n-axis vector

    // Get eye position (cubic tetrahedron center)
    center = ppatch->GetCenter();

    // Select random vector for patch view space orientation
    rv = RandomVector();

    patch_n = ppatch->GetNormal();     // Get patch normal

    do   // Get valid u-axis vector
    {
      patch_u = Cross(patch_n, rv);
    }
    while (patch_u.Length() < MIN_VALUE);

    patch_u.Norm();                           // Normalize u-axis
    patch_v = Cross(patch_u, patch_n);        // Determine v-axis

    // Rotate cubic tetrahedron view space coordinate system
    // to align it with respect to patch view space such
    // that:
    //
    //    u = a * patch_u + b * patch_v - c * patch_n
    //    v = b * patch_u + a * patch_v - c * patch_n
    //    n = c * patch_u + c * patch_v - c * patch_n
    //
    // where:
    //
    //    a = 1 / (2 * sqrt(3)) + 1 / 2
    //    b = 1 / (2 * sqrt(3)) - 1 / 2
    //    c = -1 / sqrt(3)

    c = -1.0 / sqrt(3.0);
    a = (c * -0.5) + 0.5;
    b = (c * -0.5) - 0.5;
```

(continued)

Listing 5.14 *(continued)*

```
  u = a * patch_u + b * patch_v - c * patch_n;
  v = b * patch_u + a * patch_v - c * patch_n;
  n = c * patch_u + c * patch_v - c * patch_n;
}

void CubicClip::BuildTransform( Vector3 &nu, Vector3 &nv,
    Vector3 &nn)
{
  Vector3 origin;          // View space origin

  origin = Vector3(center);

  // Set view transformation matrix
  vtm[0][0] = nu.GetX();
  vtm[0][1] = nu.GetY();
  vtm[0][2] = nu.GetZ();
  vtm[0][3] = -(Dot(origin, nu));

  vtm[1][0] = nv.GetX();
  vtm[1][1] = nv.GetY();
  vtm[1][2] = nv.GetZ();
  vtm[1][3] = -(Dot(origin, nv));

  vtm[2][0] = nn.GetX();
  vtm[2][1] = nn.GetY();
  vtm[2][2] = nn.GetZ();
  vtm[2][3] = -(Dot(origin, nn));

  vtm[3][0] = 0.0;
  vtm[3][1] = 0.0;
  vtm[3][2] = 0.0;
  vtm[3][3] = 1.0;

  // Premultiply by translation matrix
  vtm[2][3] -= 1.0;

  // Premultiply by perspective transformation matrix
  vtm[3][0] += vtm[2][0];
  vtm[3][1] += vtm[2][1];
  vtm[3][2] += vtm[2][2];
  vtm[3][3] += vtm[2][3];

  // Premultiply by normalization matrix

  vtm[0][0] = (vtm[0][0] + vtm[3][0]) / 3.0;
  vtm[0][1] = (vtm[0][1] + vtm[3][1]) / 3.0;
  vtm[0][2] = (vtm[0][2] + vtm[3][2]) / 3.0;
  vtm[0][3] = (vtm[0][3] + vtm[3][3]) / 3.0;
```

```
   vtm[1][0] = (vtm[1][0] + vtm[3][0]) / 3.0;
   vtm[1][1] = (vtm[1][1] + vtm[3][1]) / 3.0;
   vtm[1][2] = (vtm[1][2] + vtm[3][2]) / 3.0;
   vtm[1][3] = (vtm[1][3] + vtm[3][3]) / 3.0;

   vtm[2][0] = SN * vtm[2][0] + RN * vtm[3][0];
   vtm[2][1] = SN * vtm[2][1] + RN * vtm[3][1];
   vtm[2][2] = SN * vtm[2][2] + RN * vtm[3][2];
   vtm[2][3] = SN * vtm[2][3] + RN * vtm[3][3];
}

// Update cubic tetrahedron view transformation matrix
void CubicClip::UpdateView( int face_id )
{
   Vector3 nu, nv, nn;    // View space co-ordinates

   switch (face_id )      // Exchange co-ordinates
   {
     case CT_TopFace:
       nu = -u; nv = -v; nn = n;
       break;
     case CT_RightFace:
       nu = -v; nv = -n; nn = u;
       break;
     case CT_LeftFace:
       nu = -u; nv = -n; nn = v;
       break;
     default:
       break;
   }

   // Build new view transformation matrix
   BuildTransform(nu, nv, nn);
}
```

CubicClip::SetView differs from its *HemiClip* equivalent in that it aligns the cubic tetrahedron view space with respect to the polygon view space as discussed in Section 5.14 (Eqs. 5.30 and 5.31). Similarly, *UpdateView* is based on Equation 5.32, and *BuildTransform* uses Equation 5.38 for its normalization transformation.

Again, *CubicClip::BuildTransform* is not production-quality code. Like its sibling *HemiClip::BuildTransform*, it should really be rewritten to concatenate the view, translation, perspective, and normalization transformations into one matrix. Make sure, however, that you understand how it works first!

5.17 POLYGON SCAN REVISITED

We can derive polygon scan conversion classes for hemicubes and cubic tetrahedrons from our previous *PolyRender* class. Unlike *PolyClip4* and its associated classes, *PolyRender* requires relatively few modifications. In fact, all we need to do is combine the pseudodepth and frame buffers into one "cell information" buffer that holds the polygon depth and identifier for each hemicube face cell, eliminate the Gouraud shading functionality, and add a *HemiDelta* class object.

We also need to consider triangular frame buffers for our cubic tetrahedron faces. Although this is not as difficult as it might first appear, it does require an abstract class from which we can derive our two polygon scan conversion classes. Starting from P_RENDER.H (Listing 4.12), then, we have:

Listing 5.15

```
// FF_SCAN.H - Form Factor Scan Conversion Class

#ifndef _FF_SCAN_H
#define _FF_SCAN_H

#include "ff_scan.h"
#include "ff_poly.h"

static const float FF_Infinity = MAX_VALUE;
static const WORD FF_None = 0;

struct FormCellInfo       // Face cell information
{
  float depth;            // Polygon cell depth
  WORD id;                // Polygon identifier
};

struct FormVertexInfo     // Vertex information
{
  struct                  // Face cell array offsets
  {
    int x;                // Width offset
    int y;                // Height offset
  }
  face;
  Point3 posn;            // Scaled position
};

struct FormScanInfo       // Scan line intersection info
{
  double x;               // X-axis coordinate
  double z;               // Pseudodepth
};

struct FormEdgeInfo       // Edge information
{
  BOOL first;                    // First intersection flag
  FormScanInfo isect[2];         // Scan line intersection array
};

// Form factor polygon scan conversion (abstract class)
class FormScan
{
```

```
protected:
  BOOL status;                    // Object status
  int ymin;                       // Minimum y-axis co-ord
  int ymax;                       // Maximum y-axis co-ord
  int num_vert;                   // Number of vertices
  FormCellInfo **cell_buffer;     // Cell info buffer ptr
  FormEdgeInfo *edge_list;        // Edge list pointer
  FormVertexInfo v_info[8];       // Vertex info table
  WORD poly_id;                   // Polygon identifier

  virtual void DrawEdgeList() = 0;
  void GetVertexInfo( FormPoly & );
  void ScanEdges();

public:
  virtual ~FormScan() { };

  BOOL GetStatus() { return status; }
  void Scan( FormPoly & );
};
```

#endif

The cell information buffer pointed to by *elem_buffer* replaces the Z-buffer and bitmap object pointers maintained by *PolyRender*. The buffer itself will be allocated and initialized by one of the derived classes. Since the buffer size is fixed at compile time by the delta form factor resolution, *FormScan* dispenses with the *Open* and *Close* functions required by *PolyRender*.

Note that *DrawEdgeList* has been made a pure virtual function in *FormScan*. This is what makes *FormScan* an abstract class; there is no function body defined for *DrawEdgeList*. Instead, it must be defined by a derived class.

One problem with virtual functions in C++ is that they are accessed at run time through a virtual function table pointer. Although this may require only two to four additional machine instructions per function call, these additional instructions may slow an otherwise small and fast function that could otherwise be placed inline by the compiler. A second problem is that every object derived from a virtual class has a hidden pointer to the virtual function table. As a rule of thumb, virtual functions should be used sparingly and only where necessary.

DrawEdgeList is an example where a virtual function is required. It is called by *Scan*, which does not know what type of frame buffer it should draw to. The code could be rewritten to avoid this situation, but it would lose some of its elegance with no significant increase in performance.

On the other hand, the function is virtual only because we are implementing two separate form factor determination algorithms. In its completed form, our radiosity renderer will use only one of these. In terms of production-quality code, it would then make sense to merge *FormScan* with its derived class and implement *DrawEdgeList* as a nonvirtual function.

Incidentally, any base class with virtual functions should have a virtual destructor declared for it. This explains the pure virtual class destructor *~FormScan*. It ensures that the appropriate destructor will be called for any derived class.

Returning from the intricacies of C++ programming rules, we have:

Listing 5.16

```
// FF_SCAN.CPP - Form Factor Scan Conversion Class

#include "ff_delta.h"
#include "ff_scan.h"

// Scan convert polygon
void FormScan::Scan( FormPoly &poly )
{
  poly_id = poly.GetPolyId();    // Get polygon identifier
  GetVertexInfo(poly);           // Get vertex information
  ScanEdges();                   // Scan convert edges
  DrawEdgeList();                // Draw edge list
}

// Get vertex information
void FormScan::GetVertexInfo( FormPoly &poly )
{
  int i;                   // Loop index
  FormVertexInfo *pv;      // Vertex info element pointer
  Point3 posn;             // Normalized vertex position

  // Initialize polygon y-axis limits
  ymax = 0;
  ymin = FF_ArrayRes - 1;

  // Get number of vertices
  num_vert = poly.GetNumVert();

  for (i = 0; i < num_vert; i++)
  {
    pv = &(v_info[i]);  // Get vertex info element pointer

    // Get vertex normalized view space coordinates
    posn = poly.GetVertex(i);

    // Scale view space u-v coordinates
    pv->posn.SetX(posn.GetX() * FF_ArrayRes);
    pv->posn.SetY(posn.GetY() * FF_ArrayRes);
    pv->posn.SetZ(posn.GetZ());

    // Convert to cell array x-y coordinates
    pv->face.x = (int) pv->posn.GetX();
    pv->face.y = (int) pv->posn.GetY();
```

```
      // Update polygon y-axis limits
      if (pv->face.y < ymin)
        ymin = pv->face.y;
      if (pv->face.y > ymax)
        ymax = pv->face.y;
  }
}

void FormScan::ScanEdges()        // Scan convert edges
{
  int i, j;                 // Loop indices
  double dx;                // X-axis delta
  double dz;                // Pseudodepth delta
  double ix;                // Intersection X-axis coordinate
  double iz;                // Intersection pseudodepth
  double y_dist;            // Y-axis distance
  FormEdgeInfo *pedge;      // Edge info pointer
  FormScanInfo *pscan;      // Scan line info pointer
  FormVertexInfo *psv;      // Start vertex info pointer
  FormVertexInfo *pev;      // End vertex info pointer
  FormVertexInfo *psw;      // Swap vertex info pointer

  // Initialize edge list
  for (i = ymin; i < ymax; i++)
    edge_list[i].first = FALSE;

  for (i = 0; i < num_vert; i++)
  {
    // Get edge vertex pointers
    psv = &(v_info[i]);
    pev = &(v_info[(i + 1) % num_vert]);

    if (psv->face.y == pev->face.y)
    {
      continue;             // Ignore horizontal edges
    }

    if (psv->face.y > pev->face.y)
    {
      // Swap edge vertex pointers
      psw = psv; psv = pev; pev = psw;
    }

    // Get start vertex info
    ix = psv->posn.GetX();
    iz = psv->posn.GetZ();

    // Determine inverse slopes
    y_dist = (double) (pev->face.y - psv->face.y);

    dx = (pev->posn.GetX() - ix) / y_dist;
    dz = (pev->posn.GetZ() - iz) / y_dist;
```

(continued)

Listing 5.16 *(continued)*

```
    // Scan convert edge
    pedge = &(edge_list[psv->face.y]);
    for (j = psv->face.y; j < pev->face.y; j++)
    {
      // Determine intersection info element
      if (pedge->first == FALSE)
      {
        pscan = &(pedge->isect[0]);
        pedge->first = TRUE;
      }
      else
        pscan = &(pedge->isect[1]);

      // Insert edge intersection info
      pscan->x = ix;
      pscan->z = iz;

      // Update edge intersection info
      ix += dx;
      iz += dz;

      pedge++;  // Point to next edge list element
    }
  }
}
```

Once you remove the polygon color components from *GetVertexInfo* and *ScanEdges*, there is very little difference between these functions and their *PolyRender* equivalents.

5.17.1 Polygon Scan Conversion for Hemicubes

Deriving a polygon scan conversion class for hemicubes from *FormScan* completes our adaptation of *PolyRender*. In addition to implementing the minimal changes required, we need to examine the cell information buffer after scan conversion and sum the delta form factors. This results in the following C++ class:

Listing 5.17

```
// HC_SCAN.H - Hemicube Scan Conversion Class

#ifndef _HC_SCAN_H
#define _HC_SCAN_H

#include "ff_scan.h"
#include "hc_delta.h"
```

```
// Hemicube polygon scan conversion
class HemiScan : public FormScan
{
  private:
    HemiDelta dff;        // Delta form factors

  public:
    HemiScan();

    ~HemiScan();

    void InitBuffer();
    void DrawEdgeList();
    void SumDeltas( float *, int );
};

#endif
```

and:

Listing 5.18

```
// HC_SCAN.CPP - Hemicube Scan Conversion Class

#include "hc_poly.h"
#include "hc_scan.h"

HemiScan::HemiScan()     // Class constructor
{
  int row;        // Loop index

  status = TRUE;          // Initialize object status

  // Allocate edge list
  if ((edge_list = new FormEdgeInfo[FF_ArrayRes]) != NULL)
  {
    // Allocate cell information buffer
    if ((cell_buffer = new (FormCellInfo (*[FF_ArrayRes])))
        != NULL)
    {
      for (row = 0; row < FF_ArrayRes; row++)
      {
        if ((cell_buffer[row] =
            new FormCellInfo[FF_ArrayRes]) == NULL)
        {
          // Release partially allocated buffer
          row-;
          for ( ; row >= 0; row-)
            delete [] cell_buffer[row];
          delete [] cell_buffer;

          // Release edge list memory
          delete [] edge_list;
```

(continued)

Listing 5.18   *(continued)*

```
          status = FALSE;
          break;
        }
      }
    }
  }
  else
  {
    delete [] edge_list;          // Release edge list memory
    status = FALSE;
  }
}

HemiScan::~HemiScan()    // Class destructor
{
  int row;         // Loop index

  delete [] edge_list;             // Release edge list memory

  // Delete cell information buffer
  for (row = 0; row < FF_ArrayRes; row++)
    delete [] cell_buffer[row];
  delete [] cell_buffer;
}

// Initialize cell information buffer
void HemiScan::InitBuffer()
{
  int row, col;      // Loop indices

  for (row = 0; row < FF_ArrayRes; row++)
    for (col = 0; col < FF_ArrayRes; col++)
    {
      cell_buffer[row][col].depth = FF_Infinity;
      cell_buffer[row][col].id = FF_None;
    }
}

void HemiScan::DrawEdgeList()    // Draw edge list
{
  int x, y;                // Loop indices
  int sx, ex;              // Scan line x-axis co-ordinates
  double dz;               // Pseudodepth delta
  double iz;               // Element pseudodepth
  double x_dist;           // X-axis distance
  FormEdgeInfo *pedge;     // Edge info pointer
  FormScanInfo *pss;       // Scan line start info pointer
  FormScanInfo *pse;       // Scan line end info pointer
  FormScanInfo *psw;       // Swap scan line info pointer
```

```
    pedge = &(edge_list[ymin]);
    for (y = ymin; y < ymax; y++)
    {
      // Get scan line info pointers
      pss = &(pedge->isect[0]);
      pse = &(pedge->isect[1]);

      if (pss->x > pse->x)
      {
        // Swap scan line info pointers
        psw = pss; pss = pse; pse = psw;
      }

      // Get scan line x-axis coordinates
      sx = (int) pss->x;
      ex = (int) pse->x;

      if (sx < ex)          // Ignore zero-length segments
      {
        // Determine scan line start info
        iz = pss->z;

        // Determine inverse slopes
        x_dist = pse->x - pss->x;

        dz = (pse->z - iz) / x_dist;

        // Enter scan line
        for (x = sx; x < ex; x++)
        {
          // Check element visibility
          if (iz < (double) cell_buffer[y][x].depth)
          {
            // Update Z-buffer
            cell_buffer[y][x].depth = (float) iz;

            // Set polygon identifier
            cell_buffer[y][x].id = poly_id;
          }

          // Update element pseudodepth
          iz += dz;
        }
      }
      pedge++;     // Point to next edge list element
    }
}

// Sum delta form factors
void HemiScan::SumDeltas( float *ff_array, int face_id )
{
  WORD poly_id;     // Polygon identifier
  int row, col;     // Face cell indices
```

(continued)

Listing 5.18 *(continued)*

```
if (face_id == HC_TopFace)
{
  // Scan entire face buffer
  for (row = 0; row < FF_ArrayRes; row++)
    for (col = 0; col < FF_ArrayRes; col++)
    {
      if ((poly_id = cell_buffer[row][col].id) !=
          FF_None)
        ff_array[poly_id - 1] +=
            dff.GetTopFactor(row, col);
    }
}
else
{
  // Scan upper half of face buffer only
  for (row = HC_ArrayDim; row < FF_ArrayRes; row++)
    for (col = 0; col < FF_ArrayRes; col++)
    {
      if ((poly_id = cell_buffer[row][col].id) != FF_None)
        ff_array[poly_id - 1] +=
            dff.GetSideFactor(row, col);
    }
}
}
```

The cell information buffer is the equivalent of the Z-buffer and bitmap (frame buffer) used by *PolyRender*. *PolyRender::Open* is responsible for allocating and initializing a Z-buffer whose dimensions are determined by the bitmap being written to. The size of the cell information buffer, on the other hand, is determined by the hemicube resolution. This being a constant, we can allocate the buffer once at program startup through the class constructor. This replaces *PolyRender::Open*; the class destructor replaces *PolyRender::Close*.

HemiScan::HemiScan uses two arrays to allocate the cell information buffer one row at a time. This allows us to minimize the possibility of running out of memory because of memory fragmentation. It also allows us to specify hemicube resolutions in excess of 128×128 cells under MS-Windows 3.1. If there is insufficient memory available, the object status flag is set to FALSE.

InitBuffer is responsible for initializing the cell information buffer. It must be called before each polygon scan conversion.

DrawEdgeList is nearly identical to *PolyRender::DrawEdgeList*. The only significant difference is that the vertex color has been replaced with the polygon identifier.

Finally, *SumDeltas* does precisely what its name suggests. It scans the cell information buffer looking for covered face cells. When it finds one, it looks up the associated delta form factor and increments the indicated polygon's form factor by that amount. It must be called after each pass through the environment, since the cell information buffer is reused for the five hemicube faces.

5.17.2 Polygon Scan Conversion for Cubic Tetrahedrons

Deriving a polygon scan conversion class for cubic tetrahedrons from *FormScan* results in code that is a near clone of *HemiScan*. The only difference is that we now have to allocate and access a triangular cell information buffer. Fortunately, the changes are quite minor:

Listing 5.19

```
// CT_SCAN.H - Cubic Tetrahedron Scan Conversion Class

#ifndef _CT_SCAN_H
#define _CT_SCAN_H

#include "ff_scan.h"
#include "ct_delta.h"

// Cubic tetrahedron polygon scan conversion
class CubicScan : public FormScan
{
  private:
    CubicDelta dff;      // Delta form factors

  public:
    CubicScan();

    ~CubicScan();

    void InitBuffer();
    void DrawEdgeList();
    void SumDeltas( float * );
};

#endif
```

and:

Listing 5.20

```
// CT_SCAN.CPP - Cubic Tetrahedron Scan Conversion Class

#include "ff_delta.h"
#include "ff_scan.h"
#include "ct_scan.h"

CubicScan::CubicScan()  // Class constructor
{
  int row;      // Loop index
  int width;    // Scan line width

  status = TRUE;        // Initialize object status
```

(continued)

Listing 5.20   *(continued)*

```cpp
  // Allocate edge list
  if ((edge_list = new FormEdgeInfo[FF_ArrayRes]) != NULL)
  {
    // Allocate cell information buffer
    if ((cell_buffer =
        new (FormCellInfo (*[FF_ArrayRes]))) != NULL)
    {
      width = FF_ArrayRes;
      for (row = 0; row < FF_ArrayRes; row++)
      {
        if ((cell_buffer[row] = new FormCellInfo[width])
            == NULL)
        {
          // Release partially allocated buffer
          row--;
          for ( ; row >= 0; row--)
            delete [] cell_buffer[row];
          delete [] cell_buffer;

          // Release edge list memory
          delete [] edge_list;

          status = FALSE;
          break;
        }
        width--;            // Decrement scan line width
      }
    }
  }
  else
  {
    delete [] edge_list;          // Release edge list memory
    status = FALSE;
  }
}

CubicScan::~CubicScan()           // Class destructor
{
  int row;        // Loop index

  delete [] edge_list;            // Release edge list memory

  // Delete cell information buffer
  for (row = 0; row < FF_ArrayRes; row++)
    delete [] cell_buffer[row];
  delete [] cell_buffer;
}

// Initialize cell information buffer
void CubicScan::InitBuffer()
{
```

```
  int row, col;       // Loop indices
  int width;          // Scan line width

  width = FF_ArrayRes;
  for (row = 0; row < FF_ArrayRes; row++)
  {
    for (col = 0; col < width; col++)
    {
      cell_buffer[row][col].depth = FF_Infinity;
      cell_buffer[row][col].id = FF_None;
    }
    width--;     // Decrement scan line width
  }
}

void CubicScan::DrawEdgeList()  // Draw edge list
{
  int x, y;                // Loop indices
  int sx, ex;              // Scan line x-axis co-ordinates
  double dz;               // Pseudodepth delta
  double iz;               // Element pseudodepth
  double x_dist;           // X-axis distance
  FormEdgeInfo *pedge;     // Edge info pointer
  FormScanInfo *pss;       // Scan line start info pointer
  FormScanInfo *pse;       // Scan line end info pointer
  FormScanInfo *psw;       // Swap scan line info pointer

  pedge = &(edge_list[ymin]);
  for (y = ymin; y < ymax; y++)
  {
    // Get scan line info pointers
    pss = &(pedge->isect[0]);
    pse = &(pedge->isect[1]);

    if (pss->x > pse->x)
    {
      // Swap scan line info pointers
      psw = pss; pss = pse; pse = psw;
    }

    // Get scan line x-axis co-ordinates
    sx = min((int) pss->x, FF_ArrayRes - y);
    ex = min((int) pse->x, FF_ArrayRes - y);

    if (sx < ex)         // Ignore zero-length segments
    {
      // Determine scan line start info
      iz = pss->z;

      // Determine inverse slopes
      x_dist = pse->x - pss->x;

      dz = (pse->z - iz) / x_dist;
```

(continued)

Listing 5.20   *(continued)*

```
      // Enter scan line
      for (x = sx; x < ex; x++)
      {
        // Check element visibility
        if (iz < (double) cell_buffer[y][x].depth)
        {
          // Update Z-buffer
          cell_buffer[y][x].depth = (float) iz;

          // Set polygon identifier
          cell_buffer[y][x].id = poly_id;
        }

        // Update element pseudodepth
        iz += dz;
      }
    }
    pedge++;      // Point to next edge list element
  }
}


// Sum delta form factors
void CubicScan::SumDeltas( float *ff_array )
{
  WORD poly_id;      // Polygon identifier
  int row, col;      // Face cell indices
  int width;         // Scan line width

  width = FF_ArrayRes;
  for (row = 0; row < FF_ArrayRes; row++)
  {
    for (col = 0; col < width; col++)
    {
      if ((poly_id = cell_buffer[row][col].id) !=
          FF_None)
        ff_array[poly_id - 1] += dff.GetFactor(row, col);
    }
    width--;      // Decrement scan line width
  }
}
```

You have to look closely to see the differences between *CubicScan* and *Hemi-Scan*. The class constructor *CubicScan::CubicScan* allocates the cell information buffer one row at a time, as before. However, the row length is decremented with each succeeding row to allocate the necessary triangular buffer. Similarly, *Cubic-Scan::DrawEdgeList* uses the row index when calculating the scan line *x*-axis coordinates. This ensures that there is no possibility of the column index exceeding the current row length.

The only other difference is *CubicScan::SumDeltas*, which needs to access only one face type. As such, it does not need a face identifier parameter.

5.18 A HEMICUBE ALGORITHM CLASS

We now have the necessary components to implement the hemicube algorithm as a C++ class. Following the algorithm pseudocode presented in Figure 5.21, we see that the implementation becomes almost trivial:

Listing 5.21

```
// HEMICUBE.H - Hemicube Class

#ifndef _HEMICUBE_H
#define _HEMICUBE_H

#include "parse.h"
#include "hc_clip.h"
#include "hc_scan.h"

static int HemiFaceNum = 5;

class HemiCube            // Hemicube
{
  private:
    FormPoly out;         // Output polygon
    HemiClip clip;        // Polygon clipper
    HemiScan scan;        // Polygon scan conversion

  public:
    BOOL GetStatus() { return scan.GetStatus(); }
    void CalcFormFactors( Patch3 *, Instance *, float *,
        WORD );
};

typedef HemiCube FormFactor;     // Class alias

#endif
```

The function *GetStatus* should be called once to ensure that the *HemiScan* object was able to obtain enough memory for its cell information buffer. Assuming it was successful, *CalcFormFactors* can then be called to determine the form factors from a selected polygon to all other polygons in its environment. This function is implemented as:

Listing 5.22

```
// HEMICUBE.CPP - Hemicube Class

#include "hemicube.h"

void HemiCube::CalcFormFactors( Patch3 *pp, Instance *pi,
    float *ff_array, WORD num_elem )
{
```

(continued)

Listing 5.22   *(continued)*

```
int i;                  // Loop index
BOOL hidden;            // Patch visibility flag
BOOL self;             // Self patch flag
WORD j;                 // Loop index
WORD elem_id;          // Element identifier
Element3 *pelem;       // Element pointer
Instance *pinst;       // Instance pointer
Patch3 *ppatch;        // Patch pointer
Surface3 *psurf;       // Surface pointer

// Clear the form factors array
for (j = 0; j < num_elem; j++)
  ff_array[j] = 0.0;

// Set the hemicube view transformation matrix
clip.SetView(pp);

// Project environment onto each hemicube face
for (i = 0; i < HemiFaceNum; i++)
{
  // Update view transformation matrix
  clip.UpdateView(i);

  scan.InitBuffer();  // Reinitialize depth buffer

  // Walk the instance list
  elem_id = 1;
  pinst = pi;
  while (pinst != NULL)
  {
    // Walk the surface list
    psurf = pinst->GetSurfPtr();
    while (psurf != NULL)
    {
      // Walk the patch list
      ppatch = psurf->GetPatchPtr();
      while (ppatch != NULL)
      {
        // Check for self patch
        self = (ppatch == pp) ? TRUE : FALSE;

        // Determine patch visibility
        hidden = clip.BackFaceCull(ppatch);

        // Walk the element list
        pelem = ppatch->GetElementPtr();
        while (pelem != NULL)
        {
          if (hidden == FALSE && self == FALSE)
          {
```

```
                    // Clip element to face view volume
                    if (clip.Clip(pelem, out, elem_id) > 0)
                    {
                      scan.Scan(out);      // Scan convert polygon
                    }
                  }
                  pelem = pelem->GetNext();
                  elem_id++;
                }
                ppatch = ppatch->GetNext();
              }
              psurf = psurf->GetNext();
            }
            pinst = pinst->GetNext();
          }

          // Sum delta form factors
          scan.SumDeltas(ff_array, i);
        }
}
```

5.18.1 A Character-Mode Test Program

Another 1,200 or so lines of source code for our growing library of C++ classes—it is time for another character-mode test program:

Listing 5.23

```
// TEST_2.CPP - Hemicube Test Program

// NOTE: _NOT_WIN_APP must be globally defined for this
//       program to be successfully compiled

#include <stdio.h>
#include <stdlib.h>
#include <iostream.h>
#include <time.h>
#include "error.h"
#include "parse.h"
#include "hemicube.h"

// Default entity directory path
static char NoEntityDir[] = "";

static HemiCube Hemi;           // Hemicube
static Parse Parser;            // World file parser
static Environ Environment;     // Environment

double Calculate( float *, WORD, BOOL );
```

(continued)

Listing 5.23   *(continued)*

```cpp
int main( int argc, char **argv )
{
  char *pentdir;        // Entity directory path
  float *ff_array;      // Form factor array
  WORD num_elem;        // Number of elements

  // Check hemicube status
  if (Hemi.GetStatus() != TRUE)
  {
    OutOfMemory();
    return 1;
  }

  // Get entity directory path (if any)
  if (argc > 2)
    pentdir = argv[2];
  else
    pentdir = NoEntityDir;

  // Parse the environment file
  if (Parser.ParseFile(argv[1], pentdir, &Environment) ==
      FALSE)
    return 1;

  // Allocate form factor array
  num_elem = Environment.GetNumElem();
  if ((ff_array = new float[num_elem]) == NULL)
  {
    OutOfMemory();
    return 1;
  }

  // Seed the random number generator
  srand((unsigned) time(NULL));

  // Calculate and display form factors
  (void) Calculate(ff_array, num_elem, TRUE);

  // Recalculate form factors and display execution time
  cout << endl << "Resolution = " << FF_ArrayRes << " x "
      << FF_ArrayRes << " cells" << endl;
  cout << "Execution time = "<< Calculate(ff_array,
      num_elem, FALSE) << " seconds";

  delete [] ff_array;    // Delete form factor array

  return 0;
}
```

```
// Calculate form factors
double Calculate( float *ff_array, WORD num_elem, BOOL
    ff_flag )
{
  clock_t start, end;    // Execution time variables
  Instance *penv;        // Environment pointer
  Instance *pinst;       // Instance pointer
  Surface3 *psurf;       // Surface pointer
  Patch3 *ppatch;        // Patch pointer
  WORD src_id = 1;       // Source polygon identifier
  WORD rcv_id;           // Receiving polygon identifier

  // Get environment pointer
  pinst = penv = Environment.GetInstPtr();

  if (ff_flag == FALSE)
  {
    start = clock();     // Start the program timer
  }

  // Walk the instance list
  while (pinst != NULL)
  {
    // Walk the surface list
    psurf = pinst->GetSurfPtr();
    while (psurf != NULL)
    {
      // Walk the patch list
      ppatch = psurf->GetPatchPtr();
      while (ppatch != NULL)
      {
        // Calculate patch to element form factors
        Hemi.CalcFormFactors(ppatch, penv, ff_array,
            num_elem);

        if (ff_flag == TRUE)
        {
          // Report form factors
          cout << "Patch " << src_id << endl;
          for (rcv_id = 0; rcv_id < num_elem; rcv_id++)
            cout << "   FF(" << src_id << "," << (rcv_id + 1)
                << ") = " << ff_array[rcv_id] << endl;
        }

        src_id++;
        ppatch = ppatch->GetNext();
      }
      psurf = psurf->GetNext();
    }
    pinst = pinst->GetNext();
  }

  if (ff_flag == FALSE)
  {
```

(continued)

Listing 5.23   *(continued)*

```
    end = clock();        // Stop the program timer

    // Return form factor calculation time
    return (double) (end - start) / CLOCKS_PER_SEC;
  }
  else
    return 0.0;
}
```

Like *TEST_1*, this program is a character-mode application that sends its output to the user console. Once again, *_NOT_WIN_APP* must be globally defined in order to correctly compile ERROR.CPP (Listings 3.21 and 3.22).

TEST_2 will accept any valid environment file as its input. For example, you could enter:

```
TEST_2 COL_CUBE.WLD
```

to calculate the form factors between the faces of the two cubes in the COL_CUBE.WLD environment (Listing 3.17). A more useful approach, however, is to develop a simple test environment (Fig. 5.28) for which the form factors can be solved analytically as a comparison. From Siegel and Howell (1992), the form factor from dE_i to E_j is given by:

$$F_{dEi-Ej} = \frac{4H}{\pi\sqrt{1+H^2}} \arctan\sqrt{\frac{R^2-H^2}{1+H^2}} \tag{5.40}$$

where:

$$H = \frac{W}{2d}$$
$$\tag{5.41}$$
$$R = \frac{W}{d\sqrt{2}}$$

and where dE_i is parallel to and located directly below the center of E_j.

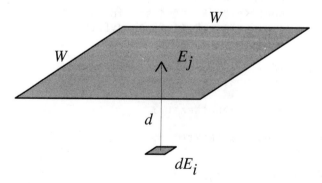

Figure 5.28   Test environment

Suppose we choose $W = d = 1.0$. Substituting these values into the above equations, we find the analytic form factor F_{dEi-Ej} to be approximately 0.2395. We can compare this with the estimated form factor values calculated by *HemiCube* by first specifying a unit area polygon, as in SQUARE.ENT (Listing 5.24).

Listing 5.24   SQUARE.ENT

```
ENTITY unit square
VERTEX
< 0.5 -0.5 0.0 >
< 0.5 0.5 0.0 >
< -0.5 0.5 0.0 >
< -0.5 -0.5 0.0 >
END_VERT
SURFACE
[ 1.0 0.0 0.0 ] [ 0.0 0.0 0.0 ]
END_SURF
PATCH
0 { 0 1 2 3 }
END_PATCH
ELEMENT
0 { 0 1 2 3 }
END_ELEM
END_ENTITY
```

With this, we can arrange two instances of the square to be parallel to and face one another at a distance of one unit, as in SQUARE.WLD (Listing 5.25).

Listing 5.25   SQUARE.WLD

```
WORLD opposing squares
COMMENT first square
square.ent
< 1.0 1.0 1.0 >
< 0.0 0.0 0.0 >
< 0.0 0.0 -0.5 >
COMMENT second square
square.ent
< 1.0 1.0 1.0 >
< 180.0 0.0 0.0 >
< 0.0 0.0 0.5 >
END_FILE
```

HemiCube::CalcFormFactors will calculate the form factor from the center of each of these polygons to the opposing polygon (It will also calculate the form factor to itself—which, of course, is always zero.) If you enter:

```
TEST 2 SQUARE.WLD
```

when both SQUARE.ENT and SQUARE.WLD are in the current directory, your output should look something like this:

```
Polygon 1
  FF(1,1) = 0
  FF(1,2) = 0.239623
Polygon 2
  FF(2,1) = 0.240574
  FF(2,2) = 0

Resolution = 100 x 100 cells
Execution time = 0.27 seconds
```

Why the different values? Remember that *HemiClip::SetView* randomly orients the hemicube about the polygon normal. The projection of the opposing polygon onto the hemicube depends on this orientation. Thus, your particular output may also vary from that shown, depending on the random numbers produced by your program's *rand* function and its seed value.

(Your timing results will also depend on how busy your machine is. The above results were obtained using an Intel 486 66-MHz machine running MS-DOS. If you run *TEST_2* in a multitasking environment, which includes MS-Windows 3.1, the results will indicate in part what percentage of the CPU's time your process has been allotted.)

5.19 A CUBIC TETRAHEDRAL ALGORITHM CLASS

Our cubic tetrahedral algorithm can be implemented as a simple variant of *HemiCube*:

Listing 5.26

```
// CUBIC_T.H - Cubic Tetrahedron Class

#ifndef _CUBIC_T_H
#define _CUBIC_T_H

#include "parse.h"
#include "ct_clip.h"
#include "ct_scan.h"

static int CubicFaceNum = 3;

class CubicTetra          // Cubic tetrahedron
{
  private:
    FormPoly out;         // Output polygon
    CubicClip clip;       // Polygon clipper
    CubicScan scan;       // Polygon scan conversion
```

```
  public:
    BOOL GetStatus() { return scan.GetStatus(); }
    void CalcFormFactors( Patch3 *, Instance *, float *,
        WORD );
};
```

```
typedef CubicTetra FormFactor;  // Class alias
```

```
#endif
```

and:

Listing 5.27

```
// CUBIC_T.CPP - Cubic Tetrahedron Class

#include "cubic_t.h"

void CubicTetra::CalcFormFactors( Patch3 *pp, Instance
    *pi, float *ff_array, WORD num_elem )
{
  int i;                 // Loop index
  BOOL hidden;           // Patch visibility flag
  BOOL self;             // Self patch flag
  WORD j;                // Loop index
  WORD elem_id;          // Element identifier
  Element3 *pelem;       // Element pointer
  Instance *pinst;       // Instance pointer
  Patch3 *ppatch;        // Patch pointer
  Surface3 *psurf;       // Surface pointer

  // Clear the form factors array
  for (j = 0; j < num_elem; j++)
    ff_array[j] = 0.0;

  // Set the cubic tetrahedron view transformation matrix
  clip.SetView(pp);

  // Project environment onto each cubic tetrahedron face
  for (i = 0; i < CubicFaceNum; i++)
  {
    // Update view transformation matrix
    clip.UpdateView(i);

    scan.InitBuffer();  // Reinitialize depth buffer

    // Walk the instance list
    elem_id = 1;
    pinst = pi;
    while (pinst != NULL)
    {
```

(continued)

Listing 5.27 *(continued)*

```
    // Walk the surface list
    psurf = pinst->GetSurfPtr();
    while (psurf != NULL)
    {
      // Walk the patch list
      ppatch = psurf->GetPatchPtr();
      while (ppatch != NULL)
      {
        // Check for self patch
        self = (ppatch == pp) ? TRUE : FALSE;

        // Determine patch visibility
        hidden = clip.BackFaceCull(ppatch);

        // Walk the element list
        pelem = ppatch->GetElementPtr();
        while (pelem != NULL)
        {
          if (hidden == FALSE && self == FALSE)
          {
            // Clip element to face view volume
            if (clip.Clip(pelem, out, elem_id) > 0)
            {
              scan.Scan(out);      // Scan convert polygon
            }
          }
          pelem = pelem->GetNext();
          elem_id++;
        }
        ppatch = ppatch->GetNext();
      }
      psurf = psurf->GetNext();
    }
    pinst = pinst->GetNext();
  }

  // Sum delta form factors
  scan.SumDeltas(ff_array);
  }
}
```

Apart from their polygon clipping and scan conversion classes, *CubicTetra* and *HemiCube* are essentially identical.

5.19.1 Another Character-Mode Test Program

We can test our cubic tetrahedral algorithm code with the following test program. More important, we can compare its form factor estimates with those produced by our hemicube implementation in *TEST_2*.

Listing 5.28

```cpp
// TEST_3.CPP - Cubic Tetrahedron Test Program

// NOTE: _NOT_WIN_APP must be globally defined for this
//        program to be successfully compiled

#include <stdio.h>
#include <stdlib.h>
#include <iostream.h>
#include <time.h>
#include "error.h"
#include "parse.h"
#include "cubic_t.h"

// Default entity directory path
static char NoEntityDir[] = "";

static CubicTetra Cubic;         // Cubic tetrahedron
static Parse Parser;             // World file parser
static Environ Environment;      // Environment

double Calculate( float *, WORD, BOOL );

int main( int argc, char **argv )
{
  char *pentdir;          // Entity directory path
  float *ff_array;        // Form factor array
  WORD num_elem;          // Number of elements

  // Check cubic tetrahedron status
  if (Cubic.GetStatus() != TRUE)
  {
    OutOfMemory();
    return 1;
  }

  // Get entity directory path (if any)
  if (argc > 2)
    pentdir = argv[2];
  else
    pentdir = NoEntityDir;

  // Parse the environment file
  if (Parser.ParseFile(argv[1], pentdir, &Environment) ==
      FALSE)
    return 1;

  // Allocate form factor array
  num_elem = Environment.GetNumElem();
  if ((ff_array = new float[num_elem]) == NULL)
  {
```

(continued)

Listing 5.28   *(continued)*

```
      OutOfMemory();
      return 1;
  }

  // Seed the random number generator
  srand((unsigned) time(NULL));

  // Calculate and display form factors
  (void) Calculate(ff_array, num_elem, TRUE);

  // Recalculate form factors and display execution time
  cout << endl << "Resolution = " << FF_ArrayRes << " x "
      << FF_ArrayRes << " cells" << endl;
  cout << "Execution time = "<< Calculate(ff_array,
      num_elem, FALSE) << " seconds";

  delete [] ff_array;    // Delete form factor array

  return 0;
}

// Calculate form factors
double Calculate( float *ff_array, WORD num_elem, BOOL
    ff_flag )
{
  clock_t start, end;    // Execution time variables
  Instance *penv;        // Environment pointer
  Instance *pinst;       // Instance pointer
  Surface3 *psurf;       // Surface pointer
  Patch3 *ppatch;        // Patch pointer
  WORD src_id = 1;       // Source polygon identifier
  WORD rcv_id;           // Receiving polygon identifier

  // Get environment pointer
  pinst = penv = Environment.GetInstPtr();

  if (ff_flag == FALSE)
  {
    start = clock();     // Start the program timer
  }

  // Walk the instance list
  while (pinst != NULL)
  {
    // Walk the surface list
    psurf = pinst->GetSurfPtr();
    while (psurf != NULL)
    {
      // Walk the patch list
      ppatch = psurf->GetPatchPtr();
      while (ppatch != NULL)
      {
```

```
            // Calculate patch to element form factors
            Cubic.CalcFormFactors(ppatch, penv, ff_array,
                num_elem);

            if (ff_flag == TRUE)
            {
              // Report form factors
              cout << "Patch " << src_id << endl;
              for (rcv_id = 0; rcv_id < num_elem; rcv_id++)
                cout << "  FF(" << src_id << "," << (rcv_id + 1)
                    << ") = " << ff_array[rcv_id] << endl;
            }

            src_id++;
            ppatch = ppatch->GetNext();
          }
        psurf = psurf->GetNext();
      }
    pinst = pinst->GetNext();
  }

  if (ff_flag == FALSE)
  {
    end = clock();        // Stop the program timer

    // Return form factor calculation time
    return (double) (end - start) / CLOCKS_PER_SEC;
  }
  else
    return 0.0;
}
```

Again, TEST_3.CPP is a clone of TEST_2.CPP. If you enter:

```
TEST_3 SQUARE.WLD
```

when both SQUARE.ENT and SQUARE.WLD are in the current directory, your output should look something like:

```
Polygon 1
  FF(1,1) = 0
  FF(1,2) = 0.23486
Polygon 2
  FF(2,1) = 0.23518
  FF(2,2) = 0
Resolution = 142 x 142 cells
Execution time = 0.22 seconds
```

There are two points of interest here. First, the estimated form factors are slightly less than those produced by our *HemiCube* class. The *HemiCube* estimates were off by an average 0.33 percent; these are off by 1.04 percent. Remember, however, that these are random values. Also, the accuracy of both algorithms will vary depending on the specific polygon-to-polygon geometry and hemicube resolution. The more important issue is the variance in their estimates for many thousands of polygons in a complex environment.

The second point is that *CubicTetra* appears to be faster than *HemiCube* in determining form factors. It was—for this particular geometry and resolution. The question is whether this will remain true when the two algorithms are applied to a large variety of complex environments.

The cubic tetrahedral algorithm should in theory be the faster of the two. Pavicic (1994) noted that it needs to perform an average of 2.75 clipping operations for small polygons, whereas the hemicube algorithm must perform 3.83 such operations on average. However, there are various programming tricks that can skew the results markedly. Suppose, for example, that we tag a polygon when we clip it against a face and find that it is (a) entirely within the view volume, (b) backface culled, or (c) behind the "eye position" defined by the view-space origin and the receiving polygon's normal. (The *flags* member of *Element3* [Listing 3.11] has some spare bits that can be used for this purpose.) We could then trivially reject the polygon when clipping it against subsequent faces.

Another possibility is to tag the faces themselves if a polygon is clipped against the boundary of an adjoining face. In this case, we then know that the polygon should be clipped against the tagged face as well. These tricks may provide marked increases in execution time for complex environments, perhaps as much as 100 percent or more. Which algorithm, then is the better one? That depends on your programming ingenuity.

This, however, misses the point. We examined the cubic tetrahedral algorithm as an interesting alternative to that of the hemicube. Certainly, we can profile the performances of the two algorithms and implement various speed-up techniques. However, our primary objective is to explore the radiosity approach. Implementing both algorithms is an ideal way of doing so. Besides, we now have two form factor determination classes to play with.

5.20   A HARDWARE ALTERNATIVE FOR HEMICUBES

Whereas the cubic tetrahedral algorithm may be faster, the hemicube offers an advantage for those with computer graphics workstations: hardware acceleration. Many of these high-end machines implement three-dimensional graphics primitives using specialized hardware graphics accelerators. Supported operations usually include backface culling, three-dimensional polygon clipping, scan conversion, Z-buffering, and Gouraud shading. A library of callable low-level graphics functions enables users to access this hardware directly.

Rushmeier et al. (1991) discussed several techniques for accelerating the hemicube algorithm. For graphics workstations they proposed the following: First, allocate a screen window to represent a hemicube face and initialize the view-transformation matrix. The vertices of each polygon in the environment are then sent to the graphics coprocessor for display, with the polygon identifier representing its "color." Once the environment has been processed, the color is read for each pixel in the window and a polygon form factor array is updated accordingly. Expressed in pseudocode, this becomes as shown in Figure 5.29.

```
Allocate graphics screen window for hemicube face
FOR each polygon E_i
  FOR each hemi-cube face
    FOR each polygon E_j
      F_ij = 0
    ENDFOR
  ENDFOR
  FOR each hemi-cube face
    FOR each polygon E_j
      F_ij = 0
      color = j
      Send polygon vertex list to graphics coprocessor
    ENDFOR
  ENDFOR
  Copy window frame buffer to item buffer
  FOR each hemi-cube face cell k
    F_ik =   F_ik + ΔF_k
  ENDFOR
ENDFOR
```

Figure 5.29   Hardware-assisted hemicube algorithm

Comparing this to our software implementation, we see clearly that we have done it the hard way! Hardware-assisted hemicube algorithms have been implemented by Cohen et al. (1988), Baum et al. (1989), and others. Rushmeier et al. (1991) reported that execution times for backface culling, polygon clipping, and Z-buffering were improved by a factor of 100 or more. On the other hand, the remaining operations of issuing vertex lists to the graphics processor and summing the delta form factors still has to be implemented in software. As a result, the overall acceleration of the hemicube algorithm over an equivalent software implementation ranged from 160 percent for a resolution of 50×50 cells to 350 percent for a resolution of 300×300 cells.

Special-purpose graphics processors dedicated solely to form factor determination have been developed (e.g., Bu and Deprettere (1987a,b) and Bu and Deprettere (1989)). However, these are so far experimental devices. Until we have commercially available graphics coprocessors designed specifically for radiosity rendering (or at least ones that can be microprogrammed to implement the necessary algorithms), we shall have to rely upon our programming skills to maximize the performance of our algorithms.

5.21   THE SINGLE-PLANE ALGORITHM

We can simplify the hemicube algorithm even further by replacing the hemicube with a single projection plane placed directly above and parallel to the differential polygon

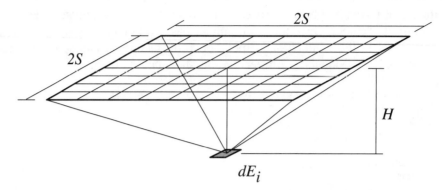

Figure 5.30 Single-plane algorithm

element dE_i (Fig. 5.30). At first, this simplification appears to offer at least one advantage: There is only one plane to clip against. It is definitely faster—Recker et al. (1990) reported a speed-up of approximately 100 percent over the hemicube algorithm. However, there are hidden costs to this approach that diminish its usefulness.

The first problem is that the plane does not cover the entire hemisphere above the element. This means that polygons in the environment near the horizon will be missed. In physical terms, this means that we may underestimate the radiant flux that is either received or emitted by dE_i when we perform our radiosity calculations. However, this may not be significant in practice. Sources near the horizon typically contribute very little to the overall flux received by a surface due to the cosine factor. Similarly, Sillion and Puech (1989) demonstrated that if dE_i is a Lambertian emitter, the amount of flux "escaping" from beneath the plane is approximately $2(H/S)^2$. If we are willing to accept an error of 1 percent, then an S/H ratio of 14:1 is appropriate.

The second problem is that the delta form factors now vary widely. If we are to avoid objectionable aliasing artifacts, the largest delta form factors should be comparable to those of the hemicube. These occur for cells directly over dE_i, and so the cell sizes should be comparable. Unfortunately, this means that the single plane, with its area of $4S^2 = 784$ square units (for an S/H ratio of 14:1) versus the hemicube's 12 square units, will have approximately 65 times as many cells as the hemicube!

Sillion and Puech (1989) solved this problem by using variable-size cells (which they called "proxels"). They subdivided the plane such that each cell would have approximately the same form factor. Unfortunately, this precludes the use of the Z-buffering algorithm for scan conversion, which requires equal-size cells. Sillion and Puech used Warnock's algorithm (e.g., Sutherland et al. 1974) to subdivide the projected polygons until each one was either fully visible or fully hidden. Although this is a more complicated approach than the Z-buffer algorithm, it does have the advantage of having a time complexity that is linear with the number of polygons in the scene being viewed. Sillion and Puech compared the execution times of their single-plane algorithm versus the hemicube algorithm for an environment of 1,152 polygons. They found both algorithms to be competitive up to a hemicube resolution of approximately 400×400 cells; thereafter their approach offered better performance.

Recker et al. (1990) proposed an alternative solution that does not require an area subdivision algorithm. First, a second plane with a higher cell resolution is centered within the first plane (Fig. 5.31). A polygon is then transformed and clipped to the view volume of the outer plane, with the clipped polygon vertices being saved for later use. The polygon is scan converted over the outer plane, ignoring the region occupied by the inner plane, and the delta form factors are summed for the covered cells. The saved polygon vertices are then clipped again to the inner plane's view volume and scan converted. The delta form factors are summed and added to those summed during the first pass.

The lower resolution of the outer plane speeds the scan conversion process, but this is mostly negated by having to clip and scan the polygon twice. In practice, this modified single-plane algorithm reduces the number of cells and delta form factors required by some 80 percent while offering approximately the same execution time as the single-plane algorithm.

The third problem is not so easily overcome. The single plane's field of view is much larger than the hemicube's top face, and so the view distance is much closer to the view-plane window. Recalling Equation 4.13, we can see that this will severely affect our pseudodepth scale for Z-buffering. That is, our three-dimensional projective transformation scales the depth p_n of a vertex from view plane according to $p'_n = p_n/(1 - p_n/d)$, where d is the view distance and p'_n is the pseudodepth. Given, for example, two points with true depths 10 and 11 units from the view plane, decreasing the view distance by a factor of 14 will decrease the pseudodepth distance between them by a factor of 166.

All we can do to counteract this problem is to increase the precision of our Z-buffer. In C++, this means going from a *float* to a *double*, doubling the size of the buffer. On the other hand, this may not be necessary. The changes to the pseudodepth scale may not pose a problem for typical environments of interest.

Interested readers might consider implementing the modified single-plane algorithm for themselves, if only to compare its performance with the hemicube and cubic tetrahedral algorithms. It should be possible to derive a single-plane class from *FormClip* and *FormScan* with relatively little effort, using *HemiClip* and *HemiScan* as prototypes.

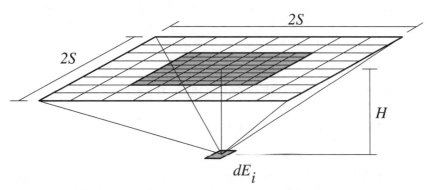

Figure 5.31   Modified single-plane algorithm (Recker et al. 1990)

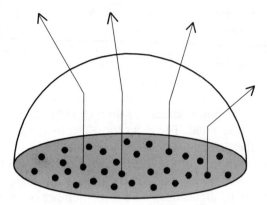

Figure 5.32   Monte Carlo form factor determination

5.22   STOCHASTIC RAY-CASTING TECHNIQUES

Ray-casting techniques offer yet another approach to form factor determination. Maxwell et al. (1986) and Malley (1988) used stochastic (Monte Carlo) techniques to shoot randomly distributed rays into the environment from the surface of a polygon. Malley's approach was to reverse Nusselt's analogy (Fig. 5.32). A hemisphere is placed over the center of a polygon, following which random points on the base are chosen and rays shot straight up. When they intersect the surface of the hemisphere, they are redirected along the surface normal at that point (i.e., radially from the hemisphere's center). Each ray is then tested for intersections with other polygons in the environment using conventional ray-tracing techniques. A polygon's form factor is given by the number of rays it intercepts divided by the total number of rays shot.

This is a valuable technique in that it can be applied to both planar and curved surfaces. It can also accommodate transparent objects and nondiffuse surfaces. The random distribution of points ensures that aliasing artifacts are minimized, and no three-dimensioanl projective transformation, polygon clipping, or scan conversion operations are required. Moreover, there are many ray-tracing techniques (e.g., Glassner 1990) that can be used to accelerate the ray-polygon intersection calculations. The only disadvantage is that a large number of rays must be shot in order to approach the accuracy provided by the hemicube algorithm and its variants.

5.23   VERTEX-TO-SOURCE FORM FACTOR DETERMINATION

Many of the problems associated with the hemicube and cubic tetrahedral algorithms can be avoided by taking a different approach to form factor determination. Wallace et al. (1989) proposed that we instead model the emitting polygon as a finite area source and determine its form factor as seen from each receiving polygon's vertex in the environment (Fig. 5.33). The source is subdivided such that its size is much

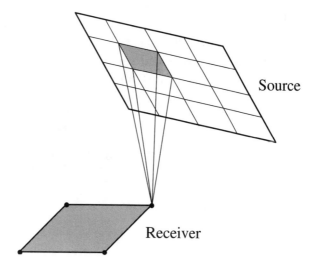

Figure 5.33   Receiver vertex-to-source form factors

smaller than the distance to the vertex. The delta form factor is then calculated for each one; the vertex-to-source form factor is their sum.

We could use contour integration (Eq. 5.6) to solve the individual delta form factors. However, this can be very time consuming, and it does not address the polygon occlusion problem. Wallace et al. (1989) instead proposed approximating each small polygon as an arbitrarily oriented disk (Fig. 5.34).

From Siegel and Howell (1992), the analytic form factor from a differential area dE_j parallel to and at a distance r from a finite disk E_i with radius a is:

$$F_{dEj-Ei} = a^2 / (r^2 + a^2) \qquad (5.42)$$

This is the geometry shown in Figure 5.34, where $\theta_i = \theta_j = 0$. Using the reciprocity relation from Section 2.5 (that is, $A_i F_{ij} = A_j F_{ji}$), we have:

$$F_{Ei-dEj} = dA_j / (\pi r^2 + A_i) \qquad (5.43)$$

where dA_j is the area of a differential element dE_j surrounding the vertex and A_i is the area of the approximated source polygon E_i.

We can generalize this result by including the cosines of the angles between the surface normals and the direction between dE_j and E_i. This is an approximation, but it is useful nevertheless:

$$F_{Ei-dEj} \approx dA_j \cos\theta_j \cos\theta_i / (\pi r^2 + A_i) \qquad (5.44)$$

If we divide the source polygon finely enough, we can model each E_i as a differential area and shoot a single ray from the receiver vertex dE_j. If the ray intersects any intervening polygons, then that portion of the source is hidden from the vertex. Assuming that the source polygon is planar and has been evenly subdivided, its total form factor as seen from the vertex is:

$$F_{ij} \approx \frac{dA_j}{n} \sum_{k=1}^{n} HID_k \frac{\cos \theta_{jk} \cos \theta_{ik}}{\pi r_k^2 + A_i/n} \qquad (5.45)$$

where n is the number of subdivided source polygons and HID_k is one if the kth source polygon is visible to the vertex; otherwise it is zero.

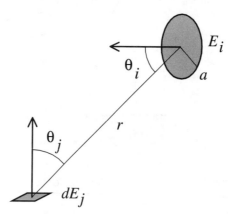

Figure 5.34   Form factor geometry between differential area dE_j and finite disk E_i

We will later be interested in the reciprocal form factor F_{ji}. Using the reciprocity relation, we see that this is:

$$F_{ji} = \frac{A_i}{dA_j} F_{ij} \approx \frac{A_i}{n} \sum_{k=1}^{n} HID_k \frac{\cos \theta_{jk} \cos \theta_{ik}}{\pi r_k^2 + A_i/n} \qquad (5.46)$$

One comment before we continue: Equation 5.44 assumes that the source polygon can be modeled as a circular disk. This approximation holds true for equilateral triangles and square quadrilaterals. However, it does not accurately model long, thin polygons. This is not a serious problem. As we shall see in Chapter 7, the polygonal elements in our environment should not be long and thin to begin with.

5.23.1 Ray-Polygon Intersections

The efficiency of the ray-casting approach depends on how quickly we can perform ray-polygon intersection calculations for possibly occluding polygons. Fortunately, there is a particularly elegant algorithm for convex polygons due to Badouel (1990) that is fast and efficient.

The first step is to define the ray (Fig. 5.35). Its origin is the receiver vertex S, while its direction is the vector $\mathbf{r}$ from the receiver vertex to a point E on the source polygon, or $\mathbf{r} = E - S$.

Expressed as a parametric equation (Section 4.8.2), this becomes:

$$p(t) = S + t * \mathbf{r} \qquad (5.47)$$

where $t \geq 0$. That is, for any positive value of t, $p(t)$ describes a point in the direc-

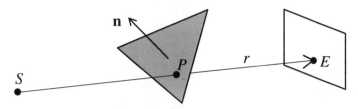

Figure 5.35   Ray-polygon intersection geometry

tion of **r**. Furthermore, a value of $0 \leq t \leq 1$ describes a point along the ray between S and E.

Now, given an arbitrary polygon, we need to determine whether it intersects the ray between S and E. The polygon vertices define a plane, so we can first ask whether the ray intersects this plane. This problem is equivalent to that discussed in Section 4.8.2, where the line between S and E represented a polygon edge. Repeating Equation 4.30, we have:

$$t = \frac{d - \mathbf{n} \cdot \mathbf{S}}{\mathbf{n} \cdot \mathbf{r}} \tag{5.48}$$

where **n** is the polygon normal, **S** is the bound vector from the world space origin to the receiver vertex S, and d is the distance from the world space origin to the nearest point on the plane. From Equation 4.27, we have:

$$d = \mathbf{n} \cdot \mathbf{p} \tag{5.49}$$

where **p** is the bound vector from the world space origin to any point on the plane. For convenience, this can be taken as the first vertex describing the polygon.

The denominator of Equation 5.48 should be evaluated first to avoid a division-by-zero error. If it is equal to zero, then the ray is parallel to the polygon and so does not intersect the polygon.

Equation 5.48 is then evaluated to find t. If it is less than zero, then the plane is behind the receiver vertex S. If it is greater than one, then the plane is behind the source point E. In either case, the ray does not intersect the polygon between S and E, and so we are done. Otherwise, we now have to determine whether the ray intersects the polygon itself and not just its plane. This is where it gets interesting.

Assume that the polygon is a triangle with vertices p_0, p_1, and p_2 and that Q represents the ray-polygon intersection point (Fig. 5.36). If we define **Q** as the bound vector from p_0 to Q, $\mathbf{v}_1$ as the bound vector from p_0 to p_1, and $\mathbf{v}_2$ as the bound vector from p_0 to p_2, vector addition shows us that:

$$\mathbf{Q} = \alpha * \mathbf{v}_1 + \beta * \mathbf{v}_2 \tag{5.50}$$

where α and β are constants. The intersection point Q will be inside the polygon if and only if $\alpha \geq 0$, $\beta \geq 0$, and $\alpha + \beta \leq 1$.

Separating Equation 5.50 into its world space axis components, we have:

$$x_Q - x_0 = \alpha(x_1 - x_0) + \beta(x_2 - x_0)$$
$$y_Q - y_0 = \alpha(y_1 - y_0) + \beta(y_2 - y_0) \tag{5.51}$$
$$z_Q - z_0 = \alpha(z_1 - z_0) + \beta(z_2 - z_0)$$

We want to solve for α and β. Suppose we project the triangle and vectors shown in Figure 5.36 onto the x-y, x-z, or y-z plane. That is, we consider only two of the three equations in Equation 5.51. We must ensure that the polygon is not perpendicular to the plane; otherwise the projection will be a straight line. We therefore need to find the dominant axis of the polygon normal (i.e., the component with the largest magnitude) and choose the plane perpendicular to it. Given the polygon normal $\mathbf{n} = \{n_x, n_y, n_z\}$, we choose an axis q such that:

$$q = \begin{cases} x & \text{if } |n_x| = \max(|n_x|, |n_y|, |n_z|) \\ y & \text{if } |n_y| = \max(|n_x|, |n_y|, |n_z|) \\ z & \text{if } |n_z| = \max(|n_x|, |n_y|, |n_z|) \end{cases} \tag{5.52}$$

We then project onto the plane perpendicular to this axis. If we define its axes as s and t, then we have:

$$s_o = Q_s - p_{0s}, \quad t_0 = Q_t - p_{0t}$$
$$s_1 = p_{2s} - p_{0s}, \quad t_1 = p_{1t} - p_{0t} \tag{5.53}$$
$$s_2 = p_{2s} - p_{0s}, \quad t_2 = p_{2t} - p_{0t}$$

Substituting these into Equation 5.51, we have:

$$s_0 = \alpha * s_1 + \beta * s_2$$
$$t_0 = \alpha * t_1 + \beta * t_2 \tag{5.54}$$

or, expressed in matrix form:

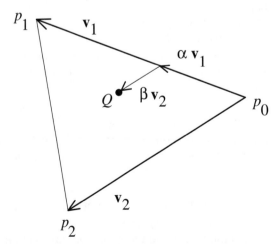

Figure 5.36   Vector representation of ray-triangle intersection point Q

$$\begin{bmatrix} s_1 & s_2 \\ t_1 & t_2 \end{bmatrix} \begin{bmatrix} \alpha \\ \beta \end{bmatrix} = \begin{bmatrix} s_0 \\ t_0 \end{bmatrix} \tag{5.55}$$

Using Cramer's rule (see any text on elementary matrix theory), we find that the solutions to this equation are:

$$\alpha = \frac{\det \begin{bmatrix} s_0 & s_2 \\ t_0 & t_2 \end{bmatrix}}{\det \begin{bmatrix} s_1 & s_2 \\ t_1 & t_2 \end{bmatrix}} = \frac{s_0 t_2 - s_2 t_0}{s_1 t_2 - s_2 t_1} \tag{5.56}$$

and:

$$\beta = \frac{\det \begin{bmatrix} s_1 & s_0 \\ t_1 & t_0 \end{bmatrix}}{\det \begin{bmatrix} s_1 & s_2 \\ t_1 & t_2 \end{bmatrix}} = \frac{s_1 t_0 - s_0 t_1}{s_1 t_2 - s_2 t_1} \tag{5.57}$$

Solving for α and β allows to us to determine whether a given ray intersects a triangular polygon. We can clearly extend this result to any convex polygon by dividing it into triangles.

Badouel's algorithm is one of several possible approaches to determining ray-polygon intersections. Two other algorithms of interest are presented by Haines (1991) and Voorhies and Kirk (1991). Also, Woo (1990) offers an acceleration technique using bounding boxes to quickly cull nonoccluding polygons before performing detailed ray-polygon intersection calculations.

One simple acceleration technique we can employ is called *shadow caching* (Haines and Greenberg 1986). The likelihood is that if a ray shot from the vertex to the source is occluded by a given polygon, then other rays shot to the source will also be occluded by the same polygon. When a shot ray is occluded, then, a pointer to the occluding polygon is cached. When the next ray from the vertex is shot, this polygon is tested first. If it occludes the ray, then there is no need to step through the rest of the environment.

5.23.2 Source Point Distribution

The accuracy of the ray-casting approach depends on the number of rays we shoot from a vertex to the source. The question is, how should we choose points on the source such that we adequately sample the environment for occluding polygons?

One approach is to use the element vertices that define the source patch. Depending on the distance of the source from the receiver, this may or may not provide adequate sampling resolution. In either case, the uniform spacing of the element vertices may cause form factor aliasing problems. Wallace et al. (1989) show that any aliasing artifacts will be particularly noticeable at shadow edges. What should be soft-edged shadows will have a jagged staircase appearance. The effect is similar to that of hemicube aliasing, except that it can be more noticeable.

A second approach is to calculate the vertex radiant exitances and then average each one according to its nearest neighbors. Our *Vertex3* class allows us to do this because each vertex has a pointer to a linked list of shared polygons.

The best approach, however, is to choose a set of uniformly random points on the source polygon. The more rays we shoot from the receiver, the better the form factor estimate will be. The resultant random ray directions will tend to minimize any form factor aliasing, much as jittering the orientation did for the hemicube algorithm.

This requires yet another algorithm. Turk (1990) describes a simple technique for triangles and convex polygons. Given a triangle with vertices p_0, p_1, and p_2 (Fig. 5.37) and two random numbers s and t between 0 and 1, a random point Q inside the triangle is given by:

```
IF s + t > 1
   s = 1 - s
   t = 1 - t
ENDIF
a = 1 - s - t
b = s
c = t
Q = a*p₀ + b*p₁ + c*p₂
```

where the vertices **p** and the intersection point **Q** are expressed as bound vectors from vertex p_0.

We can extend this algorithm to convex polygons by dividing them into triangles and using a third random number to choose which triangle should be considered. To maintain a uniform distribution, the probability of choosing a given triangle should be determined by its area relative to that of the polygon.

There is one final consideration: What is an appropriate number of rays to shoot? With each successive ray, the form factor estimate determined by Equation 5.46 becomes more accurate. We could continue to shoot rays until the difference between successive estimates is less than some predetermined criterion. (This being a random process, several more rays should be shot to ensure that the difference is not a statistical fluke.) Since the total number of rays appears in Equation 5.46, it would have to be recalculated with each new ray shot.

The problem with this approach is that it becomes increasingly inefficient as the distance between the source and the receiver vertex decreases. When they are very close and the true form factor approaches unity, rays shot toward the horizon of the receiver vertex's hemispherical field of view will have very little effect.

Wallace et al. (1989) solved this problem by adaptively subdividing the source polygon such that each subdivided area had approximately the same analytic form factor when seen from the receiver vertex. In this sense, it is similar to Sillion and Puech's (1989) single-plane algorithm, except that the plane is overlaid on the source

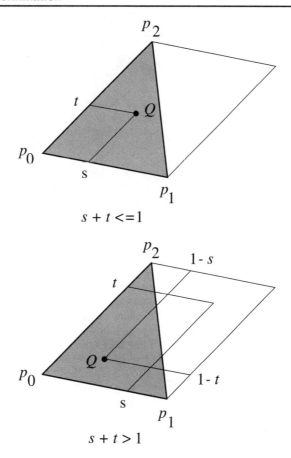

Figure 5.37 Generating a random point inside a triangle

polygon. Wallace et al. then shot a ray to the center of each subdivided polygon. Excellent results were obtained using as few as 16 rays per receiver vertex. Unfortunately, there is a considerable amount of overhead involved in subdividing arbitrary polygons in this manner. Wallace et al. used uniform subdivision for the more complex images in their paper.

Another possible solution is to estimate the unoccluded form factor of the source patch and scale the number of rays to be shot according to this estimate. A small or distant source patch will require relatively few rays, say a minimum of four. A large or very close patch will require a large number of rays, perhaps as many as several thousand for a patch that nearly fills the hemispherical field of view of the receiver vertex.

Suppose we enclose the source patch in a *bounding sphere* that is centered on the patch's center and whose radius r is equal to the distance to the furthest vertex (Fig. 5.38).

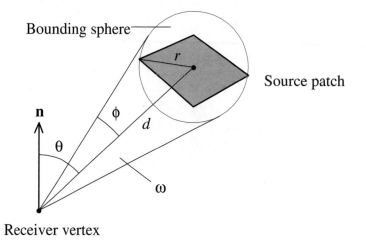

Figure 5.38   Unoccluded form factor estimate geometry

Knowing the distance d of the patch center from the receiver vertex, we can calculate the half-angle ϕ subtended by the sphere as:

$$\phi = \arctan(r/d) \tag{5.58}$$

and the corresponding solid angle ω as:

$$\omega = 2\pi(1 - \cos\phi) \tag{5.59}$$

(e.g., Hall 1989). From this, the form factor of the bounding sphere is approximated by (Cohen and Wallace 1993):

$$F_{vertex-source} \approx \frac{\cos\theta}{\pi}\omega \tag{5.60}$$

We should be careful when implementing this solution. Solving the radiosity equation involves more than simply obtaining reasonable form factor estimates. A small but highly luminous light source located near the vertex's horizon may provide most of the incident flux at the vertex. In this case, we shall want to determine whether another patch occludes even a small portion of the source patch. We need to shoot some minimum number of rays—say four—in order to ensure accurate form factor estimates for all sources, regardless of their position and orientation relative to the receiver vertex.

A second consideration is that we will likely be subdividing our surfaces into patches and elements such that the five-times rule (Section 5.5) is satisfied. There will be occasions where this assumption must fail—surfaces that join at right angles, for example—but then there will likely be no intervening patches. Given this, it is reasonable to use a constant number of rays that adequately sample source patches with a maximum half-angle ϕ of 0.1 radians (5.7 degrees). Again, four rays will usually provide adequate results.

5.23.3 Ray-Casting Advantages and Disadvantages

Before implementing a C++ class for our ray-casting algorithm, we should review the advantages offered by the ray-casting approach. First and foremost, it efficiently samples the environment. Rays are cast only in the precise direction of the source for each vertex.

Second, ray casting mostly avoids the aliasing problems caused by a uniform sampling of the environment. In particular, the plaidlike shading artifacts that are sometimes evident when the hemicube algorithm is used are no longer a concern.

Third, the ray-casting approach ensures that all sources are considered, regardless of their size. Unlike the hemicube algorithm and its derivatives, there is no possibility that a small and distant light source will be missed. This allows the user to include point light sources in the description of the environment.

Related to this advantage is the ability to include physically realistic light sources in the environment description. Most light sources have non-Lambertian flux distributions (e.g., Ashdown 1993, Verbeck and Greenberg 1984, Warn 1983). A theater spotlight is an extreme but still common example–its flux is emitted primarily in one direction. Most light fixture manufacturers provide *goniophotometric diagrams* that represent the fixture as a point source and show or tabulate its luminous intensity for various vertical and horizontal angles (e.g., IESNA 1993).

Ray casting allows us to readily incorporate these sources in our radiosity solutions. This includes not only theoretical point sources (Warn 1983), but also physically accurate area sources (Verbeck and Greenberg 1984) and complex volume sources (Ashdown 1993). All that is required is a C++ object for the light source that encapsulates its three-dimensional flux distribution and returns the luminance of a ray leaving the source in a given direction.

Fourth, we need to know the vertex exitances in order to perform Gouraud shading of the visible elements in a scene. We shall see in the next chapter that the hemicube algorithm provides exitances only for the element centers; the vertex exitances must be obtained through interpolation. In contrast, the ray-casting algorithm provides the vertex exitances directly.

A fifth advantage comes from our ability to model complex surfaces as a mesh of polygon patches and elements. Wallace et al. (1991) used a quadratic spline to model a complex curved surface. This was then represented by a mesh of 1,176 elements for radiosity and rendering purposes. However, the ray-occlusion tests were performed using the implicit quadratic spline equation for the surface. Rather than testing for occlusion against each element for each vertex and each ray (five rays per vertex were used), the test function had to solve only a fairly simple equation.

A final advantage is that ray casting determines one form factor at a time. Unlike the hemicube algorithm, there is no need to provide storage for the form factors of every element in the environment.

Compared to these advantages, the two disadvantages of ray casting are minor but still noteworthy. First, the hemicube algorithm processes each element in the environment once for each patch. Given m patches and n elements, this results in an algorithmic time complexity of $O(mn)$. (See Section 2.6 for an overview of the meaning of time complexity.) A naive implementation of the ray-casting algorithm, on the other hand, processes each patch in the environment once for each vertex for the ray-occlusion tests. However, it must also process every element in the environment for each source patch to test for possible occlusion. This gives a time complexity of $O(mn^2)$. Thus, ray casting becomes increasingly more expensive relative to the hemicube approach as the complexity of the environment grows. Fortunately, this situation improves dramatically when ray-tracing acceleration techniques (e.g., Arvo and Kirk 1989) or implicit surface equations (e.g., Wallace 1989) are used.

The second disadvantage is that the ray-casting algorithm requires the vertex normal for its ray-occlusion test calculations. This adds an additional 12 bytes to every *Vertex3* object. Without it (and the hemicube algorithm does not need it), the size of *Vertex3* could be reduced by over 25 percent. This can be a significant amount of memory for complex environments.

Vilaplana and Pueyo (1992) noted a corollary to these disadvantages. An extremely complex environment can in theory be stored in virtual memory. However, we shall see in Chapter 6 that both the hemicube and ray-casting algorithms continually cycle through the entire environment as the radiosity equation is being solved. This means that portions of the environment will be repeatedly paged from virtual memory. In practical terms, this means a nearly continuous stream of data will occur to and from the hard disk or network server. The polite term for this behavior is "thrashing"; network system administrators and other frustrated users often use more colorful terminology.

This is where the inner loop of the ray-occlusion test becomes important. Accessing every patch for every vertex may greatly increase the amount of virtual memory paging. In situations where virtual memory usage is unavoidable, ray casting may not be the algorithm of choice.

5.24   A RAY-CASTING ALGORITHM CLASS

We can assemble the above algorithms into a class that, stated in pseudocode, performs as indicated in Figure 5.39.

```
Select source patch s
Select vertex v
Form factor estimate Fvs = 0
IF source patch is not backface
  FOR number of rays
    Select random point on source patch
    IF point visible from vertex
      Shoot ray from vertex to source point
      FOR all other patches in environment
        Check for ray occlusion
    ENDFOR
```

```
      IF ray not occluded
        Update form factor estimate F_vs
      ENDIF
    ENDIF
  ENDFOR
ENDIF
```

Figure 5.39   Ray-casting algorithm pseudocode

Given a source patch *s*, this algorithm is repeated for every vertex in the environment. Unlike the hemicube algorithm, it returns a single form factor estimate.

Expanding the pseudocode into C++, we have:

Listing 5.29

```cpp
// RAY_CAST.H - Ray Cast Form Factor Class

#ifndef _RAY_CAST_H
#define _RAY_CAST_H

#include "parse.h"

// Maximum number of rays to be cast
static const int RC_NumRays = 4;

class RayCast    // Ray cast form factor determination
{
  private:
    double ray_area;           // Intersection area
    double src_area;           // Source patch area
    double selector;           // Triangle selector
    Patch3 *psrc;              // Source patch pointer
    Patch3 *pcache;            // Last occluding patch
    Vector3 end;               // Intersection vector
    Vector3 ray_dir;           // Ray direction
    Vector3 src_center;        // Source patch center
    Vector3 src_norm;          // Source patch normal
    Vector3 start;             // Receiver vertex vector
    Vector3 v0, v1, v2, v3;    // Vertex vectors

    void Select( Vector3 * );
    BOOL CheckOcclusion( Instance * );
    BOOL TestPatch( Patch3 * );

  public:
    void Init( Patch3 * );
    double CalcFormFactor( Vertex3 *, Instance * );
};

#endif
```

Init is called once for each source patch to initialize the *RayCast* private members with several of its attributes. The environment is then processed one vertex at a time. Recalling that each *Instance3* object has a pointer to its linked list of vertices, we can access each vertex exactly once. *CalcFormFactor* is then called to estimate the vertex-to-source form factor.

Note that *RC_NumRays* is set to 4. This will produce satisfactory results for most environments. However, it should be increased for environments where the vertex-to-source distance is expected to be small in comparison to the source patch width.

The remainder of the class consists of:

Listing 5.30

```
// RAY_CAST.CPP - Ray Cast Form Factor Class

#include "ray_cast.h"

double RayCast::CalcFormFactor( Vertex3 *pvertex, Instance
    *penv )
{
  int i;              // Loop index
  double ff;          // Vertex-source form factor
  double ray_len;     // Ray length
  Vector3 nv;         // Vertex normal
  Vector3 n_ray;      // Normalized ray direction
  Vector3 r_ray;      // Reverse normalized ray direction
  Vector3 view;       // Source patch view vector

  start = Vector3(pvertex->GetPosn());
  nv = pvertex->GetNormal();
  view = start - src_center;

  // Determine whether source patch is backface
  if (Dot(src_norm, view) < MIN_VALUE)
    return 0.0;

  ff = 0.0;
  for (i = 0; i < RC_NumRays; i++)
  {
    // Select random point on source patch
    Select(&end);

    // Generate ray to shoot from vertex to source
    ray_dir = end - start;

    // Check for source point behind vertex
    if (Dot(nv, ray_dir) < MIN_VALUE)
      continue;

    // Test for ray-element intersection
    if (CheckOcclusion(penv) == FALSE)
    {
```

```
        // Calculate ray length
        ray_len = ray_dir.Length();

        // Calculate normalized ray direction
        n_ray = ray_dir;
        n_ray.Norm();

        // Determine reverse normalized ray direction
        r_ray = -n_ray;

        // Update form factor estimation
        ff += Dot(n_ray, nv) * Dot(r_ray, src_norm) / ((PI *
            ray_len * ray_len) + ray_area);
    }
  }

  // Multiply by ray-source patch intersection area
  ff *= ray_area;

  return ff;
}

// Initialize parameters for source patch
void RayCast::Init( Patch3 *ppatch )
{
  double a1, a2;        // Triangle areas
  Vector3 temp;         // Temporary 3-D vector
  Vector3 e0, e1, e2;   // Edge vectors

  psrc = ppatch;
  pcache = NULL;
  src_area = psrc->GetArea();
  src_norm = psrc->GetNormal();
  src_center = Vector3(psrc->GetCenter());
  ray_area = src_area / RC_NumRays;

  // Get patch vertex vectors
  v0 = Vector3(ppatch->GetVertexPtr(0)->GetPosn());
  v1 = Vector3(ppatch->GetVertexPtr(1)->GetPosn());
  v2 = Vector3(ppatch->GetVertexPtr(2)->GetPosn());
  v3 = Vector3(ppatch->GetVertexPtr(3)->GetPosn());

  // Calculate patch edge vectors
  e0 = Vector3(v1 - v0);
  e1 = Vector3(v2 - v0);

  // Calculate first triangle area
  temp = Cross(e0, e1);
  a1 = temp.Length() / 2.0;

  if (ppatch->IsQuad() == TRUE)
  {
    // Calculate patch edge vector
    e2 = Vector3(v3 - v0);
```

(continued)

Listing 5.30   *(continued)*

```
    // Calculate second triangle area
    temp = Cross(e1, e2);
    a2 = temp.Length() / 2.0;
  }
  else
    a2 = 0.0;

  // Calculate fractional area of first triangle
  selector = a1 / (a1 + a2);
}

// Select random point within source patch area
void RayCast::Select( Vector3 *ppoint )
{
  double s, t;        // Random point parameters

  // Get random point parameters
  s = GetNormRand();
  t = GetNormRand();

  // Ensure random point is inside triangle
  if (s + t > 1.0)
  {
    s = 1.0 - s;
    t = 1.0 - t;
  }

  // Calculate random point coordinates
  if (GetNormRand() <= selector)
  {
    // Locate point in first triangle
    *ppoint = (1.0 - s - t) * v0 + s * v1 + t * v2;
  }
  else
  {
    // Locate point in second triangle
    *ppoint = (1.0 - s - t) * v0 + s * v2 + t * v3;
  }
}

// Check for ray occlusion
BOOL RayCast::CheckOcclusion( Instance *pinst )
{
  Patch3 *ppatch;       // Patch pointer
  Surface3 *psurf;      // Surface pointer

  // Test cached patch for ray-patch intersection
  if (TestPatch(pcache) == TRUE)
    return TRUE;

  // Walk the instance list
  while (pinst != NULL)
  {
```

```
      // Walk the surface list
      psurf = pinst->GetSurfPtr();
      while (psurf != NULL)
      {
        // Walk the patch list
        ppatch = psurf->GetPatchPtr();
        while (ppatch != NULL)
        {
          if (ppatch != psrc)      // Ignore source patch
          {
            // Test for ray-patch intersection
            if (TestPatch(ppatch) == TRUE)
            {
              // Cache occluding patch
              pcache = ppatch;

              return TRUE;
            }
          }
          ppatch = ppatch->GetNext();
        }
        psurf = psurf->GetNext();
      }
      pinst = pinst->GetNext();
  }

  return FALSE;
}

// Check for ray-patch intersection (Badouel's Algorithm)
BOOL RayCast::TestPatch( Patch3 *ppatch )
{
  BOOL i_flag;           // Intersection flag
  int i;                 // Loop index
  int i0, i1, i2;        // Projection plane axis indices
  double alpha;          // Scaling parameter
  double beta;           // Scaling parameter
  double dist;           // Patch plane distance
  double d, t;           // Temporary variables
  double isect[3];       // Ray-patch intersection
  double n_mag[3];       // Patch normal axis magnitudes
  double vert[4][3];     // Patch vertices
  double s0, s1, s2;     // Projected vector co-ordinates
  double t0, t1, t2;     // Projected vector co-ordinates
  Point3 *pvp;           // Vertex position pointer
  Vector3 normal;        // Patch normal
  Vector3 temp;          // Temporary 3-D vector

  // Check for valid patch
  if (ppatch == NULL)
    return FALSE;

  // Get patch normal
  normal = ppatch->GetNormal();
```

(continued)

Listing 5.30   *(continued)*

```
// Calculate divisor
d = Dot(normal, ray_dir);

// Determine whether ray is parallel to patch
if (fabs(d) < MIN_VALUE)
  return FALSE;

// Calculate patch plane distance
temp = Vector3(ppatch->GetVertexPtr(0)->GetPosn());
dist = Dot(normal, temp);

// Calculate ray hit time parameter
t = (dist - Dot(normal, start)) / d;

// Check whether patch plane is behind receiver vertex or
// source patch point
//
// NOTE: MIN_VALUE offsets are required to prevent
//       interpretation of adjoining surface vertices as
//       occlusions
if (t < MIN_VALUE || t > (1.0 - MIN_VALUE))
  return FALSE;

// Calculate ray-patch plane intersection
temp = start + (ray_dir * t);

// Get intersection axes
isect[0] = temp.GetX();
isect[1] = temp.GetY();
isect[2] = temp.GetZ();

// Get patch normal axis magnitudes
n_mag[0] = fabs(normal.GetX());
n_mag[1] = fabs(normal.GetY());
n_mag[2] = fabs(normal.GetZ());

// Get patch vertex axes
for (i = 0; i < ppatch->GetNumVert(); i++)
{
  pvp = ppatch->GetVertexPtr(i)->GetPosnPtr();
  vert[i][0] = pvp->GetX();
  vert[i][1] = pvp->GetY();
  vert[i][2] = pvp->GetZ();
}

// Find patch normal dominant axis
if ((n_mag[0] > n_mag[1]) && (n_mag[0] > n_mag[2]))
{
  i0 = 0; i1 = 1; i2 = 2;      // X-axis dominant
}
else if ((n_mag[1] > n_mag[0]) && (n_mag[1] > n_mag[2]))
{
```

```
      i0 = 1; i1 = 0; i2 = 2;        // Y-axis dominant
   }
   else
   {
      i0 = 2; i1 = 0; i2 = 1;        // Z-axis dominant
   }

   // Calculate projected vertex #0 coordinates
   s0 = isect[i1] - vert[0][i1];
   t0 = isect[i2] - vert[0][i2];

   // Check for intersection (consider quadrilateral as two
   // adjacent triangles
   i = 2;
   i_flag = FALSE;
   do
   {
      // Calculate projected vertex coordinates
      s1 = vert[i - 1][i1] - vert[0][i1];
      t1 = vert[i - 1][i2] - vert[0][i2];

      s2 = vert[i][i1] - vert[0][i1];
      t2 = vert[i][i2] - vert[0][i2];

      // Determine vector scaling parameters
      if (fabs(s1) < MIN_VALUE)     // Is s1 == 0 ?
      {
         beta = s0 / s2;
         if ((beta >= 0.0) && (beta <= 1.0))
         {
            alpha = (t0 - beta * t2) / t1;
            i_flag = ((alpha >= 0.0) && ((alpha + beta) <=
                1.0));
         }
      }
      else
      {
         beta = (s1 * t0 - s0 * t1) / (s1 * t2 - s2 * t1);
         if ((beta >= 0.0) && (beta <= 1.0))
         {
            alpha = (s0 - beta * s2) / s1;

            // Test for intersection
            i_flag = ((alpha >= 0.0) && ((alpha + beta) <=
                1.0));
         }
      }
      i++;      // Advance to next triangle (if any)
   }
   while (i_flag == FALSE && i < ppatch->GetNumVert());

   return i_flag;
}
```

Although somewhat lengthy, the code in Listing 5.30 is mostly a straightforward rendition of the preceding algorithms. You might compare it with the total amount of C++ code needed to implement the hemicube and cubic tetrahedral algorithms.

The only implementation issue of note is *TestPatch*, where a small value (*MIN_VALUE*) is added to the tests that determine whether the patch intersects the ray between the receiver vertex and the source. Remember that adjoining surfaces do not share vertices because they will likely have different *Spectra* exitance values. The off-sets are necessary to prevent these vertices from being seen as occluding the ray.

Note also that *RayCast* does not implement the bounding sphere heuristic. Instead, it always shoots *RC_NumRays* rays (defined in RAY_CAST.H, Listing 5.29). Implementation of Equations 5.58 through 5.60 is left as an exercise for the reader.

5.24.1 Yet Another Character-Mode Test Program

We can test *RayCast* with the following test program:

Listing 5.31

```
// TEST_4.CPP - Ray Casting Test Program

// NOTE: _NOT_WIN_APP must be globally defined for this
//       program to be successfully compiled

#include <stdio.h>
#include <stdlib.h>
#include <iostream.h>
#include <time.h>
#include "error.h"
#include "parse.h"
#include "ray_cast.h"

// Default entity directory path
static char NoEntityDir[] = "";

static RayCast Ray;             // Ray casting
static Parse Parser;            // World file parser
static Environ Environment;     // Environment

int main( int argc, char **argv )
{
  char *pentdir;          // Entity directory path
  Instance *penv;         // Environment pointer
  Instance *pinst_1;      // Instance pointer
  Instance *pinst_2;      // Instance pointer
  Surface3 *psurf;        // Surface pointer
  Patch3 *ppatch;         // Patch pointer
  Vertex3 *pvert;         // Vertex pointer
  WORD src_id = 1;        // Source patch identifier
  WORD rcv_id;            // Receiving vertex identifier
```

```
// Get entity directory path (if any)
if (argc > 2)
  pentdir = argv[2];
else
  pentdir = NoEntityDir;

// Parse the environment file
if (Parser.ParseFile(argv[1], pentdir, &Environment) ==
    FALSE)
  return 1;

// Seed the random number generator
srand((unsigned) time(NULL));

// Get environment pointer
pinst_1 = penv = Environment.GetInstPtr();

// Walk the instance list
while (pinst_1 != NULL)
{
  // Walk the surface list
  psurf = pinst_1->GetSurfPtr();
  while (psurf != NULL)
  {
    // Walk the patch list
    ppatch = psurf->GetPatchPtr();
    while (ppatch != NULL)
    {
      // Initialize the ray casting object
      Ray.Init(ppatch);
      cout << "Patch " << src_id << endl;

      // Walk the instance list
      rcv_id = 1;
      pinst_2 = penv;
      while (pinst_2 != NULL)
      {
        // Walk the vertex list
        pvert = pinst_2->GetVertPtr();
        while (pvert != NULL)
        {
          cout << "  FF(" << rcv_id++ << "," << src_id <<
              ") = " << Ray.CalcFormFactor(pvert, penv)
              << endl;
          pvert = pvert->GetNext();
        }
        pinst_2 = pinst_2->GetNext();
      }
      src_id++;
      ppatch = ppatch->GetNext();
    }
```

(continued)

Listing 5.31   *(continued)*

```
      psurf = psurf->GetNext();
    }
    pinst_1 = pinst_1->GetNext();
  }

  cout << endl << "Number of rays = " << RC_NumRays;

  return 0;
}
```

TEST_4 can be used with any environment (*.WLD) file. To verify the results, however, we can use:

Listing 5.32   **RAY_TEST.WLD**

```
WORLD opposing squares
COMMENT first square
square.ent
< 0.0001 0.0001 1.0 >
< 0.0 0.0 0.0 >
< 0.0 0.0 -0.5 >
COMMENT second square
square.ent
< 1.0 1.0 1.0 >
< 180.0 0.0 0.0 >
< 0.0 0.0 0.5 >
END_FILE
```

This is essentially the same geometric arrangement as that shown in Figure 5.28, where $W = d = 1$. The differential element is approximated by a square measuring 0.0001 units across. From Equations 5.40 and 5.41, the analytic form factor is approximately 0.2395.

Since the vertices are relatively close to the source patch (more so than they would likely be in a typical environment), *RC_NumRays* (Listing 5.29) should be defined as 16 for the purposes of this test program. A sample run of *TEST_4* will then produce something like:

```
Patch 1
  FF(1,1) = 0
  FF(2,1) = 0
  FF(3,1) = 0
  FF(4,1) = 0
  FF(5,1) = 0.243623
  FF(6,1) = 0.232016
  FF(7,1) = 0.230337
  FF(8,1) = 0.222784
```

```
Patch 2
  FF(1,2) = 1.4147e-009
  FF(2,2) = 1.41473e-009
  FF(3,2) = 1.4147e-009
  FF(4,2) = 1.41466e-009
  FF(5,2) = 0
  FF(6,2) = 0
  FF(7,2) = 0
  FF(8,2) = 0

Number of rays = 16
```

Again, remember that these values were produced by a random process. This explains why the four largest form factors differ slightly. On the other hand, note that the form factors to the differential patch #2 are calculated. If you run *TEST_2* and *TEST_3* on RAY_TEST.WLD, you will see that the hemicube and cubic tetrahedral algorithms miss these values entirely.

5.25 VISIBILITY PREPROCESSING

We have so far used backface culling to eliminate those polygons that face away from the source patch (hemicube algorithm) or receiver vertex (ray-casting algorithm). This still leaves us with the task of examining each and every polygon in the environment for each source patch or receiver vertex. Since the underlying patch effectively divides the environment into two half-spaces, we should consider possible techniques for eliminating those polygons (and portions thereof for boundary cases) in the half-space we cannot "see" from the hemicube or vertex as quickly and efficiently as possible.

We need not look far; the ray-tracing literature is replete with *visibility preprocessing* algorithms. The basic principle is to divide the environment into a hierarchy of nested subspaces. One example is *octree encoding*, where the volume of space enclosing the environment is recursively divided into eight subspaces called *octants* (Fig 5.40). A data structure such as:

```
struct OctreeNode
{
  Element3 *pelem;           // Element pointer
  OctreeNode *pchild[8];     // Child node pointers
};
```

is then used to link these subspaces into an *octree*. Each leaf node of the tree points to exactly one patch element; the subspace representing the node forms a spatial bounding box around the element. Traversing the tree from root to leaf allows us to determine the position of each element to within the limits of the bounding box. It also allows us to cull large portions of the tree without having to examine each element.

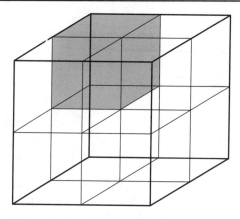

Figure 5.40   Subdividing a three-dimensional space into octants

A more efficient technique for representing the hierarchy of octants is *binary space partitioning*. The environment is recursively divided into half-spaces by planes, where three perpendicular planes form eight octants. Each node requires less memory, and the depth of the tree is typically smaller than the octree.

Wang and Davis (1990) presented a visibility preprocessing algorithm based on a binary space partitioning (BSP) tree that specifically addresses hemicube requirements. They used a priority list structure to order the partitioning planes in front-to-back order as seen from the hemicube center. By traversing this list, they managed to avoid having to perform Z-buffering for the elements.

BSP trees are also very useful for ray casting vertex-to-source form factors. Sung and Shirley (1992) examined a variety of spatial subdivision algorithms and concluded that the BSP offers the best performance for ray-tracing applications. Included with their presentation is an extensive and well-documented implementation written in C.

Finally, Ng and Slater (1993) provided a wealth of information on BSP trees and bounding boxes relating to their study of a multiprocessor-based radiosity renderer. By enclosing the source and receiver patches in an axis-aligned *bounding box* (Fig. 5.41), they were able to cull most nonoccluding polygons by checking whether any of their vertices were inside the box. Constructing the box for each pair of polygons and checking vertices against it can proceed very quickly, because the bounding planes of the box are parallel to the world space axes.

The advantage of the bounding box approach is that it eliminates the need to build, store, and manipulate a BSP tree or other auxiliary data structure. Ng and Slater (1993) found that using bounding boxes alone resulted in execution speeds nearly twice those of implementations based on BSP trees for small environments of less than 500 polygons.

More information on bounding boxes and related techniques can be found in Marks et al. (1990), Haines and Wallace (1991), and Zhang (1991). In addition, an excellent source of ray-tracing acceleration techniques is Arvo and Kirk (1989).

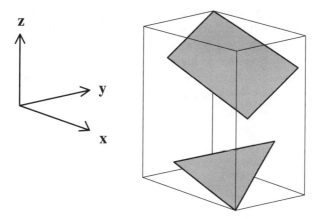

Figure 5.41   Bounding box approach to culling nonoccluding polygons

5.26   CONCLUSIONS

Form factor determination is a major component of any radiosity-rendering program, and so it is entirely appropriate that we have devoted so much space to the topic. It is also frustrating not to have the space to address the topic in even greater depth. Interested readers are strongly encouraged to investigate the following references: Baum et al. (1989), Cohen and Wallace (1993), Max and Troutman (1993), Max and Allison (1992), Pietrek (1993), Recker et al. (1990), Rushmeier et al. (1991), Sbert (1993), Sillion and Puech (1989), Spencer (1992), Sun et al. (1993), Tampieri (1992), Vilaplana and Pueyo (1992), Wallace (1989), Wang et al. (1992), Wang and Davis (1990), Emery et al. (1991), and Zhou and Peng (1992).

A visibility preprocessing algorithm should be included in any production-quality radiosity renderer. The bounding box approach is almost trivial to implement. Readers interested in the BSP tree approach will find an excellent example and implementation in Sung and Shirley (1992) that can with relatively little effort be adapted to vertex-to-source ray casting. It can also be used for the hemicube algorithm, although this will require more work and some ingenuity.

It should also be noted that the code presented in this chapter was written with the reader, not execution time, in mind. Despite our concern for a "carefully crafted C++ implementation," no attempt has been made to optimize this code.

Optimizing compilers will improve matters to some extent by assigning register variables, unrolling loops, inlining functions, and so forth. However, obtaining the best performance often requires hand optimization and even assembly language programming for the most time-critical functions. This comes at a considerable cost: Highly optimized code is difficult to document clearly and even more difficult to understand.

Nevertheless, the performance-minded reader is encouraged to consider hand optimization of the source code. Following standard software engineering practices, you should: (a) fully understand the underlying algorithms before you begin, (b)

perform a careful analysis with a source code profiler to pinpoint execution bottle-necks, (c) clearly document all changes for later reference.

This, however, should be a project for the future. We have no less than three form factor determination methods in hand and a fourth that can be implemented with a few hours of work. Still to come is the final component of our radiosity renderer: solving the radiosity equation.

REFERENCES

Airey, J. M., and M. Ouh-Young. 1989. *Two Adaptive Techniques Let Progressive Radiosity Outperform the Traditional Radiosity Algorithm*. Department of Computer Science, University of North Carolina, Technical Report TR89-020.

Arvo, J., ed. 1991. *Graphic Gems II*. San Diego, CA: Academic Press.

Arvo, J., and D. Kirk. 1989. "A Survey of Ray Tracing Acceleration Techniques," in Glassner (1989), pp. 201–262.

Ashdown, I. 1988. "Dynamic Multidimensional Arrays in C," *Computer Language* 5(6):83–88 (June).

Ashdown, I. (1993). "Modeling Complex 3-D Light Sources," *ACM SIGGRAPH '93 Course 22 (Making Radiosity Practical) Notes*.

Badouel, D. 1990. "An Efficient Ray-Polygon Intersection," in Glassner (1990), pp. 390–393, 735.

Baum, D. R., H. E. Rushmeier, and J. M. Winget. 1989. "Improving Radiosity Solutions through the Use of Analytically Determined Form Factors," *Computer Graphics* 23(3):325–334 (ACM SIGGRAPH '89 Proc,).

Beran-Koehn, J. C., and M. J. Pavicic. 1991. "A Cubic Tetrahedral Adaptation of the Hemi-Cube Algorithm," in Arvo (1991), pp. 299–302.

Beran-Koehn, J. C., and M. J. Pavicic. 1992. "Delta Form Factor Calculation for the Cubic Tetrahedral Algorithm," in Kirk (1992), pp. 324–328, 575–576.

Bian, B. 1992. "Hemispherical Projection of a Triangle," in Kirk (1992), pp. 314–317, 569–574.

Bian, B., N. Wittels, and D. S. Fussell. 1992. "Non-Uniform Patch Luminance for Global Illumination," *Graphics Interface '92*, pp. 310 –318.

Bouatouch, K., and C. Bouville, eds. 1992. *Photorealism in Computer Graphics*. Berlin, Germany: Springer-Verlag.

Bu, J., and E. F. Deprettere. 1987a. "A VLSI System Architecture for High-Speed Radiative Transfer 3D Image Synthesis," *Eurographics '87* (Proc. European Computer Graphics Conference and Exhibition), G. Marechal, ed., Amsterdam: Elsevier Science Publishers B.V. (North-Holland), pp. 221–235.

Bu, J., and E. F. Deprettere. 1987b. "A VLSI Algorithm for Computing Form-Factors in Radiative Transfer Computer Image Synthesis," *Computer Graphics 1987* (Proc. CG International '87), T. L. Kunii, ed., London, England: Springer-Verlag, pp. 181–193.

Bu, J., and E. F. Deprettere. 1989. "A VLSI System Architecture for High-Speed Radiative Transfer 3D Image Synthesis," *The Visual Computer* 5(2):121–133.

Cherry, V. H., D. D. Davis, and M. K. Boelter. 1939. "A Mechanical Integrator for the Determination of the Illumination from Diffuse Surface Sources," *Transactions of the Illuminating Engineering Society* 34(11):1085–1094.

Cohen, M. F., and D. P. Greenberg. 1985. "The Hemi-Cube: A Radiosity Solution for Complex Environments," *Computer Graphics* 19(3):31–40 (ACM SIGGRAPH '85 Proc.).

Cohen, M. F., D. P. Greenberg, D. S. Immel, and P. J. Brock. 1986. "An Efficient Radiosity Approach for Realistic Image Synthesis," *IEEE Computer Graphics and Applications* 6(3):26–35.

Cohen, M. F., C. Puech, and F. Sillion, eds. 1993. *Proc. Fourth Eurographics Workshop on Rendering*. Aire-la-Ville, Switzerland: Eurographics Technical Report Series EG 93 RW.

Cohen, M. F., and J. R. Wallace. 1993. *Radiosity and Realistic Image Synthesis*. San Diego, CA: Academic Press.

Emery, A. F., O. Johansson, M. Lobo, and A. Abrous. 1991. "A Comparative Study of Methods for Computing the Diffuse Radiation Viewfactors for Complex Structures," *Journal of Heat Transfer* 113:413–422.

Glassner, A. S., ed. 1989. *An Introduction to Ray Tracing*. San Diego, CA: Academic Press.

Glassner, A. S., ed. 1990. *Graphic Gems*. San Diego, CA: Academic Press.

Goral, C. M., K. E. Torrance, D. P. Greenberg, and B. Battaile. 1984. "Modelling the Interaction of Light between Diffuse Surfaces," *Computer Graphics* 18(3):212–222 (ACM SIGGRAPH '84 Proc.)

Haines, E. 1991. "Fast Ray-Convex Polyhedron Intersection," in Arvo (1991), pp. 247–250.

Haines, E., and D. P. Greenberg. 1986. "The Light Buffer: A Ray Tracer Shadow Testing Accelerator," *IEEE Computer Graphics & Applications* 6(9):6–16.

Haines, E., and J. Wallace. 1991. "Shaft Culling for Efficient Ray-Traced Radiosity," *Proc. Second Eurographics Workshop on Rendering*, Barcelona, Spain.

Hall, R. 1989. *Illumination and Color in Computer Generated Imagery*. New York: Springer-Verlag.

Howell, J. R. 1982. *A Catalog of Radiation Configuration Factors*. New York: McGraw-Hill.

IESNA. 1993. *IESNA Lighting Handbook*, 8th ed. New York: Illuminating Engineering Society of North America.

Kirk, D., ed. 1992. *Graphic Gems III*. San Diego, CA: Academic Press.

Kokcsis, F., and J. F. Böhme. 1992. "Fast Algorithms and Parallel Structures for Form Factor Evaluation," *The Visual Computer* 8:205–216.

Lambert, J. H. 1760. *Photometria sive de mensura et gradibus luminus, colorum et umbrae*. German translation with annotations by E. Anding (1892), *Ostwalds Klassiker der Exakten Wissenschaften,* Nos. 31–33. Leipzig.

Malley, T. J. 1988. *A Shading Method for Computer Generated Images*. Master's thesis, Department of Computer Science, University of Utah.

Marks, J., R. Walsh, J. Christensen, and M. Freidell. 1990. "Image and Intervisibility Coherence in Rendering," *Graphics Interface* '90, pp. 17–30.

Max, N. 1992. *Optimal Sampling for Global Illumination*. Lawrence Livermore National Laboratory UCRL-JC-112598.

Max, N., and M. J. Allison. 1992. "Linear Radiosity Approximation Using Vertex-to-Vertex Form Factors," in Kirk (1992), pp. 318–323.

Max, N., and R. Troutman. 1993. "Optimal Hemicube Sampling," in Cohen et al. (1993), pp. 185–200 and addendum.

Maxwell, G. M., M. J. Bailey, and V. W. Goldschmidt. 1986. "Calculations of the Radiation Configuration Factor Using Ray Casting," *Computer-Aided Design* 18(7):371–379.

Meyer, G. W., H. E. Rushmeier, M. F. Cohen, D. P. Greenberg, and K. E. Torrance. 1986. "An Experimental Evaluation of Computer Graphics Imagery," *ACM Transactions on Graphics.* 5(1):30–50.

Murdoch, J. B. 1981. "Inverse Square Law Approximation of Illuminance," *Journal of the Illuminating Engineering Society* 11(2):96 –106.

Ng, A., and M. Slater. 1993. "A Multiprocessor Implementation of Radiosity," *Computer Graphics Forum* 12(5):329–342.

Nishita, T., and E. Nakamae. 1984. "Continuous Tone Representation of Three-Dimensional Objects Taking Account of Shadows and Interreflections," *Computer Graphics* 20(4):125–132 (ACM SIGGRAPH '84 Proc,), 125–132.

Nusselt, W. 1928. "Grapische Bestimmung des Winkelverhältnisses bei der Wärmestrahlung," *Zeitschrift des Vereines Deutscher Ingenieure* 72(20):673.

O'Brien, P. F. 1963. "Pleijel's Globoscope for Lighting Design," *Illuminating Engineering* 58(3):131–138.

Pietrek, G. 1993. "Fast Calculation of Accurate Formfactors," in Cohen et al. (1993), pp. 201–220.

Pueyo, X. (1991). "Diffuse Interreflections. Techniques for Form Factor Computation: A Survey," *The Visual Computer* 7:200–209.

Recker, R. J., D. W. George, and D. P. Greenberg (1990). "Acceleration Techniques for Progressive Refinement Radiosity," *Computer Graphics* 24(2):59–66 (1990 Symposium on Interactive 3D Graphics).

Rogers, D. F. 1985. *Procedural Elements for Computer Graphics.* New York: McGraw-Hill.

Rushmeier, H., D. R. Baum, and D. E. Hall. 1991. "Accelerating the Hemi-Cube Algorithm for Calculating Radiation Form Factors," *Journal of Heat Transfer* 113:1044–1047.

Saraiji, R. M. N., and R. G. Mistrick. 1992. "Calculation Methods, Error Tendencies, and Guidelines for Finite Element Flux Transfer," *Journal of the Illuminating Engineering Society* 21(1):92–102.

Sbert, M. 1993. "An Integral Geometry Based Method for Fast Form-Factor Computation," *Computer Graphics Forum* 12(3):C-409–420 (Proc. Eurographics '93).

Schröder, P., and P. Hanrahan. 1993. "On the Form Factor between Two Polygons," *Computer Graphics Proceedings*, pp. 163–164 (ACM SIGGRAPH '93).

Shirley, P. 1991. "Radiosity via Ray Tracing," in Arvo (1991), pp. 306–310.

Siegel, R., and J. R. Howell. 1992. *Thermal Radiation Heat Transfer* (3rd ed.). Washington, DC: Hemisphere Publishing.

Sillion, F., and C. Puech. 1989. "A General Two-Pass Method Integrating Specular and Diffuse Reflection," *Computer Graphics* 23(3):335–344 (ACM SIGGRAPH '89 Proc.).

Sparrow, E. 1963. "A New and Simpler Formulation for Radiative Angle Factors," *Journal of Heat Transfer* 85(2):81–88.

Sparrow, E., and R. Cess. 1978. *Radiation Heat Transfer.* Washington, DC: Hemisphere Publishing.

Spencer, S. N. 1992. "The Hemisphere Radiosity Method: A Tale of Two Algorithms," in Bouatouch and Bouville (1992), pp. 127–135.

Sun, J., L. Q. Zou, and R. L. Grimsdale. 1993. "The Determination of Form-Factors by Lookup Table," *Computer Graphics Forum* 12(4):191–198.

Sung, K., and P. Shirley. 1992. "Ray Tracing with the BSP Tree," in Kirk (1992), pp. 271–274, 538–546.

Sutherland, I. E., and G. W. Hodgman. 1974. "Reentrant Polygon Clipping," *Communications of the ACM* 17(1):32–42.

Sutherland, I. E., R. F. Sproull, and R. Schumacker. 1974. "A Characterization of Ten Hidden-Surface Algorithms," *Computing Surveys* 6(1):1–55.

Tampieri, F. 1992. "Accurate Form Factor Calculation," in Kirk (1992), pp. 329–333.

Tellier, P., E. Maisel, K. Bouatouch, and E. Languénou. 1993. "Exploiting Spatial Coherence to Accelerate Radiosity," *The Visual Computer* 10:46–53.

Verbeck, C. P., and D. P. Greenberg. 1984. "A Comprehensive Light-Source Description for Computer Graphics," *IEEE Computer Graphics & Applications* 4(7): 66–75.

Vilaplana, J., and X. Pueyo. 1992. "Exploiting Coherence for Clipping and View Transformations in Radiosity Algorithms," in Bouatouch and Bouville (1992).

Voorhies, D., and D. Kirk. 1991. "Ray-Triangle Intersection Using Binary Recursive Subdivision," in Arvo (1991), pp. 257–263.

Wallace, J. R., K. A. Elmquist, and E. A. Haines. 1989. "A Ray Tracing Algorithm for Progressive Radiosity," *Computer Graphics* 23(3):315–324 (ACM SIGGRAPH '89 Proc.).

Wang, M., H. Bao, and Q. Peng. 1992. "A New Progressive Radiosity Algorithm through the Use of Accurate Form Factors," *Computers & Graphics* 16(3): 303–309.

Wang, Y., and W. A. Davis. 1990. "Octant Priority for Radiosity Image Rendering," *Proceedings of Graphics Interface '90*, pp. 83–91. Canadian Information Processing Society.

Warn, D. R. 1983. "Lighting Controls for Synthetic Images," *Computer Graphics* 17(3):13–21 (ACM SIGGRAPH '83 Proc.).

Woo, A. 1990. "Fast Ray-Polygon Intersection," in Glassner (1990), p. 394.

Zhang, N. 1991. "Two Methods for Speeding Up Form-Factor Calculations," *Proceedings of the Second Eurographics Workshop on Rendering*, Barcelona, Spain.

Zhou, Y., and Q. Peng. 1992. "The Super-Plane Buffer: An Efficient Form-Factor Evaluation Algorithm for Progressive Radiosity," *Computers & Graphics* 16(2):151–158.

Solving the Radiosity Equation

We have one last major . . . and surprisingly easy . . . task before us: solving the radiosity equation (Fig. 6.1). Once we have the tools to accomplish this, we will finally be able to render photorealistic images of our environments.

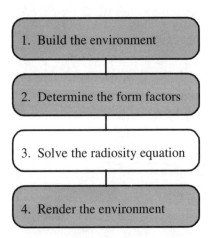

Figure 6.1 Radiosity-based rendering program outline

This is the central component of the radiosity approach. Having suffered through photometric and radiometric theory, radiosity theory, three-dimensional projective transformations, polygon clipping in four dimensions, polygon scan conversion, and form factor determination mathematics as a prelude, you might expect this to be the most difficult chapter in the book. If so, you will be pleased to learn that it is exactly the opposite.

> Again and again: do not let the mathematics deter you! The following two sections are dense reading, but none of the equations require more than a basic understanding of matrix theory and high school algebra. Moreover, you can ignore the details if you so choose. The equations are necessary only to lay a firm mathematical foundation for what follows.

6.1   FULL RADIOSITY

We saw in Chapter 2 that the radiosity equation is a system of n linear equations of the form:

$$
\begin{bmatrix} M_{o1} \\ M_{o2} \\ \dots \\ M_{on} \end{bmatrix} =
\begin{bmatrix}
1-\rho_1 F_{11} & -\rho_1 F_{12} & \dots & -\rho_1 F_{1n} \\
-\rho_2 F_{21} & 1-\rho_2 F_{22} & \dots & \dots \\
\dots & \dots & \dots & \dots \\
-\rho_n F_{n1} & -\rho_n F_{n2} & \dots & 1-\rho_n F_{nn}
\end{bmatrix}
\begin{bmatrix} M_1 \\ M_2 \\ \dots \\ M_n \end{bmatrix}
\tag{6.1}
$$

where n is the number of elements in the environment. We know the initial exitance vector; its entries M_{oi} will be mostly zeroes. The only nonzero entries are for those elements representing light sources. We also know the reflectivity ρ_i of each element, and we can estimate the form factor F_{ij} between any two elements i and j. All we have to do to obtain the final exitances M_i is to solve these equations.

Most environments result in linear systems that are far too large to solve using direct methods such as Gaussian elimination. The classic alternative is to use iterative techniques such as the Gauss-Seidel method. This was the original approach taken by Goral et al. (1984), Cohen and Greenberg (1985), and Cohen et al. (1986). Baum et al. (1989) referred to it as the "full radiosity algorithm."

We also saw in Chapter 2, however, that this gives us a radiosity algorithm with $\mathbf{O}(n^2)$ time and space complexity. A large and complicated environment with 50,000 elements can easily consume 1 to 10 gigabytes of memory for its form factors and take days of CPU time to compute a single image. We clearly need a better approach.

What we really want is an algorithm that consumes a minimal amount of memory and that generates a reasonable approximation of the final image almost immediately. More generally, we need to maintain a careful balance between the requirement for photorealistic images and the demands of interactive computing. Waiting a day or more to see whether we chose the right balance of light sources for an image is not exactly interactive!

In a perfect world, our algorithm would generate a reasonable first approximation and then progressively and gracefully refine the image until it reaches its final form. This essentially describes how iterative techniques work, except that we need a much more effective algorithm than the Gauss-Seidel method.

The great surprise is that such an algorithm actually exists. Before examining it, however, we should review the basic principles of iterative techniques.

6.2 ITERATIVE TECHNIQUES

Expanding on Equation 2.25, we can express Equation 6.1 more succinctly in matrix notation as:

$$\mathbf{M}_o = (\mathbf{I} - \mathbf{T})\mathbf{M} \tag{6.2}$$

where $\mathbf{I}$ is the identity matrix and $\mathbf{T}$ is:

$$\mathbf{T} = \begin{bmatrix} \rho_1 F_{11} & \rho_1 F_{12} & \cdots & \rho_1 F_{1n} \\ \rho_2 F_{21} & \rho_2 F_{22} & \cdots & \cdots \\ \cdots & \cdots & \cdots & \cdots \\ \rho_n F_{n1} & \rho_n F_{n2} & \cdots & \rho_n F_{nn} \end{bmatrix}$$

$$= \begin{bmatrix} \rho_1 & 0 & \cdots & 0 \\ 0 & \rho_2 & \cdots & 0 \\ \cdots & \cdots & \cdots & \cdots \\ 0 & 0 & \cdots & \rho_n \end{bmatrix} \begin{bmatrix} F_{11} & F_{12} & \cdots & F_{1n} \\ F_{2n} & F_{22} & \cdots & \cdots \\ \cdots & \cdots & \cdots & \cdots \\ F_{n1} & F_{n2} & \cdots & F_{nn} \end{bmatrix} = \mathbf{RF} \tag{6.3}$$

where $\mathbf{R}$ is the (diagonal) reflectance matrix and $\mathbf{F}$ is the form factor matrix.

If we consider $(\mathbf{I} - \mathbf{T})$ as an $n \times n$ matrix—call it $\mathbf{K}$ for convenience—we have a linear system of the form:

$$\mathbf{M}_o = \mathbf{KM} \tag{6.4}$$

which can be solved using any one of several iterative techniques.

A quick review of iterative techniques for solving linear systems may be in order. Suppose we are given a system of linear equations such as:

$$\mathbf{b} = \mathbf{Ax}$$

where $\mathbf{x}$ is the unknown $n \times 1$ vector, $\mathbf{A}$ is a square $n \times n$ matrix, and $\mathbf{b}$ is a known $n \times 1$ vector. Most iterative techniques convert this system into an equivalent system with the form:

$$\mathbf{x} = \mathbf{Qx} + \mathbf{c}$$

where the $n \times n$ matrix $\mathbf{Q}$ and the $n \times 1$ vector $\mathbf{c}$ are derived from $\mathbf{A}$ and $\mathbf{b}$. The details of the derivation depend on the particular iterative technique.

To solve for $\mathbf{x}$, we start with an initial $n \times 1$ vector $\mathbf{x}^{(0)}$ that hopefully approximates the final solution. At worst, it can have entirely random values for its elements. With it, we can generate a sequence of vectors $\mathbf{x}^{(k)}$ by repeatedly computing:

$$\mathbf{x}^{(k)} = \mathbf{Q}\mathbf{x}^{(k-1)} + \mathbf{c}, \quad k = 1,\ldots$$

This is the iterative component of the technique. The sequence of vectors $\mathbf{x}^{(k)}$ will be such that the elements of the vector either *converge* to those of the unknown vector $\mathbf{x}$ or else *diverge* into some random vector as k increases.

Although it is unlikely that $\mathbf{x}^{(k)}$ will exactly equal $\mathbf{x}$ for any finite value of k, the error between them will tend to grow progressively smaller as k increases (and if the sequence converges). This means that we can stop when:

$$\frac{\left| \mathbf{x}_i^{(k)} - \mathbf{x}_i^{(k-1)} \right|}{\left| \mathbf{x}_i^{(k-1)} \right|} \leq threshold, \quad i = 1,\ldots,n$$

for some "threshold" value. At this point, the approximate solution vector $\mathbf{x}^{(k)}$ such that the fractional error between it and the unknown vector $\mathbf{x}$ is guaranteed to be equal to or less than this value for each of its elements. The iterative method is then said to have *converged* to an acceptable solution.

Of critical importance to the user is the *convergence rate*. That is, what value of k is needed in order to attain an acceptable solution? This is determined by the characteristics of the chosen iterative method, the choice of $\mathbf{x}^{(0)}$, and the particular problem being solved.

There are two issues of concern here. First, there are linear systems where the solution vector diverges rather than converges to a solution. Fortunately, the radiosity equation is guaranteed to converge to a solution using either the Jacobi or Gauss-Seidel iterative methods.

(For those familiar with advanced matrix mathematics: The sum of any row of form factors is equal to or less than unity by virtue of the summation relation (Eq. 2.18), and each form factor is multiplied by a reflectance value ρ that is less than unity. Also, the main diagonal term of $\mathbf{K}$ in Equation 6.4 is always unity, since $F_{ii} = 0$ for all planar or convex elements. Thus, $\mathbf{K}$ is strictly *diagonally dominant*, which guarantees convergence for any choice of $\mathbf{M}^{(0)}$ using either Jacobi or Gauss-Seidel iteration.)

Second, we need to consider what our choice of $\mathbf{M}^{(0)}$ should be. The closer it is to the unknown final exitance vector $\mathbf{M}$, the more quickly our chosen iterative method will converge. Of course, the only a priori information we have concerns the initial exitances of the elements representing light sources. In other words, our best choice is to assign the initial exitance vector $\mathbf{M}_o$ to $\mathbf{M}^{(0)}$. Interestingly enough, this choice has some physical significance.

6.2.1   Follow the Bouncing . . . Light

Returning to Equation 6.2, suppose we rearrange it slightly to solve for $\mathbf{M}$. We then have:

$$\mathbf{M} = (\mathbf{I} - \mathbf{T})^{-1}\mathbf{M}_o \qquad (6.5)$$

Again, we cannot solve this equation directly, since calculating the inverse of a matrix is rarely an easy task. However, we can approximate it with a *MacLaurin power series expansion*. It can be shown that:

$$\frac{1}{(1-x)} = \sum_{n=0}^{\infty} x^n = 1 + x + x^2 + x^3 + \ldots \qquad (6.6)$$

which converges for $-1 < x < 1$. There is a similar series expansion for matrices (e.g., Golub and Van Loan 1983):

$$(\mathbf{I} - \mathbf{T})^{-1} = \mathbf{I} + \mathbf{T} + \mathbf{T}^2 + \mathbf{T}^3 + \ldots \qquad (6.7)$$

which gives us:

$$\mathbf{M} = \mathbf{M}_o + \mathbf{T}\mathbf{M}_o + \mathbf{T}^2\mathbf{M}_o + \mathbf{T}^3\mathbf{M}_o + \ldots \qquad (6.8)$$

that converges if the *spectral radius* of $\mathbf{T}$ (i.e., the absolute value of its largest *eigenvalue*) is less than one. Fortunately, this condition is true for any physically possible radiosity equation (e.g., Heckbert 1991). This means that we can safely ignore the somewhat abstruse mathematics behind the spectral radius and eigenvalues of a matrix.

There is an important physical significance to Equation 6.8 (e.g., Kajiya 1986). Each successive term $\mathbf{T}^k\mathbf{M}$ represents the kth bounce of the initially emitted light. The term $\mathbf{M}_o$ represents the initial flux (i.e., the direct illumination), $\mathbf{T}\mathbf{M}_o$ represents the first bounce component, $\mathbf{T}^2\mathbf{M}_o$ the second bounce, and so on. We can intuitively see this by observing that the element reflectances ρ are multiplied with each successive bounce. This represents the accumulating light losses due to absorption.

We can express Equation 6.8 in its iterative form as:

$$\mathbf{M}^{(k)} = \mathbf{T}\mathbf{M}^{(k-1)} + \mathbf{M}_o, \quad k > 0 \qquad (6.9)$$

In other words, the behavior of light flowing through an environment is itself an iterative method! Moreover, the initial exitance vector $\mathbf{M}_o$ serves as its initial "guess" to the final exitance vector $\mathbf{M}$.

Comparing Equation 6.9 to iterative techniques for solving linear systems, it becomes clear why the radiosity equation always converges to a solution when we apply these techniques. To do otherwise—that is, for the approximate solution vector $\mathbf{M}^{(k)}$ to diverge with increasing values of k—would require the total quantity of light in an environment to *increase* with each successive bounce. This would in turn contravene the energy balance discussed in Section 2.6.1.

There is, in fact, only one iterative technique that faithfully models the physical reality of light's behavior as expressed by Equation 6.9. It is the *Jacobi iterative method*, the simplest iterative technique for solving systems of linear equations.

Although it may not be necessary for our development of a practical algorithm for solving the radiosity equation, we should ask how the Jacobi method works for two reasons. First, it will provide us with a better understanding of how and why iterative techniques work. More important, however, the Jacobi method offers a fascinating and instructive insight into the physical reality of the radiosity equation.

6.2.2   Jacobi Iteration

The Jacobi method splits (or *decomposes*) an $n \times n$ matrix $\mathbf{A}$ into a *diagonal* matrix $\mathbf{D}$, a strictly *lower diagonal* matrix $-\mathbf{L}$, and a strictly *upper diagonal* matrix $-\mathbf{U}$. Written in matrix form, this becomes:

$$
\mathbf{A} = \begin{bmatrix} a_{11} & a_{12} & \cdots & a_{1n} \\ a_{21} & a_{22} & \cdots & a_{2n} \\ \cdots & \cdots & \cdots & \cdots \\ a_{n1} & a_{n2} & \cdots & a_{nn} \end{bmatrix} = \mathbf{D} - \mathbf{L} - \mathbf{U}
$$

$$
= \begin{bmatrix} a_{11} & 0 & \cdots & 0 \\ 0 & a_{22} & \cdots & 0 \\ \cdots & \cdots & \cdots & \cdots \\ 0 & 0 & \cdots & a_{nn} \end{bmatrix} - \begin{bmatrix} 0 & 0 & \cdots & 0 \\ -a_{21} & 0 & \cdots & 0 \\ \cdots & \cdots & \cdots & \cdots \\ -a_{n1} & -a_{n2} & \cdots & 0 \end{bmatrix} - \begin{bmatrix} 0 & -a_{12} & \cdots & -a_{1n} \\ 0 & 0 & \cdots & -a_{2n} \\ \cdots & \cdots & \cdots & \cdots \\ 0 & 0 & \cdots & 0 \end{bmatrix}
$$

(6.10)

From this, we get:

$$
\mathbf{A}\mathbf{x} = (\mathbf{D} - \mathbf{L} - \mathbf{U})\mathbf{x} = \mathbf{b} \tag{6.11}
$$

which becomes:

$$
\mathbf{D}\mathbf{x} = (\mathbf{L} + \mathbf{U})\mathbf{x} + \mathbf{b} \tag{6.12}
$$

and so:

$$
\mathbf{x} = \frac{(\mathbf{L} + \mathbf{U})}{\mathbf{D}}\mathbf{x} + \frac{\mathbf{b}}{\mathbf{D}} \tag{6.13}
$$

The Jacobi iterative method is thus:

$$
\mathbf{x}^{(k)} = \frac{(\mathbf{L} + \mathbf{U})}{\mathbf{D}}\mathbf{x}^{(k-1)} + \frac{\mathbf{b}}{\mathbf{D}} \tag{6.14}
$$

or, expressed in its more familiar form:

$$
x_i^{(k)} = \frac{\sum_{j=1, j \neq i}^{n}\left(-a_{ij}x_j^{(k-1)}\right) + b_i}{a_{ii}}, \quad i = 1, \ldots, n \tag{6.15}
$$

In plain English, this equation states that we can solve each element $x_i^{(k)}$ of our approximate solution vector $\mathbf{x}^{(k)}$ by using the values of all the other elements $x_j^{(k-1)}$ of our previously calculated solution vector.

6.2.3   Modeling Light

The Jacobi iterative method models the flow of light in an environment. We can confirm this by deriving Equation 6.9 in terms of the Jacobi iteration. Following the development of the Jacobi method above, we start with Equation 6.2 and decompose $\mathbf{T}$ into a diagonal matrix $\mathbf{T}_D$, a strictly lower diagonal matrix $-\mathbf{T}_L$ and a strictly upper diagonal matrix $-\mathbf{T}_U$ to get:

$$(\mathbf{I} - \mathbf{T}) = \mathbf{I} - \mathbf{T}_D + \mathbf{T}_L + \mathbf{T}_U \tag{6.16}$$

and thus:

$$\mathbf{M}_0 = (\mathbf{I} - \mathbf{T}_D + \mathbf{T}_L + \mathbf{T}_U)\mathbf{M} \tag{6.17}$$

This becomes:

$$(\mathbf{I} - \mathbf{T}_D)\mathbf{M} = -(\mathbf{T}_L + \mathbf{T}_U)\mathbf{M} + \mathbf{M}_o \tag{6.18}$$

and:

$$\mathbf{M} = \frac{-(\mathbf{T}_L + \mathbf{T}_U)}{(\mathbf{I} - \mathbf{T}_D)}\mathbf{M} + \frac{\mathbf{M}_o}{(\mathbf{I} - \mathbf{T}_D)} \tag{6.19}$$

This is equivalent to the Jacobi iterative method presented in Equation 6.14. However, the form factor F_{ii} for planar or convex patches is always zero, which means each diagonal element of $\mathbf{T}$ equals zero, and so $(\mathbf{I} - \mathbf{T}_D) = \mathbf{I}$. Also, $\mathbf{T} = -(\mathbf{T}_L + \mathbf{T}_U)$. Thus:

$$\mathbf{M} = -(\mathbf{T}_L + \mathbf{T}_U)\mathbf{M} + \mathbf{M}_o = \mathbf{T}\mathbf{M} + \mathbf{M}_o \tag{6.20}$$

which results in the Jacobi iterative method:

$$\mathbf{M}^{(k)} = \mathbf{T}\mathbf{M}^{(k-1)} + \mathbf{M}_o, \quad k > 0 \tag{6.21}$$

for solving the radiosity equation. This is identical to Equation 6.9. Referring to Equation 6.3, we have:

$$\mathbf{M}^{(k)} = \mathbf{M}_o + \mathbf{R}\mathbf{F}\mathbf{M}^{(k-1)} \tag{6.22}$$

which, expressed in the form of Equation 6.15, is:

$$M_i^{(k)} = M_{oi} + \rho_i \sum_{j=1}^{n} F_{ij} M_j^{(k-1)}, \quad i = 1, \ldots, n \tag{6.23}$$

This is the radiosity equation that we saw in Chapter 2 (Eq. 2.21), expressed as an iterative method.

6.2.4   Gauss-Seidel Iteration

The problem with Jacobi iteration is that it is often slow to converge to a solution. The *Gauss-Seidel iterative method* takes a simple but effective approach to improving this situation. We saw in Equation 6.15 that the Jacobi method calculates the value of each element $x_i^{(k)}$ in sequence by using the values of the other elements from $\mathbf{x}^{(k-1)}$. Since the elements $x_j^{(k)}$ (where $j < i$) have already been calculated and are presumably closer approximations to the final solution vector elements than their $x_j^{(k-1)}$ counterparts, why not use these values instead when calculating $x_i^{(k)}$?

This is exactly what the Gauss-Seidel method does. Its iterative equation is:

$$\mathbf{x}^{(k)} = \frac{\mathbf{U}}{(\mathbf{D}-\mathbf{L})}\mathbf{x}^{(k-1)} + \frac{\mathbf{b}}{(\mathbf{D}-\mathbf{L})}, \quad k > 0 \tag{6.24}$$

or, expressed in its more familiar form:

$$x_i^{(k)} = \frac{\displaystyle\sum_{j=1}^{i-1} -a_{ij}x_j^{(k)} + \sum_{j=i}^{n} -a_{ij}x_j^{(k-1)} + b_i}{a_{ii}}, \quad i = 1,\ldots,n \tag{6.25}$$

A derivation of Equation 6.24 can be found in most elementary linear algebra and numerical analysis texts (e.g., Burden and Faires 1985).

The Jacobi method can be seen in terms of modeling light bouncing from surface to surface in an environment. This is not the case for the Gauss-Seidel method. In a sense, it tries to anticipate the light each surface will receive from the next iteration of reflections. There is no physical analogue to this process, but it does work in that the Gauss-Seidel method usually converges more quickly than the Jacobi method does. Cohen and Greenberg (1985) found that the Gauss-Seidel method solved the radiosity equation for typical environments in six to eight iterations.

6.2.5   Full Radiosity Disadvantages

When it was first presented by Goral et al. (1984) and Nishita and Nakamae (1985), radiosity rendering was for the most part viewed as an interesting mathematical curiosity. The Jacobi and Gauss-Seidel methods have a time complexity of $\mathbf{O}(n^2)$ for each iteration. That is, doubling the number of elements in an environment quadruples the CPU time required to solve its particular radiosity equation. Given the available computer technology at the time, this made the full radiosity algorithm an impractical rendering technique for all but the simplest of environments.

Another disadvantage of full radiosity is that it requires storage for $n^2/2$ form factors. This means that the memory space complexity of the full radiosity algorithm is $\mathbf{O}(n^2)$ as well. We could possibly avoid this requirement by recomputing form factors on the fly for each element during each iteration. However, the high cost of form factor determination means that we would have to wait much longer between each iteration. This is exactly what we are trying to avoid. We need to obtain an initial image as quickly as possible.

We can gain some relief by substructuring the environment into patches and elements (Cohen et al. 1986). This brings both the time and space complexities down to $\mathbf{O}(nm)$ for n patches and m elements. Substructuring is a useful technique, but we can do better.

6.3 SHOOTING VERSUS GATHERING

There is an interesting and instructive physical interpretation of the Jacobi and Gauss-Seidel methods. We can think of each execution of Equation 6.15 (Jacobi) or 6.25 (Gauss-Seidel) as being one *step*; it takes n steps to complete one *iteration* of the method. At each step, we are updating the estimated exitance of one element by processing one row of the radiosity equation. For the Jacobi method, this is Equation 6.23, repeated here as:

$$M_i^{(k)} = M_{oi} + \rho_i \sum_{j=1}^{n} F_{ij} M_j^{(k-1)}, \quad i = 1, \ldots, n \tag{6.26}$$

We can show this diagramatically as:

$$\begin{bmatrix} \cdot \\ x \\ \cdot \\ \cdot \end{bmatrix} = \begin{bmatrix} \cdot \\ x \\ \cdot \\ \cdot \end{bmatrix} + \begin{bmatrix} \cdot & \cdot & \cdot & \cdot \\ x & x & x & x \\ \cdot & \cdot & \cdot & \cdot \\ \cdot & \cdot & \cdot & \cdot \end{bmatrix} \begin{bmatrix} x \\ x \\ x \\ x \end{bmatrix} \tag{6.27}$$

The physical interpretation of this process is straightforward: We are simply summing the contribution of flux from all the other elements in the environment to the exitance of the current element. Looking at Figure 6.2 and referring to Equation 6.26, we see that each element E_j has an exitance M_j and an area A_j. Referring to Equation 6.26, we find the portion of the flux Φ_j emitted by E_j that is received by E_i to be :

$$\Phi_{ij} = M_j A_j F_{ji} \tag{6.28}$$

The amount of exitance ΔM_i of E_i that is due to this flux subsequently being reflected by E_i is thus:

$$\Delta M_i = \rho_i \Phi_{ji} / A_i = \rho_i M_j A_j F_{ji} / A_i \tag{6.29}$$

However, we can apply the reciprocity relation $A_i F_{ij} = A_j F_{ji}$ (Section 2.5.1) to obtain:

$$\Delta M_i = \rho_i M_j F_{ij} \tag{6.30}$$

More colloquially, this can be seen as the current element E_i *gathering* exitance from all of the elements E_j in the environment in order to determine its exitance due

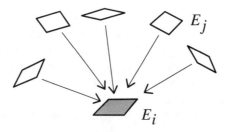

Figure 6.2 Gathering flux from the environment

to these elements. The term M_{oi} in Equation 6.26 simply accounts for any initial exitance of E_i. This will be nonzero only if E_i is a light source.

It may be somewhat difficult to visualize exitance being transferred between elements. It becomes clearer when we multiply both sides of Equation 6.30 by A_i to obtain:

$$\Delta\Phi_i = \Delta M_i A_i = \rho_i M_j F_{ij} A_i \qquad (6.31)$$

Again applying the reciprocity relation, we get:

$$\Delta\Phi_i = \rho_i M_j F_{ji} A_j = \rho_i F_{ji} \Phi_j \qquad (6.32)$$

which shows that we are, in fact, gathering and subsequently reflecting radiant flux. Equation 6.30 is more useful in terms of Equation 6.26, however, and so we "gather" exitance to E_i. The difference is solely semantic.

A number of authors have loosely referred to this process as gathering "energy." However, the physical quantity being discussed is radiant exitance (i.e., watts per unit area) times area. This is *power*, or radiant flux. Energy is "gathered" only in the sense that solving the radiosity equation balances the *flow* of energy (which is power) between elements in the environment.

The problem with this approach is that it can be excruciatingly slow. Consider a complex environment with perhaps 50,000 elements. Using the Jacobi or Gauss-Seidel method, we must perform one complete iteration before we have an image of the first bounce of light from the environment. That means we must execute Equation 6.26 50,000 times! This clearly does not satisfy our requirement for an "immediate but approximate" image.

This is where the physical interpretation becomes useful. If we think for a moment about how light flows in an environment, it becomes evident that we should be interested in those elements that emit or reflect the most light. It logically does not matter in what order we consider the distribution of light from element to element, as long as we eventually account for its being completely absorbed.

This leads to an entirely different paradigm. Given an environment with one or more light sources, we can think of them *shooting* flux to the other elements (Fig. 6.3). These elements then become, in effect, secondary light sources, shooting some of the flux they receive back into the environment. By always selecting the element

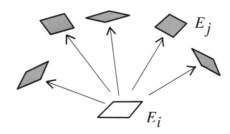

Figure 6.3   Shooting flux into the environment

that has the greatest amount of flux to "shoot," we will drastically improve our convergence rate. Again, it makes intuitive sense that the more quickly the light is absorbed, the more quickly our as-yet-unspecified iterative method will converge to a solution.

It also becomes evident that this idea answers our need for both an immediate image and progressive convergence to the final solution. By shooting flux from one element to all other elements in the environment, we immediately obtain an initial estimate for all element exitances. This occurs in one step rather than in a complete iteration. In fact, the concept of an iteration no longer applies, for we may end up choosing one element several times before we cycle through the entire set. It all depends on which element currently has the greatest amount of flux to shoot.

Of course, we also obtain improved estimates for all the element exitances at each step. This means that the rendered image will continuously and gracefully converge to the final photorealistic image.

Now, all we have to do is express this idea in the form of a practical algorithm.

6.4   PROGRESSIVE REFINEMENT RADIOSITY

What we are looking for is the *progressive refinement* radiosity algorithm (Cohen et al. 1988). Based on the concept of shooting flux, it offers not only an immediate image with continuous and graceful convergence but also $\mathbf{O}(n)$ time and space complexity. Given an environment with n elements, it requires memory space for only n form factors. Even better, it can generate an initial image almost immediately, and can generate if necessary updated images after each step (as opposed to each iteration).

So how does it work? To shoot flux or exitance back into the environment, we simply reverse the subscripts of Equation 6.30. For exitance, this becomes:

$$\Delta M_j = \rho_j M_i F_{ij} \frac{A_i}{A_j} = \rho_j M_i F_{ji} \qquad (6.33)$$

Multiplying both sides of this equation by the area of element E_j gives us the equation for shooting flux.

Unlike the full radiosity algorithm (Eq. 6.26), this equation acts on one column of the radiosity equation at a time. Shown diagramatically, this is:

$$\begin{bmatrix} x \\ x \\ x \\ x \end{bmatrix} = \begin{bmatrix} x \\ x \\ x \\ x \end{bmatrix} + \begin{bmatrix} \cdot \\ x \\ \cdot \\ \cdot \end{bmatrix} \begin{bmatrix} \cdot & x & \cdot & \cdot \\ \cdot & x & \cdot & \cdot \\ \cdot & x & \cdot & \cdot \\ \cdot & x & \cdot & \cdot \end{bmatrix} \quad \text{for all elements } E_j \qquad (6.34)$$

This means we can now display an image of the environment whenever one column of the radiosity equation has been processed. This has a time complexity of $\mathbf{O}(n)$ as opposed to $\mathbf{O}(n^2)$ or the basic radiosity algorithm.

The progressive refinement radiosity algorithm proceeds as follows. First, we assign an "unsent exitance" value ΔM_i^{unsent} to each element in the environment. This is in addition to its final exitance M_i, which we are trying to determine. The amount of flux each element has to shoot is ΔM_i^{unsent} times its area, A_i. Initially, only the elements representing light sources will have nonzero values of flux, and so ΔM_i^{unsent} is initialized to M_{oi}. The final exitance values M_i are also initialized to M_{oi}.

Choosing the element E_i with the greatest amount of flux (not exitance) to shoot, we execute Equation 6.33 for every other element E_j in the environment. Each of these elements "receives" a delta exitance ΔM_j; this value is added to both its unsent exitance ΔM_j^{unsent} and its final exitance M_j.

After the flux has been shot to every element E_j, ΔM_i^{unsent} is reset to zero. This element can shoot again only after receiving more flux from other elements during subsequent steps.

This process continues until the total amount of flux remaining in the environment is less than some predetermined fraction ε of the original amount, or:

$$\sum_{i=1}^{n} \Delta M_i^{unsent} A_i \leq \varepsilon \tag{6.35}$$

At this point, the algorithm is considered to have converged to a solution.

Expressing this in pseudocode, we have Figure 6.4.

FOR each element i

$\quad M_i = \Delta M_i^{unsent} = M_{oi}$

ENDFOR

WHILE $\displaystyle\sum_{i=1}^{n} \Delta M_i^{unsent} A_i > \varepsilon$

$\quad$ Select element i with greatest unsent flux $\Delta M_i^{unsent} A_i$
$\quad$ Calculate all form factors F_{ij}
$\quad$ **FOR** each element j

$\quad\quad \Delta M = \rho_j F_{ij} \Delta M_i^{unsent} \dfrac{A_i}{A_j}$

$\quad\quad \Delta M_j^{unsent} = \Delta M_j^{unsent} + \Delta M$

$\quad\quad M_j = M_j + \Delta M$

$\quad$ **ENDFOR**

$\quad \Delta M_i^{unsent} = 0$

ENDWHILE

Figure 6.4 Progressive refinement radiosity algorithm

Progressive refinement radiosity does not—repeat, *does not*—require any less time to *completely* solve the radiosity equation to some vanishingly small margin of error. It is an iterative approach that, like full radiosity, progressively refines the element exitances as it converges to a solution. However, its overwhelming advantage is that usable images can be displayed almost immediately, and that each succeeding image takes much less time to calculate.

We still have the form factors to contend with. However, we only need to calculate the n form factors F_{ij} from the current element E_i to all other elements E_j between displaying images. This is exactly what our hemicubes and cubic tetrahedrons provide when centered over a given element. Yes, we have to recompute these form factors on the fly for each step of the progressive radiosity algorithm. However, the convergence rate is *much* faster than it is for full radiosity. Cohen et al. (1988) compared progressive refinement and full radiosity algorithms using an environment consisting of 500 patches and 7,000 elements. The progressive radiosity implementation converged to a visually acceptable image after approximately 100 steps. At this point, the full radiosity implementation was only 20 percent of its way through its first iteration.

Incidentally, Gortler and Cohen (1993a) established that the progressive refinement radiosity algorithm is a variant of the *Southwell* iteration method (e.g., Gastinel 1970). Like the Jacobi and Gauss-Seidel methods, Southwell iteration will always converge to a solution for any radiosity equation.

6.5 AMBIENT EXITANCE

The progressive refinement radiosity algorithm described above has one minor problem. When the flux is first shot from the light sources, only those elements visible to them are illuminated. The rest of the environment will be in shadow. This will quickly change as the flux bounces from surface to surface during subsequent steps. Nevertheless, it may be somewhat disconcerting to have the first few images appear relatively dark as the light sources are shot one by one.

Cohen et al. (1988) resolved this problem by introducing an *ambient term* that simulates the effect of a completely diffuse light source evenly illuminating every surface of the environment. The contribution of this term to the exitance of each element is gradually diminished as the radiosity algorithm converges to its final solution, thereby maintaining a reasonably constant average exitance for the environment. This term is added for display purposes only; it does not participate in solving the radiosity equation. With the term added, the visual differences between successive images can become almost unnoticeable.

To calculate the ambient exitance, we first need to define the *average reflectance* of the environment. This is the area-weighted average of the individual element reflectances, given as:

$$\rho_{avg} = \sum_{i=1}^{n} \rho_i A_i \bigg/ \sum_{i=1}^{n} A_i \tag{6.36}$$

where ρ_{avg} must be calculated for each color band.

If we think of the environment as being an empty room with no obstructions and whose surfaces have a reflectance of ρ_{avg}, then we can see that the light will bounce back and forth within this room until it is completely absorbed. From this, we can derive the following *interreflection factor*:

$$R = 1 + \rho_{avg} + \rho_{avg}^2 + \rho_{avg}^3 + \ldots = \frac{1}{1 - \rho_{avg}} \tag{6.37}$$

We also need to estimate the area-weighted average amount of unsent exitance. This is simply:

$$M_{avg}^{unsent} = \sum_{i=1}^{n} M_i^{unsent} A_i \Big/ \sum_{i=1}^{n} A_i \tag{6.38}$$

Of course, this will decrease whenever flux is shot from an element into the environment. This ensures that the ambient term decreases to zero as the radiosity algorithm converges to a solution.

From this, we can define the ambient exitance as:

$$M_{ambient} = RM_{avg}^{unsent} \tag{6.39}$$

For *display purposes only*, the estimated exitance of an element E_i is then:

$$M_i' = M_i + \rho_i M_{ambient} \tag{6.40}$$

Cohen et al. [1988] demonstrated that the ambient term improves the initial convergence rate as well as the visual appearance of the image. Using the area-averaged error metric:

$$error_{rms} = \sqrt{\sum_{i=1}^{n} \left(M_i^{(\infty)} - M_i^{(k)} \right)^2 A_i \Big/ \sum_{i=1}^{n} A_i} \tag{6.41}$$

where $M_i^{(\infty)}$ is the converged (i.e., final) exitance of each element E_i after an infinite number of steps and k is the number of steps actually performed, they found that adding the ambient term decreases the error from 40 to 30 percent after 15 steps for a typical environment of 500 patches and 7,000 elements. After 70 steps, the ambient term became negligible, leaving the progressive refinement radiosity algorithm to converge to a solution on its own after some 100 steps. At the same time, the error for the full radiosity algorithm using the Gauss-Seidel method after 100 steps was approximately 98 percent.

6.6 A PROGRESSIVE REFINEMENT RADIOSITY ALGORITHM

We can combine the ambient exitance with our previous progressive refinement radiosity algorithm. At the same time, we can take advantage of the hierarchical arrangement of patches and elements in our environments. This gives us Figure 6.5.

```
Calculate initial ambient exitance M_ambient
FOR each patch i
    ΔM_i^unsent = M_oi
ENDFOR
```

(continued)

Figure 6.5   *(continued)*

WHILE $\displaystyle\sum_{i=1}^{n} \Delta M_i^{unsent} A_i > \varepsilon$

    Select patch *i* with greatest unsent flux $\Delta M_i^{unsent} A_i$
    Calculate all patch-element form factors F_{ik}
    FOR each patch *j*
      FOR each element *k* of parent patch *j*
        // Determine increase in exitance of element *k* due to patch exi-
        // tance ΔM_i^{unsent}

$$\Delta M = \rho_k F_{ik} \Delta M_i^{unsent} \frac{A_i}{A_k}$$

$$M_k = M_k + \Delta M$$

        // Add area-weighted increase in element *k* exitance to parent
        // patch *j*

$$\Delta M_j^{unsent} = \Delta M_j^{unsent} + \Delta M \frac{A_k}{A_j}$$

    ENDFOR
    ENDFOR
    $\Delta M_i^{unsent} = 0$

    Recalculate ambient exitance $M_{ambient}$
ENDWHILE
FOR each element *k*
    // Add initial and ambient exitance contributions
    $M_k = M_k + M_{ok} + \rho_k M_{ambient}$

ENDFOR

Figure 6.5   Progressive radiosity algorithm with ambient exitance

6.7   PROGRESSIVE REFINEMENT CONVERGENCE BEHAVIOR

Shao and Badler (1993b) presented a detailed and informative discussion of the convergence behavior of the progressive refinement radiosity algorithm. They observed that while the algorithm may quickly converge to a visually appealing image, many more steps are often required to capture the nuances of color bleeding and soft shadows. They demonstrated that it took 2,000 or more steps to achieve full convergence in a complex environment of some 1,000 patches and 25,000 elements. Many of the radiosity-based renderings published to date were completed using far fewer steps, implying that their apparent realism may be due to part to ambient exitance.

    Much of the problem lies in how progressive refinement works. By always selecting the patch with the most flux to shoot, it concentrates first on the light sources. Most of their flux will be shot to what Shao and Badler (1993b) called *global* patches—those patches that are relatively large and can be seen from much of the environment. For an architectural interior, these are typically the walls, floor, and ceiling of a room. Their elements receive most of the flux from the light sources and consequently shoot it to the other global patch elements.

The *local* patches are those patches that are small, possibly reflective in only one color band, and usually hidden from much of the environment. Their flux will not be shot until that of the global patches has been exhausted. This is undesirable for two reasons. First, their small areas mean that they will receive relatively little flux in comparison to the global patches. It may take several hundred steps before they shoot for the first time.

The second reason is that when these local patches do shoot, much of their flux often goes no further than their immediate neighbors. While this does not affect the global environment to any great extent (and so does not appear in the error metric defined in Equation 6.41), it does account for the color bleeding and soft shadow effects we are trying to achieve. In this sense, a better error metric is the worst-case difference between the estimated and converged element exitances. In their experiments, Shao and Badler (1993b) observed that it took twice as many iterations as there were patches (not elements) in the environment.

One strategy to overcome this problem involves de-emphasizing the contributions due to the global patches, ensuring that all patches shoot their flux in a reasonable number of steps. This requires a modification of the progressive refinement radiosity algorithm that is described next.

6.8 POSITIVE OVERSHOOTING

Convergence of the Gauss-Seidel algorithm can often be accelerated by using one of several techniques known as *successive overrelaxation* (e.g., Noble 1969). Applied to the radiosity equation, these techniques can be interpreted as "overshooting" the amount of flux from a patch into the environment. That is, the amount of flux shot from the patch is more than the amount of unsent flux the patch actually has. The flux shot in subsequent steps by the receiving patches will tend to cancel this overshooting. In the meantime, the total amount of unsent flux in the environment is shot and absorbed more quickly. This tends to result in faster convergence rates.

Shao and Badler (1993b) presented a modified version of the progressive refinement radiosity algorithm that incorporates *positive overshooting* to accelerate the convergence rate by a factor of two or more. At the same time, it tends to prioritize the ordering of patches being shot such that the local patches are shot sooner, thereby enhancing the rendering of subtle lighting effects such as color bleeding and soft shadows.

The modification to the radiosity algorithm (Fig. 6.4), based on an earlier proposal by Feda and Purgathofer (1992), is given in Figure 6.6.

...

```
Select element i with greatest positive unsent flux ΔMᵢᵘⁿˢᵉⁿᵗAᵢ
Estimate overshooting parameter ΔMᵢᵒᵛᵉʳˢʰᵒᵒᵗ
Calculate all form factors Fᵢₖ
FOR each patch j
  FOR each element k
        // Determine increase in exitance of element k due to patch exi-
        // tance ΔMᵢᵘⁿˢᵉⁿᵗ and area-weighted positive overshoot
```

$$\Delta M = \rho_k F_{ik} \left(\Delta M_i^{unsent} + \Delta M_i^{overshoot} \right) \frac{A_i}{A_k}$$

$$M_k = M_k + \Delta M$$

```
        // Add area-weighted increase in element k exitance to parent
        // patch j
```

$$\Delta M_j^{unsent} = \Delta M_j^{unsent} + \Delta M \frac{A_k}{A_j}$$

ENDFOR

ENDFOR

$$\Delta M_i^{unsent} = -\Delta M_i^{overshoot}$$

...

Figure 6.6   Progressive refinement radiosity algorithm with positive overshooting

As with ambient exitance, the amount of positive overshooting and its contribution to the shooting patch's unsent exitance must be determined independently for each color band.

Feda and Purgathofer (1992) based their calculation of the overshooting parameter $\Delta M_i^{overshoot}$ on the ambient exitance of the environment. However, Shao and Badler (1993b) noted several problems with this approach and instead suggested the following:

$$\Delta M_i^{overshoot} = \rho_i \sum_{j=1}^{n} \Delta \tilde{M}_j^{unsent} F_{ij} \qquad (6.42)$$

where:

$$\Delta \tilde{M}_j^{unsent} = \begin{cases} \Delta M_j^{unsent} & if \quad \Delta M_j^{unsent} > 0 \\ 0 & otherwise \end{cases} \qquad (6.43)$$

This essentially sums the amount of unsent flux the patch will later receive from the elements in the environment and multiplies it by the reflectance of the patch. The patch effectively *gathers* the unsent flux it would otherwise receive in later steps and shoots it along with its own unsent flux.

Equation 6.43 ensures that the patch will never receive a negative amount of flux from any element. Thus, only positive overshooting can occur. On the other hand, the patch may shoot a negative amount of flux; this serves to cancel the overshot flux in later steps.

Since we can now have both positive and negative unsent flux, we need to modify our convergence criterion. Equation 6.34 becomes:

$$\sum_{i=1}^{n} \left| \Delta M_i^{unsent} A_i \right| \leq \varepsilon \qquad (6.44)$$

Experiments performed by Shao and Badler (1993b) on two complex environments demonstrated that the convergence rate with positive overshooting can be accelerated by a factor of two or more over that of conventional progressive radiosity. There was also strong evidence that the appearance of subtle color bleeding and soft shadow effects may appear as much as three to five times more quickly. Positive overshooting is clearly a useful addition to the basic progressive radiosity algorithm.

Other overrelaxation techniques for solving the radiosity equation are described by Gortler and Cohen (1993a) and Greiner et al. (1993).

6.9 A PROGRESSIVE REFINEMENT RADIOSITY CLASS

Having explored the mathematical techniques needed to solve the radiosity equation, we can encapsulate these ideas in a C++ class. First, however, we need to complete our *RadEqnSolve* class that we began in Chapter 4. We defined a number of several "stub" functions in RAD_TMP.CPP (Listing 4.19). Following the above discussions on progressive refinement radiosity and ambient exitance, we can replace them with:

Listing 6.1

```
// RAD_EQN.CPP - Radiosity Equation Solver Base Class

#include "rad_eqn.h"

// Initialize patch and element exitances
void RadEqnSolve::InitExitance()
{
  int i;                  // Loop index
  int num_vert;           // Number of element vertices
  Instance *pinst;        // Instance pointer
  Element3 *pelem;        // Element pointer
  Patch3 *ppatch;         // Patch pointer
  Surface3 *psurf;        // Surface pointer
  Spectra emit;           // Surface emittance
  Vertex3 *pvert;         // Vertex pointer

  total_flux = 0.0;

  // Walk the instance list
  pinst = penv->GetInstPtr();
  while (pinst != NULL)
  {
```

(continued)

Listing 6.1 *(continued)*

```
    // Walk the surface list
    psurf = pinst->GetSurfPtr();
    while (psurf != NULL)
    {
      // Get surface emittance
      emit = psurf->GetEmittance();

      // Walk the patch list
      ppatch = psurf->GetPatchPtr();
      while (ppatch != NULL)
      {
        // Set patch unsent exitance
        ppatch->SetExitance(emit);

        // Update total environment flux
        total_flux += ppatch->GetUnsentFlux();

        // Walk the element list
        pelem = ppatch->GetElementPtr();
        while (pelem != NULL)
        {
          // Initialize element exitance
          pelem->GetExitance().Reset();

          num_vert = pelem->GetNumVert();
          for (i = 0; i < num_vert; i++)
          {
            // Get element vertex pointer
            pvert = pelem->GetVertexPtr(i);

            // Initialize vertex exitance
            pvert->GetExitance().Reset();
          }
          pelem = pelem->GetNext();
        }
        ppatch = ppatch->GetNext();
      }
      psurf = psurf->GetNext();
    }
    pinst = pinst->GetNext();
  }
}

// Update unsent flux statistics
void RadEqnSolve::UpdateUnsentStats()
{
  double curr_unsent;     // Current unsent flux
  double max_unsent;      // Maximum unsent flux
  Instance *pinst;        // Instance pointer
  Patch3 *ppatch;         // Patch pointer
  Surface3 *psurf;        // Surface pointer
```

```
  // Initialize unsent flux values
  total_unsent = 0.0;
  max_unsent = 0.0;

  // Walk the instance list
  pinst = penv->GetInstPtr();
  while (pinst != NULL)
  {
    // Walk the surface list
    psurf = pinst->GetSurfPtr();
    while (psurf != NULL)
    {
      // Walk the patch list
      ppatch = psurf->GetPatchPtr();
      while (ppatch != NULL)
      {
        // Get current unsent flux value
        curr_unsent = ppatch->GetUnsentFlux();

        // Update total unsent flux
        total_unsent += curr_unsent;

        // Update maximum unsent flux and patch pointer
        if (curr_unsent > max_unsent)
        {
          max_unsent = curr_unsent;
          pmax = ppatch;
        }
        ppatch = ppatch->GetNext();
      }
      psurf = psurf->GetNext();
    }
    pinst = pinst->GetNext();
  }

  // Update convergence value
  if (total_flux > MIN_VALUE)
    convergence = fabs(total_unsent) / total_flux;
  else
    convergence = 0.0;
}

// Calculate interreflection factors
void RadEqnSolve::CalcInterReflect()
{
  Instance *pinst;  // Instance pointer
  Patch3 *ppatch;   // Patch pointer
  Spectra sr;       // Surface reflectance
  Spectra sum;      // Sum areas times reflectances
  Surface3 *psurf;  // Surface pointer
```

(continued)

Listing 6.1   *(continued)*

```
  irf.Reset();
  sum.Reset();
  total_area = 0.0;

  // Walk the instance list
  pinst = penv->GetInstPtr();
  while (pinst != NULL)
  {
    // Walk the surface list
    psurf = pinst->GetSurfPtr();
    while (psurf != NULL)
    {
      // Walk the patch list
      ppatch = psurf->GetPatchPtr();
      while (ppatch != NULL)
      {
        // Update sum of patch areas times reflectances
        sr = ppatch->GetParentPtr()->GetReflectance();
        sr.Scale(ppatch->GetArea());
        sum.Add(sr);

        // Update sum of patch areas
        total_area += ppatch->GetArea();

        ppatch = ppatch->GetNext();
      }
      psurf = psurf->GetNext();
    }
    pinst = pinst->GetNext();
  }

  // Calculate area-weighted average reflectance
  sum.Scale(1.0 / total_area);

  // Calculate interreflection factors
  irf.SetRedBand((float) 1.0 / ((float) 1.0 -
      sum.GetRedBand()));
  irf.SetGreenBand((float) 1.0 / ((float) 1.0 -
      sum.GetGreenBand()));
  irf.SetBlueBand((float) 1.0 / ((float) 1.0 -
      sum.GetBlueBand()));
}

// Calculate ambient exitance
void RadEqnSolve::CalcAmbient()
{
  Instance *pinst;   // Instance pointer
  Patch3 *ppatch;    // Patch pointer
  Spectra sum;       // Sum areas times unsent exitances
  Spectra unsent;    // Patch unsent exitance
  Surface3 *psurf;   // Surface pointer
```

```
    sum.Reset();

    // Walk the instance list
    pinst = penv->GetInstPtr();
    while (pinst != NULL)
    {
      // Walk the surface list
      psurf = pinst->GetSurfPtr();
      while (psurf != NULL)
      {
        // Walk the patch list
        ppatch = psurf->GetPatchPtr();
        while (ppatch != NULL)
        {
          // Update sum of unsent exitances times areas
          unsent = ppatch->GetExitance();
          unsent.Scale(ppatch->GetArea());
          sum.Add(unsent);

          ppatch = ppatch->GetNext();
        }
        psurf = psurf->GetNext();
      }
      pinst = pinst->GetNext();
    }

    // Calculate area-weighted average unsent exitance
    sum.Scale(1.0 / total_area);

    // Calculate ambient exitance
    ambient.SetRedBand(irf.GetRedBand() *
        sum.GetRedBand());
    ambient.SetGreenBand(irf.GetGreenBand() *
        sum.GetGreenBand());
    ambient.SetBlueBand(irf.GetBlueBand() *
        sum.GetBlueBand());
}
```

These four functions do more or less what their names suggest. *InitExitance* initializes the patch unsent exitances with that of their parent surfaces and resets the element and vertex exitances to zero. *UpdateUnsentStats* finds the patch with the maximum unsent flux and also calculates the convergence value as a fraction of the total unsent flux to the total environment flux. *CalcInterReflect* calculates the environment interreflection factors (one for each color band), whereas *CalcAmbient* calculates the ambient exitance terms.

With this, we can derive a progressive refinement radiosity class from *RadEqnSolve* as follows:

Listing 6.2

```cpp
// PROG_RAD.H - Progressive Refinement Radiosity Class

#ifndef _PROG_RAD_H
#define _PROG_RAD_H

#include "environ.h"
#include "rad_eqn.h"

// NOTE: Either _HEMI_CUBE or _CUBIC_TETRA must be defined
//       in order to specify the appropriate form factor
//       determination class for FormFactor. This will
//       typically be done from the command line or through
//       the integrated development environment (IDE).

#if defined(_HEMI_CUBE)
#include "hemicube.h"
#elif defined(_CUBIC_TETRA)
#include "cubic_t.h"
#else
#error Either _HEMI_CUBE or _CUBIC_TETRA must be defined
#endif

// Progressive refinement radiosity equation solver
class ProgRad : public RadEqnSolve
{
  protected:
    float *ff_array;          // Form factor array pointer
    BOOL over_flag;           // Overshoot flag
    BOOL status;              // Object status
    FormFactor ffd;           // Form factor determination
    Spectra overshoot;        // Overshooting parameters

    void AddAmbient();
    void CalcOverShoot();

  public:
    ProgRad() : RadEqnSolve() { over_flag = TRUE; }

    ~ProgRad() { Close(); }

    BOOL Calculate();
    BOOL OverShootFlag() { return over_flag; }
    BOOL GetStatus() { return ffd.GetStatus(); }
    BOOL Open( Environ * );
    void Close();
    void DisableOverShoot() { over_flag = FALSE; }
    void EnableOverShoot() { over_flag = TRUE; }
};

#endif
```

Note that *ProgRad* can use either the *HemiCube* or *CubicTetra* class for form factor determination. If you forget to define either *_HEMI_CUBE* or *_CUBIC_TETRA* at compile time, your compiler will issue an appropriate error message via the *#error* directive.

Since *ProgRad* is derived from *RadEqnSolve* (Listing 4.18), we already have a mechanism for toggling the ambient exitance feature on and off via *RadEqnSolve::EnableAmbient* and *RadEqnSolve::DisableAmbient*. The functions *EnableOverShoot* and *DisableOverShoot* provide the same functionality for positive overshooting. Our *HELIOS* program provides the necessary user interface for both these features through its *Convergence Parameters* dialog box. This allows you to experiment with various environments to see exactly how the ambient exitance affects the image quality and how much faster the radiosity algorithm (usually) converges with positive overshooting enabled.

The remainder of our *ProgRad* class consists of:

Listing 6.3

```cpp
// PROG_RAD.CPP - Progressive Refinement Radiosity Class

#include "prog_rad.h"

// Open progressive radiosity renderer
BOOL ProgRad::Open( Environ *pe )
{
  penv = pe;              // Save environment pointer
  step_count = 0;         // Reset step count
  convergence = 1.0;      // Convergence
  InitExitance();         // Initialize exitances

  if (amb_flag == TRUE) // Ambient exitance required ?
  {
    CalcInterReflect(); // Calculate interreflection factor
    CalcAmbient();      // Calculate initial ambient term
  }

  // Allocate form factor array
  if ((ff_array = new float[penv->GetNumElem()]) == NULL)
    return FALSE;

  return TRUE;
}

// Close progressive radiosity renderer
void ProgRad::Close()
{
  // Release form factor array
  if (ff_array != NULL)
  {
```

(continued)

Listing 6.3 *(continued)*

```cpp
    delete [] ff_array;
    ff_array = NULL;
  }

  if (penv != NULL)
  {
    // Interpolate vertex exitances
    tone.Interpolate(penv->GetInstPtr());

    // Normalize vertex exitances
    tone.Normalize(penv->GetInstPtr());
  }
}

// Calculate element exitances
BOOL ProgRad::Calculate()
{
  float rff;                 // Reciprocal form factor
  BOOL self;                 // Self patch flag
  WORD ff_index = 0;         // Form factor array index
  Element3 *pelem;           // Element pointer
  Instance *pinst;           // Instance pointer
  Patch3 *ppatch;            // Patch pointer
  Surface3 *psurf;           // Surface pointer
  Spectra delta;             // Delta exitance
  Spectra reflect;           // Surface reflectance
  Spectra shoot;             // Shoot exitance

  // Check for maximum number of steps
  if (step_count >= max_step)
  {
    if (amb_flag == TRUE)
    {
      AddAmbient();          // Add ambient exitance
    }
    return TRUE;
  }

  UpdateUnsentStats();    // Update unsent flux statistics

  // Check for convergence
  if (convergence < stop_criterion)
  {
    if (amb_flag == TRUE)
    {
      AddAmbient();          // Add ambient exitance
    }
    return TRUE;
  }
```

```
// Calculate form factors
ffd.CalcFormFactors(pmax, penv->GetInstPtr(), ff_array,
    penv->GetNumElem());

if (over_flag == TRUE)
{
  CalcOverShoot();    // Calculate overshooting parameters
}

// Walk the instance list
pinst = penv->GetInstPtr();
while (pinst != NULL)
{
  // Walk the surface list
  psurf = pinst->GetSurfPtr();
  while (psurf != NULL)
  {
    // Get surface reflectance
    reflect = psurf->GetReflectance();

    // Walk the patch list
    ppatch = psurf->GetPatchPtr();
    while (ppatch != NULL)
    {
      // Check for self patch
      self = (ppatch == pmax) ? TRUE : FALSE;

      // Walk the element list
      pelem = ppatch->GetElementPtr();
      while (pelem != NULL)
      {
        if (self == FALSE)    // Ignore self
        {
          // Check element visibility
          if (ff_array[ff_index] > 0.0)
          {
            // Compute reciprocal form factor
            rff = (float) min((double) ff_array[ff_index]
                * pmax->GetArea() / pelem->GetArea(),
                1.0);

            // Get shooting patch unsent exitance
            shoot = pmax->GetExitance();

            if (over_flag == TRUE)
            {
              // Add overshoot exitance
              shoot.Add(overshoot);
            }
```

(continued)

Listing 6.3   *(continued)*

```
                    // Calculate delta exitance
                    delta.SetRedBand(reflect.GetRedBand() *
                        rff * shoot.GetRedBand());
                    delta.SetGreenBand(reflect.GetGreenBand() *
                        rff * shoot.GetGreenBand());
                    delta.SetBlueBand(reflect.GetBlueBand() *
                        rff * shoot.GetBlueBand());

                    // Update element exitance
                    pelem->GetExitance().Add(delta);

                    // Update patch unsent exitance
                    delta.Scale(pelem->GetArea() /
                        ppatch->GetArea());
                    ppatch->GetExitance().Add(delta);
                  }
                }
              pelem = pelem->GetNext();
              ff_index++;
            }
          ppatch = ppatch->GetNext();
        }
      psurf = psurf->GetNext();
    }
    pinst = pinst->GetNext();
  }

  if (over_flag == TRUE)
  {
    // Subtract shot exitance from patch unsent exitance
    pmax->GetExitance().Subtract(shoot);
  }
  else
  {
    // Reset unsent exitance to zero
    pmax->GetExitance().Reset();
  }

  if (amb_flag == TRUE)
  {
    CalcAmbient();        // Recalculate ambient exitance
  }

  step_count++;           // Increment step count
  return FALSE;           // Convergence not achieved yet
}

void ProgRad::AddAmbient()      // Add ambient exitance
{
```

```
    Element3 *pelem;       // Element pointer
    Instance *pinst;       // Instance pointer
    Patch3 *ppatch;        // Patch pointer
    Spectra delta_amb;     // Delta ambient exitance
    Spectra reflect;       // Surface reflectance
    Surface3 *psurf;       // Surface pointer

  // Walk the instance list
  pinst = penv->GetInstPtr();
  while (pinst != NULL)
  {
    // Walk the surface list
    psurf = pinst->GetSurfPtr();
    while (psurf != NULL)
    {
      // Get surface reflectance
      reflect = psurf->GetReflectance();

      // Walk the patch list
      ppatch = psurf->GetPatchPtr();
      while (ppatch != NULL)
      {
        // Walk the element list
        pelem = ppatch->GetElementPtr();
        while (pelem != NULL)
        {
          // Calculate delta ambient exitance
          delta_amb.SetRedBand(ambient.GetRedBand() *
              reflect.GetRedBand());
          delta_amb.SetGreenBand(ambient.GetGreenBand() *
              reflect.GetGreenBand());
          delta_amb.SetBlueBand(ambient.GetBlueBand() *
              reflect.GetBlueBand());

          // Update element exitance
          pelem->GetExitance().Add(delta_amb);

          pelem = pelem->GetNext();
        }
        ppatch = ppatch->GetNext();
      }
      psurf = psurf->GetNext();
    }
    pinst = pinst->GetNext();
  }
}

// Calculate overshooting parameters
void ProgRad::CalcOverShoot()
{
```

(continued)

Listing 6.3   *(continued)*

```
BOOL self;              // Self patch flag
WORD ff_index = 0;      // Form factor array index
Element3 *pelem;        // Element pointer
Instance *pinst;        // Instance pointer
Patch3 *ppatch;         // Patch pointer
Spectra spr;            // Shooting patch reflectance
Spectra unsent;         // Patch unsent exitance
Surface3 *psurf;        // Surface pointer

overshoot.Reset();      // Reset overshooting parameters

// Walk the instance list
pinst = penv->GetInstPtr();
while (pinst != NULL)
{
  // Walk the surface list
  psurf = pinst->GetSurfPtr();
  while (psurf != NULL)
  {
    // Walk the patch list
    ppatch = psurf->GetPatchPtr();
    while (ppatch != NULL)
    {
      // Check for self patch
      self = (ppatch == pmax) ? TRUE : FALSE;

      // Walk the element list
      pelem = ppatch->GetElementPtr();
      while (pelem != NULL)
      {
        if (self == FALSE)     // Ignore self
        {
          // Get unsent patch exitance
          unsent = ppatch->GetExitance();

          // Ensure unsent exitance is positive in each
          // color band
          if (unsent.GetRedBand() < 0.0)
            unsent.SetRedBand(0.0);
          if (unsent.GetGreenBand() < 0.0)
            unsent.SetGreenBand(0.0);
          if (unsent.GetBlueBand() < 0.0)
            unsent.SetBlueBand(0.0);

          // Multiply unsent exitance by patch-to-
          // element form factor
          unsent.Scale(ff_array[ff_index]);

          // Update overshooting parameters
          overshoot.Add(unsent);
        }
```

```
            pelem = pelem->GetNext();
            ff_index++;
        }
        ppatch = ppatch->GetNext();
    }
    psurf = psurf->GetNext();
  }
  pinst = pinst->GetNext();
}

// Get shooting patch reflectance
spr = pmax->GetParentPtr()->GetReflectance();

// Multiply overshooting parameters by shooting patch
// reflectance
overshoot.SetRedBand(overshoot.GetRedBand() *
    spr.GetRedBand());
overshoot.SetGreenBand(overshoot.GetGreenBand() *
    spr.GetGreenBand());
overshoot.SetBlueBand(overshoot.GetBlueBand() *
    spr.GetBlueBand());
}
```

Most of Listing 6.3 is a straightforward implementation of the preceding algorithms. The only item not discussed so far is the calculation of the reciprocal form factor in *Calculate*. If this value is greater than unity, it indicates that hemicube (or cubic tetrahedron) aliasing has occurred. When this happens, we should in theory subdivide the shooting patch and shoot the exitance again. Here we take the simpler approach of silently clipping the reciprocal form factor to unity. (See Section 7.5.2 for further details.)

With *ProgRad*, we have all the code we need to render photorealistic images. Before doing so, however, we should look at how easily we can accommodate vertex-to-source form factors within the progressive refinement radiosity paradigm.

6.10 A RAY-CASTING RADIOSITY ALGORITHM

From Section 5.23 we know that ray casting allows us to determine the form factor from an element vertex v to a source patch i. Repeating Equation 5.46 here (with a change of subscripts to avoid confusion), we have:

$$F_{vi} = \frac{A_i}{n} \sum_{t=1}^{n} HID_t \frac{\cos \theta_{vt} \cos \theta_{it}}{\pi r_t^2 + A_i/n} \tag{6.45}$$

which is calculated by our *RayCast* class (Listings 5.29 and 5.30).

We want to shoot exitance from each vertex to the source patch. Repeating Equation 6.33 with another change of subscripts, we have:

$$\Delta M_v = \rho_v M_i^{unsent} F_{vi} \tag{6.46}$$

With this, our progressive refinement radiosity algorithm (Fig. 6.4) becomes as in Figure 6.7.

FOR each element i

 $\Delta M_i^{unsent} = M_{oi}$

ENDFOR

WHILE $\displaystyle\sum_{i=1}^{n} \Delta M_i^{unsent} A_i > \varepsilon$

 Select element i with greatest unsent flux $\Delta M_i^{unsent} A_i$
 FOR each element j

  $\Delta M = 0$

  FOR each vertex v

   $\Delta M_v = \rho_j F_{vi} \Delta M_i^{unsent}$

   $M_v = M_v + \Delta M_v$

  ENDFOR

  $\Delta M_j^{unsent} = \Delta M_j^{unsent} + \Delta M / num\_vertices$

 ENDFOR

 $\Delta M_i^{unsent} = 0$

ENDWHILE

Figure 6.7 Progressive refinement radiosity algorithm with ray casting

Note that we no longer have to calculate and store the form factors for each selected shooting element. This makes the ray-casting radiosity algorithm more efficient with respect to memory usage. On the other hand, Equation 6.42 requires the shooting patch-to-receiving element form factors before the exitance is shot into the environment. This means that we can no longer calculate the amount of positive overshooting required for each pass.

We can, however, take advantage of our patch-element hierarchy and ambient exitance enhancements. From Figure 6.5, we have Figure 6.8.

Calculate initial ambient exitance $M_{ambient}$
FOR each patch i

 $\Delta M_i^{unsent} = M_{oi}$

ENDFOR

WHILE $\displaystyle\sum_{i=1}^{n} \Delta M_i^{unsent} A_i > \varepsilon$

 Select patch i with greatest unsent flux $\Delta M_i^{unsent} A_i$
 FOR each patch j

  FOR each element k of parent patch j

   $\Delta M_k = 0$

```
    FOR each vertex v
        // Determine increase in exitance of vertex v due to patch
        // exitance ΔMᵢᵘⁿˢᵉⁿᵗ
```

$$\Delta M_v = \rho_j F_{vi} \Delta M_i^{unsent}$$

$$M_v = M_v + \Delta M_v$$

$$\Delta M_k = \Delta M_k + \Delta M_v$$

```
    ENDFOR
        // Add area-weighted increase in element k exitance to parent
        // patch j
```

$$\Delta M_j^{unsent} = \Delta M_j^{unsent} + \frac{A_k \Delta M_k}{A_j * num\_vertices}$$

```
  ENDFOR
ENDFOR
```

$$\Delta M_i^{unsent} = 0$$

```
Recalculate ambient exitance M_ambient
ENDWHILE
FOR each element k
  FOR each vertex v
    // Add initial and ambient exitance contributions
```

$$M_v = M_v + M_{ok} + \rho_k M_{ambient}$$

```
  ENDFOR
ENDFOR
```

Figure 6.8   Ray-casting radiosity algorithm with ambient exitance

Once again, using *RadEqnSolve* as the base class, we can derive the following:

Listing 6.4

```cpp
// RAY_RAD.H - Ray Casting Radiosity Class

#ifndef _RAY_RAD_H
#define _RAY_RAD_H

#include "environ.h"
#include "rad_eqn.h"
#include "ray_cast.h"

// Ray casting radiosity equation solver
class RayRad : public RadEqnSolve
{
  private:
    RayCast ffd;          // Form factor determination

    void AddAmbient();

  public:
    RayRad() : RadEqnSolve() { }
```

(continued)

Listing 6.4 *(continued)*

```
    ~RayRad() { }

    BOOL Calculate();
    BOOL Open( Environ * );
    void Close() { tone.Normalize(penv->GetInstPtr()); }
};

#endif
```

and:

Listing 6.5

```
// RAY_RAD.CPP - Ray Casting Radiosity Class

#include "ray_rad.h"

// Open ray casting radiosity renderer
BOOL RayRad::Open( Environ *pe )
{
  penv = pe;              // Save environment pointer
  step_count = 0;         // Reset step count
  convergence = 1.0;      // Convergence
  InitExitance();         // Initialize exitances

  if (amb_flag == TRUE) // Ambient exitance required ?
  {
    CalcInterReflect(); // Calculate interreflection factor
    CalcAmbient();      // Calculate initial ambient term
  }

  return TRUE;
}

// Calculate element exitances
BOOL RayRad::Calculate()
{
  int i;                 // Loop index
  int num_vert;          // Number of element vertices
  float vsff;            // Vertex-to-source form factor
  BOOL self;             // Self patch flag
  Element3 *pelem;       // Element pointer
  Instance *pinst;       // Instance pointer
  Patch3 *ppatch;        // Patch pointer
  Surface3 *psurf;       // Surface pointer
  Spectra p_delta;       // Patch delta exitance
  Spectra v_delta;       // Vertex delta exitance
  Spectra reflect;       // Surface reflectance
  Spectra shoot;         // Shoot exitance
  Vertex3 *pvert;        // Vertex pointer
```

```
// Check for maximum number of steps
if (step_count >= max_step)
{
  if (amb_flag == TRUE)
  {
    AddAmbient();      // Add ambient exitance
  }
  return TRUE;
}

UpdateUnsentStats();  // Update unsent flux statistics

// Check for convergence
if (convergence < stop_criterion)
{
  if (amb_flag == TRUE)
  {
    AddAmbient();      // Add ambient exitance
  }
  return TRUE;
}

// Initialize form factor determination object
ffd.Init(pmax);

// Walk the instance list
pinst = penv->GetInstPtr();
while (pinst != NULL)
{
  // Walk the surface list
  psurf = pinst->GetSurfPtr();
  while (psurf != NULL)
  {
    // Get surface reflectance
    reflect = psurf->GetReflectance();

    // Walk the patch list
    ppatch = psurf->GetPatchPtr();
    while (ppatch != NULL)
    {
      // Check for self patch
      self = (ppatch == pmax) ? TRUE : FALSE;

      // Walk the element list
      pelem = ppatch->GetElementPtr();
      while (pelem != NULL)
      {
        if (self == FALSE)    // Ignore self
        {
          // Get shooting patch unsent exitance
          shoot = pmax->GetExitance();

          // Reset patch delta exitance
          p_delta.Reset();                    (continued)
```

Listing 6.5 *(continued)*

```
            num_vert = pelem->GetNumVert();
            for (i = 0; i < num_vert; i++)
            {
              // Get element vertex pointer
              pvert = pelem->GetVertexPtr(i);

              // Get vertex-to-source form factor
              if ((vsff = (float) ffd.CalcFormFactor(pvert,
                penv->GetInstPtr())) > 0.0)
              {
                // Calculate vertex delta exitance
                v_delta.SetRedBand(reflect.GetRedBand()
                    * vsff * shoot.GetRedBand());
                v_delta.SetGreenBand(reflect.GetGreenBand()
                    * vsff * shoot.GetGreenBand());
                v_delta.SetBlueBand(reflect.GetBlueBand()
                    * vsff * shoot.GetBlueBand());

                // Update vertex exitance
                pvert->GetExitance().Add(v_delta);

                // Update patch delta exitance
                p_delta.Add(v_delta);
              }
            }

            // Update patch unsent exitance
            p_delta.Scale(pelem->GetArea() / ((double)
                num_vert * ppatch->GetArea()));
            ppatch->GetExitance().Add(p_delta);
          }
          pelem = pelem->GetNext();
        }
        ppatch = ppatch->GetNext();
      }
      psurf = psurf->GetNext();
    }
    pinst = pinst->GetNext();
  }

  // Reset unsent exitance to zero
  pmax->GetExitance().Reset();

  if (amb_flag == TRUE)
  {
    CalcAmbient();        // Recalculate ambient exitance
  }

  step_count++;          // Increment step count
  return FALSE;          // Convergence not achieved yet
}
```

```
void RayRad::AddAmbient()          // Add ambient exitance
{
  int i;                   // Loop index
  int num_vert;            // Number of element vertices
  Element3 *pelem;         // Element pointer
  Instance *pinst;         // Instance pointer
  Patch3 *ppatch;          // Patch pointer
  Spectra delta_amb;       // Delta ambient exitance
  Spectra reflect;         // Surface reflectance
  Surface3 *psurf;         // Surface pointer
  Vertex3 *pvert;          // Vertex pointer

  // Walk the instance list
  pinst = penv->GetInstPtr();
  while (pinst != NULL)
  {
    // Walk the surface list
    psurf = pinst->GetSurfPtr();
    while (psurf != NULL)
    {
      // Get surface reflectance
      reflect = psurf->GetReflectance();

      // Walk the patch list
      ppatch = psurf->GetPatchPtr();
      while (ppatch != NULL)
      {
        // Walk the element list
        pelem = ppatch->GetElementPtr();
        while (pelem != NULL)
        {
          // Calculate delta ambient exitance
          delta_amb.SetRedBand(ambient.GetRedBand() *
              reflect.GetRedBand());
          delta_amb.SetGreenBand(ambient.GetGreenBand() *
              reflect.GetGreenBand());
          delta_amb.SetBlueBand(ambient.GetBlueBand() *
              reflect.GetBlueBand());

          num_vert = pelem->GetNumVert();
          for (i = 0; i < num_vert; i++)
          {
            // Get element vertex pointer
            pvert = pelem->GetVertexPtr(i);

            // Update vertex exitance
            pvert->GetExitance().Add(delta_amb);
          }
          pelem = pelem->GetNext();
        }
        ppatch = ppatch->GetNext();
      }
```

(continued)

Listing 6.5　　*(continued)*

```
        psurf = psurf->GetNext();
    }
    pinst = pinst->GetNext();
  }
}
```

As you can see, the differences between *RayRad* and *ProgRad* are minimal. Apart from their form factor determination requirements, the two *Calculate* functions differ only in their innermost loops. The same holds true for *UpdateUnsentStats* and *AddAmbient*. For the effort of developing a few dozen additional lines of code, we now have two radiosity algorithms to play with. Each has its advantages and disadvantages in rendering photorealisitc images, as we shall soon see.

6.11　*HELIOS:* PUTTING IT ALL TOGETHER

C'est fini! After nearly 7,000 lines of source code and fifty C++ classes, we are done. All we need to do now is to compile and link a new version of *HELIOS*. With it, we can render photorealistic images of an environment.

> *HELIOS* is designed for Microsoft Windows 3.1 and Windows NT (see Chap. 4). If you are developing for another target environment, you will need to port the user interface portion of *HELIOS* to that environment. See Section 4.19 for details.

The first step is build a make file or a project file from within an integrated development environment (IDE). This leads to a minor complication: We must choose among one of three versions of *HELIOS* to compile and link. There is a different list of source code files and conditional compilation directives required, depending on whether we want to use the progressive refinement or ray-casting radiosity algorithms. If we choose the former, we then have to decide between hemicubes and cubic tetrahedrons.

Then again, there should be no choice. Having expended the effort in developing the code, we might as well compile, link, and experiment with all three versions. To avoid the otherwise inevitable confusion and frustration, it is probably best to set up make or IDE project files in three separate subdirectories. There is nothing more exasperating than debugging what appears to be a successfully compiled and linked program, only to discover that an incorrect object file was used.

With this in mind, we can start with the *Helios* version given in Figure 6.9. Note that for 16-bit Windows 3.1, the memory model *must* be specified as LARGE. As was explained in Section 3.13, the *WinText* class assumes that its functions use *_far* pointers.

Also, the compilation directive *_HEMI_CUBE* must be globally defined. This can usually be done from a make file or through the compiler preprocessor options.

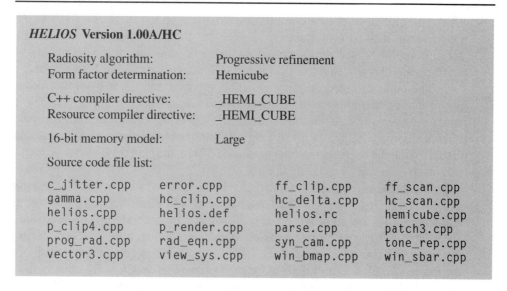

Figure 6.9 HELIOS (hemicube) project files

Furthermore, it must be separately defined for the C++ compiler *and the resource script compiler*.

Once you successfully compile and link this version, you can run it and display the *About* dialog box. The version number should read "1.00A/HC," where "HC" stands for "Hemi-Cube."

Our next version is given in Figure 6.10.

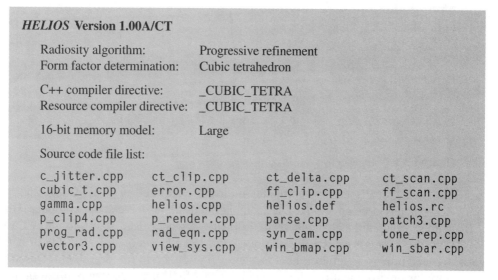

Figure 6.10 HELIOS (cubic tetrahedron) project files

The globally defined compilation directive to use here is _CUBIC_TETRA. Once again, it must be separately defined for the C++ compiler and the resource script compiler. Once you successfully compile and link this version, its version number should read "1.00A/CT," where "CT" stands for "Cubic Tetrahedron."

The cubic tetrahedron and hemicube versions are, apart from the form factor determination methods used, identical. There are also few if any discernible differences between the images they produce. If anything, the cubic tetrahedron might offer a slight advantage in alleviating aliasing problems for environments with primarily parallel and perpendicular surfaces. There may also be slight differences in execution time when rendering images.

Given these minimal differences, you might ask "why bother?" The answer is that neither *HemiCube* nor *CubicTetra* has been optimized. Section 5.19.1 offers several suggestions for improving the performance of both algorithms, and the references cited in Chapter 5 offer a variety of acceleration techniques. Since form factor determination consumes most of the CPU time needed to generate a radiosity rendering, these two classes and their associated classes (*HemiClip* and others) should be prime candidates for optimization efforts. Having two separate algorithms to work with can only improve the chances for success.

On the other hand, we also have our ray-casting approach to consider (Fig. 6.11).

***HELIOS* Version 1.00A/RC**

Radiosity algorithm:	Ray casting (progressive refinement)
Form factor determination:	Ray casting
C++ compiler directive:	_RAY_CAST
Resource compiler directive:	_RAY_CAST
16-bit memory model:	Large

Source code file list:

```
c_jitter.cpp    error.cpp      gamma.cpp      helios.cpp
helios.def      helios.rc      p_clip4.cpp    p_render.cpp
parse.cpp       patch3.cpp     rad_eqn.cpp    ray_cast.cpp
ray_rad.cpp     syn_cam.cpp    tone_rep.cpp   vector3.cpp
view_sys.cpp    win_bmap.cpp   win_sbar.cpp
```

Figure 6.11 HELIOS (ray-casting) project files

The globally defined compilation directive required is _RAY_CAST, and it must be separately defined for the C++ compiler and the resource script compiler. The program's version number should read "1.00A/RC," where "RC" stands for "Ray Casting."

With three successfully compiled and linked versions of *HELIOS* in hand, all we need now is an environment to view . . . and therein lies a problem. Describing a complex environment requires *many* lines of ASCII text. Do you really want to enter 100,000 lines by hand?

6.12   A SIMPLE TEST ENVIRONMENT

In a few years, books like this one will likely be published on CD-ROM. It would be wonderful to have megabytes of space available to include a collection of complex and interesting environments to play with. Until then, we have the printed page and the diskette accompanying this book.

The diskette includes several moderately complex environments that demonstrate the capabilities of *HELIOS*. The best that can be done in print is to present a very simple environment—a bench and two suspended lights in an otherwise empty room. Although this setup may seem rather mundane, the color plates demonstrate that it can offer some surprising subtleties.

We first need an entity file for the bench:

Listing 6.6   BENCH.ENT

```
ENTITY bench
VERTEX
< 0.0 0.0 2.5 >
< 2.5 0.0 2.5 >
< 2.5 2.5 2.5 >
< 0.0 2.5 2.5 >
< 5.0 0.0 2.5 >
< 5.0 2.5 2.5 >
< 5.0 0.0 0.0 >
< 5.0 2.5 0.0 >
< 5.0 2.5 2.5 >
< 5.0 0.0 2.5 >
< 0.0 0.0 0.0 >
< 0.0 0.0 2.5 >
< 0.0 2.5 2.5 >
< 0.0 2.5 0.0 >
< 4.8 0.0 0.0 >
< 4.8 0.0 2.3 >
< 4.8 2.5 2.3 >
< 4.8 2.5 0.0 >
< 0.2 0.0 0.0 >
< 0.2 2.5 0.0 >
< 0.2 2.5 2.3 >
< 0.2 0.0 2.3 >
< 5.0 0.0 0.0 >
< 5.0 2.5 0.0 >
< 5.0 2.5 2.5 >
< 5.0 0.0 2.5 >
< 0.0 0.0 0.0 >
< 0.0 2.5 0.0 >
< 0.0 2.5 2.5 >
< 0.0 0.0 2.5 >
END_VERT
```

(continued)

Listing 6.6   *(continued)*

```
SURFACE
[ 0.5 0.2 0.7 ] [ 0.0 0.0 0.0 ]
[ 0.0 0.8 0.3 ] [ 0.0 0.0 0.0 ]
[ 0.0 0.8 0.3 ] [ 0.0 0.0 0.0 ]
[ 0.0 0.3 0.0 ] [ 0.0 0.0 0.0 ]
END_SURF
PATCH
 0 {  0  4  5  3 }
 1 {  6  7  8  9 }
 2 { 10 11 12 13 }
 3 { 14 15 16 17 }
 3 { 18 19 20 21 }
 3 { 21 20 16 15 }
 3 { 17 16 24 23 }
 3 { 16 20 28 24 }
 3 { 19 27 28 20 }
 3 { 14 17 23 22 }
 3 { 10 27 19 18 }
 3 { 14 22 25 15 }
 3 { 21 15 25 29 }
 3 { 26 18 21 29 }
END_PATCH
ELEMENT
  0 {  0  1  2  2 }
  0 {  0  2  3  3 }
  0 {  4  2  1  1 }
  0 {  4  5  2  2 }
  1 {  6  7  8  8 }
  1 {  6  8  9  9 }
  2 { 10 11 12 12 }
  2 { 10 12 13 13 }
  3 { 14 15 16 17 }
  4 { 18 19 20 21 }
  5 { 21 20 16 15 }
  6 { 17 16 24 23 }
  7 { 16 20 28 24 }
  8 { 19 27 28 20 }
  9 { 14 17 23 22 }
 10 { 26 27 19 18 }
 11 { 14 22 25 15 }
 12 { 21 15 25 29 }
 13 { 26 18 21 29 }
END_ELEM
END_ENTITY
```

The color scheme is a bit garish—a mauve top, sea green sides, and dark green edges. If you prefer something more contemporary, you can always change the surface reflectance values in the SURFACE section.

The top surface is divided into two square patches, and each patch is divided into two equal triangles (Fig. 6.13). A finer mesh of patches and elements would allow us to display more shading details in the rendered image. (Adding the necessary patch, element, and especially vertex description lines to BENCH.ENT is left as a typing exercise for the masochistic reader.)

There are two identical light fixtures, so we need only one common entity file to describe them:

Listing 6.7   LIGHT.ENT

```
ENTITY light
VERTEX
< 0.0 0.0 0.02 >
< 0.2 0.0 0.02 >
< 0.4 0.0 0.02 >
< 0.6 0.0 0.02 >
< 0.8 0.0 0.02 >
< 1.0 0.0 0.02 >
< 1.0 1.0 0.02 >
< 0.8 1.0 0.02 >
< 0.6 1.0 0.02 >
< 0.4 1.0 0.02 >
< 0.2 1.0 0.02 >
< 0.0 1.0 0.02 >
< 0.0 0.0 0.0 >
< 1.0 0.0 0.0 >
< 1.0 0.0 0.02 >
< 0.0 0.0 0.02 >
< 1.0 0.0 0.0 >
< 1.0 1.0 0.0 >
< 1.0 1.0 0.02 >
< 1.0 0.0 0.02 >
< 1.0 1.0 0.0 >
< 0.0 1.0 0.0 >
< 0.0 1.0 0.02 >
< 1.0 1.0 0.02 >
< 0.0 1.0 0.0 >
< 0.0 0.0 0.0 >
< 0.0 0.0 0.02 >
< 0.0 1.0 0.02 >
< 0.0 0.0 0.0 >
< 0.2 0.0 0.0 >
< 0.4 0.0 0.0 >
< 0.6 0.0 0.0 >
< 0.8 0.0 0.0 >
< 1.0 0.0 0.0 >
< 1.0 1.0 0.0 >
< 0.8 1.0 0.0 >
< 0.6 1.0 0.0 >
< 0.4 1.0 0.0 >
< 0.2 1.0 0.0 >
< 0.0 1.0 0.0 >
END_VERT
```

(continued)

Listing 6.7 *(continued)*

```
SURFACE
[ 0.0 0.0 0.0 ] [ 1.0 1.0 1.0 ]
[ 0.0 0.0 0.5 ] [ 0.0 0.0 0.0 ]
[ 0.0 0.0 0.5 ] [ 0.0 0.0 0.0 ]
[ 0.0 0.0 0.5 ] [ 0.0 0.0 0.0 ]
[ 0.0 0.0 0.5 ] [ 0.0 0.0 0.0 ]
[ 0.0 0.0 0.0 ] [ 0.5 0.5 0.5 ]
END_SURF
PATCH
0 { 0 1 10 11 }
0 ( 1 2 9 10 }
0 { 2 3 8 9 }
0 { 3 4 7 8 }
0 ( 4 5 6 7 }
1 { 12 13 14 15 }
2 { 16 17 18 19 }
3 { 20 21 22 23 }
4 { 24 25 26 27 }
5 { 28 39 38 29 }
5 { 29 38 37 30 }
5 { 30 37 36 31 }
5 { 31 36 35 32 }
5 { 32 35 34 33 }
END_PATCH
ELEMENT
0 { 0 1 10 11 }
1 ( 1 2 9 10 }
2 { 2 3 8 9 }
3 { 3 4 7 8 }
4 ( 4 5 6 7 }
5 { 12 13 14 15 }
6 { 16 17 18 19 }
7 { 20 21 22 23 }
8 { 24 25 26 27 }
9 { 28 39 38 29 }
10 { 29 38 37 30 }
11 { 30 37 36 31 }
12 { 31 36 35 32 }
13 { 32 35 34 33 }
END_ELEM
END_ENTITY
```

LIGHT.ENT describes the light fixture as a unit square, which is definitely not what is shown in Figure 6.13 and the color plates. Remember, however, that we can scale, rotate, and translate an entity as required, depending on the parameters we specify in the environment file. In this case, we can stretch LIGHT.ENT into a semblance of a linear fluorescent lighting fixture that emits light from both its top and bottom faces.

Figure 6.13 shows the light fixtures suspended below the ceiling plane. Accordingly, the top and bottom faces of LIGHT.ENT consist of five patches. This is an attempt to comply with the five-times rule (Section 5.5), again within the limits of the size of text file that can be reproduced here. LIGHT.ENT will be rotated 180 degrees on its horizontal axis to properly orient it in the environment.

Finally, we need to define the floor, ceiling, and walls of our room. Each of these surfaces consists of one patch and a square grid of 25 elements. This is far from optimal with respect to the five-times rule, especially where the surfaces meet at the corners. On the other hand, it will serve to demonstrate both the strengths and weaknesses of our radiosity methods.

We can use the following entity file as a template to define these surfaces:

Listing 6.8   W_WALL.ENT

```
ENTITY white wall
VERTEX
< 0.00 0.00 0.00 >
< 0.20 0.00 0.00 >
< 0.40 0.00 0.00 >
< 0.60 0.00 0.00 >
< 0.80 0.00 0.00 >
< 1.00 0.00 0.00 >
< 0.00 0.20 0.00 >
< 0.20 0.20 0.00 >
< 0.40 0.20 0.00 >
< 0.60 0.20 0.00 >
< 0.80 0.20 0.00 >
< 1.00 0.20 0.00 >
< 0.00 0.40 0.00 >
< 0.20 0.40 0.00 >
< 0.40 0.40 0.00 >
< 0.60 0.40 0.00 >
< 0.80 0.40 0.00 >
< 1.00 0.40 0.00 >
< 0.00 0.60 0.00 >
< 0.20 0.60 0.00 >
< 0.40 0.60 0.00 >
< 0.60 0.60 0.00 >
< 0.80 0.60 0.00 >
< 1.00 0.60 0.00 >
< 0.00 0.80 0.00 >
< 0.20 0.80 0.00 >
< 0.40 0.80 0.00 >
< 0.60 0.80 0.00 >
< 0.80 0.80 0.00 >
< 1.00 0.80 0.00 >
< 0.00 1.00 0.00 >
< 0.20 1.00 0.00 >
< 0.40 1.00 0.00 >
< 0.60 1.00 0.00 >
< 0.80 1.00 0.00 >
< 1.00 1.00 0.00 >
END_VERT
```

(continued)

Listing 6.8   *(continued)*

```
SURFACE
[ 0.8 0.8 0.8 ] [ 0.0 0.0 0.0 ]
END_SURF
PATCH
0 { 0 5 35 30 }
END_PATCH
ELEMENT
0 {  0  1  7  6 }
0 {  1  2  8  7 }
0 {  2  3  9  8 }
0 {  3  4 10  9 }
0 {  4  5 11 10 }
0 {  6  7 13 12 }
0 {  7  8 14 13 }
0 {  8  9 15 14 }
0 {  9 10 16 15 }
0 { 10 11 17 16 }
0 { 12 13 19 18 }
0 { 13 14 20 19 }
0 { 14 15 21 20 }
0 { 15 16 22 21 }
0 { 16 17 23 22 }
0 { 18 19 25 24 }
0 { 19 20 26 25 }
0 { 20 21 27 26 }
0 { 21 22 28 27 }
0 { 22 23 29 28 }
0 { 24 25 31 30 }
0 { 25 26 32 31 }
0 { 26 27 33 32 }
0 { 27 28 34 33 }
0 { 28 29 35 34 }
END_ELEM
END_ENTITY
```

W_WALL.ENT describes the three white walls of our room. The surface reflectance is described by the surface identifier, which is:

```
   .  .  .
SURFACE
[ 0.8 0.8 0.8 ] [ 0.0 0.0 0.0 ]
END_SURF
   .  .  .
```

(This actually describes a light gray surface that reflects 80 percent in each of the three color bands. Looking at the surface in real life, we would probably say it is off-white in color.)

To create the red wall, we only need to change the above to:

[0.95 0.0 0.0] [0.0 0.0 0.0]

and name the modified file R_WALL.ENT. Similarly, the floor becomes:

[0.2 0.3 0.3] [0.0 0.0 0.0]

which we name FLOOR.ENT. (This will look like a rather pleasant gray carpet with a blue-green tinge. We can blame the furnishings on the interior decorator.)
    Finally, the ceiling is a sparklingly clean white:

[0.95 0.95 0.95] [0.0 0.0 0.0]

which we name CEILING.ENT. That done, we can arrange our room and its furnishings with:

Listing 6.9   ROOM.WLD

```
WORLD room
COMMENT floor
floor.ent
< 1.0 1.6 1.0 >
< 0.0 0.0 0.0 >
< 0.0 0.0 0.0 >
COMMENT ceiling
ceiling.ent
< 1.0 1.6 1.0 >
< 180.0 0.0 0.0 >
< 0.0 1.6 1.0 >
COMMENT red wall
r_wall.ent
< 1.0 1.0 1.0 >
< 270.0 0.0 0.0 >
< 0.0 0.0 1.0 >
COMMENT white wall
w_wall.ent
< 1.0 1.6 1.0 >
< 0.0 90.0 0.0 >
< 0.0 0.0 1.0 >
COMMENT white wall
w_wall.ent
< 1.0 1.0 1.0 >
< 90.0 0.0 0.0 >
< 0.0 1.6 0.0 >
COMMENT white wall
w_wall.ent
< 1.0 1.6 1.0 >
< 0.0 270.0 0.0 >
< 1.0 0.0 0.0 >
COMMENT light #1
light.ent
< 0.8 0.05 1.0 >
< 180.0 0.0 0.0 >
< 0.1 0.2 0.8 >
```

(continued)

Listing 6.9 *(continued)*

```
COMMENT light #2
light.ent
< 0.8 0.05 1.0 >
< 180.0 0.0 0.0 >
< 0.1 1.4 0.8 >
COMMENT bench
bench.ent
< 0.16 0.16 0.08 >
< 0.0 0.0 0.0 >
< 0.1 0.2 0.0 >
END_FILE
```

This gives us an environment with 9 instances, 22 surfaces, 48 patches, 197 elements, and 326 vertices.

6.12.1 Taking It for a Test Drive

We have an environment and three versions of *HELIOS* to examine it with. Their user interfaces are almost identical, so we can choose whichever one we please for a test drive.

To display a view of the room, we first need to ensure that the files given in Figure 6.12 are in the same directory.

```
BENCH.ENT        CEILING.ENT      FLOOR.ENT        LIGHT.ENT
R_WALL.ENT       W_WALL.ENT       ROOM.WLD
```

Figure 6.12 ROOM enviroment data files

and run *HELIOS* as a MS-Windows program. Once its main window is displayed, we can:

1. Choose *File* from the menu bar.
2. Choose the *Open...* menu item to display the *Open* common dialog box.
3. Select the ROOM.WLD file.

An *Environment Statistics* dialog box will appear with an enumeration of the instances, surfaces, polygons, and vertices in the environment.

If the entity files are not in the same directory as ROOM.WLD, an error message will appear in a dialog box. Rather than exiting *HELIOS*, we can:

1. Choose *File* from the menu bar.
2. Choose the *Directories...* menu item to display the *Directories* dialog box.
3. Enter the correct file path in the *Entities File Path* edit control and repeat the previous three steps to select the ROOM.WLD file again.

With the environment file parsed and loaded into memory, we can now:

1. Choose *Camera* from the menu bar.
2. Choose the *Set Parameters* menu item to display the *Camera Parameters* dialog box.
3. Enter "2" in the *View Distance* edit control.

This sets the camera view distance at 2.0 units, giving a field of view roughly equivalent to a 35-mm lens on a 35-mm camera. The default *Window Dimensions* values tell *HELIOS* to display the image as a horizontally oriented bitmap of 640 × 480 pixels. We can change this to whatever size we want, from a minimum of 32 to a maximum of 2,048 pixels.

The synthetic camera's position and orientation must be specified next:

1. Choose *View* from the menu bar.
2. Choose the *Specify View...* menu item to display the *View Parameters* dialog box.
3. Enter "–1.5" (note the minus sign) in the *Eye Position X-Axis* edit control.
4. Enter "1.9" in the *Eye Position Y-Axis* edit control.
5. Enter "0.5" in the *Eye Position Z-Axis* edit control.
6. Enter "–30" (note the minus sign) in the *View Direction Horizontal Degrees* edit control.

The *View Direction Vertical Degrees* and *View-Up Vector* edit controls remain unchanged.

The synthetic camera is now set up to display an image, starting with:

1. Choose *Render* from the menu bar.
2. Choose the *Wireframe* menu item.

A wireframe image of the room will be displayed (Fig. 6.13). Recalling Chapter 4, we know this image will automatically resize itself whenever the display window size is changed. We can also go back and change any of the previous entries to change the view or camera parameters; the wireframe image will update itself accordingly.

To display a full-color *shaded* bitmap image:

1. Choose *Render* from the menu bar.
2. Choose the *Shaded* menu item.

It may take a few seconds or more to display the image, depending on the CPU speed and whether a math coprocessor is present. Increasing the bitmap size in either direction increases display calculation time accordingly. Remember that we are using floating-point operations here; an integer-only version (Section 4.12) would speed this up considerably for an 80*x*86-based computer.

Now, remember that:

HELIOS needs a computer system capable of displaying at least 32,768 colors.

We can use a computer with a 256-color display, but the images as displayed by *HELIOS* will appear posterized. The diskette accompanying this book includes C++ source code and an executable file for a color quantization utility (Section 3.5.2) that converts 24-bit color bitmaps to 8-bit (256-color) bitmaps.

As an aside, it is worth noting that an MS-Windows program operating in 256-color mode does not automatically map 24-bit RGB colors to the current palette of 256 colors when the MS-Windows API function *SetPixel* is called. Unless specifically programmed to do otherwise, the Windows GDI (Graphical Device Interface) merrily maps the color to one of 20 default system colors that have been specified via the Control Panel for the window borders, title bars, menu bars, background, and so forth. This explains why 24-bit color images displayed using Microsoft Paintbrush and similar programs usually appear so garish when a 256-color display adapter is used.

Remember also that even though our computer may be capable of displaying 32,768 or more colors, the Microsoft Windows environment may be set up to use an 8-bit (256-color) display driver for speed reasons. You may have to use the Windows Setup program to change to the appropriate display driver (see your documentation for details).

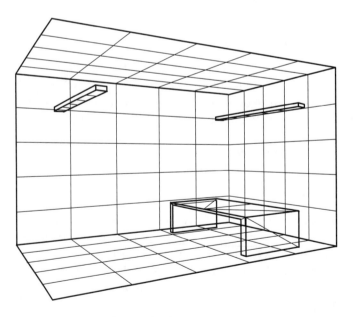

Figure 6.13   ROOM.WLD wireframe display

Ready then? Here we go:

1. Choose *Render* from the menu bar.
2. Choose the *Rendering* menu item.

and . . . wait . . . and there you have it: a photorealistic rendering of the room. The *Convergence Statistics* dialog box will tell us how many steps were required to achieve the default-stopping criterion of 0.001.

How long do we have to wait? On a typical 66 Mhz 486 machine, execution times were as follows:

HELIOS/CT:	35 seconds
HELIOS/HC:	44 seconds
HELIOS/RC:	196 seconds

which included five seconds for Gouraud shading and bitmap display calculations. Our execution times will obviously vary, depending on the CPU speed of our machine and whether it has a numeric coprocessor (which is highly recommended). Radiosity rendering is almost entirely concerned with floating-point calculations. As such, it will not matter much whether we are running under 16-bit MS-Windows 3.1 or 32-bit Windows NT. The execution times will be roughly comparable for the same CPU clock speed.

As promised, there are no discernible differences between the images produced by the hemicube and those of the cubic tetrahedral algorithm. On the other hand, there are marked differences between these images and the ray-cast image. The former clearly shows the effects of nodal averaging (Section 4.16) in smoothing out differences between element exitances, whereas the ray-cast image shows some rather obvious Mach bands.

Despite these problems, you have to admit that the images show none of the plastic surfaces we so often see in ray-traced images. Achieving similar results with an unoptimized ray-tracing program would consume hours to days of CPU time. As the color plates show, *HELIOS* is quite capable of rendering more complex environments with very aesthetic results.

There are two other points to be made here concerning the relative execution times. First, the cubic tetrahedron algorithm appears to offer approximately 25 percent better execution times than the hemicube algorithm. Remember, however, that this applies only for the particular implementations of these algorithms we have developed. The discussion at the end of Section 5.19.1 presented a number of possible acceleration techniques that may skew the performance results in either direction.

Second, the ray-casting algorithm is nearly six times slower than the cubic tetrahedron algorithm—but only for this particular environment. Section 5.23.3 noted that a naive implementation of the ray-casting algorithm has a time complexity of $O(mn^2)$ for m patches and n elements, whereas the hemicube and cubic tetrahedron algorithms have a time complexity of $O(mn)$. This means that the difference in execution times will increase with increasing environment complexity. This clearly indicates the need for implementing one or more ray tracing acceleration techniques within the *RayCast* class, again as discussed in Section 5.23.3. Remember that *HELIOS* is a test-bed for experimentation; it is not a production-quality radiosity renderer!

Having performed the radiosity calculations for the environment, we do not need to choose *Rendering* again until we load in a new environment data file. That is, we can change the camera and view parameters to look at the environment from whatever direction we choose, using the *Wireframe* display to provide a quick pre-view. Once we have what we want, we can:

1. Choose *Render* from the menu bar.
2. Choose the *Redisplay* menu item.

to redisplay a photorealistic image of the room.

We can redisplay the image in gray scale or pseudocolor by:

1. Choose *Options* from the menu bar.
2. Choose the *Set Display…* menu item to display the *Display Parameters* dia-log box.
3. Select either the *Grayscale* or *Pseudocolor* radio button.
4. Select the OK button.
5. Choose *Render* from the menu bar.
6. Choose the *Redisplay* menu item.

The *Display Parameters* dialog box also allows us to specify the gamma-cor-rection value (Section 3.5.1). The default value is 2.2; increasing it has the effect of increasing the image contrast and lightening the image. We can disable gamma cor-rection by unchecking the *Enable* checkbox.

If the display is capable of only 32,768 or 65,536 colors, there will be some noticeable color banding in the image. This is not an aliasing artifact but a slight pos-terization of the image. This is also where color reduction comes in (Section 3.5.2). It is disabled by default, but we can enable it by checking the *Enable* checkbox and redisplaying the image. The default *Noise Level* value is 1, but we can set it to any integer value from 1 to 8 (which results in a very grainy image).

We can also do the following:

1. Choose *Options* from the menu bar.
2. Choose the *Set Convergence…* menu item to display the *Convergence Para-meters* dialog box.
3. Enter an integer value between 1 and 2000 in the *Maximum Steps* edit con-trol. (The default value is 100.)
4. Enter a floating-point value between 0.0 and 1.0 in the *Stopping Criterion* edit control. (The default value is 0.001.)
5. Check or uncheck the *Ambient Exitance* checkbox as desired. (Ambient exi-tance is disabled by default.)
6. Check or uncheck the *Positive Overshoot* checkbox (positive overshooting is enabled by default. It also does not appear in the HELIOS/RC version of the dialog box.)

ROOM.WLD takes between 40 and 50 steps to converge to the default-stopping citerion of 0.001 with positive overshooting enabled. As an experiment, we might try setting the maximum steps to 1 and enabling or disabling ambient exitance. We can select *Rendering* again and see what the difference is between the images. We might also disable positive overshooting to see how long ROOM.WLD takes to converge without it.

To save the image to a BMP file:

1. Choose *File* from the menu bar.
2. Choose the *Save As...* menu item to display the *Save As* common dialog box and specify an appropriate directory and file name. The file can later be viewed using Microsoft Paintbrush or any other BMP-compatible graphics program capable of displaying at least 32,768 colors.

Finally, we can:

1. Choose *Help* from the menu bar.
2. Choose the *About Helios...* menu item to display the *About HELIOS* dialog box.

to confirm which version of *HELIOS* we are currently running.

The preface promised that radiosity is "fascinating to experiment with." This demonstration of *HELIOS* should fulfill that promise.

6.13 CONCLUSIONS

We began this chapter with a promise that solving the radiosity equation would be easy in comparison to the material presented in the preceding chapters. Looking back, you may be inclined to disagree. However, look again at the progressive refinement radiosity algorithm outlined in Figure 6.4. This is the radiosity approach in its entirety! Everything else can be considered bothersome implementation details.

More to the point, we can take some pride in having developed three functional versions of *HELIOS*. At some 7,000 lines of C++ source code, it represents a medium-sized software engineering project for one person. Seen from a different perspective, it offers a surprising amount of functionality for its size. This is due in no small part to the underlying graphical user interface provided by MS-Windows—can you imagine implementing *HELIOS* under MS-DOS?

So, we finally have our radiosity-based rendering program. True, we have to create our environment and entity data files by hand, which can be a nuisance. Do this enough times and you will be ready and willing to write your own AutoCAD DXF translator. (See the accompanying diskette for a simple example.) Before then, however, we need to determine how an environment should be meshed to produce the best radiosity rendering results.

REFERENCES

Baum, D. R., H. E. Rushmeier, and J. M. Winget .1989. "Improving Radiosity Solutions through the Use of Analytically Determined Form Factors," *Computer Graphics* 23(3):325–334 (ACM SIGGRAPH '89 Proc.).

Burden, R. L., and J. D. Faires. 1985. *Numerical Analysis*. Boston MA: Prindle, Weber & Schmidt.

Cohen, M. F., S. E. Chen, J. R. Wallace, and D. P. Greenberg. 1988. "A Progressive Refinement Approach to Fast Radiosity Image Generation," *Computer Graphics* 22(4):75–84 (ACM SIGGRAPH '88 Proc.)

Cohen, M. F., and D. P. Greenberg. 1985. "The Hemi-Cube: A Radiosity Solution for Complex Environments," *Computer Graphics* 19(3):31–40 (ACM SIGGRAPH '85 Proc.).

Cohen, M. F., D. P. Greenberg, D. S. Immel, and P. J. Brock. 1986. "An Efficient Radiosity Approach for Realistic Image Synthesis," *IEEE Computer Graphics and Applications* 6(3):26–35.

Cohen, M. F., and J. R. Wallace. 1993. *Radiosity and Realistic Image Synthesis*. San Diego, CA: Academic Press.

Feda, M., and W. Purgathofer. 1992. "Accelerating Radiosity by Overshooting," *Proc. Third Eurographics Workshop on Rendering*, Bristol, England.

Gastinel, N. 1970. *Linear Numerical Analysis*. San Diego, CA: Academic Press.

Golub, G. H. and C. F. Van Loan. 1983. *Matrix Computations*. Baltimore, MD: Johns Hopkins University Press.

Gortler, S., and M. F. Cohen. 1993a. *Radiosity and Relaxation Methods: Progressive Refinement Is Southwell Relaxation*. Princeton, NJ: Princeton University, Technical Report CS-TR-408-93.

Greiner, G., W. Heidrich, and P. Slusallek. 1993. "Blockwise Refinement–A New Method for Solving the Radiosity Problem," *Proc. Fourth Eurographics Workshop on Rendering*, Paris, France, pp. 233–245.

Heckbert, P. S. 1991. "Simulating Global Illumination Using Adaptive Meshing," Ph.D. thesis, University of California Berkeley, Technical Report UCB/CSD 91/636.

Kajiya, J. T. 1986. "The Rendering Equation," *Computer Graphics* 20(4):143–150 (ACM SIGGRAPH '86 Proc.).

Noble, B. 1969. *Applied Linear Algebra*. Englewood Cliffs, NJ: Prentice Hall.

Shao, M., and N. I. Badler. 1993a. *A Gathering and Shooting Progressive Refinement Radiosity Method*. Department of Computer and Information Science, University of Pennsylvania, Technical Report MS-CIS-93-03.

Shao, M., and N. I. Badler. 1993b. "Analysis and Acceleration of Progressive Refinement Radiosity Method," *Proc. Fourth Eurographics Workshop on Rendering*, Paris, France.

Wallace, J. R., K. A. Elmquist, and E. A. Haines. 1989. "A Ray Tracing Algorithm for Progressive Radiosity," *Computer Graphics* 23(3):315–324 (ACM SIGGRAPH '89 Proc.).

CHAPTER

7

Meshing Strategies

INTRODUCTION

Looking at our first radiosity-based images, we quickly become aware that the accuracy of the radiosity approach is very much dependent on the underlying mesh of elements used to represent each surface. Although the images may display soft shadows and subtle color bleeding effects, their details are limited by the size and shape of the underlying elements. This is particularly evident where surfaces are close to one another—there are no sharp shadow edges.

We can see this problem more clearly in Figure 7.1. The continuous curve represents the "true" exitance distribution $M(x)$ that we might measure across a surface

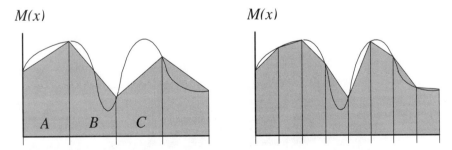

Figure 7.1 Interpolating shadow details with a closely spaced mesh

in a physical environment. Looking at this surface, we would see the steeply sloped portions of the curve as reasonably well-defined shadow edges.

Now suppose we model this surface as an array of elements. The vertical lines then indicate the positions of the element vertices, and the height of each line represents the exitance at that vertex. The shaded gray area connecting these lines represents the linearly interpolated exitance at each point on the surface. In a three-dimensional environment, this interpolation would be the result of Gouraud shading (Section 4.13).

This demonstrates the need to choose an appropriately spaced mesh of elements. If the mesh is too coarse, there may be excessive interpolation errors between the vertices (C). These become evident in the rendered image as missing shadow details (B) and unrealistically soft shadow edges. In some cases, the outlines of the elements themselves may become visible.

One brute force solution to this problem is to finely mesh each surface such that individual elements are too small to be visible in any rendered image. This works, but the cost in terms of memory requirements and execution times quickly becomes unmanageable. It is also inefficient because there is no reason to finely mesh the surface where the change in exitance is relatively constant (A).

7.1 NONUNIFORM MESHING TECHNIQUES

A better approach is to employ a nonuniform element spacing such as that shown in Figure 7.2. Here the element vertices are placed such that the interpolation error at any point on the surface does not exceed some predetermined maximum value. Large, smoothly shaded areas of the surface can be represented by relatively few elements, whereas the shadow edges and other areas where the true surface exitance $M(x)$ changes abruptly can be represented by small and closely spaced elements.

Of course, the problem with this scheme is that we need to know the distribution of shadows in the environment before we begin solving the radiosity equation. To rephrase this slightly, we need to know the solution to the radiosity equation in order to create an appropriate mesh that allows us to solve the radiosity equation.

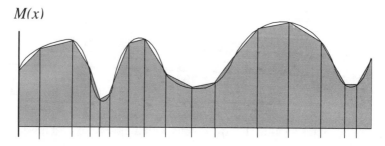

Figure 7.2 Interpolating shadows details with a nonuniform mesh

There are several solutions to this circular reasoning. We can attempt to predict a priori where the shadows will occur when we generate our initial mesh for an environment. This allows us to concentrate elements where we suspect the exitance distribution will change rapidly across a surface. We can also iteratively *refine* our mesh after each step in solving the radiosity equation. We can split or merge elements, move element vertices, or create an entirely new mesh as required.

The great advantage of these solutions is that they can be automated. That is, we can provide our radiosity renderer with a geometric description of an environment and let these *meshing algorithms* decide how to mesh each surface. There may be some touch-up work required to obtain a suitable mesh, but most of the work will have been done for us.

7.2 MESHING STRATEGIES

Having said this, there are two disadvantages that prevent us from implementing these algorithms within the context of *HELIOS*. First, they require a detailed knowledge of the geometry of each object in the environment. This information is available from our environment data structure, but it can be difficult and time consuming to obtain. A more flexible geometrical representation is generally required.

The second disadvantage is more immediate. We have a limited amount of space remaining in which to discuss both meshing techniques and other radiosity approaches. This book is about radiosity, not automatic meshing algorithms. Moreover, a detailed discussion and implementation of these algorithms properly deserves an entire book.

This leaves us with one option. We will have to create our initial meshes by hand and modify them based on our analysis of the rendered images. To this end, we need to develop a set of heuristic rules, or *meshing strategies*, that will allow us to understand and predict the cause-and-effect relationship between element meshes and what we see in the images.

HELIOS is admittedly incomplete. Entering thousands of vertices by hand is obviously impractical for truly complex environments. Also, a professional implementation should include an automatic meshing algorithm that relieves the user of having to understand the following strategies. To this end, the following discussions include numerous references for further study. *HELIOS* was designed from the beginning to be extensible; the challenge is to use it as a testbed for your own experiments and investigations.

7.3 GENERATING INPUT FILES

The easiest way to create an entity data file is to use a commercial three-dimensional CAD program such as AutoDesk's AutoCAD. As we noted in Chapter 3, these programs offer many more features than we shall ever require. On the other hand, their ability to model complex three-dimensional surfaces is essential for any truly serious radiosity-rendering efforts. Although we do not have the space here that is needed to develop a CAD file translation utility, we should nevertheless examine the issues involved in generating input files.

7.3.1   Surface Orientation

One problem common to many three-dimensional CAD programs is that they do not enforce the concept of a surface having a visible side. The user is expected to specify a surface as an ordered sequence of vertices, but the concept of a surface normal is undefined. If these vertices are imported as is into our entity files, there is no guarantee that the surfaces will be properly oriented. The popular AutoCAD DXF file format (Autodesk 1992a–c) is a good example—users must often "flip" surface normals when transferring DXF files to a more capable CAD program.

One practical solution is to display the CAD files using shaded surfaces. If a surface faces away from the camera, it should be displayed as a wireframe. A user interface command then allows the user to identify and interactively "flip" incorrectly oriented surfaces by reordering their vertices. Smith (1991), Baum et al. (1991, which is an expanded version of Smith 1991), and Blinn (1993) offer several practical suggestions on how to perform this interactive preprocessing of CAD files.

7.3.2   Surfaces versus Solids

Another problem—and this also applies to our own entity data files—is that a physical surface has two sides. There is no problem in an exterior wall of our test environment room (Section 6.12), for example, having only one visible side. The radiant flux in the room will never encounter the invisible side of these surfaces. Similarly, each surface of our solid light fixtures and bench need only one visible side. However, consider a sheet of paper suspended in midair. (This is, after all, virtual reality.) While we may see its visible side from our camera position in the room, we must remember that light is flowing though the environment in all directions. The paper may cast a shadow on the floor, which is reasonable. However, the light subsequently reflected from within this shadow will pass right through the invisible side of the paper if it is modeled as a single surface. To avoid this anomaly, we need to model the paper as having two visible sides; that is, with two identical and coplanar surfaces facing in opposite directions.

This highlights an important point: The radiosity approach interacts with solid objects in an environment. The implication is that the environment data file should be created with a solid modeling program that intrinsically enforces this concept.

Until such programs become widely available, however, we shall have to expect data input from less capable three-dimensional CAD programs.

7.3.3 Coplanar Surfaces

Coplanar surfaces present yet another problem. Suppose we have a (single-sided) sheet of paper lying on a desktop surface. Unfortunately, our vertex coordinates and Z-buffering algorithm have a finite depth precision. It may well be that the two surfaces are no longer exactly coplanar after their vertex coordinates have been independently scaled, translated, rotated, and interpolated during perspective projection and clipping. At worst, the paper may appear to be partially embedded in the desktop when the two surfaces are rendered.

It is not always evident which of two coplanar surfaces should be visible. Baum et al. (1991) adopted the heuristic that the smaller of the two surfaces should remain visible. The larger, underlying surface is then topologically modified by "cutting a hole" in it to accommodate the visible surface.

7.3.4 Merging Surfaces

A CAD user will often build a complex surface piece by piece. Although the final result may look correct when rendered as a shaded image, it may be that adjoining vertices are almost but not quite coincident (e.g., Segal 1990). Baum et al. (1991) simplified these surfaces by first determining whether adjoining surfaces consisted of the same material (i.e., they had the same reflectance properties). If so, then any vertices whose three-dimensional coordinates were less than some minimum distance apart are merged. (Vertex coordinates were stored in an octree data structure to simplify their comparison.) Once this was done, the edges were then merged as well to create a contiguous set of surfaces (e.g., Fig. 7.3).

Baum et al. (1991) also found it convenient to merge complex surface sets into single (but possibly topologically complex) surfaces (e.g., Fig. 7.4). This made sub-

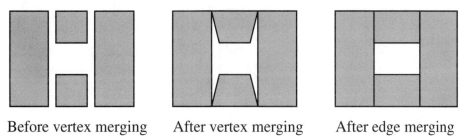

Before vertex merging   After vertex merging   After edge merging

Figure 7.3 Vertex and edge merging for complex surfaces

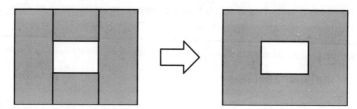

Figure 7.4   Merging surfaces

sequent division of these *maximally connected* surfaces into a mesh of elements a more controllable process with fewer geometric constraints.

7.3.5   T-Vertex Elimination

A second reason to merge complex sets of common surfaces is that it eliminates *T-vertices* (Fig. 7.5). As Baum et al. (1991) observed, these vertices create several problems. For example, the additional vertex along a common edge between two elements can create discontinuities when they are Gouraud shaded. In Figure 7.5, the calculated exitance at vertex C will likely differ from the exitance interpolated at that point from the vertices A, D, and E (see Section 4.13 for details). The resultant differences in shading may be visible as a line extending from vertices A to D.

   A more serious problem may occur due to the finite precision of the floating-point arithmetic used to manipulate the vertex coordinates. Suppose in Figure 7.5 that vertices A, D, and E represent one element. If the T-vertex C is not exactly coincident with the edge defined by A and D, there may be a noticeable gap between the elements in the rendered edges. (as shown in Fig. 7.6).

   T-vertices are less of a problem when they occur on the edges separating different surfaces because each surface is independently shaded. However, gaps between these surfaces (also referred to as pixel dropouts) may still occur due to floating-point roundoff. These gaps will also occur between elements of the same surface.

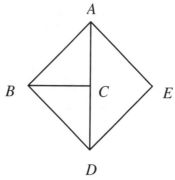

Figure 7.5   Vertex C, a T-vertex

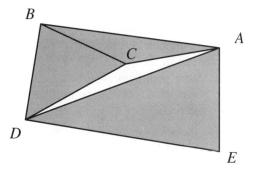

Figure 7.6 Gap between elements created by T-vertex

They are never more than a single pixel wide, which makes them easy to distinguish from errors in the entity data files.

Baum et al. (1991) proposed that edges of adjoining polygons be "ziplocked" by using identical sets of vertices for each edge. For example, if the triangle *A-D-E* in Figure 7.5 were a different surface from *A-B-C* and *B-D-C*, ziplocking would change it into the quadrilateral *A-C-D-E*. (The addition of vertices may require that the original elements be split into quadrilaterals and triangles to limit their number of edges to four. Alternatively, ziplocking can be done immediately before displaying the image if the three-dimensional graphics package supports more complex polygons.)

While eliminating T-vertices from a mesh is highly recommended, it is not essential. Cohen and Wallace (1993) describe their use as *slave* vertices. A mesh is developed with T-vertices and solved using one of the radiosity algorithms presented in Chapter 6. However, the exitances of the T-vertices are not used when it comes time to display the elements using Gouraud shading. Instead, they are linearly interpolated from those of the edge endpoint vertices (e.g., *A* and *D* in Fig. 7.5). This may introduce some small amount of error into the radiosity solution. However, it ensures that the Gouraud-shaded elements of a surface do not exhibit any visible discontinuities at their edges.

7.3.6   Preprocessing CAD Files

Baum et al. (1991) incorporated the rules just given in a series of filter programs that preprocessed AutoCAD DXF files for radiosity-rendering applications (see also Smith 1991). Although such programs are undeniably useful, they represent a major software development effort that clearly extends beyond the scope of this book. Fortunately, much of the discussion just presented can be applied equally well to input files that are generated by hand.

A much simpler but still useful approach is to use a three-dimensional CAD program to create initial surface meshes for our entity files. AutoCAD, for instance, can be used to model the surfaces as polygon meshes and generate DXF files. Creating a program that reads these files and generates an output file of surfaces, patches, and elements is straightforward. The technical details of the DXF file format are described in Autodesk (1992a–c), and an example DXF file parser is included on the diskette accompanying this book. This relieves much of the tedium involved in creating entity files by hand using a text editor.

One problem inherent in the AutoCAD DXF and similar CAD file formats is that they do not include the geometrical information needed by automatic meshing algorithms. However, Baum et al. (1991) found that this information can be derived from such files during the process of merging vertices, edges, and surfaces and storing the files in a winged-edge data structure. Thus, although they are by no means ideal, most CAD file formats can be used to represent environments for radiosity-based rendering programs.

7.4   MESHING CONSIDERATIONS

There are many ways in which light can interact with a mesh of elements. We have already seen some examples. For example, (a) a nonuniform mesh is needed to capture exitance gradients efficiently; (b) aliasing effects can occur at shadow edges if the mesh is too coarse; and (c) small shadow details can be missed entirely by a coarse mesh. We need to consider these and other interactions and from them develop more heuristic rules for our mesh design strategies.

7.4.1   Aliasing Effects and Discontinuity Meshing

Aliasing effects require further explanation. Consider a sharply defined shadow edge that is diagonal to a set of elements (Fig. 7.7). There are two related problems here. First, the expanded view of one element indicates that the surface exitance should be zero inside the shadow and 100 otherwise. However, the screen scan line drawn across the element indicates that Gouraud shading would show a continuous decrease in screen luminance from left to right. Looking at the set of elements in a rendered image, we would see the shadow as having a staircase appearance that clearly indicates the underlying element mesh.

This problem has an obvious but difficult solution: Orient the elements such that their edges follow the shadow boundaries. This allows Gouraud-shaded elements

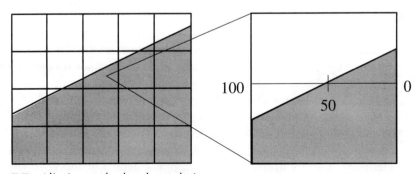

Figure 7.7   Aliasing at shadow boundaries

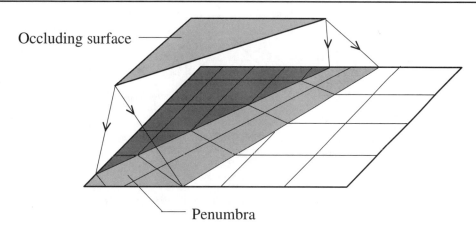

Figure 7.8   Minimizing shadow aliasing artifacts with discontinuity meshing

to accurately follow the contours of the shadow edges. We ideally want the boundaries to follow the edges of soft shadows as well (Fig. 7.8). The trick is to determine where these boundaries occur.

This is where automatic meshing algorithms are useful. We can perform an *a priori* geometrical analysis of the environment to determine where shadows will most likely occur. Nishita and Nakamae (1985) and Campbell and Fussell (1990) did this by shooting "shadow rays" from the light sources to project silhouettes of objects onto surfaces. This defines both the umbrae (shadows) and penumbrae (literally, "almost shadows") cast by the object onto the surfaces, much as our ray-casting radiosity algorithm determines vertex-to-source form factors. These silhouettes provide the geometrical information needed to align surface elements with the penumbra boundaries.

Heckbert (1991) referred to these boundaries as "discontinuities" in the surface exitance distribution. Efficient *discontinuity meshing* algorithms for determining optimal element meshes are presented in Heckbert (1992), Lischinski et al. (1992), and Tampieri (1993). (See also Cohen and Wallace 1993 for a detailed summary.) Unfortunately, these algorithms are too involved to discuss or implement here.

One problem with discontinuity meshing is that it can identify only shadows due to direct illumination from light sources. There may be circumstances in which well-defined soft shadows are a result of indirect lighting from highly reflective surfaces. These generally cannot be identified until the radiosity equation has been at least partially solved.

7.4.2   Gouraud-Shading Anomalies

The second aliasing problem has to do with Gouraud shading in general. Remember that this is done in screen space. That is, we are really interpolating pixel luminances rather than surface exitances. Every time we reorient the quadrilateral element shown in Figure 7.9, the scan line has a different pair of endpoint pixel luminances to inter-

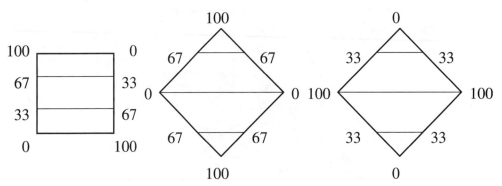

Figure 7.9 Gouraud-shading anomalies due to screen-space orientation

polate between. From this, we can see that the appearance of the element will change as we change our camera view position and orientation in an environment.

Note that this problem applies only to quadrilateral elements; it does not occur when triangular elements are rendered. This suggests the simple solution of splitting quadrilaterals into triangles. Since the problem occurs only during the shading process, we can perform this triangulation in screen space immediately before Gouraud interpolation.

Airey et al. (1990) and Haines (1991) recommended splitting quadrilaterals such that the endpoints of the diagonal edge have the least exitance difference (averaged over all three color bands). If, for example, a quadrilateral element has average vertex exitances values of 1.0, 2.0, 3.0, and 7.0, it would be split with a new edge extending from the first to the third vertex. This tends to smooth out aliasing at shadow boundaries and alleviate other shading problems.

A more rigorous (and computationally expensive) solution is to perform bilinear interpolation of exitances in world space directly on the surface of each element (e.g., Cohen and Wallace 1993). This also solves another problem with Gouraud shading. The perspective projection of an element's coordinates from world space to screen space results in the element depth coordinates being distorted (Section 4.3). Thus, linear interpolation between two points of an element's edge is not entirely correct because the element depth along the scan line may change in a nonlinear fashion. On the other hand, linear interpolation is itself an approximation, and so we can generally ignore this problem. (See Blinn 1992 for another approach.)

7.4.3   Mach Banding

Mach banding is another issue that is exacerbated by Gouraud shading. The human visual system is acutely sensitive to edges in its field of view. When we look at an edge between a dark gray and a white surface, we often perceive the gray as being darker and the white as being whiter adjacent to the edge. This is a purely physiological effect— measuring the surface luminance at these points would show no such anomalies.

The problem is that Gouraud shading creates sudden changes in surface luminance at element edges (e.g., Fig. 7.1). We perceive these changes as being edges within what should be smoothly shaded surfaces. The edges become more noticeable when the surfaces are large in the rendered image. They also occur where the slope of the exitance distribution changes rapidly across the surface, such as within soft shadows.

Mach banding problems can be minimized by using a finer element mesh. Another approach is to perform a higher-order interpolation between vertex exitances. Referring to Figure 7.1, we can replace the straight lines connecting the vertices with curves that are described by quadratic or cubic equations. In two dimensions, this is equivalent to modeling a curved surface with Bézier or B-spline surfaces (e.g., Foley et al. 1990), except that the two-dimensional "surface" we are trying to model is the true exitance distribution $M(x)$. A detailed review of these interpolation techniques is presented in Cohen and Wallace (1993).

7.4.4 Mesh Grading and Aspect Ratios

Mach banding problems can also be alleviated by ensuring that the mesh *grading* is relatively smooth. That is, the difference in areas between adjacent elements should be kept as small as possible. This produces a mesh like that shown in Figure 7.10 (where T-vertices have been allowed for illustrational clarity).

One consequence of a smooth mesh grading is that the individual elements tend to have a small *aspect ratio*, which is defined as the ratio of the inner and outer bounding circles (Fig. 7.11) for the element vertices (e.g., Baum et al. 1991). Such elements are referred to as being *well shaped*. This has three advantages. First, it maximizes the element area and thereby minimizes the number of elements needed to mesh a surface. Second, it produces elements that approximate circular disks; this is one of the assumptions of the ray-casting radiosity algorithm (Section 5.23). Third, it improves the accuracy of the form factor determination process and through it the radiosity solution (Baum et al. 1989).

Baum et al. (1991) suggested subdividing quadrilaterals and triangles into four by placing new vertices at the midpoint of each element edge, as shown in Figure 7.12. If the parent element is well shaped, then each of its child elements will also be

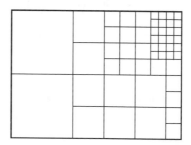

Figure 7.10 Smooth mesh grading

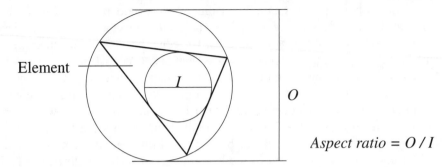

Figure 7.11   Element aspect ratio determination

well shaped. This is particularly convenient when it comes to subdividing elements with an automatic meshing algorithm.

7.4.5   Light and Shadow Leakage

Finally, we need to recognize the consequences of randomly placing one entity on top of another. Consider a flat surface with a vertical partition dividing it (Fig. 7.13). The two gray elements on the flat surface receive flux that is shot from the light source. However, these elements are divided by the partition. When they later shoot their flux, it will be sent to both sides of the partition. In other words, there is *light leakage* through the partition (Bullis 1989 and Campbell and Fussell 1990).

Suppose the partition is a wall that divides two rooms. If only one of the rooms is illuminated, we will see in the rendered image that the wall apparently has a gap between it and the floor, with light spilling through to illuminate the darkened room. This is an interesting effect, but definitely not what was intended! Similarly, this light is lost from the illuminated room. The floor elements adjacent to the wall will appear darker than they should, so that we also have *shadow leakage* from the darkened room.

The solution is to ensure that element boundaries are aligned not only with the shadow boundaries (as in discontinuity meshing) but also with the surface boundaries of other entity surfaces. Baum et al. (1991) performed this alignment automatically using algorithms presented in Segal (1990) and Segal and Séquin (1988).

This is perhaps the most difficult and frustrating aspect of meshing, since one or

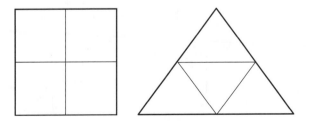

Figure 7.12   Four-to-one subdivision of well-shaped elements

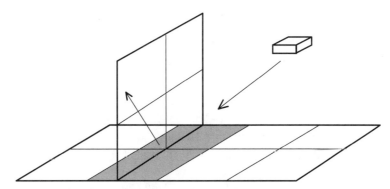

Figure 7.13 Mismatched element boundaries allowing light and shadow leakage

more surfaces usually need to be remeshed whenever an object is moved in the environment. On the other hand, it should be recognized that remeshing is not necessary in each instance, nor will light and shadow leakage be significant in many cases. It is largely a matter of experience, subjective judgment, and most important, trial and error.

7.5 ADAPTIVE SUBDIVISION

Most of the meshing considerations just discussed can be implemented manually as a set of rules to follow when designing an initial mesh. However, there are limits to how many patches and elements we can expect a user to generate. A better solution is to begin with a coarse mesh and let an automatic meshing algorithm iteratively refine it after each step in solving the radiosity equation. This allows the program to develop a mesh that concentrates elements at shadow boundaries and other regions where the exitance distribution changes rapidly.

Again, we do not have the space to implement an automatic meshing algorithm within the context of *HELIOS*. However, it is instructive to review how we might implement one.

There are several possibilities for mesh refinement (e.g., Cohen and Wallace 1993 and Ho-Le 1988). We can, for example, reposition the element vertices to align them with the shadow boundaries (e.g., Aguas et al. 1993). This is useful to some extent, but it assumes that the mesh spacing is such that the number of elements is sufficient to represent the shadow details. It can also result in thin elements that are not well shaped.

A second possibility is to subdivide the elements. This *adaptive subdivision* allows us to generate new elements only where they are most needed. Following the heuristic rules presented above, we ideally want to:

1. Minimize element aspect ratios.
2. Minimize element vertex-to-vertex exitance differences.
3. Avoid T-vertices.
4. Ensure a smooth mesh grading.

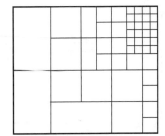 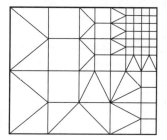

Figure 7.14a A balanced mesh   **Figure 7.14b** A balanced and anchored mesh

When should an element be subdivided? One criterion is to compare the element vertex exitances and subdivide only if they differ by more than some predetermined amount in any color band with respect to the range of reflected vertex exitances in the environment. There are more involved criteria that result in fewer elements being subdivided (e.g., Cohen and Wallace 1993), but this criterion is usually sufficient.

We also need some sort of stopping criterion. This is relatively easy: We stop when the subdivided element area becomes too small to be significant in a rendered image. Since each subdivision produces four child elements such that each has approximately one-quarter of the parent element's area (Fig. 7.11), the process will likely stop at third or fourth level.

If we begin with a smooth mesh grading, subdividing elements according to Figure 7.12 will ensure that the mesh remains smoothly graded. It will also tend to minimize the subdivided element aspect ratios. Baum et al. 1991 suggested that the initial mesh should be *balanced* by ensuring that each element of a surface should be adjacent to no more than two other elements along any of its edges (Fig. 7.14a).

Every subdivision will unavoidably generate new T-vertices. Baum et al. 1991 also suggested that neighboring elements should be *anchored* to these vertices. That is, the neighboring elements are further subdivided by connecting the T-vertex to another vertex in the same element (Fig. 7.14b). Assuming that only triangular and quadrilateral elements are allowed and ignoring symmetry, there are only six possibilities for anchoring (Fig. 7.15). This simplifies the development of an automatic meshing algorithm that supports balanced and anchored mesh elements.

7.5.1 Winged-Edged Data Structures

So what is the mystique behind creating a meshing algorithm? It certainly looks simple enough: Add a few new elements and vertices to the environment data structure and the problem is mostly solved.

The real problem is in those minor implementation details. If we use one of the progressive refinement radiosity algorithms from Chapter 6, we need to know which elements share a vertex in order to interpolate its exitance. We also need to know this information before we can interpolate a vertex's normal. This is the reason why each

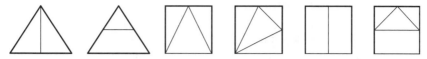

Figure 7.15   Element anchor morphology

of our *Vertex3* objects maintains a linked list of pointers to the *Element3* objects that share it.

Now, suppose we want to subdivide a parent element to create four child elements. The first step is to insert new vertices midway between each pair of existing vertices (which define the element edges). This is easy enough, although we should check beforehand to see whether a T-vertex belonging to an adjacent element of the same surface is already at that position. If it is, then we must use it instead.

This poses a question: Which other elements of the surface share this edge of the parent element? If T-vertices are allowed, there could be any number of elements. We would have to check every edge of every other element in the *Instance* object to determine whether it is collinear with current edge and whether the new vertex intersects it.

We have to repeat this process for every vertex we consider when subdividing an element. This includes existing T-vertices, since we have to update their element lists when we split the parent element at that point. The process clearly becomes unmanageable for even moderately complex environments.

The proper solution to this situation is to redesign our environment data structures from *Vertex3* upward as a winged edge data structure. These are described in detail in Baumgart (1974, 1975). Further details are provided by Glassner (1991), Hanrahan (1982), Mäntlyä and Sulonen (1982), Weiler (1985), and Wilson (1985).

The advantage of the winged-edge data structure is that it provides a wealth of geometric connectivity information concerning the vertices, edges, and polygonal faces of a three-dimensional solid object. The above question becomes trivial, since the winged-edge data structure directly encodes information about which elements share an edge.

The disadvantage is that the winged-edge data structure can be difficult to implement properly. For example, an implementation described in part by Glassner (1991) requires 19 algorithmic steps to insert a new edge between two existing vertices. Glassner punctuates his description of the data structure with such disclaimers as, "You have to make sure you do things in just the right order, or disaster will ensue" and, "I have provided only some signposts around what I found to be the most twisting parts of the road." Comments like these indicate that designing a robust and efficient winged edge data representation is not without its own perils.

Winged-edge data structures have been used in many radiosity-rendering programs (e.g., Cohen et al. 1986, Baum et al. 1991, and Lischinski et al. 1992), and with good reason. They offer an elegant means of accessing the geometrical information needed by both adaptive subdivision and discontinuity meshing algorithms. It is unfortunate that their complexity precluded their description in this book.

7.5.2   Patches and Form Factors

We have so far discussed the adaptive subdivision of element meshes. Cohen et al. (1986) noted that there are two occasions where patches may need to be subdivided as well. For example, subdivision is required when the differences between patch vertex exitances in any color band exceed some predetermined limit, similar to the criterion we used for subdividing elements.

The second occasion is less obvious. Recalling the progressive refinement radiosity algorithm presented in Figure 6.4, we calculate the form factor F_{ij} from a patch E_i to all other elements E_j in the environment. This can be done using either the hemicube or cubic tetrahedral algorithm from Chapter 5. However, we then calculate the delta exitance ΔM to be sent to each of these elements as:

$$\Delta M = \rho_j F_{ij} \Delta M_i^{unsent} \frac{A_i}{A_j} = \rho_j F_{ji} \Delta M_i^{unsent} \qquad (7.1)$$

since the reciprocity relation (Section 2.5) states that $A_i F_{ij} = A_j F_{ji}$.

The problem is that we obtain an approximate value of F_{ij} by modeling E_i as a differential element located at the center of the patch. If the area of E_i is much larger than that of E_j, the calculated value of the reciprocal form factor F_{ji} can clearly exceed unity at some point. This is a serious error because it implies that the element E_j will receive more exitance than the patch E_i has sent into the environment!

There are several possible solutions. First, we can ensure that the range of element sizes does not become excessive. The minimum value of F_{ij} is that of the smallest delta form factor for the hemicube or cubic tetrahedron. By limiting the ratio A_i/A_j, we can guarantee that F_{ji} will never exceed unity.

Subdividing the patch is a second possibility that has the same effect. Its advantage is that the process becomes transparent to the user. On the other hand, it will require a number of modifications to both the element meshing and form factor determination algorithms.

The third possibility was suggested by Chen (1991) and was used in our implementation of the progressive refinement radiosity algorithm (Listing 6.3). The reciprocal form factor is simply (and silently) clipped to unity.

7.6   CONCLUSIONS

This chapter has outlined the issues involved in developing suitable meshes for the radiosity equation. Although we did not have the space to develop an adaptive subdivision algorithm, we now have a much better understanding of the cause-and-effect relationship between an element mesh and the rendered images. The meshing strategies developed in this chapter should help in improving the images that *HELIOS* creates.

There is a deep and fundamental relationship between the radiosity approach and *finite element* methods. These are extremely important tools for scientists and engineers in a number of fields ranging from fluid mechanics and structural engineering to cosmology. The radiosity approach models the field of light in an environment. Finite element methods have been used to model everything from stresses in steel and concrete structures to the magnetic fields of galaxies. The literature on this topic is vast and multidisciplinary. Nevertheless, many of the techniques developed for finite element analysis can be applied to the automatic generation and modification of element meshes for radiosity. Recommended reading includes Baehann et al. (1987), Bank et al. (1983), Chew (1989), Frey (1987), Heckbert and Winget (1991), Hugues (1987), Lalonde (1993), Schuierer (1989), and Watson (1984).

There are numerous challenges here for the ambitious reader. First, *HELIOS* would benefit from a utility that automatically preprocesses CAD files. This could be modeled after the filter programs described in Baum et al. (1991). Full technical details for the AutoCAD DXF file format are presented in Autodesk (1992a–c).

A more challenging project is to redesign the environment data structure presented in Chapter 3 to incorporate the winged-edge data structure. Unfortunately, the few complete sources of information on this topic (e.g., Baumgart 1974, 1975) may be difficult to obtain unless you have access to a large university library or an interlibrary loan service.

With this in place, you could implement one or more adaptive subdivision or discontinuity meshing algorithms (e.g., Lischinski et al. 1992). With these, *HELIOS* would be well on its way to becoming a professional-quality radiosity rendering tool.

Meshing is a difficult problem for which there are no easy solutions. Although it is somewhat incidental to the radiosity equation, a well-shaped mesh is essential to obtaining an accurate approximation to the true radiosity solution, and from it truly photorealistic images. The best we can do for now is to develop our initial meshes, modify them through trial and error, and in general practice what Heckbert (1991) aptly called the "black art" of finite element meshing.

REFERENCES

Aguas, M. P. N., and S. Müller. 1993. "Mesh Redistribution in Radiosity," *Proc. Fourth Eurographics Workshop on Rendering*, Paris, France, pp. 327–335.

Airey, J. M., J. H. Rohlf, and F. P. Brooks, Jr. 1990. "Towards Image Realism with Interactive Update Rates in Complex Virtual Building Environments," *Computer Graphics* 24(1):41–50 (ACM Workshop on Interactive Graphics Proc.).

Arvo, J., Ed. 1991. *Graphic Gems II*. San Diego, CA: Academic Press.

Autodesk. 1992a. *AutoCAD Release 12 Reference Manual*. Sausalito, CA: Autodesk Inc., Publication #100186-02.

Autodesk. 1992b. *AutoCAD Render Reference Manual (Release 12)*. Sausalito, CA: Autodesk Inc., Publication #100190-01.

Autodesk. 1992c. *AutoCAD Development System Programmer's Reference Manual (Release 12)*. Sausalito, CA: Autodesk Inc., Publication #100192-01.

Baehann, P. L., S. L. Wittchen, M. S., Shepard, K. R. Grice, and M. A. Yerry. 1987. "Robust, Geometrically Based, Automatic 2D Mesh Generation," *International Journal of Numerical Methods in Engineering* 24:1043–1078.

Bank, R. E., A. H. Sherman, and A. Weiser. 1983. "Refinement Algorithms and Data Structures for Regular Local Mesh Refinement," in Stepleman (1983), pp. 3–17.

Baum, D. R., S. Mann, K. P. Smith, and J. M. Winget. 1991. "Making Radiosity Usable: Automatic Preprocessing and Meshing Techniques for the Generation of Accurate Radiosity Solutions," *Computer Graphics* 25(4):51–60 (ACM SIGGRAPH '91 Proc.).

Baum, D. R., H. E. Rushmeier, and J. M. Winget. 1989. "Improving Radiosity Solutions through the Use of Analytically Determined Form Factors," *Computer Graphics* 23(3):325–334 (ACM SIGGRAPH '89 Proc.).

Baumgart, B. G. 1974. "Winged-Edge Polyhedron Representation." Palo Alto, CA, Stanford University, Technical Report STAN-CS-320.

Baumgart, B. G. 1975. "A Polyhedron Representation for Computer Vision," *Proc. National Computer Conference '75*, pp. 589–596.

Blinn, J. F. 1992. "Hyperbolic Interpolation," *IEEE Computer Graphics & Applications* 12(4):89–94.

Blinn, J. 1993. "Jim Blinn's Corner: Backface Culling Snags," *IEEE Computer Graphics & Applications* 13(6):94–97.

Bullis, J. M. 1989. *Models and Algorithms for Computing Realistic Images Containing Diffuse Reflections*. Master's thesis, Univeresity of Minnesota, Minneapolis.

Campbell, A. T. III, and D. S. Fussell. 1990. "Adaptive Mesh Generation for Global Diffuse Illumination," *Computer Graphics* 24(4):155–164 (ACM SIGGRAPH '90 Proc.).

Chen, S. E. 1991. "Implementing Progressive Radiosity with User-Provided Polygon Display Routines," in Arvo (1991), pp. 295–298, 583–597.

Chew, L. P. 1989. "Guaranteed-Quality Triangular Meshes." Department of Computer Science, Cornell University, Ithaca, NY, Technical Report 89-893.

Cohen, M. F., S. E. Chen, J. R. Wallace, and D. P. Greenberg. 1988. "A Progressive Refinement Approach to Fast Radiosity Image Generation," *Computer Graphics* 22(4):75–84 (ACM SIGGRAPH '88 Proc.).

Cohen, M. F., D. P. Greenberg, D. S. Immel, and P. J. Brock. 1986. "An Efficient Radiosity Approach for Realistic Image Synthesis," *IEEE Computer Graphics and Applications* 6(3):26-35.

Cohen, M. F., and J. R. Wallace. 1993. *Radiosity and Realistic Image Synthesis*. San Diego, CA: Academic Press.

Foley, J. D., A. van Dam, S. K. Feiner, and J. F. Hughes. 1990. *Computer Graphics: Principles and Practice* (2nd ed.). Reading, MA: Addison-Wesley.

Frey, W. H. 1987. "Selective Refinement: A New Strategy for Automatic Node Placement in Graded Triangular Meshes," *International Journal of Numerical Methods in Engineering* 24:2183–2200.

George, P. 1991. *Automatic Mesh Generation*. New York, NY: John Wiley & Sons.

Glassner, A. S. 1991. "Maintaining Winged-Edge Models," in Arvo (1991), pp. 191–201.

Haines, E. 1991. "Ronchamp: A Case Study for Radiosity," *ACM SIGGRAPH '91 Frontiers in Radiosity Course Notes.*

Hanrahan, P. 1982. "Creating Volume Models from Edge-Vertex Graphs," *Computer Graphics* 16(3):77–84 (ACM SIGGRAPH '82 Proc.).

Heckbert, P. S. 1991. "Simulating Global Illumination Using Adaptive Meshing," Ph.D. thesis, University of California Berkeley, Technical Report UCB/CSD 91/636.

Heckbert, P. S. 1992. "Discontinuity Meshing for Radiosity," *Proc. Third Eurographics Workshop on Rendering*, Bristol, England.

Heckbert, P. S., and J. M. Winget 1991. "Finite Element Methods for Global Illumination, " University of California Berkeley, Technical Report UCB/CSD 91/643.

Ho-Le, K. 1988. "Finite Element Mesh Generation Methods: A Review and Classification," *Computer-Aided Design* 20:27–38.

Hugues, T. J. R. 1987. *The Finite Element Method.* Englewood Cliffs, NJ: Prentice-Hall.

Lalonde, P. 1993. "An Adaptive Discretization Method for Progressive Radiosity," *Graphics Interface '93*, Toronto, Ontario, pp. 78–86.

Languénou, E., K. Bouatouch, and P. Tellier 1992. "An Adaptive Discretization Method for Radiosity," *Computer Graphics Forum* 11(3):C-205–C-216 (Eurographics '92 Proc.).

Lischinski, D., F. Tampieri, and D. P. Greenberg 1992. "Discontinuity Meshing for Accurate Radiosity," *IEEE Computer Graphics and Applications* 12(6):25 –39.

Mäntylä, M., and R. Sulonen 1982. "Gwb —A Solid Modeler with Euler Operators," *IEEE Computer Graphics & Applications* 2(7):17–31.

Nishita, T., and E. Nakamae. 1985. "Continuous Tone Representation of Three-Dimensional Objects Taking Account of Shadows and Interreflection," *Computer Graphics* 19(3):23–30 (ACM SIGGRAPH '85 Proc.).

Samet, H. 1989. *The Design and Analysis of Spatial Data Structures.* Reading, MA: Addison-Wesley.

Schuierer, S. 1989. "Delaunay Triangulations and the Radiosity Approach," *Eurographics '89* (Proc. European Computer Graphics Conference and Exhibition), W. Hansmann, F. R. A. Hopgood, and W. Strasser, eds. Amsterdam: Elsevier Science Publishers B.V. (North-Holland), pp. 345–353.

Segal, M. 1990. "Using Tolerances to Guarantee Valid Polyhedral Modeling Results," *Computer Graphics* 24(4):105–114 (ACM SIGRRAPH '90 Proc.).

Segal, M., and C. H. Séquin. 1988. "Partitioning Polyhedral Objects into Non-Intersecting Parts," *IEEE Computer Graphics & Applications* 8(1):45–52.

Shephard, M. S. 1988. "Approaches to the Automatic Generation and Control of Finite Element Meshes," *Applied Mechanics Review* 41(4):169–185.

Sillion, F. 1991b. "Detection of Shadow Boundaries for Adaptive Meshing in Radiosity," in Arvo (1991), pp. 311–315.

Smith, K. P. 1991. "Fast and Accurate Radiosity-Based Rendering," master's project report, University of California Berkeley, Technical Report UCB/CSD 91/635.

Stepleman, R. S., ed. 1983. *Scientific Computing: Applications of Mathematics and Computing to the Physical Sciences.* New York: North-Holland. IMACS Trans. Scientific Computation, Vol. 1.

Tampieri, F. 1993. *Discontinuity Meshing for Radiosity Image Synthesis*, Ph.D. thesis, Cornell University, Ithaca, NY.

Toussaint, G. 1991. "Efficient Triangulation of Simple Polygons," *The Visual Computer* 7:280–295.

Watson, D. F., and G. M. Philip. 1984. "Systematic Triangulations," *Computer Vision, Graphics and Image Processing* 26(2):217–223.

Weiler, K. 1985. "Edge-Based Data Structures for Solid Modeling in Curved-Surface Environments," *IEEE Computer Graphics & Applications* 3(1):21–40.

Wilson, P. R. 1985. "Euler Formulas and Geometric Modeling," *IEEE Computer Graphics & Applications* 5(8):24–36.

Looking to
the Future

INTRODUCTION

For all the effort we have put into developing *HELIOS*, it is only the beginning. The
full scope of radiosity extends well beyond the limits of this book. We do not have
the space to implement or even discuss many important topics and techniques,
including:

- Modeling complex area and volumetric light sources (Ashdown 1993a, b,
  Bao and Peng 1993, and Languénou and Tellier 1992).
- Semispecular and specular reflections (Chen et al. 1991, Hall and Rushmeier
  1993, Immel et al. 1986, Jessel et al. 1991, Kok et al. 1990, Le Saec and
  Schlick 1990, Rushmeier and Torrance 1990, Sillion and Puech 1989, Sillion
  et al. 1991, and Wallace et al. 1987).
- Bump mapping (Chen and Wu 1990, 1991).
- Participating media (Rushmeier 1988 and Rushmeier and Torrance 1987).
- Parallel processor implementations (Airey et al. 1990, Baum and Winget
  1990, Bu and Deprettere 1987a, b, Chalmers and Paddon 1991, Chen 1991,
  Feda and Purgathofer 1991, Guitton et al. 1991, Hermitage et al. 1990, Jessel
  et al. 1991, Ng and Slater 1993, Price 1989, Purgathofer and Zeller 1990, and
  Shen et al. 1992).
- Higher-order radiosity basis functions (Bian et al. 1992, Cohen and Wallace
  1993, Gortler et al. 1993, Lischinski et al. 1991, Schröder et al. 1993,
  Tampieri and Lischinski 1991, Troutman and Max 1993, and Zatz 1993).
- Other radiosity approaches and related global illumination algorithms (Aup-

perle and Hanrahan 1993, Baranoski 1992, DiLaura and Franck 1993, Dretakkis and Fiume 1991, Greiner et al. 1993, Heckbert 1990, Kawai et al. 1993, Kok 1992, Kok et al. 1993, Liere 1991, Lischinksi et al. 1991, Neumann and Keleman 1991, Neumann and Neumann 1989, 1990, Rushmeier et al. 1993, Salesin et al. 1992, Shao et al. 1988a, b, Tampieri and Lischinksi 1991, Wang et al. 1992, Xu et al. 1989, and Zhou and Peng 1992).

Some of the techniques discussed in these papers are interesting from a theoretical perspective but too demanding in terms of execution time and memory requirements to be of practical use. Others are practical and useful and may have important roles to play in future radiosity developments.

Fortunately, we do have the space to discuss, however briefly, some possible extensions to *HELIOS* that you might consider. They vary from simple modifications to major programming projects.

8.1 Ray-Tracing Techniques

One of the disadvantages of *HELIOS* and the radiosity algorithms discussed in this book is that they can model only opaque and diffuse surfaces. Moreover, these surfaces are intrinsically featureless within each surface. The only details we see are in their shading, due to the field of light in the environment.

This is in sharp contrast to the ray-tracing paradigm, which can model specular and semispecular reflections and transparent or semitransparent objects with relative ease. Texture mapping and Phong illumination techniques—to name a few—offer the possibility of richly detailed images that radiosity methods by themselves can never equal.

8.1.1 Texture Mapping

There is no reason, however, why we cannot borrow these techniques for our radiosity-based images. *Texture mapping* is an excellent example. Suppose that we want to model an office environment as seen from above a wooden desk. Using ray tracing, we would map an image of wood grain to the surface of the desk. The details of this technique can be found in any book on advanced ray-tracing algorithms such as Wilt (1993). (See also Cohen et al. 1986, who discuss it in relation to radiosity-based rendering, and Heckbert 1986 for a comprehensive survey.)

Using radiosity methods, we can model the surface by computing its average spectral reflectance ρ_{avg}. That is, we average the spectral reflectance of each pixel in the texture map image (for each color band) and use this to represent the desktop as an otherwise featureless surface. Clearly, the details of the wood grain will have a mostly insignificant effect on the global radiosity solution.

Once we have solved the radiosity equation for the room and rendered (but not displayed) a preliminary bitmapped image, we can perform a pixel-by-pixel texture mapping of the wood grain to the desk in the image. This requires two operations. First, we need to warp and scale the rectangular wood grain image to the three-dimensional view of the desktop (e.g., Foley et al. 1990). This can become somewhat involved, especially where there are intervening objects between the surface and the synthetic camera position. Fortunately, we have already implemented most of the necessary algorithms in our viewing system.

Second, we need to incorporate the shading details we obtained from our radiosity solution. This is the easy part. Given the Gouraud-interpolated radiant exitance for each color band and visible pixel of the surface, its texture-mapped exitance is simply:

$$\hat{M}_{xy} = M_{xy} \frac{\rho_{xy}}{\rho_{avg}} \tag{8.1}$$

where M_{xy} is the Gouraud-interpolated spectral exitance for a pixel with screen coordinates x and y, ρ_{xy} is the interpolated surface reflectance as determined from the texture map, and M_{xy} is the pixel's texture-mapped spectral exitance.

There is one caveat to this procedure: We cannot always assume that the effect of a texture-mapped surface on the environment can be accurately approximated with a featureless surface having its average spectral reflectance. A surface with large and prominent changes in texture (a black-and-white tiled floor, for example) may locally affect the environment by reflecting patterns of light onto adjacent surfaces (such as a wall). In cases like these, we may have to consider each textured area as a separate surface and model its average reflectance accordingly.

Incorporating texture mapping in *HELIOS* is not exactly a "simple modification." Balanced against this, however, is the marked increase in realism that the technique offers. If you do decide to attempt this extension, the rewards should more than repay the effort.

8.1.2   Phong Illumination Model

One characterization of Gouraud shading is that the surfaces it renders appear uniformly lifeless. This is due to the lack of specular highlights that we subconsciously expect to see in photorealistic images.

In ray tracing, one popular solution to this problem is the *Phong illumination model* (Phong 1975). If we consider the reflection of a ray of light from various surfaces (Fig. 8.1), we realize that a semispecular surface reflects some but not all of the light in a given direction. The more specular the surface, the more light there will be reflected in the general direction of the specularly reflected ray.

Referring to Figure 8.2, we find Phong illumination models semispecular reflections as:

$$L_v = \rho_s L_i \left(\mathbf{u}_v \cdot \mathbf{u}_r \right)^f \tag{8.2}$$

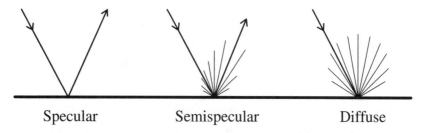

Specular   Semispecular   Diffuse

Figure 8.1 Reflection from specular, semispecular, and diffuse surfaces

where L_i is the luminance of a ray i emitted by a white light point source, L_v is the luminance of the ray v seen by the viewer, ρ_s is the specular reflectance of the surface (which can differ from the surface reflectance), $\mathbf{u}_v$ is a normalized vector pointing in the direction of the viewer, $\mathbf{u}_r$ is a normalized vector pointing in the direction of the reflected ray r, and f is a constant that determines the degree of specularity and that typically ranges from 1 (diffuse) to 200 or so (highly specular).

If the specular reflectance is equal for all three color bands, the resultant reflection will have the same spectral distribution as the light source. This will give the surface a plastic-looking finish. Alternatively, the specular reflectance can be made the same as the surface reflectance. The surface will then appear to have a metallic finish.

The Phong illumination model can be combined with our ray-casting radiosity algorithm as follows: Solving the radiosity equation gives us the diffuse exitance component for each vertex in the environment. Using the existing code in our *Ray-Cast* class, we can determine the visibility of each light source as seen from each vertex. By modeling each source element as a point source located at the element's center, we can solve Equation 8.2 for any given viewpoint within the environment. This solves for the specular exitance component at each vertex. Combining the diffuse and specular components for each vertex, we can then use our Z-buffer and Gouraud-shading algorithms as before to render an image.

As an alternative, and assuming that we have sufficient memory, we can store a linked list of light source visibilities for each vertex when we perform our vertex-to-

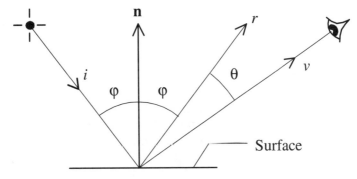

Figure 8.2 Phong illumination model parameters

source form factor calculations. We normally do not need much precision for the visibility value, so that one byte or even one bit could be used for each source.

It is important to note that the Phong illumination model does not consider semispecular reflections within the environment. This means that the resultant image will be somewhat ad hoc in that the radiosity solution does not take these reflections into account. On the other hand, the amount of radiant flux represented by the specular highlights is minuscule compared to the total amount of flux in the environment, and so it has little if any effect on the radiosity solution. Indeed, the only reason for incorporating Phong illumination is to provide the specular and semispecular highlights that add to the realism of the final image.

Some high-end workstations support both texture mapping and Phong illumination in hardware (see Cohen and Wallace 1993 for implementation details). For the rest of us, we must replicate these features in software. Although it may be a nontrivial programming project, the increased realism of the rendered images should more than repay the effort.

8.2 Radiosity in Motion

Given the ease and speed with which simple radiosity environments can be rendered, you might consider something more challenging. Creating a full-color image with subtle color bleeding effects and realistic soft shadows is impressive enough. However, think of the possibilities in creating a "walkthrough" that can be displayed in full motion on a multimedia computer.

Modifying *HELIOS* to generate a sequence of images according to a script file of camera positions and orientations is trivial. Once the radiosity equation has been solved for a given environment, you can repeatedly call the various *SynCamera* member functions to update the camera viewpoint and shoot images.

From here, it is mostly an issue of recording the images in some suitable form. Given the appropriate software and hardware, they can be written to a motion-compressed digital video file or sent frame by frame to a video recorder. Depending on the supporting software provided by the hardware manufacturers, this can be an evening-long programming project or a major software development effort.

Of course, this assumes that the radiosity equation needs to be solved only once for a static environment. The true challenge comes when the environment is dynamic.

8.2.1 Changes In Lighting

Suppose we want to change the lighting as our camera moves through the environment. The form factor matrix remains unchanged, but this is little consolation where progressive refinement radiosity is concerned. In general, we have to solve the radiosity equation, form factors and all, whenever the initial exitance of a light source is changed.

There are some shortcuts we can consider, however. To begin with, an environment with a single light source will require no recalculation at all—we only need to dim or brighten the entire environment accordingly when its initial exitance is changed. Of course, this will require a minor change to *ToneRep::Normalize* to ensure that the bitmap pixel luminances are properly calculated.

A complex environment will likely have more than one light source. Changing the initial exitance of one source will require us to find a new solution to the radiosity equation. However, we already have a good approximation with the current solution. We can model the change in initial exitance as an additional quantity of unsent exitance. This requires a minor change to *RadEqnSolve::InitExitance* to prevent it from resetting the final vertex exitances. *ProgRad::Calculate* or *RayCast::Calculate* will then simply calculate the changes in exitance and add them to the current solution. In most situations, the radiosity algorithm will converge to a solution much more quickly, since the stopping criterion is still based on the total quantity of flux in the environment.

Of course, if the light source is dimmed, this implies a *negative* quantity of unsent exitance (Chen 1990). Several minor changes to the radiosity equation solver functions will be needed to accommodate this physically impossible but eminently useful possibility.

If there are many lighting changes to be modeled—theater lighting, for example—it may be useful to calculate separate solutions for each individual group of light sources (Airey et al. 1990). These solutions are independent of one another. You can scale and sum them to represent any possible combination of light sources and their initial exitances. Dorsey et al. (1991) and Dorsey (1993) describe a similar approach, except that images are prerendered for a fixed camera position and each group of light sources. Lighting changes can then be represented at interactive rates by simply blending the rendered images.

8.2.2 Changes in Surface Reflectance

A second challenge comes when the surface reflectances are changed. One typical example is in architectural design, where the viewer may want to compare the visual appearance of different wall or floor finishes. Again, the form factor matrix remains unchanged. However, the solution may change drastically if the surface area is large and its spectral reflectance in one or more color bands is changed by any significant amount.

Once again, we have to solve the radiosity equation whenever a surface reflectance is changed. Chen (1990) noted that the current solution often provides a good starting point, particularly when the number of surfaces that have changed is small in number. From Equation 2.21, we know that the exitance of an element is given by:

$$M_i = M_{oi} + \rho_i \sum_{j=1}^{n} M_j F_{ij} \tag{8.3}$$

If we define M'_{oi} as the new initial exitance and ρ'_i as the new reflectance of the element, then the incremental change in final exitance is given by:

$$\Delta M_i = M'_{oi} - M_{oi} + (\rho'_i - \rho_i) \sum_{j=1}^{n} M_j F_{ij} \qquad (8.4)$$

Substituting Equation 8.3 into this equation gives us:

$$\Delta M_i = M'_{oi} - M_{oi} + \frac{(\rho'_i - \rho_i)(M_i - M_{oi})}{\rho_i} \qquad (8.5)$$

where the current surface reflectance ρ_i is assumed to be greater than zero. We can add this value (which may be negative) to the current calculated element exitance M_i and also the unsent exitance of the parent patch. From this, we can shoot the exitance until the radiosity algorithm converges to a new solution.

This technique becomes less helpful as the number of surfaces with changed reflectances or initial exitances increases. Another, more general approach to this problem—*eigenvector* radiosity—is described by DiLaura and Franck (1993). It has the distinct advantage that its solution to the radiosity equation is independent of the surface reflectances. In other words, the radiosity equation for a given environment has to be solved only once. The effects of changing the surface reflectances or initial patch exitances can be trivially solved thereafter. Unfortunately, it is a full radiosity method in that the entire form factor matrix must be precalculated and stored in memory while the radiosity equation is being solved.

8.2.3   Changes in Environment Geometry

Changes to the geometry of the environment, even something as simple as moving one small object, can have global effects on the radiosity solution. It can be difficult to predict these effects, especially when the objects are close to a light source. Moving an object or modifying its geometry changes the form factor matrix, and so a new solution to the radiosity equation is required.

As before, there are advantages in beginning with the current solution. If the changes to the radiosity equation are small, convergence to a new solution will proceed rapidly.

There are other possibilities. Baum et al. (1986) present an algorithm for situations where the changes to the geometry are known in advance and can be precomputed. More general approaches are taken by Chen (1990) and George et al. (1990), who discuss several techniques for isolating those portions of the environment whose form factors are affected by moving, modifying, adding, or deleting objects. Positive or negative exitance is then shot as required to account for these changes. The discussions include practical implementation details and pseudocode for algorithms that are, unfortunately, beyond the scope of this book. If you need to account for geometric changes in the environment, however, these two references are definitely worth investigating.

8.3 Monte Carlo Radiosity

Most radiosity-based rendering programs use either progressive refinement or ray casting to solve the radiosity equation. While these are certainly the two most popular algorithms, there are others. They range from simple probabilistic ray-tracing techniques to bleeding-edge research in higher mathematics.

Monte Carlo radiosity takes a brute force approach to radiosity rendering. Like progressive refinement radiosity, it begins by dividing surfaces into arrays of elements. It then shoots rays of light in random directions from the light sources. Each ray is followed until it intersects a surface, at which point it is multiplied by the surface reflectance and reshot. Again, a set of random rays is used. This is continued until most of the radiant flux has been absorbed.

Monte Carlo radiosity is essentially a variant of progressive refinement radiosity, where the form factors are implicitly calculated using ray casting. In pseudocode, the algorithm becomes as in Figure 8.3 (adapted from Shirley 1991a):

FOR each element i

$$\Phi_i = \Delta\Phi_i^{unsent} = \Phi_{oi}$$

ENDFOR

WHILE $\sum_{i=1}^{n} \Delta\Phi_i^{unsent} > \varepsilon$

    Select element i with greatest unsent flux $\Delta\Phi_i^{unsent}$
    Send $\Delta\Phi_i^{unsent}$ to other elements

    $\Delta\Phi_i^{unsent} = 0$

ENDWHILE
FOR each element i

    $M_i = \Phi_i / A_i$

ENDFOR

Figure 8.3 Monte Carlo radiosity algorithm

Recalling that $\Phi_i = M_i A_i$, this can be seen to be identical in outline to our progressive refinement radiosity algorithm pseudocode in Figure 6.4. The only difference is the line "Send $\Delta\Phi_i^{unsent}$ to other elements." Monte Carlo radiosity does this by dividing the flux into a number r of equal "packets" and shooting each as a ray in a random direction from the element into the environment. The origin of the ray is chosen at random across the sending element's surface.

The number r depends on the quantity of unsent flux. By ensuring that each ray has an approximately constant amount of flux, r will depend on the value of $\Delta\Phi_i^{unsent}$. This results in each ray having an approximately equal effect on the environment.

The random direction of the ray is weighted by the flux distribution or reflectance characteristics of the source or reflecting surface. A Lambertian surface, for example, reflects flux in a cosine distribution (i.e., Lambert's cosine law, Eq. 1.9).

Thus, the probability of a ray being shot at a vertical angle θ from the surface normal is proportional to cos (θ).

In pseudocode then, "Send $\Delta\Phi_i^{unsent}$ to other elements" becomes as in Figure 8.4.

```
FOR each ray
    Choose a random origin
    Choose a weighted random direction
    Shoot ray in random direction
    Find nearest intersecting element j
```

$$\Delta\Phi = \rho_j \Delta\Phi_i^{unsent} / r$$

$$\Phi_j = \Phi_j + \Delta\Phi$$

$$\Phi_j^{unsent} = \Phi_j^{unsent} + \Delta\Phi$$

```
ENDFOR
```

Figure 8.4 Sending flux between two elements

Further implementation details are presented in Shirley (1991a). Also, Ashdown (1992) presented an implementation of the above pseudocode (written in C) as part of an overview of radiosity methods.

Monte Carlo radiosity offers several important advantages in comparison to progressive refinement and ray-casting radiosity. First, there is no need to calculate form factors. This is done implicitly when the rays are shot into the environment.

Second, the Monte Carlo radiosity algorithm is not limited to modeling Lambertian light sources and surfaces. The random ray-direction weighting approximates the flux distribution or reflectance characteristics of the light source or surface. This allows us easily to model semispecular surfaces and non-Lambertian light sources. There is a variety of illumination models (e.g., Foley et al. 1990) that can be directly represented within the context of the Monte Carlo radiosity algorithm. Even transparent and fully specular surfaces such as glass and mirrors can be accommodated.

Given these advantages, why do we even bother with other radiosity methods? The answer is that it can take a *very* large number of rays to model accurately the lighting of a complex environment. We are trading the simplicity of ray tracing for long (and sometimes *very* long) execution times.

Feda and Purgathofer (1993) present an adaptation that adds an outer loop to the pseudocode shown in Figure 8.3. More rays are shot at each iteration, thereby incrementally increasing the overall accuracy of the solution while generating increasingly accurate intermediate images as the algorithm progresses. This makes Monte Carlo radiosity somewhat more competitive with progressive refinement and ray casting radiosity in terms of user interaction.

Further information and discussions of Monte Carlo radiosity can be found in Kajiyama and Kodaira (1989), Pattanaik and Mudur (1992), Rushmeier (1986), Shirley (1990a–c), Shirley (1991b), Shirley et al. (1991), Shirley and Wang (1991), Stanger (1984), Tregenza (1983), and Ward et al. (1988).

Finally, no discussion of Monte Carlo radiosity is complete without mentioning *RADIANCE*, a superlative ray-tracing program that incorporates a wide variety of shading and illumination models aimed at producing photorealistic images of physically based phenomena. It also features the view-dependent Monte Carlo radiosity algorithm presented in Ward et al. (1988).

RADIANCE was developed by Greg Ward of Lawrence Berkeley Laboratory under the sponsorship of the U.S. Department of Energy. Originally written for UNIX-based platforms, it has since been ported to the 80x86 and Amiga environments. It is production-quality software with features that rival those of the best commercial products.

The source code to *RADIANCE* is freely distributed and is currently available on the Internet via anonymous ftp from hobbes.lbl.gov and the ACM SIGGRAAPH '94 Conference Proceedings on CD-ROM (Ward 1994).

8.4   Other Radiosity Algorithms

There are several other important but mathematically complex algorithms for solving the radiosity equation. They are at the forefront of radiosity research and well beyond the scope of this text. Nevertheless, a few brief comments are in order regarding their advantages and significance.

Hierarchical radiosity extends the concept of patches and elements to its logical limit. Recall from Section 5.10 that patches were divided into elements in order to limit the number of element-to-element form factors that must be calculated while solving the radiosity equation. As long as the five-times rule (Section 5.5) is satisfied, we can group elements and calculate the form factor from an element to each group. Each patch constitutes a group of elements.

Suppose, however, that elements are grouped such that *each element* sees a minimum number of groups where the five-times rule is still satisfied for each group. The two-level hierarchy of patches and elements is extended to whatever depth is needed to link individual elements to appropriate groups of other elements in the environment.

At first, this suggests the need for a truly gargantuan data structure of linked lists, possibly one for each element. It also implies that every form factor has to be precomputed in order to group the elements seen by each element.

Hanrahan and Salzman (1990a, b) and Hanrahan et al. (1991) demonstrated that this is not the case. (See also Cohen and Wallace 1993 for a more accessible discussion and detailed pseudocode.) An "oracle" function can be used to quickly estimate form factors and indicate which elements should be grouped together. Furthermore, surfaces are adaptively subdivided into a hierarchy of elements, thereby minimizing the number of elements needed to represent an environment. (Each element is subdivided into at most four child elements.) In a test environment consisting of 98 polygons, their hierarchical radiosity algorithm (Hanrahan et al. 1991) created 4,280 elements arranged in a quadtree with 5,674 nodes and computed 11,800 element-to-element interactions. By comparison, a naive radiosity algorithm would have required as many as 175,000 elements and computed some 15 *billion* interactions.

There is a deeper mathematical basis to hierarchical radiosity than that of simply minimizing the number of element-to-element form factor calculations. It can be described in terms of hierarchical "basis functions" (e.g., Cohen and Wallace 1993) that have interesting parallels with the mathematics of the Fast Fourier Transform and various lossy image compression algorithms (such as the Discrete Cosine and Haar transforms). This has led to the development of *wavelet* radiosity (Gortler et al. 1993b) and *Galerkin* radiosity (Zatz 1993). These in turn are related to the independently derived *eigenvector* radiosity algorithm (DiLaura and Franck 1993).

Finally, there is *importance-based* radiosity (Smits et al. 1992), which borrows its inspiration from the nuclear physicist's neutron transport theory. This radiosity method differs from those previously described in that it generates view-dependent solutions. Although this may limit its usefulness in some applications, it offers an important advantage when extremely complex environments must be rendered. Importance-based radiosity identifies those components of a scene that will significantly affect the radiosity solution for a given viewpoint. This brings the number of elements that must be considered in form factor calculations down to manageable levels.

These advanced radiosity algorithms have been introduced only within the past two years and are for the most part ongoing research projects. Given time, they may lead to practical and useful radiosity-rendering techniques that outperform any algorithms currently in use.

8.5 Conclusions

Shenchang Eric Chen (Chen 1991) was right: Implementing a radiosity program is indeed "an enormous task." It has taken us more than 500 pages and over 7,000 lines of C++ source code to develop *HELIOS*. Even so, there are numerous finishing touches—in particular, antialiasing, integer-based polygon fill, ray-casting acceleration techniques, winged-edge data structures, and adaptive subdivision—that had to be left as those infamous "exercises for the reader."

Despite these shortcomings, we can be proud of *HELIOS*. It opens the door to new opportunities in computer graphics. It was not designed to be a "user-friendly" (whatever that means) program for the madding crowd. Rather, it is a software development platform, a testbed for *your* ideas and experiments with radiosity.

The radiosity approach has been the domain of a small coterie of academic researchers for the past ten years. We must thank these people for their interest in what was at first a mathematical curiosity and their dedication to transforming the technique into a powerful computer graphics tool. We must also encourage them to continue their studies, for there are undoubtedly other fascinating and useful radiosity techniques still waiting to be discovered.

For us, however, the excitement is here and now. This book has given you a lengthy and practical introduction to the radiosity approach. If you want to learn more, begin with Cohen and Wallace 1993—there is no better introduction to the intricacies of advanced radiosity methods. Beyond this, there are many excellent academic papers that cover all aspects of radiosity. The Bibliography lists most (but certainly not all) of those that have been published to date. While some of them may be difficult to obtain, they all have something to offer.

More to the point, however, we have *HELIOS*. This program—and this book—were written to bring radiosity into the wider world of computer science students and those who love to program. Remember: radiosity is easy to understand and fascinating to experiment with. Try *HELIOS* and see for yourself.

8.6   POSTSCRIPT

At the risk of communication overload, the author extends an invitation to readers interested in sending e-mail messages regarding the contents of this book. Bug reports, comments, questions, and suggestions for a *possible* second volume (*Radiosity: Advancing the Art*) are welcomed. (Please recognize, however, that questions regarding porting the code to different environments and compiler-related problems are often difficult to answer.)

The author's current e-mail address is:

Ian Ashdown (72060.2420@compuserve.com)

This address may change in the future as the vaunted "information superhighway" evolves from political rhetoric into a viable reality. If so, please contact the publisher, John Wiley & Sons, Inc., for the correct address.

REFERENCES

Airey, J. M., J. H. Rohlf, and F. P. Brooks, Jr. 1990. "Towards Image Realism with Interactive Update Rates in Complex Virtual Building Environments," *Computer Graphics* 24(1):41–50 (ACM Workshop on Interactive Graphics Proc.).

Arvo, J., ed. 1991. *Graphic Gems II*. San Diego, CA: Academic Press.

Ashdown, I. 1992. "Radiosity and Realism," *The C Users Journal* 10(8):33–42 (August).

Ashdown, I. 1993a. "Near-Field Photometry: A New Approach," *Journal of the Illuminating Engineering Society* 22(1):163–180 (Winter).

Ashdown, I. 1993b. "Modeling Complex 3-D Light Sources," *ACM SIGGRAPH '93 Course 22 (Making Radiosity Practical) Notes*.

Aupperle, L., and P. Hanrahan. 1993. "A Hierarchical Illumination Algorithm for Surfaces with Glossy Reflections," *Computer Graphics Proceedings* (ACM SIGGRAPH '93). pp. 155-162.

Bao, H., and Q. Peng. 1993. "Shading Models for Linear and Area Light Sources," *Computers & Graphics* 17(2):137–145.

Baranoski, G. V. G. 1992. "The Parametric Differential Method: An Alternative to the Calculation of Form Factors," *Computer Graphics Forum* 11(3):C193–C-204 (Eurographics '92 Proc.).

Baum, D. R., J. R. Wallace, M. F. Cohen, and D. P. Greenberg. 1986. "The Back-Buffer Algorithm: An Extension of the Radiosity Method to Dynamic Environments," *The Visual Computer* 2:298–306.

Baum, S. E., and J. M. Winget 1990. "Real Time Radiosity through Parallel Processing and Hardware Acceleration," *Computer Graphics* 24(2):67–75 (1990 Symposium on Interactive 3D Graphics).

Bian, B., N. Wittels, and D. S. Fussell 1992. "Non-Uniform Patch Luminance for Global Illumination," *Graphics Interface '92*, pp. 310–318.

Bouatouch, K., and C. Bouville, eds. 1992. *Photorealism in Computer Graphics*. Berlin, Germany: Springer-Verlag.

Bu, J., and E. F. Deprettere. 1987a. "A VLSI System Architecture for High-Speed Radiative Transfer 3D Image Synthesis," *Eurographics '87* (Proc. European Computer Graphics Conference and Exhibition), G. Marechal, ed. Amsterdam: Elsevier Science Publishers B.V. (North-Holland), pp. 221–235.

Bu, J., and E. F. Deprettere. 1987b. "A VLSI Algorithm for Computing Form-Factors in Radiative Transfer Computer Image Synthesis," *Computer Graphics 1987* (Proc. CG International '87), T. L. Kunii, ed. London, England: Springer-Verlag, pp. 181–193.

Chalmers, A. G., and D. J. Paddon. 1991. "Parallel Processing of Progressive Refinement Radiosity Methods," *Proc. Second Eurographics Workshop on Rendering*, Barcelona, Spain.

Chen, H., and E. Wu. 1990. "An Efficient Radiosity Solution for Bump Texture Generation," *Computer Graphics* 24(4):125–134 (ACM SIGGRAPH '90 Proc.).

Chen, H., and E. Wu. 1991. "Radiosity for Furry Surfaces," *Eurographics '91* (Proc. European Computer Graphics Conference and Exhibition), F. H. Post and W. Barth, eds. Amsterdam: Elsevier Science Publishers B.V. (North-Holland), pp. 447–457.

Chen, S. E. 1989. *A Progressive Radiosity Method and Its Implementation in a Distributed Processing Environment*. Master's thesis, Program of Computer Graphics, Cornell University, Ithaca, NY.

Chen, S. E. 1990. "Incremental Radiosity: An Extension of Progressive Radiosity to an Interactive Image Synthesis System," *Computer Graphics* 24(4):135–144 (ACM SIGGRAPH '90 Proc.).

Chen, S. E. 1991. "Implementing Progressive Radiosity with User-Provided Polygon Display Routines," in Arvo (1991), pp. 295–298, 583–597.

Chen, S. E., H. E. Rushmeier, G. Miller, and D. Turner. 1991. "A Progressive Multi-Pass Method for Global Illumination," *Computer Graphics* 25(4):165–174 (ACM SIGGRAPH '91 Proc.).

Cohen, M. F., D. P. Greenberg, D. S. Immel, and P. J. Brock. 1986. "An Efficient Radiosity Approach for Realistic Image Synthesis," *IEEE Computer Graphics and Applications* 6(3): 26–35.

Cohen, M. F., and J. R. Wallace. 1993. *Radiosity and Realistic Image Synthesis*. San Diego, CA: Academic Press.

DiLaura, D. L., and P. J. Franck. 1993. "On Setting Up and Solving Large Radiative Transfer Systems," *Journal of the Illuminating Engineering Society* 22(2):3–7 (Summer).

Dorsey, J. O'B. 1993. *Computer Graphics Techniques for Opera Lighting Design and Simulation*. Ph.D. thesis, Program of Computer Graphics, Cornell University, Ithaca, NY.

Dorsey, J. O'B., F. X. Sillion, and D. P. Greenberg. 1991. "Design and Simulation of Opera Lighting and Projection Effects," *Computer Graphics* 25(4):41–50 (ACM SIGGRAPH '91 Proc.).

Dretakkis, G., and E. Fiume. 1991. "Structure-Directed Sampling, Reconstruction and Data Representation for Global Illumination," *Proc. Second Eurographics Workshop on Rendering*, Barcelona, Spain.

Feda, M., and W. Purgathofer. 1991. "Progressive Refinement Radiosity on a Transputer Network," *Proc. Second Eurographics Workshop on Rendering*, Barcelona, Spain.

Feda, M., and W. Purgathofer. 1993. "Progressive Ray Refinement for Monte Carlo Radiosity," *Proc. Fourth Eurographics Workshop on Rendering*, Paris, France, pp. 15–25.

Foley, J. D., A. van Dam, S. K. Feiner, and J. F. Hughes. 1990. *Computer Graphics: Principles and Practice* (2nd ed.). Reading, MA: Addison-Wesley.

George, D. W. 1990. *A Radiosity Redistribution Algorithm for Dynamic Environments*. Master's thesis, Program of Computer Graphics, Cornell University, Ithaca, NY.

George, D. W., F. X. Sillion, and D. P. Greenberg. 1990. "Radiosity Redistribution in Dynamic Environments," *IEEE Computer Graphics and Applications* 10(6):26-34.

Gortler, S. J., P. Schröder, M. F. Cohen, and P. Hanrahan. 1993b. "Wavelet Radiosity," *Computer Graphics Proceedings,* pp. 221–230 (ACM SIGGRAPH '93).

Greiner, G., W. Heidrich, and P. Slusallek. 1993. "Blockwise Refinement—A New Method for Solving the Radiosity Problem," *Proc. Fourth Eurographics Workshop on Rendering*, Paris, France, pp. 233–245.

Guitton, P., J. Roman, and C. Schlick. 1991. "Two Parallel Approaches for a Progressive Radiosity," *Proc. Second Eurographics Workshop on Rendering*, Barcelona, Spain.

Hall, D. E., and H. E. Rushmeier. 1993. "Improved Explicit Radiosity Method for Calculating Non-Lambertian Reflections," *The Visual Computer* 9:278–288.

Hammersley, J. M., and D. C. Handscomb. 1964. *Monte Carlo Methods*. London, England: Methuen.

Hanrahan, P., and D. B. Salzman. 1990a. *A Rapid Hierarchical Radiosity Algorithm for Unoccluded Environments*. Princeton, NJ: Princeton University, Technical Report CS-TR-281-90.

Hanrahan, P., and D. Salzman. 1990b. "A Rapid Hierarchical Radiosity Algorithm for Unoccluded Environments," in Bouatouch and Bouville (1992), pp. 151–170.

Hanrahan, P., D. Salzman, and L. Aupperle. 1991. "A Rapid Hierarchical Radiosity Algorithm," *Computer Graphics* 24(4):197–206 (ACM SIGGRAPH '91 Proc.).

Heckbert, P. S. 1986. "Survey of Texture Mapping," *IEEE Computer Graphics & Applications* 6(11): 56–67.

Heckbert, P. S. 1990. "Adaptive Radiosity Textures for Bidirectional Ray Tracing," *Computer Graphics* 24(4):145–154 (ACM SIGGRAPH '90 Proc.).

Hermitage, S. A., T. L. Huntsberger, and B. A. Huntsberger. 1990. "Hypercube Algorithm for Radiosity in a Ray Traced Environment," *Proc. Fifth Distributed Memory Computing Conference*, IEEE Society Press, pp. 206–211.

Immel, D. S., M. F. Cohen, and D. P. Greenberg. 1986. "A Radiosity Method for Non-Diffuse Environments," *Computer Graphics* 20(4):133–142 (ACM SIGGRAPH '86 Proc.).

Jessel, J. P., M. Paulin, and R. Caubet. 1991. "An Extended Radiosity Using Parallel Ray-

Traced Specular Transfers," *Proc. Second Eurographics Workshop on Rendering*, Barcelona, Spain.

Kajiyama, H., and S. Kodaira. 1989. "An Illuminance Analysis in Partitioned Spaces Using the Monte Carlo Method," *Journal of the Illuminating Engineering Society* 18(2):93–108 (Summer).

Kawai, J. K., J. S. Painter, and M. F. Cohen. 1993. "Radiooptimization–Goal Based Rendering," *Computer Graphics Proceedings* (ACM SIGGRAPH '93 Proc.), pp. 147–154.

Kok, A. J. F. 1992. "Grouping of Patches in Progressive Radiosity," *Proc. Fourth Eurographics Workshop on Rendering*, Paris, France, pp. 221–231.

Kok, A. J. F., F. W. Jansen, and C. Woodward. 1993. "Efficient, Complete Radiosity Ray Tracing Using a Shadow-Coherence Method," *The Visual Computer* 10:19–33.

Kok, A. J. F., A. C. Yilmaz, and L. H. J. Bierens. 1990. "A Two-Pass Radiosity Method for Bézier Patches," in Bouatouch and Bouville (1992), pp. 115–124.

Languénou, E., and P. Tellier. 1992. "Including Physical Light Sources and Daylight in Global Illumination," *Proc. Third Eurographics Workshop on Rendering*, Bristol, England, pp. 217–225.

Le Saec, B., and C. Schlick. 1990. "A Progressive Ray Tracing Based Radiosity with General Reflectance Functions," in Bouatouch and Bouville (1992), pp. 101–113.

Lischinski, D., F. Tampieri, and D. P. Greenberg. 1993. "Combining Hierarchical Radiosity and Discontinuity Meshing," *Computer Graphics Proceedings* (ACM SIGGRAPH '93), pp. 199–208.

Neumann, L., and A. Neumann. 1989. "Photosimulation: Interreflection with Arbitrary Reflectance Models and Illumination," *Computer Graphics Forum* 8:21–34.

Neumann, L., and A. Neumann. 1990. "Efficient Radiosity Methods for Non-Separable Reflectance Models," in Bouatouch and Bouville (1992), pp. 85–97.

Ng, A., and M. Slater. 1993. "A Multiprocessor Implementation of Radiosity," *Computer Graphics Forum* 12(5): pp. 329–342.

Pattanaik, S., and S. Mudur. 1992. "Computation of Global Illumination by Monte Carlo Simulation of the Particle Light," *Proc. Third Eurographics Workshop on Rendering*, Bristol, England.

Phong, B. 1975. "Illumination for Computer Generated Images," *Communications of the ACM* 18(6):311–317.

Price, M., and G. Truman. 1989. "Parallelism Makes Light Work," *Computer Graphics '89*, November, London, England, pp. 409–418.

Purgathofer, W., and M. Zeller. 1990. "Fast Radiosity by Parallelization," in Bouatouch and Bouville (1992), pp.171–181.

Rushmeier, H. 1988. *Realistic Image Synthesis for Scenes with Radiatively Participating Media*. Ph.D. thesis, Program of Computer Graphics, Cornell University, Ithaca, NY.

Rushmeier, H., C. Patterson, and A. Veerasamy. 1993. "Geometric Simplification for Indirect Illumination Calculations," *Graphics Interface '93*, Toronto, Ontario, pp. 227–236.

Rushmeier, H., and K. Torrance. 1987. "The Zonal Method for Calculating Light Intensities in the Presence of a Participating Medium," *Computer Graphics* 21(4):293–302 (ACM SIGGRAPH '87 Proc.).

Rushmeier, H. E., and K. E. Torrance. 1990. "Extending the Radiosity Method to Include

Specularly Reflecting and Translucent Materials," *ACM Transactions on Computer Graphics* 9(1):1–27.

Salesin, D., D. Lischinski, and T. DeRose. 1992. "Reconstructing Illumination Functions with Selected Discontinuities," *Proc. Third Eurographics Workshop on Rendering*, Bristol, England.

Shao, M., and N. I. Badler. 1993. "Analysis and Acceleration of Progressive Refinement Radiosity Method," *Proc. Fourth Eurographics Workshop on Rendering*, Paris, France.

Shao, M., Q. Peng, and Y. Liang. 1988a. "Form Factors for General Environments," *Eurographics '88* (Proc. European Computer Graphics Conference and Exhibition), D. A. Duce and P. Jancene, eds. Amsterdam: Elsevier Sciences Publishers B.V. (North-Holland), pp. 499–510.

Shao, M., Q. Peng, and Y. Liang. 1988b. "A New Radiosity Approach by Procedural Refinements for Realistic Image Synthesis," *Computer Graphics* 22(4) (ACM SIGGRAPH '88 Proc.), pp. 93–101.

Shen, L., E. Deprettere, and P. Dewilde. 1992. "A New Space Partitioning for Mapping Computations of the Radiosity Method onto a Highly Pipelined Parallel Architecture," *Advances in Computer Graphics V*. Berlin, Germany: Springer-Verlag.

Shirley, P. 1990a. *Physically Based Lighting Calculations for Computer Graphics*. Ph.D. thesis, Department of Computer Science, University of Illinois, Urbana-Champaign.

Shirley, P. 1990b. "Physically Based Lighting Calculations for Computer Graphics: A Modern Perspective," in Bouatouch and Bouville (1992), pp. 73–83.

Shirley, P. 1990c. "A Ray Tracing Method for Illumination Calculation in Diffuse-Specular Scenes," *Graphics Interface '90*, pp. 205–212.

Shirley, P. 1991a. "Radiosity via Ray Tracing," in Arvo (1991), pp. 306–310.

Shirley, P. 1991b. "Time Complexity of Monte Carlo Radiosity," *Eurographics '91* (Proc. European Computer Graphics Conference and Exhibition), F. H. Post and W. Barth, eds. Amsterdam: Elsevier Science Publishers B.V. (North-Holland), pp. 459–465.

Shirley, P., K. Sung, and W. Brown. 1991. "A Ray Tracing Framework for Global Illumination Systems," *Graphics Interface '91*, pp. 117–128.

Shirley, P., and C. Wang. 1991. "Direct Lighting Calculations by Monte Carlo Integration," *Proc. Second Eurographics Workshop on Rendering*, Barcelona, Spain.

Sillion, F. X., J. R. Arvo, S. H. Westin, and D. P. Greenberg. 1991. "A Global Illumination Solution for General Reflectance Distributions," *Computer Graphics* 25(4):187–196 (ACM SIGGRAPH '91 Proc.).

Sillion, F. X., and C. Puech. 1989. "A General Two-Pass Method Integrating Specular and Diffuse Reflection," *Computer Graphics* 23:(3):335–344 (ACM SIGGRAPH '89 Proc.).

Smits, B. E., J. R. Arvo, and D. H. Salesin. 1992. "An Importance-Driven Radiosity Algorithm," *Computer Graphics* 26(4):273–282 (ACM SIGGRAPH '92 Proc.).

Stanger, D. 1984. "Monte Carlo Procedures in Lighting Design," *Journal of the Illuminating Engineering Society* 13(4):368–371.

Tampieri, F., and D. Lischinski. 1991. "The Constant Radiosity Assumption Syndrome," *Proc. Second Eurographics Workshop on Rendering*, Barcelona, Spain.

Tregenza, P. R. 1983. "The Monte Carlo Method in Lighting Calculations," *Lighting Research & Technology* 15(4):163–170.

Troutman, R., and N. Max. 1993. "Radiosity Algorithms Using Higher Order Finite Element Methods," *Computer Graphics Proceedings* (ACM SIGGRAPH '93), pp. 209–212.

Van Liere, R. 1991. "Divide and Conquer Radiosity," *Proc. Second Eurographics Workshop on Rendering*, Barcelona, Spain.

Wallace, J. R., M. F. Cohen, and D. P. Greenberg. 1987. "A Two-Pass Solution to the Rendering Equation: A Synthesis of Ray Tracing and Radiosity Methods," *Computer Graphics* 21(4):311–320 (ACM SIGGRAPH '87 Proc.).

Wang, M., H. Bao, and Q. Peng. 1992. "A New Progressive Radiosity Algorithm through the Use of Accurate Form-Factors," *Computers & Graphics* 16(3):303–309.

Ward, G. J. 1994. "The Radiance Lighting Simulation and Rendering System," *Computer Graphics Proceedings* (forthcoming).

Ward, G. J., F. M. Rubinstein, and R. D. Clear. 1988. "A Ray Tracing Solution for Diffuse Interreflection," *Computer Graphics* 22(4):85–92 (ACM SIGGRAPH '88 Proc.).

Wilt, N. 1993. *Objected-Oriented Ray Tracing in C++*. New York: John Wiley & Sons, Inc.

Xu, H., Q. S. Peng, and Y. D. Liang. 1989. "Accelerated Radiosity Method for Complex Environments," *Eurographics '89* (Proc. European Computer Graphics Conference and Exhibition), W. Hansmann, F. R. A. Hopgood, and W. Strasser, eds. Amsterdam: Elsevier Science Publishers B.V. (North-Holland), pp. 51–61.

Zatz, H. 1993. "Galerkin Radiosity: A Higher Order Solution Method for Global Illumination," *Computer Graphics Proceedings,* pp. 213–220 (ACM SIGGRAPH '93).

Zhou, Y., and Q. Peng. 1992. "The Super-Plane Buffer: An Efficient Form-Factor Evaluation Algorithm for Progressive Radiosity," *Computers & Graphics* 16(2):151–158.

Photometric and Radiometric Definitions

INTRODUCTION

The photometric and radiometric definitions presented in Chapter 1 are those commonly used in illumination engineering and are in accordance with the American National Standards Institute publication *Nomenclature and Definitions for Illuminating Engineering* (ANSI/IES 1986). This booklet is a veritable encyclopedia of photometric and radiometric terminology. However, interested readers are forewarned: It is anything but light bedside reading!

As noted in Chapter 1, the photometric and radiometric terminology presently used by the computer graphics community differs somewhat from that promoted by ANSI/IES (1986). The concepts are the same; the differences are in name only. It is to be hoped that this situation will change in the future—ANSI/IES (1986) offers a consistent and useful set of definitions for both the computer graphics and illumination engineering communities.

The following definitions have been excerpted (with some minor editing) from ANSI/IES (1986) with the kind permission of the Illuminating Engineering Society of North America.

ANSI/IES DEFINITIONS[1]

2. Electromagnetic Radiation

2.1 Radiant energy, *Q*. Energy traveling in the form of electromagnetic waves. It is measured in units of energy such as joules or kilowatt-hours.

 2.1.1 Spectral radiant energy, $Q_\lambda = dQ/d\lambda$. Radiant energy per unit wavelength interval; e.g., joules per nanometer. $Q_\lambda(\lambda) = dQ/d\lambda$ at wavelength λ.

2.4 Radiant flux (radiant power), $\Phi = dQ/dt$. The time rate of flow of radiant energy. It is expressed preferably in watts.

 2.4.1 Spectral radiant flux, $\Phi_\lambda = d\Phi/d\lambda$. Radiant flux per unit wavelength interval at wavelength λ; e.g., watts per nanometer.

2.5 Radiant flux areal density, $d\Phi/dA$ (at a point on a surface). The quotient of the radiant flux incident on or emitted by an element of surface area at the point, by the area of the element. Radiant flux density emitted from a surface has been called emittance (a deprecated term). The preferred term for radiant flux density leaving a surface is exitance, (*M*). Radiant flux density incident on a surface is irradiance, (*E*).

 2.5.1 Spectral radiant exitance, M_λ, and irradiance E_λ. Spectral concentration of radiant exitance, $M_\lambda = dM/d\lambda$, and spectral concentration of irradiance, $E_\lambda = dE/d\lambda$.

2.6 Radiant intensity, $I = d\Phi/d\omega$ (in a given direction). The radiant flux proceeding from a source per unit solid angle in the given direction; e.g., watts per steradian.

 Note: Mathematically, a solid angle must have a point at its apex; the definition of radiant intensity, therefore, applies strictly only to a point source. In practice, however, radiant energy emanating from a source whose dimensions are negligible in comparison with the distance from which it is observed may be considered as coming from a point. Specifically, this implies that with change of distance (1) the variation in solid angle subtended by the source at the receiving point approaches $1/(\text{distance})^2$; and that (2) the average radiance of the projected source area as seen from the receiving point does not vary appreciably.

 2.6.1 Spectral radiant intensity, $I_\lambda = dI/d\lambda$. Radiant intensity per unit wavelength interval; e.g., watts per (steradian-nanometer).

2.7 Radiance, $L = d^2\Phi/[d\omega(dA \cdot \cos\theta)] = dI/(dA \cdot \cos\theta)$ (in a given direction at a point on the surface of a source, of a receiver, or of any other real or virtual surface). The quotient of the radiant flux leaving, passing through, or arriving at an element of the surface surrounding the point, and propagated in directions defined by an elementary cone containing the given direction, by the product of the solid angle of the cone and the area of the orthogonal projection of the element of the surface on a plane perpendicular to the given direction.

 Note: In the defining equation θ is the angle between the normal to the element of the surface and the given direction.

---

[1]©1986 by Illuminating Engineering Society of North America, New York, in *Nomenclature and Definitions for Illuminating Engineering (IES RP-16).*

2.7.1 Spectral radiance, L_λ. Spectral concentration of radiance:

$L_\lambda = d^3\Phi/[d\omega(dA \cdot \cos\theta)d\lambda]$.

2.10 Radiant sterisent, $L^*(x)$ (at a point along a ray path). Rate of increase in radiance, per unit path length, at the point and in the direction of the ray, due to "generated" (emitted or scattered) radiance, or the "generated" radiant intensity per unit volume, at the point and in the direction of the ray, by which a distributed source can be characterized. $L^* = dL_g/dx = dI_g/dV$, where dx is an element of distance along the ray path, dV is an element of volume at the point, and the subscript g denotes a "generated" quantity.

2.10.1 Spectral radiant sterisent, L^*_λ. Spectral concentration of sterisent, $L^*_\lambda = dL^*/d\lambda$.

3. Light

3.1 Light. Radiant energy that is capable of exciting the retina and producing a visual sensation. The visible portion of the electromagnetic spectrum extends from about 380 to 770 nanometers.

3.2 Luminous flux Φ. Radiant flux (radiant power); the time rate of flow of radiant energy, evaluated in terms of a standardized visual response.

$$\Phi_v = K_m \int \Phi_{e\lambda} V(\lambda) d\lambda$$

where

Φ_v	= lumens
$\Phi_{e\lambda}$	= watts per nanometer
λ	= nanometers
$V(\lambda)$	= spectral luminous efficiency
K_m	= maximum spectral luminous efficacy in lumens/watt (lm/W)

Unless otherwise indicated, the luminous flux is defined for photopic vision. For scotopic vision, the corresponding spectral luminous efficiency $V'(\lambda)$ and the corresponding maximum spectral luminous efficacy K'_m are substituted in the above equation. K_m and K'_m are derived from the basic SI definition of luminous intensity and have the values 683 lm/W and 1754 lm/W respectively.

3.2.1 Lumen, lm. SI unit of luminous flux. Radiometrically, it is determined from the radiant power. Photometrically, it is the luminous flux emitted within a unit solid angle (one steradian) by a point source having a uniform luminous intensity of one candela.

3.3 Luminous flux density at a surface, $d\Phi/dA$. The luminous flux per unit area at a point on a surface.

Note: This need not be a physical surface; it may also be a mathematical plane.

3.3.1 Illuminance, $E = d\Phi/dA$. The areal density of the luminous flux incident at a point on a surface.

3.3.1.1 Illumination. An alternative, but deprecated, term for illuminance.

3.3.1.2 Lux, lx. The SI unit of illuminance. One lux is one lumen per square meter (lm/m^2).

3.3.1.3 Footcandle, fc. A unit of illuminance. One footcandle is one lumen per square foot (lm/ft^2).

3.3.2 Luminous exitance, $M = d\Phi/dA$. The areal density of luminous flux leaving a surface at a point. Formerly, *luminous emittance* (deprecated).

3.4 Luminous intensity, $I = d\Phi/d\omega$ (of a point source of light in a given direction). The luminous flux per unit solid angle in the direction in question. Hence, it is the luminous flux on a small surface centered on and normal to that direction divided by the solid angle (in steradians) which the surface subtends at the source. Luminous intensity may be expressed in candelas or in lumens per steradian (lm/sr).

Note: Mathematically, a solid angle must have a point at its apex; the definition of luminous intensity, therefore, applies strictly only to a point source. In practice, however, light emanating from a source whose dimensions are negligible in comparison with the distance from which it is observed may be considered as coming from a point. Specifically, this implies that with change of distance (1) the variation in solid angle subtended by the source at the receiving point approaches $1/(distance)^2$; and that (2) the average luminance of the projected source area as seen from the receiving point does not vary appreciably.

The word intensity as defined above is used to designate luminous intensity (or candlepower). It is also widely used in other ways. . . . Intensity has been used to designate the level of illuminance on a surface or the flux density in the cross section of a beam of light. In physical optics, intensity usually refers to the square of the wave amplitude.

3.4.1 Candela, cd. The SI unit of luminous intensity. One candela is one lumen per steradian (lm/sr). Formerly, *candle*.

Note: The fundamental luminous intensity definition in the SI is the candela. The candela is the luminous intensity, in a given direction, of a source that emits monochromatic radiation of frequency $540 \cdot 10^{12}$ Hertz that has a radiant intensity in that direction of 1/683 watt per steradian.

3.4.2 Candlepower, cp. Luminous intensity expressed in candelas.

3.5 Luminance, $L = d^2\Phi/(d\omega dA \cdot \cos\theta)$ (in a direction and at a point on a real or imaginary surface). (See Fig. A.1.) The quotient of the luminous flux at an element of the surface surrounding the point, and propagated in directions defined by an elementary cone containing the given direction, by the product of the solid angle of the cone and the area of orthogonal projection of the element of the surface on a plane perpendicular to the given direction. The luminous flux may be leaving, passing through, and/or arriving at the surface. Formerly, *photometric brightness*.

By introducing the concept of luminous intensity, luminance may be expressed as $L = dI/(dA \cdot \cos\theta)$. Here, luminance at a point on a surface in a given direction is interpreted as the quotient of luminous intensity in the given direction, produced by an element of the surface surrounding the point, by the area of the orthogonal projection of the element of surface on a plane, perpendicular to the given direction. (Luminance may be measured at the receiving surface by using

$$L = dE/(d\omega \cdot \cos \theta)$$

This value may be less than the luminance of the emitting surface due to attenuation of the transmitting media.)

3.5.1 SI unit of luminance. Candela per square meter (cd/m^2).

3.5.2 Inch-pound (formerly English [USA]) unit of luminance. Candela per square foot (cd/ft^2).

3.8 Luminous sterisent, $L^*(x)$ (at a point along a ray path). Rate of increase in luminance, per unit path length, at the point and in the direction of the ray, due to "generated" (emitted or scattered) luminance, or the "generated" luminous intensity per unit volume, at the point and in the direction of the ray, by which a distributed source can be characterized. $L^* = dL_g/dx = dI_g/dV$, where dx is an element of distance along the ray path, dV is an element of volume at the point, and the subscript g denotes a "generated" quantity.

3.9 Quantity of light (Luminous energy, $Q = \int \Phi dt$). The product of the luminous flux by the time it is maintained. It is the time integral of luminous flux.

3.10 Spectral luminous efficacy of radiant flux, $K(\lambda) = \Phi_{v\lambda}/\Phi_{e\lambda}$. The quotient of the luminous flux at a given wavelength by the radiant flux at that wavelength. It is expressed in lumens per watt.

3.10.1 Spectral luminous efficiency of radiant flux. The ratio of the luminous efficacy for a given wavelength to the value at the wavelength of maximum efficacy. It is dimensionless.

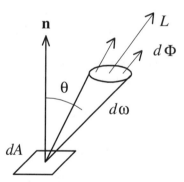

Figure A.1   Luminance

REFERENCE

ANSI/IES. 1986. *American National Standard Nomenclature and Definitions for Illuminating Engineering*, ANSI/IES RP-16-1986. New York: Illuminating Engineering Society of North America.

Memory-Management Issues

INTRODUCTION

Memory, memory, and more memory. It always seems that our applications require more memory than we currently have available. This curse of the computer is nowhere more evident than in radiosity rendering. Depending on the radiosity methods we employ, we may need to store both vertices and form factors as floating-point data types for thousands to hundreds of thousands of polygons. Tens of megabytes can disappear in the blink of an eye as a complex environment is read into memory.

While we may not be able to avoid these requirements, we can at least curb our programs' appetite for memory by carefully examining how memory is allocated, used, and released. Dynamic memory allocation is an obvious and well-documented candidate; other software engineering techniques include dynamic multidimensional arrays, nonrectangular array allocation, and class-specific memory managers.

For whatever reason, most C and C++ programming texts dismiss multidimensional arrays and memory-management in a few paragraphs. This is unfortunate in the extreme, since dynamic multidimensional arrays and class-specific memory-management techniques are essential to many computer graphics and scientific programming applications. Thus, although they may not be directly related to radiosity-rendering methods, we are advised to examine them carefully. The effective use of memory can make the difference between a demonstration program and a production-quality application.

THE DEFAULT MEMORY MANAGER

Calling *new* in C++ or *malloc* in C invokes the default memory manager provided by the compiler. This gives us convenient and nearly transparent access to dynamically allocated memory blocks of almost any size. It also, however, brings with it some hidden costs in terms of execution time and memory requirements.

When your program first starts, its memory manager receives a pointer to a large block of memory (called the *heap* or *free store*) from the operating system. The memory manager then typically initializes this block with a header similar to:

```
struct BlockHeader
{
  size_t size;   // Block size (less block header)
  void *pnext;   // Next block pointer
};
```

where *size* is set to the size of the block in bytes (less that occupied by the *BlockHeader* structure) and *pnext* is set to *NULL*. It then saves a global *FreeMemoryList* pointer to this header.

A call to *new* or *malloc* with a request for *n* bytes results in the following sequence of events:

1. The *size* member of the block header pointed to by the *FreeMemoryList* pointer is compared to the requested size *n*.
2. If *size* is greater than *n*, then a null pointer is returned, indicating memory allocation failure.
3. The *size* member is set to *n*; the *n* bytes following the block header will become the allocated memory block.
4. Another block header is initialized, starting at *n* + *sizeof(BlockHeader)* bytes beyond the current block header. The current header's *pnext* pointer and the *FreeMemoryList* pointer are both set to point to this new header.
5. The new header's size member is set to the size of the remaining block in bytes, less *sizeof(BlockHeader)*. Its *pnext* pointer is again set to *NULL*.
6. If the call was to *new*, the class constructor (if any) is executed to initialize the allocated block.
7. A pointer to the allocated block (*not* the block header) is returned.

Successive calls to *new* or *malloc* result in the same sequence being repeated until the heap is exhausted, in which case it stops at the second step.

Calling *delete* or *free* is more interesting. The pointer received is to the allocated block, but of course the block header immediately precedes it in memory. The memory manager sets *pnext* to point to the block header currently pointed to by *FreeMemoryList*, then sets *FreeMemoryList* to point to the allocated block. This effectively frees the block by adding it to the linked list of free memory blocks. (If the next free block in the list immediately follows the current block in memory, the memory manager will likely coalesce the two blocks into one by setting the current *pnext* to the value of the following block's *pnext* pointer.)

Further calls to new or delete will now execute the above sequence of events with the exception of the second step. It becomes:

2. If *size* is greater than *n*, then check the block header pointed to by *pnext*; continue doing so until either *size* is less than or equal to *n* or *pnext* is *NULL*. If *pnext* is *NULL,* return a null pointer (no suitably sized block is available); otherwise continue to the next step.

The memory manager effectively walks the linked list of free memory blocks looking for a free block large enough to satisfy the allocation request.

There are several problems with this scheme. First, a hidden header block is used for every successful allocation of memory. This may be only eight bytes or so in size, but it quickly adds up when many small objects must be allocated.

Second, it takes time to scan the free memory list looking for suitably sized blocks, particularly when a large number of blocks have already been allocated. (This is more important in real-time systems, where some functions may have to execute within specific and guaranteed time limits.)

Third, and most important, randomly allocating and releasing blocks of memory of varying sizes quickly fragments the heap. The memory manager first looks for memory on the free memory list. If it finds one that is larger than necessary, it simply splits it into two, allocating one block and adding the second to the free memory list. The result is that each free block tends to become smaller and smaller until adjacent blocks are released, whereupon they are coalesced into a larger block.

Finally, dynamically allocating large contiguous blocks of memory creates a certain amount of havoc for the memory manager. To begin with, it may not be able to satisfy the allocation request if the heap is too fragmented. There may be plenty of memory available, but only in small, scattered blocks. (Some programming languages—Lisp, for example—support "garbage collection," where the blocks of allocated memory in the heap are physically copied to other locations such that the resulting free blocks can be coalesced. This is impractical in C and C++, since it means that every pointer to dynamic memory has to be somehow updated at the same time.)

Even if one or more large contiguous blocks (one or two megabytes for a Z-buffer, for example) can be allocated, this drastically limits the ability of the memory manager to allocate other blocks without running into memory-fragmentation problems.

There are two solutions to these problems. The simpler one involves a close look at how C and C++ address multidimensional arrays; the second is to write our own memory manager.

B.2   DYNAMIC MULTIDIMENSIONAL ARRAYS

Multidimensional arrays are often required in computer graphics and scientific programming. With access to megabytes of RAM, it becomes possible to solve large and complex problems quickly and efficiently. However, both C and C++ make it difficult to dynamically allocate and access multidimensional arrays unless the array dimensions are known at compile time. The general lack of documentation on programming in C and C++ using multidimensional arrays only exacerbates the problem.

The solution is to understand in detail how C and C++ access multidimensional arrays at runtime. Consider this quote from *The Annotated C++ Reference Manual* (Ellis and Stroustrup 1990):

> A consistent rule is followed for multidimensional arrays. If E is an n-dimensional array of rank $i \times j \times \ldots \times k$, then E appearing in an expression is converted to a pointer to an $(n-1)$-dimensional array with rank $j \times \ldots \times k$. If the * operator, either explicitly or implicitly as a result of subscripting, is applied to this pointer, the result is a pointed-to $(n-1)$-dimensional array, which itself is immediately converted into a pointer.
>
> For example, consider

```
int x[3][5];
```

> Here x is a 3×5 array of integers. When x appears in an expression, it is converted to a pointer to (the first of three) five-membered arrays of integers. In the expression $x[i]$, which is equivalent to $*(x + i)$, x is first converted to a pointer as described; then $x + i$ is converted to the type of x, which involves multiplying i by the length of the object to which the pointer points, namely five integer objects. The results are added and indirection applied to yield an array (of five integers), which in turn is converted to a pointer to the first of the integers. If there is another subscript the same argument applies again; this time the result is an integer.
>
> It follows from all this that arrays in C++ are stored row-wise (last subscript varies fastest) and that the first subscript in the declaration helps determine the amount of storage consumed by an array but plays no other part in subscript calculations.

This explanation also applies to ISO Standard C (ISO/IEC 1990) and the original Unix C (Kernighan and Ritchie 1988). Hidden in the jargon is the key phrase:

"$x[i]$ . . . is equivalent to $*(x + i)$"

Suppose we have a one-dimensional array F of n values. The data type doesn't matter, but let's make it *float* for convenience. It can be dynamically allocated with a call to *new* or *malloc* (followed by casting to a pointer to *float*). Unfortunately, we can access F only as a one-dimensional array of *float* values . . .

Not true! Suppose we also have a one-dimensional array D of m pointers to *float* and that each points to an element in F. Given an integer index i for D, we could access the element in F that $D[i]$ points to as:

```
value = *(D[i]);
```

However, this is equivalent to:

```
value = D[i][0];
```

We could also use a second index j to access the jth element in F beyond $D[i]$. This can be expressed as:

```
value = *(D[i] + j);
```

or even:

```
value = *(*(D + i) + j);
```

However, the most succinct expression is:

```
value = D[i][j];
```

In other words, we can use two one-dimensional arrays to simulate a two-dimensional array. Each pointer in *D* points to a fixed span of values in *F* (Fig. B.1). Furthermore, we never have to explicitly access the second array *F*. Generalizing this approach, we can use $n - 1$ one-dimensional arrays of pointers and a single one-dimensional array of values to simulate an *n*-dimensional array (e.g., Ashdown 1988).

True multidimensional arrays are those that are statically allocated and optionally initialized at compile time. They fill a contiguous block of memory and form part of the executable program that must be loaded from disk along with the program code. The arrays themselves are stored in contiguous blocks of memory. The compiler must be told the sizes of the first $n - 1$ dimensions of a static *n*-dimensional array. With these, it can calculate array offsets using integer multiplication and addition. These calculations can be performed very quickly, especially if the code ends up being cached by the CPU.

The interesting point here is that whereas a multidimensional array subscript expression such as $D[i][j]$ can be interpreted in terms of pointers and pointer arithmetic, the compiler needs to access only the address of *D*; the rest is integer arithmetic.

Dynamically allocated multidimensional arrays are a different story. The compiler doesn't know the array dimensions, and so it must generate code to physically read each pointer implied by the expression $*(*(D + i) + j)$. This may lead to slightly slower array access times if the necessary pointers aren't stored in the CPU's internal cache. Usually, however, the difference in performance will be negligible.

What does make a difference—a *big* difference—is that there is no requirement for *F* to be a single contiguous array. In other words, each pointer in *D* can point to a separate one-dimensional array of values. This allows the memory manager to allo-

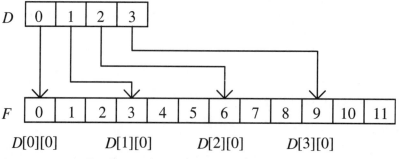

Figure B.1 Dynamically allocated two-dimensional array

cate memory in small chunks, one row at a time. It's the perfect solution to the problem of dynamically allocating large arrays. It's even better for MS-Windows 3.1 applications because it allows us to evade the 64-Kbyte maximum array size limitation without declaring the array as a _huge data type and suffering the considerable expense of _huge pointer arithmetic.

Another advantage of dynamically allocated multidimensional arrays is that the memory manager considers each allocated row to be an independent block of memory. This allows truly gargantuan arrays to be stored in virtual memory while still providing reasonably fast and efficient access to their row elements.

We used these techniques without fanfare in our *PolyRender, HemiClip,* and *CubicClip,* classes to dynamically allocate depth buffers and delta form factor arrays. In *PolyRender*, it allowed us to allocate arrays larger than 64 Kbytes under MS-Windows 3.1. CubicClip made use of yet another advantage of dynamic allocation: nonrectangular arrays.

B.3 TRIANGULAR ARRAYS

A seeming disadvantage of the cubic tetrahdral algorithm (Section 5.8) is that it requires a triangular array in which to store delta form factors. We could, of course, use a square array and simply not use half of it. However, this is an unnecessary waste of memory, particularly for high cubic tetrahedron resolutions.

Figure B.1 shows each pointer in *D* pointing to a fixed span of values in *F*. In other words, each of the "rows" in *F* has the same length. Clearly, however, this does not need to be the case. Each row can be whatever length we choose. If we decrement the row length by one for each successive pointer in *D*, we can simulate a triangular array with no wasted space other than the array of pointers needed for *D* itself. We need to know the length of each row in *F* when we access it through *D*, but this is no different from our need to know the number of rows and columns in a rectangular two-dimensional array.

A clear understanding of pointers and pointer arithmetic allows us to effectively manage dynamic multidimensional arrays in C and C++. It's only unfortunate that most programming texts fail to adequately address these capabilities.

B.4 CLASS-SPECIFIC MEMORY MANAGEMENT

From our perspective of writing an efficient radiosity renderer, the default memory manager underlying the global *new* and *malloc* operators has the undesirable trait of using a block header for every object it allocates. It would be much better if we could allocate small objects (such as polygon vertices) as arrays and eliminate the hidden headers.

Fortunately, we can, and on a per-class basis. When it comes to memory management, C++ provides the ultimate solution: If you don't like how the default memory manager works for a particular class, replace it with one of your own design by overloading *new* and *delete*.

Write your own memory manager? It's not as onerous a project as you might think. Following an example presented in Stroustrup (1991), a user-defined class with its own built-in memory manager can be as simple as in Listing B.1.

Listing B.1   A simple example of class-specific memory management

```
// Class-specific new and delete operators - EXAMPLE ONLY

#include <stdlib.h>

static int ObjectsPerChunk = 128;

class MyClass
{
  private:
    ... class-specific data

    static MyClass *FreeListPtr;    // Free list pointer

    MyClass *pnext;      // Next object pointer

  public:
    ... class-specific data access functions

    void *operator new( size_t );
    void operator delete( void * );
};

// Global free object list pointer
MyClass *MyClass::FreeListPtr = NULL;

void *MyClass::operator new( size_t size )
{
  int i;                          // Loop index
  MyClass *pfree = FreeListPtr;    // Free object pointer

  if (pfree != NULL)    // Free object available ?
  {
    // Update free object list pointer
    FreeListPtr = FreeListPtr->pnext;
  }
  else
  {
    // Allocate new chunk
    pfree = new MyClass[ObjectsPerChunk];

    // Link chunk to free object list
    FreeListPtr = pfree;
```

```
      // Link objects in chunk
      for (i = 1; i < ObjectsPerChunk; i++)
      {
        pfree->pnext = pfree + 1;
        pfree++;
      }
      pfree->pnext = NULL;      // Terminate free list

      // Point to first free object in chunk
      pfree = FreeListPtr;
   }

   return pfree;
}

void operator delete( void *pobj )
{
   MyClass *pcurr = (MyClass *) pobj;

   // Link object to free object list
   pcurr->pnext = FreeListPtr;
   FreeListPtr = pcurr;
}
```

The basis of this class is almost self-explanatory. Each *MyClass* object consists of user-defined data and a pointer to the next object. There's also a global *MyClass* object pointer called *FreeListPtr* that is initialized to *NULL* at program startup.

When the overloaded *new* operator is first called, it allocates an array of uninitialized *MyClass* objects in a block of memory called a "chunk." The call to *new* is not recursive; the default (i.e., global) *new* operator is always called when arrays of objects are to be allocated.

As shown in Listing B.1, there are 128 objects in a chunk. In practice, *ObjectsPerChunk* would be defined such that the chunk is reasonably sized, say 4 Kbytes. The object pointers are initialized to form a linked list of objects within the chunk, with the last object's pointer set to *NULL*. The first object in the chunk is linked to *FreeListPtr*, and a pointer to it is returned by *new*.

Successive calls to *new* simply advance the *FreeListPtr* pointer and return a pointer to the next object in the list. If the free object list is exhausted (i.e., the chunk is full), another chunk is allocated and the process is started over.

Calling *delete* links the object to be deleted to the head of the free object list, ready for the next call to *new*. This means that after a while, the linked list of free objects may span several allocated chunks in possibly random order.

This is a *very* simple memory manager. Once a chunk has been allocated, there is no mechanism to delete it short of program termination. You also can't derive anything from *MyClass* without providing a rewritten *new* operator, and even then you end up with multiple free memory lists, one for each class. It would be more useful to have a generic memory manager that allocates several sizes of chunks for various classes, depending on the size parameter passed to *new*. It should also indicate memory allocation failure and delete chunks that are no longer in use.

More comprehensive memory-manager classes that perform intelligent chunk allocation are occasionally presented in computer programming magazines. Examples include Burk and Custer (1992), Peterson (1992), and Weller (1990). The discussion provided by Burk and Custer is very informative and well worth reading. Despite its title, their generic "chunk allocator" is applicable to any environment that supports a C++ compiler.

Our radiosity-rendering program doesn't need a chunk allocator, but it could benefit from a class-specific memory manager for *Vertex3* and *Element3*. Relying on the default memory manager incurs a memory overhead of approximately 20 percent for each allocated object. The (incomplete) code in Listing B.1 outlines how these classes can be extended to include built-in memory management. The implementation details are left to the interested reader as an exercise.

REFERENCES

Ashdown, I. 1988. "Dynamic Multidimensional Arrays in C," *Computer Language* 5(6):83–88 (June).

Burk, R., and H. Custer. 1992. "A Reusable C++ Chunk Allocator for DOS and Windows," *Windows/DOS Developer's Journal* 3(2):5–13 (February).

Ellis, M. A., and B. Stroustrup. 1990. *The Annotated C++ Reference Manual*. Reading, MA: Addison-Wesley.

ISO/IEC 1990. *International Standard for Programming Language C*. New York: American National Standards Institute, ISO/IEC 9899, 1990.

Kernighan, B.W., and D.M. Ritchie. 1988. *The C Programming Language* (2nd ed.). Englewood Cliffs, NJ: Prentice Hall.

Peterson, M. E. 1992. "WINMEM: An Efficient Subsegment Memory Allocator for Windows 3.x," *Windows/DOS Developer's Journal* 3(7):5–11 (July).

Stroustrup, B. 1991. *The C++ Programming Language* (2nd ed.). Reading, MA: Addison-Wesley.

Weller, S. 1990. "Fast Memory Allocation Scheme," *The C Users Journal* 8(4):103–107 (April).

Bibliography

Aguas, M. P. N., and S. Müller. 1993. "Mesh Redistribution in Radiosity," *Proc. Fourth Eurographics Workshop on Rendering,* Paris, France, pp. 327–335.

Airey, J. M., and M. Ouh-young. 1989. "Two Adaptive Techniques Let Progressive Radiosity Outperform the Traditional Radiosity Algorithm." Department of Computer Science, University of North Carolina, Technical Report TR89-020.

Airey, J. M., J. H. Rohlf, and F. P. Brooks, Jr. 1990. "Towards Image Realism with Interactive Update Rates in Complex Virtual Building Environments," *Computer Graphics* 24(1):4–50 (Proc. ACM Workshop on Interactive Graphics).

Anderson, A., and M. Grant 1991. "VISULUX: A Radiosity Based Lighting Design Tool," *Proc. Second Eurographics Workshop on Rendering,* Barcelona, Spain.

Arnauldi, B., X. Pueyo, and J. Vilaplana. 1991. "On the Division of Environments by Virtual Walls for Radiosity Computation," *Proc. Second Eurographics Workshop on Rendering,* Barcelona, Spain.

Arvo, J., ed. 1991. *Graphic Gems II.* San Diego, CA: Academic Press.

Asensio, A. F. 1992. "A Hierarchical Ray-Casting Algorithm for Radiosity Shadows," *Proc. Third Eurographics Workshop on Rendering,* Bristol, England, pp. 179–188.

Ashdown, I. 1992. "Radiosity and Realism," *The C Users Journal* 10(8):33–42 (August).

Ashdown, I. 1993a. "Near-Field Photometry: A New Approach," *Journal of the Illuminating Engineering Society* 22(1):163–180 (Winter).

Ashdown, I. 1993b. "Modeling Complex 3-D Light Sources," *ACM SIGGRAPH '93 Course 22 (Making Radiosity Practical) Notes.*

Aupperle, L., and P. Hanrahan. 1993a. "Importance and Discrete Three Point Transport," *Proc. Fourth Eurographics Workshop on Rendering,* Paris, France, pp. 85–94.

Aupperle, L., and P. Hanrahan. 1993b. "A Hierarchical Illumination Algorithm for Surfaces with Glossy Reflections," *Computer Graphics Proceedings* (ACM SIGGRAPH '93), pp. 155–162.

Bao, H., and Q. Peng 1993a. "Shading Models for Linear and Area Light Sources," *Computers & Graphics* 17(2):137–145.

Bao, H., and Q. Peng. 1993b. "A Progressive Radiosity Algorithm for Scenes Containing Curved Surfaces," *Computer Graphics Forum* 12(3):C-399–C-408 (Proc. Eurographics '93).

Baranoski, G. V. G. 1992. "The Parametric Differential Method: An Alternative to the Calculation of Form Factors," *Computer Graphics Forum* 11(3):C193–C-204 (Proc. Eurographics '92).

Bastos, R. M., A. A. de Sousa, and F. N. Ferreira. 1993. "Reconstruction of Illumination Functions Using Bicbic Hermite Interpolation," *Proc. Fourth Eurographics Workshop on Rendering,* Paris, France, pp. 317–324.

Baum, D. R., S. Mann, K. P. Smith, and J. M. Winget. 1991. "Making Radiosity Usable: Automatic Preprocessing and Meshing Techniques for the Generation of Accurate Radiosity Solutions," *Computer Graphics* 25(4):51–60 (ACM SIGGRAPH '91 Proc.).

Baum, D. R., H. E. Rushmeier, and J. M. Winget. 1989. "Improving Radiosity Solutions through the Use of Analytically Determined Form Factors," *Computer Graphics* 23(3):325–334 (ACM SIGGRAPH '89 Proc.).

Baum, D. R., J. R. Wallace, M. F. Cohen, and D. P. Greenberg. 1986. "The Back-Buffer Algorithm: An Extension of the Radiosity Method to Dynamic Environments," *The Visual Computer* 2(5):298–306.

Baum, S. E., and J. M. Winget. 1990. "Real Time Radiosity through Parallel Processing and Hardware Acceleration," *Computer Graphics* 24(2):67–75 (1990 Symposium on Interactive 3D Graphics).

Beran-Koehn, J. C., and M. J. Pavicic. 1991. "A Cubic Tetrahedral Adaptation of the Hemi-Cube Algorithm," in Arvo (1991), pp. 299–302.

Beran-Koehn, J. C., and M. J. Pavicic. 1992, "Delta Form-Factor Calculation for the Cubic Tetrahedral Algorithm," in Kirk (1992), pp. 324–328, 575–576.

Bhate, N. 1993. "Application of Rapid Hierarchical Radiosity to Participating Media," *First Bilkent Computer Graphics Conference,* ATARV-93, Ankara, Turkey.

Bhate, N., and A. Tokuta. 1992. "Photorealistic Volume Rendering of Media with Directional Scattering," *Proc. Third Eurographics Workshop on Rendering,* Bristol, England, pp. 227–245.

Bian, B. 1990. *Accurate Simulation of Scene Luminance.* Ph.D. thesis, Worcester Polytechnic Institute, Worcester, MA.

Bian, B. 1992. "Hemispherical Projection of a Triangle," in Kirk (1992), pp. 314–317, 569–574.

Bian, B., N. Wittels, and D. S. Fussell. 1991. "Accurate Image Simulation by Hemisphere Projection," *Proceedings of the SPIE/IS&T,* Vol. 1453, San Jose, CA.

Bian, B., N. Wittels, and D. S. Fussell. 1992. "Non-Uniform Patch Luminance for Global Illumination," *Graphics Interface '92,* pp. 310–318.

Borel, C. C., and S. A. W. Gerstl. 1991. "Simulation of Partially Obscured Scenes Using the Radiosity Method," *Proceedings of the SPIE on Characterization, Propagation, and Simulation of Sources and Backgrounds,* Vol. 1486, pp. 271–277.

Borel, C. C., S. A. W. Gerstl, and B. J. Powers. 1991. "The Radiosity Method in Optical Remote Sensing of Structured 3-D Surfaces," *Remote Sensing of the Environment* 36:13–44.

Bouatouch, K. and C. Bouville, eds. 1992. *Photorealism in Computer Graphics.* Berlin, Germany: Springer-Verlag.

Bouatouch, K., and P. Tellier. 1992. "A Two-Pass Physics-Based Global Lighting Model," *Graphics Interface '92,* pp. 319–328.

Bouville, C., K. Bouatouch, P. Tellier, and X. Pueyo. 1990. "A Theoretical Analysis of Global Illumination Models," in Bouatouch and Bouville (1992), pp. 57–72.

Bu, J., and E. F. Deprettere. 1987a. "A VLSI System Architecture for High-Speed Radiative Transfer 3D Image Synthesis," *Eurographics '87* (Proc. European Computer Graphics Conference and Exhibition), G. Marechal, ed. Amsterdam: Elsevier Science Publishers B. V. (North-Holland), pp. 221–235.

Bu, J., and E. F. Deprettere. 1987b. "A VLSI Algorithm for Computing Form-Factors in Radiative Transfer Computer Image Synthesis," *Computer Graphics 1987* (Proc. CG International '87), T. L. Kunii, ed. London, England: Springer-Verlag, pp. 181–193.

Bu, J., and E. F. Deprettere. 1989. "A VLSI System Architecture for High-Speed Radiative Transfer 3D Image Synthesis," *The Visual Computer* 5(2):121–133.

Buckalew, C. 1990. *Illumination Networks.* Ph.D. thesis, University of Texas at Austin.

Buckalew, C., and D. S. Fussell. 1989. "Illumination Networks: Fast Realistic Rendering with General Reflectance Functions," *Computer Graphics* 23(3):89–98 (ACM SIGGRAPH '89 Proc.).

Buckalew, C., and D. S. Fussell. 1990. *An Energy-Balance Method for Animation.* Department of Computer Sciences, University of Texas at Austin, Technical Report TR-90-06.

Bullis, J. M. 1989. *Models and Algorithms for Computing Realistic Images Containing Diffuse Reflections.* Master's thesis, University of Minnesota, Minneapolis.

Campbell, A. T., III. 1991. *Modeling Global Diffuse Illumination for Image Synthesis.* Ph.D. thesis, University of Texas at Austin.

Campbell, A. T. III, and D. S. Fussell. 1990. "Adaptive Mesh Generation for Global Diffuse Illumination," *Computer Graphics* 24(4):155–164 (ACM SIGGRAPH '90 Proc.).

Carter, M. B., and J. L. Gustafson. 1993a. *The Symmetric Radiosity Formulation.* Ames Laboratory, Technical Report IS-J 4880.

Carter, M. B., and J. L. Gustafson. 1993b. *An Improved Hierarchical Radiosity Method.* Ames Laboratory, Technical Report IS-J 4881.

Chalmers, A. G., and D. J. Paddon. 1991. "Parallel Processing of Progressive Refinement Radiosity Methods," *Proc. Second Eurographics Workshop on Rendering,* Barcelona, Spain.

Chen, H., and E. Wu. 1990a. "An Efficient Radiosity Solution for Bump Texture Generation," *Computer Graphics* 24(4):124–134 (ACM SIGGRAPH '90 Proc.).

Chen, H., and E. Wu. 1990b. "An Adapted Solution of Progressive Radiosity and Ray-Tracing Methods for Non-Diffuse Environments," in Chua and Kunii (1990), pp. 477–490.

Chen, H., and E. Wu. 1991. "Radiosity for Furry Surfaces," *Eurographics '91* (Proc. European Computer Graphics Conference and Exhibition), F. H. Post and W. Barth, eds. Amsterdam: Elsevier Science Publishers B. V. (North-Holland), pp. 447–457.

Chen, S. E. 1989. *A Progressive Radiosity Method and Its Implementation in a Distributed Processing Environment.* Master's thesis, Program of Computer Graphics, Cornell University, Ithaca, NY.

Chen, S. E. 1990. "Incremental Radiosity: An Extension of Progressive Radiosity to an Interactive Image Synthesis System," *Computer Graphics* 24(4):135–144 (ACM SIG-GRAPH '90 Proc.).

Chen, S. E. 1991. "Implementing Progressive Radiosity with User-Provided Polygon Display Routines," in Arvo (1991), pp. 295–298, 583–597.

Chen, S. E., H. E. Rushmeier, G. Miller, and D. Turner. 1991. "A Progressive Multi-Pass Method for Global Illumination," *Computer Graphics* 25(4):165–174 (ACM SIG-GRAPH '91 Proc.).

Christensen, P. H., D. H. Salesin, and T. D. DeRose. 1993. "A Continuous Adjoint Formulation for Radiance Transport," *Proc. Fourth Eurographics Workshop on Rendering*, Paris, France, pp. 95–104.

Chua, T. S., and T. L. Kunii. 1990. *CG International '90: Computer Graphics Around the World*. Tokyo, Japan: Springer-Verlag.

Cohen, M. F. 1985. *A Radiosity Method for the Realistic Image Synthesis of Complex Environments*. Master's thesis, Program of Computer Graphics, Cornell University, Ithaca, NY.

Cohen, M. F. 1991. "Radiosity," in Rogers and Earnshaw (1991), pp. 59–90.

Cohen, M. F., and D. P. Greenberg. 1985. "The Hemi-Cube: A Radiosity Solution for Complex Environments," *Computer Graphics* 19(3):31–40 (ACM SIGGRAPH '85 Proc.).

Cohen, M. F., D. P. Greenberg, D. S. Immel, and P. J. Brock. 1986. "An Efficient Radiosity Approach for Realistic Image Synthesis," *IEEE Computer Graphics and Applications* 6(3):26–35.

Cohen, M. F., S. E. Chen, J. R. Wallace, and D. P. Greenberg. 1988. "A Progressive Refinement Approach to Fast Radiosity Image Generation," *Computer Graphics* 22(4):75–84 (ACM SIGGRAPH '88 Proc.).

Cohen, M. F., and J. R. Wallace. 1993. *Radiosity and Realistic Image Synthesis*. Cambridge. MA: Academic Press Professional.

DiLaura, D. L. 1992. "On the Development of a Recursive Method for the Solution of Radiative Transfer Problems," *Journal of the Illuminating Engineering Society* 21(2):108–112 (Summer).

DiLaura, D. L., and P. Franck. 1993. "On Setting Up and Solving Large Radiative Transfer Systems," *Journal of the Illuminating Engineering Society* 22(2):3–7 (Summer).

Dorsey, J. O'B. 1993. *Computer Graphics Techniques for Opera Lighting Design and Simulation*. Ph.D. thesis, Program of Computer Graphics, Cornell University, Ithaca, NY.

Dorsey, J. O'B., F. X. Sillion, and D. P. Greenberg. 1991. "Design and Simulation of Opera Lighting and Projection Effects," *Computer Graphics* 25(4):41–50 (ACM SIGGRAPH '91 Proc.).

Dretakkis, G., and E. Fiume. 1991. "Structure-Directed Sampling, Reconstruction and Data Representation for Global Illumination," *Proc. Second Eurographics Workshop on Rendering*, Barcelona, Spain, pp. 189–201.

Dretakkis, G., and E. Fiume. 1992. "Concrete Computation of Global Illumination Using Structured Sampling," *Proc. Third Eurographics Workshop on Rendering*, Bristol, England.

Dretakkis, G., and E. Fiume. 1993. "Accurate and Consistent Reconstruction of Illumination Functions Using Structured Sampling," *Computer Graphics Forum* 12(3):273–284 (Eurographics '93).

Drucker, S. M., and P. Schröeder. 1992. "Fast Radiosity Using a Data Parallel Architecture," *Proc. Third Eurographics Workshop on Rendering*, Bristol, England, pp. 247–258.

Emery, A. F., O. Johansson, M. Lobo, and A. Abrous. 1991. "A Comparative Study of Methods for Computing the Diffuse Radiation Viewfactors for Complex Structures," *Journal of Heat Transfer* 113:413–422.

Feda, M., and W. Purgathofer. 1991. "Progressive Refinement Radiosity on a Transputer Network," *Proc. Second Eurographics Workshop on Rendering,* Barcelona, Spain.

Feda, M., and W. Purgathofer. 1992. "Accelerating Radiosity by Overshooting," *Proc. Third Eurographics Workshop on Rendering,* Bristol, England, pp. 21–32.

Feda, M., and W. Purgathofer. 1993. "Progressive Ray Refinement for Monte Carlo Radiosity," *Proc. Fourth Eurographics Workshop on Rendering,* Paris, France, pp. 15–25.

Foley, J. D., A. van Dam, S. K. Feiner, and J. F. Hughes. 1990. *Computer Graphics: Principles and Practice* (2nd ed.). Reading, MA: Addison-Wesley.

Franck, P. 1990. *Mathematical Approaches to Solving the Luminous Radiative Transfer Problem.* Department of Civil and Architectural Engineering, University of Colorado, Boulder, independent study report.

Gatenby, N., and W. T. Hewitt. 1991. "Radiosity in Computer Graphics: A Proposed Alternative to the Hemi-cube Algorithm," *Proc. Second Eurographics Workshop on Rendering,* Barcelona, Spain.

George, D. W. 1990. *A Radiosity Redistribution Algorithm for Dynamic Environments.* Master's thesis, Program of Computer Graphics, Cornell University, Ithaca, NY.

George, D. W., F. X. Sillion, and D. P. Greenberg. 1990. "Radiosity Redistribution in Dynamic Environments," *IEEE Computer Graphics and Applications* 10(6):26–34.

Goldfeather, J. 1989. *Progressive Radiosity Using Hemispheres.* Department of Computer Science, University of North Carolina at Chapel Hill, Technical Report TR89-002.

Goral, C. 1985. *A Model for the Interaction of Light between Diffuse Surfaces.* Master's thesis, Program of Computer Graphics, Cornell University, Ithaca, NY.

Goral, C. M., K. E. Torrance, D. P. Greenberg, and B. Battaile. 1984. "Modeling the Interaction of Light between Diffuse Surfaces," *Computer Graphics* 18(3):213–222 (ACM SIGGRAPH '84 Proc.).

Gortler, S., and M. F. Cohen. 1993. *Radiosity and Relaxation Methods: Progressive Refinement Is Southwell Relaxation.* Princeton, NJ: Princeton University, Technical Report CS-TR-408-93.

Gortler, S. J., P. Schröder, M. F. Cohen, and P. Hanrahan 1993. "Wavelet Radiosity," *Computer Graphics Proceedings* (ACM SIGGRAPH '93), pp. 221–230.

Greenberg, D. P., M. F. Cohen, and K. E. Torrance. 1986. "Radiosity: A Method for Computing Global Illumination," *The Visual Computer* 2(5):291–297.

Greenberg, D. P., and F. Sillion. 1991. *Global Illumination Algorithms.* Aire-la-Ville, Switzerland: Eurographics Association, Eurographics Technical Report EG 91 TN 7.

Greene, N., M. Kass, and G. Miller. 1993. "Hierarchical Z-Buffer Visibility," *Computer Graphics Proceedings* (ACM SIGGRAPH '93), pp. 231–240.

Greiner, G., W. Heidrich, and P. Slusallek. 1993. "Blockwise Refinement–A New Method for Solving the Radiosity Problem," *Proc. Fourth Eurographics Workshop on Rendering,* Paris, France, pp. 233–245.

Guitton, P., J. Roman, and C. Schlick. 1991. "Two Parallel Approaches for a Progressive Radiosity," *Proc. Second Eurographics Workshop on Rendering,* Barcelona, Spain.

Haines, E. 1991. "Radiosity Bibliography," in Greenberg and Sillion (1991), pp. 55–60.

Haines, E., and J. Wallace. 1991. "Shaft Culling for Efficient Ray-Traced Radiosity," *Proc. Second Eurographics Workshop on Rendering,* Barcelona, Spain.

Hall, D. E. 1990. *An Analysis and Modification of Shao's Radiosity Method for Computer Graphics Image Synthesis.* Master's thesis, School of Mechanical Engineering, Georgia Institute of Technology.

Hall, D. E., and H. E. Rushmeier. 1993. "Improved Explicit Radiosity Method for Calculating Non-Lambertian Reflections," *The Visual Computer* 9:278–288.

Hall, R. 1989. *Illumination and Color in Computer Generated Imagery.* New York: Springer-Verlag.

Hamid, T. P. 1988. *The Radiosity Model.* Department of Computer Science, University of Glasgow, Scotland, Project Report.

Hanrahan, P., and D. B. Salzman. 1990a. *A Rapid Hierarchical Radiosity Algorithm for Unoccluded Environments.* Princeton, NJ: Princeton University, Technical Report CS-TR-281-90.

Hanrahan, P., and D. Salzman. 1990b. "A Rapid Hierarchical Radiosity Algorithm for Unoccluded Environments," in Bouatouch and Bouville (1992), pp. 151–170.

Hanrahan, P., D. Salzman, and L. Aupperle 1991. "A Rapid Hierarchical Radiosity Algorithm," *Computer Graphics* 24(4):197–206 (ACM SIGGRAPH '91 Proc.).

Heckbert, P. S., 1990. "Adaptive Radiosity Textures for Bidirectional Ray Tracing," *Computer Graphics* 24(4):145–154 (ACM SIGGRAPH '90 Proc.).

Heckbert, P. S,. 1991. *Simulating Global Illumination Using Adaptive Meshing.* Ph.D. thesis, University of California Berkeley, Technical Report UCB/CSD 91/636.

Heckbert, P. S. 1992a. "Discontinuity Meshing for Radiosity," *Proc. Third Eurographics Workshop on Rendering,* Bristol, England, pp. 203–226.

Heckbert, P. S. 1992b. "Radiosity in Flatland," *Computer Graphics Forum* 11(3):C-181–C-192 (Proc. Eurographics '92).

Heckbert, P. S., and J. M. Winget. 1991. "Finite Element Methods for Global Illumination," University of California Berkeley, Technical Report UCB/CSD 91/643.

Hermitage, S. A., T. L. Huntsberger, and B. A. Huntsberger. 1990. "Hypercube Algorithm for Radiosity in a Ray Traced Environment," *Proc. Fifth Distributed Memory Computing Conference.* IEEE Society Press, pp. 206–211.

Immel, D. S., M. F. Cohen, and D. P. Greenberg. 1986. "A Radiosity Method for Non-Diffuse Environments," *Computer Graphics* 20(4):133–142 (ACM SIGGRAPH '86 Proc.).

Jessel, J. P., M. Paulin, and R. Caubet. 1991. "An Extended Radiosity Using Parallel Ray-Traced Specular Transfers," *Proc. Second Eurographics Workshop on Rendering,* Barcelona, Spain.

Jones, G. R., C. G. Christou, B. G. Cumming, A. J. Parker, and A. Zisserman. 1993. "Accurate Rendering of Curved Shadows and Interreflections," *Proc. Fourth Eurographics Workshop on Rendering,* Paris, France, pp. 337–347

Kajiya, J. T. 1986. "The Rendering Equation," *Computer Graphics* 20(4):143–150 (ACM SIGGRAPH '86 Proc.).

Kajiyama, H., and S. Kodaira. 1989. "An Illuminance Analysis in Partitioned Spaces Using the Monte Carlo Method," *Journal of the Illuminating Engineering Society* 18(2):93–108 (Summer).

Kawai, J. K., J. S. Painter, and M. F. Cohen. 1993. "Radiooptimization—Goal Based Rendering," *Computer Graphics Proceedings,* pp. 147–154 (ACM SIGGRAPH '93 Proc.).

Kirk, D., ed. 1992. *Graphic Gems III.* San Diego, CA: Academic Press.

Kok, A. J. F. 1992. "Grouping of Patches in Progressive Radiosity," *Proc. Fourth Eurograph-*

ics Workshop on Rendering, Paris, France, pp. 221–231.

Kok, A. J. F., and F. W. Jansen. 1992. "Adaptive Sampling of Area Light Sources in Ray Tracing Including Diffuse Interreflection," *Computer Graphics Forum* 11(3):289–298 (Eurographics '92), pp. 289–298.

Kok, A. J. F., F. W. Jansen, and C. Woodward. 1993. "Efficient, Complete Radiosity Ray Tracing Using a Shadow-Coherence Method," *The Visual Computer* 10:19–33.

Kok, A. J. F., A. C. Yilmaz, and L. H. J. Bierens. 1990. "A Two-Pass Radiosity Method for Bézier Patches," in Bouatouch and Bouville (1992), pp. 115–124.

Kok, A. J. F., C. Yilmaz, and L. H. J. Bierens. 1991. "Source Selection for the Direct Lighting Computation in Global Illumination," *Proc. Second Eurographics Workshop on Rendering,* Barcelona, Spain.

Kokcsis, F., and J. F. Böhme. 1992. "Fast Algorithms and Parallel Structures for Form Factor Evaluation," *The Visual Computer* 8:205–216.

Kwok, B. 1992. *Analysis of Radiosity Techniques in Computer Graphics.* Master's thesis, York University, Toronto, Ontario.

Lalonde, P. 1993. "An Adaptive Discretization Method for Progressive Radiosity," *Graphics Interface '93,* pp. 78–86, Toronto, Ontario.

Languénou, E., K. Bouatouch, and P. Tellier. 1992. "An Adaptive Discretization Method for Radiosity," *Computer Graphics Forum* 11(3):C-205–C-216 (Proc. Eurographics '92).

Languénou, E., and P. Tellier. 1992. "Including Physical Light Sources and Daylight in Global Illumination," *Proc. Third Eurographics Workshop on Rendering,* Bristol, England, pp. 217–225.

Le Saec, B., and C. Schlick. 1990. "A Progressive Ray Tracing Based Radiosity with General Reflectance Functions," in Bouatouch and Bouville (1992), pp. 101–113.

Lewis, R. R. 1992. "Solving the Classic Radiosity Equation Using Multigrid Techniques," *Proc. 1992 Western Computer Graphics Symposium,* Banff, Alberta, pp. 157–164.

Lischinski, D., F. Tampieri, and D. P. Greenberg 1991. *Improving Sampling and Reconstruction Techniques for Radiosity.* Department of Computer Science, Cornell University, Ithaca, NY, Technical Report 91-1202.

Lischinski, D., F. Tampieri, and D. P. Greenberg. 1992. "Discontinuity Meshing for Accurate Radiosity," *IEEE Computer Graphics and Applications* 12(6):25–39.

Lischinski, D., F. Tampieri, and D. P. Greenberg. 1993. "Combining Hierarchical Radiosity and Discontinuity Meshing," *Computer Graphics Proceedings* (ACM SIGGRAPH '93), pp. 199–208.

Magnenat-Thalmann, N., and D. Thalmann. 1987. *Image Synthesis: Theory and Practice.* Tokyo, Japan: Springer-Verlag.

Max, N. L., and M. J. Allison. 1992. "Linear Radiosity Approximation Using Vertex-to-Vertex Form Factors," in Kirk (1992), pp. 318–323.

Max, N., and R. Troutman. 1993. "Optimal Hemicube Sampling," *Proc. Fourth Eurographics Workshop on Rendering,* Paris, France, pp. 185–200 and addendum.

Maxwell, G. M., M. J. Bailey, and V. W. Goldschmidt. 1986. "Calculations of the Radiation Configuration Factor Using Ray Tracing," *Computer-Aided Design* 18(7):371–379.

Meyer, G. W., H. E. Rushmeier, M. F. Cohen, D. P. Greenberg, and K. E. Torrance. 1986. "An Experimental Evaluation of Computer Graphics Imagery," *ACM Transactions on Computer Graphics* 5(1):30–50.

Michelin, S., G. Maffies, D. Arques, and J. C. Grossetie. 1993. "Form Factor Calculation: A

New Expression with Implementations on a Parallel T.Node Computer," *Computer Graphics Forum* 12(3):421–432 (Eurographics '93).

Mistrick, R. G., and D. L. DiLaura. 1987. "A New Finite Orthogonal Transform Applied to Radiative Transfer Calculations," *Journal of the Illuminating Engineering Society* 16(1):115–128 (Winter).

Neumann, L., and C. Kelemen. 1991. "Solution of Interreflection Problem for Very Complex Environments by Transillumination Method," *Proc. Second Eurographics Workshop on Rendering,* Barcelona, Spain.

Neumann, L., and A. Neumann. 1989. "Photosimulation: Interreflection with Arbitrary Reflectance Models and Illumination," *Computer Graphics Forum* 8:21–34.

Neumann, L., and A. Neumann. 1990. "Efficient Radiosity Methods for Non-Separable Reflectance Models," in Bouatouch and Bouville (1992), pp. 85–97.

Ng, A., and M. Slater. 1993. "A Multiprocessor Implementation of Radiosity," *Computer Graphics Forum* 12(5):329–342.

Nishita, T., and E. Nakamae. 1985. "Continuous Tone Representation of Three-Dimensional Objects Taking Account of Shadows and Interreflection," *Computer Graphics* 19(3):23–30 (ACM SIGGRAPH '85 Proc.).

Nishita, T., and E. Nakamae. 1993. "A New Radiosity Approach Using Area Sampling for Parametric Patches," *Computer Graphics Forum* 12(3):385–398 (Eurographics '93).

Paddon, D. 1993. "Multiprocessor Models for the Radiosity Method*,"* *First Bilkent Computer Graphics Conference,* Ankara, Turkey, ATARV-93.

Pattanaik, S. 1990. *Computational Methods for Global Illumination and Visualization of Complex 3D Environments.* Ph.D. thesis, Birla Institute of Technology and Science, Pilani, India.

Pattanaik, S., and S. Mudur. 1992. "Computation of Global Illumination by Monte Carlo Simulation of the Particle Light," *Proc. Third Eurographics Workshop on Rendering,* Bristol, England, pp. 71–83.

Pattanaik, S., and S. Mudur. 1993a. "Efficient Potential Equation Solutions for Global Illumination Computation," *Computers & Graphics* 17(4):387–396.

Pattanaik, S., and S. Mudur. 1993b. "The Potential Equation and Importance in Illumination Computations," *Computer Graphics Forum* 12(2):131–136.

Perry, R. L., and E. P. Speck. 1959. "Geometric Factors for Thermal Radiation Exchange between Cows and Their Surroundings*,"* *Journal of the American Society of Agricultural Engineering,* Technical Report 59-323.

Pietrek, G. 1993. "Fast Calculation of Accurate Formfactors," *Proc. Fourth Eurographics Workshop on Rendering,* Paris, France, pp. 201–220.

Price, M., and G. Truman. 1989. "Parallelism Makes Light Work," *Computer Graphics '89,* pp. 409–418 (November), London, England.

Priol, T., K. Bouatouch, and D. Menard. 1993. "Parallel Radiosity Using a Shared Virtual Memory," *First Bilkent Computer Graphics Conference,* Ankara, Turkey, ATARV-93.

Puech, C., F. Sillion, and C. Vedel. 1990. "Improving Interaction with Radiosity-Based Lighting Simulation Programs," *Computer Graphics* 24(1):51–57 (Proc. ACM Workshop on Interactive Graphics).

Pueyo, X. 1991. "Diffuse Interreflections. Techniques for Form-factor Computation: A Survey," *The Visual Computer* 7:200–209.

Purgathofer, W., and M. Zeller. 1990. "Fast Radiosity by Parallelization," in Bouatouch and Bouville (1992), pp. 171–181.

Recker, R. J. 1990. *Improved Techniques for Progressive Refinement Radiosity.* Master's thesis, Program of Computer Graphics, Cornell University, Ithaca, NY.

Recker, R. J., D. W. George, and D. P. Greenberg. 1990. "Acceleration Techniques for Progressive Refinement Radiosity," *Computer Graphics* 24(2):59–66 (1990 Symposium on Interactive 3D Graphics).

Reichert, M. 1992. *A Two-Pass Radiosity Method Driven by Lights and Viewer Position.* Master's thesis, Program of Computer Graphics, Cornell University, Ithaca, NY.

Rogers, D. E., and R. A. Earnshaw. 1991. *State of the Art in Computer Graphics: Visualization and Modeling,* New York: Springer-Verlag.

Rushmeier, H. 1988. *Realistic Image Synthesis for Scenes with Radiatively Participating Media.* Ph.D. thesis, Program of Computer Graphics, Cornell University, Ithaca, NY.

Rushmeier, H., D. R. Baum, and D. E. Hall. 1991. "Accelerating the Hemi-Cube Algorithm for Calculating Radiation Form Factors," *Journal of Heat Transfer* 113:1044–1047.

Rushmeier, H., C. Patterson, and A. Veerasamy. 1993. "Geometric Simplification for Indirect Illumination Calculations," *Graphics Interface '93*, pp. 227–236,Toronto, Ontario.

Rushmeier, H., and K. Torrance. 1987. "The Zonal Method for Calculating Light Intensities in the Presence of a Participating Medium," *Computer Graphics* 21(4):293–302 (ACM SIGGRAPH '87 Proc.).

Rushmeier, H. E., and K. E. Torrance. 1990. "Extending the Radiosity Method to Include Specularly Reflecting and Translucent Materials," *ACM Transactions on Graphics* 9(1):1–27.

Salesin, D., D. Lischinski, and T. DeRose. 1992. "Reconstructing Illumination Functions with Selected Discontinuities," *Proc. Third Eurographics Workshop on Rendering,* Bristol, England.

Sbert, M. 1993. "An Integral Geometry Based Method for Fast Form-Factor Computation," *Computer Graphics Forum* 12(3):C-409–420 (Proc. Eurographics '93).

Schröder, P. 1993. "Numerical Integration for Radiosity in the Presence of Singularities," *Proc. Fourth Eurographics Workshop on Rendering,* Paris, France, pp. 177–184.

Schröder, P., S. J. Gortler, M. F. Cohen, and P. Hanrahan. 1993. "Wavelet Projections for Radiosity," *Proc. Fourth Eurographics Workshop on Rendering,* Paris, France, pp. 105–114.

Schuierer, S. 1989. "Delaunay Triangulations and the Radiosity Approach," *Eurographics '89* (Proc. European Computer Graphics Conference and Exhibition), W. Hansmann, F. R. A. Hopgood, and W. Strasser, eds. Amsterdam Elsevier Science Publishers B. V. (North-Holland), pp. 345–353.

Shao, M., and N. I. Badler. 1993a. *A Gathering and Shooting Progressive Refinement Radiosity Method.* Department of Computer and Information Science, University of Pennsylvania, Technical Report MS-CIS-93-03.

Shao, M., and N. I. Badler. 1993b. "Analysis and Acceleration of Progressive Refinement Radiosity Method," *Proc. Fourth Eurographics Workshop on Rendering,* Paris, France, pp. 247–258.

Shao, M., Q. Peng, and Y. Liang. 1988a. "Form Factors for General Environments," *Eurographics '88* (Proc. European Computer Graphics Conference and Exhibition), D. A.

Duce and P. Jancene, eds. Amsterdam: Elsevier Sciences Publishers B. V. (North-Holland), pp. 499–510.

Shao, M., Q. Peng, and Y. Liang. 1988b. "A New Radiosity Approach by Procedural Refinements for Realistic Image Synthesis," *Computer Graphics* 22(4):93–101 (ACM SIGGRAPH '88 Proc.).

Shen, L., E. Deprettere, and P. Dewilde. 1992. "A New Space Partitioning for Mapping Computations of the Radiosity Method onto a Highly Pipelined Parallel Architecture," *Advances in Computer Graphics V,* Berlin, Germany: Springer-Verlag.

Shirley, P. 1990a. *Physically Based Lighting Calculations for Computer Graphics.* Ph.D. thesis, Department of Computer Science, University of Illinois, Urbana-Champaign.

Shirley, P. 1990b. "Physically Based Lighting Calculations for Computer Graphics: A Modern Perspective," in Bouatouch and Bouville (1992), pp. 73–83.

Shirley, P. 1990c. "A Ray Tracing Method for Illumination Calculation in Diffuse-Specular Scenes," *Graphics Interface '90,* pp. 205–212.

Shirley, P. 1991a. "Radiosity via Ray Tracing," in Arvo (1991), pp. 306–310.

Shirley, P. 1991b. "Time Complexity of Monte Carlo Radiosity," *Eurographics '91* (Proc. European Computer Graphics Conference and Exhibition), F. H. Post and W. Barth, eds. Amsterdam: Elsevier Science Publishers B. V. (North-Holland), pp. 459–465.

Shirley, P., K. Sung, and W. Brown. 1991. "A Ray Tracing Framework for Global Illumination Systems," *Graphics Interface '91,* pp. 117–128.

Shirley, P., and C. Wang. 1991. "Direct Lighting Calculations by Monte Carlo Integration," *Proc. Second Eurographics Workshop on Rendering,* Barcelona, Spain.

Siegel, R., and J. R. Howell. 1992. *Thermal Radiation Heat Transfer* (3rd ed.). Washington, DC: Hemisphere Publishing.

Sillion, F. X. 1991. "Detection of Shadow Boundaries for Adaptive Meshing in Radiosity," in Arvo (1991), pp. 311–315.

Sillion, F. X., and C. Puech. 1989. "A General Two-Pass Method Integrating Specular and Diffuse Reflection," *Computer Graphics* 23(3):335–344 (ACM SIGGRAPH '89 Proc.).

Sillion, F. X., and C. Puech. 1994. *Radiosity and Global Illumination.* San Mateo, CA: Morgan Kaufmann.

Sillion, F. X., J. R. Arvo, S. H. Westin, and D. P. Greenberg. 1991. "A Global Illumination Solution for General Reflectance Distributions," *Computer Graphics* 25(4):187–196 (ACM SIGGRAPH '91 Proc.).

Smith, K. P. 1991. "Fast and Accurate Radiosity-Based Rendering." Master's project report, University of California Berkeley, Technical Report UCB/CSD 91/635.

Smits, B. E., J. R. Arvo, and D. H. Salesin. 1992. "An Importance-Driven Radiosity Algorithm," *Computer Graphics* 26(4):273–282 (ACM SIGGRAPH '92 Proc.).

Spencer, S. 1990. "The Hemisphere Radiosity Method: A Tale of Two Algorithms," in Bouatouch and Bouville (1992), pp. 127–135.

Sturzlinger, W. (1992). "Radiosity with Voronoi Diagrams," *Proc. Third Eurographics Workshop on Rendering,* Bristol, England, pp. 169–177.

Sun, J., L. Q. Zou, and R. L. Grimsdale. 1993. "The Determination of Form-Factors by Lookup Table," *Computer Graphics Forum* 12(4):191–198.

Tampieri, F. 1990. *Global Illumination Algorithms for Parallel Computer Architectures.* Master's thesis, Program of Computer Graphics, Cornell University, Ithaca, NY.

Tampieri, F. 1991. "Fast Vertex Radiosity Update," in Arvo (1991), pp. 303–305, 598.

Tampieri, F. 1992. "Accurate Form-Factor Computation," in Kirk (1992), 329–333, 577–581.

Tampieri, F. 1993. *Discontinuity Meshing for Radiosity Image Synthesis.* Ph.D. thesis, Cornell University, Ithaca, NY.

Tampieri, F., and D. Lischinski. 1991. "The Constant Radiosity Assumption Syndrome," *Proc. Second Eurographics Workshop on Rendering,* Barcelona, Spain.

Teller, S. J. 1991. *Computing the Antipenumbra of an Area Light Source.* University of California Berkeley, Technical Report UCB/CSD 91/666.

Teller, S. J. 1992. "Computing the Antipenumbra of an Area Light," *Computer Graphics* 26(4):139–148 (SIGGRAPH '92 Proc.).

Tellier, P., E. Maisel, K. Bouatouch, and E. Languénou. 1993. "Exploiting Spatial Coherence to Accelerate Radiosity," *The Visual Computer* 10:46–53.

Troutman, R., and N. Max. 1993. "Radiosity Algorithms Using Higher Order Finite Element Methods," *Computer Graphics Proceedings* (ACM SIGGRAPH '93), pp. 209–212.

van Liere, R. 1991. "Divide and Conquer Radiosity," *Proc. Second Eurographics Workshop on Rendering,* Barcelona, Spain.

Varshney, A. 1991. *Parallel Radiosity Techniques for Mesh-Connected SIMD Computers.* Master's thesis, Department of Computer Science, University of North Carolina at Chapel Hill, Technical Report TR91-028.

Varshney, A., and J. F. Prins. 1992. "An Environment-Projection Approach to Radiosity for Mesh-Connected Computers," *Proc. Third Eurographics Workshop on Rendering,* Bristol, England, pp. 271–281.

Vedel, C., and C. Puech. 1991. "A Testbed for Adaptive Subdivision in Progressive Radiosity," *Proc. Second Eurographics Workshop on Rendering,* Barcelona, Spain.

Vedel, C. 1992. "Improved Storage and Reconstruction of Light Intensities on Surfaces," *Proc. Third Eurographics Workshop on Rendering,* Bristol, England, pp. 113– 121.

Vilaplana, J. 1992. "Parallel Radiosity Solutions Based on Partial Result Messages," *Proc. Third Eurographics Workshop on Rendering,* Bristol, England, pp. 259–270.

Vilaplana, J., and X. Pueyo. 1990. "Exploiting Coherence for Clipping and View Transformation in Radiosity Algorithms," in Bouatouch and Bouville (1992), pp. 137–149.

Wallace, J. R. 1988. *A Two-Pass Solution to the Rendering Equation: A Synthesis of Ray Tracing and Radiosity Methods.* Master's thesis, Program of Computer Graphics, Cornell University, Ithaca, NY.

Wallace, J. R., M. F. Cohen, and D. P. Greenberg. 1987. "A Two-Pass Solution to the Rendering Equation: A Synthesis of Ray Tracing and Radiosity Methods," *Computer Graphics* 21(4):311–320 (ACM SIGGRAPH '87 Proc.).

Wallace, J. R., K. A. Elmquist, and E. A. Haines. 1989. "A Ray Tracing Algorithm for Progressive Radiosity," *Computer Graphics* 23(3):315–324 (ACM SIGGRAPH '89 Proc.).

Wang, M., H. Bao, and Q. Peng. 1992. "A New Progressive Radiosity Algorithm through the Use of Accurate Form-Factors," *Computers & Graphics* 16(3):303–309.

Wang, Y. 1990. *Image Synthesis Using Radiosity Methods.* Ph.D. thesis, University of Alberta, Calgary.

Wang, Y., and W. A. Davis. 1990. "Octant Priority for Radiosity Image Rendering," *Graphics Interface '90,* pp. 83–91.

Wanuga, P. H. 1991. *Accelerated Radiosity Methods for Rendering Complex Environments.* Master's thesis, Program of Computer Graphics, Cornell University, Ithaca, NY.

Ward, G. J, F. M. Rubinstein, and R. D. Clear. 1988. "A Ray Tracing Solution for Diffuse Interreflection," *Computer Graphics* 22(4):85–92.

Ward, G. J., and P. Heckbert. 1992. "Irradiance Gradients," *Proc. Third Eurographics Worskhop on Rendering,* Bristol, England, pp. 85–98.

Watt, A. 1990. *Fundamentals of Three-Dimensional Computer Graphics.* Reading, MA: Addison-Wesley.

Watt, A., and M. Watt. 1992. *Advanced Animation and Rendering Techniques.* Reading, MA: Addison-Wesley.

Xu, H., Q. S. Peng, and Y. D. Liang. 1989. "Accelerated Radiosity Method for Complex Environments," *Eurographics '89* (Proc. European Computer Graphics Conference and Exhibition), W. Hansmann, F. R. A. Hopgood, and W. Strasser, eds. Amsterdam: Elsevier Science Publishers B. V. (North-Holland), pp. 51–61.

Zatz, H. 1993. "Galerkin Radiosity: A Higher Order Solution Method for Global Illumination," *Computer Graphics Proceedings* (ACM SIGGRAPH '93), pp. 213–220.

Zhang, N. 1991. "Two Methods for Speeding Up Form-Factor Calculation," *Proc. Second Eurographics Workshop on Rendering,* Barcelona, Spain.

Zhang, X. 1987. *The Finite Fourier Transform for Radiative Transfer Analysis in Complicated Geometries.* M.Sc. thesis, University of Colorado, Boulder.

Zhao, Z. H., and D. Dobkin. 1993. "Continuous Algorithms for Visibility: The Space Searching Approach," *Proc. Fourth Eurographics Workshop on Rendering,* Paris, France, pp. 115–126.

Zhou, Y., and Q. Peng. 1992. "The Super-Plane Buffer: An Efficient Form-Factor Evaluation Algorithm for Progressive Radiosity," *Computers & Graphics* 16(2):151–158.

How to Use
the Diskette

The diskette accompanying the book/desk edition of this book contains C++ source code and MS-Windows 3.1 executable files for *HELIOS*, a fully functional radiosity-based rendering program for the Microsoft Windows 3.1 environment. It also contains several sample environment files, a color quantization utility for MS-Windows Paintbrush-compatible BMP files (*BMP_TEST*), and a sample AutoCAD DXF file parser (*DXF_TEST*).

There are four versions of *HELIOS* included on the diskette:

1. HELIOS_C.EXE—uses the cubic tetrahedral algorithm for form factor determination (see Chaps. 5 and 6).
2. HELIOS_H.EXE—uses the hemicube algorithm for form factor determination (see Chaps. 5 and 6).
3. HELIOS_R.EXE—uses the ray-casting algorithm for vertex-to-source form factor determination (see Chaps. 5 and 6).
4. HELIOS_S.EXE—displays full-color shaded images only (see Chap. 4).

HARDWARE REQUIREMENTS

All four versions of *HELIOS* require:

1. An IBM PC-AT clone with an 80386 CPU and a math coprocessor (an 80486 or Pentium CPU is recommended).
2. A color video display capable of displaying at lcast 32,768 colors.
3. Microsoft Windows 3.1.

489

HELIOS will run on a computer equipped with a 256-color video display adapter. However, the photorealistic images displayed by *HELIOS* will appear posterized. Nevertheless, the computer can be used to display wireframe and full-color shaded images. It can also be used to save the photorealistic images to disk as 24-bit color BMP files.

The MS-DOS utility program *BMP_TEST* included on this diskette can be used to convert 24-bit color BMP files into equivalent 8-bit (256-color) BMP files. These files can be displayed on a computer equipped with a 256-color video display adapter using the Paintbrush application program that is provided with Microsoft Windows 3.1.

Remember that even though your computer may be capable of displaying 32,768 or more colors, your Microsoft Windows environment may be set up to use a 4-bit (16-color) or 8-bit (256-color) display for speed reasons. (The default setup for MS-Windows 3.1 is for a 16-color VGA display.) You may have to use the Windows Setup Program to change to the appropriate display driver. (See your Microsoft Windows documentation for details.)

SOFTWARE INSTALLATION

HELIOS requires approximately 1.2 megabytes of free disk space on your personal computer's hard drive.

To install *HELIOS* and its associated files, follow these steps:

1. Make a backup copy of the diskette and store it in a safe place.
2. Insert the diskette into any available 3½-inch disk drive on your personal computer.
3. Start MS-Windows.
4. Choose "Run" from the Windows Program Manager File pull-down menu.
5. In the "Command Line" edit box, enter the diskette drive name and the program name as follows:

drive:\SETUP

For example, if your diskette drive is drive A, enter:

A:\SETUP

6. Select the "OK" button or press the "Enter" key. The *HELIOS* Installation dialog box will be displayed.
7. Follow the instructions on the screen to install *HELIOS*. The following files will be copied to your hard drive:

   • README.TXT.
   • Borland C++ 4.0 IDE files.

- Microsoft Visual C++ V1.5 MAKE files.
- HELIOS C++ include files.
- HELIOS C++ source code.
- HELIOS executables.
- HELIOS icon files (binary).
- Sample environment and entity files.
- Sample AutoCAD DXF file parser (executable, source code, and documentation).
  - Octree color quantization utility (executable, source code, and documentation).

8. After you have finished installing the software, the SETUP program asks whether you want to display the README.TXT file after exiting the program. You should read this file for any last-minute changes or instructions.
9. To remove *HELIOS* and its associated files from your computer, select the *UNINSTALL* program icon from the *HELIOS* program group and follow the instructions on the screen.

OPERATING INSTRUCTIONS

Operating instructions for the executable programs included on the diskette are as follows:

1. HELIOS_C—see Section 6.12.1.
2. HELIOS_H—see Section 6.12.1.
3. HELIOS_R—see Section 6.12.1.
4. HELIOS_S—see Section 4.19.5.

Further information regarding recommended camera and viewing parameters for the sample environments is presented in the README.TXT file on the diskette.

Operating instructions for the octree color quantization program (*BMP_TEST*) and the sample AutoCAD DXF file parser (*DXF_TEST*) are included in text files on the diskette.

Index

493

CREDITS

Listings 3.8 and 3.9 adapted from D. Bragg. 1992. "A Simple Color Reduction Filter." In D. Kirk, ed. Graphics Gems III. San Diego, CA: Academic Press.

ANSI/IES Definitions, Appendix A, © 1986 by Illuminating Engineering Society of North America, New York, in *Nomenclature and Definitions for Illuminating Engineering* (IES. RP-16).

Color Plate 6 courtesy of Stuart Feldman. © 1994 by Lightscape Technologies, Inc.

Color Plates 7, 8, and 9 courtesy of Donald Schmitt. © 1994 A. J. Diamond, Donald Schmitt and Company.

Color Plates 10, 11, 12 courtesy of David Munson. © 1993 by Hellmuth, Obata and Kassabaum, Inc.